from

Nixon Agonistes

"He is the least 'authentic' man alive, the late mover, tester of responses, submissive to 'the discipline of consent.' There is one Nixon only, though there seem to be new ones all the time —he will try to be what people want."

"For him, American history stood still while he learned the method of his current game. History ended in 1921, with the death of his hero, Wilson, and did not start up again until 1946. Neither the Depression nor the New Deal had any discernible effect on him."

"History never rests, never leaves alone the thing it makes; and there are signs that history, having made ours a great nation, may now be in the process of unmaking it. . . . Nixon's victory was the nation's concession of defeat, an admission that we have no politics left but the old individualism, a web of myths that have lost their magic. . . . Our archetypal 'self-made man' is not only self-effacing but almost self-obliterating."

MENTOR and SIGNET Titles of Interest

(0451)

NIXON AGONISTES

The Crisis of the Self-Made Man

by

Garry Wills

UPDATED AND EXPANDED

A MENTOR BOOK

NEW AMERICAN LIBRARY

NEW YORK AND SCARBOROUGH, ONTARIO

To Mayno Collins Wills
who lived for others

Library of Congress Catalog Card Number: 72-80426

Some material here reshaped appeared earlier in *Esquire*, *National Review*, *The New Politics*, and *The Saturday Evening Post*.

This is an authorized reprint of a hardcover edition published by The Houghton Mifflin Company.

MENTOR TRADEMARK REG. U.S. PAT. OFF. AND FOREIGN COUNTRIES
REGISTERED TRADEMARK—MARCA REGISTRADA
HECHO EN WINNIPEG, CANADA

SIGNET, SIGNET CLASSIC, MENTOR, PLUME, MERIDIAN AND NAL BOOKS are published *in the United States* by New American Library, 1633 Broadway, New York, New York 10019, *in Canada* by The New American Library of Canada Limited, 81 Mack Avenue, Scarborough, Ontario M1L 1M8.

First Mentor Printing, September, 1971

10   11   12   13   14   15   16   17   18

PRINTED IN CANADA

O lastly over-strong against thy self!
> —Milton, *Samson Agonistes*

When you're alone like he was alone . . .
> —Eliot, *Sweeney Agonistes*

Preface to the 1979 Edition

THIS BOOK appeared two years before the Watergate break-in that led to Nixon's resignation. Naturally, I have been asked if anything in Nixon's downfall surprised me, and one thing did—the venality he showed in office, the growing importance of the cash nexus in all his dealings. I think that was not pronounced in Nixon's earlier career; but I should have expected it. The man of the classical liberal marketplace measures other things, and is measured himself, in terms of financial authentication. Worth is established by its symbol, money. Even that would complete the picture of Nixon as the last liberal of the social Darwinian school.

I have let the book stand as written, adding only a brief Afterword. The often-told Watergate story is implicit, I think, in Nixon's whole career—the inability to trust others, even in his own government; the continued sense of grievance, even at the pinnacle of success; the overkill reaction to any challenge. The competitive human market opens anew every day. One can win or lose everything at once. The mechanism of barter has no memory. Individualists assure us "It is a jungle out there," speaking from their own inner jungle. Nixon's pure expression of that creed made him an eccentric at the center of our national experience, the *individual* as a *social measure,* our aberrant norm.

GARRY WILLS

PREFACE

THIS BOOK grew out of a series of reportorial assignments that led me to watch the American people make Richard Nixon President, then led me to reflect upon this man elected, these people electing him, the relation of country to President as he took up and wielded powers they had granted him. To say the two deserve each other will, I suppose, be taken as an insult (to one or the other), though I mean the remark in several ways, some complimentary (to both). What is best and weakest in America goes out to reciprocating strength and deficiencies in Richard Nixon. In the dialogue of such a ruler with the ruled—traced in air, as it were, between them as they try to communicate—an older America can be seen struggling back toward life, an older set of hopes and doubts, including an older sense of what can only be called *liberalism*.

An older sense, perhaps confusing at first; but one that must be relearned if we are to grasp that thing in its original shape so named, see how it lingers in our institutions, haunts our language, forms our assumptions. Liberalism clearly was—covertly (I shall argue) still *is*—the philosophy of the marketplace, and America is distinguished by a "market" mode of thought in all its public (and even private) life, a mode that is Nixon's through and through. This pattern in our thinking is both more and less than a defined philosophy; it is a huge sunken body of historical aspirations which, now ill-formulated when we frame them at all, are nonetheless implicit in much of what we say and do, are the substance of our half-forgotten dreams, of goals we hardly aspire to anymore, of words now used almost to meaninglessness. They provide moral standards which we rather defer to than adhere to; yet, as originally voiced, these aspirations formed a large system of linked influences, very powerful in our past, now only partly alive.

It is Nixon's hope that he can resurrect this moldering system (for he knows it, its original force, and serves it in his way). The odds are against him. The sheer size of the thing, which has kept it from dying out in all its limbs, makes it improbable that we can lift it up again. And some will deny that it deserves a second life. Still, Nixon must make the effort; this is his *agon,* his struggle; for without a borrowed life from that old set of values and aspirations, he cannot succeed, cannot be judged by norms congenial to him. He may fail, as his favorite predecessor failed— as Wilson failed. But the struggle, even if doomed, is an honorable one, and Nixon must be assessed in its terms, by his own standards, loftier than men give him credit for.

I have tried to repeat the order of my own observation and reflection as I wrote the book, which therefore moves— both from part to part, and within each part—from observed particulars to argued generalities. Though the particulars are less than "evidence" (in the strict sense) for my generalizations, they are not mere occasions for them either. One's judgment of a nation's ideals and performance depends on a "feel" for that nation, both for the attributes its people share and for its internal diversity, as these are revealed (not often deliberately) in the train and pattern of salient events, a "feel" to be tested by the reader as he recovers those events in memory. For this reason I continually start from, and appeal back to, that "feel" as Americans have acquired it in their reaction, over the years, to Nixon's career, campaign, and presidency. I would keep the argument, so far as I can, based cumulatively upon observed detail, on small things widely known and discussed, analyzed and shared, things summonable still to the mind's inquest. What Americans instinctively value or believe cannot be demonstrated *a priori,* nor taken from official protestations; it can only be observed "close up" in the weave of communal life, then tested as men trade their observations, noting congruences, sharing insights, comparing others' selection and use and juxtaposition of "clues" to the national style. The whole will at last be found implied in the parts, or it will not be found at all.

Besides, the book takes up what Frost would have called "a lover's quarrel with my country"; and lovers take delight, even when quarreling, in the particular features of the beloved.

GARRY WILLS

Contents

Part ONE

THE MORAL
MARKET

(Ralph Waldo Emerson)

1. The Loneliness of
the Long Distance Runner

*"All I knew was that you had to run, run, run, with-
out knowing why you were running, but on you
went through fields you didn't understand and into
woods that made you afraid, over hills without knowing you'd been up and down, and shooting across
streams that would have cut the heart out of you had
you fallen into them. And the winning post was no
end to it, even though crowds might be cheering you
in, because on you had to go . . ."*
—Smith (The Runner)

FEBRUARY 1968: It is early morning in Wisconsin, in
Appleton, air heavy with the rot of wood pulp. This is the
place where Joe McCarthy lived and was buried—a
place, once, for Nixon to seek out on campaign; then,
for a longer time, a place to steer shy of. He has out-
lived both times, partially. And it is too late to care
in any event: the entire American topography is either
graveyard, for him, or minefield—ground he must walk
delicately, revenant amid the tombstones, whistling in histrionic unconcern.

Not that Appleton wishes to remind him; the towns-
people are busy pressing wood into paper, and all they
want from Nixon is a boost for the local product. Fair
enough. Romney, after all, is milking cows in the cheese
towns of Wisconsin. The least Nixon can do is fiddle with
wood pressings.

Appleton's Conway Hotel is offering coffee on one side
of its banquet room, but the crowd has already curdled to
a standstill half an hour before Nixon's scheduled "remarks." Those standing on the floor cannot see Nixon
when he edges through the crowd onto a low platform

and says, "Good morning." I am off to one side, where I see nothing but shadow bent distortedly onto the wall by insistent television lights—shadows, rather, since the angled lights give him one dark silhouette and a lighter "ghost" askew of it. Doubled hands rise and dip beside the haloed body, or flail in ghost gestures through it—six dim grades of shadow weaving elusive canons, visual echoes like the sound of "Tricky Dicky," fiction pictures. Six crises endured—six Nixons, which do not seem to add up or solidify. The hands move in jerky quick apparitions, dark ones unable to escape the haunting light ones, nimble pianist fingers, prestidigitating shadow.

His speech is the standard one of this campaign, but with a bit more partisan bite in it than those delivered in frosty New Hampshire. "Give 'em hell," someone shouts from the floor. "I don't need to," Nixon snaps back. His right hand shadows out, shaking nemesis: "They have given themselves hell." His pitch is to party loyalty: "I have been campaigning twenty years" (it is twenty-two). "I have campaigned in seven national elections" (three times for himself). "I have never campaigned against another Republican, and I'm not going to start it now. The way for a Republican to win is not to show how he can take on other Republicans, but to show how he can take on Lyndon Johnson." (Translation: "I will not accept yesterday's challenge to debate George Romney.")

He goes briskly toward the morning's business. "I'm glad to join the papermakers; but"—his right forefinger waggles its double plumes of shadow—"I want it understood that when we get to Washington we'll cut *down* on the paper work!" He moves to the papermaking gadget, presses a plunger, "couches" the excess water out of his paper disc, then dries it in a curved toaster. The master of ceremonies, meanwhile, tells him he will be the second President of the United States to have made paper (George Washington was the first). Appleton applauds. On to Stevens Point.

Each of Nixon's stops today will be in different congressional districts—Appleton, eighth; Stevens Point, seventh, largely Democrat, Polish, Catholic. I make my way up the press bus, to Charlie McWhorter, a custodian of Republican lore and ask why this district was put so high on Nixon's list of places to visit. "Well, it's Mel Laird's district." (Laird, who will be Nixon's Secretary of

Defense, got a federal water-pollution laboratory for the university—Wisconsin State—where Nixon will be speaking today.) McWhorter, a veteran of earlier Nixon campaigns, is riding the bus because there is still no press secretary at this stage of Nixon's campaign. Pat Buchanan, acting press secretary, has other duties which make him fly with Nixon in the rented DC–3 while our bus pants along on the ground. "I'm here on pretty short notice myself," Charlie says. "I got the call last Wednesday"— two days before the campaign began. McWhorter is a good mixer—one of the mainstays of the Newport Jazz Festival, a bachelor who lives in the Village. On a first-name basis with hundreds of party regulars everywhere, he is supposed to be Nixon's guide to the local situation at these stops.

I used to have a friend in Wisconsin politics; I ask Charlie if he remembers the man. "No. But I'll bet Dick would." (I asked him later; he did.) "There's not much I can tell that man about Republican politics." McWhorter, who has an elfin pinched nose and chin, pushes his glasses up onto his bald head, perches them behind a tongue-of-flame wisp of remaining hair, and lifts his left eyebrow in a tight *circonflexe:* it is his trademark expression—the wise old Kewpie doll: "Dick knows almost everything there is to know about the party's inner workings and geography."

12 NOON, STEVENS POINT: An hour before the talk, the school's gymnasium is almost full. It has the fresh-staleness of lacquer, basketball, young bodies. About half of the university's six thousand students will eventually squeeze into the gym or be clotted at its entries. I ask a dozen students, here and there, if they ever heard of the Hiss case. "Hess?" One thinks she heard *something* about it. What? "I don't know; just something." The sophomores were born in 1948. Here, at least, Nixon should be able to shed his past. But he isn't. I ask the students what they know about the man. The most frequent answer: "He was the Vice-President, once." (Way back, their voices say.) The second most common answer: "He is called Tricky Dick." Do you know why? "No." But the ghost is there. The third answer: "He was spit on in South America." Do you know why? "No."

It is typical of Nixon that the *indignity* inflicted at his

most courageous moment should be remembered. He has
called his life a series of crises. He might have said a series
of disasters. Even the victories hurt. He made his one
real charge stick—Hiss was convicted, before Joe Mc-
Carthy ever made an accusation. But this charge was
mingled with all the wild ones that followed, and his role
in the Hiss case gave him the reputation of a proto-
McCarthy. He vindicated himself in the "Checkers speech."
But to do so he had to violate his own privacy; and the
experience left him with a permanent air of violation, not
of vindication. No one remembers what he said to
Khrushchev, only that he said it in a kitchen. He walked a
fine line of reserve and calm during Eisenhower's ill-
nesses; yet that only contributed to the view that he was
Ike's errand boy. Kennedy's election in 1960 is attributed
to his eloquence and "style," Nixon's loss is put down to
bad makeup. There is a genius of deflation that follows
Nixon about. He has been strong many times; but fate
gets photographers to him when he collapses on Bill
Knowland's shoulder in tears, or when he snarls at journalists. There were many attempts to "dump Nixon" over
the years, but he would not bow out gracefully, leave well
enough alone, disappear.

That gaucheness of a man lingering on when he is no
longer wanted becomes, at a certain point, the crazy proof
of his importance. He survived. He was often a leftover,
but he always found some job to perform in that capacity. He represented the marginally salvageable past.
A part of the McCarthy mood, he could contribute to
Ike's kind lobotomy of the electorate: Nixon would do
the cutting, Eisenhower the curing—gall and honey. He
mobilized the party while the General stood above par-
tisanship. And when he was not mere spear carrier in the
regime, he could be the hatchet wielder. The symbolism
of McCarthy's exorcism was appropriate: Ike had Nixon
repudiate him. Above party himself, apparently unaware
of storms in the lower atmosphere, the General could still
have "his" party, in the person of Nixon, disown Mc-
Carthy. Then, when reelection time came around, Ike tried
to rise to new peaks on Olympus by disowning the dis-
owner. He told his unhappy running mate to "chart his
own course" when everyone knew Nixon had no other
course to steer but that traced in air by Ike's elusive
coattail, swept up daintily now, a skirt not to be soiled

with Nixon's touch. But Eisenhower had made too much use of the identification "Nixon = Party" to get rid of him. That would be not only rising above the party, but attacking it. Again, Nixon's past made him marginally useful —by just the margin that kept him from being jettisoned.

Nixon's people in Wisconsin were trying once again to turn his leftover state to advantage. He was not only a leftover from the Eisenhower administration. The Nixon staff was even calling his defeat at the hands of Kennedy an advantage: there is something glamorous about being a survivor of Camelot, even if one played the role, in it, of Mordred. Nixon's people like to tell the story of the little girl whose memory of the 1960 debate is that Nixon was "President Kennedy's friend." If one must be a ghost, he might as well be the ghost of Camelot past.

But the approach at Stevens Point cannot be ghostly. It is all about the future: he comes down hard on a major theme of his new campaign, the "last third of the century" theme. "You can *change* the world. By 2000 A.D. we can wage a successful war against poverty, hunger, misery, and most disease. It is a challenging world, yes! But what an exciting time to be alive!" There is a Camelot in your future.

That is the substance. But much of the speech is mere games that politicians play. "Mel Laird told me . . ." and "As I told Mel Laird . . ." Stroke. Stroke. The president of the university, Lee Sherman Dreyfus, is a swinger, proud of the fact that his initials are L.S.D. "We're going on a trip together," he told students last fall, when he took office. When he rises to introduce Nixon, he warns the students that what they do will be picked up by national TV. "We will be judged by the community of scholars." The meeting is of global concern. (Here he casually puts his hands in his pockets and reveals his own large globe covered with red sweater, a key chain dangling almost to his knees—he must have become a swinger in the forties.) He introduces those on the platform, including his wife: "Cool it," he growls over the applause, "I've got to live with her." The remark is much appreciated by the students—if not by the community of scholars. L.S.D. is as popular with his students as L.B.J. is unpopular.

So Nixon, skilled at this sort of thing, maneuvers deftly onto the president's coattail with his opening words. "I asked your president, who I know is a professor of com-

munications, if that included television. He said it does.
Maybe if I'd known him in sixty, I'd be in the White
House now." Yesterday in Green Bay he said that if
Vince Lombardi had been coaching him in '60, he might
be in the White House. At TV appearances he says to
everyone, from the makeup man and the camera crew to
the producer and interviewer, "If only . . ." Much of the
population will soon think Richard Nixon needs *them*, and
if only he had known them in 1960 . . . When he is not
flattering the school's president, during this speech, he
works on the students: "In the last third of the century,
great advances will be made in fields like automation and
cybernetics (on which you know far more than I do) . . .
You, as students of history, know better than I . . ."
Stroke. Stroke.

The question period goes well. "Mr. Vice-President,"
begins the first student. "No, Hubert's coming next week."
"I mean Mr. former Vice-President." "That's all right; I've
been called everything" (a line he used regularly in the
'62 campaign—even his jokes are risen ghosts). A Eugene
McCarthy group has passed out hard questions to be
asked; when the first of these is brought up, Nixon unfolds
a petition the McCarthy group brought for him to sign,
and answers its three requests point by point, disposing of
the hard questions all at once. A voice shaky with anger
says Nixon is a liar unless he is willing to support revolution in Latin America. Nixon, after deploring Castroite
violence, calmly ticks off four ways to "revolutionize"
Latin America—its economy, agriculture, education, and
aid programs. When he finishes, to applause rivaling that
of L.S.D., President Dreyfus rises, puts his red globe
against the microphone stand, and confirms the success:
"Just in case, in November, you're looking for a job—
you're a pretty good lecturer; just give me a call."

The students mob him in the corridor, fluttering papers
at him for his autograph. The curly black hair, with erod-
ing blunt headland of widow's peak, ducks down as he
surrenders that little bit of himself that politicians pay out
in ink and energy to every passerby—his name scrawled
across I.D. cards, agriculture textbooks, Gene McCarthy
questionnaires. When two girls push irritably at the spongy
ball of people rolling and breathing all around him, one
stops, in mid-struggle, to say, "Boy, he's getting *manhandled*." The other shrugs loftily, "Let's face it, he likes

it," and huffs her way in. The odd thing about this athletic ceremony is that there is so little respect for it on either side—with the hounds or with the hare.

3:15 P.M., OSHKOSH: The bus rolls into an improbably luxurious motel. In the press room, typewriters cautiously, oh-so-tentatively meditate student response at Stevens Point. *Is* there, then, a *new* new-Nixon—Nixon-Seven, nearing the cat's allotment of lives? Those who have to file stories are on the phone; most of those who don't are at the makeshift bar. McWhorter is there, brooding, under raised left triangle of eyebrow, on districts and registrations and voter margins. Then the "real" (well, *pro tem*) press secretary comes in, Pat Buchanan. As usual, he has a black overcoat on, with the collar wrapped up around his lumpy raw face—forty-year-old torpedo, hands on the iron in his pockets? No, he is twenty-nine, a writer, one of Nixon's fresh batch of intellectuals. Pat was, indeed, the very first. He climbed aboard in time to make the '66 campaign swing with Nixon and to accompany him on his '67 tour of the Middle East. Earlier, he caddied for the Vice-President at Burning Tree Club when Nixon had to trudge around the links, a glorified caddy for Ike. Pat was nine at the time of the Hiss case. After a turn as editorial writer on the conservative St. Louis *Globe-Democrat* and some dabbling in the conservative activism of Young Americans for Freedom, he made overtures to Nixon, was invited to New York for a three-hour interview, and became the first of the '68 crop of bright young men. He has proved himself in the interval; he keeps the briefing file on all current affairs, called "the Q and A" (Nixon likes to use lawyer jargon, his talks are full of phrases like "self-serving evidence" and "adversary procedure"). With Ray Price's help, Pat drew up the first version of Nixon's *Pueblo* statement. But, old-timer that he is on this new staff, he was not with "the Boss" (as the staff calls him) in 1960, the presidential year Pat became old enough to vote—so, while performing a thousand duties by day, he reads up on the '60 campaign at night, using Theodore White's book as his basic text.

Pat has come to the press room to tell me I can ride the plane with Nixon to Chicago tonight; I should get my luggage out of the bus and into one of the staff cars. He also wants to know what the press is making of the

Stevens Point performance. Several reporters ask him if
the four points Nixon rattled off are part of a position
paper on Latin America. "No. He surprised me. I had
heard some of that dam-stuff from him in private, but not
all put together just this way. That's what's so dam-
amazing about this dam-guy; he's got all the dam-infor-
mation stored up there, and if you touch any dam-subject
out it comes." (Pat uses his idiosyncratically turned prefix
much as the ancient Greeks scattered particles, to distribute emphases.) Before the campaign began, Buchanan
described for me his Middle East trip, during which the
Israeli war broke out: "The Boss was talking to all these
dam-officials in Israel, and he knew as much of the dam-
position of the Arabs and Russians as they did. He sat
there sketching all the dam-possibilities, and amazed the
officials. That's the way he is. Take any political situation
in the dam-world, and he has war-gamed it this way and
that, considering every which way it might go."

7:00 P.M., FOND DU LAC: Ill-omened name for a
town that manufactures outboard motors. But another
solid Republican district (the sixth, Congressman Steiger's
district)—good spot for a Lincoln Day dinner, perhaps
the twentieth at which Nixon has had a speech to give
(his first was delivered in 1948, at Bill Scranton's invitation, in Pennsylvania). Charlie McWhorter is at the press
table, but he keeps bouncing up to greet old friends as
they mount the dais or drift by it—young Bill Steiger,
plump Ody Fish, Joe this and Jim that. While "Los Ban-
ditos" tootle their imitation Tijuana, the Nixons arrive,
she ducking her tight nods of acknowledgment, he with his
fixed smile behind which the eyes burrow and surface,
war-gaming the situation; flash up and move back down—
down somewhere, to chambers that *must* exist but have
not been plumbed. He has the effrontery, for which he
may never be forgiven, of carrying out before the public
an embarrassingly private set of eyes, eyes unable to rest
vacuously on the pomp of Fond du Lac's Lincoln Day
bunting.

I am sitting, now, just below the dais; I see him and not
his shadow. There are no multiple images crossing, com-
plicating, in some measure canceling each other. Yet in the
very motions of the man there seems some unintended
syncopation—not mere duplicity (Tricky Dick), but mul-

tiplicity (new Nixons to the *n*th degree, and each old one jerking still at one part of his frame or face, giving a lack of focus to him even when he stands, in his customary dark suit, before the lights and cameras).

It is easy to fall prey to Herblockism—the reverse of being star struck. Kennedy was prettier than Nixon— which should not matter to anyone but adolescent girls. Nixon has a pear face, advancing at you about the mouth and jowls, receding from you about the brow and eyes; yet it is worse than phrenology, it is some weird prosopology, to blame ideology on genes, or try to read character from facial contour. Nixon's physical reflexes are not very good; he was a clumsy second-string player on the Whittier College football team. Some of his poor focus is probably nothing but poor reflexes.

The introduction of the honored guest is standard fare, like our slices of meat glued soggily together: Lincoln "bound up the nation's wounds after the war" (he didn't, he didn't live to). "Even his foes said he was a man of unquestioned integrity" (on the contrary, some of his friends wondered at times if he was a crook). Then something about "illusions of grandeur," and "attributes of computence," and—moving on to Nixon—"simularities between he and the Great Emancipator." It is a speech that could not be given without notes—all *studied* clusters of cliché.

Nixon, on the contrary, rarely speaks from notes, and he likes everyone to know this: after the introduction, men move the bulky wooden podium away, and Nixon stands there gesturing stiffly, shielded by nothing but the bar of microphone stand. There is no obvious simularity between he and the Great Emancipator. Nixon is (relatively) short and glib, not the kind to swap pungent stories in the back room. But there are some resemblances. Two big posters with Lincoln's features flank Nixon. The Emancipator, too, was a caricaturist's dream, an ugly fellow easily Herblockized. Both men, despite a natural reticence, were successful courtroom pleaders. Both learned the electoral process inside and out, clean side and dirty, and were proud of the fact that they could play this dangerous game with the best and with the worst—though it was not easy for either of them. Tricky Abe.

But Lincoln, though unimpressive as an orator, knew how to convey some of his private vision in words. He was a classical rhetorician, familiar with all the schoolboy tropes. Yet, like all poets, he used the standard techniques to speak what was original in him. "Bind up the nation's wounds"—the bleeding body politic is an old worn image; but Lincoln made it, irrevocably, his. Nixon, up there, pivots and rattles words impressively; but they have no core. It is not because he has not "made them his" at a certain level. The newsmen have heard them all before. It is easy to take notes (few of the reporters know shorthand): "Let the time . . ." stands for, "Let the time never come when the forces that desire victory have a military superiority over the forces that desire peace." "Some courts . . ." stands for, "Some of the courts have gone too far to weaken the peace forces as against the criminal forces." "Ground . . ." stands for, "There is no ground more important than the ground we stand on . . ." The words are well-organized, well-rehearsed, carefully weighed. Nixon thinks any basic speech through for almost as many weeks as he spends reciting it. He has infuriated many speech writers by tearing all their threads out and restitching a talk in his own idiom, resolutely nonheroic. Even his final draft of "the campaign speech" was too formal for him. Following the text the first time he gave it, in New Hampshire, you could see at first hand his impatience with periodicity, unwillingness to build toward a climax. He kept breaking his own written sentences down into smaller units, piecing them out with "Ands" and "Buts." He shies—as Lincoln did not—from the portentous statement. Yet this personal characteristic does not express personality. It gives his words a stiff matter-of-factness, a disjointedness despite the speech's careful structure. One feels it could break off at any moment, there is no long climb up to a concluding height. The speech does not "swing." It has no rhythm. Its reflexes are faulty.

At this point, I was in danger, once again, of thinking in terms of a beauty contest. The disjointedness of the talk seemed expressed in his face as he scowled (his only expression of thoughtfulness) or grinned (his only expression of pleasure). The features do not quite work together. The famous nose looks detachable. In pictures, its most striking aspect is the ski-jump silhouette ("Bob Hope and I would make a great ad for Sun Valley"), but the aspect that awes one when he meets Nixon is its distressing *width,* accentuated by the depth of the ravine running down its center, and by its general fuzziness (Nixon's "five-o'clock shadow" extends all the way up to his heavy eyebrows, though—like many hairy men—he is balding above the brows' "timberline"). The nose swings far out; then, underneath, it does not rejoin his face in a straight line, but curves far up again, leaving a large but partially screened space between nose and lip. The whole face's lack of *jointure* is emphasized by the fact that he has no very defined upper lip (I mean the lip itself, the thing makeup men put lipstick on, not the moustache area). The mouth works *down* solely, like Charlie McCarthy's—a rapid but restricted motion, not disturbing the heavy luggage of jowl on either side. When he smiles, the space under his nose rolls up (and in) like the old sunshades hung on front porches. The parts all seem to be worked by wires, a doomed attempt to contrive "illusions of grandeur."

One feels guilty noticing such things. It is embarrassing to feel oneself sinking to the level of Mitch Miller at a Miss America contest. And yet that very sensation increases the difficulty of listening to Nixon's words: one does not like to feel embarrassed by a candidate. That must explain a good deal of the popular antipathy to Nixon. One is *embarrassed* to keep meeting the dog one kicked yesterday.

Dwight Chapin adds to the air of a Miss America contest: he looks like a young Bert Parks, with regular, lifeless features and patent-leather hair. He was seven at the time of the Hiss case, and still a student during Nixon's last campaign (in '62). After some time spent in the J. Walter Thompson advertising agency, he became Nixon's personal aide, in charge of extracting him from affairs like this and sorting his staff out into cars. Now he tells me where those cars are, and I go to the one behind Nixon's, accompanied by Ray Price.

If Buchanan, with his Y.A.F. background, is the right wing of Nixon's traveling brain trust, Price—who was in charge of the late *Herald Tribune* editorial page—is the left wing. While Buchanan keeps up the Q and A file, Price works on longer-term projects. Like Buchanan, he went with the Boss on one of his study trips, this one to the Orient. Price drew up the Nixon article on Asian policy that appeared in *Foreign Affairs* last fall—a compound of specifics (SEATO is obsolete, we should strengthen ASPAC) and slogans (China should be treated with "creative counterpressure," "dynamic detoxification" —and so, evasively, through the alphabet).

Price, a handsome young man, is almost a senior citizen on the new staff. He was seventeen during the Hiss case. He is working, now, on the problems of the cities. What, I ask him, does Nixon mean when he says *some* of the courts have weakened the forces of law? "Well, he doesn't want to place all the blame on the Supreme Court." What other courts does he have in mind? "I don't know for sure. Have the courts convicted many rioters?" No. (Riots are not the best time or place in which to collect the hard evidence that leads to convictions.) But is that what Nixon meant? "You'll have to ask him." That is: since the Birchers have preeempted criticism of the Supreme Court, Nixon must try vaguely to attack the court without sounding as if he planned to impeach Earl Warren. Tricky, eh?

I ask Price who Nixon's advisers are—on, say, Asian affairs. "Well, he still has many contacts in the government. I can't name names, of course, since they are still employees of the United States government, and their position can't be used for partisan purposes by a candidate. Most of his contacts are in the foreign service." How about the academy? "Fewer there; I am trying to get him together with some people. But, primarily he is his own expert."

Nixon, despite his vast knowledge, makes few overtures to intellectuals at this stage of his campaign. Those around him are younger than he is; and most of them either came to him on their own (like Buchanan) or were recruited by Len Garment, a silky-smooth lawyer in Nixon's firm. In September of 1967, he arranged interviews with Nixon for Martin Anderson and Richard Whalen. Anderson (eleven years old when Hiss was investigated) is the author of *The Federal Bulldozer;* he drew up Nixon's plan for abolishing the draft (after a Vietnamese settlement) and establishing a computer job-bank for handling unemployment. Whalen—about the same age as Anderson—is the biographer of Joseph Kennedy, the writer-in-residence at Georgetown University's Center for Strategic Studies. He is, as well, prickly and independent. After Miami, he will leave Nixon because the candidate's speeches fail to go beyond slogans. Other recruits for the team were closer at hand; John Mitchell, Frank Lincoln, John Sears, and Tom Evans were all, like Garment himself, members of Nixon's law firm.

10:00 P.M., OSHKOSH: A blowy airport, and the weathered DC-3 that has been tilted up and down in short hops from district to district all day. Mrs. Nixon goes up into the private section with her husband; the rest of the staff fills the twenty seats left in the rear. Rose Mary Woods is in the first seat—the redheaded secretary who joined Nixon's staff when he came to the Senate in 1951 (she had been secretary to a congressman). Rose is the channel through which everyone communicates with the Boss, heroine of the thousand crises that flare up and are extinguished around a public man, who cannot be distracted by them; and villainess to many disgruntled veterans of these crises. She is protective, devoted, inclined to hold a grudge (as newsmen find out when they say bad things about the Boss). Len Hall calls her "the mother hen"— though others add that she has no power Nixon does not want to give her. Hall's criticism of the 1960 campaign, which he was supposed to be managing, is that the Boss made all decisions, kept everything in the palm of his hand, wanted to know everything, do everything, "war-game" everything. The instrument for such total control was the indefatigable Rose.

The DC-3's motors pop and backfire in the moist Wisconsin winter—"Where did you dig this one up, Dwight?" The banter of people traveling together, never more than half-relaxed, pops and backfires as the plane rocks over runways, settles down to serious roaring, gets itself determinedly into the air. After we have been airborne for several minutes, Pat Buchanan, muttering about the dam-winds, leans and does stiff-legged involuntary curtsies down the aisle: the Boss will see me now.

Up in the forward cabin, only two lights are on—those picking out the seats on either side of a card table. Mrs. Nixon's unflamboyant red hair, in a cotton-puff hairdo, glitters dully under one light. The other picks out her husband's great declivity of nose. Murmuring politely, she puts out a hand to brace herself (it is a redhead's hand, full of freckles) and goes back to talk with Rose. I slide in under the little forward spotlight, as Nixon clicks his own light off, sinks his head back into shadow, and pulls his overcoat around him (the plane is cold as well as noisy, I have to lean forward out of my little pool of light toward his darkness, straining to hear him).

I had been told that Nixon's technique, in these midair interviews, is to filibuster on the first question, so I should ask what I really want to know at the outset—"Give him your high hard one right off"—or I might never get him around to it. Unfortunately, I had no high hard one. Besides, how does one outtrick Tricky? I knew that for the most intricate Q, he would have a well-prepared A. So I did not fool with Vietnam and stuff. What I would like was some insight into the man muffled in the dark across from me. I remembered that Nixon has referred quite often to Theodore Roosevelt. Sometimes men's heroes reveal their aspirations. I asked if he felt any special affinity to the Republican Roosevelt. "Not so much in ideas." Pause. His answer was quiet, and there was none of that nervous speed of reply that characterizes him in public. "I guess I'm like him in one way only: I like to be in the arena. I have seen those who have nothing to do—I could be one of them if I wanted—the people just lying around at Palm Beach. Nothing could be more pitiful." His voice had contempt in it, not pity.

Two things surprised me—the nature of the emotion that showed through, and the fact that it *did* show. His voice had a different timbre to it—a resonance of selfhood, a little unguardedness (very little, he is a politician twenty-four hours a day). Out in the light, he had splintered into shadows. Here in shadow he solidified, drew himself together, stopped gesturing. The first time I saw him was at a reception, where he sailed resolutely through sticky clusters of people, using his hands, out front, for prow; clasping them, sweeping them to make a point (and make a path), making the rounds. On the platform, he keeps his hands in a ball over his stomach—there is no podium to rest them on, and he would have to lift them too far to get a gesture launched if they hung at his sides. His motions are standardized—using the fingers on his right hand to count off points on his left hand; hammering balled hand into cupped hand; "on the one hand" (left arm woodenly out from the elbow), "on the other" (right arm out). But he mixes one special gesture in—a fluttering of the fingers that suggests confetti falling (he uses it for comic denial, along with a grimace that turns his eyes up in his head—both are comic in ways not intended).

I had wondered if he keeps his hands so protectively before him in private. I heard conflicting reports: Pat Buchanan said no, but a political figure who had a friendly recent conference with Nixon told me he put his hands together in a prayer-clasp, then flipped them back and forth all through the conversation, saying, "But the *other* side of the coin . . ." War games.

In the plane, he wrapped his arms around him in the cold and did not gesture at all. There was no fence out in front of him. And no face. Perhaps they come to much the same thing. It is unfair to judge Nixon as the least pretty of the candidates. But, as he talked without the gesticulating accents in his voice, with no movement of his hands or (so far as I could see into the shadow) of his caricature features, it seemed that the face *does* matter, because it affects the man behind it. Perhaps a Rockefeller, or Romney, or Reagan, or Percy, or Lindsay does not live entirely on the surface; still, each one could do so if he wanted—it is a very pleasant surface. And if none of them lives *entirely* there, it pays each to do a good deal of commuting to that pleasant locale. It would not pay Nixon at all. He must be aware that people vote for him despite his appearance; he speaks, always, across a barrier. To carry that barrier about with one, to *be* that barrier, must introduce a painful complexity into one's approach toward fickle things like television and reporters and New Hampshire voters. One gets the impression, watching Nixon's brain turn rapidly in public behind the slowly working mask, that he is challenging one, saying, "Which are you going to advert to? What is important to you?" While he is being tested as a candidate, he feels he is a test of others' seriousness.

Seriousness. Responsibility. He has no respect for those "lying around at Palm Beach." The Republican candidates who had hopes for the nomination in 1968 were all extravagantly serious, bad at small talk, not known for their ability to relax. Nixon plays golf, but dutifully. Romney hits three balls and runs from shot to shot on the golf course, so he won't waste any time playing *golf.* Rockefeller indulges in art-collecting as a form of philanthropy. Percy exercises feverishly in his private swimming pool. Only Reagan seems able to play—but then, he *is* a player.

If all of them were locked in a room, forbidden to talk about politics, they would bore each other to death within a week.

Nixon, Percy, and Reagan worked their way through college in the thirties, when a college degree was still hard to get, and still worth getting. (Romney tried several times and could not make it through.) The Depression even affected Rockefeller, up in his financial stratosphere: he wanted to be a "regular fellow" (the very language he used) at Dartmouth, and asked for a campus job; but he was gently convinced that he would be depriving some poor student of a job. All the future candidates were ambitious: they dutifully participated in one sport (the minimum required of campus leaders in the thirties): football for Nixon and Reagan, soccer for Rockefeller, water polo for Percy. Nixon, Reagan, and Percy were made class or student body presidents. But only Nixon, in this dreary club, consistently got high grades. In a serious field, he outseriously them all. Locked in that room, under the drone of boredom, he would probably die last. (Romney would go first, singing Mormon hymns of horror at men's shallowness.) Nixon would survive by studying the signs of disintegration in the others. He was known, in law school, for his "iron butt." He "studies" everything—even the procedure for ordering properly sliced tomatoes in a restaurant (a process he described at great length before Mark Harris, to avoid the ordeal of spontaneous small talk).

Our conversation in the plane moved from Palm Beach into "the arena." I asked Nixon if he thought he could handle the presidency in this period. "Yes. It is a time when a man who knows the world will be able to forge a while new set of alliances, with America taking the lead in solving the big problems. We are now in a position to give the world all the good things that Britain offered in her Empire without any of the disadvantages of nineteenth-century colonialism." You think we have a kind of manifest destiny? "No, not in Beveridge's sense—though Bowers' book on Beveridge is one of the most instructive I have read." (Score one for Nixon, the grind. I wonder if any of the other candidates ever heard of Claude Bowers? We'll charitably give them Albert Beveridge.) "You asked me if Teddy Roosevelt is my hero. Not in the sense that Wilson is. I think he was our greatest President of this

century. You'll notice, too, that he was the best-educated."
(Score two for Nixon; he knows he is the only Republican candidate who maintained high grades in school, and who stayed in school after his four years of college.)
"Wilson had the greatest vision of America's world role. But he wasn't practical enough. Take his 'open agreements openly arrived at.' That is not the way diplomacy is conducted. The Vietnamese war, for instance, will be settled at secret high-level negotiations. The Johnson administration has boxed itself in where it can't undertake these. But a new administration could and would."

What about the home front? Do you think you could talk to militant black leaders, bring peace back to our cities? "Well, you have to be conceited to be in this business; and this will sound conceited. But I think I could do it as well as any man. I'm very good at one-to-one relationships. You'll notice that I don't have any witnesses here; I never have Pat [Buchanan] take notes on my private interviews. I think that when a third person is present, one is distracted, wondering what *his* reaction is. Or people sometimes show off to the third man. But if there are just two of you, you can concentrate totally on each other." Not on "image." Not on "face." Nixon would like to carry on all his dealings away from the public—he *does* like darkness; he can only be personal where "personality" is not an issue. Revelations like the Checkers speech were violations; and he has all the scars of a violated man. A friend close to him in his vice-presidential days says he came back from humiliating talks with Eisenhower almost in tears, wanting no one to see him.

This led to my next question: "Don't you feel it demeaning that you have to get out and shake hands and grin; that you have to worry about makeup and lighting?" "Well, on the television thing, yes. Isn't that a hell of a thing—that the fate of a great country can depend on camera angles? I get so impatient with the whole process that I refuse to take coaching. But as to shaking hands, I like to do that—it brightens people's lives to meet a celebrity; and, as you may have noticed, I'm rather good at it." He is not. I watched him, close up, shaking hands for three hours as an endless line passed by him in New Hampshire. Behind the polite ducking nods, empty jokes, forced amiability, Nixon's mind was almost visibly fidgeting, worrying about the multiple journalistic "third person" that was photographing him, studying him over the line's crawl, criticizing every move. Beside him his wife stood the three hours in high heels, her face chilled with smiles, her mouth puckering as the ninetieth child went by and had to be admired with a long-distance kiss. Her eyes are not like her husband's, here, there, and everywhere; they follow each person who moves by her, some coming close to whisper, some straying wide to size her up—left to right, she keeps them each in focus; but, for the split second when she turns back, right to left, to greet a new face, the eyes blur momentarily, blanking out all unnecessary sensation connected with this ordeal. She is saving herself, in split seconds, all the long afternoon that she spends herself. On her way to the school where these crowds waited for her, newsmen caught Mrs. Nixon and asked how she felt at the outset of another long campaign. She bravely answered, "I love it; one meets so many old friends again." But I watched her hands as she said it; the freckled hands were picking at each other, playing with gloves, trying to still each other's trembling. There is one thing worse than being a violated man. Being a violated man's wife.

It intrigued me that Nixon, otherwise very conscious of his public handicaps, should think he is good at handshaking. I asked what he meant: "I am able to treat each person as an individual. I have more sympathy with the so-called unimportant people than many intellectuals have. I guess that's why you guys in the press say I do better in the small towns than in the big cities. I admit it. That's true. But some liberals who claim to have so much 'concern' don't give a damn about the individual." That is the answer: it is part of his "one-to-one" philosophy. "The last person who should be arrogant is the intellectual, who *should* know better, but . . ." He broke off; the contempt had come back into his voice. Palm Beach idlers, arrogant intellectuals. No wonder he thinks he can talk to the common men. He feels—whether happily or not—a special bond with them. I recalled a memorandum he composed just after the Hiss case (Earl Mazo was allowed to consult it): Hiss, Nixon wrote, "was rather insolent toward me from the time that I insisted on bringing Frankfurter's name in, and from that time my suspicion concerning him continued to grow." Hiss was not only a perjurer; he was "rather insolent toward me." The arrogant intellectual. It was Johns Hopkins and Harvard Law against Whittier College. That helps explain early Nixon outbursts like: "If the American people understood the real character of Alger Hiss, they would boil him in oil."

Romney and Percy and Reagan are Midwesterners. But all three made a great deal of money comparatively early in life, and moved in wide circles. Percy picked out his Kenilworth mansion when he was still an impoverished teen-ager. Romney was an "operator" in Washington lobbyist circles (aluminum, automobiles) long before he went to American Motors. And Reagan, destiny's tot, was sipping his soda in the right drugstore before he was out of his twenties. Nixon, who worked even harder than single-minded men like Percy and Romney, never had real money until 1960; of the available Republicans he had been, for years, the most provincial.

Whittier was a Quaker town when Nixon was growing up in it, Whittier College a Quaker school. And Nixon's family had such a Quaker tradition that Jessamyn West wrote *The Friendly Persuasion* about his (and her) great-grandfather. After Nixon's successful career in the little Quaker college, his faculty adviser could still recommend him to the Duke Law School in these terms: "If he has any handicap, it is his lack of sophistication." The lack was a militant one. Even little Whittier had its (comparatively) high society—the Franklins, a college social club affecting formal dress among the citrus trees. Nixon founded an underdog group, symmetrically non-Franklinian, called the Orthogonians (squares), with a four-square slogan of "Beans, Brawn, Brains and Bowels." One has difficulty imagining Alger Hiss's initiation into the Orthogonians. Nixon's first great successes were in debate, at which he excelled—by the triumph of content over style. The square would outsmart the smart guys, with the help of his "iron butt."

The desire to win was there early—to meet the smart guys, to get out of Whittier. He has described several times the way he yearned after Union Pacific trains that passed near his home. He listened for those trains at night. His attempts to get out of the town began early: in his final year at Duke's law school, he went to New York and applied to two major firms for a job (one of them was John Foster Dulles' firm); but neither wanted him. Then he lowered his sights considerably and, with his fresh law

degree, tried to become an FBI agent. The Bureau had
just undergone a budget cut, and it did not want him. So
he went back to Whittier as a lawyer till Pearl Harbor,
when he went to Washington to apply for war work (he
eased over slowly to the Navy, a difficult transition for a
Quaker). Back to Whittier for a political base, and the
campaign of a veteran returned from war. Back again to
California, after his defeat in 1960. As soon as he thought
he was washed up in politics (and so did not need "a
base"), he went to New York and a large law firm—the
fulfillment of his trip that last year at Duke. Yet he told
people he liked New York because it gave him privacy,
not for the city's society or high life or art. Nixon was
alien there, and liked that. His footloose habits are not
merely part of his determined study of world affairs. In
1960, on Election Day, he drove into Mexico while returns
were coming in. On the day of his Senate election, he held
a disconsolate picnic by the sea—keeping on the move,
trying to distract himself. He escapes, not to his home but
into anonymity and distance—down the Union Pacific
track.

Not one of the "smart guys," he always felt challenged
to win the victory of content over style. And he does his
homework. The great example was the Hiss case. In 1946,
"the Communist issue" was just being born. (Nixon later
claimed it had *not* arisen.) The Dies Committee—or Rankin Committee as it was then being called—was already
controversial. Eleanor Roosevelt was saying that communists should not be allowed to teach in American schools
—but that she would fear for the health of a campus that
had no communist students. A schizophrenia was developing toward our World War II allies. Nixon, who had won
Congressman Jerry Voorhis' seat by an attack on his "left-
wingism," did not know much about communism, but he
soon put his "iron butt" to work on the subject. In that
1947 class, he sat on the Labor Committee with two other
freshmen who were interested in the issue, two conservative Roman Catholics, Jack Kennedy of heavily Catholic
Massachusetts and Charles Kersten of heavily Catholic
(Polish) Wisconsin. Kersten came from Milwaukee, where
the communist infiltration of unions was a burning issue;
he and Kennedy held some Labor Committee hearings in
Milwaukee.

Nixon, sizing up his colleagues, decided Kersten knew

a great deal about communism (more, clearly, than young Jack Kennedy); so he formed an alliance with him to study the problem. I asked Nixon about those days when he was new in Washington. "Charlie Kersten is a deeply religious man, whose anti-communism is of a philosophical sort. It's too bad he came from that terrible district (the old fifth), where he couldn't get reelected after his third term. He taught me most of what I know about communism." Later, I asked Kersten if this was true: "Not really. I led him to the people who really taught him—especially Father Cronin. But Dick was very curious about communism even before I met him. After some hearing in which he noticed the line of my questioning, he came over and asked me where I had obtained my information. So we tackled the problem together."

Their investigation was simultaneously naive and sophisticated. The two young congressmen trudged from embassy to embassy of the Iron Curtain lands, asking whether there was a free press, or free speech, in each country. Kersten told me: "I remember the Czechoslovak ambassador was very nervous while we were questioning, and we didn't know why. The next day we heard about the coup that had put Gottwald in power—what the ambassador, clearly, had been hearing the day before, at the very time when we were asking all those questions about freedom and communism in his country. That was in February of forty-eight."

Kersten, a courtly Milwaukee lawyer, had been doing his own homework, and he took Nixon to see his teachers. "I introduced Dick to the then Monsignor Fulton Sheen, who had just finished a book on communism. We spent a long evening discussing it, and he gave us autographed copies. The book had not yet appeared. Then I took him to see Father Cronin." That meeting, in 1947, determined the outcome of the Hiss case. Nixon was about to stumble on information that made the encounter of Whittier College with Harvard Law a kind of rigged bout between David and Goliath.

Father John Cronin was a student of John A. Ryan, the pioneer of Catholic social thought. He followed Ryan into the union movement during the forties, and he has remained true to this heritage by working with civil rights groups in the sixties. In the interval—through most of the fifties, while he was formally employed by the National Catholic Welfare Conference in Washington—he devoted himself to Richard Nixon, as a kind of one-man brain trust. The relationship grew out of their work on the Hiss investigation.

I went to see Father Cronin, who is now a teacher behind the scrolled Renaissance façade of St. Mary's Seminary in Baltimore. He is a white-haired, pink-faced, very gentle man, known as a sympathetic adviser to seminarians with problems. "Most of the walking wounded make it as far as my door." I asked him how he got involved with Nixon and Hiss. "Early in the forties, when I was working with the dockside unions in Baltimore, some of my friends came to me with complaints that they were being voted out of union offices by suspiciously packed meetings. I did a little investigating and found these were communist cadres at work. About that time the FBI approached me to find out what I knew about this. Soon I was in touch with Bill Sullivan [now an assistant director of the FBI]. I kept track of what was going on for them. And I got to know many agents intimately. Cardinal—then Archbishop —Mooney heard of my knowledge in this area; so he asked me to prepare a secret report on communism for the American bishops, and I was able to use classified material that had come my way." Did the bishops take any action on your report? "About the only immediate recommendation I made was that the bishops take steps to save China, by countering our shift of sympathy from the Nationalists. Oddly enough, that was blocked by the inaction of Cardinal Spellman. But by this time I was known, in Catholic circles, as something of an expert on communism. Charlie Kersten heard this, and came to see me. Later, he brought Nixon, and I told them about certain Communists in atomic espionage rings and in the State Department." Did you name names? "Yes." Was one of the names Alger Hiss? "Yes." This was a year and a half before Whittaker Chambers was called by the House committee to confirm testimony given by Elizabeth Bentley—when Hiss was first named publicly as a communist.

There were three things about this episode that interested me in my conversation with Father Cronin: that Nixon did not name Hiss himself (or any of the other people mentioned by Father Cronin); that, when Hiss was brought into the public investigation by Chambers, Nixon did not betray his prior knowledge, or its source; and that, nonetheless, acting on that knowledge, he pursued Hiss with great determination. Just how good his homework had been is revealed by an incident Nixon alluded to during my interview with him on the plane. "Charlie Kersten was the one who told me to go put the evidence before John Foster Dulles." He was referring to a threat that arose at the very outset of the Hiss case. Thomas Dewey was the Republicans' presidential candidate that year, and his foreign-policy expert was Dulles. Dulles, the Chairman of the Carnegie Endowment for International Peace, had supported Alger Hiss's appointment as president of that organization; he still thought Hiss innocent of the charges being made against him. Nixon heard that Dulles was going to defend Hiss publicly, committing the Republican Party. He mentioned this to Kersten: "I suggested we go up to New York that very night," Kersten recalls, "and present the evidence to Dulles. We went, and over a period of several hours Dick persuaded not only John Foster Dulles but Allen Dulles too, who was with him."

Nixon made another important convert early on—Bert Andrews, chief of the *Herald Tribune*'s Washington bureau. Andrews had just won a Pulitzer Prize for reporting the inequities of security-clearance; yet Nixon, using his intense homework, convinced him, too, that Hiss was lying, and had his help all through the investigation. The preparation was paying off. When Nixon—a first-term congressman, as lowly a creature as exists in Washington —pushed the Hiss case, he seemed to be taking a great risk. It was less than it looked. He had cards all up and down his sleeves, and inside his vest.

Father Cronin tells the story: "Ed Hummer was one of the FBI agents I had worked with. He could have got in serious trouble for what he did, since the Justice Department was sitting on the results of the Bureau's investigation into Hiss—the car, the typewriter, etc. But Ed would call me every day, and tell me what they had turned up; and I told Dick, who then knew just where to look for things, and what he would find."

Nixon, the hardworking lawyer, was a hot political property after Hiss's conviction. In 1952 Ike wanted him. Nixon had McCarthy's issue; but, as Father Cronin puts it, he used a rifle instead of a shotgun. Besides, he was young (thirty-nine) and partisan—to balance elderly Ike's ambiguous party background. "After the Hiss case," Father Cronin says, "I didn't see much of Dick. As a senator, he concentrated more on his state's problems. But then, when he became Vice-President, I began writing speeches for him. In fact, from 1953 to 1960, I was his only speech writer." How much of your time did you spend on this? "Most of it. I take credit for what was called the new Nixon *that* time around. I was able to give a little background to his treatment of social questions, which I had been studying all my life. Naturally, he tore my speeches apart and remade them in his style; but occasionally he was too busy, and had to deliver the text as I had written it, and that's when he would get the full text printed in the *New York Times*. There is something in Nixon that will not let well enough alone."

Nixon began his '68 campaign with a big political dinner in Concord, New Hampshire. After he had come in, but before his speech, the M.C. was having microphone trouble. Nixon leaped up and tossed one of his standard comments over the lectern: "I don't mind Johnson's turning the lights off in the White House, but you'd think he'd leave us alone up here in New Hampshire." Then, as the M.C. introduced Nixon's two daughters with a feeble joke, the candidate popped up again, but got to the microphone too late for his topper—the M.C. had moved on to another subject. Later he made another lunge, also aborted. As a member of the second string at Whittier, Nixon rarely got into a football game: he cost the team too much by his eagerness, which regularly made him leap offside. In interviews, he answers rapidly, yet corrects himself just as rapidly; when an interviewer is beginning his second question, Nixon cuts him off with, "To put it in a nutshell . . ." or, "Let me answer it this way . . ." He boils his answer down, refines it, reworks it three times. Father Cronin says that his speeches always got worse from one draft to another: "He keeps simplifying, simplifying. He can't leave things alone."

Nixon is not indecisive; it is just that he makes five decisions as he sees fifty new possibilities. He always hears an objector over his shoulder, shifts his weight to meet attack from some new quarter. Len Hall claims Nixon had decided not to debate Kennedy in 1960; then he decided he should; then he regretted the decision—"I could win the debate and lose the election"—so that, having accepted the challenge, he did not debate. "He leaned over backwards being obsequious to Kennedy." He tried too hard. He ran so fast after the train that he fell on his face.

And he takes his falls hard. People forget that he is Irish, both sides of his family—a black Irishman, melancholy, prone to despondency. "He went into a deep depression early in nineteen sixty," Father Cronin recalls, "as soon as it was clear that Rockefeller would not be a rival. Instead of organizing his campaign, putting together position papers and all that, he brooded on the responsibility. I think he was overcome by the thought of it." Father Cronin struggles with his pipe, and with an unwillingness to say anything critical of a friend: "Dick has great physical and moral courage, but there is an element of self-doubt very deep in him." Again the uneasiness: "I don't think that Pat helps him." Why not? "Well, in the nineteen fifty-six campaign, Dick prepared the last draft of a speech on a tape recorder; but some aide had not fixed the recorder properly, so nothing was on the tape. After all that work, he had to deliver an earlier draft—mine. His heart was not in it, so he gave it a poor delivery. And Pat chewed the hell out of him in front of the staff." At one point, Earl Mazo revealed, Mrs. Nixon made her husband put an agreement to give up politics in writing. Then, when he told her at a dinner party that he meant to run for governor of California, she "chewed him out" again in public.

Yet, even alone, Nixon goes on. I asked about his reasons for running as our plane neared Chicago: "There is an awful mood abroad—a desire to just blow everything up. There must be a new vision of America's role if we are to shake ourselves out of this nihilism." He hugs himself almost as if he felt the chill of the world's mood. He has an extraordinary empathy with despondent people—which helps justify his surprising claim that he is "good with people." Pat Buchanan first learned of this after the 1966 tour of duty, when Nixon helped elect many Republicans to office. "I woke up the day after the election," Pat told me. "We had won a big victory, but I felt let down, I couldn't understand why, I guess it was just not having that next day's deadline to work at. The Boss called me and must have noticed something in my voice, because he said: 'Are you feeling blue? I know what it's like. Don't stop working altogether, or you'll feel miserable and useless. Taper off gradually, over a week or so, and *then* take a vacation.'"

Another example of this empathy occurred right after the invasion of the Bay of Pigs. Earl Mazo had an appointment with Nixon, who had just returned from seeing Kennedy. "You remember," Mazo told me in Washington, "that was when Kennedy was reaching out for help from everybody—Eisenhower, Nixon, Republicans on the Hill." Mazo went into Nixon's office and found him on the phone. "He kept making call after call, while I waited for nearly an hour. He was calling Republican officials. Some he asked, others he begged, some he even threatened. He was telling them not to attack Kennedy on this thing. When he finally got to me, I said, 'What is this? Here's the perfect issue for your party. Why aren't you using it?' He told me, 'I just saw a crushed man today. He needs our help. I told him to go upstairs and have a drink with his wife, and avoid making any decision until things brighten up a bit.'"

It is advice he has not always followed himself. He has done things in his black moods—dictated a resignation from the ticket in '52, yielded precipitately in '60 (hurting others on the ticket in areas where votes were still being counted), nagged at the press in '62. He pushes himself very hard, on principle. He thinks, erroneously, that he performs best out on the borderline of fatigue, when he has worried a thing to its bitter end. There is a Celtic strain of asceticism in him. His wife says, "Neither Dick nor I care a bit for creature comforts." And Nixon complained when he was put in a soft chair for a TV interview: "One has to be uncomfortable to do one's best thinking. I don't sleep before a big decision; yet I am at my best then."

All those who were considered, early in 1968, for the Republican nomination had fundamentalist backgrounds—strict Baptist for Rockefeller, Mormon for Romney, Christian Scientist for Percy, Quaker for Nixon, Goldwaterism for Reagan. In fact, most had been, at one time or another, lay preachers. Romney did his missionary work. Rockefeller and Nixon both taught Sunday school. Reagan gave the major revivalist speech of 1964. This background showed in the fact that none of the Republicans who aspired to the presidency was a smoker; and, though Romney and Percy were the only strict teetotalers, Rockefeller and Nixon rarely take a drink (wine for Rockefeller, beer for Nixon). One might rashly conclude from this that politics is a godly occupation. Or, nearer the truth, that it is a fanatic one. Or that it is a *substitute* for religion. (Or that the candidates' backgrounds were mere coincidence.) But, for whatever reason, there *was* a similarity to them all (all but Nixon)—a straightforwardness and lack of mystery that goes with fundamentalist simplicities. Romney and Percy are theological true believers; Reagan is a political one. It gives uncomplicated vigor to their efforts and impact. Rockefeller is an example of a more subtle, but still common type—the self-made man's philanthropic descendant. First-generation millionaires tend to give us libraries. The second and third generation think they should give us themselves. (Naturally, some people want to look this gift horse in the mouth —which may be the reason Rockefeller keeps his teeth on display.)

Only in Nixon does fundamentalism lead to complexity. I asked him—in a plane getting more and more buffeted by winds, uncomfortable, good for his thinking—what effect his Quakerism had on him. "Oh, I suppose it is the stress on privacy. Friends believe in doing 'their own thing,' not making a display of religion. That's why I never use God's name in speeches, or quote the Bible." But some Quaker meetings have the open prayer. "Yes, but that's not our branch. We have silent prayer—even the silent grace. I have a great respect for other people's privacy. That's why I can't go out and grab people and hug them and carry on. I suppose the Quakerism just strengthened my own temperament here. I'm an introvert in an extrovert profession."

I asked if he thought he could convey his private vision of America's future to public crowds—and I remarked on his lack of rhetorical "grandness," his whittling away at ambitious effects. "Well, there will be some lift in later speeches; but these primaries are not the place for it. I'll have some later. Sure, some is needed. But, you know, people have known me too long for me to come on all of a sudden talking like Adlai Stevenson. If I am to convince people, it will be in simple declarative sentences, by the force of the facts." Content over style.

11:30 P.M., CHICAGO: We are on the ground, after nudging slowly through bad weather onto Midway Field (the original plan, to go to O'Hare, was changed). Nixon keeps talking while the plane empties; walks abstractedly down the aisle, trying to remember a book on Wilson he would recommend; turns at the door—"I'll send you the title. Does Pat Buchanan have your address?" Rose Woods's brother, the Sheriff of Cook County, has cars waiting to take us to the Blackstone. I ride with Bob Ellsworth, the interim campaign manager; then, at the hotel, rush to my room and spend two hours copying down everything I can remember of the conversation with Nixon.

I took no notes. I watched him all the time, trying to let him lead the talk, to see where he would take it. He returned most often to Wilson, to the student as President. "But Wilson was not practical enough." Nixon takes great pride in knowing the nuts and bolts of the electoral game; *he* can be as tough and shrewd as the next guy. He has hurt his small reputation for candor by showing newsmen how he tailors his approach to different audiences. But he is not just the calm technician he pretends to be—if he were, he would have been more successful in the past, quieter under stress, surrounded by other old pros from old battles. He is, instead, a brooding Irish puritan. And a lonely man. These qualities might be handicaps for a President (though Lincoln was even more melancholy, and downright neurotic); but they made Nixon the most interesting candidate of his party. He still heard trains in the night. It seemed unlikely, in the first months of 1968, that he would ever catch them. But after years of drudgery and setback, he could still hear them.

2. The Center Cannot Hold

"Some of them think they are seeing a mirage, but it isn't a mirage they're seeing."

—George Wallace

THERE WAS A SENSE EVERYWHERE, in 1968, that things were giving. That man had not merely lost control of his history, but might never regain it. That palliatives would not serve, and nothing but palliatives could be found. That we had slipped gears somewhere, and a train of mismeshings was chewing the machinery up. There was something in the atmosphere that made it seem faintly obscene for a presidential candidate, in a country that admires "happy warriors" and the banishing of fear, to use the phrase "politics of joy." The cities were in danger, and the college campuses, and the public schools.

And the President. Lyndon Johnson traveled nowhere, toward the end, for fear. He was allowed to run out his term because he had, in effect, abdicated. It was the year of the Secret Service men, their faces variously angled out across the crowd as it faced in, each trained pair of eyes raking an assigned arc. A time of *mutual* surveillance, when those of different races, when young and old, when policemen and ordinary citizens passed, if possible, on opposite sides of the street, warily; or—too late to cross over—went by each other with eyes down. A time of locking up and closing in, of "How to Defend Yourself." Michigan housewives pushing baby buggies down to the pistol range for practice.

When assassination made commissions—and even men —ask why America is sick. (Not that a Sirhan or Ray or whoever is "America." The point, all along, was that we welcomed the excuse for asking such questions—and assassination gave us too good an excuse.) When one of the

43

first major cities to elect a black mayor became the first to have a full-scale ambush laid for police (because palliatives will not serve). When nonrioting blacks—men layers of oblivion down below the "forgotten American"—wondered whether they should show up for work at parking lots on the night of a Wallace rally. When a middle-aged woman delegate to the Chicago convention, herself a liberal marching out of sympathy with the beaten demonstrators, chose to take a Negro with her through police lines and be arrested, rather than walk off through part of the ghetto ("I'm more afraid of the streets than of jail").

Even the lack of large destructive riots—after the spilled-fire spread of those in April when King was murdered—seemed the result of fear, of edginess about lighting any match lest the whole enterprise go up. And, always, all the year, Wallace. The temptation will be strong to look back on dire predictions of what Wallace might do—throw election into the House of Representatives, capture northern states, get 25 percent of the vote—and say they were exaggerated. The true cause for concern, however, is not what Wallace might have done, but what he did. When Wallace said *he* had made both the major parties talk his own language of law and order, he was wrong. They would have done it without him. He was not the cause but an effect; he was one way of measuring the growth of resentment. His was a weird "third party" —no party at all. It lacked platform, personnel, history, future, or program. It was a one-man phenomenon. At the last minute, General LeMay was pulled only partially in—he could not appear on most states' ballots—and then pushed almost totally back out: his sketch of a partial program in foreign affairs damaged the purity of Wallace's appeal, which was not meliorative, but nihilist. Wallace offered neither palliative nor real cure; just a chance to scream into the darkness. It was a kind of perverse exercise in honesty—a proclamation that the darkness is *there*.

A nihilist vote is something new in America, the home of boosters. In a land of "uplift" it was "downletting," vertiginously so, to realize that this man, this symbol, despite his lack of any real party, or organization, of staff, of funds, of roots, of respectability, nonetheless captured over 13 percent of the national vote. The Wallace voter felt that "the system is breaking down"—that it could no longer protect the citizen (perhaps did not want to), that the citizen was alone and vulnerable, of no concern to the courts, the pointyheads, the diplomats. So throw them out, with their bicycles, briefcases, umbrellas. Tear them down. It was a tortured cry, echoed from unlikely corners: young blacks and students, too, felt that The System was impervious to their concerns. They did not participate any longer, and some thought the way to achieve "participatory democracy" must lie through a prior "destruction of The System as presently constituted." For man had lost control of his history.

Each grievance fed on another. In Chicago, resentment of kids for cops; resentful cops' retaliation; the anger of delegates over this show of naked force; press reaction, followed by a backlash, all across the land, of sympathy for Mayor Daley. In New York, all the resources of our progressive liberal society were set to work upon the school system: federal and state and local money and staff and wisdom; the Ford Foundation; the teachers' union; the community. All this sophistication made the problem worse (some gear had slipped, and the resulting shudder through the works was a measure of the machine's delicacy); and, from below, vestiges of the darkest things in man, of racism and vendetta, sent up minatory exhalations. The very process of discourse was misted over, poisoned, with distrust—there was not only "the credibility gap" in Washington, but a wide resentment toward the vehicles of what must be bad news, or false news. In 1964 many thought it shocking that, at the Republican Convention, delegates turned to the press booths and shook their fists in anger after Eisenhower's criticism of reporters. But by the 1968 convention, cops beat newsmen and broke their cameras. What is more interesting, the demonstrators in the parks were often hostile to the press, suspecting them of being plainclothesmen, or—after their credentials had been established—demanding loyalty to "the revolution" before they would talk. Meanwhile, newsmen who followed Wallace said they felt like patsies, straight men for the candidate's act, so much did he use them to elicit boos and jeers from his crowds. Spiro Agnew got a similar response when he held up a copy of the *New York Times* and mocked it. Disturbed by the angry wash of criticism after Chicago, Reuven Frank, head of NBC News, said of the American viewer: "The

world as reported by television threatens him. It is a short
and understandable step for him to conclude that television threatens him." There was, back of all these localized complaints, basic sense of futility in attempts to
communicate. What one said would be distorted; what
one heard had been confected. We had miles of cables,
batteries of cameras, bouquets of microphones under every nose. And we could not talk to each other.

Each election year is a revelation—in the way the electorate is consulted, wooed, or baffled; in the way issues
are chosen, presented, or evaded; in the demands and
promises made, compromises struck, strains felt tacitly or
voiced. The nation at once celebrates and mourns itself. It
was precisely this period of self-revelation that some men
feared as we entered upon 1968. What would the mirror
show? There was slim hope we could avoid trouble in
the cities, on the campus, in Washington, in Vietnam, during the fevered time of primaries and convention and
campaign and election. The democratic process itself was
considered dangerous, offering as it does so many opportunities for demagogy and demonstration, riot and assassination. Should the Democratic Convention be moved
from Chicago? Be held at all? (There was a moment when
the expected death of Eisenhower, who was struggling in
an oxygen tent after another heart attack, seemed to
offer an excuse for postponing the convention, dashing the
plans and timetable of disrupters.) Could the President of
the United States safely attend the convention of his
party, no matter *where* it was held? Would the riot in
Miami be serious enough to make the causeways go up,
isolating Miami Beach? Were there enough Secret Service
men to go around?

What is hard, and essential, to convey is the *interaction*
of resentments. The bitterness moved in crossing tides, an
acid weave of right and left, old and young. Each shock
deepened a fear, unsettled a hope. When, in the space of
two short weeks, Rockefeller withdrew (again, though
temporarily) from the race for President, Johnson withdrew (temporarily, many thought at first) from the same
race, Dr. King was slain, riots broke out, and Spiro Agnew
shouted at moderate black leaders, a complex weave of
apprehension went forward in each segment of the population. This was a time when some black leaders began
making plans for departure from the country. Men said,

with a forced laugh, that anything could happen, and no one laughed back. It seemed, after the tumult of late March and early April, that the worst had happened. But by June, Senator Kennedy's death made men realize that worse can follow worse indefinitely, no terminal worst in sight.

The year's character is not adequately grasped, however, by looking only at scenes of major disruption— Memphis when King marched the first time and tried to march the second; Washington with machine guns ringing the Capitol while a nearby ghetto burned; Columbia University during the rebels' occupation; strike after strike in New York City; the kitchen in Los Angeles that was meant to be Kennedy's escape route; rioting and three deaths in Miami while convening Republicans looked the other way; Chicago's convention; Ocean Hill–Brownsville and the birth of a new anti-Semitism; San Francisco State College under siege. Eddies of fear, widening from these crises, intensified local and obscure conflicts. Perhaps the best way to suggest the *train* of cumulative anxieties is to look at the sequence of events during two weeks of the fall campaign in one spot—in the city that gave Republicans their vice-presidential candidate (after experiencing the race disturbance that *made* him a candidate).

All through the first weekend in October, demonstrators were arriving in Baltimore for the federal trial of nine Roman Catholics who had burned draft records in a little suburb of the city, Catonsville. This "Catonsville Nine" was in many ways an attractive group. It included two talented brothers—diminutive crewcut Daniel Berrigan, a poet and a Jesuit priest, and tall Philip Berrigan, writer and activist, also a priest, in a religious order founded to do work among the American Negroes. Two "lay brothers," an ex-priest and ex-nun (married to each other), a registered nurse, a volunteer in the Alliance for Progress, an artist—all had done missionary duty of a more conventional sort before they burned the files. Five had been in Latin America on charitable projects, four had spent considerable time working for black equality before they entered the peace movement. Young people, talented, the "Peace Corps types" America was proud of early in the sixties, now indicted as criminals: enemies of society. They had destroyed the records with napalm they

mixed up themselves, from the recipe in an Army handbook ("Burn paper, not men").

Here, in striking form, was the plight of a nation un-
willingly, half-wittedly at war. Self-determination for the
South Vietnamese had been our justification. Yet there
were other reasons all along, reasons unconfessed, more
important; more consistent, without reaching the stage of
open calculation that would make them entirely consistent
—a desire to help the French get off the hook (which we
did, clumsily, by impaling ourselves); a desire to maintain
"presence in Asia" by preventing a tilt and domino-fall of
countries toward China. As usual, we had self-interest at
heart, yet we felt obliged to profess simple altruism (up-
lifters, always)—and each posture, half-adopted, canceled
the other out, giving us a policy not truly in our interest
or in that of the South Vietnamese. We hoped to muddle
through and, instead, muddled farther in.

We staggered from one absurdity to another. Mythical
"advisers" that became an army. A government we helped
unseat mainly because of "religious persecution" adver-
tised by Buddhists who wrote their message in fire, themselves the fuel—though a UN commission later found, on
the scene, that there had been no persecution. All along
we argued that we wanted South Vietnamese independence, yet, in the last weeks of the 1968 campaign, when
the South's elected officials objected to the makeup of
Johnson's peace talks in Paris, we threw off the mask and
said, in effect, that it was our war to dispose of as we
would. We had been telling lies to them all the time, not
deliberately, but as the side effect of lying to ourselves,
pretending we were in command, when accident had
trapped us, when we had lost control of our own history.
There was nothing in the long war's lesion of our best
youth and self-confidence to satisfy any type of man—not
hard anti-communists, nor irenic accommodationists; neither the partisans nor the enemies of Diem, Ky, or the
rest; not guardians of our self-interest, not generals looking
only to the military aspect, not politicians, not moralists,
not anybody.

The resulting anomalies were too painful to look at, so
the nation ignored the war as far as it could (the families
of those dying there could not). It was a war endlessly
written of, photographed, debated—yet it left no image in
the American mind. The reportage was all paddling in

water. The national psyche refused to take any impression. Part of the Catonsville Nine's offense was that they made us remember. This was a war we did not sing songs about, or spin myths for. There was no outpouring of chauvinist movies to stiffen our resolve, making us kill with jolliness. When John Wayne patriotically forced a movie onto the screen with his own money, its iconography was all wrong —an overrefined Nazi-type general and a pretty girl of the resistance thought to be collaborating, yellow updated Dana Wynter and Helmut Dantine playing slant-eyed roles. We had no contemporary image of the war, not even a simplistic one.

How, for a war like this, about which the nation felt so shamefaced, could our legal system prosecute men of the Berrigan sort? Here was one source of widespread resentment. Yet how could we not prosecute? Two of the Nine, Philip Berrigan and artist Thomas Lewis, had been part of "the Baltimore Four" who poured rabbit blood over draft files in the city; they were actually out on bail when they went to Catonsville. Others would later join the "D.C. Nine" to destroy Dow Chemical records. The Nine had, in its turn, inspired another group, the "Milwaukee Fourteen," to burn other records. Most of the Nine had destroyed their draft cards or counseled others to do so. And the way they acted threw doubt on their willingness to let others act freely. The only clerks in the file room they rifled were women; the nine advocates of nonviolence ordered these two not to resist, not to preserve the files entrusted to them—not, in effect, to follow their consciences. When the women tried to hold on, the files were taken away forcibly; one of the women, fifty-nine years old, had her hand cut as the basket was twisted from her; the other woman had to break a window with her telephone receiver to call for help.

The nation was at war; trying ineffectually to extricate itself, but still a nation, and still at war—with laws that should, in equity, bind all. The Nine were not conscientious objectors refusing service when asked, but preachers of strategic disobedience, intent, as they admitted, on maximum harassment of governmental procedure. Even their trial was to be used as a rallying point for further action. Father Dan Berrigan issued a country-wide invitation in the newspapers: "We promise all who come a good time in the company of love and courage, 'legal' proceedings that will blow your mind and open your heart . . . a defense that defends you, a prosecution that prosecutes. What more could one ask, after Chicago, before November 5?" Even if the Nine were not traitors and cowards, or any of the things men called them who did not know them, they were breakers of the law, however conscientious, who should submit to the penalties of law for the sake of conscience—or so it seemed to many. Yet William Kunstler, the famous civil rights lawyer, was on hand to claim the Nine should escape all punishment. New sources for resentment.

And there was more. Flyers sent out by the Peace Action Committee, which ran demonstrations during the trial, invited people to "Agnew Country." There was an implicit connection between what happened here and the hopes of the vice-presidential candidate. He was running as a spokesman for law and order. What if law and order should break down in his own city (while he was far off, campaigning)? That was the reason some demonstrators came. The flyers said: "'Agnew Country' is not as placid as Mr. Agnew would like to believe. The guv's recent campaign statements concerning 'subversives,' academic freedom and dissent, as well as his vendetta against H. Rap Brown and his abysmal attitudes toward the black community in general will be challenged." Challenged how? The flyers listed such things as "mass distribution of printed material in downtown areas during rush traffic." Policemen recognized, naturally, this challenge to what is called "confrontation," the planned brush with law under conditions of maximum tension. The Baltimore *Free Press* got out a special edition for incoming demonstrators: "We demand the Nine be set free. We demand an end to injustice. But because the Nine will not be freed, and because injustice will not cease simply because we voice these demands, we see more and more clearly the path we and our allies must take. And this path does not lead through the courts." The possibilities for conflict were, some thought, exhilarating.

That same weekend, Dan Berrigan, the poet, went out to the area where Agnew had lived, and addressed students of Towson State College. He was invited by people calling themselves the campus chapter of SDS, though they were only a small group of friends who meant, some day, to affiliate themselves with SDS. But police intelligence agents, wandering in dazed incognito over the campus, had taken them at their word and marked them down, with shaking hands, as a local arm of the student SMERSH. The agents were apprehensive because Agnew was going to risk his closest appearance to Baltimore on this campus, one week from the day Berrigan spoke.

It was not a campus that cared much for Agnew; no state campus did. Even staid good Republicans were mad at him. Towson, a little teachers' college, had almost doubled its enrollment and faculty in the process of becoming a liberal arts college; yet teachers' salaries remained scandalously low, and faculty turnover led to a precarious scramble from one year to the next. A faculty organization had for months been trying to reach the governor (who was not yet, when they began, a nominee for Vice-President), without success. Surrounding this (the most receptive) group, there were students and faculty members resentful of Agnew for his cavalier treatment of protestors at another school, Bowie State, and angry at his charge that communist instigators had led the students in Chicago.

But they were not thinking of Agnew as they listened to quiet Dan Berrigan, a master of contoured rhetoric. Question from the floor: "Why aren't you obliged to wear a Roman collar?" (He wears a clerical suit with a black turtleneck pullover, like an ecclesiastical U-boat commander.) "By whom? By Jesus Christ?" Afterward, someone asked about the fish-skeleton medallion on his peace necklace. "The fish is a sign of Christ. And this is what He looked like after the Church had picked Him bare." After the speech was finished, county police came up quietly and arrested the priest. While in town to answer the federal charge and stand trial, he was taken into custody by order of Samuel Green, the aggressive state's attorney in Baltimore County, to make sure he would show up at a later trial for county charges against him. The students, angry, went fluid with the scene's possibilities, flowed around the cops' car, hardened there to hold it back. But Berrigan discouraged them, and went in peace.

The anger did not die; it smoldered all weekend and was still hot Sunday night when the Action Center held its first rally, at the hall of St. Ignatius Church (the downtown Jesuit parish). It was much like other New Left meetings—semimilitant banners proclaiming love (the artist, Tom Lewis, had paintings hung in two rows from the ceiling, like flags in a medieval throne room), speakers late, entertainers filling up the aimless gaps. Wisps of stray muddy hair and music, rasp of guitar and harmonica, politely received. There is little self-criticism in these social critics—doing one's thing is what matters, and perhaps one's thing is fourth-hand mimickry of folk rock. Poets read their odes to the Nine in a sweat of ingratiating creativity, dry-throated, thirsting to be eloquent. The main difference here is the concentration of priests and nuns, sudden white borders around faces not bearded or tangled in hair. The nuns, as by drill, listen and clap hard at everything, responding with more enthusiasm if guitars are clumsily pawed. They are trained to encourage pupils.

There is much talk of the Berrigans, both of them in jail now. Kunstler, at the microphone, calls their imprisonment a trick of the prosecution—he must go out to the county jail to consult his clients; bond there is almost eight times what it was for the federal charge. Others wonder if county or city police will try to arrest the two members of the Nine who have made it through rain to this hall. A proposal is made and applauded to form a "human sanctuary" around the defendants when they leave.

Grenville Whitman, in charge of the next day's march, gives instructions. "Don't talk to reporters. We have people instructed to do nothing but talk with them. Let them handle it." It is true. A volunteer PR man hunts down each journalist and feeds him names and facts. Whitman explains that the city has granted a permit for the march to go through town, past the Post Office Building (where the federal court is), to the nearby War Memorial (snickers for the name). But the sidewalk around the Post Office has been interdicted, and "We mean to take that sidewalk" (rebel yells at this—the Southern music of lost causes has moved to a strange new Confederacy). Whitman alternates toughness and placation: "We'll march right through the shopping district during lunch hour." But: "This is not a march against the police. Police are people. If you want to shout something about police, yell 'More pay for cops.'" Some boos. Different parts of the audience respond to the hard and soft lines. There are middle-aged Catholics and Quakers here, the old liberal peace demonstrators, uneasy at talk of revolution. Only the nuns clap at everything. One priest, a Jesuit down from New York, looking at mimeographed assaults on Agnew, says, "I didn't come here to stage a riot, or embarrass a candidate, but to support my brother in his time of need." The room is full of strange allies—some who had worked for Gene McCarthy; but McCarthy's name is booed by many. "Oh yeah, McCarthy," Gren Whitman smiles. "He was one of those who tried to act through the System. Remember him?"

County police in plain clothes have been spotted in the crowd, pointed at, ridiculed. General Gelston, of the National Guard, is also there. The demonstrators' parade marshals have gone out as scouts into the rain and found unmarked cars around the corner, their inhabitants waiting, keeping dry. This means the two defendants will be arrested; so a human chain is thrown around them and moves into the rain, oozing through doorways like a fast amoeba, a thing of changing outline but amorphous tight cohesion. Police sentries have squished back and forth around the corner, relaying intelligence to the cars, and a cluster of plainclothesmen is debating on the street. "Let them go." It would take a little war to extricate them. The amoeba breaks up at a Volkswagen, disgorging its core; and the little car speeds off. One plainclothesman, rain running down his face along with tears of anger, shouts brokenheartedly at General Gelston: "I never backed off in my life. I've gone into buildings against armed men—fourteen years in the service, and I never backed off. Well, tomorrow I hand in my resignation." So many resentments converging.

The marchers congregated next morning in champagny air that made flags snap and placards sparkle: "Our Cats Have Nine Lives." Just north of the little park they stood in was Johns Hopkins University; just south, row houses, agglutinated out of mutual need—leaning, dilapidating, on each other. The men are at work, only their women out on the street, incredulous as the march goes by—250 rows of six, marshals spaced every ten rows. First Indian beads and bare feet. "She's got no *shoes*," one matron gasps; and another screams, "Where yew-all from, honey?" Bare feet mean hillbillies in the ladies' anachronistic demonology. They are innocent of Hippies. "Ho-Ho-Ho-Chi-Minh! The NLF Is Going to Win!" And SDS with its banners: "Two-Four-Six-Eight! Organize and Smash the State!" These cries do not shock the women as much as the next group—lines of priests and nuns still singing they will overcome: "Black and white togeh-eh-ther" (there are no blacks in the march). "We shall end the war-or-er." As they pass the women shout bitterly: "I suppose *you'll* tell *us* how to live next Sunday, from the pulpit!" "It's indecent," the women buzz to each other with reassuring bitterness, a cluster of three, one in her forties, two in their twenties, one of these holding a child—a pretty two-year-old smeared with smiles and snot, all softness, hardening toward a fourth in their chorus, suckled on resentment. "Well," the young mother smiles acid: "They'll meet their match tonight." Wallace was due in town that night.

Meanwhile the trial had begun, with courtesy and formal manners at first. Dan Berrigan groaned, "I can see we are in for five days of flyshit." Kunstler waived *voir dire,* disdaining legal niceties to rely on moral eloquence. Berrigan said of the jurors, "They go round with a butterfly net to the Rotary Clubs to find such people. They're all from the Washington-Baltimore military-industrial set. They've been in three wars, and arranged them all." The judge, old and courtly, impeccably cooperative, did not impress him either: "If you're going to be hanged, it's better to have Grandpa do it. But I confess I feel like the man on the whaler, who fell into the whale's head, where they get the oil for perfume, and drowned in that syrupy brain. Death by Karo."

By one o'clock the marchers were at the Memorial, being heckled by old men out for lunch and young men out for trouble. The young ones had a taste for ghoulish signs. "Peace Creeps Go Home." "We Need Mayor Daley." "Gas the Nine Swine." Macabre gas-chamber humor, feeding a belief in the marchers that they walk everywhere in the midst of fascists. After some indecisive milling and oratory, the civil-disobedience group went over to claim the Post Office sidewalk, and everybody else tagged along. To the dismay of the marchers, police fell back. The kids owned the sidewalk, without a fight. By the ninth time around, the whole thing was a bore. Only one thing added surprise as people rode this slow merry-go-round. A young man from Washington softly and wittily heckled people as they circled by. He said he had served in the Air Force under Curtis LeMay, and he was all for George Wallace. His polite articulateness and youth were odd enough in a bigot; his color was even more startling. He was black.

Oscar Levant says that *Porgy and Bess* is the perfect folk opera—*Jewish* folk opera, that is. This strange heckler seemed to have wandered in from such a world of ethnic transformation—Sportin' Life, the slick Jewish boy gone bad in blackface. He handed out bars of soap to the shaggier hippie-types. When he gave one to a girl, the boy beside her looked as if he had been poleaxed; he circled back several times before he thought up an answer: "Lay off, *whitey*." But nothing disturbed the insouciant soap-peddler, who was in town checking on courses at the University of Baltimore. He blew mocking kisses at boys who looked effeminate in long hair ("Hi, honey!").

As the afternoon passed, sheer tedium melted the march down. Round one to the police. But the real trouble, if it came, would come that night. A few blocks away from St. Ignatius, Wallace would be speaking to his faithful, eight thousand of them, who risked downtown streets at night (about which they like to tell horror stories) to see their hero. A large group of the peace demonstrators risked the streets also, crossing to the Civic Center from their church. It was a typical stroll they had to make across an inner city—boarded-up lots (marred with craters and mounded with dirt), excavated streets, shiny out-of-scale buildings, all the federal bulldozer's cosmetic efforts on a place bombed senseless by civilization. Tall sterile buildings stand in the debris unacclimated, products of reverse "extraction," gleaming molars stuck in the rotten maw. The buildings look as much out of place as if they had come from Mars—big isolated boxes brought dangling from Martian helicopters like Christ dangling incongruous across the first shots of *La Dolce Vita*. The center cannot hold. The jumble of alien things poured into the dark heart of our cities is an attempt to fill a vacuum, to grow things artificially inward to the dead core of our lives.

The Civic Center was one of the first things to "renew"—i.e., Martianize—Baltimore. Outside, oddly finned and louvered, it has all the beauty of an air conditioner made for some unimaginable giant's window. Inside, it is a study in human engineering—broad ramps crisscrossing up and around the auditorium like pedestrian turnpikes. Now the turnpikes are heavily patrolled, checked, mar-

shaled by police in and out of uniform. Black kids get in,
if at all, after being bumped, scrutinized, frisked, challenged. About a hundred blacks make it nonetheless, and
go to the hecklers' heaven of this campaign year—a side
balcony (left one in this case), as close to the stage as
possible, rival podium in view of all, whence the protestors
can shout down at the stage or out at the audience.
(Nixon's advance men were careful to fill such positions
with their own; what heckling he got was from the back,
way back.) While the crowd waits for Wallace's epiphany,
and the black kids limber up their voices, the peaceniks
from St. Ignatius stay outside picketing and singing. A
band, made up of young boys, is on the stage, brassily
laboring the year's omnipresent campaign song, "When
the Saints Come Marchin' In." Over on the right side, on a
high side bench, exhibitionists' heaven, a plump thirtyish
woman stands up and jiggles in her place, flipping her
Wallace skimmer like a gypsy's tambourine. The crowd's
eyes and cigars roll synchronously toward her, and applause spreads out across the hall. That was all Bubbles
needed. Now she's out in the aisle, wiggle-stepping her
thin calves and thick active fanny up ten steps, then turn
and *down* the stairs ("An American Beauty"), blubber
jerked and tossed, caught and thrown in the thresh of her
hammock-brassiere. This middle-aged group, so critical of
the hippies' four-letter words and "immorality," had already, at eight o'clock, donned the ten-o'clock faces of an
all-night party at the Elks Club.

　　Then Wallace came, wafted out fast, all energy and
strut as if held off the floor by will power. The crowd is
ripe. He radiates a gritty nimbus of piety, violence, sex.
Picked-on and self-righteous, yet aggressive and darkly
venturous, he has the dingy attractive air of a B-movie
idol, the kind who plays a handsome garage attendant.
But he is getting past his prime, pouty about the lips and
eyes, on his way to character roles, parts rejected by
Edward G. Robinson. He comes rubbing his hands on invisible garage rag (most of the pit grease out of his
nails), smiling and winking, Anything-I-can-do-for-you-
pretty-girl? His hair is still wet from careful work with
comb and water in the gas station's cracked mirror (main
panel in the men's room triptych, rubber machine on one
side, comb-and-Kleenex dispenser on the other). He gives
little-boy salutes, snapped off at the end, Wash-your-wind-

shield? Keeps on the move, back and forth, drinking the
cheers, with quick turns and darts toward camera, jocular,
pointing out newsmen he knows, best attendant in the
station, can't do enough for you, Fill-your-tank-Ma'am?

The ritual struggle with the hecklers begins at once—
his good-humored bows and waves played carefully against
their mounting frenzy. He toys with them, invites them,
does little matador tricks with their blind snorts and
trampling. This is only the first, or *Y'all-good-fellows-
underneath* stage. He will not escalate till they do. They
are the aggressors; he gives an impression of control even
while they make it impossible for him to speak. The second stage is entered gradually, as he gets the crowd quiet.
He sounds his allies as well as enemies. Will they sing
"Dixie"? (No, they will not, they are too busy shouting up
at hecklers' heaven.) Oh-ho, so that's it; tonight his people want the rough stuff. Start slow, though; pious. "You
young people seem to know a lot of four-letter words."
(Tsk-tsk, what's the world coming to? That nice young
man at the gas station doesn't carry on so when out with
his friends.) "But I have two four-letter words you don't
know: S-O-A-P and W-O-R-K." Work is the magic word.
Most of the traveling celebrities Wallace has with him
are union leaders—just-plain-folks celebrity.

Still at the piety stage: "I was fighting Nazis before you
folks was born." But hotting up: "You jes' cum up t' the
platform aftawuhd, an' I'll autygraph your sandals." His
diction declines, in an artfully calibrated way, as the
crowd's inhibitions degenerate. They know the "autograph your sandals" line, but love it, for familiarity; im-
plore him for other tunes in his repertoire. "Yew an-
archists bettuh have yewuh day now." The crowd puffs,
rocks, explodes with a euphoric wrath—happy with
dream-visions of revenge on all the rebel children, a cos-
mic spanking when George takes over. It is a great parental tantrum. "Wuah they teaching in those colleges, anyway?" His own people cry back: "Communism!" They
said it; he does not need to (he keeps one eye, always, on
those cameras). Blats of air horns in the crowd leave a
flatulent rubbery smell after each honk. The crowd is
being George-Groszed, made itchy with unconfessed lusts;
but never, in its own eyes, more beautiful. They are walking vindications of America—as rebellious blacks and
hippies are a walking profanation. George understands.

"The press says weuh some kind of uncivilized racists." Shaken fists and voices at the press section. "Oh, not these boys. Theyuh hard-workin' reporters. Ah love these folks." Magnanimous George steps up (on-camera) to save cameramen-murderers from the mob (Don't lynch 'em; we'll hang 'em right and proper when the Judge gets here). "It's theyuh *editors*, back in *offices*, that write all that stuff. But who is uncivilized? Jes' look at the folk heuh supporting *me*, and then look at those who are *not* with me."

He can't give them enough. The Edward G. Robinson lips stretch out and square themselves, a horizontal figure eight. "Some people wonderin' about *'Unidentified Flying Objects.'* Well, it's some of these ol' editors been so upset at me they got a runnin' fit like some ol' houn' dog and just went into *oabit*." Give it to 'em, George. The inner flesh of the lips is purple, like bricks inside a thick wall: "Yew-know, after ah appeared on 'Meet the Press,' they didn't sen' me their certificate of thanks . . . Ah told them they could take their li'l ol' certificate, and they knew wuah they could do with it." Seegar was calling to seegar, warm in the gas station's office, under a fly-specked pinup's twin pendants. He'll have to go the whole way to satisfy this audience. "Ah hadn' meant to say this tonight, but *yew*-know, if one of those hippies lays down in front of mah car when *Ah* become President . . ." They drown out the punch line in happy fulfilled anger. Refrain of some favorite song, it is too longed-for to be audible when it comes.

Their happiness is enough to break the heart. They vomit laughter. Trying to eject the vacuum inside them. They are not hungry or underprivileged or deprived in material ways. Each has, in some minor way, "made it." And it all means nothing. Washington does not care. The children do not care. They have worked, and for what? As I looked through the crowd—the very young, and then a jump to middle age, no college students there but the protesting peaceniks—I wondered if the young mother from the street corner was there (someone watching her bright smear of baby), the one who screamed at the marching priests. Had the policeman come, the one who said last night that he did not back off in fourteen years? Had he turned in his resignation that day?—the kids had made a mockery of his life. They *must* not get away with it. The desire for "law and order" is nothing so simple as a code word for racism; it is a cry, as things begin to break up, for stability, for stopping history in mid-dissolution. Hammer the structure back together; anchor it down; bring nails and bolts and clamps to keep it from collapsing. There is a slide of things—queasy seasickness in these laughing tortured faces, vomiting emptiness.

Yet the blacks and the Berrigan demonstrators, looking down on this crowd from their balcony, could see nothing but hypocrisy in its praise of law and order. It seemed all pretense and phoniness—Chicago police feigning shock at the sound of words that are scrawled in precinct jakes and johns, used as much by cops as robbers; cabdrivers and bartenders who alternate dirty jokes with hatred of the demonstrators who "screw in our parks"; the Civic Center jiggly with Bubbles as the saints march in, then swooning at the hair-oil piety of George. Were the demonstrators obscenely "provocative" at the Chicago convention? Right now, below the stage, the soap-peddling heckler of the afternoon march is on his feet, shouting obscenities at his fellow blacks. He is weary and smeared, his natty clothes rumpled, his fingers stained with red ink as he improvises insults on the back of Wallace placards. He turns, at intervals, and gives the balcony his one-finger *fico* sign. The Wallace audience loves it, congratulates him, reaches for his hand to shake it. They are obviously not against obscenity as such.

It does look hypocritical, inconsistent, all things young people mean by their broad term of accusation, "middle class." But there is no hypocrisy. Only anguish. The issue of law and order reflects moral yearnings, though it has itchy George, the B-movie idol, in charge of its louder expressions. These are people infinitely tolerant of the recognized immoralities, the release and relapse of the Elks Club, of the Christmas office party, the clandestine affair, the hocused expense account, the tax dodge. All of these are countenanced as failures within the framework of their life; none of them challenge that framework. What frenzied the police in Chicago was not the fact that kids were screwing in the parks, but that they *proclaimed* they were doing so; said they *should* do so. Screwing in the grass had become a political act. "Getting away with it" was a challenge, like some whip across the face, since it was deliberately meant to raise the question, Why *not* get away with it?

And the parents had no answer. That was what brought out cruelty in the solid burghers of America. They had "done everything for the children"—except answer them. And that failure was enough to undo all they had done. They are angry not so much at their children as at themselves for failing the children. And it is anger at oneself that eats into the mind. Their faith—in hard work, good manners, obedience to law, success, self-reliance—was being challenged. And their *grounds* for faith have, through the years, evanesced. All their religions are empty—beginning with the religion of religion. After that, the religion of progress (civilization had bombed our cities senseless). The religion of success (*they* had succeeded, and had ashes in their mouths). The religion of prosperity (for America has had a spirituality of materialism, with millionaire saints now losing their faith). Finally, the last great belief, education. America had said, like the man in Chesterton, "I do not know what good is, but I shall give it to my children." The parents might not be able to defend "the American way"; but that was only because they were not educated. Their children would do it; teachers had been hired to show them how. Yet the children, taught to doubt, far from defending their parents' way of life, question it with new rigor, mercilessly. Under that questioning, these parents fall back on a mindless faith in George's "good old America." But the faith is a desperate one, grown defensive. These people have neither an examined certitude nor a soothing oblivion. They do not have the comforting simplicities of the rebel. They defend an establishment they do not really feel part of, without weapons or joy, getting little for their effort. Caught between complacency and protest, their anger is a sterile thing, ejaculations into air.

When people talk of lancing the nation's sores, they tend to think of localized sharp conflicts—in the ghetto, on the campus, in and around striking public workers. But these problems we could handle, were it not for a quiet sour fear at the center of American life. We have now a vast middle range of the comfortable discontented. They are not, as Nixon knows, the kind who march or riot. They just lock their doors. And they vote. They do not, most of them, go to Wallace rallies; but those who do go speak for them in growing measure. This is the vague unlocalized resentment that had such effect in the 1968 campaign, tainting all the air around talk of law and order. America itself, like her major cities, has blight at the core, not in limbs and extremities. As I stood, bewildered like most reporters, in the insane din of that Wallace rally, saw a crowd of eight thousand tormented by a mere few hundred, I realized at last what had not sunk in at Miami's riot, or Chicago's. I realized this is a nation that might do anything. Even elect Nixon.

3. The Politics of Resentment

"I find the people strangely fantasied;
Possess'd with rumours, full of idle dreams,
Not knowing what they fear, but full of fear . . ."
—King John

AND THE NIGHT was not over. Inside the Civic Center, while Wallace spoke, fights had been controlled. As the crowd left, minor clashes were broken up at first: Wallace backers, black kids, and peace marchers brushed each other, some aching for trouble, others aching for escape, all tense. Police, roving yet restrained, played umpire; the crowd was turning against itself, not united against them. Yet police decision here, as so often, was a delicate matter of timing and gradation. There is an infinite slide of variables into unstable combination. Each factor acts chemically on others, making crowds peaceful or hostile in minutes. Are they to be soothed or threatened, "moved along" or ignored? Should leaders be taken away? Should counterpicketing be allowed? To move in may scare the crowd, turn it against the police. To wait may mean things slip past the manageable point. And each decision is dated as soon as made; the conditions have, in a minute, changed.

When the flow of people away from the Civic Center began to slow, diked in various places by "confrontations" that reached out toward each other and formed writhing peninsulas of battle between Wallace and anti-Wallace zealots, the cops moved fast. Mounted police made a sudden appearance, in ranks, sweeping the sidewalks, prying out those who tried to stay behind in alleys or cling together in doorways. Sweeps by car or on foot could not have done this so smoothly, obviating chances of resistance—there is no arguing with six feet of trained horse hock bumping you down a brick wall, with a cop and his club high above, surveying, not subject to the mass of men on foot. Then backup teams fanned out, coming raucous down parallel streets, dogs everywhere. It was the first time dogs were turned on crowds since the days of Bull Connor down South. It is easy to see why their use was discontinued: primordial things are loosed in the corridors of the mind when dogs run undiscouraged out to their leashes' limit, jerk themselves by the run's sheer impact partway around, loud and hoarse and latrant all the while, then do it again, aimed at you, all froth and fang and trained menace, seeming to drag their trainers. Dogs of such disciplined savagery inflict on men the indignity of their own fear, something not easily forgiven the men who use them.

But there is no happy way to send crowds off when they mean to stay and fight. This was not a Chicago riot—police and demonstrators both frightened, both fighting. with kicks, obscenity, blood. I saw one policeman command a group of eight young men who were fighting each other to stop and line up in a doorway. He came at them, and they shrank back, their eyes on the dog, hypnotized. When the van came, that one cop took each prisoner in turn by the arm and put him in while the others waited. There was no resisting. His dog, on short leash, was at his other hand, quieted to growls; but every ear heard that animal motor running, no matter how soft. Which way is better? Is there *any* good way to deal with men gone nobly berserk for ideals? It is just another of the decisions police must make, crisis by crisis, day by day.

Back at St. Ignatius Hall, headquarters of the demonstration, the decision to use dogs looked mistaken. By the time I got back there, the church auditorium was almost as raucous as the Civic Center had been. Most of those supporting the Catonsville Nine had stayed in the hall to share in the New Left's main activity—heated delivery of orations to each other. Only some had made the trip to the Civic Center. And as these travelers returned, breathless and frightened, they gave a lurid version of the ordeal they had been through. Dogs scattered loose into the crowd, innocent people bitten, cops "freaked out" and urging their beasts on, clubbing and Macing people the while. Each bearer of dispatches from the front was invited to the microphone and prompted by groans and curses to give as dramatic an account as he could manage. Since the fear they had experienced went beyond the bare fact—that dogs on leashes had made them run— there was symbolic truth to their stories. These visions and worse had snapped at their heels as they scampered; and description of an inner vision is the basic mode of discourse in companies like this. It is extraordinary how little those in the juvenile Left question each other's vivid but varying accounts of reality. For people who make a cult of honesty, who accuse The System of telling lies to flatter itself, they are casual about their own reports—in the underground press, in their perfervid nonstop speeches to each other, in the demonology they have constructed around "the military-industrial complex." A brilliant man like Dan Berrigan can, in this way, claim that anyone who lives in Baltimore must be employed by a government firm in Washington, and therefore be responsible for three wars. He will be believed. The New Left regularly passes the White Queen's before-breakfast test. Horror stories have an aesthetic appeal that recommends them even when they run counter to New Left ideology—e.g., Berrigan had a very "unradical" view of the economic condition of his jurors, compared with the income of those who help our government be benevolent with armies. Berrigan's analysis, like the description of the Baskerville Hounds at large in Baltimore's streets, was one of the "symbolic truths" the New Left lives with. Needless to say, The System is not allowed such symbols. Over on that side, they become lies.

Father Berrigan, it must be admitted, balances things off with superb equity: he is as ready to believe the rest as they are to take his word. Though he was not at the Civic Center, he springs into action after news of the dogs is relayed. At the microphone, he muses with husky emotion: "I think we should be on the street tonight. I'll see you there." Everyone realizes the generosity of this gesture

—he has most to lose by courting trouble while out on bail (while actually on trial). But others are more prudent, and perhaps afraid—the streets have, after all, been described as if they were one great kennel.

There is a great deal of debate on and off the stage. Some are for going to the jail and solacing those arrested. Some want to march against the police. Or stay in the hall all night. Or find a way to get people to their homes or hotels. George Mische, one of the Nine, tries to quiet this increasingly violent group of love-not-war-makers: he says that he and the rest of the Nine are ready to take to the streets in protest, but only if the protestors are determined on restraint in their own ranks. "Anybody who wants to call Wallace a pig, and cops pigs, should stay here and not go down. If we get caught in this, we're playing the same game they are . . . Anybody who wants to get out of hand and spoil the whole thing is going to have to walk over some of the Catonsville Nine to do it."

That brings it to a head. A boy mutters angrily, "If they had talked like this in Chicago, we would not have had a Chicago" (Chicago being the New Left's great victory, the archetypal Confrontation). One girl, shaking with urgency and sense of mission, went around among the yeastier groups: "Do you *want* kids to get beat up?" she asked, almost in tears. "I was out there. The police did not start the fighting. The crowd was fighting with itself, our people and the Wallace audience." (Wallace people far outnumbered the Berrigan people.) "There was no clubbing or Macing. The cops were uptight, of course. Everybody was. That's why, if we go out there now, our people are going to get hurt." She was eloquent—a graduate student of French at the Hopkins—but the audiences she picked were unreceptive.

The crowd was intensely active yet paralyzed. The Wallace throng was getting revenge of a sort for *its* static frenzy in the Civic Center. The young tormentors in the Civic Center balcony were now tortured on their own home ground. Like the police, they had to escalate carefully, fitting each move to the situation, not outrunning public sympathy too far, or they would hurt their cause. And this situation was difficult to gauge. There were no solid reports coming in, of the numbers arrested, the extent of injuries, the movements of the police. Scouts were sent out. Marshals from the morning's march were asked to convene in a runway between the hall and the church.

That was a mistake. Since the marshals had no orders yet, they were only authorized to do—what? Authorized to speak, of course, more importantly than each had in the crowded hall. The keepers of order were soon engaged in a disorderly shouting match, several giving speeches simultaneously while the nonorating waited their chance and, characteristically, called, "Cut the goddam *rhetoric!*" Opposing sides tried to outnoble each other ("Who's-afraid?" vs. "Think-of-the-others"). Which course would serve the Cause best? There was no answer; the marshals, tiring of the din, drifted back to less authorized and more interesting exchanges inside.

That was a model for the rest of the evening: exasperation increasing, then easing off. Villains were denounced, tactics debated, ideals enunciated, brilliant maneuvers invented and criticized, wars fought in hypothesis, bloodshed enacted or avoided. Martyrdoms were righteously sought, in imagination suffered, then warmly applauded. The crowd talked itself violently into peace and, after midnight, went home, cheated of confrontation; staled by emotions half-vented, in unsatisfying ways. Ejaculations in air.

Resentments stranger than those of the Wallace rally had been loose in St. Ignatius Hall. Resentments not so much against the war, as against the judge and jurors who would enforce the law. Against the police who had let them parade, not satisfying their vision of police swinishness; and who had used dogs and "got away with it." Not, really, against any one act on the part of The System, but against The System itself, the thing that seems so impersonal, impervious to appeal, set on a course of deliberate destructiveness. Deliberate. That is the key point. Wallace's people have lost their faith in education. The "pointyheads" are not so much evil as befuddled by the mind's vain efforts—educated morons made stupid by sophistication. But the kids still believe in education—not, of course, the kind they are being given, but the kind they try to give themselves. They do not know what the good is, but they could find out if others (like their parents, or teachers, or draft board) would stop interfering with their lives.

For the demonstrators, then, the crime of The System

is not intelligence, but immoral uses of intelligence. In a way, these kids are back where the Wallace people were ten years ago, before they lost all faith in the mind. The Right's villains in the fifties were not tragicomic pointy-heads with ridiculous briefcases and professorial bicycles, but cool educated Achesons engaged in clever treason. McCarthyism of this older sort was not voiced in 1968 by Wallace and his followers, but by the New Left. Instead of Acheson, we got a round-faced Peter-Lorre villain, Rusk. Traitors no longer accomplished our retreat from China, but our involvement in Vietnam. Instead of a communist Eisenhower, we had a superpatriot-murderer, "MacBird," guilty of a Dallas-type accent and mind and war. The maker of international mischief was no longer the UN, but the CIA. The chemical that poisoned the world was no longer fluoridated water but Dow Chemical napalm. Instead of Roosevelt's treachery at Pearl Harbor, we had the CIA's plot to kill Kennedys. The point of McCarthyism, old or new, is that whatever has gone wrong was *planned* to go wrong. It was treason, conspired at. The uncovering of this labyrinthine plot or plots is almost hopeless, so encased in protective secrecy is The System, so deeply has it brainwashed the public; but virtuous citizens must make the effort. This conspiratorial view exactly reflects what Richard Hofstadter, analyzing McCarthyism, called the paranoid style in politics: "When it argues that we are governed largely by means of near-hypnotic manipulation (brainwashing), wholesale corruption, and betrayal, it is indulging in something more significant than the fantasies of indignant patriots: it is questioning the legitimacy of the political order itself."

Confluent poisons, intermingling; conflicts within groups and between them—that was the legacy of Monday's march, and trial opening, and picketing at the Post Office, and rally of the Right, and quandary of the Left. No one was satisfied—not hot-headed cops who had to back off, not picketers or antipicketers, not hecklers or antihecklers, not priests trying to enact sermons, not people trying to lock the priests inside their churches. More and more this kind of experience touches the average American. Has one's city rioted, or walked the edge of riot? Has a campus been troubled? Were you there? Was your neighbor? Your son or daughter? Was a member of your family called up for National Guard duty? Has your priest or rabbi marched or demonstrated? Your postman? Did your policeman riot? And *if* one was there, which side did he take? (*Whose* riot?) How did it change the person involved? Change the attitude of others toward that person? These are the kinds of emotional half-questions that moved through Baltimore as crowds broke up and spread out, going home, Monday night. The rest of the trial went rasping down its foreseen track without violent incident, but the whole proceeding was made edgy by the clashes of the first day.

And the week was not over. As one crisis wound down unresolved, another was building, back where the week started, on the campus of Towson State College. For several reasons, this had been chosen as the spot where Governor Agnew would make his one "home" appearance and speech. It was not in the city itself, a danger area for him after his offended its black (and much of its white) population. Nixon's "urban expert" was expert enough to stay out of Baltimore. Agnew's daughter had gone to Towson State. The college is near his old home, where he first held elective office (as county executive). The campus is small, and had always been placid (till Berrigan's arrest). It has a nice large gymnasium, Burdick Hall, that could be rented with Republican funds.

Several things were taking place on campus throughout the week of Berrigan's trial. Colonel Lally of the State Police, Agnew's favored adviser on law and order, was disturbed over the "SDS chapter" that invited Berrigan to speak. The police were also checking a professor of philosophy, who had nothing to do with the SDS but had been active in the Peace Action Center's demonstrations for Berrigan. Professor James Hill says that Dan Berrigan "politicized" him, so he decided to make a theater-of-the-absurd "happening" out of Agnew's appearance on campus. A group of about a hundred students and several faculty members agreed on a series of short, nonsensical sounds and gestures to be made, on signal, during Agnew's speech—they would laugh fifteen seconds too long at his jokes, bark like dogs, hold books up in their right hands, shout "Necktie" and, toward the end, throw confetti and blow horns while parading ecstatically for Agnew. They would become idiots to demonstrate the idiocy of the political process. Part of the fun seems to have been the choice of elaborate signals to start and stop each out-

burst: no single gesture was to last long—their aim was
not to prevent Agnew from speaking, but to give him
what they considered the appropriate inane accompani-
ment.

There is a special tang in conspiracy when it is silly.
There was solemn debate on how long the laughing and
barking should last. *Which* book should one hold up? (Not
that anyone would see the title, this was conscientious
artistry, like sculpting the back of statues meant for
niches.) Other members of the faculty were trying to
prevent disturbance of any sort—not simply from disinterested love of peace; they did not want to jeopardize
their efforts to get funds and salaries out of the governor.
Three faculty groups, including the campus AAUP, asked
students to preserve decorum. Parents in the area had
heard a suppressed giggle of preparation for the happening, and phone calls came in to the president and dean,
protesting the idea of protest during the governor's
"homecoming" (as it had been billed). Others were calling
Agnew's office. The magic word "necktie" had been
breathed abroad. The story newsmen had by the time of
the talk was that someone would take off his necktie and
a riot would begin. Police intelligence officers were hot on
the track of these rumors, and Agnew was told to be
ready for the worst. As one of his campaign organizers
put it later, with bureaucratic euphemism, "The Governor
was overbriefed on the subject of student trouble at that
meeting." And for Agnew, student trouble meant one thing
—SDS. (The so-called SDS group was not even involved
in the great Necktie Plot.)

Some attempt was made to head trouble off. On the
morning of the governor's talk, faculty representatives at
Towson State finally got their meeting with the governor
on the subject of proper funding for the school. Agnew
was affable, attentive, cooperative; he gave his side of the
story, complete with statistics supplied him by Mel Cole,
his education assistant. He was trying out the theme of his
address for that evening—all the things his administration
had done for education. Still, he saw the faculty's problem,
he said, and would do what he could about it (meaning,
presumably, get out of the state by becoming Vice-President). The faculty members left in good humor, with
hopes for the future, anxious that no troublemakers should
spoil things that night.

One of this group called Hill and asked him to cancel the happening. Hill said he did not want to, and perhaps could not. At first the plan had been for him to give the signals. But as knowledge of his part in the affair was leaked, he decided it would be too easy to stop the whole thing simply by rushing him out. So he gave the task to various students. They meant to station themselves at visible points near the front of the auditorium. In order to draw less attention to themselves, these students were told to get haircuts and dress "straight." As Professor Hill said after the event, "We were incredibly naive. The last political rally I had been to was one for Adlai Stevenson." The Nixon technique, carried over to Agnew by skilled advance men like Nick Ruwe, was to pack the front of the auditorium with loyalists, then surround the candidate with cheering girls cued to shout favorable chants. They would drown out any hecklers. Placards, strategically lined up, were used as a wall to cut off the back of the auditorium, a screen between dissidents and TV cameras. In a crowd of three thousand people, Hill's hundred actors were lost. One boy, who was to cue the barking, worked himself forward into a group of kids so straight and righteous that he lost his nerve and never uttered a whelp. Even if people could hear or see the Hill group, there was little chance they would understand the deliberate absurdities for what they were. After the confetti-and-horns little bash, Mrs. Hill was confronted in the women's rest room by a bulky middle-aged woman with a bulging handbag. As soon as the woman saw confetti in Mrs. Hill's hair, she said, "I suppose you're one of them." "Of who?" "Of *them*." "Oh. You mean of *us*." "Yes, you communists," and she lifted the bag to hit her. Mrs. Hill ran out. Confetti was part of the communist plot for the nonlady in the ladies' john.

As it turned out, the Hill Happening was thrice buried. His chosen hundred actors were not as noisy as a group of people from the Peace Action Center downtown and from various neighboring schools, principally the University of Maryland. And this larger group of protestors, perhaps six hundred in number, was kept outside the placard wall, drowned out by bunny cheers from the Agnew girls. There was never any threat to the speaker's microphone-dominance of the crowd. But Agnew was "over-briefed," ready for battle the minute a cough rang out from his presumably hostile audience. He rose above the podium squinting and lidded, like a friendly mole, all smiles; then he seized each chance to answer heckling, threw out prepared "ad-libs," forced a showdown. The warnings he had received become self-fulfilling prophecies.

"I suppose you're all from SDS?" he asked. A thin scatter of kids cried "Yes," while more roared "No!"— and Agnew triumphed, "I thought so. Mao supplies the philosophy while Daddy supplies the money." In the Nixon format, he had gone into a Wallace act, making the hecklers part of his show—but not with the shrewd nihilism of Wallace; with an indomitable naiveté. *He* was heckling *them,* angry at the mere thought that such kids exist in our neat society—as the thought of black militants had obsessed him for over a year. The neutral students were amused and then exasperated by this overkill and official heckling. Berrigan had, just a week before this, "politicized" a few on the campus; Agnew was politicizing hundreds.

There was an undercurrent of responsiveness between antagonists all this week, an urgency to *find* one's enemy —which is the meaning of the New Left's favorite word, "confrontation." Hunt the enemy down, make him show himself, drag him into the light of day. Those in the grip of resentment have a need to justify their feelings by making the object of it clear. Thus Agnew *had* to give hecklers the stage, though his aides labored to prevent this. Professor Hill, who refers to himself as "a very learned man," had to "identify" the kooks in the crowd even if it meant creating them—sending his hundred kids out with kook-konfetti. Wallace woos his hecklers into spectacles of hate. The kids have visions of dogs, and give them substance for their audience. They are all fulfillers of each other's nightmares.

The week was over, but its effects would last. As a result of the heckling at Towson State, County Attorney Sam Green issued a statement that those who disrupt a public gathering would be subject to arrest. Crying "necktie" or barking on signal could be dangerous occupations now. The SDS group at Towson finally joined national SDS under the title of "The Spiro T. Agnew Memorial Chapter of Students for a Democratic Society." The chapter called a rally shortly after the governor's address, and two thousand came; they went in candlelight procession to the jail where Dan Berrigan awaited his sentence. When all local SDS chapters looked for a place to assemble on Election Day, Towson State was chosen as a place of honor for the New Left.

Many kinds of animosities linger from that week. The head of the lay board of St. Ignatius Church resigned, along with other members of the board, because the hall had been used by the Peace Action Center. These men agreed with the Baltimore women on street corners: priests should stay in their pulpits (and demonstrators should stay out of them). The Nine were sentenced in November—three years for the Berrigans, two for most of the others. That was just the federal sentence. They were still liable to state charges rising out of the same action. In Sam Green's territory. And Towson State's.

Each campus has its story to tell now, as each ghetto does. As each city does. Each police force. It is no wonder Walter Lippmann, looking at the growth of resentment in the nation, wrote in September of 1968 that "the country has entered a period of revolutionary change of which no one can foresee the course or the end or the consequences. For we are living in a time when the central institutions of the traditional life of man are increasingly unable to command his allegiance and his obedience." The great voices of authority—family, church, school, country—are silenced, confused, or not listened to. The center cannot hold. "Thus," Lippmann wrote, "there will probably remain a considerable body of irreconcilable revolutionary dissent. There are no easy and there are no quick solutions for the discontent that will have to be dealt with, and we would be hiding our heads in the sand if we refused to admit that the country may demand and necessity may dictate the repression of uncontrollable violence." It was for this reason that Lippmann endorsed Nixon. Let repression be done by those to whom it comes naturally: "It is better that Mr. Nixon should have the full authority if repression should become necessary in order to restore peace and tranquillity at home . . . Repression of some sort may be unavoidable. If that is what the country is going to face, it is better that the Republicans should have the clear responsibility for the measures that are taken, and that the Democrats should be out of office and free to play the indispensable role of the opposition party." He did not flinch from the conscious choice that many were unconsciously making—Nixon as the right man for a period of resentment.

If a politics of resentment was taking shape in 1968, no one knew that fact better than the man who would, at each stage of the year, prove himself master of the situation. His time, as he put it, had come. He was in his favored position—the challenger, attacking. Humphrey had to defend the record, just as Nixon did in 1960 (when he felt his hands were tied): "I say that when a team has struck out four times, it is time to let the other side come up to bat . . . There is nothing wrong with this country that a good election cannot cure." The safest and most universal expression of resentment in American politics was working with Nixon—a desire to throw the rascals out. And Nixon, like Humphrey, would venture as far as he could in using the sticky "law and order" issue. But that issue illustrated the problem faced by anyone who would profit from the explosive state of American society: fanning one resentment too hard would ignite other equally violent hostilities, and frighten men with the prospect of all-out conflict. People might favor a degree of repression—but only that degree which did not threaten their own safety. The trick was to orchestrate resentments, getting maximum advantage from each while minimizing the inevitable backlash.

That Nixon conceived the problem in these terms is clear from an ambitious speech he gave on May 16, while he was still running the gantlet of state primaries. Like all his serious "position papers" of the campaign, the talk was given on radio, then widely distributed in booklet form. It was called "A New Alignment for American Unity." The terminology is important. Alignment, not consensus. The raw atmosphere of 1968 made talk of consensus, so popular in the last campaign, seem escapist: "We will not seek the false unity of consensus, of the glossing over of fundamental differences, of the enforced sameness of government regimentation." Lyndon Johnson's politics of consensus had clearly failed, and Nixon talked as if he meant to reengage the realities of American politics: our nation is designed to be governed, not by unanimity, but by a majority, and majorities have been achieved, within the two-party structure, by working toward wide stable coalitions. Nixon cites the classic modern example, Franklin Roosevelt's architectural majority, built of strategically joined and mutually buttressing minorities; immigrants, labor, ethnic groups, the South. The Democrats have been the majority party over the last three decades, so durable was that coalition. But in 1968, Nixon claimed, history was accomplishing another of its large realignments—that year would be for Republicans what 1932 was for the Democrats.

Not consensus, then, but a new coalition? No, coalition is a thing of the past, too. We must substitute "an alignment of ideas over the coalition of power blocs." The coalition offered a reward for each bloc, something for labor, something for the South, and so on. Nixon's speech claimed he would not get trapped into this bribing of individual sectors. It said, rather loftily, that those days are gone forever, though politicians "are reluctant to abandon the old power alliances that have served them so well in the past." Such politicians are faced with a serious new choice: "whether to cling to the old power-bloc alliances of the middle third of this century, or to join the new alignment of ideas that will shape the final third of this century." What is an alignment of ideas? It is the cooperation of people who support the same principle for different motives: thus "we will forge a unity of goals, recognized by men who also recognize and value their own diversity." This seems a rather bloodless, abstract scheme. It is unlikely that people will stop asking "What's in it for me?" and ask only for fidelity to the unifying goal of principle.

But Nixon, of course, had something up his sleeve. To see that, we need only look at the principle his minorities are supposed to agree on: "People come first, and government is their servant." Sounds harmless—if rather unspecific, like most platitudes. But the goal was carefully chosen with reference to the slogans of the five types "aligned" in Nixon's new majority. These were (1) the traditional Republican—i.e., the proponent of free enterprise, (2) the new Liberal, asking for "participatory democracy" which puts "personal liberty ahead of the dictates of the State," (3) the new South, "interpreting the old doctrine of states' rights in new ways," (4) the black militant who wants opportunity, not the dole, a "piece of the action," not degrading welfare, and (5) "the silent center, the millions of people in the middle of the American political spectrum who do not demonstrate, who do not picket or protest loudly."

If Roosevelt threw odd buttresses up over society in a Gothic structure of tension that produced stability, Nixon seems to be building with fire and straw instead of mortar and bricks: considered as a positive principle, his grab bag goal of "People First" would promote the conflict of groups. In the new South, the term indicates a strengthening of traditional representative units—not only the state as a unit, but all the local structures that preserve regional identity. For the advocate of participatory democracy, "people first" means an emphasis on spontaneity and the prophetic voice, outside (or, in a Marcusian sense, against) the arbitrary units of past representation. For the black militant, the same phrase means anything that leads to racial identity, "people first" is *my* people first; and this cancels regional considerations far more drastically than one-man one-vote liberalism ever did (a brother is a brother, no matter where he comes from), while it confines the prophetic voice within racial units. For the free enterprise Republican, the idea of people over government means the right to unfettered economic advantage, without regard to social service. For the silent center, the opposition of people to government means that federal authority should not extend to areas like prayer in the schools and local obscenity laws.

Nothing positive unites Nixon's five groups. Their common note is resentment of government, not only from different motives (as Nixon admits) but conflicting motives. Urged on, these resentments are bound to collide. Application of Nixon's "one principle" to such diverse opposed groups can only intensify hostility. Yet Nixon plays this cynical game to its end: "My point is this: these voices—the Republicans, the New Liberals, the new South, the black militants—are talking the same language [by a studied nicety, he does include the silent center in this formulation, since silence does not talk any language] . . . despite the differences in appearance, despite the differences in ways and means, despite the lack of community, despite all the pains of realignment, the fundamental agreement is there." Is where? Between Ocean Hill–Brownsville and Prince Georges County? Between Rhody McCoy and Strom Thurmond? Between Rap Brown and Barry Goldwater? Between Milton Friedman and Michael

Harrington? Who could be deceived by talk of such "alignment"?

Many people. James Reston, for instance. After Agnew was named the vice-presidential candidate, Mr. Reston found the Deeper Meaning of that move in Nixon's May 16 radio speech. In a *New York Times* article called "New Coalition: A Nixon Gamble," Reston posed the problem: "There is obviously something wrong or at least something missing in most of the explanations of why Richard Nixon chose Gov. Spiro T. Agnew of Maryland as the Republican Vice-Presidential nominee. Mr. Nixon won the nomination and blew the election all in one day, according to some of these explanations, by appeasing the South with Agnew and affronting the urban North." And then he answered the problem this way: "If he is not a prisoner or a fool, then, what is the explanation of his decision? It may be that he gave the explanation himself in a nationwide radio speech last May 16": Agnew was simply a catalyst for the "New South" in the "new alignment." And Nixon's desire to please this part of the alignment did not signify any wish to write off the other parts: "The outlook, therefore, is for a very hard Nixon campaign appealing to all the dissident elements Mr. Wallace is now gathering and to all others in what Mr. Nixon calls the 'new coalition'—the people who are sore at big government, big unions, costly wars, etc. Maybe he can do it and maybe he can't."

"Maybe he can do it?" He never meant to do it. He did not make a real effort to get the new liberal or the black militant into his camp. What he meant to do was throw up a protective screen around his actions; and Reston's article shows how well he succeeded. The May 16 speech gave him a framework within which he could operate. He could, for instance, try to neutralize some of the opposition from the black community—whence his "black capitalism" program. Yet such a gesture did not alienate people in other parts of "the alignment," since his use of the overarching formula "less government interference" allowed him to use rhetoric congenial to each sector's grievances. Much of this rhetorical adjustment was done, of course, at the local level, by his lieutenants—like Thurmond, Callaway, and Tower in the South. All Nixon had to supply was a setting, in which nuanced states' rights arguments (against, for instance, federal withhold-

ing of funds to segregated schools) seemed to be conso-
nant with other demands for local control.

It was a bold approach, which drew attention by its
very cheekiness: "You can be sure," the original speech
said by way of anticipation, "that the members of the old
power blocs will try to dismiss this new majority as just
an assortment of strange bedfellows" (the best defense
is an aggressive offense). The "new majority" scheme did
not accomplish any real alignment. It was not meant to.
What interested Nixon was the *idea* of alignment: it gave
the Restons of this world a Tinkertoy to play with. And
while they played, Nixon worked, reaping maximum advantage from the troubles of the year, using a coolly
orchestrated politics of discontent. In a low-keyed campaign, this is how he spoke to the "forgotten man"
and his disquietude, to those who attended Wallace rallies, to those who feared the rallies, to all who were
resentful.

4. The Denigrative Method

> *"It is not a smear, if you please, if you
> point out the record of your opponent."*
> —*Murray Chotiner*

NIXON WAS KNOWN, during World War II, as "Nick"
—and did better, at that, than his fellow officer in the
Navy, also stationed in the Pacific, John Kennedy, who
was known as "Shafty." Although Nixon has never been
what he calls, contemptuously, a "buddy-buddy boy," he
told political backers when he returned from the war, "I
believe the returning veterans—and I have talked to many
of them in the foxholes—will not be satisfied with a dole
or a government handout." The foxholes seem to be
poetic license, since his most obliging biographer, Bela
Kornitzer, admits "his group was not exactly a combat

unit." It is true that Bougainville was bombed while he was there, but his assignment was to move from island to island *behind* the line of advance, part of the lengthening umbilical cord of supply. He got to know his fellows, not in foxholes but across the table, during endless wartime poker games.

His Quaker mother did not approve of gambling, but he had eased his way into the military past her scruples. The war became a moral hiatus. Besides, motive is what matters, and Nick's motive was pure, was puritan. He was not playing games; with him it was a business. Lock your true Horatio Alger in a brothel, with no chance of leaving it, and he will improve management, streamline method, and raise income; his moral drive must find *some* outlet. Nick, as always, did his homework. He found poker's local theoreticians, men willing to play and discuss, re-play and debate, out of sheer analytic zeal. "I had a theory for playing draw poker," an officer named Stewart told Kornitzer. "Nick liked what I said . . . We played two-handed poker without money for four or five days, until he had learned the various plays. Soon his playing became tops." The iron butt was at work again, and with results. Here is Kornitzer's summary of the episode: "Out there Nixon passed over the traditional Quaker objections to gambling. Why? He needed money. He learned poker and mastered it to such a degree that he won a sizable amount, and it became the sole financial foundation of his career."

After the war, he gave up poker entirely. It had served its purpose. The essential Nixon traits are all here. First, the justification. "He needed money." To some men it would seem wrong to be playing for anything but amuse-ment—or at least to be playing without amusement. But for Nixon, the "self-improving" note is a moral necessity. And if you are going to do anything at all, you should make it useful; the devil's playground can become the saint's joyless field of exercise. It helps, watching Nixon's "ruthless" singlemindedness when bigger pots have been at stake, to remember those poker days.

It is also like him to have mastered a method before he risked real games. He "war-gamed" everything before-hand, with a passion for analysis, a search for what is constant in the variables, a reduction to basic patterns and technique. That, too, informs his political style. He makes no unexamined move. In fact, we can best understand his reaction to the 1960 campaign against Kennedy if we imagine "Nick," in the South Pacific, staking all his wartime winnings on one hand he was sure of, and then losing. What would he do? Get back, obviously, to the old drawing board. Repeatedly play, replay the game; tease out, mentally, what went wrong.

That is just what he did. Seven months of the year 1961 were spent reliving his career before a dictaphone, working on his book; and the longest, most intense time went into the chapter he wrote himself—one of six crises covered, though it takes up almost a third of the book. The treatment of the 1960 race is, in fact, a small book in itself, with a separate introduction devoted to Nixon's boyhood and the symbolic train that ran through Whittier and his mind.

Why did he lose in '60? He describes the bad breaks (e.g., the staph infection that hospitalized him for precious weeks) and some tactical errors (the effort to campaign in all states); but he disagrees with those who think he made a major error in debating Kennedy. The one thing, he argues, that crippled him in 1960 was his position as the "in" man challenged by an "out" man. Nixon was the hostage of an incumbent administration, made responsible for all discontent felt in the last eight years. That fact takes on overriding importance in Nixon's account of the election: "Kennedy was attacking a record and I was defending it. I don't mean to suggest that I was not perfectly willing to defend the record of the Administration of which I had been a part. But I knew from long experience that in debate, the man who can attack has a built-in advantage that is very hard to overcome. Almost automatically, he has the initiative and is the aggressor." Later, describing the crucial first debate, he says that Kennedy "did exactly what I would have done under similar circumstances: he attacked." In the second debate, Nixon tries to turn the tables and put his foe on the defensive: "At the very end of the debate, I had again been able to attack very sharply, this time on Kennedy's contention that the offshore islands of Quemoy and Matsu be surrendered." But this advantage, he claims, was taken from him: Chester Bowles, at the Kennedy camp, called Fred Seaton on the Nixon side to arrange a moratorium on

discussion of the islands. Nixon complied, lo........
weapon.

He hints that the natural difficulty of defe........
record was made insuperable because Kennedy........
exploited his "outsider" role. The principal example . this
is Kennedy's attack on the Republicans for letting Castro's
regime stand. Nixon claims the CIA had briefed Kennedy
on the contingency plan for a Cuban invasion; but Kennedy
was certain Nixon would not reveal this. When Nixon
sums up the experience, he returns to the point that seems
to have bothered him most in the whole campaign: "the
incumbent—or whoever represents an incumbent administration—will generally be at a disadvantage in debate
because his opponent can attack while he must defend."

He lost, then, because of an inbuilt disadvantage in his
position, one which Kennedy was clever enough (and,
sotto voce through the chapter, unscrupulous enough)
to exploit. It is not true that Nixon's book lacks self-
criticism. There is a good deal of humble confession in
earlier chapters; his taste for formulae even makes him
find the same flaw in four of the six crises (lapse from
control in their aftermath). These admissions, made earlier, call attention to the last chapter's distinguishing feature: Nixon discovers no major error in his 1960 campaign. He went down before an alliance of history and
"tricky Jack."

That is an important conclusion. It meant to Nixon, in
1961, that he was not basically a loser. Anyone, put on the
defensive as he was, would have lost; and, even more
important, the incumbent would be at the mercy of a
skilled challenger—e.g., himself—in the next round.

Nixon's chapter almost makes it sound as if an incumbent cannot win. But he is coming to grips with his
personal defeat. The very core of his electioneering technique had been a refusal to be put on the defensive;
training, environment, and experience all gave a special
meaning to his concept of "aggression." He was a Californian, trained by Murray Chotiner, who came to office in
1946. Any one of these circumstances would have made
Nixon a professional thrower of rascals out; in conjunction, they made him a virtuoso manipulater of discontents.

California is to America what America used to be to the
world—a nation of immigrants. And the influx of outsiders is matched by a restless internal circulation of in-

..oitants. The state is, like its freeways, a clotting of men and machines in constant (partial) motion. Its politics, too, is fluid. There is no stable party system. Cross-filing, a huge swing vote, a changing electorate, make it possible for leaders to tumble instantly down trapdoors (Goodwin Knight, Bill Knowland, and in 1962, Dick Nixon) or pop up out of nowhere (Ronald Reagan, George Murphy). There is no latticework of party structure to catch men's fall or slow their climb. It is a state with a million more registered Democrats than Republicans, which swept Reagan into office by a million votes.

Given this politics of overnight stardom and eclipse, a special campaign style was bound to emerge in California —though on this point, as on others, California is merely the vanguard of change throughout the country. Where an electorate (made up in great measure of new arrivals) knows little of a candidate's party record or performance (if any), techniques of publicity must be contrived—a thing easily done in the land of show business press agentry. Where party loyalty is comparatively insignificant, the "image" of the candidate as a person must be stressed. And where so many people have come to the state as a way of protesting conditions in the place they left, there must be a readiness to blame, change, and seek the new.

We speak, by the old synecdoche, of Madison Avenue methods in merchandizing a candidate. We really mean California methods. The initial steps toward the packaging of candidates were taken there. By 1930, Clem Whitaker had begun the work that made Whitaker and Baxter America's first large campaign-management firm. In 1934, the company played a leading part in the ten million dollar campaign to defeat Upton Sinclair. The sophisticated tools of that race included staged movies of "Bolshie" stampedes toward the state. The firm came, in time, to manage nationwide accounts—like the AMA's expensive attacks on federalized medicine. And, back in California, other firms followed this trailblazer—Baus and Ross, then Spencer and Roberts. There are also some individual publicists, like Hal Evry and the maverick Richard Tuck. And lawyer Murray Chotiner.

When Nixon turned to politics, he was bound to seek out this new game's theoreticians. Good fortune (or bad) made it unnecessary for him to seek far. His promoters had already hired the services of Mr. Chotiner, the victorious manager of Warren and Knowland elections. Chotiner found in this hardworking beginner an ideal pupil, and Nixon found a teacher whose mind tended, like his, toward the rigor of formulae. Stewart had a system for draw poker. Chotiner had a system for elections. The method was simple, tested, and ideally suited to California —as native as the clock-face cuff links worn by Chotiner. If you were one of Murray's candidates, you let the public know as little as possible about the whole range of your own opinions, and you forced it to know everything possible about a select portion of your opponent's views. The scheme depends, obviously, on the insight that people vote *against,* not *for.* The less of your own position you expose, the less the populace has to be against. This leaves you free to focus on the part of your opponent's life or record that people are most disposed to resent.

Nowhere can this method work so well as in California, a land of hopes half-broken, of visions going sour. It still draws men in continual slow-motion Gold Rush toward worked-out lodes. As one of the best students of the area, Joan Didion, says: "California is a place in which a boom mentality and a sense of Chekhovian loss meet in uneasy suspension; in which the mind is troubled by some buried but ineradicable suspicion that things better work here, because here, beneath that immense bleached sky, is where we run out of continent." The land promises escape; since it cannot (nor can any place) *keep* that promise, men live in fear. An embittering dawn of reality impends, always, over professionally chipper Californians. Their resentment is easily triggered—by someone who came to the state after them, or just before, crowding new kids into schools or trying to keep new kids out, clogging the freeways or fighting their extension. By "carpetbaggers" or exclusionists. By a man in flight from things they want to retain, or one trying to preserve a thing they came west to escape. A candidate's chances for error, if he makes a statement on anything, are marvelously broad in California.

There is nothing esoteric about Chotiner's basic insight. It is a maxim all politicians live by. Nor is Chotiner the only one to have grasped its special usefulness in California. Hal Evry, for instance, says that the most specific thing to say about one's own candidate is "Three cheers for Joe Smith," while the approach to one's adversary should be "End the Parking Meter Racket!" (Let the other fellow explain, in ridiculous detail, that there is no such thing as a parking meter racket. Everyone will suspect him of a cover-up.) What set Chotiner apart was an obsessive refinement of this insight, making it the center of all campaign wisdom. Asked why he insisted on starting a campaign at least one year before the election, he answered: "Because you need that time to deflate your opposition . . . There are many people who say we want to conduct a constructive campaign and point out the merits of our own candidate. I say to you in all sincerity that, if you do not deflate the opposition candidate before your own candidate gets started, the odds are that you are going to be doomed to defeat." It is the denigrative method: find the opposition's weak point and then just *lean* on it all through the race. In such a contest, the first blow means a great deal. Once a man is on the defensive, he must explain—and explanation is not nearly as effective as accusation. Besides, by the time your opponent has explained A, you can have B and C ready for him to explain.

What if one's opponent is launching attacks on you? Refuse to be put on the defensive. Just don't answer. If, after a while, that becomes impossible, contrive a way to turn the tables and make an *attack* out of your explanation: "May I suggest to you that I think the classic that will live in all political history came on September twenty-third, nineteen fifty-two, from Los Angeles, California, when the candidate for the vice-presidency answered, if you please, with an attack against those who had made one on him." Nixon, forced to reveal his earnings because of suspicion about his financial probity, made the fact that his opponents had not opened their books a proof that they had something to hide. It made Chotiner glow with all the teacher-pride of Mr. Chips. All but two of Nixon's campaigns for himself have been "classics" to a connoisseur of the Chotiner style. The two failures—1960 and 1962—came when (and because) Nixon was forced onto the defensive, where all his expertise seemed useless.

If California and Chotiner were combining to edge Nixon into a politics of resentment, so was history. He came to politics at a time when one of the century's great shifts was beginning, a rumble of displacement whose scale and direction were not visible then. It was a shift, though no one knew it, toward Nixon—a vague accumulating lean westward, inward, and backward. What had begun in 1946, when he had been elected to Congress, was fully accomplished in 1968 by his election as President. It was the end of the New Deal.

Nixon is a postwar man. Politically, he does not preexist the year 1946. Though he showed an early interest in American history, it was centered moralistically in semi-myth—Lincoln and Wilson, the Calvinist saviors who failed. He does not seem to have made the obvious connection between Wilson's domestication of "populism" and Franklin Roosevelt's domestication of "radicalism." For Nixon, the thirties seem not to have taken place. He lived through the Depression, studying, working, going to school. He was then at a formative age. Yet neither the Depression nor the New Deal, neither cause nor cure, had any discernible effect on him. This is another example of his total concentration on the task of the moment—in this case, college, law school, the problems of starting a new practice and business. For him, American history stood still while he learned the method of his current game. History ended in 1924, with the death of his boyhood hero Wilson, and did not start up again until 1946.

Nixon's cousin told me, in Whittier, that he vaguely recalls Dick's "talking politics" from an early age; but there is only one memory of specific judgment on "current affairs"—and that is probably a result of his father's eloquence against politicians and lawyers. Frank Nixon sounds, in the anecdotes of those who knew him, like the fabled Irishman washed up on a strange shore, who wades out of the surf shouting "Who's the government here? I'm against 'em." In 1929, the Teapot Dome scandals broke, involving the Elk Hill oil reserves of California. Frank Nixon, who was within an ace of owning rich oil fields himself, went into a rapture of recrimination for days and weeks, as new disclosures drove at least one prominent lawyer to suicide. Young Richard, then twelve years old, went to his mother in this period and told her, "I will be an old-fashioned kind of lawyer, a lawyer who can't be bought." (This is still one of Poor Richard's maxims: early in 1968, he enjoyed telling newsmen he liked his young staff members because "They are the kind of men you cannot buy.") But the revelation of crime in Harding's administration did not prompt any of the obvious political judgments in Nixon—did not make him suspicious of his family's traditional party or of big business. After his Depression schooling, he went to New York to seek employment in Wall Street firms, but failed in the attempt. He went home to Whittier and used his law practice as the means for launching a new corporation, Citra-Frost, which also failed. His early political speeches were of the Rotary Club and junior executive type. He did not even register to vote during the first four years of his majority. In 1940, he did some local speaking, in Republican Whittier, for Wendell Willkie. But when the president of Whittier's Bank of America, offering him the chance to run for Congress, asked whether he was a Republican (the banker did not *know* this, though he knew Nixon), the best Nixon could answer was: "I guess so. I voted for Dewey."

He was, politically, a blank slate (great attraction for a Chotiner). He began his career in 1946 with a total attunement to that year's issues. And there was only one issue—eloquently captured in the Republican campaign slogan "Had Enough?" The press called 1946 a year of frustration. The nation wanted to get out of uniform. It wanted rapid demobilization, removal of controls, the end of rationing. It wanted to forget the war and everything connected with it. This was the mood that had ended Wilson's high-minded regime after the earlier war. Across the ocean, a similar mood swept Winston Churchill from office. It seemed certain, when the time came, to oust Harry Truman. Some people, in fact, were not willing to wait for this time to come. J. William Fulbright suggested publicly that Truman should resign, after appointing Senator Vandenberg his Secretary of State and heir. It seemed to the Democrat from Arkansas that there was no hope for a Democratic administration to govern the country.

But the nation could not ease its memories of war by eliminating Harry. The Bomb and its control, peace terms and new alliances, divided-occupation duties, the UN, ominous little bristlings against Russia at the Paris peace talks, Wallace's break with Truman on the treatment of our Soviet allies—all these proved the nation could not go on a binge and forget, as it had after Wilson's war. And domestic troubles, set aside "for the duration," were being taken out of storage—e.g., troubles between labor and management, conflicts between security and civil rights.

Truman had seized the railroads and threatened to draft the workers. His atomic policy involved peacetime secrecy, introducing new rules and challenges. As veterans returned, demanding instant deserved rewards, people found school space, consumer goods, living accommodations as hard to come by as they had been in the war. The war had ended without ending—and who was to blame?

No one, of course. History. The gods. But there is enough truth to the Chotiner insight to make it clear who would *get* the blame. Democrats. It was a year of national unrest and Republican happiness. For the first time since 1928, since the pre-Crash euphoria of Hoover, a Republican Congress was elected, Truman's hated Eightieth.

Had enough? That was the atmosphere of Richard Nixon's entry into politics. And his opponent was a natural target. Jerry Voorhis, of a wealthy family, Phi Beta Kappa from Yale, had been a romantic twenties radical, going off to try life as a laborer, open an orphanage, mix with populists and socialists. During the Depression he supported Upton Sinclair's California race for governor, and picked up some of the "funny money" schemes of that Townsendite era. But he was also a perfect example of the New Deal's ability to recruit radicals and tame them. He went to Congress in 1936 as an FDR man, and stayed on for ten years, even sponsoring a 1940 bill to register communists.

But if the New Deal's strength before the war came from its ability to bring a Jerry Voorhis aboard, its weakness afterward was revealed by the presence of so many people with compromising radical pasts. The New Deal and the war had, between them, restored America's individualist system to economic power—and that system would be used, first of all, to attack the rescuer. Controls and cohesion, ideals and uplift, the government as a social worker not a cop on the beat—all these things chafed, as they had when Johnny came marching home in 1919 to start the individualist jazz age.

In the 1946 campaign, Voorhis was made a symbol of big government's meddlesomeness (he even wanted, the story went, to limit grain used for booze), of its support for radical unions (wartime alliance with Russia led some unions to become openly communist), of its cordial attitude toward Russia (Henry Wallace was still considered by many the true heir and spokesman for the New Deal).

It was easy for Nixon to fulfill Chotiner's directive, that the foe be deflated well ahead of time. His early circulars even described Voorhis as one who "stayed safely behind the front in Washington" while Nixon was a "clean, forthright young American who fought in defense of his country in the stinking mud and jungles of the Solomons."

The principal weapon used against Voorhis was the CIO's Political Action Committee (PAC), which even Voorhis said was communist-directed. The Nixon literature claimed Voorhis was PAC's puppet. Voorhis said he did not have PAC's endorsement and would not seek it. But that did him little good. He had been endorsed by the National Citizens' PAC, some of whose officers were also on CIO-PAC letterheads. This was the select part of the Voorhis record Chotiner decided to spotlight. The whole campaign would revolve around PAC. Voorhis' denials simply added to the discussion and awareness of PAC's activities. He was now linked with it, and nothing he did would help him much. If he denounced PAC, he could either do it in terms that looked namby-pamby next to Nixon's red-blooded yodeling, or, swinging harder and wilder than Nixon, he might drive off Democrats and Independents who were his base of support. It was a perfect trap constructed by the denigrative method.

Nixon got his opportunity to use the weapon with maximum effect as a result of his first child's birth—Tricia. The Voorhis office sent out a government pamphlet on child care to each family that had a baby in the congressman's district. Someone in the office must have thought it piquant that Voorhis should be sending a book to his rival, and drew it to the attention of the congressman, who scrawled on the book, "Congratulations! I look forward to meeting you soon in public." Nixon publicized this as a commitment to formal debate. Voorhis, who had won his own 1936 race by debating the incumbent, let himself be lured into the trap. The first debate (of five) took place before a small audience, but it had great impact, and increased the crowds that came to hear other sessions. Nixon put his man on the defensive, recalling his Left-Wing past, quoting from his writings on monetary reform, and—most important—contending he was a creature of PAC. When the congressman denied this, Nixon whipped out a paper on which the National Citizens' PAC was asked by its local chapter to sponsor Voorhis. The victim was now left with the unpleasant task of distinguishing between CIO-PAC and NC-PAC, saying he was *not* endorsed by the former, that he did not *want* to be endorsed by either —and yet that he *did* want the support of organized labor. He was off balance, explaining, splitting hairs all the rest of the campaign, which reached a climax in the fifth debate at San Gabriel Mission. Nixon, of course, went to Congress, to the Un-American Activities Committee, to Hiss.

In 1948, fresh from the Hiss case, young co-sponsor of the Mundt-Nixon Bill against subversion, Nixon was easily reelected. But Dewey, fated to win, lost. And, doing so, confirmed Nixon's belief in the Chotiner technique. Dewey believed that the Democrats were finished anyway; further attacks on them would lead to national disunity. Long before the election he was acting like a bipartisan President instead of the challenger. The incumbent's record looked *too* vulnerable. Dewey broke all the Chotiner rules —something Nixon would remember, for years later, when he referred to the Dewey team, now handling Eisenhower's bid, as a bunch of amateurs. And Dewey had most spectacularly failed in the use of Nixon's own issue, communism—an omission with special meaning for the Californian. The man who tried to shape the '48 campaign along anticommunist lines was also the party leader who backed Nixon in his first obscure race against Voorhis. It was Harold Stassen. An odd rivalry-alliance existed, ever after, between Stassen and his protégé. When Stassen tried, in '48, to wrest the nomination from Dewey, the Mundt-Nixon Bill was his favored instrument. During the Oregon primary, he drew the front-runner into a nationwide radio debate on the subject of outlawing the Communist Party. That was the logic, he maintained, of the Mundt-Nixon Bill, heavily favored by Republicans. If he could get Dewey to attack the bill, he would have a hot issue to take to the convention. But Dewey had put his staff to work, and he argued convincingly that the Mundt-Nixon Bill would not make the Communist Party illegal in itself. Dewey won the debate, and the primary, but he passed the word that communism would not be an issue in his campaign; and he lost the election. Several people learned from that experience—especially a young man Stassen had brought to the radio studio as his assistant, Senator Joseph McCarthy of Wisconsin. (Nixon first met

McCarthy at a party put on by Stassen supporters.) Dewey's loss had, for Stassen and McCarthy and Nixon, all the symmetry of earned nemesis.

When Nixon decided, two years later, to move up from the House to the Senate, every omen confirmed his analysis of the party's error in 1948. The time was ripe for questioning the loyalty of left-Democrats. The man whose seat he wanted in the Senate was Sheridan Downey, a veteran of Upton Sinclair's campaign, who knew the time to bow out. By February of '50, Stassen's debating assistant had opened his attack on communists with a speech delivered in Wheeling, West Virginia; and McCarthy's first outspoken foe, Millard Tydings, lost his Senate primary in Maryland as the price of opposition to him. The Cold War had finally, in Korea, become hot. Nixon joined the cry of his party for Secretary of State Dean Acheson's head. Even Democrats were using the "reds in government" issue to eliminate rivals: George Smathers, an early friend of Nixon's (his Florida home would later be part of the presidential compound on Key Biscayne), won a Senate primary in '50 by calling his opponent, Claude Pepper, the "Red Pepper." Nixon admits he studied the Smathers campaign, which was run by Florida's Murray Chotiner, PR man Dan Crisp, on the du Pont funds of Florida boss Ed Ball. Fall of 1950 in California thus repeated spring of '50 in Florida, with "Red Pepper" becoming "The Pink Lady."

The lady in question was a bright Irish actress, Helen Gahagan, who had gone into politics and been elected congresswoman—the earliest of the Murphy-Reagan breed of Hollywood attractions at the polls. In the House she had served, like Nixon, on the Un-American Activities Committee, and, like her colleague, she decided to move up from one chamber to the other. Unlike him, however, she had come out of the primary badly scarred by her Democratic rival, who lumped her with conspirators against America. What is more, she was married to actor Melvyn Douglas; and Mr. Douglas—seducer of Ninotchka from her Leninist ways, suave idol of a Depression era that yearned for white tie and tails—was part Jewish (real name, as Mr. Rankin found occasion to inform his committee, Melvyn Hesselberg). So Gerald L. K. Smith was on hand during the campaign to "help Richard Nixon get rid of the Jew-Communists." Probably all that Nixon had to do, in order to win, was pick up the Democrats' own primary charges against her and add some "Pink Lady" frills. But Chotiner also found an equivalent, for this campaign, of the PAC charge that had done in Jerry Voorhis. By a little skillful play with vote-counts in the House, Mrs. Douglas' record could be made to sound almost the same as that of Vito Marcantonio, the East Harlem congressman called by Walter Goodman the period's "exemplary fellow traveler." Mrs. Douglas had joined Marcantonio in criticism of Rankin's methods as chairman of the Un-American Committee. From such facts Chotiner's famous "Pink Sheet" constructed a "Douglas-Marcantonio Axis." (Nixon himself had been appointed to the committee through the intervention of Harlem congressman Adam Powell, with instructions to keep a watch on Rankin—a Nixon-Powell axis?) Mrs. Douglas was now left, like Voorhis before her, with the task of extricating herself from the implied alliance without alienating her own Left-Wing support. She had to profess her anticommunism, but in paler terms than Nixon's. As Chotiner put it: "She made the fatal mistake of attacking our strength instead of sticking to attacking our weaknesses." Chotiner's memo to campaign workers at this junction, marked "Important Strategy," read: "Helen Douglas is trying to portray a new role as a foe of Communism. Do not let her get away with it! It is a phony act."

Joe McCarthy came into the state to support the Republican campaign, and spoke on TV from Los Angeles with typical flair: "Ask the basket-cases if they agree that Acheson is an 'outstanding American.' I am sure the mothers of America will notify the administration this fall that there is nothing 'outstanding' about washing away with blood the blunders and traitorous acts of the crowd whom the Democrat candidates have pledged to protect if they are elected . . . The chips are down . . . between the American people and the administration Commicrat Party of Betrayal." Nixon went to the Senate, to the Chicago convention, to Ike.

Every campaign had taught Nixon the same lesson: mobilize resentment against those in power. When his turn came, in 1952, to make up for Truman's escape from doom four years earlier, he brought to the national scene techniques he had perfected at the state level. Running for Vice-President, he had two nation-wide television shows allotted to him by the National Committee. The first one he used, of necessity, to get back on the ticket—his "Checkers" appearance. But the second one could be devoted entirely to attack. After describing his investigation of Hiss, he contrasted Eisenhower's military staff, which "never had an instance of infiltration," with the Democratic administration: "We can assume because of the cover-up of this administration in the Hiss case that the Communists, the fellow-travelers, have not been cleaned out of the executive branch of government." In the course of his campaign, Nixon called the Democratic candidate "Adlai the appeaser . . . who got a Ph.D. from Dean Acheson's College of Cowardly Communist Containment."

The Republicans more than made up, in 1952, for Dewey's shrinking ways in 1948. It is often said that Nixon did all the attacking, while Eisenhower smiled on paternally; that a high-road vs. low-road division of labor was made between the candidates at their meeting in Denver. Even Nixon fosters this impression: "The plan was for General Eisenhower to stress the positive aspects of his 'Crusade to Clean up the Mess in Washington.' I was to hammer away at our opponents on the record of the Truman administration, with particular emphasis on Communist subversion because of my work on the Hiss case." But the real campaign was even more denigrative than such a description implies. Eisenhower, in his own calm way, had to suggest that there was a great deal to be cleaned up in Washington. What that meant, in practice, was that Nixon went after the commies, Ike went after the crooks. The presidential candidate, a model of probity, kept referring to the mink coat and deep freezer scandals of the Truman regime as the object of his crusade, promising to end "shady and shoddy" government by "crooks and cronies"—all code words for the Democratic administration. He said that America's troubles could be traced to government by men "too small for their jobs." In a sense, Eisenhower campaigned against the outgoing President, and left his actual opponent—Adlai Stevenson—to the mercies of his running mate.

It worked. But it was the last time Nixon had an unambiguous opening for his Chotiner method—until 1968. In the off-year election of 1954, he campaigned hard against the inherited ills of the Democrats' long reign; but from within the administration, no longer an outsider. By

1956, when Eisenhower and he ran again, Nixon had lost Chotiner. The lawyer had been hauled before the McClellan (formerly McCarthy) Committee, on suspiciously vague suspicions of influence-peddling, by the committee's ardent and partisan counsel, Robert Kennedy. He who lives by the sword . . .

Without Chotiner, who had become an embarrassment, Nixon had to face Stassen's "Dump Nixon" movement of '56 by getting a firm fistful of Ike's coattail, closing his eyes, and just hanging on. In 1958, the party workhorse went out to stump again on the off-year. He tried again to suggest that the Democrats did not take a hard enough line against Russia, until a telegram from Papa in the White House sternly told him to leave foreign affairs alone.

That was the record as Nixon went, debilitated, into his race with Kennedy. His last three times out as campaigner for the administration had been unspectacular. The party took stunning defeats on the off-years. The "new Nixon" was a post-Chotiner Nixon who, holding office, was forced onto the defensive. *Six Crises* tells us what influence that role had on his attempt to counter Kennedy's aggressive style (which, in its hammering on a fictitious "missile gap" and on Ike's alleged "softness toward Castro" could have taught even Chotiner a thing or two). Nixon could do nothing but fall back on his dogged thoroughness—being photographed individually with every delegate to the Republican Convention, flying off to every state—campaign equivalents of his hypercautious "homework." He flew by the iron seat of his pants that year.

Nixon's book does not list all the efforts he made to put Kennedy on the defensive. In the first television debate, he used a ploy from the Checkers speech, appealing for sympathy as one less wealthy than his opponent: "I know what it means to be poor. I know what it means to see people who are unemployed." In the second debate, he went back to his old whipping boy, Harry Truman, and tried to make Kennedy responsible for the artillery-corps language of the last Democratic President: "I can only say that I'm very proud that President Eisenhower restored the dignity and decency and, frankly, good language to the conduct of the Presidency of the United States."

The stab at Governor Brown's job in 1962 left Nixon still defending; he had to protest repeatedly, without conviction, that he did not mean to use the governorship to stay aloft in a "holding pattern" over the White House. Inclination led him, too often, toward discussion of foreign policy. All he could do at the domestic level was make Ike-promises to clean up "the mess in Sacramento." At last, he fell back on *the* topic, hinting he would chase new Hisses out of California, since Governor Brown was "not capable of dealing with the Communist threat within our borders." After all, he had not introduced "a single item of antisubversive legislation in four years."

And then there was '64. The race was hardly worth the run, with Johnson riding a postassassination wave of national sentiment; but Nixon the warhorse hears trumpets even on his off day, and chafes and foams toward the field. Nixon came and went trying to look nubile, conciliatory as could be, since his chances depended on stalemate among the others.

It had been a long hard decade and a half, from Checkers to the kickoff of 1968's campaign. His loser image had grown at the same time that, hands tied, he stiffened into a noncombative "new Nixon." No wonder he rejoiced to newsmen, at the beginning of 1968, that *he* would be attacking now, with Humphrey in the role of Johnson's defender. He crafted a Chotiner campaign, but "updated," modified, sophisticated. He was helped by the fact that Johnson's peace efforts made it possible for him to maintain a stance of watching-and-waiting on the toughest foreign issue (make the public know as little as possible about your own position). To feed the several resentments of government he invented the hippocampine "new alignment." But he did more than that. On the law and order issue, he concentrated his attack on the Attorney General, making Ramsey Clark this campaign's Vito Marcantonio—the damaging ally, the albatross. And he criticized Supreme Court decisions, making them the new PAC policy. It worked. Chotiner, who had been quietly rehabilitated in the New York campaign office of John Mitchell, then added to the White House staff, could still be proud of his pupil.

5. Checkers

*"One other thing I probably should tell you, because
if I don't they'll probably be saying this about me
too, we did get something—a gift—after the election.
A man down in Texas heard Pat on the radio mention
the fact that our two youngsters would like to have
a dog. And, believe it or not, the day before we left
on this campaign trip we got a message from Union
Station in Baltimore saying that they had a package
for us. We went down to get it. You know what it
was? It was a little cocker spaniel dog in a crate that
he sent all the way from Texas. Black and white
spotted. And our little girl—Tricia, the six-year-old
—named it Checkers. And you know the kids love
that dog and I just want to say this right now, that
regardless of what they say about it, we're going to
keep it."*

                               —the Checkers speech

RIDING IN THE STAFF BUS during Nixon's 1968
campaign, I talked with one of his speech writers about
the convention in Miami. Nixon's wooing of Strom Thurmond had been much criticized. But Nixon's man now
said the acceptance speech eclipsed everything that went
before: "That was so clearly the major event of the
convention—a brilliant job. To talk about that convention
is, simply, to talk about that speech. What did *you* think
of it?" I answered that it reminded me of the Checkers
speech. The comment seemed to horrify my interlocuter;
and Professor Martin Anderson, traveling with Nixon as
an adviser on urban matters, turned around in the seat
before us to object: "People forget that the Checkers
speech was a political master stroke, an act of political
genius!" But I had not forgotten: that was, I assured
him, my point.

Professor Anderson's defensiveness was understandable. Nixon has often been sneered at, over the years, for his television speech in the campaign of 1952. The very term "Checkers speech," reducing the whole broadcast to its saccharine doggy-passage, is a judgment in itself. But that broadcast saved Nixon's career, and made history. By the beginning of the 1968 campaign, sixteen years later, it was a journalistic commonplace that Nixon did not appear to advantage on television. His wan first TV encounter with John Kennedy had dimmed the public's earlier impression. But Nixon only risked that debate with Kennedy because he had such a record of success on the TV screen: in the history of that medium, his 1952 speech was probably a greater milestone than the presidential debate that came eight years later. Nixon first demonstrated the political uses and impact of television. In one half hour Nixon converted himself from a liability, breathing his last, to one of the few people who could add to Eisenhower's preternatural appeal—who could gild the lily. For the first time, people saw a living political drama on their TV sets—a man fighting for his whole career and future—and they judged him under that strain. It was an even greater achievement than it seemed. He had only a short time to prepare for it. The show, forced on him, was meant as a form of political euthanasia. He came into the studio still reeling from distractions and new demoralizing blows.

Nixon, naturally, puts the Checkers speech, along with the whole "fund crisis," among the six crises he survived with credit. It belongs there. He probably displayed more sheer nerve in that crisis than in any of the others. As a freshman in Congress, he did not stand to lose so much by the Hiss investigation. He had, moreover, an unsuspected hoard of evidence in that encounter; and he was backed by dedicated men like Father Cronin, while backing another dedicated man, Whittaker Chambers. In the crises he deals with after 1952, he was a Vice-President, in some way speaking for the nation, buoyed by its resources, defending it as much as himself; never totally without dignity. But at the time when he went onto the TV screen in 1952, he was hunted and alone. Nine years later he would write of that ordeal, "This speech was to be the most important of my life. I felt now that it was my battle alone. I had been deserted by so many

I had thought were friends but who panicked in battle when the first shot was fired." It was, without exaggeration, "the most searing personal crisis of my life." It was also the experience that took the glitter out of politics for Mrs. Nixon.

To say Nixon was alone by the time he gave his speech is to understate the matter badly. The whole aim of the speech, as that ordeal had been proposed, was to accomplish his isolation—to make him stand or fall (presumably the latter) on his own, without affecting the bright fortune of The Star. From Nixon's point of view, Eisenhower, after picking him up, had at the first opportunity dropped him. This was particularly trying because Nixon's fund scandal arose in the first place from support for Ike. Going into the 1952 Republican Convention in Chicago, Nixon was in heavy demand. Because of his tough line on subversion and espionage, he was considered part of the Republicans' conservative wing, whose hopes were with Robert Taft. Yet this very fact made him useful to other candidates; and he had been approached by two of them. Harold Stassen, whose presidential aspirations were not yet a joke, dangled the vice-presidency before Nixon, something to be given in return for Nixon's delivery of the California delegation. But Stassen, a boy genius in other ways, was already far advanced in political senility. Nixon could not deliver the California delegation, which was led by his old enemy Earl Warren.

Meanwhile, in Taft, the party's Eastern Establishment faced the most serious threat so far to its control of the convention. It countered this challenge by producing the prize candidate of the century—one the ADA had drooled after, four years earlier, in its attempt to rescue Democrats from what seemed to be Truman's kamikaze dive. With Ike, the Establishment could knock off anybody, even Taft. And, after Taft's defeat, the brokers could bind up the party's wounds by adding a conservative, a strong anticommunist, to the ticket. That was the plan of Eisenhower's men in May of 1952, when Dewey first approached Nixon with the idea of becoming Vice-President. It was a heady proposal for a thirty-nine-year-old just finished with his first year in the Senate.

Yet it put him in a difficult position. The leader of his own delegation, Earl Warren, had aimed at the presi-

dency four years before, but only reached the second
spot (as Dewey's running mate). This year he still had a
chance, if Taft could tie up Eisenhower, of becoming a
compromise candidate. Warren, as California's favorite
son, was therefore officially neutral in his dealings with
Taft and Eisenhower, but he hoped Taft would pick up
support. Nixon was pledged to his state's favorite son,
and he kept the letter of his pledge. But several of his
moves worked to undercut Warren. Before the convention, he did something no senator had tried in California
—sent out a questionnaire asking 23,000 California voters
who their first choice for President would be (i.e., their
real choice, as opposed to the state party's official stance
of having chosen Warren). The result, which became
known to the public, was a clear majority for Eisenhower.
Then, after Nixon (who had traveled ahead to the convention's platform hearings) joined the California delegation's train in Denver, his people spread the word that
Ike was a sure thing. As the train rolled into Chicago
and Warren was given his favorite-son reception, there
was a notable absence among delegates—Nixon had left
the train at a suburban stop. This "treachery" angered a
number of Californians. When Nixon ran for governor
in 1962, Warren's son Earl Jr. publicly switched his registration and became a Democrat, saying Nixon had
"wronged my father and the whole state" by "back-door
tactics" undertaken "for political gain for himself."

That flare-up ten years later suggests the intensity of
the Warren people's resentment in 1952. It was so great
that disaffected California delegates, who had been among
those canvassed for Nixon's fund, sought out newsmen
and suggested they check these private moneys collected
in his name. By backing Ike, Nixon lit a fuse which led,
by way of a sputtering train of news stories, to Ike's
repudiation of him.

The first news story broke on Thursday, September 18.
There had been warnings in the Nixon camp all the four
preceding days. A newsman in Washington asked Nixon
about the fund on Sunday. Monday, three other reporters
checked facts with Dana Smith, the administrator of the
fund. By Wednesday, Jim Bassett, Nixon's press secretary,
heard something was brewing from his old reporter
friends. The candidate had just begun his first major tour
—a whistlestop north through California; when the train

stopped for water around midnight, a worried staff man waited with more rumors. Thursday, it broke: the New York *Post* had a story with the headline, SECRET RICH MEN'S TRUST FUND KEEPS NIXON IN STYLE FAR BEYOND HIS SALARY. The story did not justify that sensational summary, and neither did subsequent investigation. The fund was public, independently audited, earmarked for campaign expenses, and collected in small donations over two years by known Nixon campaign backers. It was neither illegal nor unethical. And the press soon discovered that the Democratic nominee, Adlai Stevenson, had similar funds, only larger in their amount and looser in their administration. Why, then, was so much made of Nixon's fund, and so little of Stevenson's?

Nixon's official explanation, at the time, was his standard charge: the commies were behind it all. By Friday morning, the day after the charge was published, there were hecklers at his train stops to shout "Tell us about the sixteen thousand!" At a town called Marysville, he did tell them. His own version of that speech, included in his book, is more moderate than some others; but even his excerpts seem gamy enough: "You folks know the work that I did investigating Communists in the United States. Ever since I have done that work the Communists and the left-wingers have been fighting me with every possible smear. When I received the nomination for the Vice Presidency I was warned that if I continued to attack the Communists in this government they would continue to smear me. And believe me, you can expect that they will continue to do so. They started it yesterday. They have tried to say that I had taken $16,000 for my personal use." The *they* is conveniently vague throughout. They—i.e., the New York *Post* and other papers—published the charge. Go far enough back up the paragraph, through intervening "theys," and you find that the antecedent is, more immediately, "the Communists in this Government," and, in the first place, "Communists and [broad sweep here] left-wingers." The explanation is beautifully lucid and inclusive (if a little unspecific about the machinery that makes the nation's press perform the communists' bidding): since the publicizing or nonpublicizing of fund scandals is at the disposal of communists, who were (naturally) supporting Adlai Stevenson, the Stevenson fund got (naturally) no publicity like that accorded to Nixon.

Behind this funny explanation, there are scattered but clear indications, in his book, of the true story, a sad one. At one point Nixon asks why his own statement of the "basic facts" about the fund received so little attention from the press. His answer ignores the conspiratorial explanation given eight pages earlier, and supplies four reasons, two of them technical (denials never get as big a play as accusations in the press, news travels east to west and he was in California), and two more substantive: reporters are mainly Democrats (though Nixon admits that publishers are mainly Republicans, which makes for some balance), and "the big-name, influential Washington reporters cover the presidential candidates while the less-known reporters are assigned to the vice presidential candidates." The last reason, the real one, looks like another point of newspaper mechanics—the mere logistics of press assignment; until we ask why that should matter. The answer, in Nixon's own words, is that his own press release "got lost in the welter of news and speculation over whether General Eisenhower would or would not choose to find a new running mate." *That* was the news on Eisenhower's train—because Ike's advisers were known to be searching for a way to dump Nixon, and Ike was a man who at this stage followed his advisers almost blindly. In short, the Nixon fund was a big story because Eisenhower, by his silence and hints and uneasiness, made it one. For no other reason.

It was natural for Eisenhower to acquiesce in a staff decision to drop Nixon. That staff had presented him with Nixon in the first place. (Ike's knowledge of his running mate was very slim—he thought, for instance, he was forty-two rather than thirty-nine.) The General had, in fact, learned of Nixon's choice at exactly the same time Nixon did. When Herb Brownell asked Ike what he thought of Nixon, the presidential nominee expressed surprise that the decision was his to make. He said he would leave the matter to Brownell, provided the latter consulted "the collective judgment of the leaders of the party" (the top man, in military politics, protects himself by putting a subordinate in charge of the operation, under staff scrutiny). So Brownell called a meeting of the party's leaders, and went through the form of considering Taft and others. But then Dewey got up, to speak for the winning camp. Nixon he said, and Nixon it was. That decision made, Brownell went to the phone, dialed Nixon, and had him listen in while, on another phone, he told Eisenhower that the choice had been made.

As the fund story broke, Nixon wondered where Ike stood. Thursday went by, and Friday. No word from the General—to the public, or to Nixon. But the Establishment was at work: the very thing that had made Nixon good "for balance" made him unpalatable in himself, seen through Establishment eyes. He was there to draw in the yokels. If there was any doubt about his ability to do that, no one would feel compunction at his loss: Ike was too valuable a property to be risked with anyone who might hurt him. This was the attitude on Eisenhower's train, and it spread to Nixon's as newsmen jumped over from the main tour to watch the death throes in the smaller one. The machinery of execution made itself visible Saturday morning, when the New York *Herald Tribune*—the voice of the Eastern Establishment—asked for Nixon's resignation from the ticket. It was, Nixon realized, an order. The same voice that had summoned him was now dismissing him. A waiting game had been played for three days to see if he would go without having to be ordered, and Nixon had not gone. The Saturday editorial (written Friday), following so close on the *Post*'s revelation, appearing before Nixon had conferred with Eisenhower, was the first of several "hints" that he was not wanted. Despite his studied deference toward Eisenhower, Nixon makes it clear he was not dense: "The publishers and other top officials of the *Tribune* had very close relations with Eisenhower and" (for which read, *I mean*) "with some of his most influential supporters. I assumed that the *Tribune* would not have taken this position editorially unless it also represented the thinking of the people around Eisenhower. And, as I thought more about it, it occurred to me" (the little light bulb above a cartoon character's head—Nixon must play this role straight) "that this might well be read as" (*obviously had to be*) "the view of Eisenhower himself, for I had not heard from him since the trouble began, two days before."

At ten o'clock Friday night, a reporter told him the next day's *Herald Tribune* would ask him to resign. Nixon, who had not heard this, was stunned. He summoned his closest advisers, Chotiner and Bill Rogers (who would, after more of Nixon's crises, at last be his Secretary of State). These two had received the editorial an hour and a half earlier, but they were not going to tell him about it till morning—afraid he would lose sleep if he saw it (a judgment events confirmed). He asked for the editorial and read: "The proper course of Senator Nixon in the circumstances is to make a formal offer of withdrawal from the ticket." So that was it. Nixon is quite candid here: "I knew now the fat was in the fire. That sounded like the official word from Eisenhower himself." He spent four hours discussing his options with Chotiner and Rogers. Then, at two in the morning, he told his wife, and went through the whole discussion again with her.

The next day, Saturday, three days after the story broke, with newsmen plaguing him for his decision, he had to brace himself for defiance of the Establishment. It was an all-day job. He asked Chotiner and Rogers to get the ultimatum spelled out, if they could, from Ike's inner circle—Chotiner tried to reach Dewey, Rogers called Fred Seaton. They got no direct answer. But the indirect command was growing more insistent; sharper and sharper "hints" were thrown to the public (and, by this round-about path, to Nixon). Sherman Adams had summoned a man all the way from Hawaii to join the Eisenhower train, and the man was all too obviously a second-string Nixon: Bill Knowland, tough anticommunist and Californian. Eisenhower had finally spoken too, off the record. The newsmen on his train had taken a poll that came out forty-to-two for dumping Nixon; news of this was passed along to Ike's press secretary (Dewey's press man in the last campaign, Jim Hagerty), along with the newsmen's opinion that Ike might be stalling to arrange a whitewash job for Nixon. Ike did not like such talk; it questioned not only Nixon's honesty, but his. He invited the newsmen into his compartment for a talk off the record—but the main part of it was soon made public. "I don't care if you fellows are forty-to-two against me, but I'm taking my time on this. Nothing's decided, contrary to your idea that this is all a setup for a whitewash of Nixon. Nixon has got to be clean as a hound's tooth." Again, Nixon got the point: "Our little group was somewhat[!] dismayed by reports of Eisenhower's attitude. I must admit it made me feel like the little boy caught with jam on his face."

By Saturday night, then, the issue was clear: knuckle under, or defy the closest thing modern America has had to a political saint. Nixon, here as in all his crises, claims the decision was made on purely selfless grounds: he was thinking of Ike's own welfare—switching men in mid-campaign might make the General unpopular. (This is like worrying that the Milky Way might go out.) Not that Nixon is insincere in his claim. Politicians are very deft at persuading themselves that the world's best interests just happen to coincide with the advancement of their own careers. He says he put the question to his four advisers (Chotiner, Rogers, Bassett, and Congressman Pat Hillings) this way: "Forget about me. If my staying on the ticket would lead to Eisenhower's defeat, I would never forgive myself. If my getting off the ticket is necessary to assure his victory, it would be worth it, as far as any personal embarrassment to me is concerned. Looking at it this way—should I take the initiative and resign from the ticket at this time?"

But Nixon does not feel obliged to present his friends as men crippled by nobility. Chotiner, for instance, plays straight man here, saying all the "natural" things Nixon is too lofty for: "How stupid can they be? If these damned amateurs around Eisenhower just had the sense they were born with they would recognize that this is a purely political attack . . . This whole story has been blown up out of all proportion because of the delay and indecision of the amateurs around Eisenhower." Not even good old Murray, though, blunt fellow as he is, can be described in this book as attacking the Big Man himself —just the little men around him. When Nixon's friends start criticizing Eisenhower, the veil of anonymity must be lowered over them: "But now, some were beginning to blame Eisenhower, for not making a decision one way or the other." Nixon himself would never dream of questioning his leader: "What had happened during the past week had not shaken my faith in Eisenhower. If, as some of my associates thought, he appeared to be indecisive, I put the blame not on him but on his lack of experience in political warfare and on the fact that he was relying on several equally inexperienced associates. I could see his dilemma."

The decision to be made at this session was simple: obey the order relayed by the *Herald Tribune*, or risk

disobedience. But, after a full day of campaigning through
Oregon, he sat up with his inner circle, in Portland,
debating the matter till three in the morning. Then, left
alone, he went over the whole thing in his mind for two
more hours. By five o'clock Sunday morning, he had set
himself on a course he meant never to abandon: he would
not resign. Sunday brought blow on blow meant to shake
that resolution. First, there was a long telegram from
Harold Stassen, still trying to clear some path for himself. He recommended, for Nixon's own good ("it will
strengthen you and aid your career"), that a resignation
be sent right off to Ike. Then, that afternoon, Dewey
called to give Nixon the decision of "all the fellows
here in New York." Dewey had a plan for breaking the
stalemate caused by Nixon's refusal to resign and Eisenhower's refusal to back him: Nixon must plead his cause
before the people. If the response was big enough, he
could stay. And when Dewey said big enough, he meant
the impossible—near-unanimity. Nixon reports the ultimatum this way: "You will probably get over a million replies, and that will give you three or four days to think
it over. At the end of that time, if it is sixty percent
for you and forty percent against you, say you are getting
out, as that is not enough of a majority. If it is ninety
to ten, stay on." It is no wonder Nixon—or, rather, "some
of the members of my staff"—felt wary of this offer: "They
feared a concerted campaign might be put under way to
stack the replies against me." The whole plan was stacked
against him. It started with the presumption that Nixon
was through, and with feigned generosity gave him a
chance to climb back onto the ticket. If Nixon took the
offer and (as was expected) lost, then he must abide by
the consequences. It was a brilliant way of forcing resignation on a man who was determined not to resign.

    Nixon said he would consider it. Chotiner got in touch
with Party Chairman Arthur Summerfield, to find out how
the broadcast would be handled. Summerfield said they
had offers from some TV sponsors to give Nixon one
of their spots. Chotiner naturally protested: Nixon could
hardly go on the air to defend himself against the charge
of being a messenger boy for California businessmen, and
explain this on time given him by some large corporation! He told Summerfield the National Committee would
have to buy the time, if they expected any show at all.

(Money had already been set aside for two half-hour appearances by the vice-presidential candidate. But now Summerfield was in the unfortunate position of not knowing who would be the candidate: if he gave one of the periods to Nixon, and Nixon failed, that left only one spot for his successor. At $75,000 a throw, these were not shows to be granted easily.)

Nixon had to deliver a scheduled speech that night (Sunday) at the Portland Temple Club. He was still considering the TV broadcast when he came back to his hotel. He knew this contest was not what it appeared—Nixon against the press, or the Democrats, or the people. It was Nixon against Ike—a contest that, as Stevenson would learn twice over, no one can expect to win. Candidates simply do not get 90 percent victories in America —and Nixon was being told to produce that figure or get lost. He was asked to do it in circumstances that told against him. Eisenhower had been presented by his managers as the voice of a purgative honesty meant to remedy corruption. The very fact that this arbiter of morals was silent, that Nixon was sent out to argue on his own, was an implied judgment on him. He would be guilty until proved innocent, and he could not call on the one character witness who, in this set of circumstances, mattered.

Meanwhile, the Eisenhower camp had received no answer to its "offer." Now was the time to turn the screw. No escape was to be left him. The phone rang in Portland. Ike. For the first and last time during the crisis. Giving the ultimatum all his personal weight: "I think you ought to go on a nationwide television program and tell them everything there is to tell, everything you can remember since the day you entered public life. Tell them about any money you have ever received." The public self-revelation for which Nixon would be blamed in later years was being forced on him, against all his own inclinations, personal and political. By temperament and conditioning, Nixon is reserved, with Quaker insistence on the right of privacy. Nixon's mother, a woman of tremendous self-control, later said of the Checkers speech: "At the point when he gave that itemized account of his personal expenditures, I didn't think I could take it."

Nixon asked Eisenhower if he meant to endorse him. The response was put in a particularly galling way: "If I issue a statement now backing you up, in effect people

will accuse me of condoning wrongdoing." Ike knew, and
Nixon knew he knew, that the results of a vast survey of
Nixon's affairs would be available in a matter of hours.
This study had been going on for three days; Sherman
Adams, at the outset of the scandal, called Paul Hoffman, one of the architects of Eisenhower's candidacy, and
ordered a thorough inquest into Nixon's finances. Hoffman
went to the best. He put Price Waterhouse to work checking Nixon's accounts, and the law firm of Gibson, Dunn
and Crutcher went over all legal aspects of the matter.
Fifty lawyers and accountants worked on a round-the-
clock basis. The results of this scrutiny were being com-
piled Sunday night. No wrongdoing would be found. The
objective moral evidence would soon be in Eisenhower's
hands. But he refused to make his own judgment based on
this evidence. He wanted the people, who could not know
as much as he did, to decide whether Nixon was honest,
and he would follow them. The people, meanwhile, were
waiting to hear Ike's decision so they could follow *him*.
Nixon was caught between two juries, each of which was
waiting for the other to reach a verdict before it would
move.

He tried to strike a bargain: if Eisenhower was satisfied
with the TV broadcast, would he *at that point* make a
decision to endorse Nixon? (If he did not, then a victory
scored on the TV screen would be subject to attrition, as
lingering or renewed doubts worked on a situation inex-
plicably unresolved.) But Ike was not making bargains: he
said he would need three or four days (the same period
Dewey had mentioned) for the popular reaction to be
accurately gauged—during which time, Nixon would presumably be stalled in Los Angeles waiting for the response, his campaign tour all too noticeably suspended.
Nixon finally blew: "There comes a time when you have
to piss or get off the pot!" But Seraphim piss not, neither
Cherubim. The great Cherub sat blithely there, enthroned
on his high pot. Nixon sculpts and prettifies the unyielding
refusal: "One of Eisenhower's most notable characteris-
tics is that he is not a man to be rushed on important
decisions."

There was nothing he could do now but go ahead with
the show. And if so, the sooner the better. Chotiner was
back on the phone getting clearance for the $75,000.
Sherman Adams and Arthur Summerfield finally yielded

that point around midnight. The press corps had been alerted, an hour before, that there would be an announcement. It was one o'clock in the morning when Nixon came down; newsmen thought this must be it—his resignation. He deliberately built up suspense by saying he was breaking off—tense pause—his campaign tour. To make a statement over television. Two days from now. Tuesday night. He let them think it might still be his resignation he would announce. The more interest he could generate in the next two days, the bigger his audience on Tuesday night.

That was Monday morning. He got little sleep before he boarded a plane for Los Angeles that afternoon; during the flight, he drafted the first of a series of outlines for his talk. In Los Angeles, he got the reports from Price Waterhouse and Gibson, Dunn in time to put their findings in presentable summary. After midnight, he called his old English and history teachers at Whittier College, with a request that they find some suitable Lincoln quotes for the speech. They phoned two quotes to him by ten o'clock that morning—one witty and one maudlin (he used the latter). Nixon walked the streets with Bill Rogers, discussing approaches he might take. He was keyed up, and thought he just might bring it off.

And then the last blow fell. Tuesday, after a mere four hours of sleep, he kept at his outline resolutely, as is his way. He did not go to El Capitan Theater to check the TV set or props or lighting; he wanted every minute for his preparation—it was a pattern familiar to those who have watched Nixon key himself up for a crisis by mood-setting spiritual exercises. And then, with less than an hour before he must leave for the studio, the cruel blow came, shattering his schedule, his carefully programmed psychological countdown. It was Dewey on the phone again, with a last demand: "There has been a meeting of all of Eisenhower's top advisers. They have asked me to tell you that it is their opinion that at the conclusion of the broadcast tonight you should submit your resignation to Eisenhower." The Establishment was taking no chances that its scheme might misfire. Nixon asked if that was the word from the General's own mouth. Dewey answered that the men he spoke of would not have commissioned him to make such a call at such an hour unless they were speaking for the master. (But, as usual, Ike was protected: afterward he could write, "Just before

the broadcast Governor Dewey telephoned him from New
York reporting the conviction of some of my supporters
there"—two can play at that "some of the staff" game—
"that he should resign, which the young Senator later said
he had feared represented my views." Poor Senator, so
fearful, so young, so avuncularly cared for in this retro-
spective benediction. Those who have called Nixon a
master of duplicity should contrast his account of the fund
crisis with the smoothed-over version in Eisenhower's book,
which does not even mention the "hound's tooth" remark.)

Nixon stalled on the line to Dewey, stalled and
wriggled. He said it was too late to change his prepared
speech. Dewey said he could, of course, deliver his personal defense and accounting; all he had to do was tack
on, at the end, a formal resignation offered to Ike. Nixon
said he had to leave for the studio. Dewey: "Can I say
you have accepted?" Nixon: "You will have to watch
the show to see—and tell them I know something about
politics too!"

Nixon had a half hour to tell his staff of this new light-
ning bolt, get their reaction, shower, shave, dress for the
show, making meanwhile his own decision—and trying to
collect his wits and memory over the notes for his talk.
It had been five days full of pressure, sleeplessness, betrayal, ultimatums—climaxed with the most unsettling
demand of all, made when he was at a poise of tension
and could be knocked off balance so easily. A whole series
of crises. Thursday: answer the charges? Friday: dodge
newsmen, or face them; rely on the formal answer or return to the defense again and again; stall or throw oneself upon Ike's mercy? Saturday: heed the *Trib* and resign? Sunday: do the TV show? Monday: what to say on
the show? And now, at the last minute, Tuesday: defy
Dewey (and, through him, Ike)? Already the strain had
shown in Nixon. Sunday in Portland, when Hillings brought
a wire from Nixon's mother with the Quaker understated
promise of prayers WE ARE THINKING OF YOU, Nixon
broke down and cried. "I thought I had better leave the
room," Hillings said, "and give him time to compose himself." Chotiner, busy calling party people to get money
for the show, remembered "I was more worried about
Dick's state of mind than about the Party. He was edgy
and irritable."

Even the inner circle could not tell for sure whether

Nixon would stand up to the pressure, or give in while he spoke. After reporting Dewey's call, he was silent, his mind working desperately at the problem. During the twenty-five-minute ride to the studio, he went over his notes (on debater-type cards). He had withdrawn to his last ditch, to make an entirely lone stand there. The one thing he demanded in studio arrangements was that even Chotiner and Rogers be kept out. Only his wife would be present, within camera range, visible to Nixon. It is as if he were dramatizing, to himself more than others, the isolation he stood in at this dying moment of defiance.

One of the criticisms made of Nixon's television speech is that the hoarse voice and hurt face, hovering on the edge of tears, were either histrionic or (if unfeigned) disproportionate and "tasteless." But no one who knows the full story can suspect Nixon of acting, or blame him for the tension he felt and conveyed—it would be like blaming a recently flayed man for "indecent exposure." Nixon was deserted, in more ways than he could tell. And he was fighting back with more nerve than anybody knew. Besides concentrating fiercely on his appeal to the audience, which had to succeed if anything else were to follow, he was reaching out across their heads to touch swords in a secret duel with Ike.

And Eisenhower understood. Stewart Alsop, in his useful little book *Nixon and Rockefeller,* quotes from an interview with one who watched Eisenhower's reactions throughout the TV show. The General had to give a speech in Cleveland as soon as Nixon went off the air; the audience for that talk was watching a large screen in the auditorium, while Eisenhower and thirty of his people clustered by the TV set in a backstage office. Even this entourage, predominantly opposed to Nixon, was touched as the show progressed; some wept openly. But Eisenhower was calm, tapping a yellow pad with his pencil, ready to jot down comments on the speech. He took no notes while the talk was in progress, though the tapping stopped twice. Nixon, forced to act like a criminal who must clear himself, deftly made his actions look like those of a man with nothing to fear. And he issued a challenge: the *other* candidates must have something to fear, unless they followed his example. He devoted much of his half hour to this challenge, dictating terms to his accusers.

(It is this part of the speech—moving onto the offensive—
that so pleased Chotiner.)

Now I'm going to suggest some courses of conduct.

First of all, you have read in the papers about
other funds. Now, Mr. Stevenson, apparently, had
a couple—one of them in which a group of business people paid and helped to supplement the salaries of state employees. Here is where the money
went directly into their pockets.

I think what Mr. Stevenson should do is come
before the American people, as I have, and give the
names of the people who have contributed to that
fund, and give the names of the people who put
this money into their pockets at the same time they
were receiving money from their state government,
and see what favors, if any, they gave out for that.

I don't condemn Mr. Stevenson for what he did.
But, until the facts are in there, a doubt will be
raised.

As far as Mr. Sparkman is concerned, I would
suggest the same thing. He's had his wife on the
payroll. I don't condemn him for that. But I think
he should come before the American people and indicate what outside sources of income he has had.

I would suggest that under the circumstances both
Mr. Sparkman and Mr. Stevenson should come before the American people, as I have, and make a
complete statement as to their financial history. If
they don't it will be an admission that they have
something to hide. And I think you will agree with
me.

Because, remember, a man who's to be President
and a man who's to be Vice President must have
the confidence of all the people. That's why I'm doing what I'm doing, and that's what I suggest that
Mr. Stevenson and Mr. Sparkman, since they are
under attack, should be doing.

Eisenhower stopped tapping with his pencil—jabbed it,
instead, down into the yellow pad—when Nixon said
any candidate who did not reveal his finances must have
something to hide. Of course, Nixon did not mention

Eisenhower, and his phrase about other candidates joining him "since they are under attack" left a loophole for the General. But the overall force of the passage could not be missed. All candidates, he was arguing, should act as he had. That meant *Eisenhower, too*— as Ike realized, and events were to prove. After this all the candidates did make their statements.

There were reasons why it was inconvenient for Eisenhower to make his books public—e.g., the special tax decision on earnings of his *Crusade in Europe*. Besides, as Alsop delicately puts it, "the military rarely get into the habit of making charitable contributions . . ." More important, Nixon was turning the tables on Ike. Eisenhower had brought him to this revelation. Nixon would force the same hard medicine down his mentor's throat.

Yet an even defter stroke followed. Dewey had been vague on how the speech should be judged. He told Nixon to have telegrams addressed to Los Angeles, and measure the talk's impact by their content. This arrangement, besides tying Nixon down for several days, still left the matter with Eisenhower. The real decision would be made by the General, assessing news reaction. Nixon would be left to play games with his switchboard and his mail, unable to vindicate himself if Eisenhower decided the show had not cleared him.

But when it came time for Nixon to mention the sending of telegrams, he said: "I am submitting to *the Republican National Committee* tonight, through this television broadcast, the decision *it is theirs to make* . . . Wire and write *the Republican National Committee* whether you think I should stay or whether I should get off; and whatever *their decision* is, I will abide by it." (Italics added.) The General stabbed again, pencil into pad, a sword struck down as he fenced that image on the screen, and lost. Nixon has always been a party man; his strength lay there. Karl Mundt and Robert Humphreys, manning the Washington headquarters of the National Committee while Chairman Arthur Summerfield traveled with Ike, had routinely issued statements backing Nixon from the very first day of his troubles. Now, by a cool disarming maneuver, Nixon was taking the matter away from the Eastern Establishment and putting it in the hands of men sympathetic to the regulars, to grassroots workers—people who respond in a partisan way to partisan attacks upon one of their own, people most vulnerable to the planned schmaltz and hominess of the Checkers reference, people with small debts of their own and Republican cloth coats. If the decision was theirs to make, then —the real point of the broadcast as Nixon had reshaped it—*it was not Ike's*. It is no wonder that, while others in Cleveland wept, the man who had directed OVERLORD, the largest military operation in the world's history, the *General,* made an angry stab. He knew enough about maneuver to see he was outflanked. Alsop's informant said: "Before that, I'd always liked and admired Ike, of course, but I'd often wondered how smart he really was. After that, I knew Ike got what Dick was getting at right away."

The importance of that decision, redirecting the appeal to the National Committee, explains Nixon's breakdown when he saw he had gone off the air. Under the pressure of the performance, undertaken without rehearsal, using sketchy notes, he had done something rare for him—missed the countdown toward sign-off by a minute or two: "Time had run out. I was cut off just as I intended to say where the National Committee was located and where the telegrams and letters should be sent." He had based everything on this point; he needed every wire that would reach Washington. What if the telegrams were diffused ineffectually about the country, sent to him, to Ike, to TV channels and local campaign offices? He needed a crushing weight of response all directed to one point, and now (he thought) he would not get it. (The wires in fact did go everywhere, but in such breathtaking numbers that all doubt was swept before them.) He threw his cards to the floor in a spasm, told Pat he had failed; when Chotiner came into the studio, elated by the skilled performance, Nixon just shook his head and claimed, "I was an utter flop." Outside the theater, as his car pulled away, an Irish setter friskily rocked alongside barking: Nixon turned, Bill Rogers would remember, and twisted out a bitter, "At least I won the dog vote tonight." The end, he thought, of the Checkers speech. He was touching bottom. That night he would finally, after all his earlier resistance, resign.

But it took more kicks and blows to bring him to it. During the first hours after his broadcast, others were jubilant and support poured in; but no call came from the General (a wire had been sent off, but was stuck in the traffic-jam of them at Nixon's hotel switchboard— no one called from the Cleveland camp to give Nixon its message). The first notice he had of the telegram came over the news wires—and it brought word of still another ultimatum. Eisenhower did not often lose wars of attrition. They were his kind of battle.

The crowd waiting for Ike in Cleveland was hoarse with shouts and praise for the TV show they had witnessed. Eisenhower's own first comment was to Chairman Summerfield, about the $75,000: "Well, Arthur, you got your money's worth." Hagerty came back from the auditorium and told Eisenhower he could not deliver his prepared talk on inflation with this crowd. He would have to speak to the Nixon issue. The General knew. He had already chosen his strategy. He fashioned its main lines on the yellow pad, and tried it on his advisers. First, a sop to the crowd: "I like courage . . . Tonight I saw an example of courage . . . I have never seen anyone come through in such a fashion as Senator Nixon did tonight . . . When I get in a fight, I would rather have a courageous and honest man by my side than a whole boxcar full of pussyfooters."

All the praise was a cover, though. Eisenhower was a master of the basics—supply, firepower, and retention of position. After praising Nixon for courage, Ike added that he had not made his mind up on the main subject —whether Nixon would remain on the ticket: "It is obvious that I have to have something more than one single presentation, necessarily limited to thirty minutes, the time allowed Senator Nixon." But if Eisenhower, who had chosen him as his running mate, who had access to the research of the lawyers and accountants, to the advice of top politicians in the party, could not make up his mind after watching the TV show, then how could anyone in the public do so? There is only one explanation for this performance: Ike was determined not to let Nixon take the decision out of his hands. "I am not going to be swayed by my idea of what will get most votes . . . I am going to say: Do I myself believe this man is the kind of man America would like to have for its Vice President?" That is, at one minute he will not be swayed by what the people want and would vote for, and the next minute he is accepting the sacred pledge of finding out what the public wants and will vote for!

Then Eisenhower read them his telegram to Nixon, which shows the real thrust of his remarks: "While technically no decision rests with me, you and I know the realities of the situation require a pronouncement which the public considers decisive." (Or: Get your National Committee support, and see how far it carries you without me.) "My personal decision is going to be based on personal conclusions." (Or: I won't judge you by reaction to your talk—which is what he had promised he *would* do.) "I would most appreciate it if you can fly to see me at once." (Or: Here, Rover.) "Tomorrow evening I will be at Wheeling, W. Va." (Or:Tomorrow *you* will be at Wheeling, W.Va.) Not only was Eisenhower reasserting the personal jurisdiction Nixon had challenged; he wanted a public dramatization of the lines of authority. Having cleared himself with the public, Nixon must appear before a superior tribunal, summoned there to make his defense again, in greater detail, while judgment was pointedly suspended.

Nixon could not submit; yet, once the demand was made public, he could not go further in public defiance, either. He gave in. Rose Woods took down his dictated telegram of resignation.

But he would get in one last blow of his own. The wire was not directed toward Eisenhower, as Dewey had insisted it should be. He addressed it to the National Committee! As Rose Woods went out of the room to send the message, Chotiner followed her and tore off the top sheet of her pad. Rose said she could not have sent it anyway. Nixon is, by his own admission, subject to sharp lapses and lowering of his guard in the emotional depletion that follows on conflict. In four of his book's six crises he finds an example of that pattern: and the example for the fund crisis is his telegram to the National Committee. His loss of grip began the minute the show went off the air and he threw his cards to the floor. " 'What more can he possibly want from me?' I asked . . . I didn't believe I could take any more of the suspense and tension of the past week." Chotiner went to work on him, however, and persuaded him that he could avoid both of the unpalatable things being forced on him

—resignation, or compliance with Eisenhower's summons. If he just resumed his interrupted campaign-schedule (next step, Missoula, Montana), the General would have to back down. The wave of public response was already seismic. Nixon reports Chotiner's counsel this way: "Chotiner, particularly, insisted that I not allow myself to be put in the position of going to Eisenhower like a little boy to be taken to the woodshed, properly punished, and then restored to a place of dignity." At this point, there was a call from Ike's camp. Arthur Summerfield, pleased that things had turned out well, was asking for Chotiner —who soon dashed his spirits. Murray said Nixon had just dictated his resignation; he admitted, when Summerfield gasped, that the telegram was torn up—"but I'm not so sure how long it's going to stay torn." Summerfield said things could be smoothed over when Dick reached Wheeling. But Dick was not going to Wheeling: "We're flying to Missoula tonight." Summerfield wanted to know how to head off this disaster—so Chotiner set terms: Nixon will not come unless he is sure of a welcoming endorsement, without further inquisition. This was, of course, a demand that Eisenhower back down on the stated purpose of the summons, which was to go into greater detail than thirty minutes would allow.

Eisenhower, realistic about cutting his losses, saw when this news reached him that the idea of further investigation could not be sustained. He let Summerfield give Nixon's camp the proper assurances. But Nixon would still be answering a humiliating public call. Just before the plane took off for Missoula, Bert Andrews, who had worked with Nixon all through the Hiss affair, called from the Eisenhower press room in Cleveland: Ike would have no choice now but to receive Nixon warmly; Nixon would have to lose a little face in order to avoid flouting the General's summons. Nixon agreed, and let his staff arrange a flight to Wheeling after the stop at Missoula. Ike was at the airport, to throw his arm around him and call him "my boy"—looking gracious, kind, generous, as if supporting an embattled man rather than picking up strength from a victorious one. The only thing that could resolve the crisis—Ike's blue-eyed smile of benediction—had been bestowed.

But they did not forget the night when they touched

swords. There would never be any trust between them. And Nixon had begun a tutelage that would gall him and breed resentment through years of friction and slights.

6. The Hero

"And remember, folks, Eisenhower is a great man. Folks, he is a great man, and a vote for Eisenhower is a vote for what is good for America."
—the Checkers speech

THE SOLE PLACE, during the 1968 campaign, where Nixon appeared with his opponent Hubert Humphrey was the Al Smith dinner in New York. President Johnson also made one of his rare public appearances. Nixon, speaking first of the three, said, "This is an unprecedented event. Not only do we have here the current President of the United States and both men seeking his office. More than that, all three men have served as Vice President of the United States." As he said it, I looked at Humphrey, unlucky poulter at the low point of his race; at Johnson, ending his reign in confessed failure; and at Nixon himself, who has lived much of his public life off scraps from the table of Eisenhower. Yes, they had all three been Vice-President—three of the office's victims.

Johnson, master of Senate maneuver and coercion, had been a displaced person in the bright transplanted Boston of the New Frontier. And then, as President, he had to repay the slights of the Frontiersmen with unctuous servility to his martyred predecessor. Oswald had put the legend beyond any hope Johnson might have of equaling it. And, with cruel irony, he would be blamed by Jim Garrison and Barbara Garson for the deed that crippled him—Kennedy's death.

Poor Hubert lived in the shadow-casting ego of Johnson, a man hated by the very people who made up Humphrey's constituency, liberals (academic and semiacademic) of an ADA sort. Caught between the two, his President and his supporters, Humphrey had to watch his old strengths become weaknesses. His passion now seemed a vain fluttering on the verge of hysteria, his effusiveness looked like sycophancy. Within striking distance of his life's goal—the presidency—he found the years spent near that office were his main obstacle.

But even in this sad company there was something unique about Nixon's servitude. Humphrey had a domineering master, but an unpopular one. Johnson had to cope with a legend, but a dead one. Nixon had to live for years as the acolyte to a living miracle of popularity. He had to bear with this bright sun's neglect, praise the light that shone indifferently on just and unjust, but never (or rarely) on him. He rose in Miami, to accept his own nomination, and asked that he might win in another man's name: "Let's win this one for Ike!"

That Pat O'Brien line was excised from the acceptance speech as printed in the new edition of *Six Crises*. Such delicate touches—a pinch of praise given here, taken back there, a perpetual fiddling with the scales—occur regularly in *Six Crises*. The balance threatens to swing decisively one way, but always tilts back in time:

—Ike seemed cold when Nixon met him (but of course wasn't): "Despite his great capacity for friendliness, he also had a quality of reserve which, at least subconsciously, tended to make a visitor feel like a junior officer coming in to see the commanding General."

—Ike seemed to disown Nixon (but of course didn't): "The impression I got was that he was really trying to tell me he wanted me off the ticket when, in 1956, he said Nixon should 'chart his own course' . . . 'That's not what he meant at all,' said [Len] Hall. He declared that I was judging Eisenhower's statements by standards which should be applied to a political sophisticate." This implies, of course, that—

—Ike seemed unsophisticated (but of course wasn't): "He would sometimes make what would seem to be completely outlandish and politically naive remarks, just to test them, perhaps even believing in some of them momentarily."

—Ike seemed to neglect Nixon's advice (but of course didn't): "President Eisenhower had just dispatched airborne troops to Caracas to insure our protection. This took me completely by surprise. No one had consulted me or my party . . . communications between Washington and our Embassy were cut."

—Ike seemed not to be supporting Nixon's 1960 campaign (but of course was): "He felt it was important for me to establish my own identity as the new leader of the party . . . He also expressed the conviction that his great influence with the American people was due in substantial part to his image of being President of all the people, and not just a partisan as Truman had been."

—Ike seemed, in such stands, to be selfishly calculating (but of course wasn't): "He was far more complex and devious than most people realized, and in the best sense of those words."

—Ike even looked slippery (but of course was not really): "An Eisenhower characteristic was never to take direct action requiring his personal participation where indirect methods could accomplish the same result."

Of such careful tightrope-walking Nixon made a political career. We may be sure these minutely calibrated bits of praise and hints of criticism were among the passages he checked and rephrased most carefully in the work of his book's ghost writer, Al Moscow. For Nixon's relationship with Eisenhower was like a Calvinist's relation to God, or Ahab's to the whale—awe and fascination soured with fear and a desire to supplant; along with a knowledge, nonetheless, that whatever nobility one may aspire to will come from the attention of the Great One. Even the 1968 campaign leaned heavily on Eisenhower. Part of the wearily repeated stump speech was, "I had a good teacher. I am proud to have been part of an administration that ended one war and kept us out of others." And a fixture of the campaign was Eisenhower's grandson, with a proto-Ike smile and charm, and a face that was pure fifties—Howdy Doody come back from the days of Uncle Miltie and the Checkers speech to lend a hand.

It is a pity that Nixon, given his dependence on Eisenhower, has always misunderstood the General. In the Nixon scheme of things, Ike was the embodiment of rule by the common man. He had been, admittedly, the commander of great armies in the field; yet he was, in his style and mode of thought, a "basic American," avatar of the fifties' "Mid-Cult," cursed as such by the sophisticates, honored as such by "the common folk." The central American tastes and moral insights were enough, in Nixon's eyes, to compensate for Eisenhower's political simplicity. Nixon usually quotes others—especially Chotiner and Len Hall—to plant the notion that Eisenhower was a political *naïf*. But some passages make it clear that Nixon shared their view: "If, as some of my associates thought, he appeared to be indecisive, I put the blame not on him but on *his lack of experience in political warfare* and on the fact that he was relying on several equally inexperienced associates . . . And, *new as he was to politics,* the overwhelmingly hostile reaction of the press must have raised some very grave questions in his mind. The further fact that the majority of *his friends from the business, professional, and military worlds* were urging him to put me off the ticket could not have had anything but a considerable effect on his thinking."

Nixon is judging by the mechanistic norms of Chotiner. Eisenhower was as superior to those rules as Renoir to a Paint-by-Numbers set. Eisenhower was not a political sophisticate; he was a political genius. It is no mere accident that he remained, year after year, the most respected man in America. Nixon, just after his election as President, climbed to the number five spot on the Gallup poll, still below his old boss, who led the list. William Buckley, casting about for a way to get Barry Goldwater elected President in 1964, decided there was one way, which he publicly advocated: have Eisenhower run on the same ticket, for Vice-President. Then it would not matter who led the ticket.

The cult of the common man makes Americans think of their heroes as rising almost by magic, rather than by ambition, hard effort, and shrewd calculation. As great men enter our pantheon of history, all the less noble traits slip from them. Even so rough-and-tumble a figure out of Illinois politics as Abe Lincoln becomes one of the holy fools of our popular legend. It was this mythologizing that led Mencken to write: "Imagine a man getting on in American politics, interesting and enchanting the boobery, sawing off the horns of other politicians, elbowing his way through primaries and conventions, by the magic of

virtue! As well talk of fetching the mob by hawking exact
and arctic justice! Abe, in fact, must have been a fellow
highly skilled at the great democratic art of gum-shoeing.
I like to think of him as one who defeated such politicians
as Stanton, Douglas, and Sumner with their own weapons—deftly leading them into ambuscades, boldly pulling
their noses, magnificently hamstringing and horn-swaggling
them—in brief, as a politician of extraordinary talents,
who loved the game for its own sake, and knew the
measure of the crowd . . . It is a matter of unescapable
record that his career in the State Legislature was indis-
tinguishable from that of a Tammany Nietzsche."

Eisenhower came up in as rough a school as Lincoln's.
He rose in the peacetime professional army, where ambition is thwarted of its natural object (excellence in
war) and falls back on jealousy and intrigue. Eisenhower
climbed that slippery ladder of bayonets with a sure step
and rare instinct for survival. His basic shrewdness came
out in many ways. In his great success at poker and
bridge, for instance. Like Nixon, he made large sums of
money in the long games at military bases. Unlike Nixon,
he was so good he had to stop playing with enlisted men;
he was leaving too many of them broke.

The survival instinct shows, also, in his concern for
being properly armed at all times. In his autobiography,
he claims that he learned this lesson as a child in a
barnyard: a goose used to attack and torment him, until
he learned that a broom in his hand would make the
bird keep its distance. From that time he never went
out the door without a broom in his fist: "I quickly
learned never to negotiate with an adversary except from
a position of strength." Years later he recalled, quite
casually, that as President of Columbia he did not venture onto the streets of New York at night without his
service revolver in his pocket. His life in the interval had
been studiously devoted to keeping the right broom in
his hand at all times.

He was master of the essentials. The most successful
warrior in the modern world, he never romanticized war.
His head was not dizzied with MacArthur's visions of glory.
There were no screaming trumpets in his rhetoric. He
preferred drums; and even his interest in those did not
date from West Point parades, but from high school days
in Kansas: "They used a drum to rally us in ranks for re-

entering the school after play time. The drummer could turn the tumult of a recess crowd into some semblance of quiet, orderly movement. I've always admired the drum since and despised the siren. The drum communicates a message and calms as it warns. The siren is an assault on the senses. In later years, when well-intentioned escorts elected to use a siren on my behalf, I asked—or ordered —that it be stopped."

As an athlete, he was efficient rather than spectacular: "I was good at bat, trained by my coach as a 'chop hitter' —to poke the ball, in effect, at selected spots in the field, rather than swinging freely away." Speaking of the rigors of plebe year at the Point, he writes: "I suppose that if any time had been provided to sit down and think for a moment, most of the 285 of us would have taken the next train out. But no one was given much time to think—and when I did it was always, 'Where else could you get a college education without cost?' " No love affair with the uniform or his trade's glamour. Asked at the end of his course to list the three assignments he most aspired to, in order of preference, he put down "*Infantry* first, *Infantry* second, and *Infantry* third." He volunteered for cook's school, and first distinguished himself as a supply officer. The second thing he became known for in the army was a series of assignments to coach football teams.

His third, and major, specialty may surprise those who think of him as tongue-tied and vague. The disjointed syntax of Eisenhower's press conferences and aphasia after his stroke in 1957 helped to create the picture of Eisenhower as a benevolent but rather goofy, grandfatherly type. Yet his principal army work, before the war, was as a writer. Not much for books during his days at West Point, he became a student of military history afterward, while stationed in Panama. This led him to General Staff School at Fort Leavenworth in 1925. Though he had been low in his class at the Point, he ranked high in this "graduate school" of ambitious young officers seeking promotion. The commandant of the school wanted him to stay on as an instructor. Instead, he was sent to France, to write a guidebook on American action there during World War I. That is how he came to know the continent he would later invade. Then his writing duties were extended to the drafting of speeches and letters—and even of two chapters of autobiography—for General Pershing. After that, he served briefly with the Assistant Secretary of War, before Douglas MacArthur asked for his services as a writer of letters and memoranda.

Eisenhower opposed MacArthur's plan to make a personal appearance in the rebuff of Coxey's Army from Washington; but despite this difference, and a general clash of temperaments, MacArthur requested Ike's further services when he went to the Philippines. While he was there, Eisenhower learned to fly and logged 350 hours as a pilot. Even after World War II, he used to go up and take over the controls of planes—until the advent of jets. He had always been an excellent horseman; and earlier, he and George Patton had pioneered, on their own, some experiments in the maneuver and servicing of tanks. Eisenhower also helped direct the first transcontinental convoy of army trucks. He found time, somewhere along the line, to learn at first hand the use of all his professional tools—from the galley stove to airplane carburetors.

Looking back on his days in the Philippines, Eisenhower told Arthur Larson: "You know that General MacArthur got quite a reputation as a silver-tongued speaker when he was in the Philippines. Who do you think wrote his speeches? I did." Both Larson and Emmet Hughes spent hours with Eisenhower, working over successive drafts of the presidential speeches; and they both, despite very different political estimates of the man, agree that he had rare discrimination in the use of the written word. He hated imprecision and was a stickler for grammatical niceties. He disliked gaudy and inflated phrases, and had a disconcerting way of asking political speech writers, who tend to get carried away by their own rhetoric, what a high-sounding phrase might *mean*. When Hughes opened a speech with "The world and we have passed the mid-century point of a century of continuing challenge," Eisenhower penned in the margin: "I hate this sentence. *Who* challenges *whom? What about?*" Emmet Hughes is a professional journalist, used to the ministrations—blunt or subtle—of professional editors. It is interesting, then, that he found Eisenhower a particularly good editor: "The man whose own sense of syntax, as displayed over years of presidential press conferences, would invite smiles and jokes, possessed, nonetheless, a remarkably quick and exacting faculty for editing."

What, then, is one to make of those famous meanderings at press conferences? They were a proof of Eisenhower's sense of priorities. He was intensely briefed by twenty or thirty staff experts before each press conference. He went into each session with certain things clearly in mind—things he was determined to say, and the way they should be said; things he was determined not to say, and ways to circle around them. And he got the job done. The rest was fluff and filler—but fluff under control. Even Hughes, Eisenhower's critic, grants that he "made not one politically significant verbal blunder throughout eight years of press conferences and public addresses." And Larson points out that the troublesome phrases of the Eisenhower regime were not blurted by the President, as in Truman's time; they were coined by the scholarly Secretary of State, who put "the brink" and "massive retaliation" and "agonizing reappraisal" in circulation.

Eisenhower revealed his conscious strategy in these matters during the tense days of the Quemoy-Matsu crisis. His press secretary, James Hagerty, advised him to take a no-comment stand on the whole issue. " 'Don't worry, Jim,' I told him as we went out the door. 'If that question comes up, I'll just confuse them.' " An example of this calculated obfuscation occurred in the 1952 race. Eisenhower, not much liking the task, was set to campaign with Senator William Jenner, who had called Ike's old friend and boss, General Marshall, a traitor. Journalist Murray Kempton, trying to put Eisenhower on the spot, asked the candidate at a press conference in Denver what he thought of men who call Marshall a traitor. Eisenhower engaged in a rare bit of public scenery-chewing: no one should even *mention* such false charges. He seemed almost to swoon with pious detestation—yet he was careful not to mention Jenner. All the onus of slander was shifted to the journalist for raising such a question. After the conference, Ike grinned and shook hands with Kempton, making him realize what a skilled performance this was.

Eisenhower's relations with Nixon cannot be estimated until we realize that his remarks, his silences were, on key matters, conscious and chosen things. The "hound's tooth" remark might have looked like a slip at the time,

not meant to do the damage it did. But Eisenhower then
went before the Checkers audience in Cleveland and,
with little preparation, delicately praised Nixon while
drawing him back into his own net of control. Even the
welcoming comment in Wheeling—"You're my boy"—
has a patronizing, condescending note. Were these mere
slips? If so, the slips form an extraordinary pattern. At
each of the next two points where Nixon was scheduled to
step up in his political career, Ike "let slip" a sentence
that helped drag him down. The timing was as damaging as the content of the remarks. It was an election year,
both times—1956, when Eisenhower fed the "Dump
Nixon" movement his "chart your own course" remark;
and 1960, when Eisenhower was asked what decisions
of the administration Nixon was responsible for. Nixon
had to spend precious minutes in his first debate with
Kennedy trying to explain away the answer Ike gave:
"If you give me a week, I might think of one. I don't
remember." Nixon could only argue lamely that the words
were "probably facetious" (quite a card, that Ike). He
spent many years paying for the secret victory he had
won in the Checkers episode.

The two never became intimates. In 1956, Eisenhower
held a picnic at his Gettysburg farm for party workers,
where he was heard to say "Did you hear that? Dick says
he's never seen the inside of the house here." Meanwhile,
Pat Nixon was tactfully reminding Mamie of the same
thing. There were parts of the White House that Nixon
did not see until President Johnson showed him around
in the fall of 1968. And Nixon had been Vice-President
for six years before Eisenhower entered his home in
Washington. Memoirs of the fifties recall times when Nixon
came on business to Denver or other places where Eisenhower was holding social gatherings. Nixon was summoned
during business hours and sent off before the socializing
was resumed.

Even in business hours, Nixon was not treated as an
important adviser. James Reston wrote, during Nixon's last
year in office with Eisenhower, that the Vice-President
watched football games while the President was making
his decisions on a summit meeting. Eisenhower simply
was not interested in Nixon's view of things. He told Arthur Larson he thought Nixon was good at summarizing

alternatives and boiling down other men's opinions, but that he did not supply anything original himself.

Nixon's famous trip to Russia reveals Ike's lack of interest in the views of his subordinate. This was not a trip Nixon had been asked to make. He volunteered for it, and not directly to Ike. He first applied for permission to the U.S. Information Agency, which was conducting an active cultural-exchange program at the time. (If the country was sending artists, journalists, professors, and businessmen to Russia, how could it turn down the Vice-President?) Nixon had his eye on the next year's campaign. He knew he might score points (as in fact he did) that would help him in the 1960 convention and election. But he had to score the points alone. Eisenhower gave him no help at all.

Once he had wangled permission to go, Nixon did his homework—a saturation course in Khrushchevology and all things Russian:

> For months before the trip I spent every spare moment studying reports and recommendations from the State Department, the Central Intelligence Agency, the Joint Chiefs of Staff, and the White House staff.
>
> I talked for hours with every person I could find in Washington who had met and knew Khrushchev. I was briefed on more than a hundred different issues which might arise in my conversations with him.
>
> As soon as final arrangements for the trip had been approved in Moscow and Washington, I began the most intensive series of briefings I had had for any of my trips abroad . . . I sought out men who had studied Soviet affairs and men who had met Khrushchev. I saw Hubert Humphrey and Averell Harriman; I met with journalists who had interviewed him in Moscow, such as Bill Hearst, Bob Considine, Walter Lippmann, and Turner Catledge . . . Britain's Prime Minister Harold Macmillan and Chancellor Konrad Adenauer of Germany gave me their personal appraisals of the Soviet Premier . . . The most memorable briefing I received came from John Foster Dulles, the man I had sought out for advice throughout my career since the night in 1948 when

I had gone to see him in connection with the Alger
Hiss case. Mrs. Nixon and I took a crash course in
learning some common Russian expressions from
Alexander Barmine.

The interesting thing about this course of preparation
is that, in all his briefings, Nixon was not given one sniff
of important negotiations under way. Preparations for
Khrushchev's visit to America had long been debated,
and were actively carried on for ten days before Nixon
left. Despite all his study for the Russian trip, the Vice-
President's advice was not sought. He was not even aware
of the matter until the eve of his takeoff; then he was
informed, to prevent his stumbling on the plan and unconsciously botching it. Eisenhower later put it this way
in a press conference, "I told him, and I said 'So that
you will not be astonished or surprised and feel let down
by your government, should they [references to Khrushchev's trip] be opened up by the other side, you are not,
yourself, and of course will not open this subject."

The nation at large was as ignorant of the proposed
visit as Nixon had been till his departure; so editors and
pundits hoped for diplomatic gains—e.g., at the stalled
Geneva Conference—from Nixon's meeting and discussion with Khrushchev. But Eisenhower threw cold water
on this, too, when asked about Nixon's role in Russia.
He said the Vice-President "is not a part of the diplomatic processes and machinery of this government." That
fact was stressed by the announcement of Khrushchev's
visit. On August 3, while Nixon was still abroad, the
White House completed its diplomatic exchanges. Eisenhower could have waited two days for Nixon's return, on
August 5, to make the plan public. This would give the
appearance, at least, that Nixon had taken some part in
the project, that his views on Russia and her ruler had
been consulted. But instead of waiting the two days, Ike
announced his plan on August 3. He was asked, of course,
whether the Vice-President was aware of the future visit
when he left for Russia. That is when Ike explained that
Nixon *was* told—lest he "open" the matter. Nixon's politically useful debate with Khrushchev was thus deempha-
sized. His return to America was given an air of anticlimax in the speculation over Khrushchev's visit. The
White House, because of the nondiplomatic nature of

Nixon's journey, did not even arrange for a report to the nation. Nixon had put together his own trip; let him put together his own TV time.

And then, the crowning slight: Nixon, methodical as always, drew up a set of recommendations on how to treat Khrushchev in America. They boiled down, of course, to the way Nixon had treated him in Russia—argumentative, on the offensive. Eisenhower ignored the advice himself and, where it was being heeded, countermanded it. (Henry Cabot Lodge had been chosen to follow Khrushchev around, correcting him, as a one-man "truth squad." The scheme was discontinued.)

The Vice-President's party in Russia had contained one maker of policy, a man who participated in White House discussions of Khrushchev's visit, and whose opinion would privately be sought and heeded when he returned—for Eisenhower always sought and heeded it. In that sense, the most important person in the Nixon entourage was not Nixon himself, but scholarly Milton Eisenhower, the President's favorite academician. He had been sent along as the President's man on what Nixon had hoped would be his trip, his chance, on the other side of the world, to represent the President at last.

Eisenhower's periodic deflations of Nixon did not arise from mere vindictiveness. It seems clear from his actions, and from things he told many intimates, that he did not consider Nixon a statesman. There were contributing reasons for the distance between them. The gap between their ages was almost a quarter of a century—a difference that worked to Eisenhower's disadvantage as well as Nixon's (the President's view of civil rights for the Negro was, by comparison with Nixon's, paternalistic, straight out of the nineteenth century). The training of the two men could not have been more disparate. And it would have taken an unusual generosity, on both sides, to achieve rapport after their first passage-of-arms in the fund crisis. That rapport was never achieved. Eisenhower has been recorded, by various interlocutors, remarking that Nixon did not grow or mature in office; that he was not presidential timber; that he had no roots; that he was "too political."

That last phrase, perhaps, best sums up Ike's attitude toward one who, in turn, thought him an amateur in politics. The one thing Eisenhower regularly entrusted to

Nixon was housekeeping work in the Republican Party.
The Vice-President was given the thankless task of campaigning for every Republican in America on off-years,
when the ticket, without Eisenhower's magic name at the
top, took woeful beatings. If Eisenhower needed Right-
Wing support, Nixon was dispatched to round it up.
That was true at the time of the Korean peace settlement, which Senator Knowland attacked as a "peace
without honor." It was true in debates over the Bricker
Amendment and foreign aid. It was especially true when
the White House had to deal with Joseph McCarthy.

McCarthy's investigation of communists in the government was one thing when the government was Democratic; it became quite another when a Republican administration moved in. Nixon tried to head off trouble
from the start, turning to Bill Rogers, who had been
close to McCarthy (the Senator asked Rogers to serve as
his lawyer before the Tydings Committee). Right after
the inauguration, Nixon set up a meeting with McCarthy
at Rogers' home, where they tried to work out a policy
of nonaggression between all sectors of the party. Later,
Nixon invited McCarthy to come see him and Rogers in
Key Biscayne, so that new areas of investigation could
be found, gently easing Joe away from the issue of
"commies." When McCarthy said he was going to investigate the CIA, Nixon headed him off by calling the three
Republicans on the subcommittee to a private dinner,
where he persuaded them to join Democrats in blocking
the plan. When McCarthy sent Eisenhower a letter
(drafted by Robert Kennedy) asking for strong criticism
of allies who trade with communists, Nixon begged Mc-
Carthy to back down, and he did.

Of course, Nixon had this leverage with the man because he and Rogers tried to help him, tried to keep
him in the fold. Nixon had already loaned McCarthy
his files on communism during the Tydings Committee investigation; and it was Nixon who broke up Joe's famous
cloakroom scuffle with Drew Pearson (then spent a half
hour searching for the car McCarthy had misplaced).
When Stassen, whose career was becoming the shadow-
side of Nixon's, attacked McCarthy for meddling in Greek
trade arrangements with China, Nixon got Dulles to issue
a statement praising McCarthy's efforts. He tried, as well,

to make administration officials consult McCarthy on appointments.

But when it became clear that McCarthy was not going to stop his attacks on the party, Nixon helped those laboring to bring him down. When McCarthy's newly appointed director of investigations, J. B. Matthews, said "the largest single group supporting the Communist apparatus in the United States today is composed of Protestant clergymen," White House anti-McCarthyites saw a chance to mobilize their big gun, Ike, who had so far refused to "get down in the gutter with that fellow." Emmet Hughes and Bill Rogers (who said his friend Nixon would join in the attack) arranged for a group of clergymen to send a wire of protest to Eisenhower, and Hughes drafted a response from the President. But Rogers heard McCarthy was about to drop Matthews on his own. Hughes saw his chance fading, and a close race began. The telegram from the National Conference of Christians and Jews had to be speeded from New York; Sherman Adams had to take in that wire, and Hughes's draft of a reply, for Ike's approval; the prepared stencil for a press release had to be recut, since Eisenhower made some minor changes—all this before McCarthy made his move.

Rogers was calling periodically from Nixon's office to check on the progress of the plan when—luckily—who should walk into the Vice-President's room but Joe McCarthy himself. Nixon and Rogers tempted him with talk of investigating the CIA, a plan they had heretofore opposed. Anything to keep him there. Hughes quotes the account Rogers gave him later that day: "McCarthy wandered into Dick's office just after I put down the phone from talking with you the last time. Dick and I kept on and on asking him all kinds of thoughtful questions about how he was going to investigate the CIA. He even looked a little puzzled at our sudden interest. As he was rambling on, of course, your message got to the press, which he had no way of knowing. So as he headed for the door finally, he said with a big grin, 'Gotta rush now—I want to be sure I get the news of dumping Matthews to Fulton Lewis in time for him to break it on his broadcast.'" McCarthy was about an hour too late; not only had the reprimand been extracted from Eisenhower in this interval, but McCarthy's action now seemed like a contrite response to the President's criticism.

Nixon was intimately involved in the administration's attempt to bring peace between McCarthy and the army. In fact, his memory of involvement makes him say the famous fried-chicken lunch of reconciliation took place in his office (actually it was next door, in Senator Dirksen's room). When the terms of that agreement broke down, Nixon helped draft the Secretary of the Army's response.

All this was covert. Nixon did not want to attack McCarthy openly, and lose his own importance as courier between the poles of Republican sentiment. He told Len Hall this in 1954, when the White House staff was looking for a man to answer Adlai Stevenson's charge that Eisenhower had sold out to McCarthy. But the staff knew there would be little impact if a liberal Republican attacked Joe. The denunciation had to come from the right, so Eisenhower himself gave Nixon the job. The resulting television speech was written with great care; Nixon secluded himself in a hotel room to labor on it, balancing veiled praise and criticism as nicely as he could. Then he had to let Eisenhower go over it, checking and making changes. After that, all ties with McCarthy were severed. When a select committee of the Senate was appointed to investigate grounds for censuring McCarthy, Nixon chose its personnel and, in Richard Rovere's words, "arranged McCarthy's humiliation by appointing hanging judges." Roy Cohn listed Nixon among the severest critics of McCarthy to show up at his funeral.

Nixon realized these were dirty missions he was sent on, but necessary ones. His complaint was that Eisenhower did not seem to grasp their crucial nature, or value the man who could accomplish them. That is why he continued to think Eisenhower a professional soldier and an amateur politician. But Eisenhower was almost the opposite of "a plain blunt soldier." What he grasped was that partisan loyalty, the essential source of reward or punishment at lower levels, can be an encumbrance at the very top—useful at times, of course, but also dangerous. He retained loyalty through the action of subordinates; but protected himself from any danger by keeping those subordinates at arm's length, always ready to sacrifice them. He was just as willing to drop Sherman Adams, or undercut the proud rhetoric of Foster Dulles, as he had been to dump Nixon in 1952 and 1956.

A difference in attitude toward "politics" is only one

aspect of the barrier that existed between Eisenhower and Nixon, preventing mutual understanding (for Eisenhower as surely underestimated Nixon as Nixon did his boss). The Vice-President of the fifties was a "hard worker," not merely in the obvious sense that he worked hard; he wanted the work to show; he needed to convince people of his earnestness and effort. This not only impressed others, it convinced *him* that he had earned what he aimed for.

By comparison, Ike looked sybaritic and staff-punishing. This does not mean that Eisenhower did not work (though, of necessity, he kept a slower pace than Nixon). But Eisenhower had the true professional's instinct for making things look easy. He appeared to be performing less work than he actually did. And he wanted it that way. An air of ease inspires confidence. The singer's hard work on scales should all be done at home. On the stage, the voice should soar as by natural gift. Eisenhower had, over the years, done his army homework thoroughly—and not only in the narrow sense. Though he was not given to boasting or superlatives—Larson says he cut anything out of speech drafts that sounded like "I always" or "I never"—Eisenhower nonetheless told Emmet Hughes: "The fact remains that he [John Foster Dulles] just knows more about foreign affairs than anybody I know. In fact, I'll be immodest and say that there's only one man I know who has seen more of the world and talked with more people and *knows* more than he does—and that's me." Eisenhower was often represented, during his years in office, as the captive of Dulles in foreign policy. But historical perspective and the appearance of contemporaries' accounts are making it clear that Ike weighed shrewdly the strong and weak points of Dulles. Not only did he take positions opposed to his Secretary of State's; he did it with serene confidence in his own judgment. That was true in such matters as the Korean settlement, the encouragement of cultural exchange with Russia, the treatment of the French over Indochina, and the handling of Khrushchev's visit to America. Murray Kempton, in a brilliant essay called "The Underestimation of Dwight D. Eisenhower" (*Esquire*, September 1967), puts it well: "Never thereafter could he contemplate the war in Indochina except in the frozen tones of a War College report on a maneuver by officers who can henceforth abandon all hope of promotion. The French, he instructs Foster Dulles, have committed the classic military blunder. In Geneva, Dulles is said to have hinted that the United States might use the atom bomb to save the French; there is no evidence that he would have dared transmit that suggestion to a President who plainly would not have trusted him with a stick of dynamite to blow up a fish pond."

One of the results of Eisenhower's derided staff system was that he knew how to deal with experts, to evaluate competing ones, and not to be intimidated by them. His brother, Edgar Eisenhower, tried to pull rank on the Bricker Amendment, arguing that he knew more about the law because he was a lawyer. Ike answered that this matter transcended legal niceties and moved up into the area where he, Ike, was the expert. The staff system was not a way of avoiding action, as many charged (though it allowed him to evade responsibility in the sense that, if any head had to roll, it would not be his). Emmet Hughes poses the standard argument against Eisenhower—one which resembles, in some ways, the opinion of Hughes's political enemy, Nixon. After noting that Eisenhower had more power and popularity than any recent President, he says: "Yet it had been the pattern of action, if not the purpose of the man, to husband and to guard these resources—like savings earned by the sweat of a lifetime— so that they not be spent in the rough and contaminating play of power and politics." Hughes fails to appreciate that the conservation of authority—or, rather, the reconstitution of it—deserved the high priority Eisenhower gave it. He took over a nation full of internal doubt and suspicion, summarized (often melodramatically) in the phrase "the McCarthy Era." So successfully did Ike quiet this divisive ferment that his critics would, by the end of his time in office, reproach him for running such a quiet ship. It was a substantial achievement, though not a flashy one. In his customary manner, Ike got the job done, without trumpets. In his foreign policy, he inherited the Cold War and brought a degree of stability and—once again—placidity to the handling of conflicts. He took over a nation at war, a people fearful of atomic holocaust and poisoned milk. He left office to a man who cried for more missiles and for shock troops to fight guerrilla wars by helicopter.

Arthur Larson devotes a whole chapter of his book *Eisenhower: The President Nobody Knew* to a refutation of the Hughes argument against "conserving power." He contrasts Ike's handling of the Lebanon crisis with Kennedy's Bay of Pigs fiasco and Johnson's intervention in the Dominican Republic. And he contrasts the Eisenhower attitude toward Indochina with his successor's willingness to get involved in Vietnam. In Lebanon Eisenhower combined limited aim, conciliatory rhetoric, and appeals to the UN, with massive sudden troop presence—walking far more softly than Teddy Roosevelt did, but carrying a big stick. His attitude toward the crisis was summed up in *Waging Peace:*

> The basic mission of United States forces in Lebanon was not primarily to fight. Every effort was made to have our landing be as much of a garrison move as possible. In my address I had been careful to use the term "stationed" in Lebanon . . . If it had been prudent, I would have preferred that the first battalion ashore disembark at a dock rather than across the beaches. However, the attitude of the Lebanese army was at that moment unknown, and it was obviously wise to disembark in deployed formation ready for any emergency. As it turned out, there was no resistance; the Lebanese along the beaches welcomed our troops. The geographic objectives of the landings included only the city of Beirut and the adjoining airfield . . . The decision to occupy only the airfield and capital was a political one which I adhered to over the recommendations of the military. If the Lebanese army were unable to subdue the rebels when we had secured their capital and protected their government, I felt, we were backing up a government with so little popular support that we probably should not be there.

Once, when Eisenhower was complaining about the "tyranny" of weak nations who can pester giants with impunity, he ended his tirade with the calm shrug: "We must put up with it." There is a world of neglected wisdom in that statement. It underlies Eisenhower's warnings against a land war in Asia, his refusal to fight wars in which the enemy has choice of weapons and terrain and times. When Eisenhower moved, he made sure he had the broom in his hand—army, navy, air force, and marines to Lebanon (over 14,000 men) with backup troops assembling—or he did not move at all. He was not tortured by the fear of "losing face." His attitude toward the cover story for Francis Gary Powers was typical of him ("Cut your losses" is the motto Kempton finds for many of his actions). He had only one criticism of the Army in its fight with McCarthy; on the disastrous promotion of Peress, he advised the Army "to admit its mistake and then stand its ground." By trying to cover up the bungling, Secretary Stevens just got further entangled.

The common note in all these matters is Eisenhower's resolute lack of romanticism (it is no accident that he changed Roosevelt's name—Shangri-La—for the presidential retreat in Maryland). Contrast this realism with the sweeping pronouncements of his successors, who dealt in overkill rhetoric (Kennedy's inaugural "this hemisphere intends to remain the master of its own house") and insufficient troops (the Bay of Pigs). They walked noisily and carried little sticks. Lyndon Johnson's "We will always oppose the effort of one nation to conquer another" puts us forever at the mercy of tyrannical weak nations. And this policy was simply an extension of the Wilsonian imperialism, an imperialism of ideas, that was expressed in Kennedy's inaugural address. Walter Lippmann and others find the origins of Vietnam in the swashbuckling tones of that speech: "Let the word go forth from this time and place, to friend and foe alike, that the torch has been passed to a new generation of Americans, born in this century [a hit at Ike], tempered by war, disciplined by a hard and bitter peace, proud of our ancient heritage, and unwilling to witness or permit the slow undoing of those human rights to which this nation has always been committed, and to which we are committed today at home and around the world. Let every nation know, whether it wishes us well or ill, that we shall pay any price, bear any burden, meet any hardship, support any friend, oppose any foe to assure the survival and the success of liberty."

Headier stuff, this, than the yawning years of Eisenhower. But Eisenhower must have heard the rhetoric of endless young officers, would-be MacArthurs who dashed into their own Bays of Pigs, when Kennedy orated that

"Now the trumpet summons us again." Kennedy seemed almost to long for adversity: "In the long history of the world, only a few generations have been granted the role of defending freedom in its hour of maximum danger. I do not shrink from this responsibility [another hit at the supposedly do-nothing Ike]; I welcome it." One suspects that the old man on the platform felt bemused and rather sorry for the new President who literally did not know what he was asking for. One of Kennedy's first acts when he came into office was to "free" the government from reliance on massive response to military threat; he equipped the nation to go by helicopter into jungles with the assault force Generals Gavin and Taylor had recommended, much to Eisenhower's horror as a professional soldier. (Kennedy had, after all, waged a campaign that charged Eisenhower, the military man, with leaving the country in poor military condition—missile gaps, and all that.)

Kennedy, Johnson, Nixon—all the political pros—thought Eisenhower was obsolete in 1960, that he did not know the uses of political aggressiveness. None of them realized that he had found the secret of suggesting strength without rodomontade. This posture not only displeased the romantics on his team, like Emmet Hughes, but also the realistic "dealers" like Dulles and Nixon (who was on the side of Dulles in most of the latter's disagreements with Eisenhower). For Nixon, Dulles was the pro, and Ike forever the amateur.

Nixon seems entirely to have misread the source of Eisenhower's appeal. Ike's lack of pretense, his easy charm, made him seem the fulfillment of America's ideal—Everyman suddenly put in charge of the nation's destiny, the good-hearted nonprofessional with "common sense." Nixon, laboring throughout the Checkers speech to appear that sort of man himself (though he was not), seems to have mistaken Ike as the pattern of the common man as ruler.

But Eisenhower was a leader of troops, who had to convey an impression of authority—and he did. He was a very careful student of "image," the conveying of impressions. He was, after all, the first television President. In occupied Berlin, he urged the Allies to hold less lavish feasts in the midst of a defeated and hungry people. In keeping an eye out for leaders among his young officers, he looked not only for competence but for the ability to suggest competence to others. After the Checkers speech, Eisenhower had lost his little war with Nixon; but he looked magnanimous and happy at the plane in Wheeling. Nixon, who had won, looked haggard and almost hysterical as he tottered over to Knowland and wept on his shoulder. Ike was taking the measure of his man already.

Nixon, not understanding Eisenhower's standards, thought he could ingratiate himself by doing all the regime's dirty work. He thought this was the way to rise. All it did was convince Ike that he was not made for higher things. His one chance of growing in the President's esteem might have come from a refusal to run such errands. What followed is a comedy of errors—Nixon working harder and harder to please, yet falling lower and lower in Eisenhower's opinion of him. In 1956 the President tried to get rid of him, just as he had in the fund crisis. But Nixon still clung to him tenaciously. Chart his own course? Good: Nixon marched to the White House and said openly that his own course was to run again for Vice-President. Ike had had the tables turned on him again, but in a way that made Nixon lose dignity, and therefore lose Ike's support for the top office. The process was circular—Nixon suffering a humiliation Ike had inflicted on him, and that very humiliation making Ike more certain that his understudy lacked stature.

If he had not lacked stature before, he would have when Eisenhower got through with him. He had to keep repeating the pattern of the Checkers speech—saving his political life by surrendering important hostages. And though all this was Eisenhower's doing, Nixon had to sing hosannas to his leader. The Ike gives, the Ike takes away. Praised be the name of the Ike. It is hard enough to maintain dignity while jumping feverishly after a set of vanishing coattails. It is twice as hard when one has to pretend that the coattails are not being whisked away deliberately. A Uriah Heep attitude was forced on Nixon: "As he held the door open with his hand, Uriah looked at me, and looked at Agnes, and looked at the dishes, and looked at the plates, and looked at every object in the room, I thought—yet seemed to look at nothing; he made such an appearance all the while of keeping his red eyes dutifully on his master."

The quiet struggle of the two will now go on in history,

thanks to Nixon's persistence. The comedy seemed ended, time after time. But up Nixon popped and grabbed the coattails for another ride. Nixon's own presidency was launched as a restoration of the Ike regime. His first act as President-elect was to make a pilgrimage to the dying General's bedside. The lines have been solemnly joined in a dynastic marriage.

And who are we to say has won?

Ike? In one sense. Nixon has had to keep up the hosannas, consecrate himself to the Eisenhower legend, despite all the indignitites inflicted on him in his eight years as Vice-President. He is caught forever in an ignominious servitude.

Or is it Nixon who won? He lost points at each encounter, but survived. Survived the Checkers speech, all the party errands, the 1956 coolness, the Russian trip, the harsh affront of 1960 ("Give me a week . . ."), all the private quips and criticisms at his expense. Survived, and wrested from Eisenhower a final recognition of Uriah as the legitimate heir and successor.

It is an extraordinary story of two extraordinary men, who could not appreciate each other's virtues, who needed each other's weaknesses; who advanced by defeating each other.

7. The Common Man

"That's what we have and that's what we owe. It isn't very much, but Pat and I have the satisfaction that every dime that we've got is honestly ours. I should say this—that Pat doesn't have a mink coat. But she does have a respectable Republican cloth coat. And I always tell her that she'd look good in anything."

—*the Checkers speech*

"DECISIVENESS" was a key issue in 1952. When Nixon told Eisenhower to piss or get off the pot, his remark was more startling for its political import and open threat than for its anguished crudity of expression. Adlai Stevenson, the Democratic candidate, was under old and increasing attack as a "Hamlet," one incapable of reaching firm decisions and acting on them. This criticism neatly turned Stevenson's very gifts and talents against him—it made "intellectual" sound like "ineffectual." And this caricature of academic dithering formed a striking contrast with the image of Eisenhower, man of action about whom Walter Bedell Smith wrote a book called *Eisenhower's Six Great Decisions*. Yet here was a young senator on the telephone, warning Ike that he must act now or become another "Hamlet" himself. Nixon reports the advice he gave Ike in these words: "This thing has got to be decided at the earliest possible time . . . The great trouble is the indecision." It was rough stuff, and meant to be.

But Nixon must report, ruefully, that all the telephone call did was bear in upon him once more the truth that Eisenhower could not be rushed. Of course Nixon cannot venture a conclusion from this fact, but he does go out of his way to remark that "Sometimes he took more time to decide an issue than some of his eager lieutenants thought necessary."

But when the fund crisis had been resolved, Nixon immediately praised Eisenhower for his leisurely way of coping with it; he made a virtue of the silence that had tortured him for days. On the very night of the two men's reconciliation, he said from a platform in Wheeling, West Virginia, that such thoughtful delay did Ike credit: "I praised Eisenhower for the way he had made the decision with regard to the charges against me. I contrasted his attitude of carefully investigating the facts before acting with Truman's policy of defending his cronies accused of wrongdoing without regard to the facts. We were back on the political campaign trail."

The rest of Nixon's chapter on the fund crisis—with its careful veiled hints of criticism directed at Ike—shows that Nixon did not believe the argument he made that night in Wheeling. How could he, after his secret war with Eisenhower? But to get "back on the political campaign trail," he had to put the best light possible on his running mate's actions. There is nothing unusual about this. As Dr. Johnson said, a man is not under oath when composing funerary inscriptions. The same license is extended to politicians on the stump. Nixon need have no qualms about the matter—and, verifiably, does not: he is after all the one who described both his views, the private and the public one, in the same chapter.

What is unusual is Nixon's candor in acknowledging that distinction which all politicians observe between their actual opinions and those they can express in public. An even more striking instance of this candor shows up in the chapter on 1960's campaign. Kennedy directed heavy fire at Republicans, during that race, for letting Castro maintain a communist regime in this hemisphere. Nixon argues, persuasively, that this was cynical: Kennedy had been briefed on Cuba by the CIA, and presumably knew of contingency plans for Castro's overthrow. (Later, Kennedy apologists for the Bay of Pigs would argue that Eisenhower was *too* tough on Castro when he began these preparations.) Nixon says: "For the first and only time in the campaign, I got mad at Kennedy—personally. I understand and expect hard-hitting attacks in a campaign. But in this instance I thought that Kennedy, with full knowledge of the facts, was jeopardizing the security of a United States foreign policy operation. And my rage was greater because I could do nothing about it."

There is no doubt about the last sentence: it would scuttle his own career, as well as the plot against Castro, to break security himself. Nonetheless, after saying he could do nothing to reveal Kennedy's ploy, Nixon goes on to take credit for the restraint imposed on him: "What could I do? One course would be simply to state that what Kennedy was advocating as a new policy was already being done, had been adopted as a policy as a result of my direct support, and that Kennedy was endangering the security of the whole operation by his public statement. But this would be, for me, an utterly irresponsible act: it would disclose a secret operation and completely destroy its effectiveness."

What course was left for a man so hamstrung by virtuous reticence? "The covert operation had to be protected at all costs. I must not even suggest by implication that the United States was rendering aid to rebel forces in and out of Cuba. *In fact, I must go to the other extreme: I must attack the Kennedy proposal to provide such aid as wrong and irresponsible because it would vio-*

late our treaty commitments" (italics added). Strange logic: because one is unable to do one thing, one must do the exact opposite. Prevented, say, from punishing a wife-beater, one *must* punish the wife-beater's wife.

No one, admittedly, could ask for greater candor. Nixon patiently explains that he took a stand that was not only different, but at the opposite extreme, from what he actually held: "I was in the ironic position of appearing to be 'softer' on Castro than Kennedy—which was exactly the opposite of the truth, if only the whole record could be disclosed." Yet even these frank pages cannot recapture the hard assault he made on his own position. Here is what he said, in the fourth televised debate:

> I think that Senator Kennedy's policies and recommendations for the handling of the Castro regime are probably the most dangerously irresponsible recommendations that he's made during the course of this campaign. In effect, what Senator Kennedy recommends is that the United States government should give help to the exiles and to those within Cuba who oppose the Castro regime—provided they are anti-Batista. Now let's just see what this means. We have five treaties with Latin America, including the one setting up the Organization of American States in Bogotá in 1948, in which we have agreed not to intervene in the internal affairs of any other American country—and they as well have agreed to do likewise. The charter of the United Nations—its Preamble, Article I and Article II—also provide that there shall be no intervention by one nation in the internal affairs of another. Now I don't know what Senator Kennedy suggests when he says that we should help those who oppose the Castro regime, both in Cuba and without. But I do know this: that if we were to follow that recommendation, that we would lose all of our friends in Latin America, we would probably be condemned in the United Nations, and we would not accomplish our objective. I know something else. It would be an open invitation for Mr. Khrushchev to come in, to come into Latin America and to engage us in what would be a civil war, and possibly even worse than that.

One must keep reminding oneself, all through this urgently reasoned passage, that Nixon does not believe a word of it. Where another politician, unable to express his real opinion, might resort to hedging and evasion, to tactical ambiguity, or (in the last resort) to a perfunctory expression of the required opinion, Nixon throws himself enthusiastically into the task of "making a case" for the opposite side. If it is permissible to express a different view in public from the one held in private—and let us not be pharisaical about this, the practice is common in American politics—then Nixon will use that method with dogged thoroughness. As he might have said to his mother about the wartime poker games, "Everyone does it"—but few do it as well as he does. When the game is denouncing Kennedy's view, he will use treaties and precedent, arguments from self-interest and altruism, appeals to lofty morality and basic prudence. Like a lawyer, he feels licensed to make a case for his client; and this lawyer's briefs are always thorough.

A lawyer's habit of heaping arguments one on the other (if one does not sway the jury, another may), of putting the best light on things, is apparent throughout Nixon's career. In the fund crisis, for instance, he realized the money in dispute was a perfectly ethical source of aid to his career—this at the level of private opinion. But in public, he had to make it not only allowable but praiseworthy, not only useful to himself but a positive boon to mankind. So he managed to imply that the fund helped the taxpayer as much as it helped him. He asked a whole series of questions along this model: "Do you think, for example, that, when I or any other senator makes a trip to his home state to make a purely political speech, the cost of that trip should be charged to the taxpayers?" None of the things Nixon mentions in his list could be charged to the taxpayers by any addition to the senator's basic salary; so the argument was misleading. But once such a quest for the noblest possible interpretation of one's actions is begun, there is no end to the self-serving hymns that can be improvised. Moderate virtue, merely being good, is not good enough. All *real* virtue comes in one brand, labeled Heroic. Nixon points out, for instance, that he did not supplement his income by having Mrs. Nixon work in his office, on a Senate payroll. This abstention could imply several kinds of virtue—a scruple about propriety, regard for appearances, the safeguarding of taxpayers' interests —though it could arise, as well, from mere preference on his part or his wife's. But Nixon will not simply imply a virtuous motive for his act; he lays claim to the most selfless motive he can imagine—in this case, concern for the poor, as exemplified in the surplus of "government girls" around Washington: "I found that there were so many deserving Washington stenographers and secretaries who needed the work that I just didn't feel it was right to put my wife on the payroll." Mustn't let Rose Woods starve. The trouble with a public *persona*, sheerly political, is that when one cultivates it as assiduously as Nixon does, maintaining its separation from the private man and his views, the thing tends to drift farther and farther off from reality. The benevolent provider for government girls is already deep in the realms of fiction.

There is a carefully maintained contrast between the private Nixon, who thinks of himself as a Wilsonian in-tellectual, and a public Nixon who is simplistic and "just folks." This assumption of public folksiness is, of course, just another convention of American politics; but Nixon is led to extremes by his dogged methodical bent and literal-mindedness. What he intends as pleasant modesty becomes almost a form of groveling. He is just like all the rest of us, only more so. The classic attempt to make this identification was the Checkers speech, in which Nixon electronically entered the average man's home, mingled his own cares with the problems of that family living room, hung his wife's cloth coat in the closet, rustled his own mortgages in among the householder's debts and bills, parked his two-year-old car in the garage, and boarded Checkers in the backyard doghouse. Nixon told the com-mon man that he, too, owned no stocks and bonds, had no city slicker ways or rich man's arrogance. He, like Maggie and Jiggs listening to him, was just one of those people *God* cares for: "I believe it's fine that a man like Governor Stevenson, who inherited a fortune from his father, can run for President. But I also feel that it's essential, in this country of ours, that a man of modest means can also run for President. You remember what Abraham Lincoln said, 'God must have loved the common people—he made so many of them.'"

Following Chotiner's rule, he did not refer, in the speech, to his only real achievement of the war—becoming an officer. Instead he groveled: "My service record was not a particularly unusual one. I went to the South Pacific. I guess I'm entitled to a couple of battle stars. I got a couple of letters of commendation, but I was just there when the bombs were falling . . ." The tone of the speech was Uriah Heep's "Umble as I am, umble as my mother is, and lowly as our poor but honest roof has ever been . . ." As Murray Kempton wrote, "Nixon ended the 1960 campaign wandering limply and wetly about the American heartland begging votes on the excuse that he had been too poor to have a pony when he was a boy."

This formal self-deprecation fits in with Nixon's customary mood of self-discipline. And his methodical habits make him build *structures* of public humility. Even his verbal tics and formulae reflect a Heepish combination of the assertive and the mealymouthed: "Just let me say this . . ." is delivered as a request for *permission* to nail down a fact. So is "Let me make one thing very clear," or "Just to keep the record clear . . ."

There are larger patterns of public humility, too—the Out-of-the-Mouths-of-Babes statement, for instance. People are always wandering up to him with gems of wisdom on their lips. These are often children or "common folk," and it is amazing how much Nixon finds out from such encounters. A Numble Person can always learn from The People. During the 1968 campaign, for instance, Nixon kept telling the story of a couple he met. Neighborlike, he asked how things were going, and the man said "Pretty well, I'm making good pay." But the wife said that when she finished her accounts every week, she found herself with two dollars less than she had last year. What luck to have met a woman who, week after week, achieved just the statistical average of the nation, and kept books carefully enough to know this! The most famous campaign example of the Mouths-of-Babes encounter was the girl who, in Deshler, Ohio, spoke to Nixon on his train platform by waving a sign that said "Bring us together again" —giving him an inaugural theme.

A variant on this pattern is the I-Would-Never-Have-Said-That-Myself device (but since someone else did, I'll pass it along to you, simply because every scrap of wisdom from that source is worth preserving). For instance: "General Eisenhower introduced me as his running mate to the Republican National Convention as a man who has a special talent and an ability to ferret out any kind of subversive influence." At a reception for Medal of Honor winners, one of the men told Nixon that he should have the medal for his performance in South America. Nixon, judiciously umble, is not so sure: "No one knows what he is capable of until he has been tested . . ."

Not all of these came-up-and-saids are compliments. Some are in the nature of "guides," which Nixon adds to his stock of words to live by—the As-My-Guru-Told-Me formula. And it is no surprise that the guru turns out, frequently, to be Eisenhower. The pages of *Six Crises* sparkle with the wit and wisdom of Ike:

—"My personal attitude . . . can probably best be described by one of my favorite Eisenhower anecdotes."

—"I laughed and recognized that I had just experienced another example of the truth of one of Eisenhower's favorite admonitions."

—"There could not have been a more dramatic demonstration of the truth of this maxim—one of President Eisenhower's favorites—than my meeting with Nikita Khrushchev."

—"As President Eisenhower put it, 'Like all successful politicians I married above myself.' "

Another mark of the Umble Person is that he has a great deal to learn. And so, from one crisis to another, we are told how he failed here, improved there. In each crisis he applies the lessons of the last. During the fund crisis, for instance, he remembers that "I had learned from my experience in the Hiss case that what determines success or failure in handling a crisis is the ability to keep coldly objective when emotions are running high." Without that prior schooling, he would, you see, have thought hotheadedness and uncontrolled emotion were the proper response to crisis.

The whole of *Six Crises* is a saga of moral education. He may have lost an election, but he made his soul. The problems that plagued him at the outset of the book are all overcome by the end. In the first four crises, for instance, he suffers from emotional collapse when the crisis has passed. In the last two, he has learned how to prepare for this danger, and obviate it. (Unfortunately for his thesis, the book came out just before his 1962 campaign for governor, after which his most notorious lapse took place, the "last press conference.")

It might seem that the publication of a story of moral growth is not the mark of a Numble Person but of a boaster. But a man of self-esteem does not spell out the moral justification for each of his acts. He presumes that people will credit him with good intentions. Heep, however, starts with the assumption that others are *not* expecting virtue from him. He must point it out. John F. Kennedy felt no need to apologize for his World War II heroism. He winningly avoided reference to it himself; but his attitude, we can guess, was that he was decorated for bravery because he was brave. He did not feel obliged to protest that his was not, after all, a bravery that went beyond the common measure.

Nixon was forced to a public accounting of his finances. But all through his career he has given us public accountings of his moral state. A recitation of high motives for having a political fund, for not hiring his wife, for not buying mink. It is a bit embarrassing to listen to such abject pleading—David Copperfield cannot break away from Uriah too quickly. I think this explains the vague dislike for Nixon that many experience. It is not caused by any one thing he has done or omitted, but by an oppressive moralism and air of apology.

Nixon's flattery of the common man is not simply a personal trait. It is one of the permanent aspects of American politics. But Nixon has subjected it, in his normal way, to systematic exploitation. The trait has been analyzed by D. H. Lawrence in his study of American literature. Intelligence, he claims, lives always on sufferance in America, afraid of conflict with the majority, whose voice is the nation's will. Lawrence finds the classic expression of this in one of Fenimore Cooper's "white tales," *Homeward Bound*. A group of Americans sails home from Europe, reenacts ocean-baptism into America's piny innocence, into the pure forest of Cooper's Indian tales. But the novel is confused by realities that do not fit this scheme. The crass "go-getter," Steadfast Dodge, has "done" Europe, performing a raid on it out of the very heart of the American ethos. In him, therefore, the new is fouling the old, the forest corrupting the city. Dodge's doctrine of equality makes him feel, paradoxically, that his country is superior to European nations, which maintain forms of social superiority. The novel's Effingham family represents a very different America—respect-

ful toward Europe, educated by contact with it, yet loyal
to the American ideal of equality. They are not "proud of
their umbleness," and this puts them at the mercy of
Dodge. Eve Effingham cannot avoid the company of
Steadfast without denying his equality: "Eve Effingham
had pinned herself down on the *Contrat Social*," Lawrence says, "and she was prouder of that pin through her
body than of any mortal thing else." The Effinghams are
stranded in mid-ocean: they must not feel either superior
or inferior to Europe or America. They are "homeward
bound," yet leaving their home as well, unable to reach
shore in either direction. And their problem is Cooper's
own, in a book like *The American Democrat* (which
Mencken admired): "Intrinsically Fenimore Cooper was
the superior of the Dodges of his day. He felt it. But he
felt he ought not to feel it. And he never had it out with
himself."

The Effingham in Nixon—the quick mind, and puritanical concentration, and sensitivity to suffering—have for
years been at the mercy of Steadfast Dodges. As he put it
himself, "People have known me for too long for me to
come on all of a sudden talking like Adlai Stevenson."
There is a confession, deep in that statement, to a kind of
self-mutilation. The choice constantly being forced on the
American politician is to be a man of Stevenson's elegance,
but unelected, or a man who hides his own intelligence and
feeling in order to voice the sentiments of the crowd. It is
in many ways a false dilemma—the common man does,
in the end, want uncommon leaders; Stevenson was not rejected merely for his grace and wit. But the daily choices
and petty concessions of politics keep posing the dilemma
—either join the Dodges, or be an ineffectual Effingham
striving toward land. Nixon is extraordinary, here as
everywhere, for his acute self-analysis and clarity in grasping the alternatives: perhaps no one ever made this particular choice so consciously. He has gone through most of
his career knowing that he is better, brighter, more profound than he lets himself appear. That knowledge must,
in the long run, do something to one's self-esteem, leak
little acids in upon it day by day: "Through these white
novels of Cooper runs this acid of ant bites, the formic
acid of democratic poisoning. The Effinghams feel superior. Cooper felt superior. Mrs. Cooper felt superior too.
And bitten."

This is the formula for resentment in America—the conflict between deference and competitiveness, both imposed as duties. Our individualism is both emulative (you should "best" the next man) and egalitarian (without being better than the next man). One must achieve, yet remain common; excel, yet pretend not to; keep asserting, as Nixon did in his inaugural address, that "Greatness comes in simple trappings." Or, as Steadfast Dodge says in the novel: "I think you will agree with me, sir, in believing it excessively presuming in an American to pretend to be different from his fellow citizens."

8. Whittier: First Day

"When you are actually in America, America hurts."
        —*D. H. Lawrence*

NIXON SPENT the last weekend before election 1968 in Los Angeles, at the posh tiered Century Plaza Hotel, site of a big demonstration and semiriot when President Johnson stayed there (we now have many such unmonumented battlefields). Nixon was resting, readying himself for the ordeal of the campaign's last hours—the election-eve telethon; the long flight back on election day; then the eerie time he has known so often, waiting for the oracle that issues piecemeal from election booths to be put together, less and less enigmatic as the night passes, pronouncing his future.

He needed rest. He had been sliding, with quiet inevitability, down in the polls. Humphrey, who *could* not win a month ago, just *might* win now. There were hundreds of desperate last-minute plans to reverse this trend. Nixon was bombarded with them. Yet he sat there, shell-shocked. Back in New York, his strategists around John Mitchell even considered accepting Humphrey's challenge to debate; one reason for dismissing the plan was Nixon's harried state. He was getting irritable. He needed rest.

I decided to spend the two blank days of his rest in Whittier, the hometown he would not be visiting this weekend. It takes a mere forty minutes to get there when traffic is moving. Century City streets, with extravagant astral names like Galaxy Boulevard, wind almost inevitably up onto Santa Monica Freeway, which arches one on a low trajectory over the sunken metropolis. Los Angeles, thanks to earthquake legislation, is literally a topless city. It grows by creeping through valleys, up hills, stripping earth and then reclothing it in Western-pastel, a muddied blend of low Spanish and low modern styles. Up on the freeway, one crosses this discolored carpet of a town without seeing much of it. Railings, poles, signs make a tunnel. Downtown buildings are hidden by the placards that mark exits and bifurcations and irrevocable chances to weave out of one freeway to another. But these low buildings do not, as one might expect, leave a clear prospect of sky. The gray morning thickness of air was cut by many lines, by their nodes and carriers, joinings and dispersions—latticework pylons lifting this network of wires. Lanes of traffic knot and ravel out beneath a tangle of the city's nerves. It is the dreary future of McLuhan's vision—a quiver of disembodied awareness, signal and reception; America fondly creates the entity she has praised for years as a "live wire." This part of the country looks like a crush of people speeding nowhere, a jam of signals saying nothing, a great human switchboard. No wonder Nixon left it as soon as he could.

But the place he left as a boy was open land, haze of sun leaf-sieved into lemons on Leffingwell's ranch, oranges on the Murphy ranch, and—between the two, strategically placed to service workers from both farms—the Nixon grocery store. I saw little of that agrarian valley remaining as I came down off the throughway and went east out Whittier Boulevard, past the very small buildings and very large signs that trigger America's bottomless lust for hamburgers. At Whittier itself, I turned up the town's main street, which runs north toward a green side of mountain, under which Whittier College is sheltered. It seemed the place to begin.

But it was Sunday; perhaps no one would be on campus. Just before I reached the college, I saw the First

Friends Church on my left, with people streaming into it. Outside, one of those black chinked signs under glass, with white chips dropped into proper slots announcing the sermon: "The Christian and the Election." I pulled into a parking lot across the street, at the William Penn Hotel. I thought this might be Nixon's own church. Perhaps I could decide, here of all places, which man to vote for on Tuesday.

Not that I expected any candidate to be endorsed outright from the pulpit. Dr. Norman Vincent Peale merely made trouble for his friend, Dick Nixon, when he attacked Kennedy in 1960. Politics and religion are supposed to observe an oil-and-water compact in America. That is why priests at political demonstrations anger ladies on their street corners. When Kennedy said he would "do the right thing" and observe the neat division, he came as close as an American politician ever does to expressing the "true code of a gentleman." Nixon had to dissociate himself from Dr. Peale's charges. (So, in time, did Peale himself. He amiably pleaded that he had "never been too bright anyhow.")

First Friends, the largest Quaker church in the area, has a plain board meetinghouse air, but with boards cushioned and floor carpeted. Hardly Marble Collegiate, but verging on Wooden Collegiate. It has "stained-glass" windows— pale colored patterns of frame, niche, surrounding scrolls, with a large blank in the middle, watery cosmetics for some absent image.

My hope that this might be Nixon's boyhood church was soon dashed. That is a more austere affair further east on Whittier Boulevard, near the site of the Nixon store. But Nixon's relatives attend the downtown church—his Aunt Ollie is there this morning. And the pastor is an alumnus of Whittier College, as are most of the parish leaders. If one is to find survivals from the old Whittier, there is no better place to look than at First Friends on a Sunday morning. Attendance was thin, and those present seemed well above average age, handsomely wrinkled (as by Norman Rockwell's undemanding pencil)—*survivors,* hardy and at peace. The balcony level was empty, but for a ten-year-old girl in a seizure of concentration. Her bright eyes traveled intent across the faces beneath her. She seemed to be studying, trying to read answers. She did not, however, look much toward the pastor, or seem to be heeding his words.

They were eminently unheedable. The Christian will vote for Christ, and find peace. The pastor's style is Preacher's Ingratiating, rhetorical equivalent of Wooden Collegiate—the chirpy persuasiveness that made Dr. Peale one of the "Twelve Best U.S. Salesmen" for 1954. This Quaker pastor looks like Harold Lloyd grown older and more poised, bewildered goggles turned now to twinkling beacon lights of brotherhood. Every few seconds, a kindly smile helps the glasses light parishioners on their way. He can hardly finish a statement without asking for agreement or some common ground of understanding. Anecdote: "I went on a train ride . . ." Solicitation: "Have you been on a train recently?" Anecdote: "The little boy ran away . . ." Solicitation: "Did you ever try to run away?" The rhetorical questions insinuate, as painlessly as possible, a moral tone into the congregation's daily concerns. It is the cheerleader tone of Nixon trying to slip a fast one by: "Incidentally, in mentioning Secretary Dulles, isn't it wonderful, finally, to have a Secretary of State who isn't taken in by the Communists, who stands up to them?"

If you vote for Christ, you will find peace. It is the message of Nixon's own spiritual guide, Dr. Peale, who offers us a baby-sitter God: "He just puts His big arms around everybody and hugs them up against Himself." A nonpolitical Nanny-God to protect us from Kennedys. But will He? There is a contradiction in the fact that Peale, arguing for separation of church and state, fending off Rome's threat to that separation, jumped *into* politics. Nor was it the first time. He caused a stir back in 1948 by advancing MacArthur for President (he likes to include, in his edifying stories of achievers-through-prayer, the feats of executive types among the military). Peale is not really concerned to keep religion out of politics. He wants to keep *other* religions out—every kind but his. As Donald Meyer puts it in *The Positive Thinkers,* Peale's constituency is that great middle class afflicted by anomie—the kind of people drawn to Wallace rallies. They have affluence without satisfaction, privilege without style—lives empty at the center, like the pastel windows in First Friends. They are not safe in their possessions, because they are not conscious of deserving them. They do not know why they gain or retain life's chromium graces;

their own infidelity tortures them. To them Peale comes preaching acceptance. They have *not* failed themselves and their children. If they thought of themselves as failures, now they must think only of Peale's gratulatory maxims: "The Spirit Lifter that I read and committed today lies deeply imbedded in my mind. It is now sending off through my thoughts its healing, refreshing effects." Nineteenth-century Christianity urged the poor to learn contentment with their lack of money. Peale and his brethren must teach man to submit to wealth: "There was a time when I acquiesced in the silly idea that there is no relationship between faith and prosperity." A religion of the "deserving poor" has become the religion of the undeserving rich—for those uneasy because they no longer wear cloth coats.

To "vote for Christ" is to vote for oneself as Christ-like —a process of self-hypnosis that says the consumer life of middle America is, no matter what it seems, a godly life. But one can only learn such passivity toward affluence if the system blessing the nation is kept beyond question. If a man is always discussing the rules of the game, trying to change or improve them, he cannot relax into contentment with his lot. That is why Peale denounces "preachers offering intellectualized sermons on social problems." It distracts man from the search for inner joy to be always "fumbling with materialistic processes." The Pealite's main commerce with material things is peaceful enjoyment of them, putting off all doubt that they reflect God's blessing: "This world is somehow built on moral foundations. This . . . is the one lesson history teaches . . . The good never loses." Peale is the palliative that no longer served those flocking to Wallace speeches.

The little girl was right, then, to turn her eyes on the Norman Rockwell ladies. This congregation had not been summoned to accept Christ, but to accept itself. To accept itself accepting a world of sunny disorientation. The milky white center is reserved in these windows because *they,* the people, America's large blank center, are the object of their own cult. She would have to "make her decision" for—or against—them. Her problem was posed in the older women's somnolence, their wrinkles lightly penciled: would she soak up their nice thoughts, along with the sun; sweeten like an orange of this valley? It was easy, as I watched her puzzled face, to imagine Richard

Nixon at her age, wondering if this world would hold him.

After his sermon, and a song, the pastor went outside where, along with his assistant, he greeted the line of parishioners with handshakes, one last twinkle of unobtrusive inspiration. As I waited to talk with him, various people came up to say hello: "I've never seen you here before. Is there something I can do for you?" "Friends" live up to their name. We talk about the Nixons, about the town, about its other Quaker church. I look over the pamphlets and bulletins—theological blandness, with one tart touch of politics, the Quaker antiwar movement (no mention of that in the sermon on Christians and the Election). The friendly bulletin has notes on the community: "On the day the Apollo [VII] blasted off, Mr. and Mrs. X also left the launching pad for Canada . . ." Perfect oneness with the culture. All systems go.

When the pastor has pumped and twinkled his last, he leads me into his study and starts changing. "Rams game, we'll just make it. Want to come?" I say I must work all day, in Whittier. He is too broadminded to resent such antisabbatarianism. It looks like a rainy November day for the game, he is pulling on heavy pants and a sweater— back to Harold Lloyd's college days. As he becomes less and less clerical, one with the culture around him, blasting off for the game, I watched the reverse of a process I had seen, six weeks earlier, in Chicago. During the Democratic Convention, a group of clergymen was formed to act as peacemakers in the streets. Not many Roman priests took part (Chicago's Cardinal—"Louisiana Fats" to his liberal critics—does not like "activists" in his diocese), but ministers and rabbis hunted up and wore Roman collars, with black suit and dickey: they wanted to be recognized as clergymen, men set apart from the rest of society. The collar would protect them (they hoped—vain hope) from Mayor Daley's Irish Catholic cops.

In a way, Peale had been right about Kennedy. (It was typical of him, when his stand became inconvenient, to call it wrong. One should accept oneself as "not too bright" when this reduces social friction.) He was right, as the women on Baltimore's street corner had been right. It is impossible to keep religion out of politics in the age of Billy Graham and Dr. Peale. Where they preach, from Nixon's elbow, acceptance, what is left for religion of a different sort but to preach rejection? And that will seem, to the goodhearted pastor and his assistant, an "un-American" thing—the suggestion that the consumer life is not necessarily godly.

Talbert Moorehead, already dressed for the Rams game, arrives to drive his pastor to the stadium. Moorehead was in the class just before Nixon's at Whittier, and he is happy to reminisce—how Nixon helped him with a speech, how Nixon founded the Orthogonians ("pigs" to the older society of Franklins—Moorehead was a Franklin), how he ran for Congress the first time with everybody helping stuff mail. I listen until kickoff time drags them away, then Moorehead invites me to his office the next day (it is just down the street, beside the Bank of America). When they leave, I go back to the William Penn for breakfast—the hotel is just one of many ways the town reminds itself of Quaker history—of Wales (Bryn Mawr Street), of New England (Whittier College, Greenleaf Avenue), of Philadelphia (the college's "Franklins"— though Ben makes a gamy addition here, as he did to Sir William's "holy experiment" in the eighteenth century). There is a Friends Avenue, a Quaker Maid Dairy.

In the hotel lobby, one office door is marked "Christology"—a religious unity movement, the desk clerk explains. Leaflets give the schedule for community events: among them, "Karate for Teenagers, 7:30–9:00 in Gunn Park." Back on the street, I pause at the window of "The Beard," a boutique next to First Friends Church—silky mandarin jackets with Maltese crosses on chains. The closest I had come, all that Sunday morning, to reminders of the crucifixion.

Up Greenleaf, it is only a block to the college; the first building, Mendenhall—which houses the president's office. No one is here Sunday; that gives me time to study a bulletin board with clippings about Nixon. I find, later, that a second Nixon board was spattered with mud one night ("By students?" I ask—"Who knows?" the answer) and had to be moved inside the president's office. Over the mantel, in the open hall of the building, is a quote from the school's namesake:

> Early hath Life's mighty question
> Thrilled within the heart of youth,

With a deep and strong beseeching,
What and where is Truth?

Along with the school, the football team is named for
the gentle abolitionist poet: "Tigers Beat Poets" goes a
notice of last week's loss to Occidental, as if announcing
a brute fact of nature. The Quaker poet was also a Republican, one of the party's earliest supporters, an elector
in the college that chose Lincoln. But his latter-day pupils
are not true to the poet's party. In a copy of the student
paper *(Quaker Campus)*, I find a column urging Humphrey's election ("I have no particular love for R.M.N.")
and an editorial supporting Eugene McCarthy: "Nixon . . .
would lead without scruples or conscience . . . Nixon
headed off the stronger personality of Nelson Rockefeller
by kissing elephant behinds" *(O John!)*. "For God's sake,
forget the Pueblo" *(O Greenleaf!)*. "[America] is a sick,
violent, racist society intent on destroying itself" *(O Whittier!)*. A student Human Rights Commission has been
formed to make sure no Delano grapes shall make their
way onto Campus Inn tables, that no housemothers shall
enter a girl's room without search warrant ("things go on
on this campus which are in violation of the law"). It is
just as well Nixon aspired to the presidency of the United
States. He could hardly succeed as president of Whittier
College.

The college is small. The library, on crutch-shaped stilts
of poured concrete, is Modern Campus Standard (except
for the name, Bonnie Bell Wardman Library). The science
building plants its concrete crutches on Hadley Field,
where Nixon played guard as a Poet. I look for a place
where Nixon might have spent his time, an old building—
and stop by the oldest: Founders Hall. In front there is an
"Orthogonian Pond" donated by the club's early members.
This hall, built by pioneers in 1894, has on its second
floor a large room, with a stage and rows of folding chairs,
that served as chapel for services, auditorium for com-
mencements, theater for plays and debates, and meetinghouse for campus politics. Here was the hub of campus
life when the campus was the hub of community life,
when education was local and truly public—elocutionary,
a matter of performance to meet local standards. Here
Nixon's mother performed and graduated; and his cousin,
Jessamyn West. Here he debated and acted, cried real

effortful tears in *Bird in Hand,* and scored the large triumphs of a forensic senior year.

The place is ghosted with cobwebs and disanimated furniture—stuffed birds, science slides, the rags of curtain and scenery, things made for public theatrical life that all look dead in private. On the third floor, elocution is still taught; only now it is called "The Psychology of Persuasive Speech," and it uses tape recorders and the apparatus of McLuhan's age. The fourth floor has moldering stage costumes, out-of-date fedoras and slinky gowns that seem to have starved on their hangers. The stairs that wind down have built-in benches at each landing—former "student centers." There is a time lag between this solid building and the new ones perched on stilts, as if ready to take off. The lag will be remedied one month after Nixon's election, when Founders Hall goes up in flames.

If Whittier life revolved around the second story of Founders Hall, the group that held this key piece of terrain was the "Literary Society" which, for Whittier, *was* society. "Chief" Newman, full-blooded Indian who was football coach of the Poets, says, "When I came on the campus in 1929, the Franklins were the controlling force." Nixon, with Newman's help, changed that. "The Orthogonians became more aggressive, and began recruiting the best boys on campus." In the indulgent way of community colleges, which have near horizons populous with friendly onlookers, Franklins were the "brilliant" set at Whittier. There is no brilliance like a schoolboy's, since it is all promise—a thing still indefinite and opening out, therefore infinite. Every speech or poem is not so much a thing achieved as a harbinger. And this was, by most standards, the sphere Nixon belonged to. His grades were good, his debating excellent, his political skills already apparent. But there was, then as always, a deep distrust of brilliance in him. "I won my share of scholarships," he wrote later, "and of speaking and debating prizes in school, not because I was smarter but because I worked longer and harder than some of my gifted colleagues." Brilliance, like the hare, moves in spurts, unreliably over the long haul. Nixon would seek out the turtles, slower, methodical, more certain. He was first president of the Orthogonians. His uneasiness with brilliance he maintains to this day— the feelings that burst out when he talks about "intellectuals," standoffish Effinghams not at the mercy of Steadfast.

Some of this feeling undoubtedly comes from Nixon's sensitivity to the plight of the underdog, his genuine compassion. Talbert Moorehead, when he was running for class president, had to make a speech in that little life-and-death arena of schoolboy hopes, the second floor of Founders, and he felt inadequate to the task. Nixon, without being told, sensed this, and took him aside. "I can still see him now, pacing up and down, telling me how to give a speech: 'You've got to find an issue and concentrate on *it*, not on yourself.' He was a great one for 'issues.' "

He found a number of issues that made him a leader—without making him, in the customary sense, popular. He was friendly with everyone, but had no close friends or admiring circle. When he was not in class, he was at the store, working; and few boys remember going out there to see him (though they remember the large meals brought from the grocery and, in those Depression times, shared with others). He rose not so much by force of personality—he would have scorned the "buddy boy" approach, even if he were capable of it—as by finding the right issues.

Dancing, for instance—frowned on in this Quaker school. He won his race for president of the student body by promising to bring dances to the campus, though he himself did not attend them. His argument, made successfully to the trustees, was that it was better to have dancing under campus control than to let students seek it in the more sulphurous atmosphere of Los Angeles. Another campus "issue" was the annual bonfire, a point of class pride. Each year the fire was fueled with scrap wood topped by an outhouse. The competition was to see which senior chairman could top the pile of debris with the largest specimen—two-holer, say, or even three. Nixon scored an immense remembered triumph when his diligence turned up a four-holer. Picture the systematic intensity that went into this achievement. There is a Stewart method at poker, a Chotiner method at elections, and a four-holer method in campusmanship. Show him the rules, and he will play your game, no matter what, and beat you at it. Because with him it is not a game.

But the greatest "issue" of his school days was the

Orthogonians' undermining of the Franklins. The Franklins wore formal dress to their meetings and were literary. The Orthogonians were "common man" in style—and mainly made up of athletes. Chief Newman, the coach, claims he did not get involved in campus politics, and so cannot be included in the club's founders, but Moorehead claims everybody thought of the Orthogonians as "Chief Newman's boys." It is this tie, no doubt, and not the time he spent on the football bench, that makes Nixon feel so close, even now, to "the Chief." Football was also his way to remain "common" during his triumphs on the long debating tours of that time. He would not get trapped in the first-class lounge where Steadfast might make fun of his "snooty" ways.

That Sunday afternoon in Whittier, after talking to Mrs. Olive Marshburn (Aunt Ollie) and Mr. Merle West (Jessamyn's brother), I drove over to see the Chief. He lives in a fine suburban home on what used to be Murphy's ranch, the orange farm. He is slow in his movements and speech, firm, with the air of a chieftain, yet not haughty. "The Orthogonians kind of adopted me as a godfather." I asked if the stories about Nixon's tension before games were true—that he could not eat or sleep. "I guess so. He never spared himself. He used to take an awful lacing in scrimmage. He was tenacious as the dickens. When he got hold of something, he never let go." He was not much of an athlete, though? "No." Nixon was not only small, but clumsy. His wife recalls that he almost killed himself trying to rollerskate when they were first dating. Why, I asked the Chief, did he keep trying so hard? "I guess he thought it was his duty. Everyone tried to do something for the team, then—even if it was only to work as manager, a thankless task. Hubert Perry, the son of the banker who got Dick into politics, was manager of the team in Dick's day. We used to empty the town on a football day. It was a smaller world, then. Less sophisticated. You can't get anybody to volunteer for manager anymore." According to one classmate, Richard Harris, Nixon's role was even more ignominious than the manager's: Nixon and Harris served as "cannon fodder" to the team; they were tackling dummies—part of a defense line against which the first string did its practicing. There were not many available for the varsity at Whittier— Nixon's freshman team was made up of eleven men, so injuries or substitutions were plainly impossible. The coach had to take what he could get in the way of a second eleven for the varsity, and Nixon and Harris were it. After all his effort, Nixon did not get a football letter in senior year.

There is a self-punishing side to Nixon that only makes sense back in what Newman calls that smaller, less sophisticated world. It was a world where men were supposed to strive and deserve, even if they did not succeed. It became fashionable, in the years after Nixon's crushing defeat of 1962, to ask what kept him running. It was the same thing that kept him on the football field, where he did not belong—the sacredness of running, the need to *deserve* luck eventually by showing the pluck that starts at the bottom and never quits. The titles of Horatio Alger stories are very eloquent: *Making His Way, Helping Himself, Struggling Upward, Bound to Rise*. The emphasis is not on having risen, but on rising. Luck comes to many, but only pluck turns luck into a molder of character. It is the code of Emerson: "Life only avails, not the having lived. Power ceases in the instant of repose."

Andrew Carnegie thought no men should inherit money. We should all start equal, so the man of worth can *prove* his worth. Alger actually accomplished this aim in fiction; he used the Victorian plot-device of putting an heir in rags—unconscious prince among the paupers—to make him earn, at the bottom, the fortune that was his by mere inheritance. The doctrine of equality is, in Carnegie's hands, a way of clearing the field for self-assertion. But if we are to start equal each generation, why not each year, or each day? If what one's father did in the last decade gives an unfair advantage in this decade, why does what I accomplished yesterday not give me an unfair advantage today?

The poisonous thing about Horatio Alger was not that he made men aim at wealth or success—he did not: the stories' idle rich "boys with kid gloves" stay richer, for the most part, than laborious rising heroes. The hero did not aim at success but at succeeding—that is, at character formation and "self-improvement." He was a martyr to duty—Lincoln and Wilson forging their souls and losing their cause. The self-made man is the true American monster. The man who wants to make something outside himself—a chair, a poem, a million dollars—produces something. It can be praised or condemned; but it is "out there," a thing wrought or won or subdued, apart from the self. The *self*-maker, self-improving, is always a construction in progress. The man's product—his self—is never finished, not severed from him to stand on its own. He must ever be tinkering, improving, adjusting; starting over; fearful his product will get out of date, or rot in the storehouse. His lovingly worked stained window has, always, a white space at the center. To stand out "fair and square" is to stand out, by earned excellence, from the ranks of the common man. And to do that one must keep returning to the ranks, starting over. Found the Orthogonians, and when they become the fashionable society, found neo-Orthogonians—and so in an endless line of men rising but doomed to avoid having risen. (If one sheds the "Republican" cloth coat, does one not lose the Republicanism with it?)

Emerson, the Horatio Alger of the educated, felt this duty always to be starting over. He said one must become a child again each day—"unaffected, unbiased, unbribable, unaffrighted"—to achieve real independence, which is independence from one's past achievements and judgments, as well as from the rest of the race's opinions. It is not truth (the goal) Emerson is interested in, but *discovery* of truth (the process). Strike out on your own, he says, or "tomorrow a stranger will say with masterly good sense precisely what we have thought and felt all the time, and we shall be forced to take with shame our own opinion from another."

Nixon has this self-improving mania: the very choice of a framework for his book reflects it. As with most of his strategic decisions, the choice of an outline for *Six Crises* met several needs. First, it was another way to ride Ike's coattails—a citation shows he means people to think of *Eisenhower's Six Great Decisions* by Walter Bedell Smith. But, even beyond that choice, he had war-gamed the situation until he chose The Method for writing a book. On the one hand, by focusing on a limited number of situations, rather than adopting the standard framework of autobiography, he could omit certain parts of his life entirely. The names of Helen Douglas and Joe McCarthy simply do not occur in the book. On the other hand, he can watch himself in action, and "improve" himself publicly, by the elocutionary method of that second-floor platform in Founders Hall. The book is a report card on the student's progress. Mistakes in one crisis are corrected in the next, as if we were moving from semester to semester, from one course to another. Here he is, moralizing, at the height of the fund trouble:

> In such periods of intense preparation for battle, most individuals experience all the physical symptoms of tension—they become edgy and short-tempered, some can't eat, others can't sleep. I had experienced all these symptoms in the days since our train left Pomona. I had had a similar experience during the Hiss case.

He still lives through that rough day before the football game.

> But what I had learned was that feeling this way before a battle was not something to worry about—on the contrary, failing to feel this way would mean I was not adequately keyed up, mentally and emotionally, for the conflict ahead.

One must not only try one's best, but be conscious of trying; not enough to win, you must deserve the victory; deserve it by suffering for it. Easy wins are somehow tainted —the meaningless prizes of the brilliant.

> It is only when the individual worries about how he feels that such physical factors become signs of self-destruction rather than of creativity. Two of the most important lessons I have learned from going through the fire of decision is [sic] that one must know himself, be able to recognize his physical reactions under stress for what they are, and that he must never worry about the necessary and even healthy symptoms incident to creative activity.

It becomes a matter of *health* to tense up, and to watch one's tenseness, parading these symptoms of effort as one boasts of a cloth coat, or of scholarships won without any special ability. Nothing is being given *him* on a silver platter. He is, Uriah-like, proud of his umble origin and great effort. No charisma here, or Kennedy charm; no decadent kid gloves.

This spirituality of improvement is like the self-consciousness of health faddists. True men of action, Chesterton argued, know that concentration on health is unhealthy: "Even if the ideal of such men were simply the ideal of kicking a man downstairs, they thought of the end like men, not of the process like paralytics. They did not say, 'Efficiently elevating my right leg, using, you will notice, the muscles of the thigh and calf, which are in excellent order, I——' Their feeling was quite different. They were so filled with the beautiful vision of the man lying flat at the foot of the staircase that in that ecstasy the rest followed in a flash." But the self-made man has to concentrate on the thing he is making, on his product and end and whole excuse—on himself. When Nixon writes that "adversity breaks the weak but makes the strong," he is not simply repeating a platitude. Making the self strong is the task proposed to man by the Whittier of his youth, by the moral old America of Emerson.

The true significance of nineteenth-century liberalism was not so much that products are tested on the open market of free enterprise, or that truth will triumph in the free market of the academy, as that man himself must be spiritually *priced,* must establish his value ("amount to something"), in each day's trading. To experience one's worth in the real testing place, in the active trading of today's market, is the sole aim of America's moral monsters. That is why Emerson trumpets the need to "bring the past for judgment into the thousand-eyed present and live ever in a new day . . . a true man belongs to no other time or place, but is the center of things." That is the spirit of Nixon's cult of crisis—his eagerness, always, to be "in the arena," his praise of others for being cool under pressure, for being "tested in the fires."

But what if, having entered the market, one's stock falls? Who or what is there to lend support in that case? The merit, for an Emerson, is all his own if he stands independent, freed of help from the centuries. And if the merit is each man's without debt, then the failure must be one's own as well. Nixon puts it this way: "Chief Newman, my football coach in college and a man who was a fine coach but an even more talented molder of character [that's the real game, all right, mold the self, make a new little free-standing Emerson], used to say: 'You must never be satisfied with losing. You must get angry, terribly angry, about losing. But the mark of the good loser [improve oneself even in defeat] is that he takes his anger out on himself [succeed at becoming a martyr, even if you do not succeed in the vulgar sense] and not on his victorious opponents or his team-mates [stand alone even in defeat, don't admit human needs, don't lean]."

It is this morality of demonstrated daily desert—this meritocracy, with active trading in merits and demerits—that lies behind heartland America's hatred of welfare and relief and the systematic alleviation of poverty. The deserving rise; if the undeserving are also helped, what happens to the scoring in this game of spiritual effort and merit badges? The free-market of virtue and soul-making is destroyed by such "controls," such interference with incentive. Emerson knew this: "Your miscellaneous popular charities; the education at colleges of fools; the building of meetinghouses to the vain end to which many now stand; alms to sots, and the thousand-fold relief societies; —though I confess with shame I sometimes succumb and give the dollar, it is a wicked dollar, which by and by I shall have the manhood to withhold."

No wonder the victims of Whittier must collapse into Dr. Peale's smarmy embrace. What a grisly world our Emersons and Algers have bequeathed us from those days of literary and elocution societies, of calculating sermons about mastery of the soul. Think of the souls whose Dun & Bradstreet rating just keeps falling. That is when Peale must hurry in and tell men to accept themselves: "There are many people who simply can't have faith in God because they have no faith in themselves." How *can* they have, when the trading system for made and unmade selves has put a price tag on them? Therefore Peale and his associates "use psychiatry and psychology to help people love themselves." Put the brain to sleep; otherwise it can only whir endlessly on its pin. "Americans just buzz round like various sorts of propellers, pinned down by their freedom and equality"—their freedom to enter the market, their equality of opportunity, their chance to get in on the trading.

Even one day in Whittier, spent imagining the America of Nixon's childhood, is suffocating. That world has a locker-room smell, of spiritual athleticism. As I drove back toward Los Angeles that night, along Whittier Boulevard, wide lane enscrolled on either side with continuous neon scallops, the sulphur of Los Angeles seemed a better thing to breathe than the muggy air, heavy with moral perspiring, of Whittier.

9. Whittier: Second Day

> *"In the center of the field was a gigantic pile of sets, flats and props. While he watched, a ten-ton truck added another load to it. This was the final dumping ground. He thought of Janiver's 'Sargasso Sea.' Just as that imaginary body of water was a history of civilization in the form of a marine junkyard, the studio lot was one in the form of a dream dump."*
>
> —Nathanael West

ON MY WAY BACK to Whittier on Monday, I stopped off in Montebello, another town Los Angeles has absorbed in its unbuckled spread. Nixon's brother Don has an office there; and his secretary is Evelyn Dorn, Richard's secretary when he came from Duke University to practice law. I asked for her first impression of him: "He came in to see Mr. Bewley" (whose firm he was joining) "and I knew, after one glance, I had just seen a very serious young man. His grandfather had known Mr. Bewley's grandfather back in Indiana. The first thing he did was to go to work on the library of books, putting them in order. His law experience was mainly probating and oil lease contracts. He would sleep on the couch in the office some nights; after a while, he opened a branch in La Habra— it was just a desk in a real estate office. He was living above a garage in Fullerton.

"Then we all worked so hard on Citra-Frost, his idea for a frozen orange juice company. It was a great idea, as other attempts later proved, but we couldn't find the right container. We were freezing it in plastic bags, which didn't hold up. The failure of Citra-Frost was a great disappointment to him.

"When he first ran for Congress, I went to his debates with Jerry Voorhis and took everything down in shorthand, so he would have a record of it. I asked why he always repeated a question that had been asked him, before answering it. He said it gave him more time to be thinking of the answer. Mr. Nixon always spoke better before large groups than before small ones. I was sure he would go on to higher things. In fact, I told a local magazine in nineteen forty-six that I thought he would make a great President."

Mrs. Dorn took care of correspondence and the phone for Nixon's mother, Hannah, until she died. Hannah was, by unanimous memory, saintly—a neighborhood haven and confidante. Everyone who came to the Nixon grocery store, which was the "General Store" of cracker-barrel legend, sought her out. Mrs. Dorn says, "Even if they were just calling an order in by phone, they wanted to talk to Hannah, not Frank." Nixon's father was gloomy and argumentative, black Irishman moving in cloud, with frequent lightnings out of it. "I remember," Mrs. Dorn continued, "at the Ambassador Hotel, when Richard lost the nineteen sixty election, everyone else was in tears, but Hannah was calm. She just said a prayer when she heard the bad news. She was a very strong woman."

Shortly before lunch, Don Nixon came into his office, a giant man, genial, without the spatulate nose Hannah bequeathed to her youngest son, Edward, and middle son, Richard. I asked Don about life at the store. "Well, first it was a gas station, you know—the only one between Whittier and La Habra. Cars were still fairly new then, and the roads were just dirt. We used to have the customers lined up waiting for gas. After a while we put in some bread and milk in a big refrigerator. And that grew until we moved the church." He takes my pad and starts drawing: "Here was the gas station, and we built this addition onto it. Behind it, on Santa Gertrudes, was our house. We boys laid out a dirt tennis court here" (further south on Santa Gertrudes). "Later, when a bigger church was being built across the street, we bought the old one and moved it onto our property to hold the store. Dick used to go up into the bell tower, which was the store's office, to study by himself at night. That is where he had gone to Bible Class, taught by our Uncle West.

"I usually took care of the meat, and Dick handled the vegetables. He had to get up at three or four in the morning, and drive the truck into Los Angeles to market. Then, when he brought the load back, he dumped the vegetables in a big tub out back, and washed them off."

I mention his Aunt Ollie's claim that Dick had his mind on other things while he worked these long hours at chores, and was happy to get free, so he could lie in the grass daydreaming. "Yes, Dick was always a deep thinker. Some people thought he was aloof or stuck up because he walked right past them in the street without seeing them. He got totally wrapped up in his thoughts. Many's the time the delivery men who came before dawn would find him with his light still on, after studying all night. At family picnics, he would always go off by himself."

Mrs. Dorn broke in: "I used to come into the office in the morning and work around my desk for fifteen or twenty minutes before he looked up and said, 'Oh, good morning, Evelyn.' He doesn't let anything interrupt his concentration."

Don adds: "Even now, he likes to ride in the car with friends or members of his family, because we know he doesn't want to waste time talking. He can't stand small talk."

Was there much political discussion around the store? "Any time there was a campaign on, my father was involved. There was nothing he liked better than to argue. He'd take either side." Was he always a Republican? "No, his people were Democrats in Ohio. But when my father was twelve or thirteen, he had a horse he was proud of; when William McKinley came to town, campaigning, he noticed that horse and praised it. After that, my father was a solid Republican." Does his brother resemble his father? "Well, Dick is good at debate. And father gave us a lot of incentive to get out and make something of ourselves. Dick certainly did that. But he is more like my mother in sensitivity."

For instance? "Once we found out a woman in the neighborhood was stealing from us. We couldn't believe it at first. She was respected, a family woman—we had grown up with her two children. But we kept watching her and, sure enough, every day she came in and picked up something without paying us. We kept an account of it for a while, and then the whole family discussed what to do about it. Mother and Dick were the ones opposed to turning the matter over to the police." (Frank and Don, presumably, were in favor of that approach.) "They didn't want to embarrass her. So one day we asked a friend in the police to stand by, but not to do anything unless we asked. When the woman took something, mother invited her over to the house, but she wouldn't go at first. When mother asked if she would rather go with the policeman, she went in, and confessed, and they had a long talk. The woman said she would send us all the money in weekly payments." Gentle Hannah's son, taking her side in this family debate, is very far from the ruthless Nixon of myth. When a woman journalist spent several weeks with Hannah, and wrote a long complimentary article about her, young Julie Nixon said that everything written about Hannah's sympathy and humanity was also true of her father.

But Hannah not only felt sympathy; she was able to express it—the reason for her popularity in the store. Her son, by contrast, rarely talked to customers. Even with his mother he seems unable to express himself except in stilted terms—here he is as Vice-President, writing to her: "It can be a very dreary and boring thing to stay too close to the house and I hope you will always accept the invitations which I know will often come your way to attend functions that might be of interest to you." It sounds like a government pamphlet on "senior citizens." Before a crowd (the larger the better), addressing himself to "the issues," he is quick and glib. Otherwise he remains the enigmatic bright student of Whittier—silent, his mind churning at chores; lying in the grass, looking up, when chores were over; alone at school, though efficient and successful; quiet in the car, his family respecting a desire for quiet; off by himself at picnics; in the church tower studying; awake until the deliverymen came or (on market days) until he climbed into the truck for Los Angeles. When Khrushchev contrasted his background with Nixon's —hardworking miner vs. slick lawyer—Nixon said he had worked long hours as a boy in the family grocery store. Eisenhower tacitly agreed with Khrushchev: asked why he was inviting the Soviet Premier to America, Ike answered, "I would like to see him go to the little town where I was reared . . . and let them tell the story of how hard I worked . . . because he said in one of his conversations with Mr. Nixon, 'What do you know about work? You never worked.' Well, I can show him the evidence that I did."

Nixon's background haunts him, yet does not show—not, at least, in helpful ways. Eisenhower, a virtual exile to exotic places most of his active life—Panama, the Philippines, Africa, England, Paris—could still make his grin hazily fulgurant with Kansas, with the dust-prismed sun of his childhood afternoons. All recent Presidents have had the stamp of place on them—patrician Roosevelt of upper New York, raffish Harry Truman from Missouri (almost, one feels, from a Mark Twain story), Boston-Irish Kennedy thinly veneered at Harvard, and Johnson out of Texas like a walking tall tale, comic yet redolent of danger. Nixon alone, though deeply shaped by Whittier, has no attractive color of place to him. Kennedy retreated from governmental business to native salt air at Hyannis Port; Johnson, feeling dwarfed by the central seat of power in the world, went home to play cowboys and cattle baron in Texas. Nixon, from the outset, slipped off for surcease to Mexico, the Bahamas, Key Biscayne. Johnson has, in effect, cased the "log cabin" of his birth in golden accretions of history, as a mother bronzes her baby's shoes. Nixon, returning in 1968 to the house in Yorba Linda where he was born, scuffed the floor in embarrassment, ducked his head dutifully into this hole and that corner as if each were a trap, and left like one released.

Nixon won his release early, though Whittier is retentive of its own. After I left Don, and returned to Whittier College, the first faculty member I met was Dean Newsom, who went to high school and college with Nixon ("I got a low grade once in my best subject, chemistry"— Newsom went on to become a professor of chemistry— "and I felt the grade was unjust, but I would not have done anything about it. Dick was the one who got up and protested"). When I dropped into Moorehead Mortgage, there were three men present—Moorehead, his business associate, and the manager of Quaker Maid Dairy. All three were Whittier College alumni, close acquaintances of Nixon and his brothers. Though new people have poured into Whittier, the core of the city is remarkably stable, a nucleus containing the college and the church. "The Nixons were not community leaders," Moorehead says, "in the sense that they belonged to service organizations or were on the various committees"—a fact he obviously finds extraordinary in an "old Whittier family."

But Frank Nixon was a loner in this tight little world. After my stops in downtown Whittier, I drove out to East Whittier Friends Church, which replaced the frame moved over the street to Frank's land. East Whittier Friends is more modest than First Friends downtown. No plush or pink glass. It holds about three hundred people. Here Hannah Nixon was buried, and Billy Graham preached. The present pastor tells me the Nixons have not been outstanding donors to the church. A former pastor remembered how Frank used to fume when large donations were given by men delinquent in their grocery bills across the street. Frank carried them, of course, but with eloquent grumbling. And gave money to the poor, but with fierce privacy. Even his charity was recriminative. He was made for towering angers, then stranded amid lettuce and ground beef. The store's customers remember him as "tyrannical."

I crossed the street to the tyrant's grounds—now a gas station, all his buildings gone, only a dip in the ground where the tennis court used to be. Farther back, about a mile, is Lambert Road, a sport shop on the far side; on the near side, grassily decaying railroad tracks—the leg that ran through Leffingwell's ranch, taking on cargoes of fruit for inland America. Don Nixon had told me trains loaded here, often by night, were visible from the boys' bedroom over the garage. Or from Nixon's study tower. Mrs. Marshburn (Aunt Ollie) said, "There was a good friend of the family from Indiana who was a Santa Fe engineer. He lived in Needles. But he would come to visit Frank, and tell the boys about his work and travel. Richard was fascinated."

It is the classic summons, that steam hoot in the night, for American youth of this century's first decades—the yearning west toward horizons, or east (in Thomas Wolfe's case, north) toward cities. In Nixon's case, which? Not west. His father had been stung toward California by the cold; as a conductor on the open streetcars of Columbus, Ohio, he got frostbite in both feet. But technicolor clouds on vistas of prairie, the seductive gold rush, myths of frontier opportunity, meant nothing to his son. For him the west was a dirt road to the market in Los Angeles. Any further west was Ocean. He had to turn back.

East, then? If frontiers had a lure of the new, the East means, in the mind's topography, return to the old. To Europe, ultimately—as a pilgrim like Henry James, or explorer like Hemingway. The man who reaches New York from California has already crossed most of the Atlantic. But that was as unthinkable, for Nixon, as joining the Franklins. Even when he finally reached New York, it was as an outsider, perched there uncomfortably for business—the business, mainly, of politics. It too was a place to be escaped.

Toward what, then, did he yearn—desire going out footloose after trains that strode, stopped, and jangled in his mind? The freights that rolled out of California, piercing the coastal mountains, took with them loads of the exportable Southwest (lemons, oranges, pellets of sun) and moved inland, back toward the frostbite—to the heartland, where Nixon, campaigning in Indiana or Ohio, always says dutifully, "My roots are here." But the virtue of inland America resides, exclusively, in residing there; in the gyrating nuclear stability of tight town life—the small bits of nineteenth century left in Midwestern enclaves, cat's cradles of people. Disappearing places, and ones from which many, especially the young, now disappear. Nixon could not return there. He was left adrift, vaguely "heartland" in his sympathies, but unanchored; at home finally with the homeless, in Florida, with those who retire from America.

He had no goal he stretched toward, down the track, since there was nothing in Whittier he rejected. He was not a rebel, against parents or school or religion. He transcended Whittier by an act of super-Whittierism. The flame of ambition burned absolutely pure in him. He wanted more than Whittier, but not something definably different from Whittier. He had no bright alternative norms, real or delusionary, against which Whittier was tried and found wanting. His hero was the engineer throwing a switch that set things in motion—the process, not the destination; the rising, not having risen.

When he yearned away, when his mind churned, when

he drew apart, when the trains chugged, it was not the magic of a destination that moved him—the inland, the frostbite, the other coast, Europe, other worlds. It was the sheer energy of the effort—the train panting, heaving tons of weight forward; men working all night to fill its capacious maw, their dim light hitting the snorts of steam, puffs of the white whale; then, with grind and pulsation, all the "physical symptoms of tension," the engine picking up labors of a whole neighborhood to run nimbly down its preordained track; not choosing, just pulsing on, making time, racing itself, improving its past mark. Nixon, watching, listening, was not alone with saints or demons or a mad inspiring dream—to be priest, king, poet, merchant, god. He was alone with himself, the strain and grind, lift and rhythmic throw of his own gears, the need to test himself, pull hard down the track and earn (*churn*), deserve (*chug-chug*), achieve. "He did not spare himself."

He jumped onto the tracks, not for release. They imprisoned him in welcome iron lanes of effort, down which he could pound intently—where? Everywhere. Nowhere. The turn of wheel, buildup of steam is what counts, the keyed-up edgy feeling of man pushing himself to the limit. So instead of getting more *than* Whittier, he just got more *of* Whittier—of America's iron morality of rails. No goal but the time-out land, to turn around in, of Key Biscayne, and no respite but occasional collapse into Dr. Peale's bath of frothy religious soft soap, guaranteed to cleanse the pistons for even faster pumping. *Ur-Amerikaner* on his tracks, all clank of earnestness, hiss and puff of self-improvement. Nixon's portrait should have been painted by Lyonel Feininger.

As I drive on out Whittier, east toward La Habra where Nixon's branch office was, I remember Moorehead's comment: "The place is still Quaker enough to make it hard for bars to move in." Yet on Whittier Boulevard I have seen "topless" bars on my way in from Montebello and out to La Habra. I stop at one. The "go-go girls" are young, not professional enough yet for the bigger places in Los Angeles—with less to pose and distribute in timid bumps, and less art in its distribution, yet attractive in their awkwardness. Everything conspires here against glamour—no veiling or enhancing colored lights, no height of distance, just a grimy square of carpet in front of a blotchy full-length mirror, carpet on which they grind their toes in the alternate cigarette-stomp of the "go-go," piston-action going nowhere. No drummer beats shape into soft throw of hip, girlish undulations trying to fix a line of back, belly, breast. Pacing her way, step by step—bra loosed, twirled out, lowered, pulled off, flung away—the girl has her "act" deflated when the music, without warning, stops. A bathrobed "second girl" must run to the jukebox and feed it another dime.

It was November, election week, but hot in California, so I ordered a gin and tonic. "Oh no, we can't serve liquor. Only beer. Thirty cents a glass." Thirst and sobriety, no lights, drums, or glamour. A dour dissipation. This may be California, and a topless bar, but Whittier influence makes sure it is a frugal and unromantic place, with no hard liquor. Topless Quakerism.

I drove farther on, toward Fullerton (where Nixon started high school, and where he lived as a young lawyer). On through typical California fringe-of-town—concrete-block offices, off-green or dimmed-raspberry. Feininger slide of pistons, slow but tireless, in oil wells. A washed-out lime-colored building with large sign, FOUR-SQUARE CHURCH (theological Orthogonians—the common man's common god, Christologized, unity-movemented). Poor California has no principle of rejection; it just *receives*. The push of hope westward ends here, in indiscriminate litter of the fine and silly. Even Hannah Nixon, who lived above style as saints do, could not entirely keep this silt of California out of her house: her colored photo-portrait of Richard was, when one threw the switch, lit electrically from behind like a hamburger king's.

Still driving east, I begin to shake off the neon-and-lime offices, topless hutches, hamburg joints. The land appears, scruffy, baked with too much sun, tufted irregularly with palm trees. The mountains are there too, dusty gold in the slant of afternoon light, bastions of the coastal valley. This is the baked dirt that gave Frank Nixon one of his many rebuffs.

Frank was a restless talented man, one of five boys who lost their mother when they were young. He left grade school and went off to make his fortune—but never did. He acquired many skills, but their effect was canceled by a prickliness and touchy pride. He often tried to settle down on farms—e.g., on his father-in-law's after he married Hannah; on his own land farther north in California;

then on a crumbly slope in Yorba Linda, where he tried to grow oranges and avocados. There he built with his own hands the house, still standing, where Nixon was born. It is plain white clapboard, square, two-storied; not phonied up like Johnson's "log cabin"—still (when I went there) doing the job it was built for, housing a family, though destined to become a monument. The house is the one known thing, marked, that survives from Frank Nixon's struggle with life, the lone example of his skilled effort in a hundred fields—from painting Pullman cars to drilling for oil. When the farm was failing, he did odd bits of carpentry for others. Don remembers that "Mr. Herbert, a contractor, said that father was the best carpenter in the area. He would set a tough pace for others, and keep them at it. He worked us kids to death." One of his unendearing habits was to quote, constantly, the Bible verse about man having to earn his bread in the sweat of his brow.

Mrs. Dorn added to Don's recollections: "Frank was always intensely active. I think that is one reason he was so irritable when he could no longer do as many things as he used to." People in Whittier charitably attribute Frank's abrasiveness to various ailments—some to his partial deafness, some to arthritis, some to ulcers.

Novelist Jessamyn West was taught her Bible, in the East Whittier Church, by Frank Nixon, and she contends that his mind was even more incisive than his son's. But the rasp of his personality made it hard for others to listen to him; he was always running out of people to argue with. Richard never argued with him, never crossed him. He tried to shield his brothers from the black parental moods and quick wrath, but only by urging on them his own policy of disengagement: "Dad was very strict and expected to be obeyed under all circumstances. If he wanted something he wanted it at once. He had a hot temper, and I learned early that the only way to deal with him was to abide by the rules he laid down. Otherwise, I would probably have felt the touch of a ruler or the strap as my brothers did."

As it was, he did not feel the strap. And did not rebel. Did not, even, intervene on the side of others against his father. He must have understood this proud moody man. Not only had Frank failed over and over. His moderate success at feeding his family during the Depression was poisoned by the fact that his wife—a college graduate (Whittier, 1906) though he did not finish grade school, a local saint people flocked to (carefully steering around him)—was the presiding personality of the store, accounting for its popularity. It is hard to be married to a saint, even a real one. (It is impossible to be married to a spurious one.) Nixon's comments on his father continue: "Because of illness in his family he had to leave school after only six years of formal education. Never a day went by when he did not tell me and my four brothers how fortunate we were to be able to go to school. I was determined not to let him down."

It was not only education that Frank Nixon lacked. He was too abrupt, proud, independent for political life or business success—though his hauteur is winning, seen from a distance. He refused to take help from anyone, had an Irish strut in all his ways. Even when he wrote to an old hometown paper in Ohio asking for endorsement of Richard, he did it pugnaciously, as if the paper were on trial: "This boy is one of five that I raised and they are the finest, I think, in the United States. If you care to give him a lift I would say the *Ohio State Journal* is still doing some good."

Young Richard had his mother's code of turning the other cheek. But she was a saint, not easily equaled; and some of the resentful father must have been inside Hannah's son. Don told me "Dick was the peacemaker. When we had fights with neighbor boys, he would step in and talk us out of it. And he did not explode himself. He saved things up, though. Once I did something that finally got him angry, and he didn't just criticize me for that. He went back *two years,* telling me all the things I had done wrong. It really made me think, I'll tell you." That was Frank Nixon speaking out, at last, in Richard—a Frank long suppressed beneath the semblance of patient Hannah. But Frank was there, underneath, "saving things up."

Now that I had driven this far, I decided to go thirty miles farther, to the Mission Inn hotel, where Pat and Dick Nixon were married. It is a pseudo-ecclesiastical Wuthering Heights, mainly mission but also pagoda and castle. The St. Francis chapel, where big weddings are held, has an eighteenth-century Spanish altar and four big Tiffany windows. The mission style is made to accommodate gargoyles, including a "cat on a hot tile roof" (as the brochure puts it). The proprietors offer a chunk of the old California, only "more lovely than the old California ever knew"—the past cleaned up, as in Disneyland, and jumbled together. Newlyweds can have a stained-glass window, electrically lit through from behind, just outside their room—St. Francis as a hamburger king. The quietly monkish beamed cells are furnished with air conditioners, and the hotel claims all modern conveniences, "all the delights of Southern California," along with bits of art from all times and climes—a Spanish-mission dream dump.

The Market is death to style (which was the lesson of our Gilded Age). Emerson's proud insistence on starting new, on standing free, breaks that weave of emotional chains that should bind man to his own place and time. Ties of memory and tested affection cannot enmesh the self-reliant men, who get priced anew each day on their Market of effort and improvement. It is appropriate that Emerson, when he finally reached the point where he could not stand alone, should have been buried with these festivities, reported in the Boston *Herald* of May 1, 1882:

> A beautiful floral book stood at the left of the pulpit, being spread out on a stand . . . Its last page was composed of white carnations, white daisies and light-colored immortelles. On the leaf was displayed, in neat letters of purple immortelles, the word "Finis." This device was about two feet square, and its border was composed of different colored tea roses. The other portion of the book was composed of dark and light-colored flowers . . . The front of the large pulpit was covered with a mass of white pine boughs laid on loosely. In the center of this mass of boughs appeared a large harp composed of yellow jonquils . . . Above this harp was a handsome bouquet of dark pansies. On each side appeared large clusters of calla lilies.

Caramel ending for the man of iron. Victorian Norman-Pealisms. When the rugged individual totters, at last, into some recognition of human interdependence, there is nothing to do but smother him in cotton candy. There has been no *structure* of human need and textured life with others in his past. The man of the Market is an ascetic—

not physically starving himself to enter heaven, or save mankind, or bring the New Jerusalem to earth; but spiritually starving himself to "rise," to improve, to forge ahead. As Lawrence writes, "When the *Pequod* went down, she left many a rank and dirty steamboat still fussing in the seas. The *Pequod* sinks with all her souls, but their bodies rise again to man innumerable tramp steamers and ocean-crossing liners. Corpses. What we mean is that people may go on, keep on, and rush on, without souls. They have their ego and their will; that is enough to keep them going."

Nixon is a Market ascetic, and politics is his business. On it he lavishes an intensity of dedication that is literally consuming. Apart from that concentration, he can hardly be said to exist at all. His other interests—Key Biscayne, pro football, occasional golf—are either meeting places with other businessmen of his trade, or the conventional rest stops of the businessman unable to drive himself further.

It is not surprising, therefore, that he has no principle of choice outside his all-absorbing business. That is why he gravitates, for want of anything better, to the ceremonials of those who have no ceremony to call their own: marriage at Mission Inn, Billy Graham at Hannah's funeral. The serious young man, son of a Quaker saint, docilely lines up at the marriage mart, where all the gooiest extras—orange blossoms, "O Promise Me," illusion veils—cover the emptiness of the transaction. He might as well be in Las Vegas, where girls go through turnstile weddings, all tears—it is as close as they will come to church in several tries at marriage—sighing, "It was just what I always dreamed of."

The Whittier Nixon left had not yet been invaded by Los Angeles, by "go-go-girls" and all the worst aspects of Southern California. But, like Whittier itself, he was defenseless against these incursions, undefended by coherent taste. He fled *toward* the fluff—to Mission Inn, to a home in Beverly Hills, to Key Biscayne; to a wedding for his daughter presided over by Dr. Peale. That marriage featured Quaker "thee" and "thou" imported into a Dutch Reformed Church service. The organ played a song from Gary Cooper's screen version of *Friendly Persuasion*. Topless Quakerism. The fifteen-minute ceremony came complete with Broadway songs—two from *The King and I*

—chosen especially by Julie (it was just what she always dreamed of).

Nixon is, of all recent Presidents, the one with least taste, least stamp of personality. Whittier to Key Biscayne is a low trajectory. He told me, early in 1968, that his Quaker heritage made him reticent about religion. That reticence gave some promise of depth. But alas, when he does feel impelled to speak out, disjointed things float to the surface, scraps of a buried Mission Inn—as when he wrote in Billy Graham's magazine about the time his father took him to a California revival. The religious ceremonies he confected for his entry into the White House included a second viewing of the three-hour film *The Shoes of the Fisherman*. He seems always to have looked on religion through Cecil DeMille's eyes. Trying to give a sympathetic portrait of his two daughters, he wrote in 1961: "The difference in the personalities of our two girls, who are in many ways, of course, very much alike, was illustrated by their reactions to the motion picture, *King of Kings*. Julie exclaimed, 'It was wonderful! I cried so much.' Tricia said, 'I didn't cry when Christ died—He had suffered so much. I cried during the Sermon on the Mount because it was so beautiful.' "

The standard of style in the White House has not, it is true, been high—the style of a risen haberdasher, a retired general, a Boston Irishman on the make, a Senate wheeler-dealer. There was a histrionic note in the "Culture" of Kennedy's Washington that made its celebrators burble, even Samuel Eliot Morison sounding like William Manchester: Jack, with his James Bond taste, pretending to the level of Jackie—who, with her jet set taste, pretended to the level of Casals and Frost. The very name "Camelot" came close to the truth of the matter: if this was King Arthur's court, it was the Broadway version. (It is interesting that Frost, linked to Kennedy by a courtesy performance at his inauguration, was once drawn to the White House for real visits—during Eisenhower's regime, when his New England friend Sherman Adams was in power. Then Frost came and went without fanfare, though intellectuals with a crush on Kennedy felt that their man was making the White House safe again for poets.)

Yet other Presidents did have style, each his own, because they were marked with region and real likes; each had a usable background and personal tradition. The true,

very likable Kennedy was there beneath the surface pose
—Boston pol with his Irish Mafia and Navy pals. Eisenhower, it should not be forgotten, made a convincing
university president, and ran a White House of exquisite
courtesy. (Besides, he actually liked golf—he was freed
from Nixon's strain of pretending.) And Truman, though
vulgar as the Mississippi, had some of its earthy majesty.
Johnson's faults were those of a man who had fed on
power, and who seemed to grow in the time of power's
going off.

But Nixon is at the mercy of his past, without quite
possessing it. His addition to White House ceremonies has
been a prayer service, Sunday mornings, of the Graham-
Peale sort—one of the vague baptizing gestures such religion makes toward power. It gives the White House an
unpleasant touch of Mission Inn.

I turned my car back from Mission Inn toward Los
Angeles, along the San Bernardino Freeway, slowed at
nightfall to a crawl as restless Californians scuttle back
and forth, each going where the other was. Nixon is, he
tells us, a living fulfillment of the American dream—the
poor boy who made good, who longed to succeed and
did, the grocer's son who became President. Look how
much America has given him, how far he has gone, and
how fast.

Yet for some reason, after my visit to the places of his
birth and growth, I could think only of the things America
took from him—uncomplicated recognition of his code,
for instance: he has "made a self" in an age when self-
made men are not honored for the agony of their creation.
America took from Nixon all defense against empty symbol—he is at the mercy of our country's burgeoning Mission Inns. It took away the feel for region, the carriage
and easy swing of identity, of defined style: he is a self-
made man, and must observe the Market's cruel reversal
of biblical paradox, that he who would make a self must
lose it. A boy who, listening to trains in the night, became a racing engine of endeavor. A square shooter in
our Four-Square Church, remorselessly moral and empty.
A thing of pistons and pink "immortelles," iron rails and
cotton candy—our very own man, unmistakably.

He perfectly summarizes one America, an older and in
many ways noble America, made up of much sacrifice and
anger, of Hannah Nixon and Frank, of bodies driven by

sheer will and spiritual steam, survivors of the *Pequod*. He summarizes it all. But summaries come at the end. That America of men tinkered into shape like engines has run to the end of its track and, stranded there, is desperate for anodynes—Peale and Graham and, in the dark night, Wallace; caramel or heroin. The "forgotten America" is helpless, in its need, against excess and tastelessness. Quakerism-à-go-go. Bubbles and the Wallace sermons. Emerson billowed on his flowery bier down the parade route of the Tournament of Roses. Self-reliance pillowed in biblical epic.

Nixon is President of the forgotten men, of those affluent displaced persons who howled at Wallace rallies, heartbroken, moneyed, without style—called by their moral code to Horatio Alger battle against the odds, then baffled by a cushy world admitting no heroics. These "rugged individuals" are tied together in live wires, endlessly multiplying, of compulsory technological interdependence. The Natty Bumppo of free enterprise did not want community in the first place; that would have been bad enough. But this mere *entanglement,* this parody of community, is even worse. Restless in such chains, our American frontiersman, grown of necessity flabby, feels he has betrayed a trust. And not only is *he* unfaithful, corrupted by affluence, by privilege without responsibility (supreme torture to a Calvinist); he must also stand by and watch while the code's heretics rake in the good things—the slothful and undeserving, unwed welfare-mothers, the hippies screwing in parks, priests breaking the code by praising *un*made selves.

The forgotten American cannot face such abominations serene in a knowledge that his own self, at least, is made. The wires were in his way; he never got around to it, somehow. And so a shoddy thing, undesired, a second-rate self prefabricated in state schools, was foisted on him. A self controlled by environment, deprived of self-reliance, weakened at the core, no longer nourished with basic things (McGuffey's *Reader,* the woodshed, the little red schoolhouse). The Market—the *real* Market where a man can *amount* to something—is disappearing. And even if it were not, the "forgotten man" realizes he would not fetch a decent price on it anymore. He has failed, and failed his children.

But there was one hope left, a glimpse of the old code

and toughness, of salvation lubricated in all its pistons by desperate successful perspiration, a "local boy who made good" for every American locale (because he can rest in none), RICHARD NIXON steam-engining down the track, somehow un-derailed by history, cheered by those hoping he could reestablish the copybook maxims he lived by—though his type is fading now (become "forgotten"), he went on regardless, did not spare himself, this churning engine that *knew*-that-*it*-could (*rack*-it-*ty*-tack), knew it would (racky-rack) run the track's happy length, clack faster off on that endless dreamed roadbed that—ended. Grass on it.

The crumbling roadbed, that is Nixon's forgotten America. And what is he to do about it? Lay all the spiritual rails again? And if he does, will Americans run and pant along them as before? Or should he make converts to the Market ("piece of the action" for black capitalists)? Build up a head of Emersonian steam in the young? Find the old isolate ruggedness in kids growing up McLuhanized? It seems doubtful, impossible. But so did Nixon's mere survival—his *triumph,* later that week in November. He seems to keep running even without rails.

As my Hertz car, going back to Century City, tilted finally through a cut in the hills, I saw Los Angeles—the topless city's sunken glow. Wet air smeared its pattern. A homing jet hung low at a rakish angle, pushing great cotton swaths out from its landing lights. A neon sign bled fuzzy daubs of red into the darkness. My headlights, their beams liquid and defined, were like cross-eyed submarine rays as I went down in a sea of cotton candy, through a large mesh in the city's network of wires.

Part TWO

THE ECONOMIC MARKET

(Adam Smith)

1. Miami, 1968

"There seems to me at present to be great occasion for raising a United Party for Virtue."
—Benjamin Franklin

THERE WERE two conventions, just as there are two Miamis. First, Miami Beach, literal fiction, thing *made;* whither Cubans flock at dawn over Biscayne Bay, to work hotel restaurants and elevators (one's breakfast lox no longer served by black men). Second, mainland Miami, where the black men used to come from, and Cubans still do. Even Coral Gables calls fewer and fewer blacks to work in and around the George Merrick mansions. This is a post-Southern city, which does not "keep the nigra in his place." It simply *has* no place for him. The city's blacks, frightened by Chief Headley's preparations for the Republican Convention, knew better than to try the causeways over to the Beach. There were two conventions because, as the Kerner Commission put it, there are two Americas.

The Beach's convention was a dazzle of noise and light; and so, in chattering flashes, was Miami's. While the nominations went forward Thursday night, I ducked under a tree, out of the play of spotlights and glisten of pop bottles. Branches and limbs went crazy at the helicopter buzzing over (almost in) them, giant Mixmaster stirring the tree. Down the street, Claude Kirk was isolated, the lone white man, in a community center ringed with battle. The governor of Florida was, for a moment, a captive in his own state. The bottles, in this splintery light, spun with an awkward beauty. Back in Convention Hall, Rockefeller demonstrators threw styrene-foam snowballs, which sped from the hand a few feet, then slowed to dream-tempo, like the speeches arcing out across the crowd, bravely launched but landing with no impact. The bottles, alas, are not dreamed. They land and leave a rainy litter in the helicopter's thousand-watt gaze.

Balloons cascade to the floor and are punctured in deafening machine-gun fire. Meanwhile, under the tree, I listen to police debate what kind of fire that was in the next block. The chopper's lights, with each whirl of the blade, print and reprint leaf-patterns on the street. War is not beautiful; only its side products. It takes night and fear and a helicopter to make one notice leaves on Sixty-second Street. This Miami never reached the Beach, with its bristle of imported palm trees. There was a chasm between the two, wider than Biscayne Bay—between the bright leaf-etchings (bitten instantly into the street, dissolved, re-assembled, design superimposed on design) and the mock-ery machine-gun fire of the balloons. The chasm was in-tended, of course: one of the Beach's principal attractions as a convention site was its detachability from the main-land—pull up the bridges on the causeways, and the slen-der ridge raised out of swamp is, for all purposes, adrift in the Atlantic. Never more adrift, despite its intact cause-ways, than it was in August, with all its rollicking Re-publican passengers.

They arrived in the order of their chances—glamour boys first, all so bright the previous January, all suddenly dimmed: Percy everywhere, jumping in pools, churning over tennis courts (blonds do have more fun); Lindsay, tanned bemused Gregory Peck, trying to insert something in the platform to justify his being Republican; Romney, still electric with wild unexpellable poisons of his hope renounced. For four years, ever since Goldwater's defeat, they had been telling themselves—using their private West-ern Union, the *New York Times,* to transmit the message back and forth—that the future of the Republican Party, assuming it had any future, was wrapped in their shiny tresses. The Right had tried, and failed, and died. The party would mend its ways now or perish. True, contrary rumors had been stirring since the off-year election of 1966; but the glamour boys had heard about their own inevitability for so long that they could not relinquish hope. A new recruit to glamour—Dan Evans of Washing-ton—was to keynote the convention (youth, freshness, progress—all code words for the party of pre-Goldwater days). Ed Brooke would prove black is beautiful at the opening session. And the aging glamour boy from New York, patron of all the others, would be the first of the Big Three to arrive—he had, of course, been busy for months undoing himself, but he was known as a master of the late hard-sell blintzkrieg.

So they came, gamboling up the green lawn to their father's house, aghast at those who broke into it for the binge of '64, hoping they could put things back in order, once they arrived. But there in the doorway, with his scrambled-egg hair, collapsed bike-tube lips, and winding wine-cellar voice, was Dirksen, the housekeeper; and he knew—what the glamour boys could not work in past their lovely visages—who owned the silverware and cigars inside. He chatted pleasantly with the boys, but would not let them in. Just for good measure, the titular head of the family—faded now, as if Mr. Clean had grown suddenly eighty years old—sent a note saying the boys were not to be admitted. At the last convention, Eisenhower had made the mistake of inviting yesterday's glamour boy, William Scranton, in for a drink: but discreet coughings and clearings of throat made him realize that *that* title to the estate had lapsed, so Willie was sent back out to the croquet court.

Lindsay was allowed to tell the platform committee what the Kerner Commission and the peaceniks thought of everything; but Dirksen—a master of the art—made the platform say nothing, and made it say that it said it courageously. Peace with honor—which meant, in context, peace with war. A bid for the Negro vote, along with heavy winking over the phraseology of law and order—which, in context, meant votes, but not from Negroes. The platform announced, of course, that it was on the side of progress—thus laying any fear that the Republican Party would formally attack Motherhood. What the platform really said was that the glamour boys looked good out on the lawn but would not, come nightfall, be invited in for dinner.

After all his stalking horses had checked in, Nelson Rockefeller came—black comedy Falstaff, not only disastrous in himself, but the cause of disaster in others. He was personally responsible for the only major defections from the Establishment—those of potential glamour boys

Hatfield and Agnew. He was not only a late starter; he had developed a fascination with the starting gate, and kept circling through it as if it were a revolving door. But despite (and because of) his masterminding of defeat, month after month, throughout the last year, he was still the only standard the Establishment could rally to. He came to the sound of Bronx trumpets blown over his last well-publicized setback. His strategy called for a series of ads giving the graven truths of Rockefeller—truths chiseled for the ages, like his grandfather's creed on the plaque at Rockefeller Center's skating rink. They went in the style of the container ads—things like " 'Truth is better than falsehood'—Plato." So, on page after full page of the newspapers, we were assured that " 'Light is better than darkness'—Rockefeller." What it really meant to say was: winning is better than losing. The climax to this drum-roll was to be the counting of the polls, public and private—which would confirm one of those old truths that Rockefeller was calling "the new politics." The particular old truth in question was that "Nixon is a loser." But unaccountably the polls did not agree with this first article of Establishment faith. Even the Nixon people had expected something a little more challenging; they had prepared a trenchant pooh- and tendentious -pooh on all polls; but these printed scoffings were left in the warehouse, unneeded.

Still, he had to make the scheduled attempt to repossess the East's old property. Right of inheritance was stressed by his backers—e.g., all five of the last Republican national chairmen (Hugh Scott, Meade Alcorn, Len Hall, Bill Miller, Thruston Morton). Most of these sponsors set out from the Americana Hotel, Rockefeller's headquarters, to meet him at the airport. Even Scranton, a raven too pleasant to croak, was on hand to coo his Nevermore. He came out of the hotel wearing a seersucker sport coat and his baroque *putto* smile. A woman recognized him, and cried, "Governor!" He turned angelically, smiled (at the wrong lady), waved (at an empty space of driveway), and bumped the de-mothballed battleship of the convoy, Len Hall. Scranton then rebounded on a waiting car, which he tried to enter, but, as Hall insisted it was not theirs, he caromed genially round the proper car door, dove in, and drove off. It approximated Rockefeller's gyrations at, from, and into candidacy this year. In fact,

Rocky's comings and (mainly) goings, his ingenious new ways of losing support, almost made Scranton seem sure-footed.

Out at the airport, Governor Claude Kirk joined this party just as a Florida rainstorm made them run for cover. Kirk's face is plastered all over Miami, on billboards, on each elevator permit; one expects, any day, to find it on the state's liquor stamps. Today he wears a bright orange sport coat, seersucker pants, black socks, white shoes. He is noticeable. His sudden devotion to Rockefeller is a by-product, merely, of his fight with Florida State Chairman William Murfin. Rockefeller is a weapon to use against Nixon (i.e., Murfin); given the chance, Kirk would just as soon (maybe rather) use Reagan for the same purpose. The orange coat bounced, a lopsided balloon, up the stairs to the plane, and its wearer bussed Happy on the cheek; then, after others had got to her, he shouldered through the crowd to put his arm around her. He is a great hugger.

There is only a light scatter of onlookers as the plane lands (a staff memorandum said, "NAR should be greeted at the Miami airport by a major crowd"). But, despite the meager attendance, up go Rockefeller's arms, out goes the smile, as he emerges (his eyes disappear in the crinkling, his face one wide doomed rictus). Then into the buses for a motorcade to the Seventy-sixth Street Beach. Press bus first—I get to the last seat: there, behind us, is the candidate's bus; when we reach Miami he moves to the well beside the driver, stands there waving both hands in the picture-window bus windshield, shark grin in a goldfish bowl. There are few people on the street, and they do not recognize this dim man behind blue sun-shade glass; but he waves with his chrome jolliness, flings his standard patter back toward those in his bus: "Over here, lady. Yes, it's Rocky. Come and get it. Fooled you, didn't I, lady? And you—are—going—to—*yes*—have an accident." All this squeezed out through a deathclamp parody of laughter.

At the public beach, a good band was warming up its transient audience, helped by singers Gordon MacRae and Nancy Ames. Most of the crowd, young and bikini'd, has wandered up from the surf. A boy is doing trampoline leaps flashing a "Rocky" sign from ludicrous positions at the height of each bounce. Up on the platform, Mrs.

Rockefeller stands, uneasy, by a bump-and-grinding go-go girl (off-hip synchronized with alternating hand flung—*bump*—up in the V-for-Victory sign). Happy is tall, tall as her husband despite deferential low heels, broad-shouldered, athletic-looking. Her hair lifts with the motion of her head when women shout, "Happy!"

Bill Miller, Goldwater's running mate, an expert on defeat, tells the crowd Rockefeller can win. Miller has stripped to his shirt sleeves. So has Rocky, to engage in some beefy hugging and hand-waving with Claude Kirk. Now the candidate is on, the crowd in sunstruck bliss of song: "Oh, when the *Rock* comes marching *in.*" They seem to be more in love with the song than the candidate, to judge by the difficulty the latter has in displacing the former. "It's a thrill for us from New York to be in Mayah-mee" (which is, at least, better than Eisenhower's old Mee-ah-mee). The real New York is wooing New York South. The tenement spirit breathes here in the most expensive hotels, which shoulder each other aside for their disputed bit of ocean as tenement dwellers fight for every inch of frontage on street or backage on yard. Dyspeptic New York cabbies die and go to hell in Miami. The place has a stingy competitive extravagance worse than squalor, worse than the honest popcorn-vulgarity of Atlantic City. It is a place where people who lived near the Waldorf indulge in shabby mimicry of it.

Rockefeller thanked the people on the bandstand for welcoming him: "And Governor Scranton is here—he must have got lost in the crowd. You'll recognize him if you see him." Sure enough, swept around the platform, sponging through the sand, he was being shuttled back and forth by matrons recognizing him; shaking hands, Flintstone lips in their Sucaryl smile, courtly Lord Dubiety. In his speech, Rockefeller offered himself as a *winner*—with his team of men like Len Hall (last seen in the snows of New Hampshire trying to unwash Romney's brain), Bill Miller (Barry's personal choice for albatross), and William Scranton (who has been found, and is pushed through the ranks of entertainers onto the platform). All he needs now is endorsement by Harold Stassen. "Three months ago I made a commitment—to offer our party a choice. We need a new leadership to replace the old politics" (there they were, all in a row, sagely nodding, Meade Alcorn, Len Hall, Miller, Scranton—the new leaders). "The youth of the nation owes a debt to Senator McCarthy." Rocky, with all the passion of his own improbability, admires the peaceniks who made McCarthy's bid possible. "That's why I'm for eighteen-year-olds voting." Everything is pitched to this. His attitude on Vietnam? It has swallowed up "twenty-five thousand *young* Americans."

Rocky on youth is dealing with a subject near his heart. His reedy voice blats nasally, and he gives the impression, as he peace-marches vicariously through his speech, of a creaky uncle who remembers his gay days. Rocky, alone of the Republicans, is trying to turn youth into a constituency, as Bobby Kennedy did in the Democratic Party; and, like Bobby, he becomes at times a middle-aged caricature of youth. But Bobby, at least, was aping contemporary youth—Bob Dylan on the stump. In Rockefeller's case, antiseptic campus movies of the twenties vainly signaled to Haight-Ashbury of the sixties. It was a dreary beginning, ill attended. (His staff memorandum, prepared a month earlier, said he would need "the largest indoor facility in the city" for his reception.)

Ronald Reagan, a glamour boy himself, but of a different stripe, had not checked in. He will arrive late Saturday night. And Nixon will not come till the first day's proceedings are under way. Up through Saturday, then, the party's "moderates" or "progressives" had things all to themselves—and had nothing to show for it. What went wrong? A party that was theirs for the asking four years ago now hardly recognized them. Each had committed his own kind of suicide; yet they seemed to *share* some error, too. How else explain this carnage on the party's Left?

Percy's light—always a bit ethereal—was the first to dim. He rose fast, on charm; worked from the top (through Ike); concentrated on "issues" rather than on deals or power or the pork barrel. His seminars and committee manifestos (the "party goals" Eisenhower had him shape and ornament) made him seem an "idea man" to the press. He was a McLuhan phenomenon, who made the backroom work of politics obsolete. By the time he won his first election, to the Senate in 1966, articles in *Time* and *Harper's* rated him a certainty for Vice-President, should a Right-Wing candidate win the top spot (Nixon, say, or Reagan); and 1967's best book on the Republicans—by Dave Broder and Steve Hess—placed him second only to Romney among the party's Left candidates. *Newsweek*, in May of '67, predicted a last-round fight between him and Reagan.

It is no wonder, then, he landed in Washington on his feet and running, a Republican version of freshman Senator Bobby Kennedy—indeed, the first Republican to enter the Senate campaigning actively for President since Bob Taft came to Washington in 1940. Percy scheduled speeches all over the country; hired an extra-large staff; devoted his own Senate salary to his office payroll; took the mandatory candidate's tour of Vietnam, where he managed, in this war of the television set, to be pinned down by the enemy fire—five rounds from a mortar—in a bombed-out village. His friends were gathering $100,000 to finance this extracurricular campaigning, until echoes of "the Nixon fund" forced him to dissolve it.

Washington had gone to his head, while Illinois slipped out from under his feet. He had not established a base there—he built from the top down, in air. Yet it was part of sophistication in the mid-sixties to discount old talk about political "base." Robert Kennedy and Richard Nixon defied such rules by carpet-bagging into New York on their way to national campaigns. TV and the press create a national constituency, not tied to precincts and local debts—or so we are told. And Percy believed it.

But there were flaws in the argument, and in analogies used to make the argument. Nixon, it is true, had to leave California—because he had destroyed his base there with a mistaken effort at the governor's office. And he did find a national constituency. But it was built on old debts accumulated, blocs appeased, pals assiduously favored; it would not have come to him but for his diligent practice of the "old politics" year after year. Robert Kennedy had a national constituency based on his brother's magical name and the tragedy of his death. Yet the Kennedys are tough, are Fitzgeralds, under their charm—heirs of cutthroat Boston political wars; so Bobby quickly moved in and flexed muscle on the New York scene. It is impossible to imagine "back-home" operators undercutting him the way old-line Illinois workers sabotaged Percy. Senator Dirksen's administrative assistant, Harold Rainville ("Rainey"), whittled away at Chuck behind his back.

There were good reasons for bad blood between Percy and Dirksen: in 1962, Chuck had explored the possibility of knocking "old Ev" off in a Senate primary race, but withdrew when he could not stir up necessary interest. Now, in Washington, the obvious course for Percy was to use ladles and ladles of butter, basting his colleague. But this course was ruled out by his presidential hopes. He had to keep well "left of Ev" in order to maintain the glow on his progressive image. That image alone would make him (a) the proper heir to Romney should Romney's hopes founder or (b) the obvious "balance" man for a Nixon or Reagan candidacy. So, back in Illinois, Rainey kept everyone aware that most of those Percy speeches away from Washington were *not* being made in Illinois.

Percy, small but handsome, equipped with an outsize church-organ voice, is a walking package of that praised new commodity, "charisma." In 1966, the contrast between Jack Kennedy and his increasingly detested successor was often based on Lyndon's lack of charm. The job of Republicans seemed clear—pit some Mr. Clean against Mr. Credibility Gap. Nixon—old tarnished stuff—would not offer the proper contrast. He would give the country *two* candidates unable to move used cars off the lot.

Besides possessing charisma, Percy had the skills (and the cash) acquired in his successful business career. And, under it all, a passion for order. Even his declarations of religious faith emphasize tidiness: "[Christian Science] is a wonderfully organized church, and I admire organization. The publications come out regularly and are of high quality." But he was either the boss's fair-haired boy (at Bell & Howell, then with Ike) or the boss himself. After writing the 1960 party platform out of his "Goals" book, he could not handle the conflicts that arose from Rockefeller's demands upon Nixon. Chuck had to surrender his chairmanship of the committee to Mel Laird, and go off to prepare Bell & Howell "home movies" for the presentation of the platform.

This harsh experience did not make the loner Chuck become a team man. As a candidate in later races, he mounted personal campaigns that paralleled the party's effort instead of meshing with it. In 1964, he relied on an *ad hoc* volunteer structure, and tried to pretend Goldwater was not there. In 1966, he used structures he had set up himself (the New Illinois Committee) or separate groups brought over to him for the race (the New Breed). This did not endear him to party regulars. In fact, one reason the state party gave him his long-shot chance at the Senate in 1966 was to get rid of him. If he won, he would go to Washington and be counted out of state activities. If he lost (as seemed more likely, against Senate giant Paul Douglas), he was washed up for good—a two-time loser, a dabbler for years who had never won office.

Sweetly brash, Percy has a knack for offending others in the party. Despite his strong tie with the Rockefellers (he was a board member of the Chase Manhattan Bank), he refused to make Illinois appearances with Nelson during his struggle for nomination in 1964. When Mary Scranton tried to pressure him into support of the moderate coalition against Goldwater, Percy turned away. And though he did not formally dissociate himself from Goldwater during the '64 race, he did so afterward, joining the "Dump Dean Burch" group. Percy criticized Romney during the period when polls made Michigan's governor the front-runner among Republican candidates (Romney replied by calling Chuck an "opportunist"). Percy, fresh as fresh could be, allowed as how Nixon looked a little wilted. Sizing up the Republican field against presumptive opponent Lyndon Johnson, he said that the President "lacks that intangible ability to inspire people, to give them confidence . . . Now, this inspirational ability is an important quality in a President." And the one thing clean-cut Percy prides himself on, above all others, is his "inspirational ability."

But the perils of McLuhanism overtook Percy by the end of 1967. "Image" can become "power," but only if one stays interesting to the image-fashioners—and the press is fascinated, not by what it can create (image), but by what it lacks (plain political muscle). Percy, it became too obvious, had no clout; could not even count on his own delegation. He was pretty, and resonant, and politically nubile—and, by the time he reached Miami, all alone.

Throughout 1967, John Vliet Lindsay was "Percy East" —the only conceivable alternative to Percy as Vice-President on a Nixon or Reagan ticket; and liberal journals tried to keep their hopes for him alive right down to the finish. Wednesday of convention week the *New York Times* ran this headline—all in the same size type: NIXON IS NOMINATED ON FIRST BALLOT; SUPPORT FOR LINDSAY IN 2D PLACE GROWING.

If Percy is an example of the neglect of "base" in favor of "image," Lindsay typifies the use of "reform" as an issue in "the new politics." New York City has been governed for years by Democratic machine politics, a system regularly challenged by reform Democrats. The Republicans, who cannot compete with the machine in terms of a patronage-substructure, seemed to have no choice in 1965 but to outreform the reformers—so Lindsay, the Republican candidate, got the support of New York's Liberal Party, which is to the left of the Democrats, and of a custom-made "Independent Citizens Party." Then he ran a "fusion" ticket that included a Liberal and a Democrat. He was not running against the Democratic Party, but against all parties, against the very idea of party. In the transcript of a private session with the Liberals, Lindsay earned their endorsement with answers like this:

QUESTION: Will you, if elected Mayor of New York, use the office of Mayor for the purpose of building up the Republican Party?

LINDSAY: No, under no circumstances.

This superreformism gave Lindsay's campaign a purity almost oppressive. He would stand above patronage and deals, above the game of ethnical seesaw that New York politics tends to be. (But Lindsay, a Protestant, ran on the traditionally "balanced" ticket with an Irish Catholic and a Jew.) Early in his regime, Lindsay rebuked Puerto Rican and Negro groups that came to his office asking for more city appointments: didn't they realize he had run *against* judging people by their race? All his appointments would be based on merit alone. "If he can stand up under that kind of pressure," one of his assistants told a reporter from *The New Yorker,* "I think he can deal with the other obstacles to change in this city."

He quickly made enemies of other groups (especially unions) that had, by sacred usage, been given special treatment. Lindsay expressed a perpetual astonishment, during his early period as mayor, over the "layers and layers of deals" that ran the city in the past. His critics, naturally, said he simply did not know how to *make* the deals which keep New York stumbling forward. His answer was a proud restatement of his belief in Virtue: "The office of Mayor needs a lot more dignity than it's had in the past . . . The Mayor has to walk a little taller than he ever has before. Look at the Board of Estimate hearings—the way people come in and are literally rude to the Mayor. It's unbelievable. That kind of behavior wouldn't be tolerated anywhere else in the legislative or executive branches of government . . . Little by little, we'll bring dignity back to those hearings."

Thus, despite courageous tours of Harlem through two difficult summers, Lindsay found the city slipping out of his control. The man who had been hailed as "the hope of the nation" in 1966 ruled a despairing city in 1968. Men could hear, all through that summer, the ticking bomb of racial conflict in New York. Everyone knew that "local control" in the schools of Ocean Hill–Brownsville, launched in the spring term, would become a battlefield when the schools opened, one month after convention time. Reform purism may be the new politics; but Mayor Wagner, attacked by Lindsay as a type of the old style, was elected to the office three times. By 1968, Lindsay had unexpectedly come to respect that achievement.

Percy's baselessness, Lindsay's reform—each of them contained a measure of "amateurism." Glamour boys all seem to look down on professionals in their own field; they like to call on the "fresh blood" of volunteers, bright "nonpolitical" types, children crusaders on the Eugene McCarthy model. But the supreme amateur in politics has been George Romney. A year before the convention, he was his party's leading contender. Polls showed him beating the incumbent President. He had assembled a large campaign staff and taken a number of political tours, foreign and domestic. Successful Republican governor of a Democratic state, he even looked like a winner. His eyes —set off by the matching blue sweater he wore in informal press conferences—stabbed conviction at TV cameras. When he visited Alaska at the beginning of 1967, the large press entourage thought it had joined the next President of the United States. Yet he was still what he had always been, a nonpolitical "citizen candidate."

In 1956, the president of American Motors was made chairman of a citizens' commission on education in Detroit. The favorable exposure he gained there made him advocate widespread citizens' activity outside the party structures. In 1959, he formed Citizens for Michigan, which helped push a new state constitution past a recalcitrant Democratic executive and Republican legislature. Romney was so happy with the results that he proposed the formation of Citizens for America, a group to hold conventions and write platforms that would be models for the regular parties, forcing them to move beyond their narrow concerns. This made even Percy's National Goals seminar look partisan and soiled with politics. In 1960, Romney sent an open letter to the presidential candidates, Nixon and Kennedy, saying both parties had failed to address themselves to the nation's real needs (this despite the fact that Nixon had praised Romney and urged him to run for office).

When, in 1962, Romney ran for governor, he was still a citizen concerned: he worked from an independent office without Republican signs, relied on Romney Volunteers, and made few references to his party. At governors' conferences, and even at the party convention in 1964, he held himself aloof, a critic and prophet, the citizen come to judgment, not just a Republican seeking office. Of Goldwater's nomination, he said, oracularly, "I accept it but do not endorse it." And he handed down another of his epistolary verdicts on the inadequacy of the candidate.

Through all these "crusades," Romney built up a belief in his "nonpolitical" background: here was a man (men thought) who worked his way up in the business world and then—sincere novice amid deal-fettered pros—entered politics with the innocence of an outsider. The truth is that Romney *began* his career in politics, after three unsuccessful attempts (at three different schools) to get a college education. He went to Washington, in pursuit of his childhood sweetheart, the intense Lenore, and got a job as aide to Senator David Walsh of Massachusetts. He did work on tariff bills that equipped him for a new career— a lobbyist for Alcoa, he spent nine years as a Washington gladhander around Burning Tree Country Club and the National Press Club. Then he became an automobile lobbyist (on the carmarkers' Trade Advisory Commission), dealing with the National Recovery Administration. From this post he rose to become manager of the AMA (Automobile Manufacturers Association)—an office that made him, in wartime, managing director of the Automotive Council for War Production. He had now spent nineteen years fronting for big business among politicians.

His work as spokesman for Detroit led to several offers from automotive companies. The best one came from the

President of the AMA (his nominal boss), George Mason. Mason was also President of Nash-Kelvinator, about to merge with Hudson to form American Motors. The idea of a compact car (the Rambler) had been conceived by Mason for Nash, and was put into production for American Motors by Meade Moore. Romney took charge of the company, with the task of selling the little car as a "specialty item." He made it, instead, a symbol of virtue— small David-purity scooting free of bloated Goliaths.

There has always been a bond of sympathy, in America, between the preacher and the salesman. Billy Graham started out as a Fuller Brush Man. Romney, often given credit for the idea of the Rambler—or for reforms in the new Michigan constitution, or for the long-stalled tax-reform plan that made a success of his first term as governor—is just the man who *sold* other people's ideas, and sold them as installments on salvation. But the time arrived when persuasiveness was no substitute for ideas; then disillusionment set in. Robert McNamara, who urged Romney to get into politics when they were both auto men around Detroit, later came to know him better: Romney's trouble, he concluded, is that the man "has no brains."

In 1968 that insight spread, and Romney's very talents crippled him. His greatest gift had been mesmeric power to convince others because he so convinced himself. The blue eyes burn toward you under that low white cap of hair; the block of athletic face is rigid with fresh seizures of sincerity. He has a fanatic's belief in everything he says or does, and a prophet's fierce anger if anyone questions him. A desire to keep his burning conviction unsullied by earthly ties explains his later aloofness from politics and politicians. It also explains the impact of his maladroitness. His trouble is not simply that he makes mistakes, but that they are *meant* mistakes (because everything he says is, with his laser eyes and acetylene faith, intensely meant). And once he has made a blunder, his "sincerity" makes it impossible for him to admit it was a mistake. He went down, thrashing ridiculously, in 1968; yet he maintained to the end that it was a public service for him to call his Vietnam briefing a case of successful brainwashing: "The term 'brainwashing' focused attention on the fact we haven't been told the truth. Nobody paid attention when I talked about 'a snow job.' What I said has led to a general recognition of the credibility gap." Asked about his abortive attempt to supplant Agnew as the convention's choice for Vice-President, he said, "It is always good for you to get a big burp off your chest. I gave the party its burp." The amateur cannot change, cannot compromise or admit error, without becoming one of the dealer-type pols. With an eerie sensation of near-collision, the nation came to realize that 1967's "next President of the United States" had, behind his superb preaching talents of the salesman, "no brains." The polls predicted a crushing defeat in the New Hampshire primary; so he withdrew before the year's first votes were cast.

And that left, appropriately, Rocky.

2. Political Philanthropy

> *"Philanthropist: [One] who has trained himself to grin while his conscience is picking his pocket."*
> —Ambrose Bierce

NO ONE believed in Rockefeller's early support for Romney. The moderates' "unity candidate" made too good a surrogate for his sponsor: Romney could maneuver just those straits that were closed to Rocky—the party primaries, preconvention dreamings. It was only as Election Day neared, as the thirst to *win* got more and more acute, that Rockefeller's chances might increase. He, it would then be argued, could attract the votes of liberal Democrats and independents. And so, as Romney slid down in the polls, Rockefeller began to climb. By late 1967, Gallup put him ahead of the man he was supporting. He was also well ahead of President Johnson, 52 percent to 35 percent (Gallup). When he went into New Hampshire to campaign for Romney, he plugged harder for "moderate Republicanism" than for the governor of Michigan.

Nonetheless, Rockefeller came to Miami an underdog, dependent on Reagan to shake Nixon's hold on the South and stall off a first-ballot sweep. With a largess typical of the Rockefeller career in politics (on which he had spent, to that point, perhaps twenty-five million dollars), John Deardourff and other aides had ground out big stacks of a checklist for Miami assignments. This twenty-nine-page document was infelicitous in its phrasing (e.g., Rockefeller girls must be kept "walking the streets") and strangely candid about methods for finding, wooing, and pocketing any loose delegates. Copies of the list fell into reporters' hands, and were reproduced. It spelled out all the tasks each faction labored at, up and down the Beach, in secrecy. Under the heading of "Opposition Intelligence," for instance, the checklist began its items this way:

Job to be done:
1. Where feasible, monitoring radio communications, *et al.*
2. Assignment of personnel to watch the delegate hotels for reporting of movement of key political figures.
3. Assignment of personnel to cover the operations of key political figures as they move from one location to another.

What most interested newsmen, however, was the fact that a "hot line" to the Reagan communications center was "in progress." Here was the first solid proof that Rockefeller hoped for a Reagan breakthrough; that he might even have to work in conjunction with Reagan. (The press did not yet know that another "hot line" from Reagan headquarters went to the suite of Rockefeller's remaining champion among the Republican governors, Ray Shafer of Pennsylvania.)

The checklist provided some questions for the press to bring down Collins Avenue, the crooked spine of Miami Beach (then undergoing surgery), to Rockefeller's first press conference in the Americana. It was Monday morning; the conference was held in a room too small for the crowd, heated by TV lights that out-gunned the hotel's air conditioning. The screening process was more rigorous here than at other headquarters. Newsmen came bedangled, jangly with chains, plastic cards, pinned-on badges of all colors—they were Christmas trees walking—to get into the various headquarters and events. A friend of mine was there to "monitor" the session for Reagan, so I loaned her a string or two of these ornaments; but the private guards asked to see each person's press card and wallet-identification as well as his passes. It made for slow entry. Like all the Rockefellers, Nelson grew up surrounded by bodyguards. When he became a candidate, and then governor, new layers of watchfulness were superimposed on old ones.

Rocky's forces were all there—Emmet Hughes, part-time Republican Sorensen, who resigned from *Newsweek* to turn out the chiastic phrases Rocky had trouble reading; Henry Kissinger, owlish neo-Clausewitz hired to construct the candidate's five-point Vietnam "solution"; George Hinman, who succeeded the late Frank Jamieson as overall stategist and Nelson-packager; Les Slote, his wry scholarly press man, borscht circuit philhellene; David Rockefeller, boyish-looking symbol of financial empire (ten billion dollars is an empire in any man's language); the candidate's wife, shy, still overreacting to each overfamiliar shout of her first name; and, finally, the candidate himself. In the last few weeks he had jetted to meetings in over forty states, pouring out charm and energy and cash, spending himself with abandon, betraying his own claim that ambition had died in him along the way. Nixon was calling this six-million-dollar flurry "too much, too late."

The two have nurtured, over the years, an exquisite hate for each other. After heavy Republican losses in the off-year election of 1958, during which Nixon had been the party spokesman, Rockefeller answered a newsman's question in Caracas by saying, "I have nothing to do with Nixon." He kept the Vice-President away from his own race in New York. In 1960, Nixon was summoned to New York to get Rockefeller's additions to the platform, the condition of his support for the party. This was that "Treaty of Fifth Avenue" which Goldwater called a "Munich." In 1964, when Romney tried to hold a secret meeting of potential candidates to head off Goldwater, Rockefeller agreed to come only if Nixon were excluded. And now, in 1968, Rockefeller was taunting Nixon for his refusal to debate, calling him a loser who would drag the party down with him in still another defeat. "Nixon's the one, all right," he said in Springfield—"the one who lost it for us in nineteen sixty."

At his Miami press conference, Rocky carries on the

old warfare. Does he think Nixon is trying to get a "band-wagon" effect started? "For two *years*, yet!" He all but *oy wehs* it. What about the confidence being exuded by Nixon's press secretary (Herb Klein) and his floor manager (Rogers Morton)? "Well, Nixon's got to take the position, having rested for two months, that he's got it made." Does he think Nixon hurt himself by this running away? "He had some pretty tough alternatives" (namely, *me*). "But it is hard to understand, in this time of crisis, how a man who aspires to leadership should not come to discuss the key issues frankly." "Frankly" is a big word with Rockefeller. Often followed by a warm little ictus on the first name of the reporter questioning him: "Frankly, *Gabe* . . ."

What about the "hot line" to Reagan's camp? "I heard about that yesterday, and investigated. The phone line runs between two *trailers*." As if he never heard of such vulgar things being used at a convention. "I'm not really interested in being in a *trailer*." Is there any collaboration between his people and Reagan's? "He would like to get the nomination, and so would I." He is relaxed, affable, almost crooning his answers. When a young Israeli reporter, who has been badgering Nixon people at press conferences, spins out a long "question" about Rockefeller's superior electability in the big cities, Rocky breaks in, at last, with: *"You're* my *friend.* I think you've got something. If you want to speak further on that subject, go right ahead."

If you were running for governor—"I've got the of-fice." I mean if you were running for President—"I am." I mean if you were President—(pause, for another quick retort; but Rockefeller will not get downright giddy) —*if* you were, would you get rid of General Hershey (head of Selective Service)? "I don't think any one man is to be blamed for the draft's inequities; the system is at fault. If we change the system, General Hershey" (his grin broadens as the fake bureaucratic phrase rolls out) "would probably culminate his career in retire-ment."

"A *pleasure*," he smiles juicily. It is the Rockefeller style, forged at Dartmouth, Big Man on Campus, rumpled but authoritative. And Dartmouth of the twenties—an Owen Johnson upper Lawrenceville—was the perfect place for acquiring it. The intellectual demands were hardly rigorous—Nelson went there because his grades were not good enough to get him into Princeton. He had been educated at a "progressive school" set up by his father's money, where he never learned to read properly, or to spell. He still limps, with halts and labor, through the text of written speeches. And his grades at Dartmouth—perilously close to failure in freshman year—only picked up when he made an arrangement with his teachers: they would not mark off for spelling. When his roommate heard that Nelson had made Phi Beta Kappa in senior year, he said he would throw away his own key; if Rockefeller could make it, the honor meant nothing.

The Big Man on Campus has an entourage; the young are hero-worshipers, and though their heroes are "pals," down-to-earth and palpable, they also have God and the future on their side, if only in planning a prom. Idealism goes hand in hand with a winning self-importance at that age—a combination rarely found after school days. Later, the traffic in one's charm becomes—as the stock dwindles, grows less negotiable—a hard-faced calculus of quick gains, marginal deals, and losses cut. But Rockefeller escaped this process. He remains boyish in his sixties, still the big man even though this year's team is bound to be a losing one.

It is less his money that preserved him than the two main forces acting on his youth—religion and art. The religion came from his father, brought up in the original John D.'s Baptist fundamentalism. Almost a caricature of the businessman as Calvinist, John Rockefeller meant it when he said, "God gave me my money" (as a reward for character-forming hard work). All the stories of stinginess toward the Rockefeller offspring were true; the family religiosity united success, self-denial, thrift, charity, shelter to runaway slaves, large grants to Negro churches and schools in the South (especially Baptist ones)—all in one package of cleanly godliness.

This dour upbringing was assuaged in Nelson's case by the heretical aestheticism of his mother, Abby Aldrich, mischievous daughter of the governor's namesake, Senator Nelson Aldrich of Rhode Island. Young Nelson seems to have been Abby's favorite son—the one who inherited her Norman-helmet nose, her jutting chin and buried eyes. She, too, was careless about spelling; but intense about art, a taste Nelson acquired from her before he went to Darmouth. There was an inevitable conflict between Abby's "worldly" interest in beauty and the joyless code of work imposed by the Rockefeller side of the family. This made Nelson, a conscientious Sunday school teacher during his college days, insist on the element of *duty* in all things he enjoyed. In his senior year, he wrote an article on "The Use of Leisure" for the alumni magazine, defending "useless" things like art: "I have discovered the key to the door that opens out into a field of interest totally unrelated to the material side of life. And it is now up to me to unlock this door and explore the ground lying beyond." He was unwittingly repeating self-improvement stories from the nineteenth century—sentiments like T. S. Arthur's, in *The Way To Prosper and Other Tales:* "He could go up into higher regions of his mind, and see there in existence principles whose pure delight flowed not from the mere gratification of selfish and sensual pleasures."

Nelson's article makes it perfectly clear that this enjoyment of leisure can come, like leisure itself, only after long hours of hard work: "Every man that graduates from college must work at least eight hours a day, five and a half days a week from next summer on" (how easily "every man" becomes Rockefeller, facing that June's commencement)—"that is, if he ever wants to amount to anything. And, of course, the really ambitious ones will work for much longer hours than that." Shortly after he left college, Nelson became a trustee of the Metropolitan Museum. His father thought he was too young to undertake such a responsibility, but Nelson wrote him this evangelical justification: "The aesthetic side of a person's life is almost as important as his spiritual development or physical well-being." Then, true descendant of the godly cash-gatherer, he added that "the contacts which such a position offers are not to be disregarded."

Art could be indulged, once it was considered a form of service to society. In an extraordinarily revealing set of letters sent from college to his mother, "Nell" (as his classmates called him) defends, analyzes, accuses himself with a monk's watchfulness over his own spiritual state:

It is really very interesting for me to watch and see the funny way my feelings have been acting of late.

All of a sudden, like the lifting of a heavy fog, I realize for the first time how unutterably selfish and thoughtless I have been getting to be. It stands out in bold relief and glares [sic] me in the face.

From this very minute, I will lead a new life . . . that will not be centered around myself . . . I shall try in a small measure to make up for the discomfort I have caused you both in the past.

This spiritual self-scrutiny was encouraged in a family that held joint prayer sessions and "Family Councils" on moral issues. When Nelson sent his father congratulations for a speech that "Mr. Junior" had given on the need for religion, his father wrote back hoping the two would have an opportunity to go over the speech, point by point: "Such a discussion would be very helpful to me." Self-improvement is the primary goal of all activity, even of instruction given to others.

In the life of a boy so brought up, the term "do-gooder" takes on new force. Rockefeller came out of college determined to "do good" with all the zeal and fire that made his grandfather "do business." There was a natural attrition of the family's Baptist fundamentalism —Nelson took his first wife from the world of Philadelphia society, and was wed at the Episcopal church in Bala-Cynwyd. But the consequence of this was to displace the ardor, not extinguish it—to channel it toward a secular religion of work and philanthropy.

This "do-gooder" side of him explains the Right-Wing fear of Rockefeller, though his politics have been what Americans call "conservative." The young Nelson, who had been Roosevelt's wartime propagandist and PR man in South America, became Assistant Secretary of State in 1944, in charge of Latin American affairs. In this role, he was attacked for being soft on fascism and much too hard-line in his attitude toward communism. He wanted to set up a mutual defense pact for the hemisphere. Alger Hiss, working at Dumbarton Oaks on an agenda for the UN charter meeting in San Francisco, opposed this pact; he argued that regional treaties should be supplanted by the all-inclusive charter of the UN. But Rockefeller used the weapon that won him other battles (and no friends) in the State Department—after a private meeting with FDR, he waved an initialed memorandum that approved his plans.

Another point of grievance at State was Rockefeller's attempt to involve fascist-leaning Argentina in his pact —on certain conditions (which Peron did not meet). Rockefeller crammed the conference down State's resisting maw, and won his hemispheric pledge of mutual defense (the Act of Chapultepec). When the UN sessions got under way, Hiss and others were determined to keep Rockefeller out of San Francisco. But as soon as Russia's power over large blocs of votes became apparent, Rockefeller was rushed into town; he was the man who could swing Latin-America's votes to the U.S. position. But he put a price tag on his efforts: Argentina must be admitted to the UN.

Rockefeller's major antagonist in San Francisco was John Foster Dulles. The Russians had submitted a proposal that would make all regional pacts, except those directed against World War II foes, subject to the veto. Rockefeller complained of this to the Senate representatives (Vandenberg and Connelly), who announced they would not recommend approval of the charter if the Russian proposal passed. (Everyone in San Francisco was deferential to these Senate grandees, remembering the fate of Wilson's League when it reached the Hill.)

Rockefeller's liberal admirers like to remember the fact that he clashed with Dulles, but prefer to forget the issue. Rockefeller took a much harder line toward Russia than Dulles, who accused young Nelson of trying to sabotage the conference. (Years later he apologized, admitting that, without the provisions Rockefeller worked into Article 51, it would have been difficult or impossible to establish the NATO alliance.)

After this "Right-Wing" start—during which his only champions in the national press were David Lawrence and Arthur Krock—Rockefeller maintained a "hard" position on communism: he opposed Kennedy's test-ban treaty, supported Johnson's Vietnam war, and almost wrecked his career with a plan, unveiled at the 1959 governors' meeting, to put a bomb shelter in every American home. He fought to get Marxists driven out of the progressive school he attended; and he removed a Diego Rivera mural that was unkind to capitalists from Rockefeller Center. On crime, he has taken a generally Rightist stance, backing the New York police on many controversial points of legislation—wiretapping, "stop and frisk" laws, the right to enter without knocking, "shoot to kill" codes for the police, along with a 1966 proposal for the forcible internment of dope addicts. Although his welfare spending is high—like Reagan's in California—he has, with ritual care, balanced all his state budgets since 1960. He is, needless to say, a strong believer in the merits of big business; his Dartmouth thesis was a moist-eyed celebration of Standard Oil.

Given this background, why does he have so few defenders on the Right? Or—perhaps a greater mystery—why have liberals been so forgiving toward him? How does he appeal to New Yorkers in the black ghetto, who are most affected by his strict crime laws? The answer lies in his philanthropy, which is not merely a hobby, nor merely a duty, but an ambition and positive hunger, the justification for his being (for his being a Rockefeller): "You could plop me down in a small village of no more than two hundred people and in no time I'd be organizing them to attack whatever local problems existed. I am very happy when I am working with people." There was nothing arid or ideological about his tough bargaining at San Francisco. He was defending Latin America, which he had adopted as his very own "project." (The Rockefellers tend to specialize—Winthrop in Williamsburg, John D. III in Lincoln Center, Laurance in the nation's parks.) Nelson also considers Negroes one of his projects—and conveys to them the sincerity of his concern. He does not measure his actions solely by political norms, but by the feelings they arouse in him. His public pronouncements often echo those Dartmouth letters to his mother. Reporters were surprised when he kept saying, throughout 1968, that his internal mood had turned away from ambition for higher office: "There are things that happen inside. I'm not a psychiatrist or a psychologist. I can't analyze it for you exactly. I just don't have the ambition or the need or inner drive—or whatever the word is—to get in again." (*It is really very interesting for me to watch and see the funny way my feelings have been acting of late.*)

Another side of this monkish self-distrust is that Rockefeller moralizes most glibly when his hand, without his knowing it, is creeping toward the cookie jar. He kept amazing himself, in the early months of '68, with his own lack of ambition, all the while making little jumps and starts, only to pull himself back in line. His various withdrawals—including the strange April one, for which he called a special conference to announce that nothing had happened—reveal a man who keeps trying to burn his bridges, but who has (with great foresight) built so *many* bridges that he cannot get the job done. Such self-denying gestures should not have puzzled anyone so late in the game as 1968: he had done the same thing in 1959. First, he issued a public statement withdrawing from the presidential race. Then he spent a year in spasms of despondent repair work on that bridge. On the tense eve of his election in 1958, he made another of his spiritual health reports: "I've kept myself in balance, so whichever way it goes, I'm relaxed." He talked endlessly of people's goodness during the time of his divorce and remarriage, when he had vast experience of people's spite and venom. Soon after the 1968 campaign—in which he said that "satisfaction" had erased ambition—he took another look at his soul and found all satisfaction lies in achievement, so he would have to run for governor again. One does not easily escape the mark of John D. Rockefeller, of that Baptist "money-grubber plus theologian," as Mencken called him. Nelson, for all his worldliness, is still a Baptist preacher, wrestling with his conscience, justifying lapses, castigating his ambitions.

"Our prayers are with General Eisenhower." Those were his opening words at the second Miami press conference, late Tuesday afternoon, when Ike's most recent heart attack had been announced. At this press conference, Rockefeller insisted on running his own show, almost a variety act; calling people up to the platform, hugging them, shaking hands: "Governor Shafer made Phi Beta Kappa and *five* athletic letters. I'm only sorry he didn't go to Dartmouth."

There is a defeated good humor about him—the glamour boy out at the end of his tether, going no farther; still the Baptist preacher, but a wry defeated one, verging on Adam Powell's rich baritone impudence. The hopeful chatter of his bagel-and-lox arrival speech has given way to Powell's easy grinned answers, his con-

fiding orotundity. Rocky's voice, which gets reedy when
he is tense (e.g., when deciphering a written text), had
mellowed, was ripened to the edge of rot—not from
dissipation, but from working the "people are good" line
too hard too long, against the odds.

But for all his appearance of ease, there was panic
around and behind him, and growing bitterness in him.
His staff had come to Miami playing pranks—Richard
Tuck hired pregnant women to carry NIXON'S THE ONE
signs. But now the team was beginning to play dirty.
At the Tuesday press conference, Rocky's advocate in
the press section asked about an ad in Monday's Miami
Herald. It began:

> Memorandum to: Delegates to the Republican
> National Convention
> From: Black America
> Subject: The Presidential Nomination

The text, addressed to delegates, said: "We take this
opportunity to advise you that candidates with records
such as Richard Nixon and Ronald Reagan are not acceptable to black America." William Buckley, in town
for a TV contest with Gore Vidal, was asked his opinion
of the ad; he claimed its "Black America" was, in fact,
Nelson Rockefeller—that the idea and the cash and the
list of names had come from his office. Now the reporter asked Rockefeller to say it ain't so. Rockefeller
said it ain't so: "No, it is not true. I think we ought
to recognize that Mr. Buckley had an unfortunate fall on
the boat." (He had arrived late in Miami, after a yachting
accident that broke his collarbone.)

Everybody laughed. "Myself"—Buckley later wrote in
his syndicated column—"included. But as my laughter
died down I beamed at the [TV] set, 'You'll be sorry,
Governor.'" A bit of detective work on Buckley's part
turned up the fact that a young woman from Rockefeller's staff had placed the ad, paying in cash; and that
the governor's staff not only supplied the money and
names, but did so without permission from the *owners*
of those names. Over thirty of the "signers"—e.g., Charles
Evers, Lionel Hampton, Marian Anderson, Louis Armstrong—sent letters to the *Herald*, protesting this fraudu-

lent use of their names. Rockefeller's people were getting desperate.

There were other signs of panic. After Reagan became an open candidate, exposing his delegation to raids (it had been pledged to him only as a favorite son), a telegram was sent to each Californian over the signature of Marco Hellman, a prominent banker in the delegation. The telegram suggested that it was time for them all to switch their support to Rockefeller. But Mr. Hellman did not send the wire.

Finally the desperation reached Rockefeller himself. On his forlorn last day of effort, he began to babble about Nixon's "massive psychological blitz" and "desperate attempt to stampede this convention." He said the Nixon troops were using "all kinds of threats" to dragoon delegates at the last minute. (Nixon, sure of his count, had in fact instructed his team not to break into favorite-son or unit-vote states.) Rockefeller would not give newsmen the content of these threats, but he did tell a maudlin story of one woman delegate left in tears after Nixon men "mistreated her so."

Wednesday night was hard to take, but not unbearable. Thursday morning was the real blow—Nixon's choice of Spiro Agnew, Rockefeller's premier advocate once, as Vice-President. When Rockefeller made his required appearance at Convention Hall, he made no reference to Agnew; asked what he thought of the choice, he just shook his head and passed on.

At his last press conference, newsmen wondered if he knew why he had failed. "Have you ever been to a Republican Convention?" he answered, after a tense pause. Rockefeller had been to several of them, without learning much. There is a hard streak, though, in this preacher, the intense other side of his ardor. The philanthropist spurned is a merciless critic and judge. What *can* he think of those who would reject pure virtue and benevolence? Rockefeller left the convention in a mood of unselfish gloom, despondent over the nation's loss of him. And many shared that mood.

3. Republican Camelot

"I have never known much good done by those who affected to trade for the public good."
                                        —*Adam Smith*

ROCKEFELLER WAS the most formidable of the liberal Republicans; he epitomized them all. Like Romney, he entered state politics on a board for redrafting the state constitution. He found his permanent brain trust on that board—George Hinman and William Ronan. His "citizen panels" have given aid to Latin America, answers to all modern problems, and promotion to his career. Like Lindsay, he came into New York politics as one outside the "system of deals." Like Percy, he has concentrated on "image," on TV and McLuhan devices for reaching the public. (The best example was the slashing TV campaign mounted, during his ten-million-dollar 1966 race, by Jack Tinker & Partners.) And the other glamour boys are tied to him. Rockefeller has lent money and personnel to Lindsay and Romney. Not only did Jay Rockefeller marry Sharon Percy; the two met while doing volunteer work in Lindsay's campaign office. They were married in Chicago University's Rockefeller Chapel; and Romney crossed Lake Michigan to abstain from champagne with his fellow teetotaler, the father of the bride. Lindsay's roommate for two years at Yale was Frederick Lincoln Rockefeller, a relative of Nelson. The glamour boys, largely independent of party ties, were natural rivals, each fearful of the other's ambition; yet they formed, as well, a natural club, knit together by their similarities. All but one (Lindsay) are millionaires —a man needs money to address the people over and around party structure (i.e., without party funds). Most men cannot afford to be amateurs.

With the millionaire glamour boys, politics was a form of philanthropy—which made Rocky their symbol and leader. The reason for neglecting a conventional political "base," for going direct to the people, for using volunteers and citizens' groups, for working outside the grubby rules of party warfare, is a belief that fresh values can make their way without such props. The Republican "progressives" were, therefore, great optimists, who thought they could sell their position on its merits. They all believed in Ben Franklin's United Party for Virtue.

It is not surprising that such an idea should, from time to time, rear its noble addled head. What was surprising in the mid-sixties was that so shrewd a group of men believed in it. The whole thing can be explained only in terms of that acute case of Camelotitis the American intelligentsia succumbed to in 1960. Resenting the reign of Eisenhower, who somehow managed to get along without them, professors poured into Washington (actually or vicariously), rolled up their sleeves, and got ready to do good all over the place. Academicians, long the critics of "other-directedness" in salesmen and middle managers, felt new pride in themselves, and bliss to be alive, when they were listened to by proxy in Washington. One is reminded of the monk in Marcus Cheke's *Cardinal de Bernis:*

> It is recorded that there lived in Rome at this time a poor simpleminded French friar named Father Jacquier de Vitry who acquired a most tender attachment for the great Cardinal. Bernis used to invite him to dinner, but as the friar was so humble, the rules of protocol required him to sit at the bottom of the table, far removed from his host. So Bernis said to him: "When I do this (putting his finger to his nose) you can know I am thinking of you." And ever and anon during the banquet he would be seen to glance down the table along the profiles in serried rows of gobbling cardinals and scintillating duchesses, to make his little signal to the poor old man just visible through the forest of candles. And then the face of the poor toothless friar would be transfigured with joy.

The first symptom of this candle-lit dizziness in Washington was Richard Neustadt's book, *Presidential Power.*

Written at the end of Eisenhower's reign, it calls for a
return to FDR's White House activism. The style of argument is striking—narrated models of successful acts or
decisions, followed by "morals" put in slogan-form and
italicized. Exactly the mode of self-help handbooks. Indeed, Neustadt regularly urges the President of the sixties
to use "self-help"—unaware that he sounds like Samuel
Smiles. "This is the help," he explains without irony,
"that starts a man along the road to power." James
Reston called the book "the nearest thing we have in
contemporary America to *The Prince*," but it sounds
more like Dale Carnegie than Machiavelli. The chapter
Neustadt first showed to Kennedy was called "The Power
to Persuade." It reaches such climactic italics as these:
to persuade congressmen, the President must *"induce
them to believe that what he wants of them is what their
own appraisal of their own responsibilities requires them
to do in their own interest, not his."* That sounds like
Carnegie explaining how to make one's "pitch"; and it
could not come as a great revelation to any pol. True
to form for a self-help manual, the book puffs the obvious up to the portentous: "The President who sees his
power stakes sees something very much like the ingredi-
ents that make for viability in policy."

The central part of the book—also singled out by
Neustadt for Kennedy to read—is Chapter Seven, "Men
in Office," which contrasts Ike's style with FDR's. Roosevelt wanted power, reveled in it, studied ways of enhancing it. Eisenhower was deficient in this fine mania:
"His love was not for power but for duty." Neustadt
argues that only a lover of power will woo it properly,
win it, put it to work. He "baptizes" political ambition,
just as self-help manuals for businessmen baptize greed.
(Napoleon Hill, *Think and Grow Rich:* "You might as
well know, right here, that you can never have riches
in great quantities unless you can work yourself into a
white heat of *desire* for money.") Neustadt's final chapter,
"The Sixties Come Next," calls for new "vigor" and
"energy" in government, based on the President's self-
confidence and "expertise" in the ways of power. Power
purifies, and absolute power tends to purify absolutely.

Kennedy had Neustadt and Clark Clifford draw up
"transition priorities" just after his election. In this role,
Neustadt helped form the Camelot mystique. By casting

the problem of succession to Eisenhower in terms of a new Rooseveltian era, Neustadt set many of the administration's ideals. Indeed, one of the reasons Kennedy kept him on as an adviser was to have a second custodian (after Arthur Schlesinger) of the FDR–JFK myth. Everywhere Kennedy looked, he could see the historians; he was already in the books, on the great stage. The challenge of Roosevelt's One Hundred Days bred a precipitate mood (dangerously inflated on the eve of the Bay of Pigs invasion, then dangerously deflated). There were, besides, specific points in the Neustadt book that Kennedy took to heart. The book argues, for instance, that FDR kept himself informed by a constant alertness to Washington "gossip" and "espionage"; that he deftly played rumor against rumor, spy against spy. The trouble with Ike's staff-system, by contrast, was that he only knew what got pushed up to him at the top "through channels." This analysis encouraged Kennedy's neglect of channels like the National Security Council. But Kennedy was more genial and less devious than Roosevelt. Instead of setting spy on spy, he gathered a group of kindred souls round him, and the result was government by bull session.

But it would be easy to exaggerate the impact of Neustadt on Kennedy himself. It is safer to notice the book's effect on those around the President. At a time when the new regime was establishing its self-image, many people rode the clouds puffed out of Neustadt's vapor-mill in the Executive Office Building. (He likes to talk about the manipulation of "atmospherics.") And so it was launched—all the brave slogans, the rhetoric, the "vigor": "Ask not what your country can do for you, but what you can do for your country." In a less heady ambiance, people might have noticed that the famous formula is totalitarian, subjecting the citizen to his government, not the government to man. But such nit-picking tries to pick *meaning* from Sorensen's line; and it was not meant to *mean*. It was mere vapor from the Neustadt mills, its imprecision a mark of its function—which was self-hypnosis. Writing his *magnum opus* on the Kennedy regime, Sorensen could still strike this note of religiosity: "One of John Kennedy's *most important contributions to the human spirit* was his concept of the office of the Presidency." (Italics added. Not a contribution to government efficiency, or to the American nation, or to the solving of certain problems. To *the human spirit*. Along with Buddha and Christ.) In 1965, it was still a boast to say: "As President, he both expanded and exerted the full power of that office, the informal as well as the formal." Yet shortly after this, liberals would be lining up behind Senator Fulbright to claim back some of these powers from the President, reinvesting them in Congress. About the same time, Kennedy liberals like Richard Goodwin and Daniel Moynihan joined *Public Interest* liberals like Irving Kristol and Daniel Bell in lamenting the idea that centralization of power will lead to solution of problems. And the New Left concluded that songs about "what you can do for your country" end up meaning "what your country can do to you."

But such misgivings did not cloud the first effervescent days of Jack and Jackie in the White House. As Kennedy began his struggle with Congress, over expansion of the House Rules Committee, the work of the future seemed clearly laid out: the President must "break" Congress. A script for this morality play was supplied by James MacGregor Burns, another Kennedy enthusiast and biographer, when he wrote *The Deadlock of Democracy*. Burns subscribed to Neustadt's theory that power purifies. Only the man at the top has the vision, the universality of responsibility, to weigh claim against claim and make the best disposition for everyone concerned. The President scans a high plateau, where congressmen pop their heads up like moles and blunder in the sunlight. The nation has been locked in an epochal battle between Jefferson, who trusted people, and Madison, who distrusted them; and only in our day has Jefferson's trust been vindicated at last. Only now can we break democracy's deadlock, caused by checks and balances in Congress.

The deadlock, Burns argued, is caused by a paralyzing "four-party system." There are two presidential parties (Democrat and Republican), which address themselves to the nation as a whole, fashioning an inclusive philosophy of government and putting it up for debate every four years. But there are also two congressional parties (Democrat and Republican) composed of disparate local types running in staggered elections on local issues. Not only does Congress hamper the President; but each congressional party, controlling as it does the day-to-day "grass roots" machinery, keeps its own presidential party from living up to that high vision created when platform-drafting time comes round. The presidential parties, according to Burns, include all the intellectuals within the Republican or Democratic camps, and most of the governors; they draw upon the academy, the foundations, and the high-priced Eastern legal or business firms for their staff and executive advice. The congressional parties, whether Democrat or Republican, are made up of small-town businessmen and lawyers, who acquire their knowledge from lobbyists and protect their seats by taking care of interests and factions. The presidential parties are urban-oriented, addressing themselves to the present and the future, coping with modern problems, exercising all the responsibility of executive power. The congressional parties are oriented toward the past, toward rural values and small-town concepts of business. In Burns's nonpartisan scheme of things, we are given two heroes to cheer and two villains to hiss; and one of each is Republican, one Democrat.

Luckily, the villains' days in power are numbered. Kennedy and his successors will appeal to the people, and their enlightened rule will make it clear that distrust of the people was mistaken. We need no longer fear that majorities will neglect the rights of minorities: "Majority rule in a big diverse nation must be moderate" (tell that to the Jews in Hitler's big diverse nation). "No majority party can cater to the demands of any extremist group because to do so would antagonize the great 'middle groups' that hold the political balance of power and hence could rob the governing party of its majority at the next election. A democratic people embodies its own safeguards in the form of social checks and balances." Thus we need no legal or mechanical checks of the sort Madison provided. "Mass majorities provide their internal source of social health." We have been healthy all the time, without knowing it. The enlightened new presidency of mass power, initiated by Kennedy, will make us stop treating ourselves as invalids.

Furthermore, Congress draws its strength from economic issues, which, Burns tells us, are no longer the important ones. The presidential party has, in the past, set goals and dreamed dreams, while the congressional party, adding up the costs, blasted men's hopes. But with the age of affluence (which John Kenneth Galbraith had announced two years before Kennedy took office), bread-and-butter issues will no longer trouble us. Now that we can pay for our dreams, the important questions deal with the shape of those dreams. The presidential parties are obviously better equipped to formulate the relevant questions and find answers to them.

Burns does not call for a union of the two presidential parties into one. Rather, each presidential party should reduce its own congressional faction to a proper (i.e., insignificant) role. Then the enlightened parties can compete with each other, unimpeded by their respective old fogies, to see which is the *more* presidential. Burns suggests measures for weakening the congressional parties— redistricting, to cut out rural "rotten boroughs"; abolishing the seniority system (along with practices like the filibuster); abolishing off-year elections (to make senators and congressmen run only when the President is being elected, as subordinate parts of *his* party). And he adds steps to make the presidential parties stronger: instead of the discontinuous forum supplied by the national conventions, these parties should have regular committees and clubs and study groups, fashioning the parties' dreams for tomorrow. The model for these groups is to be Senator Percy's study of goals for Republicans. The document his committee produced, *Decisions for a Better America*, exhilarated Professor Burns. He is especially happy that only two congressmen took part in drawing it up (which is, for him, practically a guarantee of excellence).

By now, we are deep in glamourboyism: "The presidential party should stage an annual conference, much smaller than the national convention, where national policy could be debated and the party platform publicized and renovated." This is Romney's Citizens for America, holding its mini-convention, pushing ahead of the political system to see what is around the corner for America. Professor Burns has a touching faith in committees. He sees the future in terms of citizens' activities, organized around specific causes and crusades. The new affluent class will not work through party machinery, with its stress on "the old partisan, or economic, principles." The greatest of the crusades will be devoted to civil rights for the Negro, a crusade "which is the 'most hopeful for Republicans.' " Philanthropy has now become shrewd politics; do-goodism is the road to success. The glamour boys are born.

The book, so widely acclaimed when it came out, was ill-fated in its predictions; and a new preface added in 1967 made things worse. Burns believed Lyndon Johnson's legislative record had initiated the reign of President over Congress by its "brief period of unprecedented national power and accomplishment—a period, I will contend here, that may have foreshadowed the shape of American politics during the next decade." But already new stress was being placed on the *arrogance* of power. Burns even found cause for hope in Johnson's vigorous prosecution of the Vietnamese war (which was, at the outset, a popular move): that treatment bore out "the near certainty that continuing or deepening world tension will demand national executives capable of making peace or war or cold war without undue interference from the legislature."

Rockefeller, naturally, did not take his program from Burns's book—though he must have enjoyed being referred to as the obvious leader of one presidential party, the inevitable Republican candidate, and very likely the next President. "The more the congressional Republicans want to indulge in presidential politics, in short, the more they must coalesce with the party closest to them that was begotten and organized for such politics, the presidential Republicans . . . The main question is not whether the party of Goldwater and Mundt and Halleck needs the party of Eisenhower and Rockefeller and Cooper, but the reverse."

Rockefeller and Burns both breathed the spiked ozone of the sixties. No wonder, then, Rockefeller thought the 1968 convention would be his by right. Burns was simply reciting an article of faith when he repeated, throughout his book, that "The national party convention is the bulwark of the presidential parties." And: "All in all, the presidential party controls the convention as fully as the congressional party controls Congress." And: "The convention is the arena of the party liberals and moderates; the cards are stacked against the congressional parties." Yet the presidential party—which means, for Rockefeller, the Republicans' Eastern Establishment—had never considered Nixon its candidate; and here he was, about to put Miami in his pocket. The very linchpin of Burns's argument was pulled. He claimed that the presidential parties could, in the sixties, extend their power to *new* areas, working from their absolutely certain base, the convention. And that base had been taken from under them.

What had gone wrong? Burns's dream, it is clear, ended in Dallas. Camelot was broken up, the fabric of cloud unraveled. But it should not have faded so rapidly, if there was any substance to it. On the contrary, the loss of one magic leader should have increased the hunger for other young men of his sort. If Burns were right, Kennedy's death should have ushered in the very Eschaton of Glamour. But, in point of fact, the academy's infatuation with Kennedy did not spread to the people at large until after his death.

Nor is it sufficient to say the dream was killed by Lyndon Johnson's personal deficiencies. He was the heir, as his first success shows; he exercised enough power to please even Neustadt; he based his reign more exclusively on "expertise" than had any other President in history. He called on the foundations, on studies, on advanced techniques. His advisers in the war were Chomsky's "new mandarins" brought to Washington by the New Frontier. This was our first professors' war, the only kind Neustadt and Burns would have supported in 1960.

It was not the course of events that hurt the theories of Glamour. One thing hurt them: they were wrong. The idea of a United Party for Virtue has been around for a long time—since Ben Franklin's day. Yet the people have never been kindly disposed to the idea. Only the euphoria of the early sixties could convince a coterie of politicians, jornalists, and academicians that the thing would work. The result was the glamour boys—hothouse blossoms of that happy unreal time. When they finally returned to reality, it bore little resemblance to their dream. They had misjudged so many things—the shape of party power, the nature of presidential responsibility, the limits of "expertise," the uses of Congress. But most important of all, they had misjudged the victim they were trying to save from the congressional dragon. They misjudged, or never knew, the American people. They would not, it seems certain, recognize the American people if they ran smack into them—which, on the streets of Miami, they did.

4. They, the People

> *"The whole housed populace move as in mild and consenting suspicion of its captured and governed state, its having to consent to inordinate fusion as the price of what it seemed pleased to regard as inordinate luxury . . . . the all-gregarious and generalized life."*
>
> —*Henry James, on Florida's "hotel spirit"*

HAROLD STASSEN, still boyish under a toupee bought for this campaign, was a realist about Miami, but an idealist about the nation: "I realize the small power I have within the G.O.P., but I have confidence I can win in November." That was Rockefeller's position, too. Nobody loved them but the people, who were not, apparently, to be found in Miami. The people, in fact, are a mystical ever-receding entity. They are the supporters each candidate would have if you gave him a chance to reach them. For years those on the Right said there was a "silent vote" out there—the People's—that had never been cast because "the system" had given them no true choice, only an echo. With Goldwater, they had to prove their claim; but they argue that Kennedy's assassination, a national grief and numbness, Goldwater's own quirks, the midstream shift from a winning team (Clif White's) to a losing one (Bill Baroody's), a silly botched campaign—well, a thousand things—all obscured the choice this time out, too. Conservatives actually voted for Johnson because of Goldwater's "radical" belief that one can unwrite history, pluck, as it were, the apple of government from Eve's mouth, and start all over "from the roots." There is always an explanation for the People's failure to materialize at the polls.

In 1968, it was the Left—McCarthy and McGovern in their party, Rockefeller at Miami—who said the parties give us nothing but echoes, never a choice. At the conventions, the people were moated off from their favorites by those watery nullities, the party delegates. The press, when it moved from one convention to the other, felt that at least there were *people* in Chicago. "You never saw a beard in Miami." "You never even saw a sideburn." "Imagine Nixon in sideburns." "No blacks on the convention floor—only Negroes like Ed Brooke." "How out of it can you get? He has a white wife." "Yes, and he got her the easy way, abroad."

A vein of truth in it all: the Miami delegates—scrubbed, clipped, laundered—were hardly a "cross section" of America. But the effect of these comments was a kind of self-indoctrination. The presidential conventions are the great opportunity, presented every four years, for meeting the American people; an opportunity usually muffed. And the place to meet the People in 1968 was Miami, not Chicago. President Johnson set the tone for dismissing Miami. At a time when Democrats were whistling in the dark about threats to their own meeting place, he was asked why his party did not settle for Miami. "Miami is not an American city," he answered.

No, it is not. But only as a David Levine cartoon of Johnson is not Johnson. Miami is more American than America. According to Thorstein Veblen the typical American town grew by the booming of real estate, meant to float its prospective "use value" several miles into the air above its "real value." Mark Twain's swamp, Stone's Landing, lives off the promise that railway lines can be bribed in its direction; on that assumption men pace off the mud, lay out ghostly banks and stores, do business with these phantoms. The whole thing is a "fabrication."

Florida has been, in its ups and downs out of swamp and back into it, a paradigm of this process. It was the last frontier, opened up in the Gilded Age. It is no wonder John Ringling, the circus man, laid out Floridale, which never got beyond the Stone's Landing stage. As usual, a railroad was needed; and Rockefeller money put down the rails: Henry Flagler, a partner in Standard Oil, leap-frogged down "the Gold Coast"—he had a hotel ready for each extension of his Florida East Coast Railroad.

Airplanes, homing now on Miami, are lowered across pocked slime, a child's vision of ultimate mud-pie, for miles and miles—the Everglades. This is where the continent goes to mush; no rocks to front the ocean, just a spine of limestone and coral buried in ooze. Yet the railroad made its way all down the coast and out to Key West, providing a usable spine for Florida's development. It was a Baghdad frontierland, of Moorish arches and white Algerian walls; Florida was the first place to use poured-concrete on a large scale—there was no native rock to build with. A new Gilded Age dawned recently on Miami Beach, the work of designer Morris Lapidus, who grew up in Brooklyn, head muzzy with visions of a shabby Trianon, a dwarfed Versailles. At last, after years of apprenticeship on the façades of shoe stores, he was turned loose on the Fontainebleau hotel, the Eden Roc, the Sans Souci, the Americana.

Florida lifted itself by nonexistent bootstraps, and Miami Beach is perhaps the most obvious embodiment of this process. It was willed into being. The land was not only overpriced for the sake of things that might be built on it; it was physically nudged up out of the sea. The hotels, as it were, came first; and the strip of land is hung on them. *They* are the solid things; the streets and beach that rocked through all the heat-haze of August 1968 were tied to *them,* to the great yellowing slabs of pound cake. It was easy, moving through moist streets, or cruising them in air-conditioned cabs like mobile ice cubes, to think the ground was a mirage. But not the hotels. They are as real as "cold cash." They do not waver in the air.

"The miracle of Florida" is repeated, in the hotels, endlessly; how could places so vulgar, expensive, and uncomfortable make so much money from their supposed attractions? The only answer is that this is still Stone's Landing, where one pays for the *promise* of value. The Fontainebleau, headquarters hotel for the convention, may be the only place in the world where, if you order an Irish coffee, you must drink it through an "icing" of sugar and *lemon juice* around the glass's rim. And since people come to Florida for the climate, the hotel has ways of pushing you in and out of doors as you traverse it, moving across oil-and-water parallel streams of hot and cold, hot emitted from the omnipresent sun, cold from omnipresent air conditioning. A stay here is not a vacation but a speculation, vicarious entry into the trades and deals that built these hotels. The result is dull and unpalatable; but the prices retain their fascination. They are the basic subject of Miami conversation (with an overlay, during convention, of politics talk). The Fontainebleau, trumpeting its modesty, is the only hotel so famous that it does not put its name out front. But this restraint does not apply to money. No one is presumed to know the rules of tipping: a note in each room gives the "suggested gratuity" for maid service, and menus in the coffee shop supply the same information for gratifying waitresses. When one enters a hotel restaurant, the headwaiter asks, straightaway, which plan you are dining on—i.e., how you want to pay. The menus are dreary in their content, but ingenious in division by the paying schemes, spelling out what-you-get-with-what-without-paying-extra, how much you save in each "package."

Nothing could be more American. Having fun is spending money on fun; the symbol has replaced reality. But that also means *trading* for one's fun, making a deal, getting a bargain. Conspicuous consumption must be combined with compensatory savings. One "takes a flyer" in this speculative orgy, but only "on a good thing." In America, the land of opportunity, the middle class can have not only its own spa, its pale image of Palm Beach up the coast; the moderately successful man can, while vacationing, become a vicarious tycoon, sinking his little bit of money in Florida "land values," values still mainly on paper, more exciting for that. The consumer has become an investor, so it does not matter that he is given nothing of value to consume.

Beyond question, it works. The great middle class keeps coming. Human flotsam moves sluggishly down to the beach, to kick at weeds there and go back up for a game of cards in the cabana—little men led around by long cigars, overballasted women with eyelashes that bristle like bayonets. Sadsacks adrift in the Casbah, their Shangri-la on the cheap. Waiters and maids speak to them on all occasions, obtrusive, even chummy, to remind them of that "suggested gratuity"—delightful reminders, all day long, that the investors have "servants" for this week.

In among these slower-moving sadsacks came 1333

Republican delegates on August 5, freshets of brisk groomed *commanding* types. Gladsacks, as it were. These were not "typical Americans"—their median income was twenty thousand dollars a year. The group was laughably WASP—2 percent Negro (vs. 11 percent of the population), 2 percent Jew (vs. 3 percent of the population), 15 percent Catholic (vs. 23 percent of the population). Not only was the group 82 percent Protestant (vs. 35 percent of the population); the leading denomination was Episcopalian (16 percent, vs. 2 percent of the population), and the lowest was Baptist (7 percent, vs. 13 percent of the population)—giving a heavy preponderance to fashionable Protestantism. The pattern of privilege showed up even in terms of military service. Most of the men were veterans (81 percent)—Korea and World War II, of course, not Vietnam; and the branch best represented was the Air Force (35 percent, vs. 31 percent from the Army). These were people in the summer of their middle age (49 years old), and 85 percent of them had been to college. Almost half belonged to their local Chamber of Commerce, almost a third to the American Legion, a fourth to the Masons.

This group of delegates was younger than the one that nominated Goldwater, but it was more establishmentarian: 42 percent of 1968's delegation had held public office (vs. 29 percent in 1964). An extraordinarily high (though often exaggerated) number of the 1968 delegates—31 percent to be exact—had been at the Cow Palace, under the tinkling shower of gold foil, raising rebel yells for Barry (no other modern convention had brought back more than a quarter of the previous meeting's delegates).

An unrepresentative assembly, then? A rigged convention, as Rockefeller's people charged? These were the pampered Americans, not "real" ones. Not bearded or mustachioed, or even sideburned. Baking amid neon minarets, they might as well have come from Shangri-la, so far as their familiarity with ghettos and the poor was concerned.

But what is the typical American? Young or old, black or white, rich or poor, intellectual or proletarian— or some muddy in-between? One cannot answer that question. There is no typical American. Yet Miami contained something more useful for analysis: here were the archetypal Americans. *They* were the people *we* the people want to be. Even when the rest of America attacks them, it is with that peculiar split hatred called envy—hatred for people who possess something we do not hate at all, but want for ourselves. Affluent, educated, suburban—with exactly 2.8 children per family—roughly half of these delegates (48 percent) were businessmen, largely self-employed. Another 29 percent were lawyers. Their own bosses. Very few professors here (4 percent taught school, at one level or another). Go-getters. Regular hail-fellow guys well met ("Hi, Bud!"). The system may have pampered them, but they like to flatter themselves that they did it on their own. These are the (highly standardized) "individualists" at the center of America's ageless dream of success.

Milling through lobbies incandescent with TV apparatus, rejoining their butter-oiled wives by the pool, listening solemnly to pitchmen from the various candidates, giving their teen-agers a handful of bills for the evening, downing the inoffensive bribe of each faction's booze, these delegates were quintessential Americans. They would be anachronisms except that they exist *outside* time, as all ideals do. For decades, they have made up the visible body of Republicans. More important, they have always been the invisible center of the Democratic coalition. It was the genius of Roosevelt to grasp the usefulness of these types. He did not address himself to the limited number of men who embodied this ideal of success. Instead, he turned to those who had not reached the ideal. If America was, as the individualists taught, a land of opportunity, then he would best the few who *enjoyed* opportunity by organizing the many still *seeking* opportunity. And the strategy worked. Laborers, immigrants, Negroes wanted the opportunity to rise; a poverty-stricken South wanted an opportunity to compete with the rest of the country; intellectuals wanted, for the best of old American (i.e., individualist) reasons, to give these groups opportunity. Right-Wingers who denounced Roosevelt's "socialistic" experiments could not have been more mistaken. The New Deal was not collectivist in impulse; it was always emulative, looking toward a restoration of free competition. That was its trouble; it was, like all variations of the market system, based on envy.

To see the New Deal as a logical extension of Bentham-Mill liberalism, one need only recall Carnegie's objection to inherited wealth: rich boys should have the ennobling experience of competition. The moral market works best when everyone has a chance to compete. But there is a logical corollary to this, one instinctively grasped by boys who are not rich. If some boys have to be brought *down* to the level of real competition, others have to be *raised* to a certain level. Carnegie recognized this when he devoted his efforts to encouraging and helping young men who just "needed a chance" in order to show "what they were made of." Unselfish millionaires start Horatio Alger's heroes on their way up.

Yet the Alger formula is unsatisfactory. Entry into competition becomes a matter of sheer improbable chance: what if the boy, look he ever so diligently, finds no heroine endangered; or, having found her, arrives too late to rescue her; or, instead of rescuing her, gets beat up himself; or, having rescued her, discovers that her father is just as poor as he is; or, having discovered that her father is wealthy, never gets a chance to meet him? The key chapter in an Alger story is the chance encounter, the stroke of luck, that allows the hero to manifest his pluck. But the claim of the Market, ever since Adam Smith's time, has been that it allows merit to rise by *system,* as the result of basic *laws.*

The remedy was obvious, for those still trying to make individualism work: one must contrive the systematization of luck. The advocate of competition, the one who is truly concerned with maintaining the contest, will be most interested in giving all runners a chance. Therefore he must work out comparative handicaps. The New Deal was this attempt at systematization. Its rationale, appeal, and whole underlying metaphor were outgrowths of the emulative ethic. Some people had been dealt out of the game, or given too few cards, or cards from the bottom of the deck. To protect the game, the government would give everyone a *new deal,* making sure it was a *fair deal.* Each runner must have an equal place at the starting line. Some few, especially crippled, may even need a "head start." It was still, of course, a head start *in the race,* a fair deal *in the game.* There might be debate on questions of fact—that is, how much "activism" a referee must engage in to keep the game fair—but there was no disagreement on the principle: the game must go on. And no final disagreement on the referee's job: to provide an equitable basis for the game. Roosevelt, in his second inaugural address, stated the principle this way: "If the average citizen is guaranteed equal opportunity in the polling place, he must have equal opportunity in the market place."

This has been the great agreed-on undebated premise of our politics. Left and Right, liberal and conservative, Democrat and Republican, all work from this basis. Here is Ronald Reagan on the subject: "We offer equal opportunity at the starting line of life, but no compulsory tie for everyone at the finish." Here is Nixon: "I see a day when every child in this land has . . . an equal chance to go just as high as his talents will take him." Here is Rockefeller: "I see . . . the welfare concept . . . as a floor below which nobody will be allowed to fall, but with no ceiling to prevent anyone from rising as high as he wants to rise." Here is Humphrey: "I'll take my stand, as I always have, on equal opportunity . . . Our goal is an environment within which all types of business rivalry can flourish."

The advocates of laissez faire have not successfully challenged this concept of a "floor"—i.e., a court—on which the game is played, or of a "starting line" at which the runners are controlled (i.e., called together, lined up, kept from breaking before the starter's gun). They cannot question it, out of their own presuppositions. Even in Mill's classically harsh statement of laissez-faire doctrine, at the end of *Principles of Political Economy,* the government's function as the game's referee is expressly recognized when "the interference of law is *required,* not to overrule the judgment of individuals respecting their own interest, but to give effect to that judgment" (emphasis added—Mill is speaking of action *required,* not merely permissible, negligible, nugatory).

The past stability of American politics rested on the fact that its foundation—the emulative ethic—was not called into question. (The Right likes to charge that the "intelligentsia" has, in secret back rooms, become "collectivist" and deserted Market principles; but this is as vain as the charge that Roosevelt was a socialist. The academy is the great stronghold of Market orthodoxy. But we shall not be meeting academicians till we get to

Chicago. The most strenuous effort could not call up their image in the professor-free ozone of Miami.)

There have been points of disagreement in our politics, but they were matters of emphasis. The Left has stressed *equality* of opportunity. The Right has stressed opportunity to *achieve*. Yet each side allows for considerable adjustment. The Left, as it addresses the voter, stresses that welfare is meant to "put a man on his feet," so he can be a productive competitor; and its strongest argument for governmental intervention is that welfare should not be considered a "dole," an act of charity, but a basic right—the right, that is, to an equal place at the starting line. And the Right does not deny the need to help some men get started; it just argues points of fact (i.e., does this or that welfare scheme destroy initiative instead of creating it?). Such a debate is not only inevitable but endless, once one accepts the metaphor of the starting line. For where, when one gets down to it, is the starting line? Does a man begin the race at birth? Or when he enters school? When he enters the work force? When he attempts to open a business of his own? Or is the starting line at each of these points? And if so, then why not at all the intermediate points as well? And how does one correlate this man's starting line (or lines) with the staggered, endlessly multiplied starting lines of every other individual? How do we manage the endless *stopping* of the race involved in *starting* it so often? One second after the gun has sounded, new athletes pop up all over the field, the field itself changes shape, and we must call everybody in, to line them up once more. We never even get to surmise where, in this science-fiction world of continual starting and racing, the finish line might be. Or, rather, the staggered infinite finishing lines for each runner. The metaphor is a mess. And Roosevelt's was no better: each time the cards have been newly dealt, we must collect and reshuffle them to allow for the new players who have drifted up to the table; we are endlessly "dealing," never getting to the game.

It is a mark of our deep-needed faith in the emulative ethic that bill after bill is debated, passed, rejected on the basis of a concept so internally contradictory. And no one in the political system comes right out and says the concept is indeterminate in itself, and so cannot be a norm for determining other things. Professors still formulate, congressmen debate, Presidents enact, and bureaucrats administer things called Economic Opportunity Acts, which include things like Project Head Start. And all the parties to the proceeding maintain a naive faith that one can distinguish two extratemporal "moments" or situations—the (controlled) moment of lining up, and the (free) moment of running around the track—which have no correspondence to the real flow of time. These moments are consecutive in idea (*first* line up, *then* race), but simultaneous in fact. Which means that they are simultaneous, at each moment, and contradictory. The metaphor demands a constant rating of people on an equal standard and on an invidious standard ("invidious" in Veblen's sense), since the *raison d'être* of the starting line is equality and the *raison d'être* of the finish line is inequality (to distinguish win, place, show, and so on down the line).

Within the context of the starting-line or fair-deal metaphors, no real debate can be carried on: neither emphasis can be formulated as a consistent position. The pseudo-debate, disguised in competitive imagery, is maintained by stressing one of the poles of this metaphor's internal contradiction—stressing, that is, either *equality* of opportunity, or opportunity to *advance*. And the matter is decided by voters, not on the merits of the argument either side might advance (if they stooped to argue), but out of sympathy with one or the other aspect of the metaphor. If the majority of voters feel touched by the picture of the *race,* then you get a period of Republican hegemony like that which stretched from McKinley to Hoover, almost forty years. If, on the other hand, most voters feel themselves in the "moment" of need for a new place at the starting line, the result is a Democratic period of the sort that followed on the Depression and is just now breaking up.

The embracing fiction of the metaphor allows not only for wide distribution of emphasis, but for change in either party's attitude. The liberal can move from "fundamentalist" to "critical" laissez-faire doctrine (a shift already adumbrated in Adam Smith and Mill). Then, as he senses a shift in the people's ethos from the "starting" moment to the "running" moment, he can move back along the same track he traveled, giving renewed stress to local initiative, divided authority, decentralization. (This is what has been happening to the *Public Interest* liberals.) This return to a "purer" individualism should not be surprising. The "racing" moment has a long-term advantage over the "starting" one. In terms of logic, so far as one can apply it to a conceptual monstrosity like this, the start exists for the sake of the race, rather than vice versa. That is why the Miami delegates are the norm of American life, those who are out on the track, functioning, running, actively competing. Even when a majority of the electorate does not feel itself to be functioning yet, the promise of the politician is that he will *make* it function. In the Depression, men were jockeying for position, asking the referee for compensatory favors, for handicap positions at the starting line. But Roosevelt's coalition, if he failed to deliver on the promises, would soon break up; and it would ultimately break up if he delivered. A coalition based on the starting-line metaphor is, within the individualist framework, self-canceling. Once several large blocs of starters become runners, the politics of the starting line loses its appeal for them. If the various proletariats of the New Deal coalition become sufficiently bourgeoisified (as the labor movement has), Nixon's appeal to the forgotten American—the one who earns, pays taxes, "pays his way"—becomes irresistible.

Rockefeller's difficulty with the Miami delegates can be traced to his almost total misunderstanding of this process. His whole effort was to shift the Republican Party's psychology back to the "starting" moment. That would be difficult in any circumstances. In 1968, it was impossible. He meant to compete with Democrats in terms of New Deal rhetoric, just when the most vital elements of the Democratic Party were ready to stress, once more, the free motion of runners on their imaginary track. The glamour boys were trying to imitate John Kennedy, the new Roosevelt. But the Kennedy era had passed; no one knew that better than Kennedy's shrewder heirs. Rockefeller's attempt to become a Republicanized version of the Kennedyized version of FDR was an exercise in irrelevance.

Not only was his timing off; his weapons were poorly chosen. Could the poor be convinced that *Republicans* wanted to help them? And, more important, could Republicans be convinced that they *should* help the poor? The two tasks were interrelated; any talk of the one was wasted unless the other could be brought off. Rockefeller's men merely blinked reality when they tried to use their old arguments from '60 and '64. Yes, perhaps it was so—*if* he had been more of a party man, he might have blunted the South's effect on the convention; and if he had blunted the South's effect, he might have won the nomination; and if he had won the nomination, he might have found some way (his chosen one was a Reagan vice-presidency) to keep the regulars with him in the campaign; and if he had kept the regulars, he might have added a sizable chunk of "independents" to win the election (though wooing them and keeping the regulars would lead to contradictions he must live with all through the campaign). He might have won. Or might not. The point is that he could go nowhere *until* he won the party, the nomination, the base. Glamour is all very well; but he needed the gladsacks—not incidentally, but in the first place. By themselves, as everyone admitted, these archetypal Americans could not elect anyone. But were they one bloc in the support a Republican needed? The answer is that they were *the* one needed. Add others, it would all be to the good; but without them you had nothing to add the others to.

And Rocky would never have them. His tough stands on communism and crime, his belief in "fiscal responsibility," could not blunt their instinctive hostility. True, Rockefeller was brought up in the same constrictive save-your-cash-and-your-soul religion that Nixon was. If anything, the pecuniary theologian, John D., left a deeper mark on his whole brood than Whittier did on Nixon. The difference, of course, is that Nixon has spent his life on the way up—up a particularly jagged cliff. Nelson was *born* on top, king of the mountain, with only one moral duty, endlessly inculcated—to throw lifelines down to those stuck on the cliff. His means of *self*-improvement, of self-justification, is the offering of opportunity, not the seizing it. He is the benevolent millionaire of the Alger stories, looking for ways to help the good boy up. As such, he was acceptable to Mid-Americanus Miamiensis, so long as he stayed away from government and all its works (which was, in fact, the Rockefeller principle for three generations, until Nelson). The *referee* should not be benevolent, but neutral.

Rocky never knew how to reach the gladsacks. His efforts to do so in Miami were self-defeating. He bought or rented nine hundred hand-radio receivers, and distributed them to delegates as well as staff. Over this network his headquarters could send news, encouragement, and directions—a plan that cost him fifty thousand dollars. Yet all it did was confirm the delegates' most damning suspicion, that he is a "spender."

He made things even worse by throwing an almost continual party during his first days in Miami—the reception with entertainers Saturday, a reception and dinner for the large New York delegation on Sunday, a reception for all delegates Monday, followed by another New York delegation dinner. At the Monday "open house," 8000 people showed up—three times the number of delegates and alternates. There was too much of everything—food (prententious glues of salad and hors d'oeuvres), drink (eight bars), noise (two bands), heat (TV lights), people, and—after his arrival an hour late, from a pirate-run on the Washington state delegation— Rockefeller smarm. He was in his best Reverend Powell manner, baby—a kind of Keep-the-faith-fellah nudge about him, his grin being worked hard as a pump handle.

The delegates have nothing against—rather, they prefer—a business success in government. But Rockefeller is not, in these men's eyes, a business success. He is an *heir*, and they have some of Andrew Carnegie's suspicion about the moral fiber of such a creature. The American has an almost superstitious awe for a man who has made his fortune, and a corresponding distrust of the fortune that makes a man. Strike one against Rockefeller.

The delegates also admire benevolent millionaires. One must, after all, have a millionaire in order to have millionaire's daughters; and what would Ragged Dick do without *her*? But the millionaire's *son* tends in Alger stories to be a snob who wears kid gloves. He did not earn the money himself; he does not have fine antennae for individual worth in his bequests. His money gets dispensed by impersonal foundations, or goes to "causes" rather than plucky kids. After all, it was Nelson who persuaded

John D. Jr. to donate the Manhattan real estate on which the UN building stands. Strike two.

The businessman in government, the private benefactor—each is acceptable in the individualist framework. But never the combination. It terrifies gladsacks to have a happy millionaire, turning his pockets out, get at the controls of the luck-systematizing machinery. The obvious danger is bad enough—that he will start emptying out *their* pockets. But there is a deeper fear, that he will reverse gladsack morality itself—that masses of men will get *something for nothing*. This notion is paralyzing; it denies the law of cause and effect in its primary exemplar, the earning process. Emerson, as usual, was speaking from the core of American concern when he wrote: "All successful men have agreed in one thing—they were *causationists*. They believed that things went not by luck, but by law; that there was not a weak or a cracked link in the chain that joins the first and last of things. A belief in causality, or strict connection between every trifle and the principle of being, and, in consequence, belief in compensation—or that nothing is got for nothing—characterizes all valuable minds, and must control every effort that is made by an industrious one."

All "valuable minds"—minds that "amount to something." Good risks on the human market. Self-improvement manuals of the Alger period echo Emerson's basic law. The moral science of America is not Copernican or Galilean, Newtonian or Einsteinian. It is Emersonian. *What Is Success?* Put it this way: "The biggest thing in the world is the law of action and reaction, namely, for every action there is an equal and opposite reaction." *The Conquest of Poverty* said this: "A man by holding certain thoughts—if he knows the law that relates effect and cause on the mental plane—can actually create wealth." *Success* said: "No man can get something without earning it, unless someone also earns it without getting it."

A total disorientation comes over the American, a vertiginous fear that the law of moral gravity has been rescinded, when he thinks that someone might actually be getting something for nothing. What would then happen to the calculus of self-interest? One must grasp the essential point of America, so easily lost if the chauvinist praises only our deep sense of duty, or the satirist attacks selfishness as if it were a lapse in the system. Selfishness is a *duty* with us. The claim of the Market is that actions undertaken for self-interest are concatenated by Adam Smith's "invisible hand" to bring about universal benefit. The freer men's acts are—i.e., the more "honest" in their direction toward self-interest—the more dependably are they concatenated. It is the "random" unpredictable act of altruism that interferes with the scheme—unselfishness becomes a kind of sabotage. The way this works can be seen in the political marketplace, where the desires of the electorate must be discovered, before they can be satisfied. Robert Paul Wolff rightly says of the process: "It is essential to the success of this proposal that everyone vote selfishly. If too many people, out of a misguided concern for the general good, vote for what they think will benefit society as a whole, then the result will be an opinion about the total happiness rather than a measure of it . . . So long as everyone casts his ballot on the basis of a self-interested calculation of personal interest, something resembling a utilitarian calculus might emerge . . . The system has a chance of working only so long as politics is an expression of private interests."

Philanthropy on the scale of Rockefeller's, undertaken with his ardor, made systematic, reaching out toward public life, moving at last into the seat of elected power, would contradict this "higher selfishness." Theodore White has described how he sat amid Goldwater forces at the 1964 convention, shortly after Rockefeller's divorce from his first wife, and saw a woman rise to shake her fist at Rocky as he spoke: "You lousy *lover,*" she screamed. But a more heartfelt cry, one of anguish rather than complacency, expressed the fears of delegates in 1968; nibbling on Rockefeller's pâté and sipping his Scotch, they were all the time shrieking at a dog-whistle pitch of unheard urgency, "You lousy *giver.*"

5. The Goldwater Party

*"There is a certain satisfaction in coming down to
the lowest ground of politics, for we get rid of cant
and hypocrisy."*

—Emerson

NIXON IS MORE ATTENTIVE to danger than to
blandishments. Thus, despite his commanding lead in
Miami, he stayed alert, uneasy, until Wednesday settled
it all. He was not concerned about Rockefeller, but about
the real threat, the only one remaining. Reagan.

The weekend before the convention's first session was
streaked with showers. Yet a soggy crowd of almost a
thousand huddled near airport doors, Saturday night, to
greet the big jet bringing California's delegates and its
favorite son—the only "noncandidate" left. In the contest to see who (as *National Review*'s publisher put it)
would "chicken in," Reagan had kept his cool while
Romney and Rockefeller, in and out, competed for the
Stassen-of-the-Year award. (Stassen could no longer be
Stassen-of-the-Year. He had won the prize too often.)

Critics observed that Reagan had preeminent qualifications for noncandidacy. But he was the only answer
to the Right's main problem after Goldwater's loss. This
problem was not, as commentators first thought in 1964,
a matter of expiring with minimal decency. The Right's
concern was more prosaic—it had no candidate. Barry
gone, there was no national figure with political sex appeal. The Right, in its desperation, eyed improbable men
like John Tower. Then, in 1966, along came Ron. He
had made his political name with "the Speech," delivered
toward the end of Goldwater's campaign; then he won a
major office on his own (even asking Barry, gently, to stay
away from California while the race was on). As soon as

he was in office, Right-Wing kingmakers and moneymen turned his way. But each time they moved their hands toward their wallets, they found Nixon's hand already there, and shamefacedly apologized for letting their feelings run away with them. That was how it had gone for a year or more, and Nixon knew that wistful glances were still cast in Ron's direction.

Saturday, when Reagan's plane put down, in intermittent drizzle, the governor went up onto a platform to greet the damp crowd. His wife was introduced first, as the next First Lady of the land: she had to force her wide lovely eyes even wider—a bit less lovely for the artifice. Then it was the turn of "the next President of the United States," who expertly drew his head into his shoulders with an aw-shucks motion and a deprecating grin. That was, of course, the role assigned him, and he played it well. But the fiction was thin. The Secret Service men at his elbows; the intricately wired moving van outside Convention Hall; the schedule for the next day, when he would move from delegation to delegation giving this year's version of the Speech—all these made it clear he was running, and running hard. Still, his strategy demanded nondeclaration. His managers meant to do all their bargaining in the back room, and let Reagan come to town like Mr. Deeds, sincere, "nonpolitical," too good to be true (a double-edged phrase to be sure). The princess in her tower, torn by doubt on the eve of her wedding, respecting the heir she is pledged to but not loving him, must be given a glimpse of the handsome young knight riding by. Smitten, she cries to him; he rescues her from her tower, lifts her to the saddle, and rides off. That is the dream Reagan's friends dreamed nightly. But what if the princess were not smitten at once? Would the knight have to contrive ways to keep riding past her tower all day and all night? And what if that did not work? Then the knight would have to rein around and race up to the tower professing *himself* smitten—at which point the princess might wonder why he was so indifferent during the long process of engagement and the wedding preparations.

Those were the dangers in Reagan's situation; and they became obvious the minute he opened his mouth in Miami. "How did you know we were coming?" he asked in fake surprise. Even a professional actor could not keep up the pretense with total lack of irony, the strain was too great. In his very first sentence, he let himself peek around the mask and wink. But once he had done that, he was in trouble. Mr. Deeds cannot be Machiavellian, any more than Snow White can be a flirt.

However much he might play with the mask, Reagan could not drop it yet. He resumed his detached air, speechifying prettily: the sacred business before them all was to fashion a solid Republican Party, and his interest in the matter was as a governor who had restored California to Republican principles. Inside the airport, reporters pushed at him. Did he really think "the office sought the man" at any point in our past history? "I don't, honestly, know whether it's doing it this time." Would he consider the vice-presidency? "Definitely not." If he was not a candidate, why had he scheduled a breakneck tour of the delegations next day (the knight actually has *maps* showing him how to pass the tower at the most flattering angle for his profile)? "Well, some delegations have asked to hear my philosophy, my—approach." Tentative grand modulated to careful modest. The phrase sounded so spontaneous and sincere—until I heard that perfectly paced discovery of the right word repeated time after time through the week. It is an achievement to remain nonchalant on the fifth ride past the tower.

Yet who could doubt him, so slight in build, so unpretentious? Surrounded by reporters in that muggy airport, with TV lights on him, he was the only man not sweating. One felt that if he did, it would be orange juice. He looked theatrical as a Hirschfeld drawing—long straight lines of hair, cross-hatching at the contours, tilted bunched lines on his brow when he frowned Concern. He was wearing what would be his uniform for the next week, light sport jacket, dark slacks, and brown shoes from the forties—the kind with a white panel out in front of the laces. His wife, small despite large actress-features, gazed at him devoutly. In a husband-adoration contest with Lenore Romney, Nancy would, after hours of hard work at the awe-machine, melt first. There is an impure admixture, in Lenore's eyes, of *command* ("If you don't make it *this* time, George . . .").

There was nothing in this sincere young man, peeking through some time-seam where an older man should be, that breathed menace—still the seersuckered good guy, everyone's favorite for a tennis partner. He might even seem one of the glamour boys, and not the best of them— likable, of course, with good looks and intentions, with "charisma." But an amateur. Glamour Boy Right, who— paired in some Republicans' dreams (including Rocke- feller's) with a Glamour Boy Left (namely Rockefeller)— could sweep the nation with charm, concern, and "citizen politics." What, then, was there for Nixon to fear in this last arrival before his own? Where, in the unfortunate line, was the rest of Reagan?

The rest of him, the better part, at least the working and dangerous part, was at the center of a telephone- web on the fifteenth floor of the Deauville Hotel. That is where F. Clifton White worked his charts and boards and phones, sending men out to marked delegates, trying to do what no one thought he could do—break Nixon's hold on the convention. But no one thought White would accom- plish what he did in '64. Shortly after James MacGregor Burns's pronouncement that "the congressional party" could not capture a presidential nominating convention, *Senator* Dirksen was introducing *Senator* Goldwater as the party's nominee, and *Congressman* Miller was brought for- ward as his running mate. On this ticket, in its platform, during its campaign, the presidential party had no place.

How explain such a fluke? Well, in the first place, *as* a fluke. A clandestine operation that succeeded by a com- bination of circumstances—circumstances which included (without being exhausted by) extraordinary carelessness on the part of the presidential liberals and extraordinary care on the part of congressional conservatives. In short, a miracle. Fortunately, miracles do not come in a series. Next time, things would return to normal. The party, after 1964's disaster, would turn back chastened to its proper rulers.

The idea that '64 was a miracle was helped along by Clif White's own improbability. A shy man with a canted half-smile above his canted bow tie, White had lived for years on the edge of the party, a hovering alumnus of the Young Republicans, keeping his hand in, bringing up pro- tégés, part of Citizens for Nixon in 1960. Yet, aided by several conservative idealists who began their secret meet- ings with prayer, he set out in 1961 to make Barry Gold- water President. First, though, he would have to make him the nominee; and before that, he would have to make him

accept the nomination. The whole plan was unlikely. Even
if the congressional party could upset the presidential one,
White and his team were not powers in either party. Even
if they had been powers, it would be hard to make Goldwater trust them. And even if Goldwater had trusted them
(which he never came to do), it should have been impossible to sell politicians a surreal anticandidate like Barry.

The unique thing about Goldwater's candidacy was not
the fact that the man is a lightweight: that has never been
a bar to the presidency, much less to Senate eminence.
To reach Goldwater's perfect state of anticandidacy,
three things had to be added: (1) *A compulsion to reveal
one's inadequacy:* Instead of fading back into the protective foliage of his colleagues' ineptitude, the senator
kept dropping "tactical nukes" of defoliating tactlessness
that left his ignorance exposed, an easy target. (2) *An un-
swerving self-knowledge:* Goldwater's backers said "Barry
has an inferiority complex." He did not. He had an inferiority simplex—the plain knowledge, never shirked,
that he is a lightweight. He would not, to his honor, credit
those who told him he was qualified to rule the nation.
Men like Russell Kirk said he was intuitively bright. He
could prove only part of Kirk's thesis—first, by grasping
(on an intuition) his own ignorance; then by shrugging off
all talk of a "natural genius" built on this ignorance. (3)
A genuine patriotism: Knowledge of his own inadequacy
would not have been unsettling to Goldwater if his patriotism had been feigned or opportunist. He loved his country too much to put it in the hands of a lightweight.

All these misgivings were at work in Goldwater when
Clif White approached him. That was the time Goldwater
was saying, with a glance at his single year in Arizona
University, that a college degree is the minimum requirement for a modern President. White, a stranger to him,
scheduled an interview with difficulty, and the senator
stayed unimpressed: he thought the plan unrealistic, the
man ineffectual, and the whole thing redolent of kooki-
ness (a quality he feared, but with imprecise powers of
discernment). Still, his own advisers—men like Stephen
Shadegg—were also urging him to run; not to win the
election, necessarily, but to "reveal conservative strength"
by a decent showing (which Goldwater then defined as 45
percent of the vote). So he told White he would be an
interested, if rather skeptical, bystander.

After White's meetings with his cadre were blown to the press by a spy, Goldwater tried to shake off these embarrassing supporters. He had not heard they were raising money for the operation—printing costs and travel expenses; always inadequate, the sums collected; at one point, not enough to pay rent on Suite 3505 in New York's Chanin Building, White's unmarked cramped headquarters. The news that these persistent moles needed money for their burrowing came as a shock to Goldwater. He ordered White to break up the operation.

But Goldwater had little say in the matter. White's group had considered other candidates; none had the reputation or personal charm of Barry. It is a free country; they could put forward anyone they wanted. "We'll draft the sonofabitch," they decided. Peter O'Donnell of Texas, fronting for White, opened Draft Goldwater headquarters in Washington, and they held a Fourth of July rally (9000 people on that hot holiday, back when the D.C. Armory was not air-conditioned). Finally Goldwater gave in, responding more to his friends than to this army of strangers. When he chose a campaign team, it was made up of his "Arizona Mafia"—Kitchel, Kleindienst, Burch. He tried to elbow White aside. But too many party workers had been recruited by White, and looked to him as their leader. He had to be used still—as an assistant to Kleindienst.

A division of labor was agreed on, Kleindienst to guide the senator through primaries, White to make preparations for the convention. The primaries were a disaster: *New Hampshire*, managed by Kitchel and Kleindienst, where Goldwater hobbled around the state after a foot operation, hoisting that foot up, cast and all, into his mouth. Henry Cabot Lodge won, Goldwater a poor second, Rockefeller a close third. *Oregon*, where Stephen Shadegg was called in to make something of the mess: Rockefeller won, Cabot Lodge second, Goldwater a bad third, Nixon a close fourth. *California*, where Goldwater barely squeaked by, thanks to a last-minute effort by the whole team, under Dean Burch. But it all made little difference. White, told to take care of housekeeping details in San Francisco, had been wrapping the whole thing up. Every delegate to that convention, as soon as he was chosen in his own state, trailed a spider-filament of contact with White's men. Tugs, entanglements, coaxings, paying out of line, little thrills of attention along the filament, were doing the real work for Goldwater.

White had already discovered, in 1964, themes Nixon would use in 1968. The basis for White's approach was laid in one of Goldwater's talks, written in 1961 by attorney Michael Bernstein. The speech was called "The Forgotten American." Bernstein meant by that phrase the new majority of people being "bourgeoisified" out of the minorities of Roosevelt's New Deal. Bernstein, an old Roosevelt liberal himself, had for years observed this process in the labor unions, and he predicted—accurately, it turns out—that it would form a trend. White believed him.

The very success of Bernstein's speech told against him with the Arizona Mafia, who came to Washington intent on "dekooking" Goldwater by cutting away all his past advisers—especially L. Brent Bozell, once a ghost-writer for Joe McCarthy, who wrote Goldwater's *The Conscience of a Conservative* and the major speech on which *Why Not Victory?* was based. The campaign was an endless series of Goldwater's jokes on himself. And one of the best is that the dekooking went on under the leadership of Denison Kitchel, who hid under his shirt, throughout the campaign, a scarlet letter *B* burned into his chest. Long afterward, Clif White marveled, "If Kitchel's former membership in the [John Birch] Society had been made known during the 1964 campaign it would have blown everything to smithereens." But it never came out.

A new brain trust was gathered for Goldwater by Bill Baroody, a dark Onassis type who runs the American Enterprise Institute. He, too, was a great dekooker; so he brought into the operation one of the best living Lincoln scholars and political theoreticians—Professor Harry Jaffa, who had been Chuck Percy's intellectual coach at Chicago seminars. But irony dogged Goldwater throughout. A Jaffa memorandum for the platform committee had an epigram that impressed Baroody—he commended it to Karl Hess, a speech writer recruited from *Human Events*. Thus the infamous lines were born, making White cringe with foreknowledge of the result: "Extremism in the defense of liberty is no vice . . . Moderation in the pursuit of justice is no virtue."

After San Francisco everyone—except, of course, Goldwater—knew White was a master of Republican politics.

Romney and Nixon both made overtures to him. But he seems to have acquired a taste for working miracles. He wanted to create a candidate *ex nihilo*. He wanted Reagan. Early in 1967, he got him. Oilman Henry Salvatori, who had been finance manager for Goldwater in California, put up money for a Reagan brain trust; Tom Reed hit the road, laying a national base; and White was hired, officially to advise the California delegation on convention politics, actually to put Ron in the White House. By October of '67, White convened his top command in Miami, to survey the battlefield. When his electronic moving van rolled up to Convention Hall, its door bore the hopeful sign Suite 3505-A.

It was a long shot, admittedly. But so was White's gamble on Barry. And no one respected that effort more than Nixon, who had studied it and made its lessons his own. The '68 convention—heavily weighted toward the South —was set up precisely for White's kind of *Blitzkrieg,* and the fact that Nixon had done the setting up did not remove the possibility that the original *Blitzkrieger* might step in and reclaim his instrument. The mood of the nation was increasingly conservative. And—the main thing, perhaps —White had a better candidate this time.

Reagan may not be more intelligent than Goldwater— though that is hard to believe. But he is more cautious; he takes coaching better; he had a certain amount of administrative experience behind him; he retained his popularity in a job rigged with booby traps. Unlike Goldwater, he enjoys crowds, and plays them well; easily turns aside hostility. Reagan is tough, knows something about survival (a skill acquired, perhaps, in the macabre funhouse of Hollywood during the "red scare"—he spent six ticklish terms as president of the Screen Actors Guild).

But if Reagan was not a lightweight of Goldwater's sort, he still had the unreal quality of his old career. He does not look more like a movie star than John Lindsay or Chuck Percy. But he was a confector of screen visions, and it is hard to take such men seriously. Besides, he had not acquired all the savvy of his new trade. Asked about the Party's platform on Monday, he said he had not read it. Asked again on Tuesday, he still had not read it. (He does not like to read, his eyesight is bad; when he reads, he must supplement his contact lenses with unglamorous hornrims.)

White aimed his man at the Southern delegations—e.g., the Texans, housed in the Barcelona Hotel. From the Barcelona's ballroom on the second floor, I watched his arrival, typical of a candidate's in this year of assassination —Secret Service men leaning at Keystone angles from an escort convertible, slapping the pavement as soon as it slowed, surrounding the car from which Reagan unfolded warily, lean, coifed, toothy, with a quick shy wave, ingratiating head-ducks, tentative hand out for shaking (not Rocky's omnium-gatherum grappling). His main assignment in the movies was humility—lose the girl but keep loving the game.

Arrived in the ballroom, he tells how he found out, yesterday, that (aw shucks) maybe he was a candidate, after all. "Bill Knowland came up to my room in the hotel"—you can see the ridged Prussian back of Knowland's head and neck as Reagan speaks over them now, a rumple of iron folds like the cowl of a cast-iron monk. "Bill said our own delegation was discussing the idea of offering me as a candidate for President." He will not cool the Texans' ardor by being coy: "I spent the longest half hour in my life wondering what they were saying down there. If nothing else happens to me in my life, this will be honor enough. And if by some chance I win the nomination, I would not be a reluctant candidate. I'd be the most enthusiastic, energetic and active campaigner you've ever seen, because *they* have got to *go*." They believe him. And love it. Some veterans of the Cow Palace raise the old Barry cry, "Viva! Olé!" This is his country, and he is their man. The South will decide it.

But after the warmth of his reception, cold reality crept back: Peter O'Donnell got up to remind the delegates of their business. O'Donnell, head of the Draft Goldwater movement, had not introduced Reagan. Neither had John Tower. The man who introduced him to the Texans was not prominent in the Republican surge for Barry (in fact, Reagan got his name wrong when thanking him). O'Donnell and Tower were on the Nixon team, along with other key figures from 1964. Nixon had quietly (and early) won over the old Goldwater apparatus—the Southerners (Bo Callaway, Strom Thurmond), the moneymen (Roger Milliken, Jeremiah Milbank), the Arizona mafia (Richard Kleindienst), the celebrities (John Wayne), the late recruits (Dirksen), and—most important—Goldwater himself. In 1965 and 1966, when it looked as if Rockefeller or Romney had the nomination, Nixon was the only palatable candidate surviving on the Right. He played this role carefully, giving and getting support from all the leaderless Goldwater types still running or maneuvering to run. He earned their gratitude and prior commitment. Even Reagan had agreed that Nixon should have first crack at the prize. In a private meeting at Bohemian Grove, in July of 1967, Reagan said he would step in only if Nixon faltered.

All the true-blue Barry delegates still trailed their spider threads from '64; but while White was immobilized, waiting for Reagan to reach the level of open candidacy, Nixon had been picking up the lines. White saw his own strings drawn into other hands; all he could grab were the loose ends overlapping Nixon's hold—promises that if Nixon failed on the first round, they would turn to Ron. White hoped Nixon would stumble somewhere in his run through the primaries. But Nixon survived, and made regulars who felt sorry for him once feel proud, now, of their premier workhorse. "Our people are too loyal," one of White's aides grumbled in Miami. "When they say they'll stick for the first round, they stick." White had laughed off nervous doubts, in '64, that his tabulation of "solid" delegates, drawn up long before the convention, would melt in the excitement of the Cow Palace. Now he was in the position of trying to melt the same kind of people down. But the Nixon people were ready for this: Goldwater was sent around to Southern delegations, firming up the ranks. White had been using the threat that Nixon, with conservatives in his pocket, would placate liberals by making Rockefeller or Lindsay his running mate. Nixon people countered with hints that Reagan might be chosen. Goldwater was commissioned to work this theme: "I know Ron and he'll take the second spot." White, when he heard that, had a telegram drawn up and sent by Reagan to all fifty delegations, swearing he would never take such an offer. The battle was engaged, and Nixon had to pay a fairly high price—absolute assurance that no liberal would run with him—to keep the South. But it was his to keep. White's plan was working beautifully; but Nixon was the man working it. The loyalists who had followed their leaders happily in defeat were determined to follow again, sadly, with many a backward glance of consolation at Ron, toward victory. (Southerners think there is something vulgar about winning.) Despite White's presence at the Deauville, Reagan was not the heir to Goldwaterism in Miami. Nixon was.

6. Southern Strategy

Jam senior, sed cruda deo viridisque senectus.
—Vergil

MONDAY EVENING, on plan, Nixon's jet turned and returned through the gauzy late Miami afternoon. The trick was not to touch the runway too early—while the six-thirty TV shows were opening with their résumé stories on the first day of the convention. And not to land too late—when the slanting light would be grayed for the color cameras. The team had chosen six thirty-eight as optimum time for live coverage; so the plane circled a half hour, responsive to the intricate countdown, signaling the networks, holding, easing into its pattern, landing, sidling, disgorging staff, and—six thirty-eight—epiphany out of a pink sky.

Nixon made his way to a temporary platform and up to the mike: "This state, as many of my Florida friends know, has a special meaning for me—not only because I visit here from time to time, but because in the year nineteen sixty I made the decision to become a candidate for President while staying here." Applause—enough to key his regular refrain, "But this time there's a difference. *This* time we're going to *win!*" He looks jerkily around, to hang his words on an anticipated peg: "I notice in this crowd a number of my Cuban friends. This morning I had a very moving experience. I went down with Mr. and Mrs. Manuel Sanchez—who are members of our family in a very special way [i.e., valet and maid, found for the Nixons by Bebe Rebozo], and are Cuban refugees [not really, they come from Spain, though they were born in Cuba]—to vouch for them when they applied for citizenship. Mrs. Sanchez—Fina—said to me, 'Mr. Nixon, this is the greatest day in my life.' We must make America worthy of the love of people like that." Timing could do no more—Nixon's countdown included this last-minute swearing in of his servants as political assets. In the Checkers era, Nixon's servantlessness had been a sign of Americanism and piety; it is no wonder that, by 1968, the very servants and fur coats somehow became red, white, and blue.

Into cars and buses which move, under the helicopter-scrutiny given each candidate, toward the Hilton Plaza, where the real crowd is. Multicolored squirts of balloons go bumping up the hotel façade. There is a nervous snap in the air, set off in part by toy "grasshoppers" given the crowd so it can "click with Dick." That clicking will go on all week, the mechanical whir and tick of this perfect Nixon drive. Omnipresent music of the *fait accompli*. No trumpets. No trombones. Just Clicky Dick.

Next morning, Nixon finally appeared in his own head-quarters—the red-velvet candy-box maze of the Hilton's mezzanine. Here Herb Klein had presided for days over frequent press conferences, guest appearances, fashion shows of Nixonaires and Nixonettes—Miami is the stewardess capital of the world, and newsmen wrote miles of copy describing them, trying to invent differences in the kind of girls who danced for Nixon and those who danced for Reagan or Rocky, for Vote toothpaste or Pepsi-Cola; yet they were all the same, showgirls for a day. Here would-be Vice-Presidents came to catch the public eye. (The public eye would have little to do with choice of a running mate.) Here Nixon's floor manager—Rogers Morton—came to pooh-pooh the claims of Rockefeller (supported by Morton's brother, Thruston). Reporters were ruminated from chamber to chamber, trying to find something new to say about the candidate who had stayed away.

The morning after his arrival, Nixon held audience for all delegates in a marathon four-hour session. He did not drive up and down the Beach, working his way in and out of each state's chosen hotel as Rockefeller and Reagan had. Instead, the delegates were summoned to the Hilton on a staggered, six-session schedule. The Hilton now replaced the Fontainebleau—*de facto* convention headquarters.

Nixon began that extraordinary morning with a press conference at eight-fifteen—the only one he granted before balloting. He would tell the *New York Times* what it wanted to hear—"after an era of confrontation, an era of negotiation"; he was considering a trip abroad after the convention; he had met all the world rulers except those in Russia; he had achieved his comeback because "the man and the moment in history [have] come together." That last is a line Len Garment had been using on the press for months—Nixon as the defeated man who returns when his country needs him; Nixon as Churchill, as de Gaulle, as Lincoln. It is a very good ploy—suggesting that time and office would give Nixon the stature he so clearly lacked. But greatness was always suspected in Churchill, de Gaulle, Lincoln. One test of it was their prose, a resonance to all they said or wrote, even in defeat. Men do not sound like that if they have nothing in them. And the Nixon on the podium that morning, so exhaustively prepared, turning on well-oiled hinges from question to question, pointing to all his old friend-foes of the press as he stood there, arm lifted from his slight Ed Sullivan humpback, his eyes testing response to each joke before his mouth gave its belated jerk, eyes and mouth in perpetual counterpoint playing against each other—this Nixon was the soul of hard-earned competence, but he had no touch of greatness.

He did not need it. He gave them what they wanted. While reporters rough-sketched their palinodes, hailing a new Nixon still another time, the candidate scuttled off to waiting delegates, each region in its own candy-section, to tell them what *they* wanted to hear. Corn country first, running south from the Dakotas to Missouri, in the bon-bon section called the Jackie-of-Hearts Room. Reporters, by flattening themselves against the aromatic candy-divider wall, caught bits of the spiel: "The way to get the Vietcong to the negotiating table is to say unless you negotiate, this and that is going to happen." The era of negotiation, very short-lived, just yielded again to the era of confrontation.

After each session, Herb Klein gathered reporters around him and gave them a résumé of what had been said. But he conveniently forgot, in his report on the Corn

Belt, all talk of "the way to get the Vietcong to the negotiating table." His memory was selective all morning —especially after the talk with Southerners (ten-thirty in the Palace Room). Luckily, that most important session had been secretly tape-recorded, and the Miami *Herald* let the world in on it. Nixon told Strom Thurmond's fiefdom that he would not force an unacceptable Vice-President upon them (thus countering Clif White's talk of a Lindsay or Hatfield serving with Nixon); that he did not agree with the federal open-housing bill; that the busing of a school-child "will only destroy that child"; that he would follow Eisenhower's example and "not tolerate" a continual war in Vietnam; that he would turn the war over to the South Vietnamese and pressure the Soviets—through the Middle East, or Eastern Europe, or bomb negotiations—to end the war; that he would increase the missile program; that he would find an Attorney General "who is going to observe the law" and a Chief Justice who would "interpret the law . . . and not make it"; that he would not be interested in "satisfying some professional civil rights group" but in guaranteeing that "the first civil right of every American is to be free from domestic violence."

It was strong stuff—Strom stuff. So strong that Richard Rovere wrote: "Although it was surely a miscalculation (or aberration) of sorts that led him to talk as he did, and when and where he did, before the Southerners, it was one of the very few mistakes of the kind that he has made in the last two years." It was no more a mistake than talk of Manuel Sanchez to the Miamians, or of Russian summitry to the national press, or tough coldwar-manship to the Corn Belt. If Nixon gave more, more flamboyantly, to the South, that was because the whole convention hinged on the South. Others he could soothe or try to placate; these delegates he had to *serve*.

Only the South added Republican strength in 1964 when Goldwater ran at the top of the ticket; and convention votes are apportioned to the states according to their performance in the last national election. Moreover, each state that gave its electors to Goldwater—and only Southern states did—got a bonus of six extra votes. This meant that the Southern states had a whopping 316 votes to cast in Miami. Add Arizona and Texas, and the total came to 388 votes. If Nixon could add a border state like Maryland (by adopting its governor), he would be bargaining for a package of 414 votes (with only 667 needed to nominate him).

Nor was it only a question of Miami. The South was just as important in November. One of the weapons Clif White used to persuade Goldwater he should run in '64 was an article in *National Review,* written by William Rusher; it was the first and one of the most influential statements of Goldwater's "Southern strategy." Rusher argued that:

1) The Republicans had not been a *national* party since the end of Reconstruction. The Democrats had for years begun each race with an assured batch of delegates from the South. (By 1968, the entire South held 112 votes in the electoral college, where 270 were needed to elect. Border states bring the number up to 177—two thirds of the number needed to elect.) In the past, Democrats competed with Republicans for the rest of the country, not needing to win a majority there—only the amount that, added to the Southern bloc, would make a majority. (If the initial bloc goes as high as 112, they would need only 50 percent minus 111.)

2) The Republicans, accepting this situation, have traditionally had to "win big" in the rest of the country to offset this initial handicap. That meant they must look to the large electoral blocs in the Eastern states as their one (fairly desperate) hope— whence the power of moneyed liberals in the Eastern Establishment of the party.

3) But the Southern bloc has latterly been crumbling when it comes time to vote for a President (i.e., where prized Southern seniority in Congress is not at stake)—crumbling sometimes to Republicans (Ike in '52, some states to Nixon in '60), or to third parties (Thurmond in '48). What is more, the South has come unglued in some congressional and local races. The race issue mainly, but also suburbanization and industrialization, the loss of blind loyalty and the end of the Civil War, the increasing homogeneity of society throughout the nation, have led to this result.

4) The Republican strategy needs refiguring, given a chance to break into this bloc once denied them— that alone would make the Eastern states less vital.

5) But an even greater recalculation is necessary if one counts in the difficulty Republicans would have competing with Democrats for traditional centers of urban liberalism, weighed against the comparative ease with which a conservative Republican could woo the South. Which leads to the prospect that

6) Republicans can put themselves in the position of having the Southern bloc as a starting handicap; after gaining that, they can compete for the rest of the country, needing only that 50 percent minus (say) 111. This number can easily be made up in the old Republican areas of the Midwest and the new Republican West, without any need for the Northeast. Or so Rusher argued.

When this Goldwater strategy was announced, two objections were made to it—(a) that it could not work, a contention Nixon would invalidate, even without all the South (because of Wallace); and (b) it was immoral to "write off" the Northeast (instead of writing off the South), immoral to appeal to racists in the South (as Democrats had done for years). In short, wrong because it would not work (but it would), and wrong because it *might* work.

What is at stake, if one accepts the Southern strategy as the basis for Republican growth, is a reversal of the Democrats' reign as the majority party—a reversal that is likely to last for decades. Political scientists like Harry Jaffa and Samuel Lubell point out that the American party system has not been a matter of fairly equal seesawing. The normal situation is to have one solidly established party, to which a minority party can make only partial challenges, until an electoral revolution effects a change in their relationship, giving the minority party a new dominance. According to Jaffa, there have been only four such "electoral revolutions"—those marked by the rise of Jefferson (1800), Jackson (1828), Lincoln (1860), and Roosevelt (1932). The significance of Rusher's article —and of the Nixon campaign which, far more than Goldwater's, was based on its insights—is that Nixon's election may go down in history as such a turning point. That is clearly what the Nixon organization had in mind. There was much talk among them, all through 1968, of "new coalitions," of "the passing of the New Deal"—the meeting of their man with a great historic hinge and moment of reversal. Indeed, Nixon's fanciful speech on the "new alignment"—joining New South to new blacks—was an artful cover for the work being done on a real coalition; for one must know "where the ducks are" (as Goldwater put it), but one must not *say* where they are. One of Clif White's major errors—the kind Nixon did not repeat—was to confess his strategy. The Democrats, through their many years of bargain with the South, kept blinking innocently outside the bargaining room, denying any sinister "special relationship."

Perhaps the best place to find out about the real coalition being forged by Nixon in 1968 was at the "control tower" of the effort—John Mitchell's brain trust at 445 Park Avenue, just across the street from the formal headquarters at 450 Park. There, in a cubbyhole next to Mitchell's office, a brilliant young lawyer named Kevin Phillips served as the house expert on ethnic voting patterns. Formally, he was subordinate to Professor David Derge, the haruspex of all polling operations, but in fact he was in charge of his own specialty, which as he bluntly puts it is "the whole secret of politics—knowing who hates who."

Phillips, later an aide in Mitchell's Justice Department, is Bronx Irish, a savvy "city kid" who served his political apprenticeship working for Congressman Paul Fino. His academic record was excellent—Phi Beta Kappa at Colgate, National Merit Scholarship, cum laude from Harvard Law. But his heart has always been in the tough world of *Realpolitik*. By the age of fifteen, he was making intricate maps of voting patterns. "Here's one I did in high school," he said when I interviewed him during the campaign—and pulled out a dense little mosaic of colors and figures that seemed to divide the country not into states or counties, but almost by street.

Always animated by one ambition—to know who hates who. "That is the secret," he says with a disarming boyish grin, one that snags a bit on his front tooth, like an unmalevolent Richard Widmark's. "In New York City, for instance, you make plans from certain rules of exclusion —you can't get the Jews *and* the Catholics. The Liberal Party was founded here for Jews opposing Catholics, and the Conservative Party for Catholics fighting Jews. The same kind of basic decision has to be made in national politics. The Civil War is over now; the parties don't have to compete for that little corner of the nation *we* live in. Who needs Manhattan when we can get the electoral votes of eleven Southern states? Put those together with the Farm Belt and the Rocky Mountains, and we don't need the big cities. We don't even want them. Sure, Hubert will carry Riverside Drive in November. La-de-dah. What will he do in Oklahoma?"

In drawing up his ever more complex maps, Phillips does not rely only on ethnic considerations, but on the whole historical, social, economic picture of the electorate from one campaign to the next. He has a private set of categories. "Silk Stocking," for instance—rich enough to stay in town and live in the safe areas, or to move only to the best suburbs, "the red-hot types who go for Gene McCarthy"; they have never felt the shove of fellow proles in the same block; Nixon can count them out. "Yankees," the puritan abolitionists whose migrations westward trail special colors out from Phillips' New England. "You can get a pure Yankee type out on the West Coast—look at Dan Evans." On the Phillips plan, a presidential candidate would talk to those who voted for Evans much as he addresses a pristine Yankee in Maine. "Sunbelt," the new technocrats of Florida, Arizona, Texas, and Southern California—"skilled workers in light industry, non-Catholic, conservative," one of the fastest-growing and most important blocs on the map. The variations and combinations lead to that minute arithmetic in which Phillips delights: Non-Yankee New Englanders, urban Catholics, rural Catholics (German), Scandinavians (like the Yankees but with patterned divergences). His charts trace and retrace their settlements, their slight shiftings from one vote to the next.

I asked Phillips what he thought of Jaffa's thesis about four electoral revolutions. "The only thing wrong with it is that there have been five—you must count eighteen ninety-six, when Bryan and populism captured the Democratic Party and brought it down." Jaffa claims that each revolution was in the direction of greater equality, and therefore "from the Left" in American politics. How could that apply to the Republican Party in 1968? "The clamor in the past has been from the urban or rural proletariat. But now 'populism' is of the middle class, which feels exploited by the Establishment. Almost everyone in the productive segment of society considers himself middle-class now, and resents the exploitation of society's producers. This is not a movement *in favor of* laissez faire or any ideology; it is *opposed to* welfare and the Establishment" (a Chotiner moment in history). What makes the pattern emerge at this time? "It has been taking shape for years, but the trends were covered up by accidents—the low voter turnout that put Truman back in office in nineteen forty-eight, the belief that Eisenhower was just a one-shot freak of popularity in nineteen fifty-two, the crushing of Goldwater in the wake of Kennedy's assassination in nineteen sixty-four. But the trends have been there for years, especially in the South, in the suburbs, and among Catholics."

Catholics play a great part in Phillips' analysis (as they had in Sorensen's of 1960)—understandably, since they make up a quarter of the population. One of Phillips' basic polarities is of Catholics against Yankees. Catholics were called back to the Democratic Party by Kennedy's candidacy in 1960, when 78 percent of them voted the old way. But their labor ties are disappearing, and they are becoming a moralistic mainstay of the middle class. It was at Phillips' suggestion that, during the homestretch of the '68 campaign, Nixon headquarters released a proposal for aid to Catholic schools.

I asked Phillips if the growth of Negro registration would not recompense Southern Democrats for their losses to the Republican Party. "No, white Democrats will desert their party in droves the minute it becomes a black party. When white Southerners move, they move fast. Wallace is helping, too—in the long run. People will ease their way into the Republican Party by way of the American Independents"—just as Thurmond eased himself over by way of his Dixiecrat candidacy in 1948 and his independent write-in race in 1956. "We'll get two thirds to three fourths of the Wallace vote in nineteen seventy-two."

The demographic shifts in America have been away from the old centers of population. The big cities are declining in population, and declining even more drastically in *voting* population. The large cities now make up only 30 percent of the national population, against 35 percent suburban, and 35 percent rural and small-town dwellers. This diffusion means that economic climbers do not try to adopt Brahmin standards from old social leaders. The suburbs of the new rich are, like the Sunbelt, unashamed of their gains, unburdened by liberal conscience. Thus, when Phillips speaks of a new Republican power founded on the nation's heartland, he does not mean by that term the old Farm Belt or the Midwest, merely. His heartland bloats out toward every state that lacks a seaboard, and even toward some that have one (Florida, California). He sees a long period of Republican domination. "There will be no landslide this year, of course. No charisma. The only mystique that can be built around Nixon is a mystique of the non-mystique. This will be a realignment victory; the trends will just take him in. But you watch us in seventy-two. Our tabulations and techniques will be perfected by then; we'll have four years to work on them, and all the resources of the federal government. I'd hate to be the opponent in that race. Teddy better wait twelve or sixteen years. All those urban programs the Democrats passed to build up their big city machines—they passed them, but they won't get a chance to use them. I wrote a long critical study of those programs when I was with Fino. But I'll never publish it now. *We'll* be using them."

Since Phillips was aiming, even in '68, at a period in the Justice Department to give him the right connections for private practice and business, I asked who would be doing the kind of work he described for '72. "I don't know. Maybe Sherman Unger. You guys in the press write about Charlie McWhorter as the man who knows the party—he's nothing. We call him Baby Snookums at 445 Park. He drops all those facts and figures about each county and district—but if you look in his briefcase, you'll find he's just reciting from Unger's daily memo to Nixon's plane on the territory they will be going into the next day." Unger, in preparing those memos, had Phillips' reports on each state—five to ten pages which described key elements of the electorate in each sector, what to stress where, what to avoid and why.

Phillips seems very confident about the future. But I suggested there were some imponderables ahead. What if Nixon could not end the war? "Why not? The country is sick of it. All we need, to get out now, is a scapegoat. We'll give them one—the big D." What about urban riots? "That cycle's over. If there are any more, we might have to choose a key city, bring in the troops, and just cream 'em. That will settle it." Does he see no chance for a Democratic comeback? "How? When Hubie loses, McCarthy and Lowenstein backers are going to take the party so far to the Left they'll just become irrelevant. They'll do to it what our economic royalists did to us in 1936."

When I talked with Phillips, it was early October, and Nixon had not begun to slip in the polls. "No one here is interested in the election anymore," he said. "They've all got their knives out, trying to carve a place for themselves in Washington. I had an appointment the other day to talk something over with Sherm Unger at lunch, and we had to beat off about six people trying to climb aboard as we passed through the office." What kind of administration do you think it will be? "Irish and Jewish," he answered, sorting things instantly into his familiar categories —"just like Nixon's law firm."

Phillips has some doubts about Nixon—about his toughness, his willingness to trust the trends, to buck the Eastern Establishment when the crunch comes. After the Chicago riots, the polls showed labor-Catholic votes swinging back to Democrats, as a sign of their approval of Mayor Daley. Some Nixon advisers panicked—including Charlie McWhorter—and said the thing to do was swing Nixon's campaign to the Left so it could pick up disillusioned Democrats of the McCarthy stripe. Phillips has a massive contempt for such twinges surviving in Nixon men.

Nixon, of course, does not need a Phillips to teach him the facts of political life—though statistics help back up instinct and political feel. Besides, Phillips makes the same mistake Clif White did—he confesses his strategy. Nixon had to act on that plan while disguising his intention. But his virtuoso performance Tuesday morning in Miami—he had never been trickier—showed that he grasped the arguments made by tough young technicians like Phillips. And Phillips led back to Rusher; 1968 must build on 1964— which meant Nixon must build on the South, and on the Republican Party's major acquisition from the 1964 campaign, Strom Thurmond.

Bo Callaway was formally Nixon's campaign director for the South, but he made the mistake of saying that Wallace voters actually belonged in the Republican Party: the Right just will not learn to keep its mouth shut, to work on a strategy without confessing it. Early in 1968,

Callaway probably looked better than crusty old Strom—Bo is young, handsome, a West Point graduate. But he is also the man who managed to lose a gubernatorial race against Lester Maddox, which takes rare skill. By the time the party reached Miami, Strom had taken over. This was not only a matter of his personal following and record; it was also a reward to his state. In 1960, South Carolina's State Chairman, Greg Shorey, and the State's perambulating Republican pocketbook, Roger Milliken, put Goldwater's name in nomination (even after he asked them not to); in 1964, it was South Carolina that put him over the top in the nominating ballots; and in between those two convention moments, both Shorey and Milliken had been in Clif White's secret group for drafting the candidate. South Carolina is the honorary home of Southern Republicanism, laid on Goldwater foundations. Thus Strom was the right man to send telegrams (signed also by Barry and John Tower) to all Southern delegates, urging them to stand fast in Miami. Strom blocked the move of North Carolinians to visit with Ronald Reagan one week before the convention. It was Strom's old administrative assistant, Harry Dent, the State Chairman of South Carolina, who went everywhere through the South telling delegates he had Nixon's word "written in blood" that there would be no liberal Vice-President. Strom rushed everywhere, from delegation to delegation—twelve miles across the Bay to argue with the Floridians (who alone had the sense not to stay on the Beach); out on a Nixon yacht to bargain with the Mississippians. Few people would have believed, a week beforehand, that Thurmond would be kingmaker in Miami.

The man who did all this is a prodigy of energy; indeed, like Vergil's Charon, an almost monstrous combination of age and muscle—"divinely raw, green with his very years." His masklike face is still perched on a powerful, though wrinkled, neck—which is no wonder; he spends a great deal of time on his neck. "I lay [sic] on the floor every morning, and I throw my feet over my head twenty or thirty times to keep the blood flowing to my head. Your brain has to be fed by fresh blood, and if you don't exercise, your brain won't be supplied." Health foods and endless push-ups keep the sixty-six-year-old in shape. In 1947, he supplied *Life* with a funny picture, and his gubernatorial opponent with ammunition, when he stood on his head to prove he could marry a girl less than half his age. His first wife died in 1960, and he fell in love with an even younger girl, Miss South Carolina in 1966. But he had the political sense to hold off his marriage until Nixon was elected.

Strom, with his prune juice, health foods, teetotalism, his lay sermons (he is on the board of fundamentalist Bob Jones University), his wars upon dirty books and movies, is the champion clean old man. In 1968, his simultaneous attacks on Abe Fortas and on dirty movies were waged from the heart, and fell in line with a general sense of crusade through his career—he once accused South Carolina's Olin Johnston of immorality for letting Sally Rand attend a reception in the governor's mansion. Nixon—who spoke, all during his tape-recorded session with the South, as if he were aiming each word directly at Strom—knew what he was doing when he said he would *"open a new front . . . against the narcotics peddlers, the numbers boys, and the peddlers of filth."*

Strom is a true Southerner in his patriotism; a retired major general in the Army Reserve, he was decorated for bravery in the Second World War, and has always opposed "the muzzling of generals." At one of 1968's early meetings with Nixon, in May, he was impressed by the candidate's advocacy of an ABM system. "That grabbed Strom like nothing else," Harry Dent said. (Dent was highest-placed of the first nine South Carolinians given administration jobs by Nixon.) Just after the May meeting, Strom came out with his early endorsement of Nixon. It was thus no mistake (as Rovere called it) that the Tuesday morning tape contains these words: *"We are going to restore our strength in the missile program. We will begin with that . . . We aren't putting enough money into basic research to keep ahead of the Soviet Union. We are going to close that gap, and then create one where they are behind us all around the world."*

Crime is another of Strom's concerns. As he said, during his successful campaign to block Abe Fortas' appointment as Chief Justice, "Does not that decision, Mallory— I want that word to ring in your ears, Mallory . . . shackle law enforcement? Mallory, a man who raped a woman, admitted his guilt, and the Supreme Court turned him loose on a technicality . . . Is not that type of decision calculated to encourage more people to commit rapes and serious crimes?" No wonder Nixon said, Tuesday morning, *"The federal government has got to set an example. But instead of setting an example of law enforcement, we have been setting an example of law softness."* Strom's dark view of the Supreme Court dates to his own hardening from a fairly liberal governor to a leader of Southern resistance after the 1954 decision on school desegregation. His own view is that "the Constitution means today exactly what it meant in seventeen eighty-seven or it means nothing at all." He likes to give out a twenty-four-page cartoon book called "A Scriptographic Presentation of the Constitution." He even gave a copy of it to Robert Kennedy, at the hearing on his appointment as Attorney General, and solemnly begged him to study it. It was music for such a man's ears to hear Nixon say: *"I want men on the Supreme Court who are strict constitutionalists, men that interpret the law and don't try to make the law."*

In 1956 Strom drew up a "Declaration of Constitutional Principle" which nineteen Southern senators and ninety-four House members signed, warning judges away from things like the school system. He proudly keeps the original copy of that document in his office. Nixon was speaking that man's language when he said, *"I know there are a lot of smart judges, believe me—and probably a lot smarter than I am—but I don't think there is any court in this country, any judge in this country, either local or on the Supreme Court—any court, including the Supreme Court of the U.S.—that is qualified to be a local school district and to make the decision as your local school board."*

Strom is also the record holder for the longest single-man filibuster (twenty-four hours and nineteen minutes), against the 1957 civil rights bill. Nixon showed he could do business with such views when he said, of the federal open housing law: *"I felt then—and I feel now—that conditions are different in different parts of the country . . . [and] ought to be handled at the State level rather than the federal level."*

After Nixon's own nomination, he returned to his hotel for the decision on his running mate. Invitations had gone out for suggestions, especially to Southerners, and many people showed up to advise him, especially Southerners. On Monday, as the convention opened, the *New York Times* ran an "inside" story that said Nixon had narrowed his choice to Lindsay, Percy, or Rockefeller. A *Time* magazine reporter told me he had almost certain information from the Nixon camp that the Vice-President would be a liberal. The New York *Post* said on Wednesday that "the betting here is that Lindsay leads the field as Nixon's logical running mate." The *Times* backed up its unfortunate Wednesday headline, which put Lindsay's chance in the same size type with Nixon's nomination, by printing this head on the inside continuation of that story: NIXON STRATEGISTS ARE LEANING TO LINDSAY FOR SECOND PLACE. Nixon, when the paper reached him early Wednesday morning, threw it aside and muttered, "Blackmail." He did not believe that sophisticated reporters could swallow his aides' talk about a spot for Prince John.

How could anyone suppose that the man who despises brilliance, charisma, and "Buddy-buddy boys" might choose a Lindsay to stand beside him and lift his hand, lift *him* dangling over the Convention Hall podium? In a crowd containing tall men, Lindsay's lighthouse blue eyes still shine over all other heads, his face is clearly visible, with its bland stricken-eagle good looks. He would have dwarfed Nixon, eclipsed him, made him the ugly duckling. Nixon did not even like the faded gray handsomeness of Cabot Lodge, his lethargic running mate in 1960. There was never a chance for Lindsay in '68. (As if to seal that fact, Charlie McWhorter was his major champion at the Wednesday night and Thursday morning sessions.)

Rockefeller, also, had no chance. The two men hate each other too cordially. Yet, once again, liberal naiveté is hard to overestimate. Months afterward, James Reston was still sputtering with stunned indignation because Nixon had not made Rockefeller Secretary of State. Percy was no threat. As Harold Rainville said, "What President could be happy with Chuck warming up behind him?" On all these, Strom's veto was not really necessary—though it flattered him to think it was. But he vetoed *five* men— and his ban had weight with the others. He said no to Scranton, whom Goldwater wanted in 1964 (and whom he recommended again this time). And Strom said no to Hatfield, who thought he had the appointment sewed up.

But all Strom asked for was a veto. He did not choose Agnew over Volpe, though the South was the thing that tipped the scale in Spiro's favor. Volpe, a tanned little man with wrinkles scoring his face like an Indian's slashes,

came to Miami with his tongue hanging out. Invited by
Herb Klein to give one of the busywork press conferences in the Hilton, he spent most of the time talking about
himself. Yes, he had got one of the Nixon letters asking
for his recommendation on the vice-presidency, but no, he
had not sent his own recommendation. Instead, he had
mailed Nixon a study that demonstrated how an Italian, a
Catholic, could draw votes in the big cities—"and the
Vice-President should be chosen to attract votes he might
not otherwise get—for example, in the big cities. Er—not
that he won't get votes there." Will that paper be given to
the press? "I wouldn't be surprised if it were released in
the next few days." At least that threat was headed off.
His tongue was too far out; the Nixon people had to walk
on it wherever they moved through the Hilton candy box.
Volpe's error was in thinking the big cities mattered.
Wednesday was the South's night, not his.

Yet Nixon played the decision as if he were agonizing
all those hours till dawn, rather than agnewizing—for two
reasons: to give the impression that all views had been
consulted, and to assure himself that the choice had been
made with sufficient pain. (Nixon must have sleeplessness
before a decision, much as Romney made a ritual fast.)
So they came and went all night—advisers, friends, in-
spirers. Billy Graham was there, to say a good word for
Hatfield's Christian politics. The sessions lasted till five-
thirty in the morning, and were resumed at nine o'clock.
Nixon slept an hour in the interval. Dirksen's advocacy of
his son-in-law, Howard Baker, had to be tactfully de-
flected. Nixon had to give up his personal preference,
Bob Finch. And in the end it was Strom, old Stromboli
power man, who had done the hundred push-ups of convention musclemanship and determined the choice that
was as unforeseen as his own kingmaker role. By the
Kevin Phillips logic of Miami, Strom led straight to Spiro.

7. The Succeeder

> *"In brief, a darling of the gods. No other American
> has ever been so fortunate, or even half so fortunate.
> His career first amazed observers, and then dazzled
> them. Well do I remember the hot Saturday in Chi-
> cago when he was nominated for the Vice-Presidency
> on the ticket with Harding. Half a dozen other states-
> men had to commit political suicide in order to make
> way for him, but all of them stepped up docilely and
> bumped themselves off."*
>
> —H. L. Mencken

SPIRO AGNEW'S CAREER has about it a somnambu-
lant surefootedness, an inevitability of advance, that reminds one of Mencken's Coolidge, of the juggernaut of
snooze: "There were massive evidences of celestial intervention at every step of Coolidge's career, and he went
through life clothed in immunities that defied and made a
mock of all the accepted laws of nature." In an election-
eve TV broadcast, Hubert Humphrey proudly displayed
Ed Muskie, his monkish second-string Eugene McCarthy.
Nixon, on the same night, sat alone, remasticating answers for Bud Wilkinson, his kept TV interrogator. No
Agnew in sight. It was said that Nixon regretted his choice,
his deal with Thurmond. But Agnew was a guided missile,
swung into place, aimed, activated, launched with the minute calculation that marks Nixon. Once the missile was
fired, the less attention it drew to itself the better—like a
torpedo churning quiet toward its goal. Agnew has a neck-
less, lidded flow to him, with wraparound hair, a tubular
perfection to his suits or golf outfits, quiet burbling oratory. Subaquatic. He was almost out of sight by campaign's end; but a good sonar system could hear him
burrowing ahead, on course.

Agnew's beginnings were not much—forty undistinguished years. As Mencken said of Coolidge: "No man ever came to market with less seductive goods, and no man ever got a better price for what he had to offer." Agnew's father was a hardworking immigrant, a restaurateur in Boston, Schenectady, New York, Baltimore. Early in the Depression he lost his Baltimore place, but started it again, and scraped up enough money to put his son in Baltimore's most expensive school, the Johns Hopkins University. The Hopkins is in the city but not of it. Those with local ambitions, wanting old-school ties in the grappling chumminess of city politics, did better to attend provincial Loyola College and the University of Maryland's law school. (The incumbent mayor, descended from an old political family, did that.) The Hopkins was for outsiders, or for natives who wanted out. It was, for instance, Alger Hiss's escape hatch from Lanvale Street to Boston and New York and Washington—a route Murray Kempton later followed and described. But Agnew's father overlooked one problem: Spiro was (and is) no student. After three years he gave up the losing Hopkins effort. His doting biographer, Ann Pinchot, fuzzes over this flight from the test of senior year: "His scholastic concentration in sophomore year began to decline and he was distracted by other things than school." Agnew himself, at an American Legion dinner during the 1968 campaign, was more frank: "I was more interested in a good time than in studying." After he left college, he helped a bit in his father's store, then went to work by day, and school by night—a city law school now, though he was no more studious; he admits he "still wasn't doing anything scholastically." But at his daytime job he met his wife, an unpretentious girl in open-toe shoes, plump, winning Judy, still the most likable thing about him. And war came, rescuing him: he went to OCS and served honorably in Europe.

Back home, now father of two, he resolutely hit the law books again and, with the help of the GI bill, bought his first home out in the suburb of Loch Raven. Nixon presented him to the Miami convention as an expert in urban problems, and it is true that he early grasped and overcame what white urbanites take to be their main city problem—how to escape the city. It has been twenty-two years since Agnew lived in the city of his birth.

After getting his law degree, Agnew opened a practice,

but failed again. With his diploma on the wall, he had to go to work in a grocery store. Nixon, too, failed in his first major endeavor after college, the launching of Citra-Frost. From that time, various irons were being annealed in Nixon, but Agnew just bounced along slaphappily, as if he knew the gods had things in store. War once more lifted him from inconsequential civilian life; he sold his home, and served in Korea. Finally, when he returned, things began to fall into place. Modestly prosperous in a county law firm, Agnew, who gave up the family's religion and political party and adopted city, found roots in the rootlessness of suburbia. Not naturally gregarious, he could run this world's casual *cursus honorum*—vice-president of the Kiwanis Club, president of the PTA, president of the Loch Raven Community Council. Even retiring Judy participated in the unfrenetic politics of neighborhood and club basement, as Girl Scout leader, member of the Federation of Republican Women, and president of the Ki-Wives. Spiro, who had not taken part in collegiate sports, moved up from his city pastime (bowling) to golf. In this circle of one-generation clans, clan Agnew worshiped at the living totem, suburbia's answer to the generation gap, the family dog.

The first reward for this life of semi-civic duty was appointment (by a 4 to 3 Republican Council) to the county's Board of Appeals (whose duties included zoning). Since Baltimore was emptying out its whites, filling up with blacks, a land boom was on—modest and ambitious homes exploding slowly, in a lumber and lawn-grass circle, out from the old edges of town. Fields were cut up into lots, ribs of wood clothed overnight with brick, and the supple corkscrew of water rose from a thousand lawn sprinklers. Baltimore row houses, first meant to save city space, now ran stichically off toward country horizons. Rodgers Forge, farmland when Scott Fitzgerald lived there, became a maze of brick, each block with its garbage truck mews. Incongruous Dutch villages. The inbred "developments" whose winding roads never seem to reach an outside artery. Mini-mansions in pockets of shrubbery. Even partially to control zoning was to get an inside glimpse of the action. For Agnew, it was a sign of the whole system's beneficence (let a thousand sprinklers flower). He was all the time, in his Greek uprooted soul, a booster. Some wealthy real-estate men, largely Democrats who knew a booster's uses, put him on his way. The ties remain close even today; many of Agnew's investments have been in the county's rapidly improving property. These connections with land investors led the *New York Times* to accuse Agnew of "conflicts of interest" throughout his political career. The editors did not understand that when Agnew drove from his Loch Raven home to the county's tiny seat of power, Towson, he was entering a remnant of the past, still haunted by Will Kennicott; and if you are anybody in Gopher Prairie, you have ties with men all up and down Main Street.

Back in 1958, Baltimore County's Democratic boss had picked his successor for the office of county executive (ruler over a patchwork of housing developments and swallowed villages, Towson foremost among them). This boss thought he would still be running things out of his Dundalk business office; but the successor had ideas of his own. For four years, therefore, the boss—Michael J. Birmingham—plotted his own restoration; and though he was a septuagenarian of uncertain health, he had enough political debts to win a bitter, party-splitting primary. After his victory, supporters of the incumbent swung to the Republican candidate of 1962, and up popped—none other than Spiro Agnew. The old Democratic county had a Republican in charge for the first time in memory, a voice for the new suburbia, all real estate and new-arrived respectability.

The luck that let Agnew rise through Democrats' divided ranks seemed, at first, a momentary freak. Soon after Agnew's election, Birmingham died and the Democrats' party reknit, ready to claim its ancient seat again in 1966. But fate was readying better things. Part of the fatal weave came from Agnew's control of the county police. During the 1962 campaign the county police chief had invited his subordinates over for a social evening with Mike Birmingham, the aging candidate. Agnew, as part of his assault on the past administration, made an issue of the social evening-cum-Democratic candidate, and pledged a "housecleaning" if elected. The result: he brought in an outsider to shake up the police department—Robert J. Lally, the legendary Fordham FBI man (the FBI is a group of Fordham graduates checking on Harvard graduates). Lally keeps his close ties with Hoover's department and is a strict believer in law-and-order. Agnew began a close association with him that was to bear fruit six years later in the incident that brought him to national attention.

The county Agnew presided over is a lopsided doughnut circling Baltimore. (It does not, as John Lindsay informed the Miami convention when seconding Agnew's nomination, *include* the city.) An invisible 2.6 percent of the county's population is Negro, scattered through greenlawnville in moldy pockets. Insofar as the big American city is becoming black territory, Agnew knows nothing of it. When civil-rights groups, led by clergymen, tried to integrate an amusement park in the county, Agnew and Lally treated it simply as a law-and-order matter and arrested the priests and rabbis. This was Agnew's first experience with a major social problem. I asked Robert Lally if he seemed anxious to learn about the enforcement problem, to study other communities' ways of handling similar clashes: "No, he never had any doubt about the way things should be. He is very quick to boil things down to their essential." I asked Reverend Frank Williams, one of those arrested, if Agnew was a good learner in the area of Negro rights. "No. He simply admitted he did not know any Negroes, or much about them." It was a lack that did not disturb Agnew. By the time he ran for governor, he still knew only one prominent Negro, the Reverend Robert Newbold, who had to take him around and introduce him to the state's black leaders.

By 1966, Maryland Democrats seemed determined to commit suicide at the state level ("all of them stepped up docilely and bumped themselves off"). Two years earlier, George Wallace had won 45 percent of the votes in Maryland's Democratic primary, and those who ran up that total now laid claim to the party. The only candidate they could find was a tongue-tied unctuous millionaire, George P. Mahoney, who had for years been running unsuccessfully in every campaign he could enter. He made his slogan "Your Home Is Your Castle" (up with the castle drawbridge, let the horde of advancing niggers silt up in the moat). Red-hots turned out for the primary, and made poor George their nominee. There was nowhere for the liberals, the Negroes, the Jews to go but to the Republican candidate (who thus cheated his opponents of a reelection showdown in the county)—Spiro the Blessed.

Elected governor, Agnew had to give up his home for Annapolis, the crowded little town full of history and crumbling buildings (in which he did not show much interest). He consoled himself by giving the gubernatorial mansion a Loch Raven–style "club basement," where he could play billiards with his bodyguards. The new governor brought several things with him from the county—including Bob Lally, his police chief. First he appointed Lally "program executive" in charge of correlating all the state's law-enforcement agencies, then made him chief officer (colonel) of the state troopers. When Lally left the program executive's office, he picked his own successor from the FBI.

The city of Baltimore was now within Agnew's domain. But he could not often be lured there—except, on Sunday, to the stadium for a Colts game (and suburbanites now want to move the stadium out their way). His last Republican predecessor in Annapolis, Theodore Roosevelt McKeldin, a tireless hand-pumper and hubert-humphrey-izer at all Baltimore affairs, moans melodramatically (he is an old speech teacher and magnificent ham actor): "Ted just does not like to meet people. As governor, he refused to attend even the most important city events. When a new president was installed at the Johns Hopkins University—and that happens only once in a decade or more—presidents of other universities and men of influence came from all over America. But not the governor of Maryland." (Bad memory, those three Hopkins years?) "When the Greek Archbishop met our *g-r-e-a-t* Cardinal Sheehan—a unique ecumenical event—Spyros Skouras, who brought the archbishop down from New York, asked me, 'Where is Spiro?'" A young Greek lawyer in the legislature, Paul Sarbanes, says, "Agnew never did anything for the Greek community in Baltimore except leave it at the earliest opportunity." Rabbi Israel Goldman, a member of the Maryland Commission on Human Relations, says, "Agnew insulted the Jewish community by sending an underling to read some perfunctory statement when we invited him to our meeting of seven thousand people to protest the Arab aggression against Israel." Agnew frequently expresses his opinion of these ceremonial events. His biographer puts it this way: "He once said wryly that whenever he has a train of thought that requires concentration, 'somebody wants me to stop and glorify National Pickle Week.'"

But his main trouble was with the Negro community. It

did not start in Baltimore, but out on the antebellum Eastern Shore, over the Choptank River in Cambridge (what Mencken used to call "Transchoptankia"). After an appearance there by Rap Brown in 1967, blacks burned down two city blocks, which brought the National Guard in. For Agnew it was a time of lurid revelation. He had a police tape of Rap Brown's speech which he played over and over in his office, inviting black and white leaders in to hear it. "He paced up and down as it played," says Rabbi Goldman, "in great distress, and said, 'How can we put up with agitators like this?' I tried to tell him Cambridge was ready to go up in flames long before Rap Brown went there, but he did not understand. The trouble came from the miserable conditions, not from the man who denounced those conditions." Senator Verda Welcome, a prominent black moderate, was one of those given a private audition of the tape, and she shocked Agnew by her lack of shock at what Brown said. It was old stuff to anyone who had listened to the black community. Agnew had not. When Lally brought him intelligence reports on agitators, people malevolent enough to blame the system that had blessed Agnew and all his kind, he became obsessed with "militants." A conviction was hardening in him that no progress could be made until all moderates were forced to denounce the militants. Colonel Lally agreed: "We cannot have men going around telling people to burn their cities." They seem honestly to believe that those trapped in a ghetto would not think of starting trouble unless some signal caller came by to give instructions. The next clash with the black community came when Agnew's budget for fiscal '69 was submitted. Paul Sarbanes, in an extraordinary twenty-two-page indictment, called it an "East Coast version of the Ronald Reagan budget." Welfare mothers marched against it; black leaders and city officials told Agnew he was cutting back too drastically on programs for the poor. By this time Agnew was not listening. His one Negro aide was rarely consulted.

Agnew seemed to be living in the governor's mansion on borrowed time (as he had lived in the county's supreme post). "Republicans only get into office in Maryland when the Democrats split," says McKeldin, "and they would not be stupid enough to run another Mahoney in nineteen seventy." But Agnew was ready to move on.

If the Democrats had split two ways in the Mike Birmingham struggle, and the state party had fallen apart for a while on the race issue, he would climb the next step over a national party split *three* ways (Wallace, Humphrey, McCarthy). In his quick rise, he has never had to stand for reelection. "If he would hold still for a minute," Paul Sarbanes says, "we'd nail him. But he is always moving off to something new."

The next step took more doing; but who can stop gods? By the beginning of 1968, Agnew was moderately successful as a governor (nothing spectacular), but the Democrats were de-Mahoneyized, ready for 1970. Agnew was not nationally known, still something of a newcomer (just a decade ago his big race had been for the vice-presidency of the Kiwanis Club). He was considered a liberal Republican; he had stood with McKeldin in the 1964 Maryland delegation, working for Rockefeller. The campaign against Mahoney had given Agnew a liberal image. Besides, a public-accommodations law had been passed when he ran the county, a mild open-occupancy law when he was governor—both bringing local into line with federal practice. Agnew himself probably did not know, at this point, whether he was a liberal or a conservative, or what the words meant. Later, when he called Humphrey "soft on communism," then claimed he did not know such charges were common in the fifties and were connected with Joseph McCarthy, no man could plead ignorance so convincingly.

Agnew still thought his future lay with Rockefeller; he had not even met Richard Nixon. The new year crept in on him bearing unknown gifts, wrapped blessings all wound up and ready to go off, week after week, through the spring of 1968. It began in January, when an improbable fairy godmother waved king and prince together with her wand. Louise Gore is a billowy evasive woman, wealthy and unmarried, who has dabbled in Maryland politics for two decades, supporting others or running herself (she was a state senator in 1968). Her family owns the Fairfax Hotel and Jockey Club in Washington and the distinguished home Marwood, where Roosevelts and Kennedys have lived. She is difficult to track down—she seems to think the measure of one's importance is the number of people kept waiting, simultaneously, at points dotted across the map—and when one does meet her, she tends to be preoccupied, peacefully daydreaming despite her bitten nails. Asking her questions is like tapping a balloon; she drifts.

But the story came out: "I wanted to give a treat to the women who worked for me in my Senate race—I call them the Gore girls" (they deserve a treat). "So I took them up to New York for the National Republican Club luncheon. I arranged for them to stay in the Manhattan apartment of Mrs. Edmund Lynch Jr. As a special treat for them, I asked Mr. Nixon to drop by the apartment after the Club meeting. Then I learned Governor Agnew and his wife would be in town, so I invited them too. I wanted these two men I admire so much to meet each other." The two met formally on the luncheon podium; but they could not converse until they reached Miss Gore's party. "It was almost as if one picked up the other's thought from—well, from the other; they were so engrossed in each other that they forgot we were in the room. When I walked Mr. Nixon to the elevator, he told me, 'Your Governor—your Governor—make him speak out more. He's got a lot to say.' " Agnew, too, was impressed, and sent a long letter to Miss Gore thanking her for the opportunity of meeting Nixon. The spark had jumped. Later, in Florida, Nixon was to say, "There can be a mystique about a man. You can look him in the eye and know he's got it. This guy has got it." Not given to such outbursts, Nixon must have been remembering that warm first meeting six months before. What impressed him so? No doubt the same thing that won over real-estate men in Baltimore County. Agnew is a believer; his faith in the Establishment (as he proudly calls it) fairly shines from him, as does his horror for its critics. The year 1968 was to be a time for law and order. Nixon, just embarked on his own campaign in the New Hampshire primary, must have sensed this man could voice that theme with a fervor and innocence, a lack of racist nuance, impossible in most campaigners.

But before Nixon could recruit Agnew, two things had to happen. Agnew's hopes had to be separated from Rockefeller, and the Maryland newcomer had to get wider exposure. Both things happened in the bitter Easter season of 1968. But first, as usual, fate made its preparations. In February, Robert Moore opened a SNCC office in Baltimore, and made an overnight sensation by calling the city's war on crime a war on the black man. Senator Clarence Mitchell, a black moderate, took the senate floor in Annapolis to denounce this charge. The House of Representatives passed a resolution praising Mitchell because he did not praise Moore (the easiest way for whites to undermine the authority of blacks in their own community is to give them medals for attacking other blacks). There was a wrestle back and forth of "Uncle Tom" and "extremist" charges, followed by widespread desire in the black community to unite as a single effective bloc. With this aim, black leaders scheduled a secret meeting for March 24 at the Emmanuel Christian Community Church.

Meanwhile, three days before that meeting could take place, the governor of New York called a special press conference. Everyone expected him to announce his candidacy for President—including Agnew, who had been first in the field blowing Rocky's trumpet. The Annapolis press crew was invited into Agnew's suite to watch the show with Spiro; he would ride the very first wave of publicity. They were there when Agnew got the humiliating proof of his unimportance in Nelson's eyes; Rocky had gone out of his way to announce that he would not announce, and he had not announced this nonintention to his leading booster. This was typical of Rocky's performance in '68. Later his people would try to woo Agnew back; but Spiro is sensitive, and he was hardened against his original choice from that moment. It was an apparent setback from which, as usual, Agnew would profit.

In three days, the black unity meeting took place, unheralded. It was four days before Steve Lynton, who covered the black community for the Baltimore *Sun*, could piece together enough details of the session to write an article on it. Not even police intelligence officers had picked up the story. They had to rely on the article—as did Agnew. Here was another example of moderates consorting with militants; and Agnew, his hopes of impressing the liberal Rocky gone up in smoke, began to plan a public declaration of the responsibility black leaders have of maintaining law and order among their own. Three days after the Lynton article ran, Johnson withdrew from the presidential race. The Republican candidate—Nixon, apparently—now had an even better chance of winning in November.

That was Sunday. A week of horror had begun—the

week of Spiro's opportunities. A Negro college, Bowie State, was in turmoil, twenty miles from Annapolis, over poor campus conditions. Agnew would teach the moderates how to handle disturbances. He sent one of his real-estate men—one known for his tactlessness, Charles Bressler—over to Bowie State to take a hard line with the students. The governor was handling everything personally now. His Negro aide, Dr. Gilbert Ware, was not consulted; and Ware told me, "Even Mel Cole [the governor's administrative assistant in charge of education] did not know about the trouble on Bowie's campus until I told him about it." Agnew was already composing, with his own hand, a declaration on the duties of moderates. In the week after his break with Rockefeller, he seemed a whirlwind of righteousness over the issue of law.

On Wednesday of that week, Stokely Carmichael came to Baltimore, and though he did not do much but meet with friends in a bar, Lally's intelligence report went to Agnew; this was another thing to be used in the address. On Thursday the Bowie crisis came to a head. About 250 students marched on the statehouse and asked to see the governor. He replied, through intermediaries, that they were not on his calendar for that day; if they wanted to see him, they would have to make an appointment. The students sat down. When closing time (five o'clock) came at the statehouse, Colonel Lally, who had been standing by, moved the students down the steps, out of the building, into police vans: 227 were arrested in the next hour. Then Lally's men took to their cars, under orders from Agnew to close the school. While they were on the way, news came over their radios: Martin Luther King had just stepped out on a balcony, joked with friends in a car below, and had his jaw blown off. This gave extra urgency to Lally's mission: he must close the campus down before the imprisoned students could return, out on bail. Troops fanned out through dormitories and other buildings, ordering students to pack their things and leave. Some had no transportation, no money, no place to go at the moment. They were put on buses, or given passes to remain one night. The campus did not erupt.

But Baltimore did. The shudder moving out from Memphis put Baltimore in flames by Saturday. Sunday morning, federal troops moved in to supplement the National Guard. Dr. Ware suggested various moves to Agnew's aides, moves meant to cool things off: that he attend Dr. King's funeral (the governor, he found, had not even sent a message of condolence to Mrs. King—it was belatedly dispatched after his inquiry); that he meet with leaders in a private way to rebuild the community; that he go to the ghetto himself to show concern. But Agnew kept to his original plan, to confront moderates with their great crime, that meeting with militants from their own community back on March 24. Nothing had shaken that resolution in the interval—not Bowie, not King's death, not the Baltimore riots. Meanwhile, the moderates who had been chosen for excoriation were out on the streets, risking their lives to restore peace in the ghetto.

The incredible meeting took place on April 11, one week to the day after King had been shot, two days after his funeral. Some of the leaders summoned to the State Office Building grumbled that the governor never came to them, they were always summoned to him. But this time they agreed, once more, to come. The city was jittery, on the edge of violence, only partially recovered. They felt they owed it to their people to make every effort at restored peace; and surely that was why the governor had called them together. After they filed in, Charles Bressler, no friend of theirs since the Bowie incident, spoke in the interval before the governor's appearance. Parren Mitchell, head of the city's poverty program, told me, "Charlie gave us a little talk on how his people had worked their way up in the world by industry and thrift. I didn't think we needed that lesson in the history of minorities." Senator Clarence Mitchell, whose criticism of SNCC's Bob Moore had started the whole chain of events, says, "Bressler's speech about 'all *his* father wanted was a little place to open a business' irritated us before the governor ever arrived. We were ready to walk out then."

Upstairs, Agnew was still consulting with his experts on racial matters—Colonel Lally, Commissioner Pomerleau of the Baltimore city police, and General Gelston of the National Guard. Herb Thompson, Agnew's press secretary, searched out Dr. Ware, who was supposed to be the expert on black affairs, and said, "We'll have a few minutes with the governor before we go down." But by the time they entered, Agnew was ready to go. He said, "Gil, you won't like it," as Thompson handed Ware a copy of the statement, so long gestated. It was the first Ware knew of any prepared text. (The text had gone out to the press several hours before; some newsmen, who knew Agnew well enough to risk it, called and begged him not to let them print the statement.) Agnew entered the meeting room with his police and military escort. The TV cameras were there, the newsmen with their copies of the text. Senator Verda Welcome told me, "We did not know the cameras would be there, turning this into a show. We thought it was meant as a meeting of reconciliation, a time of planning for peace." Bressler, Agnew, Pomerleau, Gelston, and Lally took their seats at the dais. Gil Ware stood far away, in a corner. "There was not a black face up there," Senator Mitchell remembers. "It was like a white jury sitting in judgment on black folk."

Agnew began to read, his quiet voice playing its odd melodies, W. C. Fields regular rise-and-fall; the scathing assault was delivered in tones of quizzical soliloquy. Was this a meeting to plan the rebuilding of the ghetto? Hardly: "I did not request your presence to bid for peace with the public dollar." Then some more material in the Charlie Bressler vein: "Look around you and you may notice that every one here is a leader—and that each leader present has *worked* his way to the top." Flattery of a tactful sort? No. By the third paragraph Agnew was rehashing Bob Moore's February charges: "Some weeks ago a reckless stranger to this city, carrying the credentials of a well-known civil-rights organization, characterized the Baltimore police as 'enemies of the black man.'" Then that damning repeated praise for Clarence Mitchell: "Some of you here, to your eternal credit, quickly condemned this demagogic proclamation." The events of March: "But when white leaders openly complimented you for your objective, courageous action, you immediately encountered a storm of censure from parts of the Negro community . . . *And you ran.*" They did not run now, they walked; others had slipped out earlier, now the mass of the audience—eighty out of the hundred—left in stunned rage. "Nobody calls me a coward," Parren Mitchell says of that moment. "I had gone forty-eight hours without sleep, walking streets at war, trying to calm them."

Agnew, during the exodus, was describing the March 24 meeting: "You met in secret with that demagogue [Bob Moore] and others like him—and you agreed, according to published reports that have not been denied [i.e., Steve

Lynton's article in the *Sun*, which Agnew waved], that you would not openly criticize any black spokesman, regardless of the content of his remarks." (This goes far beyond what Lynton knew or wrote of the meeting.)

Agnew finally did talk about the riot, and offered this weird analysis of its cause: "The looting and rioting which has engulfed our city during the past several days did not occur by chance. It is no mere coincidence that a national disciple of violence, Mr. Stokely Carmichael, was observed meeting with local black-power advocates and known criminals in Baltimore on April 3, 1968, three days before the Baltimore riots began." But if Carmichael caused the rioting, he must have been in league with the man who shot King in the interval between that visit to the bar and the outbreak of arson on Saturday. The thing makes no sense. Agnew was determined to read his indictment of Moore and Carmichael, no matter what. If Baltimore had been half destroyed by an atomic bomb on April 1, he would still denounce the moderates for that March 24 meeting. But though the riot did not deflect him from his course, it gave his statement more nationwide publicity than he had hoped for. That reckless incredible statement of April 11 made Agnew Vice-President. (Coolidge, too, had risen to national prominence as the result of his part in a riot, the Boston police strike of 1919.)

All Baltimore—not only its blacks—staggered under Agnew's denunciation. Repeated attempts to bring him to a more conciliatory line were made in vain. Even the most moderate black leaders could not defend him now. He admitted he thought some of the leaders would walk out, but not so many. Asked, "What if everybody had walked out?" he answered, "I would simply"—simply!—"have been faced with a situation where I would have to find other Negro leaders." (From the moon?) At the conference when the few blacks who stayed rose and argued with him, he said, "Don't you know I'm committing political suicide when I sit here and do this?" If so, it was done with a peculiar relish: from that day forward, his "tough" statements—on Cadillacs in Resurrection City, on the failings of the Kerner Report, on shooting looters—were volunteered often and readily, in response to no obvious local need. His staff boasted of the favorable mail his statement brought in from all over the nation.

More important, the friendship with Nixon was ripening

in private. It had obviously passed through several stages when, just after the Southern Governors' Conference in June, Agnew disappeared from sight: Maryland newsmen thought he had gone back to Annapolis, until a *Newsweek* reporter saw him leaving Nixon's New York apartment. Shortly after, Nixon had dinner at the governor's mansion along with Louise Gore and Agnew's principal backers. These backers had meanwhile set up a fund for out-of-state travel and political activities. Agnew was giving ambitious speeches, addressing problems like the Vietnamese war. A year before the Miami convention, Baltimore political observers had supposed he was maneuvering toward the vice-presidency under Rockefeller; it seems clear now that all he did in late March was shift smoothly from one horse to another. In a New York speech delivered in July, which sounds like a first draft of the campaign speech he would give throughout the fall, he reduced all questions about law and warfare to one level of meaninglessness—a relativistic ploy, one would think; but he offered it as an *attack* on relativism (no wonder he did not risk that senior year in college): "One of the prime contributors to our age of anxiety is the insidious relativism that has crept into our thinking. Relativism is epitomized by the agonizing of a police officer who couldn't bring himself to kill a looter over a pair of shoes, or the youngster contemplating whether he will serve as a soldier in what he considers an unjust war. But where does this line of reasoning end? . . . What war is ultimately totally just?"

It had all fallen in line for him—King's death, riot, Poor People's Campaign. After Miami, he would make an issue of student revolt, the Democratic Convention in Chicago, the SDS in Maryland, the hecklers who greeted him at Towson State College. Law and order, Negroes and students—they helped the "conservative" Agnew just as Mahoney's racism had helped the "liberal" one. And all the while he was neither. Neither—either. Something more elemental. Darling of the gods, of course; yet taking his openings. Moving with an instinct for success.

There is a difference between ambition and opportunism. Leisurely "Ted" is not driven by Nixon's demons. He does not knock himself out; he does not even do his homework. But he is opportunistic—not cynically so; when lucky breaks come, one takes them, grateful. Man's function is to reap the fruits of our beneficent system. How foolish of "the kids" not to understand this. As he told them in the campaign: "You may give us your symptoms; we will make the diagnosis and we, the Establishment, will implement the cure." It is a message he did not try to take to Miami's blacks.

8. The Non-Succeeders

"A decent provision for the poor is the true test of civilization."

—Samuel Johnson

THERE WAS some deep athletic chatter behind me, on the plane. But it was not till we passed through the exit nozzle and into the airport that I recognized the man who had been speaking, now doubled nearly in half: Wilt Chamberlain. Celebrities were landing in Miami on every plane; but no one drew as much attention as Chamberlain, striding up one of the airport's octopus arms, ducking rhythmically at each beam. He rocked along at what is, for him, a very easy pace—he must let friends and attendants keep up. His head floats, as on a pole, almost dead in its resolute ignorance of the wake he forms, crowds pluming and combing, behind him, out toward either wall, where all eyes turn back, and up.

I knew he was working for Nixon; as we waited for our luggage, I asked what duties he would have in Miami. "Whatever they want me to do." The strain of talking straight up toward the ceiling is accentuated when he talks back—the ridged roof of his mouth hangs over one like a groined Gothic crypt. His answers are short and noncommittal; he scans the horizon for a sight of other giants, to release him from this pygmy conversation. "Hey, Wilt!" The push of autograph hunters is on. "Hey, Lew!" one man calls, working his scrap of paper in through others.

At last Chamberlain looks down: "What?" The man, un-abashed, flaps away: "Aren't you Lew?—Lew Alcindor?" He takes the paper, "No, I'm Bill—Bill Russell," and scribbles his name illegibly.

Over in Miami, a group called Vote Power has scheduled a meeting in the Liberty City ghetto, with a promise that Wilt Chamberlain and Ralph Abernathy will come over from Miami Beach. One of the many resem-blances between radical students and militant blacks is the belief that their celebrities are on twenty-four-hour call. Thus, if "stars" are going to be anywhere in the vicinity, one can announce their attendance to support the cause. Any failure to appear is explicable on the assumption that a more urgent call came at the last minute. Eventually, one learns to be surprised if any of the names announced show up.

It would be doubly surprising if Chamberlain went to Liberty City. He is not so much a Negro, or a Black, as a Giant. His fellows, insofar as he has any, are measured by their footage, not pigmentation. And as a politician he is mainly a businessman. His last endorsement of a candidate —Democrat Milton Shaap in Pennsylvania—had been a straight cash deal, as an entrepreneurial athlete praises a shaving cream. Waiting by the conical luggage-carousel, I asked him if other black support was being given to Nix-on. "Sure." By anyone well-known? "Maybe not to *you*." It was the perfect answer, his "Bill—Bill Russell" to my impertinence.

The other visible Negro in the Nixon camp was one of those old men whose deep black color has flecks of gray in it, flint silver-grained. He wore a solemn high hat, formal tie, and frock coat—half a preacher. But the other half—ribboned parasol, cloak of pinned-on silk strips, ripply fling-pants—was minstrel. He led a band of anachronistic "darkies" that played at the Nixon recep-tions. "Come up and meet Wilt Chamberlain in the Nixon hospitality suite," signs said. I thought I would give it an-other try. There he was, in the standard hotel room, grasshopper in a matchbox, people threading in and out through his limbs, which he lifted and placed, shifted and stirred, with great care. He was greeting people at the door, his head well above its lintel. When my turn came, my head disappeared as by amputation. He could have wrapped his hand around my shoulders. In a few minutes, there was a lull at the door, and I asked him if Nixon had anything to offer blacks beyond "black capitalism." He looked down; said nothing; his expression, though, told me "Bill—Bill Russell"; he turned to shake some other insect-hands.

A bright young man from Chamberlain's entourage moved about, offering cocktail peanuts and singing Wilt's praises. "Does he consider talk about politics inappropriate at a political convention?" I asked. "He does not talk about it much," he admitted. "But when he does, he's very knowledgeable." We talk a little politics ourselves; but not much. This man is an entrepreneur too, with several rock groups touring the country. Nixon has found some black capitalists.

The Republican Minorities Group, under its able leader Clarence Townes, kept wondering how to find black faces on the Beach—a minority to represent. Monday they held a reception—all the convention's black delegates (26), guests, and visiting celebrities. A witty black girl on Townes's staff told me how she had lived the last few days on the phone, trying to round up a crowd. Her efforts paid off. There were perhaps 300 people in the ballroom when she passed me through the guards. One group spun dream-lazily about its private maypole, Wilt. Another chatted with Senator Brooke. I walked around, one of the few white faces; listened to a young boy's oration —his hand splashed bits of highball with each gesture. He was letting a friend know that only brothers have soul, right, brother? I knew these comments were not aimed at me; his glassy eyes had not taken me in. Besides, he was giving the same spiel when I heard him from a distance, and each time I swerved past him. "Who's he?" I asked the girl. "Some kid with the SCLC. He's been here all day, waiting for his mule wagon, he says. He's only thirteen, but he's been downing our liquor as if it were water."

Clarence Townes finally went to the stage, said a few words, introduced celebrites (*he* delivers on his promises). He asked Senator Brooke for a brief speech. Brooke, up on the platform, saw Chamberlain for the first time, towering across the room, and called him over. They shook hands, eye to eye, Wilt on the floor and Brooke on the stage. Then the senator asked him to come up beside him. It was a mistake. Brooke shrank abruptly (everyone looks a little silly and toylike next to Wilt—Nixon avoided being photographed with him).

The word spread, at last, that the mule train had arrived. The party began to break up. By the time I got outside, the thirteen-year-old boy was on the wagon leading a standard litany: "I *am* a *man.*" Townes's aide groaned, "Oh, no! He'll never stop now." Traffic cops were getting restless. The mule train had blocked the Fontainebleau drive; there were cars jammed and honking all up the ramp and out onto Collins Avenue. The girl on Townes's staff went up to coveralled Hosea Williams, who was handling the mules for Abernathy. "Hosea, get that kid off of there; we don't want trouble before the mules even get started." "Yeah, just a minute. I'll get him down," he said with a scowl. Meanwhile, others looked fondly on the boy's effusion. Jimmy Breslin came out of the hotel just then and, as he wrote in his next day's column, was profoundly stirred by this litany. Deep calls to deep. "Hey, we've got to move this," a nervous cop finally told Hosea. "You want help with the traffic? Where you going?" "To the convention. How long will that take us?" "You better get started if you want to make it before dark." "Okay. Which way is it?" Williams looked impartially up and down Collins Avenue.

Wednesday, nomination night at Convention Hall, I saw a large group bumping grim-faced out toward the street— Ralph Abernathy in its midst, security men talking urgently sideways toward him but looking straight ahead. I thought he was being expelled, and knew there would be trouble then. But when I grabbed his press secretary out of the group, he said there was a riot in Miami and Ralph had been asked to help control it. After the quick march to the doors, there was indecisive milling, then the party turned and moved back, just as rapidly, to the press booths. Abernathy was taken into the NBC floor studio to make a televised appeal for calm. Rockefeller's name was being put in nomination on the TV monitor. A makeup girl dabbed at Abernathy's troubled face. At last another run is made for the doors, where cars are waiting. As the SCLC staff crowds into one car, I catch Hosea's arm and ask, "Where are you going?" "I don't know," he answers; "the hotel."

Unlikely, but they might have been asked to stand by there, since Abernathy is staying in Miami proper, at the

Four Ambassadors. I hunt up a cab—its radio is telling drivers to stay on the Beach; Miami is ablaze. "What nonsense," the cabbie says, snaps his meter-lever, and heads for the causeway. Whenever the ghetto's regular sigh is raised to a wail, Miami's whites panic. At the Four Ambassadors, I check Abernathy's suites. No one there. Back down, new cab, to the police station. A wry relaxed officer, Lieutenant Golden, gives out the official version. "I think we've got everything under control now." How did it start? "A Vote Power rally got out of hand." When? "Late afternoon." What started it? "No rhyme or reason."

I later hear the way things were at the outset from Milton Smith, a hefty disk jockey known affectionately to his audience on black station WAME ("Whammy") as Butterball. "I was about to finish my program at three in the afternoon, when I got a call from one of my sponsors —Samson's Market, just up the street from the Vote Power place. 'Buttuh,' he said—everyone calls me Buttuh —'there's trouble over here. They're throwing rocks. You better tell people, on the air, to stay away from the area.' I said I would do no such thing; that would only draw people. As soon as I finished, I rushed over to see what was going on." Smith has for years been a peacemaker and social worker without portfolio. He takes busloads of children on picnics every summer "to cool things off." But, as he says, "The trouble with that is, it's summer here all year around. That's what our politicians don't understand." When Smith got to the Vote Power office, he saw the mayor of Dade County up on a car, talking to a restive crowd through his bullhorn. "I took one look, and I knew. I went over and said, 'Chuck, you gotta get out of here.'" He knows Mayor Hall from his annual visit to Liberty City with promises of summer games for children —"and then I don't see him until *next* summer." The mayor tried to pull Butterball onto the car with him. "He figured they wouldn't shoot him with me standing beside him. I told him, 'I'm just as scared as you are. Let's get *out* of here.'" But as soon as he put Mayor Hall in his car, Buttuh went through the crowd doing his jolly disk-jockey routine, trying to break things up. "But what can you do?" he said to me. "These are kids who can't even go to the picture show unless they steal the money. Some can't even buy lunch at school unless they steal. They're out on the street all day, all year around, with no place to go. When I take them to the Seaquarium or someplace in the summer, it is the first time they have ever been outside their own neighborhood." (The Seaquarium, starring Flipper, is across the MacArthur Causeway that leads to Key Biscayne.) I asked Buttuh if he thought the convention had anything to do with the riot. (A report prepared for the President's violence commission would decide it had not.) "Well, the convention didn't exactly *cause* the trouble. Conditions caused that, and they're always here. It could start right now, while I'm talking to you. It could start any minute; the conditions never change. But when all that power was right across the Bay, well, no wonder they wanted to show people how we live."

My second cabdriver, who had been leery of venturing near Liberty City, was soothed by the calm lieutenant we met in the station; he took some flying passes at Liberty City along the North-South Expressway. Intermittently, a full moon shone.

> Moon over Miami,
> Shine on as we begin
> A dream or two . . .

There were no signs of fires, no reports of guns, so the driver dipped down onto city streets, and we followed the path of wreckage in toward the center of things—a weight machine thrown through a store window, the cash register wrestled to the floor; the window of a wig shop broken and stripped, ladies' heads bowled here and there in bald disgrace. As we got closer to Sixty-second Street, police cars were thickening, in clumps. Finally we reached a point where our car had to stop. I told the cabdriver I would walk a little way in and return. But at each corner police said Abernathy was just a block away; and soon I was at the Vote Power office, where all of it started. Across the street, in the drive of a gas station, Claude Kirk was on an improvised platform trying to make himself heard: "If you want to hear me, you've got to listen. Now so far I've been mighty quiet, and I've been listening, haven't I?" "You didn't have no choice." Which was the plain truth. The kids gathered on this corner are not in a listening mood. They jostle the few newsmen, cup their hands over TV lenses; shout obscenities at Kirk, drown him out (he has no bullhorn). The police, who are out in the street near their cars, stand cursing the governor for calling this crowd together after they spent hours dispersing it. Mayor Hall is sandwiched between Kirk and Abernathy, all three kneaded back and forth on the narrow box. Pudgy ineffectual Ralph loses the shoving contest, ducks down, almost falls. Hosea Williams is holding him up there.

Kirk keeps trying to charm them. "What do you want?" "Jobs." "I'm trying . . ." "We don't want your garbage jobs. I need a job tomorrow morning to pay the rent." "Come into my office tomorrow morning." "Give me twenty-five dollars to pay my rent and then I can get down there to you." By this time Buttuh is on the scene. "Twenty-five dollars! That kid didn't want a job," he told me later. "He was a hood. He was just trying to con the Governor." Kirk does not know who is who in the crowd. Unlike Lindsay, he has walked into a ghetto where he has no intelligence network, no friendly leaders he keeps in touch with day by day. He is at the mercy of the punks. "I don't want none of your garbage jobs. I could do what this cat is doing"—the kid turns to a TV cameraman sweating in his complex harness.

Buttuh had come to get Kirk off the street. "The Governor was just collecting all the rough kids out for trouble, and giving them an excuse to assemble. I went up to Ralph" (the two men's wives went to school together) "and told him they had to get this thing off the street. I offered to lead them down to Bernie Dyer's place." Dyer runs the Liberty City Community Council, a job and housing agency financed by the Christian Community Service Agency. He is considered "too militant" by Southern politicians and police; but they need him now. Kirk is finally pulled off the platform and shoved toward the LCCC building, three blocks away. Kirk, the great hugger, pins a succession of youngsters to him, almost cooing in their ears—which is good strategy. They are buffers in the ugly crowd. His bodyguards are mumbling to each other, and one starts slapping his pants desperately, "Those bastards dropped a lighted cigarette in my pants." Young kids bump up against me, flipping a wrist toward the keys and coins in my pockets. "You got lots of money. Why don't you donate it to us poor people," they grin with cool effrontery. When I feel a warm tickle at my side, I tear off my suit coat—the plastic press badge to Nixon headquarters is blazing away. One of those dropped cigarettes.

At the LCCC building, not everyone can get inside; as I try to squeeze through, boys at the door pat up and down for weapons, everyone is being frisked—the bodyguards, with their guns, get turned aside. So, after the first gantlet is run, do I. No whites allowed, except Kirk and Hall. Dyer later told me what happened inside.

Bernard Dyer is a natty little man who got his training as a community organizer in Harlem's HARYOU-ACT program. He came to Miami on an OEO program, but resigned to run the LCCC. He too had been out on the streets, trying to protect Stephen Clark, Mayor of the city of Miami. Now, when Buttuh brought Kirk, Abernathy, and Dade County Mayor Chuck Hall inside, a shouting match filled the storeroom of this converted storefront building. The room was jammed full (about 125 people), and the governor had trouble being heard. "But he wasn't bad," Dyer admits. "He stood his ground, and won some points. Then Chuck Hall got up and sounded blacker than the black. Man, to hear him, you'd have thought he was ready to burn down the city himself. He diagnosed, prognosed, prescribed, and cured all our ills." Hall blends with the group around him. Next day, among police, he would ask for a club and gun to help them in their work. I asked if Abernathy did anything to bring order to the meeting. "No, but Hosea was a great help. He took charge of writing our list of grievances." Dyer gives me the Outline for Change drawn up during that hectic night —a careful document asking for changes in the model cities program, the job market, housing, and economic opportunity programs.

Meanwhile, outside the Council office, things were getting ugly. Those blacks who could not get in were fuming at the door, threatening police who had also been excluded, white bodyguards, and newsmen. Two doors away, a liquor store had been broken into, but most of its stock was still there. One policeman stood guard over it, and kids made various passes at him, throwing things through the window. Finally Buttuh suggested he just move away and surrender the place. The policeman did—no one wanted to start a pitched battle outside, with the governor and mayor virtual hostages inside. I heard the bodyguards muttering to each other about the danger to Kirk if fire should break out—the storeroom was down a narrow passage. Getting out the front would be almost impossible. There might be a back door, but no white man was going to go around behind, in the dark, to explore. Just then, a cherry bomb was thrown from the house next door to the LCCC Hall. The police shot tear gas onto the building's balcony, and droves of squad cars turned into the street (they had been waiting nearby). A shower of bottles came out of windows, cops ducking through the cars that choked the street. Several cops now put on gas masks and charged apartments in the building where the cherry bomb was thrown. Down the street, we heard more reports—firecrackers, pistols, cherry bombs? No one knew for sure. They were back in the direction where I left my cab. I had the man's name (from our trip inside the police station together) and company (Checker); I presumed he would clear out when he heard explosions. I was certainly not going to walk the long blocks back toward him.

Police came out of the apartment building, their faces full of sooty rubber crumbles, rubbing their eyes—the masks are almost as bad as gas. "I thought I'd get me one," a young fellow (half-Jolsonized with "blackface") muttered. "I'd like to get me some tonight," another answered, fingering a large pepper-fog machine that lays down blankets of gas. Talk among the police was straight from a World War II movie—all those dirty Japs. The police might have been following the order of a Florida governor (Robert R. Reid) in 1839: "We are waging a war with beasts of prey; the tactics that belong to civilized nations are but shackles and fetters in its prosecution; we must fight fire with fire; the white man must in a great measure adopt the mode of warfare pursued by the red man, and we can only hope for success by continually harassing and pursuing the enemy." Continual pursuit and harassment—partly out of hate, partly out of fear, partly to avoid running away; wisecracks where everyone is frightened, and laughter covers a shaky voice. There were, after all, hundreds of families sitting home that night with the thought—one they live with constantly—that the man of the house might be guarding a liquor store against a mob, or charging into a dark apartment.

Yet other hundreds, inside these low lime-colored houses, do not even know how to cry for help. The police who should protect them fear them, think each summons may lead to an ambush. Miami's blacks, knowing this, long ago despaired of any visit from police but the hostile or accidental kind—a dash into apartments near those with the bombs and bottles, a retaliatory (frightened) canister or club or bullet. This is the system black men live with, and Agnew asks them to praise.

It was after midnight now; TV cars had come and gone taking film to studios. One pulled up and the driver said, "Did one of you guys leave a cab back there about eight blocks or so?" I asked for his name, and found it was my trusty Checker man, sending in his bill—forty-eight dollars. It was getting to be an expensive evening—one suit lost, and now fifty dollars (all I had in my wallet) sent out to the cabbie. I would have to bum a ride with a press car to get back to Miami Beach.

Finally Kirk and Abernathy came out. Reporters asked where Kirk was going—back to the Beach? He would not say. "Will you drive slow enough for us to follow?" "Sure," he answered, and his car took off like a rocket. The TV station wagon I was in went to Manor Park, the staging area for police operations in Liberty City. When we arrived there, the moon was free again of clouds, the park very peaceful. At intervals police cars brought more prisoners; they were loaded in a van, which drove off when it reached capacity. As each TV station checked in, a circle of light was formed and Mayor Clark stood there to reassure his city. After which, darkness so sudden the moon seemed gone. Police trucks came with coffee (largely ignored), and ice water (on which there was a run—these cops had not had water for hours in the hot Miami night). Clark stood under the trees chatting with his vice-mayor, a man named Christie, while the car radio brought news from Convention Hall. (Kirk was back there now, wearing a Nixon streamer and a chastened smile.) "I wish it would end," Mayor Clark said, "so we can get rid of these outsiders, and get back to normal." "Wisconsin should give it to Nixon," a newsman guessed—he was checking his delegate count by flashlight. "That will make Knowles happy," another voice said. "Who's he?"

Clark asked. A few minutes later, Wisconsin did it. In the dark, cicadas were clicking for Dick.

> A dream or two
> That may come true
> When the tide comes in.

9. Making It

> "First we see him as a small boy, light of foot, fish-
> ing for bullheads in the Rat River of Vermont . . .
> Then he leaves for the big city to make his fortune.
> All this is in the honorable tradition of his country
> and its people, and he has the right to expect certain
> rewards."
>
> —Nathanael West, A Cool Million

THURSDAY NIGHT, Nixon came to Convention Hall—its interior seen through dazzles, veils woven by the rows on rows of lights. He was proud of his acceptance speech. It would (carefully) reveal his inner self. He came to make the only moral claim that mattered to this audience. To tell them he had made it. *"You can see why I believe so deeply in the American dream."* He had risen, political-ly, from the dead. And he had done it by the route these men respected—by making money. Nixon had been a can-didate before, and a politician always; but only after his 1962 defeat did he become a wealthy man. The Checkers speech was truthful, back in 1952—he was poor; he was young, starting out, working hard to succeed. But then there had been failure, political defeat. And through it all he had not earned the money to be independent. Only when he became a Wall Street lawyer, with $200,000 a year from his practice, and with Bebe Rebozo to help him invest in Florida land, could he look his fellow Re-publicans straight in the eye at last. A campaign coordina-tor who worked with Nixon through the years put it this way: "Dick could not have made it to first base in nineteen sixty-eight without a substantial personal income. Republicans, especially those who finance the party, respect only one thing, success, and they have only one way of measuring success, money. Dick never had any money before now. He could not talk to these people as an equal, even when he was Vice-President. The thing that would have killed him with them was any suspicion that he simply needed a job. Now they knew he'd be giving up a damn good job, and good money."

Nixon had to command great sums of money in 1968; he could afford nothing but the best. After being a loser for years, he needed confidence, an organization, and cash. It was all or nothing for him. He could only run for one office now, for President—and this was his last chance. He was beaten before he began if he aimed at anything less: Americans voted into the White House the proverbial candidate who could not be elected dogcatcher. Old Nixon was a failure, a loser?—then the new one would establish his base as a successful lawyer, partner in a Wall Street firm; plead a case before the Supreme Court; build his campaign organization out from the partners and members and offices of that firm. It was impossible to sell the man who could not sell a used car?—then Wall Street would go to Madison Avenue's largest advertising firm, to Harry Treleaven of the J. Walter Thompson agency, who, with law partner Len Garment, took charge of consumer-packaging the candidate. Nixon was no good on TV?—then Madison Avenue would go directly to CBS, to Frank Shakespeare, who left a division presidency with that network to put Nixon, favorably, back on all networks. Nixon cannot relax, delegate authority, conserve and pace himself?—then New York would go to California, to the vast personnel of J. Walter Thompson's Western branch. To crew-cut Bob Haldeman, who scheduled the candidate to an austere enforced leisure. To dark slow Ron Ziegler, from the firm's Disneyland account, who relayed things to the press without a touch of personal interpretation. To waxen solicitous Dwight Chapin, who squeezed the candidate in and out of crowds. To bustling advance men who gave Nixon structured rallies the way rent-a-party firms now package celebrations for children. Nixon is a gut-fighter who takes naturally to the low road?—then Herb Klein and John Mitchell would answer the personal attacks on their candidate; and Spiro Agnew would play "old Nixon" to the new Nixon's studied attempt at playing Ike. And it all had worked, smoothly, expensively, on time.

Nixon need no longer be ashamed as he stood before the gladsacks in Miami, accepting their nomination. He too was a go-getter, a deserver, one who had made it. So true is this that he unconsciously echoed Mark Twain's satirical picture of the American go-getter type, Senator Abner Dilworthy, the promoter of Stone's Landing. Nixon's moment of self-revelation was far more revealing than he thought.

He built toward his great oratorical moment with an anaphoric refrain that aped Dr. King's "I have a dream . . ." Nixon described the America of 1976, the two-hundredth anniversary of the American Revolution: *"I see a day when Americans are once again proud . . . I see a day when every child in this land . . . I see a day when life in rural America attracts . . . I see a day when we can look back on massive breakthroughs . . . I see a day when our senior citizens and millions of others can plan for the future . . . I see a day when we will have again freedom from fear . . . I see a day when our nation is at peace."*

And then: *"I see the face of a child . . ."* A child poor and neglected, not given a chance. But he can be given a chance, and the pledge of this is the last vision of all: *"I see another child tonight. He hears the train go by at night and he dreams of faraway places where he'd like to go. It seems like an impossible dream."* (The last phrase, eructated by baritones on every radio, was from a song that would be played at his daughter Julie's wedding. It was the song in the Broadway show, *Man of La Mancha,* and Nixon hoped it would catch on as a *Camelot* for his regime, the reign of one whose resurrection seemed improbable as any dream.)

Senator Dilworthy, too, saw a child, as he spoke to a class at Sunday school: "Now my dear little friends, sit up straight and pretty—there, that's it—and give me your attention and let me tell you about a poor little Sunday School scholar I once knew. He lived in the far west, and his parents were poor. They could not give him a costly education, but they were good and wise and they sent him to the Sunday School." Or, as Nixon put it:

"He is helped on his journey through life. A father who had to go to work before he finished the sixth grade sacrificed everything he had so that his sons could go to college."

Senator Dilworthy continued, "He loved the Sunday School. I hope you love your Sunday School—ah, I see by your faces that you do! That is right." Nixon is there with him, tear for tear: *"A gentle Quaker mother, with a passionate concern for peace, quietly wept when he went to war but she understood why he had to go."*

"Well, this poor little boy was always in his place when the bell rang, and he always knew his lesson; for his teachers wanted him to learn and he loved his teachers dearly. Always love your teachers, my children, for they love you more than you can know, now." And, sure enough: *"A great teacher, a remarkable football coach, an inspirational minister encouraged him on his way."*

"So this poor little boy grew up to be a man, and had to go out in the world, and had to leave home and friends to earn his living." *"A courageous wife and loyal children stood by him in victory and also defeat."*

"And by and by the people made him governor—and he said it was all owing to the Sunday School. After a while the people elected him a Representative to the Congress of the United States, and he grew very famous." *"And in his chosen profession of politics, first there were scores, then hundreds, then thousands, and finally millions who worked for his success."*

"Well, at last, what do you think happened? Why the people gave him a towering, illustrious position, a grand, imposing position. And what do you think it was? What should you say it was, children? It was Senator of the United States! That poor little boy that loved his Sunday School became that man. That man stands before you! All that he is, he owes to the Sunday School." And, in a husky voice, Nixon reached the same climax: *"Tonight he stands before you—nominated for President of the United States of America!"*

Nixon's success was not offered in Miami as a theme for mere self-congratulation. It was a pledge to others, a pledge that he would not rob them of the fruits of their success: *"You can see why I believe so deeply in the American dream. For most of us the American Revolution has been won; the American dream has come true."*

For *most* of us—for the silent *majority*. A New Deal stress on the equal starting line was not for this affluent crowd. The majority feels it is out on the racetrack now, straining toward the prizes. It does not want the noisy minority to upset things, cause trouble, confiscate their money earned and saved. To the very end Nixon follows Clif White's 1964 strategy, basing it on the same concept, Michael Bernstein's concept of "the Forgotten American."

Here was Bernstein, writing the Goldwater speech: "These millions are the silent Americans who, thus isolated, cannot find voice against the mammoth organizations which mercilessly pressure their own membership, the Congress, and society as a whole for objectives which these silent ones do not want." And Nixon: *"It is the quiet voice in the tumult and the shouting."* Bernstein: "They thereby have become the Forgotten Americans despite the fact that they constitute the majority of our people." Nixon: *"It is the voice of the great majority of Americans, the forgotten Americans."* Bernstein: "The Republican Party in this era in which so many pressure groups are seeking to dominate the total man is the vehicle and voice for the dragooned and ignored individual." Nixon: *"The non-shouters, the non-demonstrators . . . they work, and they save, and they pay their taxes . . . America is in trouble today not because her people have failed but because her leaders have failed."*

Bernstein also knew the importance of law and order to the forgotten American: "One of the firmest pillars upon which American society rests is the proposition that law and order are an absolute essential for the preservation and improvement of our democratic way of life. A profound respect for the law and an abhorrence of disorder and anarchy are deeply ingrained in the American character." Compare Nixon's Miami speech: *"Now, there is no quarrel between progress and order—because neither can exist without the other. So let us have order in America."* The national greatness is something dear to the forgotten American, who remembers when all the shouters forget it. So Bernstein: "We believe that stimulating the national pride is even more important than increasing our national prestige." And Nixon: *"It is time we started to act like a great nation around the world."*

Just after the Miami convention, Nixon issued a Labor Day statement based entirely on Bernstein's argument:

For in a time when the national focus is concentrated upon the unemployed, the impoverished and the dispossessed, the working Americans have become the forgotten Americans. In a time when the national rostrums and forums are given over to shouters and protestors and demonstrators, they have become the silent Americans. Yet they have a legitimate grievance that should be rectified and a just cause that should prevail.

Government in recent years has broken faith with the American workingman; it has violated the terms of its unwritten contract with the American people.

In the last two years the average American worker has been on a government-operated treadmill. New taxes and rising prices have more than wiped out all the pay raises he has won since 1965. The new taxes on income, requested publicly by this administration, and the hidden tax of inflation, imposed clandestinely by this administration, have together left the purchasing power of the American worker below what it was in December of 1965 . . .

Since the last presidential election, the average American worker has lost more than $1000 in his income through inflation, more than $200 in his cash savings, more than $1000 in the value of the insurance policy he purchased for his family. More than two billion dollars of the great social security trust fund, the government-held pension fund accumulated from the paychecks of workers and their employers, has disappeared in the government-generated inflation of the middle sixties.

Compare Bernstein: "Under the Democrats inflation will run rampant, the purchasing power of the American dollar will melt away like snowdrifts in the spring sun, and our hard-working and thrifty people will watch in stupefied dismay as the value of their savings, their insurance, their pension funds diminish each day, ultimately perhaps to vanish entirely."

Nixon did not invent "the Forgotten American"—neither the phrase nor the concept; but he used it perfectly. He knew that 1968 was a time when those who had *succeeded* felt somehow cheated—forgotten, unrespected, mocked. They had worked and earned, not only for money or material things, but for a spiritual goal. They had believed in the *morality* of succeeding. And now the kids, the sophisticates, the "effete snobs" were denying them that honor. Nixon came to reassure such men, to tell them *he* believed in them, he had not forgotten, he was one of them.

The day after his acceptance speech, Nixon was off the Beach by noon—over one causeway to Miami, swerve left, back onto a causeway, past Flipper, and onto Key Biscayne, three quarters of an hour drive. He did not yet have the presidential helicopter, and had not bought his own house on the Key from Senator Smathers. He would, as so often before, be relaxing on Bebe Rebozo's yellow houseboat.

On Thursday, at noon, Buttuh Smith was sitting on a powder keg. Several of the officials out on the street the day before had promised to meet community leaders that morning at the LCCC headquarters. One of these was Mayor Stephen Clark; and he did not show up. A crowd of people had gathered in and around the LCCC building, and their mood was turning nasty. Police were moving them on, preventing congestion; sparks were regularly struck, some smothered by Buttuh, some by Bernie Dyer. At one point, Dyer went outside the headquarters, where kids and cops were skirmishing, and cops surrounded him; one said, "I've been wanting to get you, you sonovabitch, ever since you were on the Alan Courtney show" (Courtney has a Right-Wing talk show). "If you try to get out, you'll have to push your way through, and then I can get you." Perhaps it was only intimidation; at any rate, after a war of nerves, some counterintimidation came seeping out of the storefront, and the cops gave Bernie up.

Buttuh told me: "When Clark didn't show, I went over to a police car and had them radio a message to him. If he broke his promise now, there'd be hell to pay. After a while, a cop came over to me and said they had talked to him—he hadn't been able to get away yet, but he'd be here soon. So I kept telling people, 'Just wait. He'll be here by eleven o'clock, by eleven-thirty, by twelve o'clock.' But he never came. Later he told me the police would not let him through their line, but hell, he's supposed to be the policemen's *boss*."

Things were bad by eleven-thirty. Some white leaders had showed up for the announced meeting at the hall;

but the disappointed crowd outside said it would not let them leave until the mayor came. Dyer, inside, was worried about the hostages he found on his hands—seventeen concerned whites, clergy and minor officials. "I couldn't send them out front; they'd get killed. We had only one car in the back, so we had to make three trips, to take them away, crouching on the floor so they could not be seen."

"Things were awful bad," Buttuh said of his post outside the front door. "Then the armored car came, puffing gas out. I was moving kids along, and I shouted to a cop I had been talking with earlier, 'Don't gas them, they're leaving.' He turned his nozzle right in my face and let me have it. That did it. I went home. The next time, I'll listen to my wife and not go out. It does no good—no, I don't mean that. I guess I'd have to go. You can't blame these kids. And somebody has to help them."

So Buttuh on Thursday. Nixon on Thursday: *"Tonight I see a child . . . He awakens to a living nightmare of poverty, neglect and despair."* Nixon did not mention the "trouble" across the Bay in his acceptance speech—though three blacks had died of police gunfire, and many others had been wounded, by the time he rose to speak. Some people remained forgotten in his speech on Forgotten Americans.

"Are we forgotten?" Buttuh answered me. "You bet we are. This is a city with one-third blacks, and one-third Cubans. The Cubans get all kinds of federal aid, scholarships at the schools, jobs, and facilities. I don't mean skilled jobs. I mean any jobs—our jobs. I'm in show business, and when I go over to see an act on Miami Beach, I don't find any black doormen or waiters there. The jobs have been so taken over by Cubans that Spanish is required to get work in lots of places, so you can communicate with the rest of the help." Bebe Rebozo, Cuban born, who worked his way up from chauffeur to millionaire, has a Small Business Administration loan to develop a shopping center for Cuban businessmen. The loan, obtained when Rebozo's high school classmate, George Smathers, was chairman of the Senate's Small Business Committee, gives Rebozo a federal guarantee that rents will be paid for twenty years.

"We've got nothing against the Cubans," Buttuh says. "But we were here first. That doesn't mean we should be favored. But at least we should be given an equal chance. There are all kinds of Spanish newscasts on radio and TV here; yet not one of the three TV stations has a black announcer in the studio—and only one has a black broadcaster out on the street crews" (to get cameras into the ghetto). "We are just not treated as part of the community by whites. Cubans who have just arrived are taken into the community right away; but we stay outside."

Nixon, arriving at Miami airport on Monday, had said the place was dear to him, and referred to his Cuban friends. He does not refer to his black friends. He claims this would be phony and condescending—yet why is it so with blacks and not with Cubans? Does he have to find a Negro Rebozo? If so, he will not do it on Key Biscayne, where only one Negro lives, the island's "garden man," with his family.

He saw a child, poor and neglected. Yet, across the Bay, his car did not swerve an inch, on its dash through Miami, so he might say a word to that child, of comfort or of hope. He scorns such "show business," yet feels no qualms about exploiting sentiment in Dilworthy's accents. One cannot forswear condescension to the crowd, give up the abasing of oneself, and still talk of one's destiny (and therefore the country's) as shaped by "a remarkable football coach." Say, at the worst, he does not feel compassion for the blacks in Liberty City. Say it would only be a campaign gimmick to address himself to them directly— as Nixon said it was a campaign gimmick for Robert Kennedy to help Dr. King in his 1960 imprisonment. Yet when has Nixon been above campaign gimmicks?

He argues that he will not bring empty words and gestures, but substantive offerings. Jobs, an equal chance, opportunity, "black capitalism." And then, presumably, when the blacks have earned their way up, like Bebe Rebozo, he will give them the kind words, the symbolic gestures, of comfort he bestows on the "forgotten" middle class of nonshouting taxpayers. His sympathy is expressed to other classes, without canceling his determination to do "substantive things" as well.

The question that keeps posing itself, in the light of Miami, is that of Nixon's humanity—and it is important not to give too facile an answer. The "old Nixon" of Herblock is as mythical as the "new Nixon" baptized by crossing the East River. He is not an inhuman ogre; there

is no doubt, really, that he—like everyone this side of
barbarity—feels sorry for those who died in the moonlit
ironies of the Miami riot. And feels sorry for those who
lived. But what inhibits his expression of this concern?
Not, obviously, any standard of reticence that applies elsewhere. Not refusal to reap private gain from tragedy—he
had campaigned for months on the ordeal of *Pueblo* cap-
tives. Why must every approach of his to the blacks be
hedged with provisos, challenge, insensible bristlings?

He usually begins his comments on the Negro with a list
of things the Negro (he is certain) does not want—welfare
payments, free housing, a handout; "government charities," as he puts it, "that feed the stomach and starve the
soul." He argues that the problem must be approached as
a spiritual one, not simply a material one. "Government
could provide health, housing, means, and clothing for all
Americans. That would not make us a great country.
What we have to remember is that this country is going
to be great in the future to the extent that individuals
have self-respect, pride and a determination to do better."

To do better. There it is. Success is God, and Peale is
its prophet. So is Billy Graham, who says: "Too many
Christians have taken a most sinful and damaging pride in
being poverty-stricken." (We could perhaps put up with
them if they were only poor, but do they have to be
proud of it?) If prayer leads to success, then failure comes
from lack of prayer. If success is a spiritual state, so is
failure. When Graham was sent to bed by a virus in 1968,
he asked one of his fellow workers, "Can you think of
anything that I've done in my life, anything at all, to
deserve these sicknesses?" Cause and effect. If the gladsacks deserve their prosperity, then blacks must deserve
their poverty. Cancel the poverty, you rob the earners of
their hard-won eminence. In that case you invert the laws
of nature, give something for nothing, make the Market unworkable.

Part THREE

THE INTELLECTUAL MARKET

(John Stuart Mill)

1. Chicago, 1968

"When vague desire is the fire in the eyes of chicks
Whose sickness is the game they play."
                                    —The Association

FROM A HOTEL WINDOW at the Republican National
Convention, one saw only a restive rather dirty edge of the
Atlantic—slide of one color across another, with tattered-
lace slaps of gray lather, toward the smelly mini-beaches.
At the Democratic Convention, windows looked out on the
green apron of Grant Park and Lake Michigan's garish
blue. The scene had the too-real brilliance of a Kodak ad
ablaze in Grand Central Station. The lakefront museums
shone massive through their clumps of trees. Sailboats
leaned tactically in and out of the gap in a long break-
water. And, on the grassy apron, a game seemed to be in
progress—bowling, but with no click as the balls hit; all
muffled, lazy movement. Boys and girls were being
bowled, rolled, lifted, dragged, in a genial mingle of people.

As I went down into this scene, its aspect changed
from county fair to gypsy rally. The people wore rags,
but rags carefully chosen. Despite festivity, there was purpose in the talk and movements. A street theater group
was demonstrating, in a barnyard parable, that support
for Gene McCarthy perpetuates the System. These actors
have a glow of celebrity; they are fresh from performance
at The Oleo Strut, pacifist coffeehouse for GIs near Fort
Hood. (Black soldiers are in the guardhouse at Fort Hood;
they would not board planes for riot service here in Chicago.)

Further into the Park, the bowling goes on—teams attack children, throw them, beat them in pantomime with clubs of air, kick, drag, and carry them to nonexistent vans. It is done with enthusiasm and good humor, by young people who were up all last night chanting in the Park, newly won by them; they enjoy their quarters as a prize of battle—while they sharpen toward the next clash. Bystanders criticize each prisoner's conduct; debate the fine points; offer alternative views. All are agreed that the thing to do when grabbed is prepare for clubbing— fall into a fetal position, knees drawn up to protect the stomach from kicks, arms held around the face. But should one put *hands* over the head? This gives the face good protection, from one's forearms; but fingers make a brittle cage, easily broken themselves and not cushioning the pig-stick's blow. Better perhaps (much sage nodding at this) to put forearms over the skull and squeeze one's elbows in over face and nose as far as possible (bystanders try it and blunder around in peek-a-boo poses).

Then there is the question of when to go limp—clearly when lifted and carried (otherwise, the beating is resumed); but what if one is dragged? Tight, fetal clump, or in a straggle of limp arms and legs? There are pros and cons, posed and contradicted, ending always with the norm that takes precedence over others—do it *your* way. It's your thing. A teen-age girl skips up, let-me-try, light and laugh-ing as the mock pigs grab and twirl her like a top (she is from the kind of family that sends cops lumbering out to find her lost tops and toys, how quaint to be manhandled by them). No ghetto kid here, with hatred of pigs in-grained all through a bitter childhood. When the police stopped seeming benevolent to her, they gave off a whiff of Keystone—as does this whole scene. All "street the-ater." She will still be half-surprised when her game be-comes reality. But now she laughs, curls up, goes limp, tossed from one boy to another.

Very jolly. And yet serious. It is amazing that clubs could swing so much so hard in the days ahead, and yet no one be killed, or even seriously maimed. Part of the answer was being acted out here, on Tuesday afternoon, in the bright sun, on the too-real green grass. Kodak shots. These were kids who knew how to be beaten. And how to joke. All glue-and-paint sparkle in the sun, a vision of the Military came parading by, toy planes his epau-lettes, toy rockets the "scrambled eggs" on his MacArthur brim. He introduces himself as General Waste-More-Land, and inveighs in parody against traitors who would draft beer rather than boys.

One of the general's friends tells me how he came, in a caravan of Volkswagen buses and cars, from California. This friend, Morris Kight, is well over thirty; but the kids see him instinctively as one of them. Though he wears the inverted-V soft military hat of Vets for Peace, he explains that he chose a life of protest long before Vietnam. "I was a hotel man and, if I do say so myself, a rather successful one—I owned seven hotels. But I dropped out ten years ago to stop the madness." What was the madness then? "Pollution of the air, the triumph of the machine; the cold war and the arming. We are in the midst of three major revolutions. First, the social one: we now realize that we cannot mistreat those of another color, or of another religion; cannot mistreat our behavioral minorities (like the youth). Second, the cybernation revolution, by which machines do mankind's work, making mankind obsolete. Third, the weapons in the hands of a small number of unqualified men." What does one do about the machines, destroy them? "No, make them work for man, not against him. Let them make it possible for man to return to the soil. Make them *clear* the air, rather than foul it." He speaks with almost curtsying deference, with a curving of fine diction, an unhurried ease. "I have a fifteen-room house in Los Angeles designed by Frank Lloyd Wright. It was run down and in a poor neighborhood, so I was able to buy it and restore it for a very small sum." Why was the price so low? "Well, it was designed for some very eccentric executives." (He says it with micawber merriment—*imagine* it, *eccentric*.)

He describes these executives with a charitable nod, as he does the men who build our weapons complex—confident, without boasting, that he is in the center, a displaced sane voice in the muddled whirl of things.

There are other "oldsters" here, not quite at ease among the young. The manager of the communist *Daily World*, for instance, Frances Gabow, moves through the park in a clump of her coevals, distrustful of the kids.

The keynote of the kids' clothing is softness. No edges. Even last year's military jackets have the padding torn out—droopy epaulettes, wilted fronts, frayed bottoms, every sag and hang eloquent: "I ain't a-marchin' any-

more." All things tend to the shaggy—thin fringes of
adolescent bead, girls' eyes in a charcoal of lashed shadow.
Even their talk is soft—diffident, blurred, shoulder-shrug-
ging, with a mutter of disruptive rhythmic fillers ("like the
war, see, y'know"). Their clothes are all of the muffling
sort—blankets, capes, serapes, shepherd's coats, hoods,
woolly sweaters, thermal underwear like tailored mattress-
es. These are "soft sculptures" by Claes Oldenburg. Velvet,
velour, fur—on the head, Russian astrakhans, soft Indian
bead-bands, Arab turbans, Foreign Legion veils. Prophetic
bandages. The shoes are moccasins, soft boots, sandals
worn to a velvet pliancy—Paul Krassner, of *The Realist*,
wears shoes made of some carpet-stuff that looks like grass.
Better even than moccasins are bare feet. Bell-bottom
pants are mandatory for the girls, worn with light sweaters.
No bras, of course. No edges.

The hair is worn in two styles—the wavering divided
waterfall, or Elsa Lanchester's electrocuted look. Beards
are as full as they will grow—never trimmed. The gentle,
supple flow is prized when it comes naturally. ("Like J.C."
one boy nudges another as a male madonna-face goes by
under a helmet.) Hair is a sacrament of the real. Some
girls affect unshaven legs and armpits. They make a cult
of candor, sure that reality, under its paint, is grimy,
grubby—the nitty-gritty. They are willing, their chosen
symbols say, to face this reality, even in themselves; their
own sordidness, seediness, their own—well, hair. The opposite of this is the System's higher Disneyland presided
over, just up Michigan Avenue, by Hugh Hefner. The
"underground" papers, when they show nudes, feature
pubic hair. No *Playboy* here—pink ice-cream scoops of
flesh kept innocent of hair (no down or fuzz on the fore-
arm, not one stray wisp near any protuberant nipple). In
Miami, Republican candidates had Nixonaires, Reagan-
ettes, and Rocky-à-Go-Go Girls—stewardesses off-duty,
with half-hour makeup jobs. In Chicago, few girls (and
those dumpy) wear candidate costumes. Political youth is
in the Park, wearing no man's colors.

Not all the kids wear Compulsory Soft, of course. But
the style is set by those who do. They are at the center
of things, fully conscious of what they are doing. The more
I moved in the crowd the less it seemed like a county
fair, or even a gypsy camp. It was more like a meeting of
Paris beggars in the Laughton *Hunchback of Notre Dame*.

Funky boys lift and throw furry girls like thistledown (fall *soft,* fetal; go limp, survive amoeboid), then carry the girls (soft roll of young breasts under sweaters) to phantom paddy wagons. But with all the physical horseplay, there is no electricity of sex, nothing coy, no crackle of flirtatiousness. Sex, unless demystified, is a "hangup," commercial, part of the System. Cabdrivers in Chicago imagined vague orgies taking place in their sacred parks. But these were jaded kids, taking sex for granted (when they take it at all). Any gift-wrapping or tease is the Hugh Hefner thing, not reality; not hair. What boasting they do is not about "conquests," but about one's "highs." Narcotics have the aura that sex had. Mystery and gift-wrapping are allowed for a pleasure the System disapproves of.

The kids live easily, here in Grant Park, having gained it yesterday. They seem to need little food or sleep, each snatched in small amounts. No booze (though cigarettes, straight and loaded). They move with knapsacks strapped to them; soft ones, of course—things they can lean on, lie in, use for insulation.

Grant Park was gained with difficulty. For almost a week kids had been expelled, in growing numbers, from Lincoln Park, three miles to the north. Things escalated Sunday, the night before the first convention session. After eleven, when the Park was officially closed, police cars and motorcycles moved through the kids, getting them up, on their feet, on the move. The trunk cycles (with three wheels) moved in fighter squadrons, taking an area, then one by one peeling off—the kids were nudged to a corner of the park, then edged across the street, some blazing with anger, others just troubled, with frightened young faces (milk in a cup blown across)—but no one fighting. It is a slow, effective process. Soft war.

Lincoln Park was originally chosen by the "Yippies" for their Festival of Life. If the cops had let them have it, they would have kept to themselves, as they did at the Pentagon March. But as, every night, the Yippies get displaced and need shelter, two things happen, both caused by Daley's untenable first-line toughness. First, other kids, sensing this is the first battleground, flock north and swell the Yippie ranks toward nightfall. Second, the Yippies and their allies, driven out after eleven, head south toward the Loop, looking for lodging, and for trouble.

So, on Sunday night, one of the first groups to be edged over the street gathers numbers and courage at a gas station, then moves south, aspiring to the Amphitheater, willing to settle for the Hilton. At first, standby prowl cars scatter them easily, with come-and-go sirens slowed from scream to purr. Each car swivels its blue light, which seems to hypnotize the prey. When kids, rounding a corner, see that slow blue roll and blink, they swerve at once, to try a new route. The cops are like cowboys turning a stampede, but with this important difference: they have no place to herd these cattle *toward*. Dispersing a crowd has, as its final objective, the scattering of people back to their homes. But these kids have no homes, at least not in Chicago; and a crowd cannot be "kept moving" like isolated bums, harried from park bench to bus station and back. One young couple drops by the way almost immediately. She is in her early teens, her face half hidden in a floppy hat, her possessions cinched into the blanket she wears. The boy with her, slightly older, is along for her company. He holds *his* luggage, with a hook of the wrist, on six coat-hangers (think of the edges). He wants to find her a place to sleep, but she is angry, resents this "babying," runs for a nearby lobby where she pouts. "We flew in from Cincinnati this afternoon," he tells me, with nervous glances at the lobby. "She has friends at the Palmer House, but she wanted to stay in the Park." Ozzie and Harriet on the road—domestic crisis with no domus.

The kids spill into Wells Street, self-proclaimed "Village" of Chicago; boutiques tinkly with love beads, backyards turned into mews. The "swinging" shopowners, one step behind kids' fashions, have been fearful of the Yippies —with good reason. Wells Street is commercializing yesterday's fads—psychedelic posters as big business; strobe lights, instead of candles, in the dining room. The kids know this routine—matrons fresh from Arthur Murray, frugging in expensive discotheques. It is hard for the kids to stay even one step ahead—which makes that one step all-important. Fall behind an inch, lose the argot, its nuances, blunder into "in things" that are out, and you have missed the action—the action being, always, an enclosed totality, the right beat, beads, color, noise, words. Only someone who gives it his full time can keep current —and who gives full time to being kids except kids?

No wonder, then, these midde-class "mod" moms, miniskirted, frugging, insect-eyed with wide tint-glasses, turned a blank look out at "Yippies" streaming by, a look blank as the plywood they would board up shops with in the morning—for kids were breaking windows as they ran, the *only* windows broken this night. Better to be in front of them than that one step behind. On Monday the soapy-scented windows, with fake paper Tiffany lamps, were covered, and one shop hung an angry sign: "Destroying property on Wells St. is a total cop-out which we equate to marching around your own room. What you apparently fail to realize is that the shopowners and the community share many of the same views about the way things are being run in this country. May we suggest that if you were to unite with the National Mobilization, Peace and Freedom Party and the Black Panthers your voice might be heard." The generation gap is largely caused by elders who believe they have escaped it.

Meanwhile, running for the Hilton was a lark. The very young are soon in the lead. Girls with white petal faces, scuttling young Giulietta Masinas in clown pants, turn those petal-faces up and shout their giggling "Cops eat shit." Eluding police cars, splitting up, rejoining like quicksilver crushed, they make their way down parallel streets coursing south. Cars get caught in this stream; the kids demand, from drivers quickly rolling windows up, the V-for-Victory peace sign—given readily or grudgingly, by most; otherwise the kids bang hoods, hammer windows, kick the doors. People sourly illumined in a bus—dry Edward Hopper scene—look dazed, trying to ignore the kids. Anti-litter trashcans are rolled into the street, their contents scattered.

Chicago police are justly proud of their communications system. On the second floor of the State Street station, a vast room—all wires underneath, with neat pickup squares to get at the nervous system—has twenty-four illuminated consoles, three to a zone, flashing the location of police cars, receiving all radio and phone calls from that zone. There are overflow, backup, and coordinating consoles; a whole room devoted to taping calls; an elaborate quick-check system of couriers and computers. Over each console, red and amber lights summon higher officers or messengers. Orlando Wilson, the progressive police leader, cooperated with Motorola to pioneer this system. And so, as the kids ran, men at green consoles tracked them. They saw that the Sheraton Chicago could not be protected now; the best line of defense for the headquarters hotel, the Hilton, would be the Chicago River, whose Michigan Avenue bridge can be lifted. Dots begin to converge on the consoles: police cars. Meanwhile, at a staging area, buses are being filled with men in powder-blue riot helmets.

As the first kids come in sight of the bridge, there on the far side—consoled, blinked, computered into place—are Jimmy Riordan and his First District cops (they handled daily marches two summers ago, and have dealt with countless demonstrations in the Loop). These cops have known two things—"marches," arranged beforehand, tensed for trouble, but of a predictable sort; and looters, a lone one or a few, sprung free in the Loop (run them down). But what did they see now? Some winded photographers trying to keep up with grinning boys and girls at a dead run. At sight of the bridge, rinsed with the blue lights' swirl and alarm, most of the kids slow down, look back for support, with no more side streets they can duck down (the police have chosen well). But the very first runners do not stop—two teen-age girls unwinded after three miles; one, wearing buckskin, charges with semihiant singultus, yearning for political defloration. The nightsticks, too, are ready, risen. But the cops merely turn these girls around and shove them back. They save their clubs for a cameraman who filmed them manhandling the girls.

The cops advance, lower gates that block traffic for the raising of the drawbridge, and slowly work the crowd back. Riordan is on the bullhorn, threatening to use tear gas if the crowd—perhaps two hundred—does not disperse. A Yippie shouts, "Great! I get a high on that stuff." Tear gas is still a joke. Scattered kids shout "We want *pig*meat." Cops huddle around walkie-talkies—aerials stuck out at angles, an insect orgy. The crowd sticks to the façade of Colonel McCormack's cathedral (in the window are straw hats with headbands for all candidates— even John Connally, Lester Maddox, Sargent Shriver).

Suddenly five buses full of cops appear, called by the walkie-talkies. This is Riordan's technique, always—flood the area, discourage hotheads, make numbers prohibitive. The flow of blue helmets out onto the sidewalk splits the

kids, turns them around—peaceably, as in the Park. Round
One to the police.

But a pyrrhic victory. A half hour later, I went back
north toward the Park. No sign of the kids. Where had
they gone? Back at their consoles, police must have been
wondering the same thing. The cops had bumped the
Yippies out of the Park, only to drive them into the Loop
—and into the arms of the better-organized, more "political" Mobilization. The kids saw in this action a vivid
symbol: the System has no place for them. The third of
the daily bulletins put out by SDS exulted: "We are learning. We are learning how to move together. Learning the
City . . . Pretty soon, brothers and sisters. We are learning
targets, targets where the rich buy their things."

The National Mobilization Committee to End the War
in Vietnam is the group that, under David Dellinger, organized the 1967 March on the Pentagon. Every morning
this "Mobe" held a press conference, to announce the
day's activities. On Monday, after the kids' run, Dellinger
reported two atrocities—the "brutalization of newsmen" at
the bridge, and the deception by which he had been
shunted off, Sunday afternoon, to meet the deputy may-
or's deputy, rather than the deputy mayor himself. But
this afternoon, he continued, he meant to get some action
at City Hall.

By the time Dellinger arrived for his meeting with
David Stahl (the deputy mayor, now available), there was
a new grievance—the arrest of Tom Hayden, on state and
city charges, for letting air out of a police car's tires. Dellinger, accompanied by Dr. Sydney Peck, a sociologist
from Case Western Reserve, asks Stahl for Hayden's release, a march permit, and "withdrawal of the troops."
The deputy mayor temporizes with them for an hour and
says nothing, so they emerge (at four-thirty) angry and
prepared to escalate. Professor Peck says he is interested
in the situation as a sociologist, a student of collective behavior (tie, coat, objective manner, no Yippie here): "With
a high degree of predictability, anger will build up and
begin to vent itelf. The repressive actions of the city are
inciteful"—yes, he is a sociologist—"inciteful to violence."

Then it is Dellinger, middle-aged, high-voiced, mild in
demeanor but quivering with indignation: "We charge
Mayor Daley with dereliction of duty. He invited the
Democratic Convention here, and then refused to see

those who inevitably came along with it. He is available to the bosses in the back room, and to those carrying on the war in Vietnam, but not to the constituents in the street." Daley did invite to town a party whose candidates had used kids as political spear carriers. Yet now Daley pretends they do not exist; gives them no place to stay and demonstrate peacefully; chases them down toward trouble, exacerbates their edgy drive toward "confrontation"; and, to cap it all, refuses to discuss the crisis with any of the kids' representatives.

Now a third person in the delegation to Stahl's office talks with newsmen—Marilyn Katz, a tiny leader of the Marshals Squad, dressed in sneakers, sweat shirt, and slacks. "If there is trouble now, the city must be held responsible. They have given the jails and streets and skies to the military, and left no place to the kids, who have come to fight for freedom. The streets are theirs." How old are you, Miss Katz? "Twenty-three—seven years from the cut-off point."

The press conference breaks up as news goes around that kids are marching from Lincoln Park to the police station, where Hayden is. I catch a ride with Miss Katz, who takes the parking ticket off her car and tears it up: "They're always pestering us." Marilyn feels hunted. "Doesn't that make you feel good?" she says with a wave at the helicopter patrolling Michigan Avenue. Marilyn is plain and boyish, but with a fuzzy-eyed jerky charm like Shirley MacLaine's. She is even smaller, though—a mini-MacLaine. Her eyes, turned up to defy the helicopter, are wide and fuzzy as sunflower centers.

The System is everywhere, but it cannot fool her. "We even found the unmarked office of the CIA in the Federal Building, and one of our people put 'CIA sucks' on the door. The major TV networks were there to photograph the scene, but they weren't allowed to use it." What stopped them—the obscenity? Eyes wide at my innocence (who cares about *that*?)—"The CIA, of course. Or maybe the FBI." The System.

When we get to the station, the marchers are already gone; from this vantage point, they turned back up toward the Hilton. Marilyn tries to go inside, but she has no press credentials. Just then a corporation counsel (assistant city attorney) comes out and in sudden rage (real or feigned, exaggerated either way) screams, "Don't let that girl in. She has been arrested at least fifteen times." "You big liar," she answers, just as wild. Another counsel, a smooth-voiced black man, comes out and is friendly: "How did your trial go, Marilyn?" Wry MacLaine grimace: "Probation and a fine. Big lecture on the sacredness of property." I ask what she was arrested for. "I was helping organize welfare workers, and we did a sit-down protest in the welfare office. They got us for criminal trespass." Marilyn, even more than formal leaders like Dellinger, is the new revolutionary, engaged in a running guerrilla war with the System.

Grant Park, interdicted last night, has been seized from the rear, with only minor scuffles—a boy pulled off the statue of General Logan when the crowd moved up Michigan from the police station. As usual, the first-line intransigence of the cops became silly as, day after day, General Logan wore ragged kids and flags in all his metal apertures. The police had refused to give an inch, yet soon after gave a mile; they ejected people from Lincoln Park, many blocks north of the delegates, then had to surrender Grant Park across from the Hilton. So, that night, the chants went on till dawn; the Guard made its first appearance, to spell the overtaxed police. Mild-mannered General Dunn put a human barricade of brown before Grant Park, not to prevent kids from entering it, anymore, but to keep them from leaving, from crossing to the Hilton.

As night fell that Monday in Grant Park, I talked to a young couple who had come, by separate routes, from France. They knew more of their countrymen, and some Germans, who made the same trip for this occasion. The boy was twenty, the girl twenty-one, and both had engaged in the battle of the Sorbonne. I asked the girl (whose English was far better than the boy's) why she came: "Oh, one goes wherever one can. I have been to marches in England and Spain." Where do you get the money? "We work. I was a waitress for two weeks in New York. He was selling *affiches* from the Sorbonne. Besides, the bus was only thirty-five dollars round-trip from New York; and if you do not have the money they let you ride free. Once we got here, we volunteered for work on the medical teams, and they take care of all expenses." The "they" in question seem to have clothed her, too—in limp Army khaki. "Oh, this! Yes, I was told it would be hot in

Chicago, we could sleep on the beaches, so I brought no warm clothes. I have nothing under this coat and sweater." But where had she got the plane fare to New York? "My parents will pay the transportation to any foreign country, as part of my education."

At one point, while the ill-fated Wednesday march was stalled and had flopped down on the Grant Park lawn, thirty men, ranging from six-foot-one up toward neighboring treetops, came over to the line, "Police" stamped all over their sport shirts and sweaters. Why be plainclothes men, I wondered, yet make this raid so obvious? So I followed. They were the "red squad" out commie-hunting. When they saw a face they recognized, they would cluster around, peer at "the subject," and say things like: "We thought we'd see you here. We're ready when the trouble starts. You'd better not let us find you in the vicinity." These jolly square giants stopped to scowl and growl at Frances Gabow, Peter Pramm of SDS, and Chris Bernard of the Radical Organizing Committee.

The police still thought in terms of "agents" taking their orders from Moscow, then manipulating kids into town. It is a comforting interpretation—*we* did not drive the kids to Chicago, *America* did not; Moscow did. All one has to do is catch the agents, then dupes will be disillusioned. But no one duped these kids here. The few people who had been to Cuba or who pal around with the Vietcong are not mesmeric enough to cause this kind of reaction. Whatever launched them from hundreds of cities is not controlled in Moscow, or Havana, or Hanoi. Nor in America.

Indeed, the problem with "the Movement" is that it is ridiculously antiorganizational. Not only is the System evil; all systems are. Only doing one's thing is safe. Logically, this leads to the exuberant irrelevance of the Yippies. As one kid put it, "The answer to the War is no war. The answer to the draft is no draft. The answer to the System is no system." One must not be hung up on leaders, organizations, spheres of power. The ugly reality of things will provoke spontaneous opposition, shaped by the needs of the moment. One must do some planning of course— flunky work (hire the buses). But one hopes that events will overtake more extensive planning. That is what Tom Hayden wrote in a prophetic *Rat* article on Chicago: "There will be no way to mobilize action at the time without major initiative from below . . . The growing consciousness of the Movement—its justified distrust of organized leaderships, its creation of 'revolutionary gangs' or 'affinity groups,' its experience with the police and the streets—is sure to be a controlling force of some kind over the loose official hierarchies."

And so it was. The planned events lost their importance as improvised violence took on its own logic and momentum. For Yippies, *the* event was to have been a love-in at North Beach, but the kids had gone south and gained Grant Park by that time; why retreat back north and lose ground? The Mobe's two planned things were an "unbirthday party" for LBJ, which lost its charm when the real birthday party was called off, and Wednesday's march to the Amphitheater, which did not take place at all. All the important activities were reactions to Daley's intransigence: by taking no strategic initiative of his own —by not trying to deal with the demonstrators, or define their actions with permits; by forswearing diplomacy and propaganda—Daley let his cops fend for themselves, trying to treat the kids as outlaws or nonbeings. And this, in turn, let the kids release all their grievances, act out the purely "anti-world" system of opposition to the System. The New Politics, antipersonal and antiorganizational, is unworkable in the long run; but Daley made it work, beautifully, in Chicago.

The amazing—and ominous—thing is the impact this "police riot" had on the nation. Chicago saw no crowds with guns or Molotov cocktails. The kids committed no arson or looting; they broke a few windows, that was all. And whatever acts were committed with police batons, no shots were fired. The numbers in the street were far below what kids had hoped and cops had feared; the plans and scheduled protests collapsed. Compared to Miami's toll, the lacerated scalps of Chicago were insignificant: three men *died* in Miami, and others were shot. Stores were looted, property damaged, buildings burned to the ground; rioters fought back from hiding, not as unarmed marchers. Yet Miami was a "minor riot" to the press, and Chicago was everything—battle, war, slaughter—short of Armageddon.

A cynic would say, and have reason to say, that only black kids, after all, died in Miami, but (in the words of Tom Wicker) "these were our children in the streets" of

Chicago. Our children—those of the middle class. White ones. And blood from a scratch on one of these has a deeper effect than more deaths in the ghetto. Also, of course, the press got bloodied in Chicago (it is not so easy to distinguish them from *white* activists). Yet it was not only race prejudice (though racism was involved) that made for a double standard in Miami and Chicago: there *is* a difference between hatred for society expressed by society's outcasts, and hatred expressed by the darlings of society, the heirs and favored children of America. Black hatred is understandable, on the basis of wrongs done to blacks. But why should *these* kids turn on their elders? Is society so evil? Are the kids so oedipal?

Does it (for that matter) *matter* which side is wrong? If the society is so good, how did it produce such monstrous progeny? Or if, on the other hand, it is so evil, where did the wisdom of the kids come from (they are the ones most completely formed by this society)? Whichever way you come at it, the problem of the kids is central to America's agony. A nation that forfeits the allegiance of its off- spring is a nation that is dying. That was the true menace of Chicago. These *were* our children in the streets—in- dicting us.

2. Liberals

> "And the elephants are kindly but
> They're dumb."
> —Simon and Garfunkel

WE DO NOT, any of us, want to admit that the kids have reason to indict us. Wallace voters thought their children, corrupted by teachers, were attacking the bogeys imag- ined by pseudo-intellectuals. The teachers, in turn, believe student rebellion is aimed at society, at parents, at the government—at everyone but teachers. But the kids' own feeling for their teachers is suggested by James Simon Kunen, in his account of Columbia's 1968 disturbance:

> In through the window like Batman climbs Professor Orest Ranum, liberal, his academic robes billowing in the wind. We laugh at his appearance. He tells us that our action will precipitate a massive right-wing reaction in the faculty. He confides that the faculty had been nudging [Grayson] Kirk toward resignation, but now we've blown everything; the faculty will flock to support the President. We'll all be arrested, he says, and we'll all be expelled. He urges us to leave. We say no . . . Professor Allen Westin, liberal, comes and offers us a tripartite committee which he has no authority to constitute and which we don't want. He is thanked and escorted to the window.

For liberals, the young are by definition liberal—that is why good liberal parents learn from their children: the whole direction of history is toward liberation; each generation is freer than the last, more open to the truth, heir to a larger heritage. A. Lawrence Lowell, when he was President of Harvard, formulated the code this way: "You will be courteous to your elders who have explored to the point from which you may advance; and helpful to your juniors who will progress farther." The juniors will go farther because liberal professors and parents have lived through the earlier stages, testing ideas, purifying them, handing them on improved. If the enlightened new generation seems ungrateful, it is because they forget the battles fought by their elders. To the students who, in the Army, may soon kill or die for obscure reasons, or who, resisting, may go to jail or into exile, the middle-aged liberal must keep protesting that he, too, took risks once, must compulsively bring up McCarthyism, recall the *frisson* of tenured professors in the fifties. (President Pusey told friends that he called police onto Harvard's campus in 1969 to prevent a new McCarthyism. Liberal professors cannot attack anyone but Joe McCarthy, even when they are engineering an SDS bust.)

Another way of finding the familiar villain is to say, as Seymour Martin Lipset has, that the cause for rebellion is a disrespect for law brought on by the South's attempt to circumvent desegregation decisions. A fanciful reading of history: Senator Byrd's "interposition" and George Wallace's "standing in the door" were ineffectual gestures, mocked by those kids who remember them. If one must find the cause for rebellion in theories of law, the obvious place to look would be Martin Luther King's praise of civil disobedience in his Letter from Birmingham Jail—the place Spiro Agnew looks for an explanation of our troubles. Actually, student rebels feel no need for such justification, and looked to more appropriate heroes of violence like Che and Fidel, Mao and Ho. But that introduces unsettling new villains. Better stick with Joe McCarthy and Senator Byrd.

For all these reasons, liberals have created an orthodoxy on the subject of campus unrest: they hold that students are attacking society at large, and especially the government in Washington; the brunt of that attack is borne by the university simply because it is the thing at hand. Students do not really mean what they say to apply to Harvard! As Arthur Schlesinger puts it: "One wonders whether educational reform is the real reason for student self-assertion, or just a handy one. The colleges most in need of reform are ordinarily not those where the agitation takes place. The biggest troubles happen at the best institutions and often involve the most successful students. One sometimes suspects that the common cry againt Clark Kerr's 'multiversity' is a pretext." It is at the best schools—i.e., the most liberal ones—that most agitation takes place. But since the agitation cannot conceivably be against liberalism—i.e., against the best schools themselves—it must have some other more hidden target. And the best students—i.e., those on the Left—are doing the agitating; so, once again, this turmoil cannot be directed at liberalism, for liberals have never been able to believe in the scorn felt for them by the hard Left. Like Stepan Verkhovensky, Dostoyevsky's pallid liberal, they cherish the conviction that they are rebels too: "For all his life he sincerely believed that he was regarded with apprehension in certain quarters, that every step of his was known and watched, and that each of our three governors, who succeeded one another during the last twenty years, brought with him, as he arrived to rule over our province, a certain preconceived idea about him that had been suggested from above, most certainly on his appointment as governor.

Had anyone tried to convince our most fair-minded Mr. Verkhovensky by irrefutable evidence that there was nothing he need be afraid of, he would most certainly have been deeply offended."

In 1969, the defense of orthodox liberalism was, as so often, undertaken by Professor Schlesinger. His book of that year, *The Crisis of Confidence,* is typical of liberal reaction to all problems of the time, and especially to the problems of campus turmoil. Schlesinger asked why students were unhappy, what made their lot so different from that of earlier collegians? Well, for one thing, there were *more* of them—nearly half the kids of college age were *in* college (vs. 4 percent in 1900). Why did this development take place? Schlesinger answers that our technological society demands a college education. A fashionable cliché. But why should this be so? The mass of new students is not being taught to repair TV sets or install stereo systems at college. In fact, the higher one's education, it seems, the less equipped does one become with such useful knowledge. One does not learn in school how to design a new car or discover a new drug. If it is objected that one must know something about engineering to design the car, or about chemistry to discover the drug, the answer is that this knowledge can be taught more rapidly outside a traditional course of general study—a course that finally reaches graduate school and the laboratories where real technological skills are learned. The schools delay entry into this world—despite the fact that original scientific work is best done at an early age.

And apart from all this, most of the hordes now attending schools will not be among the elite expanding our technology—nor in the bright new "servant" class of technological repairmen. Most students will simply be consumers of the new technology, a "skill" acquired by watching TV from a baby crib. The plain truth is that a general education is now, what it always has been, an ornament of the privileged. We have more people than ever in school because we have a vastly expanding group of "privileged" people with leisure and money—indeed the leisure is enforced. Young people stacking up in greater numbers on campus, and staying there longer, are not wanted either at home or on the work market. There is nothing for them to *do* at home ("chores"?) and the unemployment figures would bloat disastrously if kids streamed out of the schools looking for jobs. (The draft has been useful in holding down the glut of kids on campus and on the work market.) Kids accurately sense the reality: we send them to school because we do not have anything else to do with them, or for them to do. One must grasp that fact to understand the frustration and sense of drift that comes over students held for years in a rather aimless if pleasant world of cultivated "stalling." Jerry Rubin puts the matter with Yippie vividness: "So the purpose of the universities is: to get us off the streets. Schools are baby-sitting agencies."

When Schlesinger says "the children of Hiroshima" are different because they live in a world of rapid change, he is judging that world from his vantage point—a life-span in which these changes are startling incursions. For the kids themselves, these "new" things were a given in the world they first encountered; and their own experience is of stagnation, of isolation from society, not of change or unsettlement. This explains their readiness to risk violence, to try anything, to call for revolution. They are not, like their teachers, afraid of change, uncertain of its outcome. The kids, stranded for a decade or more in the difficult years of adolescence, in a world transitory yet enclosed, not inside their parents' family yet unable to begin their own families, not responsible *for* anything or *to* anyone, suspended in a sterile world of dorms, travel, tests, of long-range decisions without quick results, facing an education that becomes more lengthy and competitive as its goals lose definition, do not care where change is tending if only it will take them *somewhere*.

How can men like Schlesinger ignore this side of the kids' experience? Apparently they *must* ignore it, because liberal dogma has converged on the maxims that education is a good thing, that it provides democracy with an enlightened citizenry, that it is thus a requisite of the good state—so everyone should be provided with a general, generally equal course of instruction. In this framework, the present situation must be judged a desirable one, despite the experience of students; indeed, our condition is *un*desirable only in that half the college-age kids are still out of college. The hard facts—that education is a mark of privilege, even in our liberal society; that this is nowhere more true than at the most liberal Ivy League schools; that giving people privilege without correlative re-

sponsibilities leads to frustration—have been systematically blinked.

Schlesinger, then, predictably concludes that what the
kids want is more of the same—more liberalism. We need
"a more humane and rational organization of American
education," he says, since "American higher education,
that extraordinary force for the modernization of society,
has failed to modernize itself—a fact which not only an-
tagonizes students but gives them a sense of moral justification." (Watch out, kids, here the professor comes, in
through the window, to join you.) "Academic government,
in most cases, is still foolishly autocratic . . . The situation
of college students today is like that of organized labor
before the Wagner Act. One can hardly overstate the
record of student submissiveness under this traditional and
bland academic tyranny." In short, the liberal schools have
not been liberal enough. We need a little trade-unionism
and FDR reform: "The key, it seems to me, lies in the
assessment of the student demands. If the demands make
sense, a college administration would be ill advised to reject them or defer their consideration even when student
manners are bad unless the provocation is indeed immense; stalling on procedural grounds only discourages the
moderates and facilitates their radicalization. If the demands don't make sense, the administration ought to be
able to explain why in terms that hold the moderate support." Persuasion, rational yielding, liberalization, reform
—that is the key. Yet earlier the professor had said that
academic reform was only a *pretext* for student rebellion.
Remember?—"The colleges most in need of reform are
ordinarily not those where the agitation takes place . . .
the common cry against Clark Kerr's 'multiversity' is a pretext." He cannot even keep his own argument straight,
much less hear what the kids are saying.

Liberals of the Schlesinger sort will never understand
student rebellion. It is not, in its real genius, a movement
of rational reform. It is opposed to gradual reform, and
even more opposed to reason. The liberation etymological-
ly promised by liberalism was from the dead weight of
the past. We were to be led toward rational self-government, in which men are instructed by teachers, not ruled
by priests or kings. Yet the students have rejected their
teachers and turned, beaded and robed, to gurus and mys-
ticism, to nostalgia and opium-priests and communes, to

astrology and the tarot cards, poets and saints—all the new monks and hermits who "drop out" of rational society. Che Guevara is not merely admired for the doctrine he professed, but as an outsize figure enacting hyperbole —Man against the System, new Simeon Stylites.

Henry Adams summed up the nineteenth-century liberalism of his upbringing in these words: "Social perfection was sure, because human nature worked for Good, and three instruments were all she asked—Suffrage, Common Schools, and Press." Yet the rebel kids called 1968's election meaningless. They attack the universities as empty things, and entertain Marcusian doubts about the central tenet of all, free speech. It is a rebellion against liberalism. To a philosophy built on compromise it offers the nonnegotiable demand. To impersonal "truths of the market," reached by consensus and group-process, it offers the primacy of "authentic" personal experience.

The funny thing is that Schlesinger, so predictable, his analyses so hedged by dogma, represents himself as the foe of ideology. "Ideas," he says, are "particular insights," whereas ideologies are "universal systems." Some people, he lectures us, have *both* ideas *and* an ideology; it is important to separate the former from the latter: "Jefferson, for example, was an expounder of both. His ideas—his defense of intellectual liberty, his sense of the relationship between politics and economics, his faith in education, his insights into the meaning of popular government—remain fertile and alive nearly two centuries later. His ideology, however, is today remote and irrelevant. As an ideologist, for example, he believed that agriculture was the only basis of a good society; that the small freehold system was the necessary foundation for freedom; that the virtuous cultivator was the only reliable citizen for democracy; that the great enemies of a free state were urbanization, industry, banking, an industrial working class and a strong national government."

Now, the interesting thing about these two lists of concepts—entirely apart from their truth or falsehood—is that the former set (the interconnection between education, freedom, and general enlightenment) is part of the network of "self-evident truths" Jefferson shared with the "Philosophes." These "ideas" were part of Jefferson's *systematic* philosophy. The second list, on the importance of rural life and the dangers of banking, is not based so much on *a priori* dictates as on Jefferson's parochial historical situation—it is more empirical, based on experience. If anything, Schlesinger's examples would prove the opposite of his point—but all his argument really proves is that "ideas" is a term of blessing to him, and "ideology" a cussword. Ideas turn out to be things Schlesinger agrees with; ideology is what he disagrees with.

But we must give him credit to get at his real, his deeper error: he calls unacceptable thoughts "ideological" by a natural (if illogical) inversion of his belief that all *systems* of thought are "bad." Already planted in his definition of an ideology was the assumption that systematic thought is not fruitful (I will not say "false," since here we are getting to the core of liberalism, where one must stay open to questions of truth or falsehood). The only good idea is the "particular insight." Make one idea capable of coupling with another, and it is already turning into a bad idea. Why? Because such combinations are like cartels, to stifle competition, in the marketplace of ideas. As long as one sticks to particular insights, one is always "open": no large segments of thought get automatically excluded, no particular segments are given even partial "monopoly."

It is the great myth of liberalism that this openness toward ideas exists in the academy; and it is the vulnerable nature of this myth that gives Marcuse's young disciples an easy target. All the institutionalized insincerities of the academy grow out of this myth—the conflict between egalitarian justification and privileged practice, between state support and disestablishmentarianism, between equal rating (to enlighten every citizen) and invidious rating (exclusion from entry, comparative grading, expulsion on academic grounds), between disinterestedness and professional competition, between dissent and conformity.

The historical context—hardly the cause—of the students' attack on the myth is the Vietnamese war. It did not matter to them that the university and the national government were interlocking institutions when it was simply a matter of research grants, of student fellowships, of Washington consulting the economics department. But on a moral issue like the war, the kids asked some difficult questions. How can the morality of the war be treated as an open question while long-term projects favoring its prosecution are conducted by the university, when the university cooperates with the draft in rating students according to their academic achievement, when military training is conducted on the campus for academic credit? A department that is three weeks into an eight-week research project for the government obviously does not assemble each morning to reconsider, objectively and *ab ovo,* whether the project is a proper activity for the university to undertake. If it did this, its failure to produce results would cut off future contracts. But if it does *not* do this, or is not prepared to do it when students raise questions, what happens to the pretense that the university is open, at any minute, to all questions? If there are ties with the government, and the academy refuses to ask these questions, over and over, then has it not lost moral responsibility, become a mere technician in servicing the government?

The answer is that the liberal university has always been a servant of the government. The whole justification for public schooling is founded on what Schlesinger rightly calls the Jeffersonian belief that an enlightened citizenry is a *political* necessity, one that pertains to the state. That is why tax money has supported colleges for years in the most obvious way—by giving them high school graduates as entrants, their whole education provided, up to that point, by the state. And that is why government support for higher education, even in so-called private institutions, has become increasingly available, and increasingly necessary.

There is, in the pure liberal vision, no problem of state domination so long as the state system is democratic and the schools operate on the principle of academic freedom. The two are corollaries, complementary; supporting aspects of a single thing. The free play of ideas will lead to a citizenry equipped to choose the best possible men and policies in the political marketplace of polls and elections and public opinion. Since the state's policies are arrived at democratically, by a competent electorate, as a result of the schools' own activity, the schools' support of the state is practically synonymous with support for themselves.

What we have, in theory, is not so much an establishment of any favored truths as a unity of method in both spheres, the educational and political. Liberalism, after all, is more a mode of working toward the truth than a set of truths. It is, in its apologists' own view, "value-free." As Schlesinger puts it, "ideas are relative"—as opposed to ideologies, which are absolute. No idea, therefore, positively and forever rules out any other idea, even its opposite. Even freedom is not defended so much as a positive "value," but as an instrument for spreading enlightenment (the market machinery for testing ideas). That is the ultimate reason for accord between government and the academy. All the interconnections, traced by busy students, between the schools and the war—trustee ties, government grants, IDA and CIA activity on campus, ROTC and Marine recruiting, contracts with firms that have government war contracts (like Dow Chemical)—all are the fruits of an original unity of aim in the two institutions.

That is why Schlesinger answers the student disrupters by defending both markets (academic and political) simultaneously, in Bentham's and Mill's terms: "The discipline of consent means that policies must triumph not through the divine right of kings or of a 'democratic educational dictatorship' but through making sense to a majority of the people; and the condition of bringing a majority along is the best guarantee that policies relate, not to private fantasy or personal power, but to the greatest good of the greatest number." He proposes this paradox: to guarantee tolerance and dissent, one must insist on conformity within "the discipline of consent." Once today's market has spoken, however provisionally, one must go along with its decision, never arrogating to oneself the right to defy it except through future market procedure. To claim that one is right, over against the decision of the majority, is, in Schlesinger's terminology (taken from Mill), a claim to "infallibility," a wish to destroy the market. Once begin with the assumption that all ideas are equally valuable —have, as it were, an equal place at the starting line— and this is easily read to mean that all ideas are equally valueless. Thus there is no intellectual corruption in bowing toward whatever idea prevails on today's market— i.e., establishes its Darwinian fitness to survive (at least temporarily). As John Stuart Mill put it, "improvement [consists] chiefly in this, that the new fragment of truth is more wanted, more adapted to the needs of the time, than that which it displaces." Thus Schlesinger does not call ideas false or wrong (nonrelative terms); he finds some procedural fault in them, and a cussword to identify the faulty procedure. He calls them "ideologies."

The academy long ago spotted contradictions in market thinking as it applies to the economy. "Social Darwinism" is not popular at Yale, as it was in the days of William Graham Sumner. But Yale's President, Kingman Brewster, still holds the doctrine of "intellectual Darwinism" in all its purity: "Perhaps the greatest contribution we can make is to reaffirm in the face of those who would seek to coerce conformity that practical progress relies most of all on the evolution of the better by the survival of the fittest among ideas tossed in the blanket of debate, dispute and disagreement." Those were his words in March of 1970. Under challenge, academicians retreat to their basic doctrine—still unaware that this intellectual "market" is as rickety with pretense as the economic one. Yet students, tortured by the contradictions involved in campus war work, are probing to more basic inconsistencies. For instance:

1) A truly value-free openness toward ideas does not, and cannot, exist in the academy, for several reasons. One of them is theoretical: certain ideas cannot be entertained, at least not seriously, because they would of their nature "close the market." Totalist systems, therefore—revealed religions, philosophies that proclaim an absolute truth, political systems (whether fascist or communist) that proscribe certain kinds of opinion—cannot in theory be advocated at public schools. These are not, notice, excluded because they are false but because they are exclusionary. Their fault is a methodological one, and can be detected and condemned on grounds of procedure, without value-prejudice. The only things that can be excluded are things that would exclude—things that reveal the evil of *system*. This value-free code of teaching—the concentration on *process*es for reaching a conclusion, with the taboo against actually *reaching* conclusions—is spelled out in the *Handbook for Faculty Members of the University of California* (that model of modern liberalism):

The function of the University is to seek out and to transmit knowledge and to train students in the processes whereby truth is to be made known. To convert, or to make converts, is alien and hostile to this dispassionate duty. Where it becomes necessary,

in performing this function of a university, to consider political, social or sectarian movements, they
are dissected and examined—not taught—and the conclusion left, with no tipping of the scales, to the logic
of the facts.

The phrasing is exquisite: facts and knowledge of the facts
are handed on; the only conclusions allowed are those
forced on one by the facts, the teacher having no responsibility for such conclusions. The teacher cannot even
teach (only "dissect"), when it is a matter of political,
social, or "sectarian" movements (the very term "religion"
is too value-laden to pass the committee's pure lips).

2) Aside from this theoretical limit to openness, there is
a practical limit. It is impossible to get up every morning
and rebuild one's conceptual world *ex nihilo,* to achieve
an Emersonian mental rebirth every day. One necessarily
assumes a great deal, working with what one believes to be
the best assumptions, which are the actual framework of
one's thinking. Beyond this personal set of ruling assumptions, there is the need to talk with others, to focus
research, to finish an eight-week project with one's colleague. What this means is that if Professor A and Professor B, in the same department, agree on the merits of
Proposition X in their field, they will try to propagate it
by persuasion, will tend to work with others who accept
it, will be in actual competition with all those who hold
Non-X, and will by their efforts be constantly discrediting
Non-X. To the degree that Professors A and B are successful in their work, Proposition X will become a practical orthodoxy within a specific department, and advocates
of Non-X will work under subtle inhibitions, with all kinds
of pressures, other than pure persuasion, to adopt Proposition X. Their own career, their communication with de-
partments and journals that have accepted Proposition X,
the future acceptability of their students, will depend on
adaptation to Proposition X. All this is normal enough;
indeed, it would be impossible to get any work done if
such practical exclusions did not take place. What is unsettling to intellectual honesty is the pretense (e.g., in the
University of California Handbook), that such inhibition,
such fostering of orthodoxies, does *not* take place, that
the play of ideas is entirely free.

3) The embracing orthodoxy within which these partic-

ular orthodoxies are nourished will, of necessity, be that set of masked values conducive to academic freedom. Freedom, which is theoretically only a methodological tool, becomes a positive value; and as such it is equated with other things made into positive values—e.g., the exclusion of "exclusionary" religions promotes a secularist orthodoxy; the exclusion of exclusionary philosophies promotes a pragmatic orthodoxy; the exclusion of exclusionary political systems promotes a democratic orthodoxy. No amount of verbal play will keep these "procedural" bans from taking on a positive coloration of orthodoxy in a supposedly value-free system. An intellectual establishment will exist—one not often questioned, because it is the democratic kind that Americans pay their taxes to support.

4) But, as a matter of fact, there will be some conflict between the academic market and the political one. In America, for instance, the political world, while observing the constitutional ban against an established religion, has had an establishment that favors religion-in-general (tax exemption for churches, the chaplain system, four clergymen being ecumenical about blessing the Nixon regime at its inauguration). But the academy, more consistent, is as open to arguments against religion as to those that favor it—in fact, "more open" to the former, since they are naturally less "absolutist." The two markets, which are supposed to mesh, actually clash—as we find when the Supreme Court must decide what to do about prayer-in-general in the schools, which are farm clubs for the universities.

5) This inconsistency between the two markets leads to the academician's special temptation in the sphere of politics: although he is supposed to function as an enlightener of the citizenry, promoting wise choices for the public by giving it the tools for making such choices at the ballot box, it seems easier to take a short cut: rather than educate the whole people, or at least a majority of them, it is quicker to get the king's ear (Schlesinger in Washington telling JFK what the people *should* want). Thus many academicians think of themselves aristocratically, as potential philosophers to the king, and have contempt for the populace they are supposed to serve and enlighten. (These aristocratic assumptions underlie Schlesinger's conviction that rebels, given a choice between reforming

the academy's mild sins and the sins of the unwashed electorate, simply *cannot* be aiming their insults at their professors.)

6) Even when the professor does not exert direct leverage on Washington, he adopts an aristocratic standard by his preference for teaching superior students, a preference enforced by the competitive grading system, which weeds out the less intelligent. There is a conflict, here, with the goal of education for an enlightened citizenry. If that is the aim, then not only should everyone be educated, but the *least* intelligent should be *preferred* (as those in greater need of help toward performance of their tasks within a democracy). Literacy and property tests for voting, which have existed through most of our history, were based on the Jeffersonian rule: an electorate must be educated if it is to make wise choices. If we abandon those tests, but retain Jefferson's norm, we should guarantee that each voter—with emphasis on the least equipped—will receive an education aimed at political wisdom. In that case, the quota system being urged by some blacks is consistent with our education's rationale: since the universities cannot (yet) educate everybody, they should at least educate people in proportion to their voting power, to give some *balance* of enlightenment to the electorate. But liberal professors oppose this conclusion from their own principles: they may "educate for democracy," but they keep their own preserve an aristocracy.

7) Despite the aristocratic code of the university, in which professors address an elite, the academy must yield, in any showdown with the mass electorate, to what Schlesinger calls the discipline of consent. There are two reasons for this, one theoretical (majority rule on the political market) and one practical (the universities' economic support comes from the political community, national, state, and local). Two contrary feelings, therefore, grow up in the academy—the sense of superior knowledge and the sense of ultimate powerlessness, a combination that makes for resentment. And resentment, according to Scheler and Camus, leads to intellectual asphyxiation, the constant rebreathing of one's own thoughts in a closed room.

8) Although the system claims to be value-free, a loose orthodoxy actually exists in each area of modern study, an orthodoxy made up of the Propositions X that are favored

by leaders of the profession. And it is precisely the claim of objectivity and openness that narrows the range of questions that can be asked about Proposition X—e.g., it cannot be challenged from "absolutist" directions. In fact, the more technical, minute, and "objective" study becomes, the more does it stand in need of an embracing, unquestioned Proposition X: to study in detail the minnow, and be rated on one's results, one needs a firm aquatic category within which, vicariously, to swim with one's subject, and send melodious, measurable bubbles up the exposed aquarium side. One not only narrows one's assumptions, structures one's professional world of exploration, but does this in order to make the assumptions *procedurally* unquestionable.

9) Measuring the bubbles becomes all-important to the academician's career. The pretense that there is no orthodoxy means that a teacher is supposedly judged only by his competence in his field. Thus "absolutists," or holders of Non-X, must be found to be, not wrong, but "incompetent." And teachers who are socially or politically unacceptable to their fellows cannot be dismissed on such grounds (often reasonable), but must also be declared incompetent. That category—which is supposed to be the only academic sin—is made to cover a number of real sins.

10) The result is that few, if any, men in America live so entirely on their professional reputations as do academicians, guard that reputation more jealously, rate it against others' with such regularity. Norman Podhoretz's "revelation" of the jealous rating of writers by writers on the literary market is tame stuff compared with the world of academic jockeying and gossip, where the range of action is more restricted, the tools of comparative measurement more developed, and physical separation from the rest of society more complete. Thus, in a world consecrated to the disinterested search for truth, envy and petty competitiveness thrive.

11) This desperate competitiveness makes academicians live more "in their field" than in the university as a community. The average professor at a large university knows a higher percent of the men in his own discipline, all across America, than of the total faculty at his home institute. If the students are an enclosed world to themselves, a subculture cutting through other social divisions,

they are brought into contact, at college, with a group of adults sealed up in a subculture of professional preoccupations, with its own standards of judgment, taste, and conduct.

12) The egalitarian side of the academy was, in principle, intellectual rather than social—openness gave each *idea* an equal chance, academic freedom gave each teacher the right to follow his research to any conclusion, and purity of research was guaranteed by the determination to impose no orthodoxy (by what Willmoore Kendall used to call "the public truth that there is no public truth"). Thus there was equality in the sphere of ideas, and (by extension) among those "dissecting" the ideas; but this equality did not extend to students. The relation of teacher to student was semiparental and authoritarian. The student, who comes to an institute to learn, proclaims by that very act that he does not know; the teacher is accredited as one who does know; and the process of teaching was to be one of transferring measurable amounts of knowledge from the clearly labeled possessor of that knowledge to one just as clearly labeled as deficient in it. The social and political market was to come into effect for the student only after he had "stepped up" (graduated) to life in the larger society, come of age, assumed full responsibility, gone out into the political marketplace where he could elect and be elected. There was a time lag, then, between the academic free play of ideas, as experienced by the student, and his own equal rights as something to be acted on. So went the theory—from which practice diverged, for several reasons: (a) Students were conscripted as allies in faculty battles with the administration over academic freedom, and they shared in the fruits of victory, where victories were won—thus making academic freedom mean not only the right of teachers to teach what they want, but the (ultimately antagonistic) right of students to study what they want. (b) Toward the limit of one's schooling, in graduate school, the teacher-student relationship gradually turns into that of co-researchers and colleagues. Once a last-year graduate student and a first-year instructor have shared the experience of being equals, that relationship is not erased by the fact that one of them gets his doctorate a few months before the other. Then, as tends to happen in American education, the pattern of the upper schools spread downward

—from graduate school to undergraduates, and even from college to high school. More and more, the good liberal teacher learns from, or at least with, his fellows and co-workers, the students. (c) The aristocratic feeling of superiority to the larger community, nurtured by faculty members, was instilled in students, setting the whole academy off from the rest of society; making students, in this separateness, similar to the faculty, if not equal to it. Ellen Willis has pointed out that the kids' hatred of cops in Chicago, more intense than their treatment of "other college kids" in the National Guard, was a matter of class resentment—and the snobbishness rubbed off on others: Jimmy Breslin wrote that cops resented the kids' literacy. (d) Ironically, one of the aristocratic roles of the student was to go into the community as an enlightener-activist, especially in the civil rights movement—a development many teachers favored. Yet these activists in reorganizing the state at large were told they must resume their client status on return to the campus—i.e., they could remake society, but not their school, a ridiculous situation. Yet (e) the real solvent of the teacher-student relationship is the fundamental doctrine of the academy, the free play of ideas. For if any *idea* is to be given equal hearing, then any idea's *advocate* must be given equal hearing. After all, how do we *know* the professor knows more than the student, once the student "dissents"—i.e., expresses a different idea? That question, too, must be kept "open," not solved *a priori;* solved only by dialogue—and dialogue is conducted by equals. Thus the parent-child, or patron-client relationship was always at war with an equal-to-equal relationship forced on the unwilling faculty by that faculty's own first principles.

13) The faculty's means of reasserting authority in this situation is to declare the student's opinion, not false, but incompetent—either as coming from one not methodologically accredited, or as an opinion absolutist and exclusionary (i.e., as one of the things that are by definition ruled out of the "free play" to be given ideas). Compare the *California Handbook:* "Essentially the freedom of a university is the freedom of *competent* persons in the classroom. In order to protect this freedom, the University assumes the right to prevent exploitation of its prestige by *unqualified* persons and by those who would use it as a platform for propaganda."

14) The result of all this is what Marcuse identified (but clumsily analyzed) as "repressive tolerance." That is, a situation exists wherein a covert set of values (whether true or not, good or not, is beside the point) is defended while official pretense is made of being "neutral" toward the masked values. And since there is (by the official myth) no orthodoxy, no specific provision has to be made for dissent from the orthodoxy. Dissent is supposed to *be* the orthodoxy—though that is far from true.

What is left, then, of Schlesinger's claim that students are in rebellion against society, not against the university? The university has been intertwined with our society from the outset, a servant to its political ideals, a partner in its procedures. In fact, the university concentrates and throws into relief the inconsistencies of society, makes them particularly striking because of the academy's claim to a superior standard of intellectual purity and consistency of behavior. Thus Paul Jacobs and Saul Landau concluded, in *The New Radicals,* that student rebellion began at Berkeley *because* of that school's liberalism, not despite it: "The university was the embodiment of liberalism. President Clark Kerr was the winner of the Meiklejohn Freedom Award, and its faculty had a corps of professional liberal social scientists who wrote about freedom and democracy praising the United States and the university itself as the noble embodiment of freedom. To the Free Speech Movement the university appeared to be the living example of the integration of liberalism with actual policy, for its physical scientists do research on behalf of the military, and the social scientists provide the government with vast amounts of material designed to implement foreign and domestic policies . . . It seemed to have defined its educational function as one of producing for society's needs as defined by government and the large corporations . . . To the students the freedom of speech they were granted was primarily a way of keeping them amused, within the context of education for democracy and citizenship, and within a framework of 'listen to all sides, etc.,' lest they be distracted by the content of their own lives, by their places in the university, and by world events."

The students are faced, in the academy, with a crucial set of contradictions; and those who are supposed to be their guides toward clarity turn out, in fact, to be fostering the contradictions, men who live by them. In the sphere of equal-opportunity politics, voters choose to stress one or the other side of their contradictory model—the equal starting line or the differentiating race—according to their mood and preference, avoiding reflection on the internal contradictions they live with. The same is true of our professors: they stress academic freedom (all ideas equal at the starting line) or practical orthodoxy (Proposition X actually prevailing out on the racetrack) as it suits their convenience. And they are no more ready than politicians to recognize the weaknesses in their conceptual framework. Schlesinger makes this clear in his defense of "ideas" as opposed to "ideology," an opposition he equates with William James's distinction between the tough-minded and the tender-minded: "In such passages James clearly defined the characteristic temper of American thought. This is not to suggest that pragmatism itself did not rest, as Hartz has argued, on a 'submerged and absolute literal faith.' *But a difference remains between a faith which is submerged and one which is formulated and codified in a body of dogma.*" The part I italicize is a priceless unintended revelation of the liberal mentality. If one is going to have principles or system, it is better to keep them submerged, half-conscious, unadmitted. In fact, one had better not investigate one's basic assumptions at all, for fear of discovering that they are consistent with each other (systematic), "ideological," and therefore ruled out of contemporary discourse on grounds of procedure. Since the liberal's market can work only on hidden premises, hiding one's premises becomes a liberal duty, the price one pays for keeping the market open. Schlesinger has let the secret out—liberalism's half-conscious always-present fear of investigating its own basis; its bland, rather winning hope that we can "muddle through" if we just do not think too logically; its putatively benevolent self-deception, based not on personal duplicity but on the structure of the academic market. The liberal is willing to make the supreme sacrifice for the common good—his own intellectual rigor and integrity.

Students are faced, at school, by a group of adults who profess the greatest openness, yet are conformist, career-conscious, enclosed in a protective semifeudal system. These men are supposed to be enlighteners of the community at large, yet they are alienated from it; supposed to be champions of equality, they have taken up a defensively aristocratic posture. Yet despite any feelings of superiority the academician may feel toward the community, he remains subject to it; he resents this submission, yet is bound in principle to perpetuate it. No wonder students are confused. They have been taught, all along, by Stepan Verkhovensky. And, like Verkhovensky, the liberal stands aghast at his own handiwork: " 'I agree that the author's fundamental idea is right,' he said to me feverishly, 'but that makes it more awful! It's just our idea —yes, ours! We were the first to plan it, to nurture it, to get it ready—and what new thing could they say after us? But, good Lord, how they have expressed it all, distorted, mutilated it!' he cried, rapping on the book with his fingers. 'Were those the conclusions we wanted to draw? Who can recognize the original idea here?' " In all justice, Verkhovensky had reason for dismay. His pupil was Stavrogin, the aesthete of violence; and his son was Peter, the nihilist.

3. Radicals

> *"Don't follow leaders,*
> *Watch the parking meters."*
> *—Bob Dylan*

THE REBELLION began moderately. In 1962 the SDS, Students for a Democratic Society, freeing itself from its parent group the League for Industrial Democracy, met in Port Huron, Michigan, and adopted what came to be called the Port Huron Statement, written by a twenty-two-year-old rhetorician (editor of his school paper in both high school and college), Tom Hayden. This was not yet the fire-breathing Hayden: *"In social change or interchange, we find violence to be abhorrent because it requires generally the transformation of the target, be it a human being or a community of people, into a depersonalized object of hate. It is imperative that the means of violence be abolished and the institutions—local, national, international—that encourage nonviolence as a conflict be developed."*

Hayden's specifically political analysis is reformist, unoriginal, derivative. It was the time of Kennedy's conflict with Congress, and Hayden, like most liberals, wanted to break James MacGregor Burns's "four party deadlock": *"A crucial feature of the political apparatus in America is that greater differences are harbored within each major party than the differences existing between them. Instead of two parties, presenting distinctive and significant differences of approach, what dominates the system is a natural interlocking of Democrats from Southern states with the more conservative elements of the Republican Party. This arrangement of forces is blessed by the seniority system of Congress which guarantees Congressional committee domination by conservatives."* This whole section is almost casual in its contradictions. On the one hand, congressional politicking splits up debate on the large issues (as Burns argued, asking for a national party with a national forum): *"The localized nature of the party system does not encourage discussion of national and international issues: thus problems are not raised by and for people, and political representatives usually are unfettered from any responsibilities to the general public except those regarding parochial matters."* But the *framer* of the deadlock theory knew its consequences—namely, that one must (a) *concentrate* power in the presidency and (b) *take* power from Congress. Hayden, by contrast, relying on his campus and civil rights experience, wants to take power from central administration and encourage participation—by weakening the presidency and strengthening the (reformed) Congress; since *"frustration is the expectancy of legislators intending liberal reform, and Congress becomes less and less central to national decision-making, especially in the area of foreign policy."*

But if Hayden's comments on congressional politics are thin, his reading of the campus mood is extraordinarily prescient. His Statement reads like a commentary on the Berkeley rebellion, which took the nation by surprise two years later. The enemy is the university, not some other part of society: *"Our professors and administrators sacrifice controversy to public relations; their curriculums change more slowly than the living events of the world;*

their skills and silence are purchased by investors in the arms race; passion is called unscholastic. The questions we might want raised—what is really important? Can we live in a different and better way? If we wanted to change society, how would we do it?—are not thought to be questions of a 'fruitful, empirical nature,' and thus are brushed aside." He is attacking the mechanics of "repressive tolerance," which does not censor ideas as "dangerous," but declares them unentertainable on the intellectual market, because too absolutist (not empirical), or too little adjusted to the present state of exchange (not fruitful), or posed by people who are not competent. The student, within this situation, does not feel exploited or repressed, but "manipulated"—made to think he has freedoms not actually exercised: *"The accompanying 'let's pretend' theory of student extracurricular affairs validates student government as a training center for those who want to spend their lives in political pretense, and discourages initiative from the more articulate, honest, and sensitive students. The bounds and style of controversy are delimited before controversy begins. The university 'prepares' the student for 'citizenship' through perpetual rehearsals and, usually, through emasculation of what creative spirit there is in the individual."* A university training must instill the "discipline of consent."

Liberalism puts all its stress on procedure, on ways of getting at truth, not on truths that are reached: *"All around us there is astute grasp of method, technique—the committee, the ad hoc group, the lobbyist, the hard and soft sell, the make, the projected image—but, if pressed critically, such expertise is incompetent to explain its implicit ideals."* The ideals must be kept "submerged," like Professor Schlesinger's; to have explicit ideals is to risk the dangers of tender-minded ideology: *"To be idealistic is to be considered apocalyptic, deluded. To have no serious aspiration, on the contrary is to be 'tough-minded.' "* Hayden has anticipated it all, including the liberal professor's claim that students *cannot* be rebelling against *him*, since he agrees with much that they say (if they would only come out of the building and stop fanning a new McCarthyism), and he would vote for more student power (so far as *he* is concerned), and, besides, I-was-for-Adlai-I-fought-McCarthy: *"It is highly fashionable to identify oneself by old categories, or by naming a re-*

spected political figure, or by explaining 'how we would vote' on various issues."

Hayden, attacking the claims of value-free liberalism, comes precisely to articulate values in three areas: *"Our own social values involve conceptions of human beings, human relationships, and social systems."* In the first area, he would oppose the depersonalization and manipulation of modern life (especially campus life) with a new individualism, not based on a hands-off attitude toward others (laissez faire), but on *"finding a meaning in life that is personally authentic."* "Individualism" is not, for him, an economic term but a word for that self-seeking, even in eccentric ways, that often leads outside accepted social norms.

In the system of human relations, Hayden says that "fraternity" is the aim of his fulfilled individuals. He ignores the dilemma that pits individualism against society. He thinks his kind of fraternity can be achieved *only* by his kind of individuals, since fraternity must be the acceptance of one whole man by another whole man, not those forms of partial contact fostered by modern life: *"Personal links between man and man are needed, especially to go beyond the partial and fragmentary bonds of function that bind men only as worker to worker, employer to employee, teacher to student, American to Russian."* This was written one year after Bernstein's "Goldwater Manifesto" on "the total man." Bernstein's paper was directed toward the students who, in 1961, were joining Young Americans for Freedom. The New Left and the New Right had some points of agreement in their criticism of official liberalism.

In the third area Hayden speaks of—social systems—he creates the phrase and the proposal he is best known for, "a democracy of individual participation." Formally, this is nothing more than the proclamation by Verkhovensky's son Peter that the future must "finally enable men to organize their society themselves, not just on paper but in real life." Yet Hayden's use of the idea must be studied genetically, to see what it meant to him and his contemporaries. The cluster of ideas labeled "participatory democracy" grew out of Hayden's experience in the civil rights movement down South. The young liberal, of necessity, assumed an aristocratic role at the outset: he was teacher, guide, enlightener to his charges, telling them what to do (e.g., register to vote) and how to do it (e.g., appeal over local law-enforcement officials to federal ones). This led to inner conflict for a student who resented the patron-client relation back on campus, where he was client rather than patron. And the aristocratic role came to be resented by young SNCC blacks, who found the situation untenable and pushed white benefactors out of what they declared, henceforth, was *their* movement.

But in the interval, in that period when Hayden wrote, the only position open to the hopeful white liberal was to say he was not leading the blacks but stimulating them to make *their own* decisions. From this rationalization came the prickly resistance, in early SDS days, to all "leadership." And from it, by a cruel bit of irony, came the students' imitation of that System they attacked: without professing leadership, the students mobilized pressures toward decision-making on the part of blacks. These decisions would not have been made but for the pressures; and engineering such pressures, while denying responsibility for them is, after all—manipulative! The kids tried to erect a change-inducing system that does not call for responsible leaders. Robert Moses, who became a leader in the fight against leadership, said of his SNCC operation: "We're just going to let the people in the community know that we're here, become involved in their daily lives, and find out what it is they want us to do." But the very presence of Moses, a Northern black philosophy teacher, was the sign of a need he had discerned before he moved down from New York. A pure leaderlessness cannot be sustained—as Moses had to confess when his very achievements made him change his name (to Robert Parris) and move out of Mississippi because a "cult of personality" was developing around him. The myth of perfect spontaneity is self-defeating: each success achieved gives one man or one plan extra leverage for the next day's effort, and this reduces the leverage that will be exerted by other men or other plans.

The problem in dealing with a people who have been discriminated against as inferior is to help them overcome an admittedly inferior performance without in any way implying that this is the result of inferior capabilities— a difficult job, as Patrick Moynihan found out with his study of the crippling nature of ghetto family structures. To offer help is to proclaim that you think the respective beneficiaries need help, a thing abrasive to black pride. From this has come all the delicacies of language and difficulties of analysis. For instance: liberals had to say, when trying to desegregate the schools, that education with other ghetto blacks hurt blacks; then they had to turn around and assure nervous parents that education with ghetto blacks would not, however, hurt whites. It was difficult for white college students to steer a middle course, in the rural South, between condescension and exaggerated self-abasement.

Despite warning signals, it still came as a jolting psychic rebuff for the young white idealist to be told he was not wanted, any longer, by the blacks. One of the early workers in the South, Paul Cowan, has described his own reaction: "I was hurt by the hatred black people were beginning to express toward people like me who believed in integration. I could accept the cultural explanation of their efforts to rid the organization of white people, but no rational argument really healed the pain of personal attacks." Served such a notice, the white students had but one defense against disillusionment—belief that they had brought about their own dismissal. Seen in this light, the reaction against them was an achievement, their victory, not a defeat; they had helped give birth to participatory democracy; they were no longer useful because all leadership in the new society will contain an element of planned obsolescence: the leader leads others toward a state of leaderlessness—to the stage where he is no longer required. This sequence—the euphoria of the early sit-ins and voter-registration drives, followed by edgy relations between blacks and whites, then by expulsion of whites from the young blacks' movement—gave the idea of participatory democracy its special urgency. Hayden tried to repeat in Newark the pure "service approach" to community organization that Moses had used in Mississippi ("If the people of Mississippi want to organize sewing clubs, we'll help them organize sewing clubs; if they want to organize cooking classes, we'll help them organize cooking classes; it's their decision, not ours"). Others, undergoing the same experience, drew the same moral; and it became a commonplace of those working "in the field" that blacks, and the poor generally, must participate in decisions made for their betterment. This whole side of the sixties is ignored in Daniel Patrick Moynihan's book on the concept of "maximum feasible participation" by the poor. He is so interested in the academic justifications offered for such participation that he does not see how demand for it arose out among the poor themselves. Hayden, the best-known popular advocate of participation, is not even mentioned by Moynihan.

It is true that Hayden's world is far from that of liberals like Moynihan and Richard Goodwin; for what his expulsion from the black movement meant for Hayden was the difficult transition from liberal to radical. Enlightened programs out of Washington were the kind of "leadership" no longer acceptable; the programs had to come from the bottom up, not by way of reform but of "restructuring." The "discipline of consent," of deference toward others, had to give way to a discipline of self-expression. This involves a new emphasis on immediacy of experience, beginning with the important experience of being "radicalized." For liberals like Goodwin, modern man's sense of powerlessness can be assuaged by making everybody partake in the governing process. He advocates a return to Jeffersonian concepts of localized, divided authority. But this is simply an extension and revision of the System; and it would still engage men only partially—as citizens, over against government—and in terms of the discipline of consent. Hayden wants to deal with the whole man, and to give him not merely "a say" in decisions that concern him, but complete *mastery* of himself. What happens to the young liberal, when he is radicalized, amounts to an interiorization of the political "market." That market was necessarily insincere because it dealt with the entire society as its basic unit. Adam Smith's individualism was more social in its conceptual orientation than many conservative philosophies (e.g., royalism) that preceded it: laissez faire means, in effect, let the *other* man do what he wants, and the whole point of liberalism was this deference to others, the elaborate arrangement that made everyone keep "hands off" everyone else. The market, in order to work, must invite people in, encourage (in that sense) participation, stimulate the widest possible competitive initiative. But all those who enter the game must abide by its outcome. The trouble with this constant deference to others is that one must, as it were, put off one's own deciding and acting until consensus has been reached, until market tests come up with the acceptable products, or presidents, or programs. One must go along with the majority, hedging one's own action in such a way that the group moves as a whole, by compromise, no one shoving or getting shoved too hard, various inhibitions working against forcible impingement by conviction or passion.

Such constant orientation toward others, toward society as a system of compromise, leads to what the kids see as a lack of "authenticity"—lack of personal responsibility for testing and adopting whatever one tests and adopts. The authentic man takes nothing on its reputation, on the word of others, on authority or at second hand. He does not wait for society at large, through a market interplay to which he makes one small contribution, to make decisions vital to him. He wants nothing premasticated. He must, therefore, avoid the conflict, in liberalism, between theoretical openness to all views and actual conformity to a majority view. The radical is "open" in the sense that he must try all things himself, and "closed" only in the sense that he alone decides, after trial, what is best for him. His deference to others is limited simply by those last two words, "for him." He does not impose on others' interior markets any more than he wants them to dictate to his. Ideally, this means that each person, on his self-seeking quest, achieves, as a result of quest, a "whole self" that engages others not through the System's machinery, one cog of his self touching one cog of another's, but in a total encounter; and out of a network of such private encounters, a public experience is built (*not* a public truth).

There are clear advantages to this radical shift in the locus of experimentation, from society at large to the individual. The whole society's hypothetical openness to anything—an openness the individual did not experience, bound as he was by the interplay of his view with that of many others working toward a compulsory consensus—is replaced by actual personal openness to each idea, each experience, at each moment. It is not so much a question, to the students, of reconstructing a conceptual world each morning, as of beginning one's *experience* fresh at each moment, ready for anything. Since students are, anyway, short on accumulated theory and in need of broadened experience, such empiricism has a strong appeal for them. Besides, this approach reproduces the experience of radicals who went south as good liberals to do something for others (mainly get Whitey to take a "hands off" policy toward persecuted blacks) and, in the process, got radicalized. They acted, and out of action came values—the experience of personal responsibility, of cooperation with their peers, of satisfying achievement and a new kind of community. When Mario Savio went back to Berkeley from his summer in the South, he and his friends were intent on maintaining that *esprit;* a cult of activism was born, in the belief that such action would beget enlightenment. The minor *casus belli* at Berkeley was an occasion sought for the preservation of this experience, an experience that answered almost magically to student problems—stagnation, lack of responsibility, yearning for social function.

But there are disadvantages to this cult of experience. One cannot possibly achieve the "whole self" on such a program—how would one know it was whole? By what norm? All norms must be dissolved in the wash of constant sensation. Doing one's thing is not such a clear goal after all; how does one discover what one's thing is? *This* moment's satisfaction is always suspect, indicted by the possibilities of an ever-receding *next* moment.

And this difficulty in defining individual satisfaction is a minor one compared with the great flaw in the students' view of things: how does one erect a social philosophy on this quest for individual authenticity? At first the question seemed to answer iself: it was precisely in their communal endeavors in the South that liberal activists became radically aware of themselves and of others. The main impression was of *fraternal* effort and satisfaction. All later attempts at a "love-ethic," at being flower children, at founding hippie communes and enclaves in Haight-Ashbury, on the Hog Farm—all these were attempts to hang on to that first experience of solidarity. The sensed oneness came back in flashes, especially in battle—a reason for seeking battle. One of those who held University Hall at Harvard wrote later, in the *Crimson:* "What was most euphoric, however, was us and what we were to each other. For those few hours we were brothers and sisters . . . We were very beautiful in University Hall, we were very human, and we were very together." Recalling such "togetherness," Tom Hayden wrote, "Is the only value in rebellion itself in the countless momentary times when people transcend their pettiness to commit themselves to great purposes?"

The promise only fleetingly realized in shared battle is held out, on a steadier basis, by the rock groups and their attendant fans, "groupies," entourage, their "extended family." As Richard Goldstein put it, "In Rock . . . every important artist pushes not only his music, but also a lifestyle for the fans to identify with." Yippie Abbie Hoffman summed up the whole social philosophy of the kids when he described the Beatles this way: "They are organized around the way they create. They are communal art. They are brothers and, along with their wives and girl friends, form a family unit that is horizontal rather than vertical, in that it extends across a peer group rather than descending vertically like grandparents, parents, children. More than horizontal, it's circular, with the four Beatles the inner circle, then their wives and kids and friends. The Beatles are a small circle of friends, a tribe. They are far more than simply a musical band."

This ideal community admits only those already united in the youth subculture—and only the white subculture at that. This is a sector of society already homogeneous. Radicalism did not *create* community here; at most it heightened the sense of togetherness, and gave kids political tasks. But this did not solve the subculture's real problem—how to reach out of impotent confinement with one's peers to affect society at large; affect, say, the war, or the electoral process, the draft boards, the university trustees, the racial mores of America. By creating all the insignia of a separate community (long hair, funky clothes, beards), the radicals deepened the obvious chasm between the world of the young and the official (Establishment) culture.

How does one act and form a community where leadership is an insult to each person's separate, authentic voice? Doing one's own thing makes it impossible to have a thing for all of society to do. These problems exist even within the homogeneous subculture. How, then, cope with the official culture? How create a "fraternity of whole men" when the dominant sector of society is defined as made up of "partial" men leading a "one-dimensional" life? Ignore them? Hardly, since they run the society's institutions, especially its wars, which are compulsorily manned by members of the subculture. Defy them? But that means interfering with *their* thing; and, besides, the guns are all on that side. The only answer is the classical revolutionary's: declare that since the System has, by its mechanism, deadened the older generation, made it incapable of authenticity, that generation cannot be given the privileges of "whole men" (allowed to do their thing): it must be either written off or, at best, *forced* to become "whole" by a series of violent confrontations meant to reveal their one-dimensionality to themselves. Enter Marcuse.

It is not a very satisfying solution, especially to a pilgrim from the Old Left like Marcuse. The problem of the Old Left was how to get started: since society shapes man, how can man reshape society?—how does one find a large group of men not formed and suborned by the capitalist matrix in which they grew up? And if one does find them, is this not a refutation of the social determinism that serves as one's intellectual foundation? The New Left's problem is just the opposite. It is easy to begin the revolution—it starts each instant, with each new experience (Abbie Hoffman says, "The revolution is where my boots hit"), but where does one go from there; how can one possibly *end* the revolution, by fixing people in a social arrangement? Marcuse, still longing for a proletariat but admitting that workers are lost to the revolution, is caught between old and new, and sees no way either to begin or to end. He has to posit a Utopian "new man," with completely rewired sensibilities, who will free us. (But if the new man is really new, how do we know ahead of time—as Marcuse pretends to—what vision he will bring with him? How, for that matter, did Marcuse escape the social determinants imprisoning lesser men around him? As usually happens, the dreamer is covertly his own superman: he imagines a Utopian race created in his own image.)

It would seem that the cult of experience has nowhere to go—a thing reflected in the oscillation between social activism and passivism, civil rights to flower children to Yippie to radical and back again—were it not for The Myth. Some of the students, with their code of creating oneself by one's acts, forging values rather than finding them, turn naturally to Existentialism, or to its dubious popularizers (Norman Mailer, Paul Goodman). Jack Newfield gives RFK the same Sartre-treatment Mailer had given to JFK. "He defined and created himself in action, and learned almost everything from experience . . .

When his brother died, he passed through a night of dread and learned about the absurd. He had the capacity to trust his instincts and become authentic. He was always in a state of becoming." But a philosophy cannot answer the students' questions, since that would be a retreat from the primacy of action to theorizing about one's acts. And, anyway, the lack of a social philosophy is the major flaw in Existentialism as well as in the student movement. No, what they needed was not philosophy, but Myth, a vicarious and validating experience of the creative nature of undirected activism. And history, with extraordinary compliance, gave it to them when their own bearded, dungareed archetypes, outsiders improvising, came down out of the Sierra Maestra and absentmindedly created revolutionary Cuba.

One of the students' major guides, C. Wright Mills, pointed the way in 1960 when he went to Cuba and wrote his scathing pro-Fidel pamphlet, *Listen Yankee* (which Stokely Carmichael would later read in jail). Tom Hayden, in graduate school at the University of Michigan, began (but did not finish) a dissertation on Mills. It was later the fashion in SDS to begin (but not to finish) dissertations on Mills. *Listen Yankee* made the points that would become so important to students in the sixties—that the revolution was born in the universities, among students, intellectuals, the middle class; that it did not begin with workers or peasants, but only later recruited them; that it did not advance by programmatic Marxist guidelines, but was a do-it-yourself action with on-the-job training, responsive to immediate needs, recognizing its goals only when it had achieved them: "If Fidel had been an army general, he'd not have been able to do what he did. His very lack of experience was of great value. Sometimes knowledge or experience is a wall that stops people, instead of a starting point." It was easy for the Savios and Haydens and Jerry Rubins to think of their own unexpected turns and advances of spirit, in America's South, as a Sierra Maestra of the mind; and coming down from the hills meant going back to the campus, and, past the campus, onto the streets.

Then came the decisive moment for modern radicalism —the Bay of Pigs. Liberals like Schlesinger cannot get into their heads the main, the incontrovertible point of campus revolt: it came about *under Kennedy,* during a liberal regime, when youth was hopeful and the Establishment looked permeable by young ideas. It is a strange experience to sympathize with the enemies of one's own country; it gives one a reorienting shock to do this when one's country is under what one thought of as (in David Halberstam's words) "the best and brightest men of a generation." The new radical was not in revolt against Eisenhower, against stagnation in the system. Far less was he defending the System against Right-Wing assaults from a Joe McCarthy. His protest arose when the System was run by liberals—when even Kennedy looked like an imperialist, when Adlai looked like a liar.

Three things retain an undue prominence in the liberal professors' analysis of campus rebellion—McCarthy, the Bomb, and Kennedy's death. McCarthy is ancient history to these kids; and his crime—of challenging a regnant liberalism—does not seem nearly so grave as it must to upholders of that system. The Bomb is ancient history, too, in the sense that concern with it was the overriding issue of the fifties. That was, after all, the time of the Silent Generation on campus, when the Bomb's lesson to politicians and teachers seemed a clear one: Don't rock the boat. Any too quick motion or touch of violence could start a chain reaction, could trigger the Doomsday Machine. It was a time for liberal professors to urge caution, while students, quietly, watched.

Kennedy, leading a rebellion against the quiet years, liberalized young people, sent them out on beneficent missions—Peace Corps kids in Africa, "advisers" in Vietnam, Green Beret counterinsurgents in training camps, and Cubans democratically reclaiming their own land. But he also radicalized the kids who saw this new activism as imperialist, however kind in its intent. Under Eisenhower, one could still claim that a person (Dulles, say) or an aberrant policy (massive retaliation) was at fault. These were lapses within the System, a System which could be tinkered with. But under Kennedy, if things went wrong, it was not because the wrong party or the wrong man was in charge of the System; the fault must be in the System itself. The distinctively modern rebellion had begun. As Jack Newfield explains, "The generation that passed through American universities during the 1960's developed their politics with liberals in power, as Presidents, as Governors, as university presidents. And they saw those liberals execute Caryl Chessman; invade Cuba and then try to lie about it; dispatch 24,000 Marines to the Dominican Republic; begin bombing North Vietnam; accept covert funds from the CIA; and order police onto campuses."

Schlesinger thinks the death of President Kennedy led to the disillusionment of the young—and it did contribute to it. But the Bay of Pigs had occurred, Mills had written, young men like Hayden had listened, SDS and SNCC were founded, the Port Huron Statement was adopted—all these things had happened *before* Kennedy's death. All the themes of the Berkeley rebellion had been anticipated. Wheels were turning. It is true that Kennedy defined the issue, but in a way that Schlesinger does not understand. Once it was decided that the main threat to world peace was guerrilla war, not the kind of challenge that can be met with massive retaliation, once Bobby Kennedy went to school under "Max" Taylor and became enthusiastic about counterinsurgency tactics, our enemies were defined as Ho, Mao, Fidel, and Che—that is, as the *heroes* of a new generation of American radicals.

Why are these particular men heroes? Jerry Rubin speaks for the new radicals when he says: "Communism? Who the hell knows from Communism? We never lived through Stalin. We read about it, but it doesn't affect us emotionally. Our emotional reaction to Communism is Fidel marching into Havana in 1959." It is not Marxism that makes Cuba crucial to the kids. It is quite a different thing. It is The Myth. Abbie Hoffman quotes a key passage from Fidel: "There are those who believe that it is necessary for ideas to triumph among the greater part of the masses before initiating action, and there are others who understand that action is one of the most efficient instruments for bringing about the triumph of ideas among the masses." Hoffman also quotes Che: "The best way to educate oneself is to become part of the revolution."

Cuba, in other words, offers the hope that action can be self-directing, can automatically beget enlightment; can lead somewhere, and create. This is the lesson taught in Regis Debray's exposition of Castroite principle. The Leninist and Trotskyite concepts of revolution agreed that military forces must be a "fist" obeying the "head" (the party). Even in Asia, Chu Teh was Mao's fist, as Giap would be Ho's. But in Cuba the fist *became* the head;

they were one, and were Fidel. And Fidel points to the future: other revolutions have presumed that politics must precede military action—but the purely political movement soon gets absorbed in the regnant political categories (co-option, the kids call it), or splinters into ideologically pure irrelevance: "Revolutionary politics, if they are not to be blocked, must be diverted from politics as such." Only when military action has opened up new possibilities can a new politics take shape—the fist thinks as it moves, hits, breaks through barriers. In this situation, ideology is simply another form of confinement: it narrows options just at the moment when action is creating unsuspected new options. Thought, therefore, is not welcomed by guerrillas: "The intellectual will try to grasp the present through preconceived ideological concepts and live it through books. He will be less able than others to invent, improvise, make do with available resources, decide instantly on bold moves when he is in a tight spot. Thinking that he already knows, he will learn more slowly, display less flexibility."

Even if guerrilla warfare accomplishes no more than the unsettling of the System, it is worthwhile: Fidel taught that no one can help create the new until the old has lost its hold on him, its air of being immovable. Each guerrilla raid helps destroy the System's sanctity, untouchable eminence: "In order to destroy the idea of unassailability— that age-old accumulation of fear and humility vis-à-vis the *patrono*, the policeman, the *guardia rural*—there is nothing better than combat."

It is a message not lost on the young. Without a stake in the past, they can gamble on the future. If theoretical subtleties, built on long reflection, were needed, the kids would have to take second place to their elders (as Old Leftist generals were supposed to take second place to the party structure). But since thought and theory are to be *avoided*, the kids are the ones in charge, the natural leaders. Even their physical qualifications are the proper ones: "In addition to the moral factor—conviction—physical fitness is the most basic of all skills needed for waging guerrilla war . . . That an elderly man should be proven militant—and possess a revolutionary training—is not, alas, sufficient for coping with guerrilla existence, especially in the early stages. Physical aptitude is the prerequisite for all other aptitudes; a minor point, of limited the-

oretical appeal, but the armed struggle appears to have a
rationale of which theory knows nothing."

If Debray's words are directed to great things, like life
in the Sierra Maestra, they apply as well to minor wars,
like those in Chicago or at Harvard. Very young newsmen
are sent into "liberated" buildings at Berkeley and Columbia, not only because they can win the confidence of the
kids, but because they alone have the stamina to last
through all-night leaderless long discussions, vigils, occupations.

No wonder the Cuban revolution has such magic for
young radicals. It speaks more intimately to their needs,
their shared urgencies, than the Russian revolution did to
men like John Reed. These are the urgencies expressed in a
Harvard *Crimson* editorial: "Action is its own reason for
existing. Rebellion can only be understood by a rebel
who knows that the only 'reason' for rebelling is the
pleasure (or whatever feeling) of rebelling itself." Admittedly, the realizations of the myth are not perfect.
Fidel, after all, is now the head of his own system, and it
is a bit odd for those who have forsworn "leadership" to
admire the one-man state in Cuba. There are nasty rumors about Debray's role in revealing Che's Bolivian hide-
out. Above all, the Cuban revolution is over—the head is
no longer a fist hitting hard at an Establishment. That is
why the revolution finds its later fulfillment in the National Liberation Front and in Che Guevara. The NLF
is not only a guerrilla force using (or thought of as using)
Fidel's methods; the system whose air of unassailability is
in fact *assailed* is that most powerful system of all—
America's military-industrial might, committed to battle in
a much more final way than at the Bay of Pigs. Batista and
the Bay of Pigs are small fry next to the NLF's enemy;
if these guerrillas can win their war, that is a pledge that
even America can be broken.

And then there is Che. Professor Schlesinger's book, in
a chapter called "Heroes and Hopes," described the
leaders young people follow. Their favorite author seemed
at the moment to be Hermann Hesse, but Schlesinger is
certain he will go the way of J. D. Salinger and William
Golding before him (there is no mention of Mills and
Camus, authors read by all the activists Jack Newfield interviewed to learn the reading habits of SDS members;
no mention of Paul Goodman, Herbert Marcuse, Frantz

Fanon, read by half of those Newfield interviewed). Finally Schlesinger comes—in this 1969 book—to the *political* heroes of the young: John F. Kennedy, Gene McCarthy, and John Lindsay. He does not refer to the most significant of the student heroes, Che, the magic humanitarian rebel doctor. I. F. Stone, the journalist most trusted in all sectors of the Left, wrote schoolgirlishly of Che: "He was the first man I had ever met whom I thought not just handsome but beautiful. With his curly, reddish beard, he looked like a cross between a faun and a Sunday School print of Jesus. Mischief, zest, compassion and a sense of mission all flashed across his features during our interview." Guevara, handsome, charismatic, was not satisfied to become a ruler. He was always the fist, off to other countries—two, three, more Vietnams (Vietnams, notice, not Cubas)— striking on to the end. Because he died a guerrilla, he will always be one—while Fidel goes over the national budget, more worried about tractors than machine guns. What the myth needed for its consummation was a martyr—and Che is the perfect one.

4. The Establishment

"You are living a reality I left years ago."
—*Crosby, Stills and Nash*

STUDENT FEELING for the Establishment was always (at its mildest) that "the elephants are kindly but they're dumb." That feeling was confirmed when kids listened to Establishment reaction to their riots. When students shout, in Chicago, "Ho-Ho, Ho-Chi-Minh; the NLF is going to win," or hang pictures of Che in their rooms, or wave the flags of Havana or Hanoi in their marches, they are said to be doing one of several things.

1) "They are responding to the propaganda of foreign agents, Marxist ideologues who have duped them with their

teaching." This thesis (which is Spiro Agnew's and John Mitchell's) sees the young Movement in terms of Old Left categories: the theoreticians must have planted Communist ideas in the kids, since ideas precede action. It is true that there are some doctrinaire Marxists among the young, and some groups began with an ideological loyalty to Russia (the Du Bois Clubs) or to Red China (Progressive Labor Party). But most of the new radicals have been intent on reversing the old order, putting action before ideology. In their eyes, Che and the NLF have destroyed the need for revolutionary *doctrine*. The revolution begins with action, and only that action can, by its progress, define the revolution. The presence of a few Old Leftists in and around the kids' activities—Frances Gabow walking through Grant Park—does not change the dominant atmosphere of the movement.

2) "They are waving the flags of our enemies simply to express hatred for America." Some hatred is there, or is growing up there. But to begin with that is misleading; it suggests that the NLF flag is used because any old stick is good enough to beat our country with. Those who make this judgment are unable to recognize how apt and appealing this *particular* stick is, and why. The origin of the matter is not in hate, but hope. The new radical is not primarily pro-Russian or anti-American. He is in sympathy with the Third World, which tries to escape the polar attraction of both "superpowers." The Third World is, to such radicals, the international equivalent of oppressed Southern blacks—the powerless, who must be given a say, must participate in the decisions of nations.

3) "They are nihilists, who simply want to destroy." Sometimes it comes down to that. But, once again, it does not begin that way. Getting radicalized is a euphoric experience, suggestive of new possibilities, a new life in community. It is all, at the outset, haloed. You do not create the revolution; the revolution creates you—that is the promise, a fizzy promise for those seeking some form of salvation. The faith may be disappointed in time. If so, the disillusionment will be sharp precisely because of the religious intensity involved in this awakening, this conversion called radicalization.

4) "They do not know what they want." Partially true, as the kids admit. But they know why they do not know. They do not, on principle, *define* what they want.

It is first grasped as only "something else." They want *out*. The present stage of cultural conditioning makes it impossible to formulate radical alternatives. Those alternatives will become a matter of organizational concern only after the obstacles of our culture have been cleared away. As Debray says: "The system of oppression is subtle: it has existed from time immemorial, fixed, entrenched, and solid." The measure of the System's success is that people, absorbed into it, are unaware of it. "Confrontation" is a strategy of placing some force over against the System; moving outside it and turning back on it; thus forcing the System to act in ways that reveal its nature, even to those wrapped up in it; so that people step forth and join the confronting band—as McCarthy workers, and even convention delegates, came out of the Hilton and joined the kids in Grant Park, or as "uninvolved" students join radicals after cops are called onto a campus to bust those holding a building. Apparently random acts of violence and insult are not simply nihilist, but have this aim of provoking the System into self-revelatory acts. They help, in Fidel's scheme, to reduce the air of unassailability given off by sacred institutions and offices—which is the reason even verbal and symbolic assault is so effective, so radicalizing. To chant "Daley sucks Hump," as the kids did in Chicago, considerably reduced the social unassailability of the Vice-President of the United States and the mayor of Chicago.

The process, if it does not begin in hatred, can easily end there. One cannot fight an impersonal System; one must single out *people*, concentrate attacks on them, channeling all kinds of personal frustrations into vivid assaults on men like Johnson and Humphrey. It is this kind of venomous outburst that startles outsiders and poses a psychic threat to those in the Movement.

Yet criticism of the radicals should not confine itself to deviations from their own ideal; it should go to the contradictions within that ideal. The trouble with the totally empirical approach is that it so drastically *limits* experience. The laboratory approach to life, which demands personal consumption or experimentation before a judgment can be made on any matter, leaves man at the mercy of his (necessarily limited) actual contacts with men and things. Techniques for breaking out of this limitation are needed, and one of the shrewdest defenders of these techniques is, ironically, Herbert Marcuse. In *One-Dimensional Man,* he points out that the demand for immediacy in all one's experiences makes man give up history, reliance on the memory of others, skilled selective use of the judgment of others, enjoyment of the abstract play of philosophy, the creation of an art that, by sublimation, transcends immediate sensory appeal. The submission of everything to a single test—one's own experience—precludes these important supplements to experience—the tests, as it were, of that test. This is not only an impoverishment in itself; it prevents the one encounter that matters most—self-encounter, which is nominally the students' aim. To be totally present in one's own spontaneity may be a way of confronting others; but it does not allow one to stand apart from the sensing and acting self and, during an experience, to *judge* both the experience and the self. Guerrilla acts of confrontation with the world leave no apparatus for confronting oneself. Seen in this light, "authenticity" becomes one-dimensional.

Marcuse's remarks were directed at the immediate satisfactions offered people by America's consumer society. The result of this constant flow of satisfactions is to "desublimate" longing, enclose men within the present, destroy their sense of history, and block all efforts at transcendence—which, of course, makes it impossible to judge society in radical ways. Yet the radicals are adopting just this kind of imprisonment in action and reaction, stimulation and response to stimuli. This reveals the main cultural link between the students and their elders. For the kids, the less guided action is, the more does it "open" one to good. Experience, tested by the free play of feelings, will sort itself out into patterns of wisdom—just as, for their teachers, the free play of ideas must lead to serviceable truths. In each case, the process is automatic, concatenated as by an invisible hand. And the code of "authenticity," with its concentration on immediate empirical contact with things, is a caricature of the promise held out by our consumer society of affluence and stimulation, of business prosperity guaranteed through maximum expansion, competition, marketplace activity. Despite the mutual misunderstanding known as our "generation gap," these kids are as clearly the sons of America's middle class as Peter Verkhovensky was, to Stepan's bewilderment (but not ours), Stepan's son.

The students' teachers cannot argue with them that "free play of feelings" will not lead to wisdom. In order to do that, they would need self-knowledge, need to know they have deceived themselves with talk of a "free play of ideas." Before they can analyze Peter, they must recognize, in the mirror, Stepan. The sinuosities of self-justification in men like Schlesinger, Pusey, Brewster, and Lipset show how far the liberal is from this self-knowledge.

Meanwhile, unable to give guidance to their pupils, academicians are forced to share their discontent. They too lose *role*, lose useful function. Unwilling to admit the student revolt is directed against them, they cannot either fight back or surrender; they must pretend this war is not theirs. Students attack them by accident, mistaking them for foes in the battle smoke. They are on the students' side—yet each time a professor pops in the window, they shove him out again. They offer more of the same, more liberal reform, and are rebuffed. They, too, resent the war, ROTC, use of the campus for tooling our war machine. Yet they cannot see that these are consequences of their liberal theory. They do not want to be part of the "military-industrial complex" (which is actually a military-industrial-academic complex), yet they demand government money to produce the scientists, Ph.D.'s, physicists, engineers, that cannot, any longer, find employment but by expanding national projects in space and defense. The professors want to sever particular ties with the government, while maintaining those select ones they prefer. They want to be "relevant," part of the action, consulted by Washington; yet unfettered, uncommitted, uncompromised. They have lived a contradiction, blind to that fact; and now all eyes are opening but theirs.

This liberal cannot even defend himself. And so Nixon will. Or Agnew will. Or Mitchell. Republicans, in any case. Not Democrats. After Robert Kennedy's death, the Democratic candidates had all three been college teachers —Humphrey, McCarthy, McGovern. All were liberals of long standing who had, at one time or another, made a strong plea to the young. They had in that sense called the kids into Chicago—though McCarthy, too late, tried to tell them not to come. Yet all three stood by helpless, making no gesture, or ineffectual ones, to help the kids when Daley tried to drive them off with clubs. Humphrey, who had been stung by tear gas drifting up to his hotel room, delivered his acceptance speech without mentioning the battle that took place outside his window. McGovern was not heard from. McCarthy surveyed the scene with his bland Ray Milland concern, and made a typical gesture of irrelevant self-sacrifice—he tried, too late, to withdraw his name from nomination.

This paralysis was a vivid symbol of the liberals' plight —wanting to join the kids, not knowing how; leading them on, then deserting them. (Donald Peterson, the liberal leader of the Wisconsin delegation, collected a large band of kids in his attempt to walk to the Amphitheater, then left them in the street when he turned back.) The Nixon regime has no such uncertainty about the kids. Its leaders, like Agnew and Mitchell, still believe fervently (professors believe half-heartedly if at all) in the moral market: kids have to *earn*—earn something; earn grades, if they cannot, yet, earn money; earn grades as a prelude to earning money. They also believe in the economic market—let colleges, like government, help business, since business *is* America's business, enriching us all. So it is not surprising that these men believe, without qualification, in the academic market. The free play of ideas can take place only in an orderly neutral atmosphere, and the first business of a school is to maintain that atmosphere. If it will not do this for itself, then the government will do it for them, policing the market. Nixon, in his first presidential blast at the kids (March 22, 1969) said he came "to reassert, in the face of student protest, the first principles of academic freedom," to prevent kids from "assaulting the processes of free inquiry." He can afford to be a true believer in the academic marketplace when even professors are having some doubts. As they dither, he will defend them—with force if need be. During his first year in office, he risked only one appearance on a campus— pastoral Beadle College in South Dakota—where he said that, if the kids want war, he will give it to them (confident that he, after all, has the atom bomb): "We have the power to strike back if need be, and to prevail. The nation has survived other attempts at insurrection. We can survive this."

Nixon had, of course, promised that his administration would listen to the kids—just as it would listen to the blacks. His approach to both groups was the same. To both he promised a piece of the action: "In a Nixon administration, students will have a better alternative than to take to the streets in protest. They are going to have a piece of the action." The mechanism that would work this miracle for blacks was "black capitalism" and the coordination of private resources. The scheme for the kids was a Youth Service Agency to coordinate the resources of "student associations, the 4-H Clubs, Jaycees, Boy and Girl Scouts, Future Farmers, YMCA and YMHA groups, the Young Republicans and the Young Democrats, ghetto youth (through the Urban Service Corps and similar organizations), and alienated and rebellious groups and individuals as well."

A token black man—Robert Brown, later made special assistant to the President—traveled on the campaign planes, dodging questions about Spiro Agnew ("It is the man at the top of the ticket who matters"). The token youth leaders on the plane were, of course, those joint heads of Youth for Nixon, David and Julie. They were a TV show from the Eisenhower era looked in on after ten years. Mr. and Mrs. Howdy Doody about to set up housekeeping. Even their clothes were out of the fifties—David's sloppy loafers and sport jacket, Julie's long skirts—and their favorite musician, in 1968, was still Dave Brubeck. Julie, asked to comment on the growing use of drugs by students, said, "It disgusts me. Just because it's more acceptable, that doesn't make it right." (David even stopped smoking *straight* cigarettes in public during the campaign.) Ike's grandson described the Next President of the United States this way: "He's really easygoing, a lot of fun, and has a good sense of humor—the perfect father for a teenage serial." These two were meant to neutralize youth hostility, make the kids dream of being piped toward Dr. Peale's altar to the strains of *The King and I.* Naturally, they only created trouble: SDS members, who ignored Nixon, prevented Julie and David from talking in Binghamton, New York, and heckled them elsewhere. It seemed cruel to make fun of such marionettes; but David was not just the equivalent, on the youth front, of Bob Brown "representing" the blacks. He was closer to the minstrel man who danced for Nixon in Miami. The Amherst student was, during the campaign, a Nephew Tom to his generation. Yet a Nixon aide, asked in 1969 how the President was keeping his promise to listen to the young, answered: "He has great input from David and Julie."

Nixon's way of listening was to watch a football game on the Saturday in November when 300,000 young people came to Washington to protest the war.

Nixon did make two appointments that promised an enlightened view on education and the campuses—Robert Finch as Secretary of HEW, and James B. Allen as Commissioner of Education. But in a series of clashes through the spring of 1969, Nixon ignored these men's suggestions and turned more and more to Agnew, Mitchell, and J. Edgar Hoover as his experts on the young. The youth problem was, for him, just a subdivision of the crime problem. The narrow vision this implies was made clear early in Nixon's term. On the eve of his first trip abroad, his February tour to Europe in 1969, Nixon rushed out a public letter of exaggerated praise for a "get tough" policy at Notre Dame. There was nothing in this policy, looked at calmly and by competent judges, to recommend it to educators. Its only merit was political; it pleased those "fed up" with campus disorders. For Nixon, that was enough. He ignored the background and effect of the policy he praised.

Here is that background. Just before Nixon's trip, the Reverend Theodore Hesburgh, president of Notre Dame University, called off the cinematic part of a campus symposium on pornography. When students went ahead and showed the movies anyway, police were sent into a building to confiscate the film. Twenty-five against two hundred and fifty, the cops had to Mace their way back to safety. A week later, Hesburgh published an unenforceable set of rules: at any disturbance, those engaged would be given fifteen minutes to meditate on their iniquity, after which they would be forced to produce student ID cards; those without cards would be arrested as trespassers, and those with them would be suspended on the spot, with five minutes to "cease and desist." When the five minutes passed, those who had not ceased would be instantly expelled from school; demoted thus from student privilege, they too could be hauled off as trespassing "outsiders." Father Hesburgh thought this a very reasonable procedure, since it gave students "three clear opportunities to remain in student status" (at the beginning, just before the fifteen-minute mark, and just before the five-minute mark). But experienced "hard-liners," like S. I. Hayakawa of San Francisco State, disagreed with him. Hesburgh had written a scenario without any relation to real campus disorder. How, in a fluid situation, does one decide which students have been there fifteen minutes, and which have just arrived? Or how conduct the showing of ID cards in a mob situation—much less get everyone to stand still for the book work of taking down the names of those suspended? And how keep track of the suspended student during his last five minutes of grace?—five minutes, by the way, from the beginning of the name-taking, or from its end, or from the moment when the individual got his name taken down? The whole scheme was ridiculous: it imagined a crowd disorderly enough to deserve arrest eventually (in twenty minutes), yet so orderly in the interval that it will line up to show cards and have names taken, in a twenty-minute version of fall registration procedures. One imagines the Notre Dame student body charging up to occupy a building, then coming to a dead halt to file by a clerk who checks them in by ID card and name.

What made things worse, Hesburgh issued his ultimatum without consulting the faculty-student committee set up to handle disciplinary procedures. (If he had consulted others, the flaws in his plan might have occurred to him.) The Student Senate passed a resolution saying that their president's defense of law and order flouted the established academic norms for enforcing campus law. Hesburgh's was an ill-considered act, to which Nixon gave ill-considered praise. And the most ominous thing about Nixon's letter was its conclusion: "I have directed the Vice President in meetings in Washington this coming week with the governors of the fifty states to discuss what action, consistent with the traditional independence of American universities, might be taken at the State and Federal levels to cope with the growing lawlessness and violence on our campuses."

In making Agnew the administration spokesman on students, Nixon was serving notice that he meant to be tough. Agnew had no qualifications for this role except a record of kid-baiting throughout the 1968 campaign, and, earlier, his inability as governor of Maryland to handle unrest at Bowie State and Towson State. Indeed, after his ill-fated appearance at Towson State, Agnew indulged in a vendetta against those who "founded" that campus's mythical SDS chapter. Campaigning in Detroit, he said of the two professors, "It's about time we began to discourage the employment of this kind of person in our colleges and universities." It was a statement that raised all kinds of interesting questions. If "we" should "discourage the employment" of such people, had *he* as head of the state school system done anything to get rid of the two men? If not, why not? Why recommend a duty to others which *he* had done nothing to meet? Had he ever brought the matter to the attention of Towson State authorities, or the State Board of Trustees? Or had he discussed it only with a political crowd in Detroit? Interesting questions, and embarrassing ones—as his aides must have realized on the spot; for late that night a telegram was rushed to the president of Towson State asking him to look into the matter, and promising to send material on the campus SDS chapter. The race was on to make the governor of Maryland catch up with the runaway rhetoric of the vice-presidential candidate—for he had *not* taken any steps to investigate or act on the charges he was airing.

The subsequent sad farce, which dragged on for months, had its setting back in Maryland; the national press, traveling with Agnew, did not cover it. (They had their hands full with his comparatively minor gaffes, like references to a "Fat Jap" and to "Polacks," or his announcement that he and Nixon did not campaign in ghettos because "Once you've seen one slum, you've seen them all.") A week after the Detroit talk, the president of Towson finally received the material on his two instructors: it was a hastily assembled scrapbook on the SDS, all its items taken from the national press. Yet aides said that Agnew's own information was from an FBI report, and one of the professors, Philip Marcus, was shown an intelligence report that purported to list the Maryland members of SDS. As it turned out, of course, the two men had not founded an SDS chapter; one of them was not even an SDS member—though apparently the police and FBI reports had called him one. The Board of Trustees docilely made the "investigation" their governor had requested; and they were careful to make their report *after* the national election: there were no grounds for dismissal. Nonetheless, both men were summoned before a grand jury in Baltimore County, and one was fired in the spring of 1969— so precipitately that the AAUP went to his defense. Agnew's wild charge, not preceded by responsible action as governor, covered up with a hastily assembled investigation made of paper (newspaper), had done a severe injustice to the two men and edged a quiet campus toward bitter activism. And this was the man who was campaigning on a promise to *cure* campus disorder.

The Towson State experience did not make Agnew more temperate in his approach to kids; and Nixon, who sent Stephen Hess flying to rein Spiro in when he called Humphrey "squishy soft on Communism," did not make him stop calling the *kids* Red-tinged and Hanoi-prompted. Agnew said, "I think a lot of them are connected with foreign powers," and have "received instruction from active Communist leaders of the world." If anything, he got stronger as he went, telling crowds that "scroungy student dissenters" should be treated "like the naughty children they are." He told hecklers, "You can renounce your citizenship if you don't like it here, so why don't you leave?" Then, equaling Wallace's promise to get rid of the disrupters—presumably by running them all over with the presidential limousine—Agnew said, in San Francisco: "I will promise you one thing, they're going to be like the diminishing man. They're going to dry up and disappear from this country very quickly." (What ever happened to that promise?) Still trying to fire people the schools had hired, he attacked the University of California for letting Eldridge Cleaver lecture there: "Trying to learn from such criminals is like trying to take a bath in a sewer." He criticized his opposite number, Senator Muskie, because he "stood passively by at Berkeley as three students burned their draft cards . . . Well, I wouldn't stand passively by like that, I can tell you." What would he have done; beat them up? Three at one blow? Adopting the kids' own insulting word as a compliment, he assured them "the Establishment" would cure their problems.

Nor, after he became Vice-President, did Agnew moderate his rhetoric on the young—or on their teachers. In fact, in a speech delivered at Lexington, Kentucky, he said that federal funds should be withdrawn not only from students but from whole colleges where riots occur (thus punishing the victim). By May of 1969, he was saying, "In my judgment, the war in Vietnam would be over today if we could simply stop the demonstrations in the streets of the United States." In June, Nixon sent Agnew to fulfill his own engagement at Ohio State's commencement— another hard-line speech, while Nixon was taking the mes-

sage to a safer campus in South Dakota. Agnew was flying
high that June, testing phrases he would later use on TV
commentators: "A society which comes to fear its children
is effete. A sniveling, hand-wringing power structure deserves the violent rebellion it encourages. If my generation
doesn't stop cringing, yours will inherit a lawless society
where emotion and muscle displace reason." Shortly after
this, Agnew said he would no longer speak on campuses,
since the kids were not willing to listen to such hard
truths.

But he kept up his assault. *This* power structure was not
sniveling or cringing: "As for these deserters, malcontents,
radicals, incendiaries, the civil and uncivil disobedients
among our young, SDS, PLP, Weathermen 1 and Weathermen 2, the Revolutionary Action Movement, the Yippies, hippies, yahoos, Black Panthers, lions and tigers alike
—I would swap the whole damn zoo for a single platoon
of the kind of young Americans I saw in Vietnam." He
promised that the administration would "separate them
from our society with no more regret than we should
feel over discarding rotten apples from a barrel."

While Agnew supplied the rhetoric, John Mitchell supplied the action. Indeed, Nixon's imitation of his hero
Woodrow Wilson seems to extend to Wilson's choice of an
attorney general. Mitchell talks much as A. Mitchell Palmer did, puffing up the Red Scare after World War I.
Early in his term of office, Mitchell told Sarah McClendon
that "these campus riot leaders make it easy for foreign
governments to make dupes of us." He also complained, in
that interview, that his department could not get college
administrators to be tough enough. Even young Republicans in the Nixon administration were critical of him—
they had said so in a Ripon Society publication. Mitchell
dismissed them as "juvenile delinquents" and plunged on.
The damn liberals would just have to be rescued in spite
of themselves.

As part of this rescue operation, Mitchell pressed a suit
against New Mobe, SDS, Black Panther, and Yippie personnel for their actions at the Chicago convention. This
was the first test of the so-called Rap Brown law against
crossing state lines with intent to foment riot, and it was
a tough case to make. In the first place, Mitchell was
given this particular assortment of *eight* conspirators by a
grand jury that was trying to balance off charges brought

by Ramsey Clark against eight Chicago policemen. In the second place, this assortment was particularly inappropriate—David Dellinger, for instance, had begged for peace and nonviolence in Chicago, while working to get permits for lawful assembly. The Black Panthers took no part in the street action. Even the two defendants closest to each other, Yippies Jerry Rubin and Abbie Hoffman, had fallen out over the handling of "Pigasus," their pig candidate; so they went their separate ways in Chicago. A third difficulty was with the law, which is vague and of dubious constitutionality—Ramsey Clark had been against prosecuting anyone under it. And then there was the final, greatest difficulty—the fact that the rioting in Chicago had been caused by one man, not eight. By Mayor Daley.

Nonetheless, the kids were given the spectacle of a political trial, one they could only think of as meant to stifle dissent, to separate the rotten apples from the rest in the barrel. Mitchell and Hoover let it be known, at the Chicago trial, how heavily the student movement is infiltrated with police spies and informers. That is the true fulfillment of Nixon's promise that his administration would be listening to the young.

5. The War on War

*"I know well how to turn, how to run,
How to hide behind the bitter wall of blue."*
—The Byrds

AS COLLEGE CAMPUSES filled up again in the fall of 1969, Nixon had not ended the war; so the kids decided to. A committee of young workers from the McCarthy campaign, led by Sam Brown, prepared to call a monthly moratorium on other activities, in order to speak and work against war. (They chose the word "moratorium" as softer and more moderate than terms like "general strike.") The first moratorium was to be held on October 15, one day out of school; the second, in November, two days; December, three days, and so on. As October 15 approached, Nixon, at his first press conference in three months, announced he would not be swayed by demonstrations. The kids responded to that challenge. They had, they felt, broken one President in New Hampshire; they could break another with marches in Washington.

After saying "Under no circumstance will I be affected by it [the moratorium]," Nixon scurried madly to steal peace headlines from the kids. In the space of a few days, he:

1) had Secretary of Defense Laird declare that our troops were no longer under orders to engage in active pursuit of the enemy,

2) called Ambassador Bunker back from Vietnam for a review of policy,

3) summoned Henry Cabot Lodge from the peace talks in Paris to confer on their progress,

4) announced the end of General Hershey's unpopular reign at the office of Selective Service,

5) invited Hubert Humphrey to the White House for a bipartisan statement on Nixon's quest for peace,

6) sent an open letter to a protesting student at Georgetown University (Nixon must have thought the boy a liberal, but reporters found his politics were monarchist—when not writing Presidents, he writes to Kings),

7) released the text of an October 12 speech on national progress,

8) announced that he would give a major address on Vietnam in three weeks (November 3), and

9) cleared the release of a Vietnam "fact sheet" to Congress.

None of these gestures worked. In fact, one of them badly backfired—announcement of the November 3 talk. Senate critics eased up on Nixon, waiting to see what new things he might propose. Nixon went into his normal seclusion to labor on the speech, which his Vice-President later called "the most important address of his administration, one of the most important of our decade." More than ordinary secrecy prevented leaks about the speech's content. Nixon composed the entire text himself, working and reworking it. It was released only half an hour before he went on camera. Thus there was a mighty crescendo drumroll of expectation and suspense, leading up to— silence. He had nothing new to say, in policy terms—just excuses (he released a letter from the recently deceased Ho Chi Minh, to show what intransigence he was up against). Commentators and critics (among them Averell Harriman, Johnson's negotiator at the Paris peace talks), who had gathered in TV studios to interpret Nixon's new proposal, were left with nothing to interpret—and they said so. This stung Nixon, who was counting on his emotional final plea to loose a flood of patriotic support, countering the kids' use of TV. The next day, with memories of the Checkers speech in the air, Nixon was photographed smiling at a jumble of telegrams on his desk— 52,000 of them, expressing support for his policy.

Still, he thought the speech was robbed of its impact by critics who went right to work on it in their studios. Pat Buchanan, who gives Nixon his daily news summary and clippings, made a package of these criticisms—Buchanan had kept some reporters from Nixon during the campaign because they criticized "the Boss," and he wanted to do something about the press. Nixon gave the plan his approval; Buchanan drafted a speech for the Vice-President; Agnew created an immediate occasion—an invitation to speak in Des Moines, earlier turned down —for delivering it. The TV networks were informed of the speech's content, and especially of this challenge: "Whether what I've said to you tonight will be heard and seen at all by the nation is not my decision, it's not your decision, it's their decision." (All three networks covered Agnew's speech live in its entirety, without commentary afterward.)

The speech was not long on logic. First Agnew attacked the men who criticized Nixon's speech for indulging in "instant rebuttal" before the President's words "can even be digested." Then he attacked them for excessive planning and prearrangement—for having an expert like Harriman "waiting in the wings" with an analysis "Mr. Harriman recited perfectly." First the newsmen are not prepared to cope with a speech the President "spent weeks in the preparation of." Then they are *too* prepared: "Those who recall the fumbling and groping that followed

358 THE INTELLECTUAL MARKET

President Johnson's dramatic disclosure of his intention not to seek another term have seen these men in a genuine state of nonpreparedness. This was not it." The real crime, it becomes clear, is not procedural—answering too fast, with too little preparation, too great preparation, or whatever—but the substantive crime of disagreeing with the President: "Where the President had issued a call for unity, Mr. Harriman was encouraging the country not to listen to him." The administration, it was clear, would prefer not to "contend with a gaggle of commentators raising doubts."

Needless to say, Agnew zeroed in on his favorite demon, the Eastern Establishment, which does not represent the good folk of America, the silent majority who raise no doubts and do not question Presidents. Agnew had earlier called such types "ideological eunuchs, whose most comfortable position is straddling the philosophical fence," men who are "effete . . . sniveling, hand-wringing" in their treatment of their own children, the willing victims of "an artificial and masochistic sophistication," of an affliction "encouraged by an effete corps of impudent snobs who characterize themselves as intellectuals." In Des Moines Agnew made it clear that a small band of these swishy New York types control what simpler, manlier America sees: "They draw their political and social views from the same sources. Worse, they talk constantly to one another, thereby providing artificial reinforcement to their shared viewpoints." This "tiny, enclosed fraternity of privileged men" hoodwinks solid citizens, poisoning the wells of their belief with "a raised eyebrow, an inflection of the voice, a caustic remark."

Agnew said the President's speech should have been accepted with unquestioning loyalty, and he gave two parallels to illustrate this kind of loyalty—the response to Winston Churchill's talks during the blitz of London and to Kennedy's appeal for unity during the Cuban missile crisis. These parallels suggested that the nation was in critical peril, its very existence at stake, and that Nixon's decisions were matters of survival, made "above politics" and not subject to political criticism. That analogy would have been dishonest if Agnew did not so clearly *believe* the country's life is at stake—not threatened by the Viet Cong or foreign enemies, but from demonstrations on the home front, demonstrations the networks should not cover:

"How many marches and demonstrations would we have if the marchers did not know that the ever faithful TV cameras would be there to record their antics?"

The October moratorium had been a great success, with heavy support from members of Congress. It is difficult to call kids freaky and unrepresentative when they are joined by their Representatives; so John Mitchell undertook a campaign of public "education" to prevent support for the November protest march. The Justice Department issued dark statements on trouble ahead for the nation's capital. Mitchell, asked whether he agreed with Agnew's attack on "impudent snobs," said there were more destructive elements at work than mere snobs. Richard Kleindienst, speaking for the Department, refused to grant a march permit to the "New Mobilization." Senators and congressmen who had supported the October moratorium refused to join in the Mobe plans, and asked for peace and calm. A war-hysteria settled over Washington. The tone of it is best conveyed in a TV interview with Mrs. John Mitchell, the wife of the attorney general: "This place could become a complete fortress. You could have every building in Washington burned down. It could be a great, great catastrophe. And this is the thing I worried about way before I came to Washington, knowing the liberal element in this country is so, so against us. As my husband has said many times, some of the liberals in this country, he'd like to take them and change them for the Russian Communists." (Agnew said TV networks spread fear when they air the wild comments of a Stokely Carmichael. He said nothing of wild comments voiced by the wife of our chief law enforcement officer.)

Finally D.C. Mayor Walter Washington interceded with the President to get a march permit for the New Mobe— on the grounds that real trouble would take place if the kids were given no legal way of expressing their dissent once they arrived in Washington. Only this last-minute injection of sense kept Mitchell from repeating Mayor Daley's tragic error in Washington—but this time with 300,000 demonstrators on hand, instead of 5000; for the buildup of repressive moves by the administration had called out the young in a way that dwarfed all earlier political gatherings. The Mobe rally was ten times as big as the last mass event in the capital, the 1967 March on the Pentagon. Agnew had said, before the election, that student demonstrators would "dry up and disappear" under a Nixon administration. Yet exactly one year after Nixon's election, a continual stream of embittered young people came from all over the nation to chant "Stop the Chicago Trial" in front of Mitchell's Justice Department, to carry "Free Kim Agnew" signs (his thirteen-year-old daughter had tried to wear a moratorium armband in October, but the Vice-President stopped her), to mutter curses at the President who, unreachable in the White House, had let it be known he would spend the afternoon of the mass rally watching football.

They came, as well, to supply an endless stream of people past the White House in a forty-hour vigil called the March Against Death. From Thursday afternoon until Saturday morning, a thousand of them every hour, protestors carried the names of dead American soldiers or destroyed Vietnam villages along a four-mile route. The celebrants were robed near Arlington Cemetery, their priestly mark—worn a bit pompously, unembarrassed—a wide cardboard plaque, neatly lettered with a name. Then they moved out, single file, not talking much, not even pairing off for company along the way, staying in line, liturgical. They knew they were the surrogate dead. Miles later, over halfway to the goal, each placard passed the White House, the sign moved across a background of the high grill fence, and at the gate each bearer turned, conscientiously underplaying his role, to whisper the lettered name, or shout it, and shuffle on a little faster, the minister dwarfed by the rite's solemnity. Nixon had said, in his November 3 speech, it was too late to ask *why* we were drawn into Vietnam. That meant these lines of men named off, these thousands, do not matter; so they came, saying nothing, only the names. Whole battlefields were rising in long procession, the war coming back accusatory to its source.

I saw them first at 2:00 A.M. Friday morning, November 14, in a light drizzle that frayed streetlights and dizzied the floodlit dome of their goal, the Capitol. They were ragged kids, comically self-important, a Halloween crew of trick-or-treaters; but the men they walked for could not be treated now, and they had no tricks to play—unless this were their last one, this haunting by proxy. Each marcher held a candle, poked through the bottom of a dixie cup, it glowed under their sheltering hands or long male locks, long female locks, part of the general flow and train of them, the robes, serapes, ponchos—a shaggy band of acolytes, young bearded Rasputins, beardless Alyoshas, the girls pubescent witches (but unmenacing, half Charles Addams' Morticia, her dress starring the ground, half Morticia's chunky girl in braces). The whole thing seemed both orderly and disreputable, a ritual conducted by mad monks. (Priests had just been arrested in the Pentagon for saying Mass.) At the Capitol grounds, the line wound toward twelve coffins—the old shaped kind, with shoulders, as in Dracula movies, of plain wood with a clean *shaved* look, like the bright ends of orange crates, familiar brightness sinister in this setting. A tall boy, in the sieved light and mist, took each placard and, working like a derrick, leaned in the coffin and lined the names up, packing them neatly, morticianer of cardboard. This protest of the young is as irrefutable in its innocence as Pierre's bewilderment in *War and Peace;* their walk suggests his, that famous stroll through cannon fire at Borodino, Pierre an absurd bulk top-hatted in the muddled shove of armies, staring at deaths obscene upon the bright field, most aware of beauty, mocked by it, numbed past anger to mere wonder, "What madness! Why don't they stop?"

In the marshal station, a church, at two-thirty in the morning volunteers were being registered, assigned to areas, shown how to reach walkie-talkie captains, drilled on contingencies by a boy at the pulpit microphone. Those who would man the walkie-talkies were in the choir, and their hoarse instructor had to work over the PA system. The noise did not bother some who had ended their shifts and slumped in the pews or on the floor to sleep. "This is the first time I've been in a church in years," one boy assured his girl; she answered, a little too loud, trying to sound wicked, "I haven't been in one since—last Christmas!" An eighteen-year-old marshal came in chilled and starving (he was given an apple—these troops lived on apples all weekend) and said, "I've been out there twelve hours, but isn't it beautiful? I just hope the crazies don't kill it."

Friday, just after noon, two para-Mobe probes were made at the Justice Department, the first one authorized by permit, the second one not. Dr. Spock led the first—tall, unflappable, Lewis Stone as Andy Hardy's father.

He gathered a crowd on the Mall, denounced the Rap
Brown law, then crossed Constitution Avenue to let
Mitchell know the law is unconstitutional. Jack Landau,
who handles the press for Justice, squeezed out of the
iron gate on the west side and asked Dr. Spock to call
some day when they were less busy (through the gate,
signs of that busyness could be seen, helmeted troops in
the courtyard—nine thousand of them had been brought
to Washington).

The crowd trailed back across the street onto the grass
to watch Dwight Macdonald, a portlier Skitch Henderson,
fight the wind for possession of dull pages from an endless
speech. Macdonald was speaking for the Philadelphia Resistance, in town to give Mitchell draft cards turned in at
their last rally. After the speech, the crowd milled back
to the same gate at Justice; Landau came out to say
Mitchell was still busy, but that he would carry the cards
to him. The Resistance kept its cards and tried to draw
the crowd off.

They were not going. They had taken over Tenth Street,
chanting "Jump! Jump!" to Justice personnel at windows.
Macdonald pleaded, through the cops' bullhorn, ineptly:
"You are making it difficult for the people inside to do
their work." Which was just what they had in mind. Mobe
kids with marshal armbands scattered through the crowd,
trying to dislodge it from the building's side. Finally bullhorned pleas broke up the chanting, and the crowd moved
off. D.C. police from the Special Operations Division were
on the scene, but did nothing except lend their horns to
Mobe. The SOD leader, a bear of a man (and black),
Owen Davis, sat plainclothed in an unmarked car across
the street. Mayor Daley should have been there, to see
how these things are done.

But those who had come would be back. "We'll need
helmets tonight," one girl said (SDS factions had promised
Mobe officials not to bring helmets or weapons). "Right,"
her partner answered. "Let's eat now; who knows when
they'll feed us after we're busted."

Four-thirty Friday afternoon, thunder drowned out the
voices at the White House gate, but the names kept coming, still clear on the sodden cardboard, and each name
was spoken, however inaudibly—each a cry for Lazarus,
who did not come out of the tomb. They marched, hierati-
cally bedraggled, in a steam of incensey breath and heat

vapor off their clothes, pairing off now, huddling into the rain.

While some prayed for more rain, skies cleared; but it was cold. One crowd shivered through an outside rally that night at George Washington University. Another got inside the National Cathedral for William Coffin's prayers and Pete Seeger's songs. But the helmets went to DuPont Circle. After a half hour of rhetoric, a thousand kids chanted their way four blocks west to the South Vietnamese Embassy, to serve an eviction notice. There was the usual milling, bullhorned warnings, thrown rocks and bottles, then tear gas. A Mobe legal adviser stepped between one cop and a girl tangled in the Embassy hedge. "We were supposed to observe, but this gas blinds you good," he said when, several blocks down, he surfaced toward sweet air. Others had stumbled apart from each other and were calling names to regroup—one experienced kid had tied a long scarf to his girl. "Did you see the look on the face of that guy with the Viet Cong flag?" the Mobe legal staffer asked. "I'll never forget it, a kind of half-smile when it started." The crowd fell back on DuPont Circle, talking itself into militancy again, then probed out along various arteries, alert to sirens that moved in lariats of sound around them. A police motorbike was burned, a prisoner-van stoned and rocked, a "pig car" cut off and surrounded (till a Mobe official talked it free). The loud kids kept running into quiet kids who opposed them. One girl who had thrown rocks at passing motorcycle cops took a heavy STOP sign and its iron post, torn down earlier and tossed aside, to the rail over DuPont Circle's underpass; she eased it onto the edge and held it for a passing car. A boy fought through her friends' resistance, took the sign away and tried (unsuccessfully) to shove it out of reach onto a store marquee, then hid it under a parked car.

The game went on for hours, as the night got colder. Just before midnight, D.C. Police Chief Jerry Wilson turned DuPont Circle over to the kids, on condition that they stay in it; and enough marshal types remained there to make the bargain stick. Earlier, when the first rocks were thrown, some kids stood at plate glass windows, protecting them. A marshal chased one boy with a pole who was poking it through glass, but the boy slipped away in the gas and confusion. The marshal, just his age, turned back screaming in disgust, tear-gassed to tears he would have shed anyway, "What madness!"

The broad lanes and levels, the lifeless big lumps of federal marble, make lower Pennsylvania and Constitution Avenues look like an Egyptian movie set, where even George Washington's obelisk is in place. Saturday morning a gaudy rabble came down the broad avenues, jostling but harnessed, as if drawing some new block toward pyramids in construction. But these were dismantlers of power, not builders. They were considerably more raucous than the single-file line had been, though they were supposed to be moving to the slow death-stammer beaten on crepe-wrapped drums. The twelve coffins, lifted on young shoulders, led the parade, all those names coming back at the White House from a new direction, this time to be left there. The stark deal boxes had sprouted flowers now that they were closed, and little flags.

Viet Cong types, swirling their flags, shoved and strutted, made little runs like a football line warming up; but this was not their show, and they were unhappy. Marshals politely hemmed them in, held them down, and they had to settle for marching like everyone else. The parade moved in clumps between moving lines of arm-linked marshals, braided edges giving definition to the motley stream. Celebrities led the first clumps off—Spock again, the tallest; Bill Coffin, still square-jawed Ivy League under the thinnest veneer of hippiedom (long hair, with-it slang), Dink Stover in middle age, Bones man ever at war with Bones; George McGovern, with his prim etched look, a grainily lithographed smile; Mrs. King, with vailed lids always, as if almost in tears.

At the rally site, there were signs everywhere of planning, preparation, hard work, of hours put in by kids with no energy left for running around DuPont Circle. Here were heated food pits, latrines, the $17,000 sound system (speakers up on vertiginous scaffolding), the stage, press tent, a labyrinth-entrance to the stage area through concentric fences (for moating off intruders), a marshal communications center in the press tent—all of them steps that would prove essential to the peace. The celebrities, finishing their march, went into the press tent. Timothy Leary, with his dissolute-priest look, had got there early and sat perfunctorily banging on a drum, aching to be interviewed (a dozen newsmen obliged).

The crowd sat on the cold ground, on flyers and signs if possible, or blankets if they had come prepared. The Viet Cong flags came through this sea of muffled people, surfing on toward the stage, all chants and pugnacity. They would be begged and ordered, all day, to sit down or lower their flags; they blocked the view of thousands seated behind them. They stood. When others waved the V-sign, they lifted the fist of resistance. The speeches, most of them ignorable, started early, and were ignored. This crowd had a short attention span—an effort at thoughtful speaking would bore it (as Mrs. King did). David Dellinger tried some old proletariat-stoking, but no fire caught. The big moments were brief—of wit (Dick Gregory), charm (Spock), cant (Rip Torn), and, above all, song (Arlo Guthrie, Pete Seeger, Richie Havens), in response to which the sea shuddered up in waves, swayed, joined the refrain, crying "More!" at the end of each act. Again and again there was the first surge (up on their feet) as the crowd rocked, danced, yelled, yearned in on itself; then a second surge as all arms went up and flickered the V-sign, a vast languid simmer.

In between such moments, people blew, breathed, and burrowed for warmth, formed mounds of ashlar work lying on each other, layer on layer; chased mimeoed handouts for brief fires (chase more warming than the fire). The program had politick balance, as at a convention— one labor leader (Harold Gibbons) and one businessman (Howard Samuels). Leonard Bernstein, a shorter Leary, pop priest, his hair less and less Beatle (as it silvers), more and more Stokowski, told the kids with 'umble deference, "You're beautiful!" The Viet Congers were getting restless; they had been on their feet for hours, first marching, then pinned in this crowd of pacific people shouting down their shouts. Marshals ducked in under the flags, asking for quiet, sounding their intentions—and some returned with news: the stage would be rushed during Senator McGovern's speech (perhaps on the assumption that any relief from such boredom would be welcomed). All the walkie-talkies crackled, and a thong of three-deep marshals was woven, shoulder to shoulder, around the Congs. By two-thirty, McGovern—after being warned of possible trouble by Sander Vanocur—was pinching oratory through his stone smile, and a heave went through the Congs; their flags ground even closer to the stage—then ground to a halt. The braided thong had held. Some marshals were called pigs, some were hit with thrown things (not stones—who could bend over?—but apples and hard scraps of lunch). But the crowd yelled "Stop throwing!" and the barrage died off. Put-on artists threw conciliatory marshmallows, to exaggerated laughter from the marshals, whose tensions were easing.

At four o'clock the flags moved back out through the surf of people seated; the militants were anticipating a five o'clock showdown at the Justice Department. The thousand or so guerrillas were trailed by other thousands of the curious—and by marshals, medics, legal advisers, and Ramsey Clark's hastily assembled group of independent observers. Up in Mitchell's office, the attorney general leaned his gentle collapse of face out the window—a general melt of sad eyes down toward jowly deliquescence—and watched the oncoming army. His wife would later recall that "My husband made the comment to me, looking out the Justice Department, it looked like the Russian revolution going on." As he scanned the ranks below, he sagely determined, *"There* is the hard core" (pointing to a line of kids with arms locked). Nixon, smearing Ramsey Clark in the 1968 campaign, said that *he* would have an attorney general skilled in law enforcement, known and respected by the whole law enforcement community. Instead, he got a municipal bond lawyer. This skirmish was on-the-job training for Mitchell, as close as he had ever been to a riot. No wonder he was panicky. It was a strange way for the nation's highest law-enforcement official to be learning the fundamentals of police work.

Luckily, there was some professional knowledge on the scene. As the Viet Cong flags, circling the building, turned the southeast corner, the "hot spot" where the legal march would end, only one cop was there, in a soft hat, no special markings on his uniform, just his badge and nameplate, J. V. Wilson. The kids did not know he was the Chief; to them he was just another "Pig!" shouted at as they rounded the corner, came to a halt in siege position at the south façade. Though his men had done well last night at DuPont Circle, Wilson told newmen they *might* have thrown the gas a little early. This time no gas would be thrown till he was personally convinced of its necessity. Rocks flew, American flags at each corner of the building were run down, a bottle landed near Wilson. Still he waited. Mobe marshals spread out along the ledge under the first floor Justice windows, and, hands up, palms out, urged calm while glass fell from windows behind them. A splot of red paint landed high on the gray façade. Finally Wilson told the marshals to get down, they were not safe, and—not bothering to put his own mask on—threw a gas grenade while cops came to his walkie-talkie summons.

The scenario took its destined course, desultory sluicings of the crowd this way and that, knots reforming then rinsed away with gas. But all through it young marshals urged the peaceful to leave, pointed upwind toward escape routes, took stones from some kids' hands. At the Internal Revenue Building, next to Justice, a flag bellied out and slipped down; two Mobe types quickly got to the lines and raised it again. Several attacks were made on them, each tending one line, but they held their post—until a band of three hit one of them, who kicked out from the flagpole base and swung like Tarzan on the line, bumping kids away with his boots. At last one foot was caught, though, and others joined the three assailants; the flag was dragged down and away.

Kids were fighting kids. The organization Mitchell had called the most dangerous to march on Washington had become the most pacific. Out of 300,000 people, maybe 3000 at most—1 percent—came for violence (to throw rocks at cops or windows). Three thousand can cause trouble; but not only were the 99 percent peaceful themselves, they were helping enforce peace. At all other such affairs, the crazies have been met with some disapproval from their own, but little resistance. At the Woodstock rock festival, held the preceding summer, kids had policed themselves, but in an apolitical situation, with no militants massed around a target like the Justice Department. Here, cops and kids worked together to keep order (despite Mitchell), with extraordinary friendliness.

After it all, Mitchell had learned little; he deepened resentment against him when he said the weekend could not be called generally peaceful. But the kids had learned something. Over and over, one heard an amazed "Those freaks are going to spoil it all." In other marches, pigs were on one side, kids on the other; all evil was concentrated in the offices of power. But here the enemy was also in one's ranks; and in some positions of power were men

like Mayor Washington, and Chief Wilson, and Owen
Davis of the SOD, and all the cops who helped kids on
street corners. The young had found stupidity, intransigence, evil where they did not expect it, where their
earlier assumptions had ruled it out—under thirty. It was
the beginning of their political education. Someday each
will find evil in himself; then they will no longer be kids.

6. Plastic Man

> *"Here comes the blind commissioner,*
> *They've got him in a trance."*
>   —Bob Dylan

AT THE 1969 INAUGURATION, the streets were full
of ashen Nixons. Kids in town to cause trouble wore
crinkly white masks with that undeniable nose. But Nixon's car sped past their jeering ranks, and, up on the reviewing stand, his face bunched in its instant. toothed
smile, so circumspect, so vulnerable. He had this in common with the kids; he wears a Nixon mask.

Yet he tried to please young people on this day. The
attempt was careful as always, clumsy and self-defeating.
But it was made. He began his campaign with a young
new staff that called him a survivor of the Kennedy regime. Now he would offer the kids a hand-me-down
speech from the New Frontier.

Nixon had locked himself away and studied past inaugural addresses. From them all he singled out Kennedy's, then painstakingly mimicked it: "Let this message
be heard, by strong and weak alike . . ." (JFK: "Let the
word go forth, to friend and foe alike.") "Let all nations
know . . ." (JFK: "Let every nation know . . .") "Those
who would be our adversaries, we invite to a peaceful
competition." (JFK: "To those nations who would make
themselves our adversary, we offer not a pledge but a re-

quest: that both sides begin anew the quest for peace.")
"But to all those who would be tempted by weakness, let us
leave no doubt that we will be as strong as we need to be,
for as long as we need to be." (JFK: "We dare not
tempt them with weakness, for only when our arms are
strong beyond doubt can we be certain beyond doubt that
they will never be employed.") "Without the people we
can do nothing; with the people we can do everything."
(JFK: "United, there is little we cannot do in a host of
cooperative ventures. Divided, there is little we can
do . . .") "We cannot expect to make everyone our
friend, but we can try to make no one our enemy."
(JFK: "We shall not always expect to find them supporting their own freedom.") "In the orderly transfer of
power, we celebrate the unity that keeps us free." (JFK:
"We observe not a victory of party but a celebration of
freedom.") "Our destiny lies not in the stars but on earth
itself, in our own hands . . ." (JFK: "Here on earth
God's work must truly be our own . . . man holds in his
mortal hands . . .")

Nixon tried to imitate Kennedy's call for a Teddy
Roosevelt "vigor": "I do not offer a life of uninspiring
ease." And he used a combination of bluff and flattery on
the young: "I know America's youth. I believe in them.
We can be proud that they are better educated, more
committed, more passionately driven by conscience than
any generation in our history." It was a typical effort on
Nixon's part to "create an input" for the young (his
computer-robot images are apt).

He was not more natural in any of his presidential
gestures. His aides, nonetheless, were soon stressing that he
liked the role of President. They welcome any sign of emotion in this man who seems mechanical (assembled in the
morning, disassembled every night). That is why they enjoy so much his enjoyment of sports. Glad announcements
that he is glad (the robot smiled this morning) recall the
party thrown in Mailer's *Deer Park* when Marty Peller
breaks his spell of impotence ("Marty made it").

A little spontaneity must, with Nixon, go a long way.
Even his interest in football has proved too obviously useful—that is what he talks about to wounded black soldiers
when he cannot touch on things that matter, on pain or
death, racism or warfare. (Better stick with end runs, with
tricky quarterbacks.) And just when aides have described

how Nixon bowls a little to unbend, the Boss comes along and says *why* he likes to bowl—it pits him against himself. Even play must be a form of self-discipline.

The occasion for instinctive response—or for its illusion —must be sought out. In 1968, Nixon's one unguarded moment seemed to come when he visited a school for the deaf in Michigan; he talked to children through sign-language interpreters, and was moved, manifestly. The news went forth: "For the first time in his campaign, Richard Nixon had succumbed to sentiment" (Don Oberdorfer in the Washington *Post*). Staff members told how he returned to the poor children's plight in his suite that evening. Billy Graham was called, to listen to how deeply Nixon felt. The candidate described his own compassion at a rally. Marty made it.

But the thing was a repeat performance. It duplicated a stop at the Iowa School for the Deaf in his 1960 campaign, where everyone marveled at Nixon's feeling for the kids. Eight years later, wouldn't it work again? Just once. At a different school, lest the link be made. And aides will be ready to relay his nighttime musings. Billy Graham will bless the new emotion. Marty will get by— with a little help from his friends.

Nixon, so ill-at-ease among strangers, remains guarded with intimates, with his very family—hiding grievances from his brother under stiff decorum, writing his mother in the tones of a geriatric manual. The closest the public has come to a glimpse of Nixon in the bosom of his family was on the night of his nomination in Miami. A CBS camera had been admitted to his suite—just as, later, it would record Humphrey's reactions in Chicago. Humphrey sat on a couch with friends, brooding fussily over a list of delegates as if he could hatch states out of the paper, clucking lost delegations away ("Oregon is zilch"). When the decisive state, Pennsylvania, broke out of its shell on schedule, Humphrey was up with a bound and crowing. When his wife's image wavered onto the TV screen, he lavished chaste kisses on the tube. But Nixon, on his night of victory, sat in a chair pulled forward from the others, communing with the TV set, with his yellow legal pad, with himself. When Wisconsin took him over the top, those behind him—Rose Woods, Pat, the girls— celebrated quietly, hardly trusting victory, fooled by it before. But some relief—some surrender to joy, however

measured—showed in all the others. Not in Nixon. His
hand, his head, did not rise from the pad. He was mo-
tionless—not, certainly, from lack of response. There was
scurry and alertness of all kinds inside him: slide of lenses,
click of tumblers, snag of safety catch. A stern internal
monitoring, a ceaseless self-correcting process, "corrected"
him into immobility. His very busyness kept him still. At
last, though, the inner wheels fell into place: he tore the
top sheet off his pad, handed it back toward empty air
(not to anyone in particular—all his bets are hedged, even
in this company), and said, "Does someone want this for
a souvenir?" After all the computer-preliminaries, this act,
too, was tentative, diffident. Finally he allowed himself a
grin, carefully, eyes scouting toward the camera, quick
surveillance raids always detected.

He is the least "authentic" man alive, the late mover,
tester of responses, submissive to "the discipline of consent." A survivor. There is one Nixon only, though there
seem to be new ones all the time—he will try to be
what people want. He lacks the stamp of place or personality because the Market is death to style, and he is the
Market's servant. His aim has always been the detached
mind, calculating, freed for observing the free play of
political ideas, ready to go with the surviving one. This
makes him stand for all that the kids find contrived, what
they call "plastic." They are the opposite; plunging, ready
to take risks. They move up as close as they can to each
experience, flow out to it, undergo it for its own sake;
only in this way will it be known, tested, given proper
weight in their intensely private evaluative process, their
inner "market."

Nixon draws back, disengages. As his priest-speech-
writer noticed, successive drafts by Nixon get more bland,
increasingly safe as they say less. In a blundering toward
confrontation with each other, Nixon and the kids are not
only masked but blindfolded, opposed twin parodies of
Market process, one the measure of the other's excess.
The "privileged" students, without having the tasks, have
some of the attitudes, of an aristocracy—mainly this: they
have no doubt of their own worth. They do not feel they
must *earn* dignity. For this reason Nixon, and Nixon's
America, cannot trust them: as Nixon told Theodore
White, "They were given too much, too easily; and this
weakened them."

The relaxed ways of the kids became, at Nixon's inauguration and the Woodstock Festival, a literally unbut-
toned and unbra'd openness, a celebration of hair and
nudity—while Nixon is the most doggedly *dressed* man
imaginable. At private meetings where others are in shirt
sleeves, Nixon stays creased and encased. He could not
appear rumpled and wrinkly, like Rockefeller or Bob
Kennedy—he would look seedy. He has not been able to
affect shirt sleeves like Romney, Percy, Lindsay—he would
seem somehow violated. With other politicians, informal-
ity exposes the man behind the office, a range of personality that extends beyond political role. But Nixon does not
exist outside his role, apart from politics: take his clothes
off, he would be invisible.

His rigid wall of decorum, in dress and manner, is one
of the means he uses to fend off the world, avoid participation in it. He speaks across the palings of stiff custom
and a tie. This armor makes his stiltedness less noticeable.
The more dressed up a man is—any man—the more he resembles a puppet. So if you are puppetlike in the first
place, you should meet men laced into formalest attire.
That is why Nixon restored white-tie ceremony to the
White House. Some, it is true, took the toy hats and
tunics added to White House police as a sign of Nixon's
imagination, of a latent romanticism. Quite the opposite.
Each added symbol of uniform, function, office makes
man's role in the social chess game clearer, his place
marked, moves limited. Clothes structure a situation,
make things predictable, reduce their menace. In that
sense Nixon's Graustark troops guard him with ceremony,
ward off the phantoms of his insecurity.

Nixon must put such barriers around him, extend the
interval between stimulus and response, gain time to consider all sides of a thing. When he came to the White
House, he said he would retire for private contemplation
to a study in the Executive Office Building: "I like to work
in a relatively small room with my papers all around.
When I have to do brainwork, I'll go over there." It was
hard to find an appropriate spot in the crowded EOB,
but Nixon pushed his project through. Even the White
House is, for him, a thing to be stepped away from, sized
up at some distance. When he cannot get over to the
EOB, he leaves the Oval Office, after advisers have given
him counsel, to ponder matters in the Lincoln Sitting

Room. He announced, shortly after his inauguration, that he would not make decisions in the presence of advisers, no matter how intimate.

This withdrawal to ever higher ground, to some lonely vantage for decision making, is meant to keep things manageable, distanced, under wide survey. Two of Nixon's favorite metaphors deal with the burner (move other things to back burners, keep one thing on the front one) and the plate (there is enough on the plate, don't add to it). His whole operation is geared to give him the right "input." All data must be sifted, filtered, processed five ways by the time it reaches him. The first thing he did when he entered the Oval Office was order Johnson's $13,000 three-screen TV console (for watching news on all networks) removed to Herb Klein's office. The AP and UPI tickers were put at Pat Buchanan's disposal. Americans have, to their dismay, participated nightly in the color-screen war of Vietnam. Nixon will not do that; he wants his news in summary capsules, mediated, boiled down to impersonal content. Nor are cameras allowed to scrutinize him as they did his predecessors. Kennedy liked to be photographed making decisions, even tough ones like the Cuban blockade. Johnson, watching his three TV screens (kept on all day so he would not have to wait for them to warm up), was constantly watched by an official photographer. But Nixon told his cameraman, Ollie Atkins, to be present only on ceremonial occasions.

The development of his staff system has been toward ever greater refinement, reduction, purification of what gets to him through his "final filter," John Ehrlichman. The movement was toward ideal unity—a striving for the one-man State Department (Kissinger), one domestic surrogate (Agnew), one "program" man (Shultz), one staff expert (Ehrlichman), one politics man (Dent), one general adviser (Mitchell), one official friend (Rebozo). One burner. One plate. One decider.

He lives in a cleared circle, an emotional DMZ, space razed and defoliated, so he cannot be "got to" unexpectedly. If it seems a lonely way of living, it is his chosen way, and long has been. What the presidency gives him is ever larger decisions to make, and more resources for concentration on that task. For years he has burned and razed this space for his mind to work in, detaching himself from his surroundings ("I developed the ability long ago to do one thing while thinking of another"). He keeps his mind at a deliberate remove from his body. In all six of the crises in Nixon's book, there is a point where he must triumph over illness, sleeplessness, fatigue. The chapter he wrote himself describes this warfare on his own flesh, which he overcomes in battle after battle:

> As I walked through the aisle to the podium, the fatigue I had felt as a result of three days with almost no sleep left me completely. As I started to speak, I could sense that this would be one of my better efforts.

> While I got very little sleep for the balance of the night, I was able to get up at seven and proceed to the Kiel Auditorium for the scheduled meeting. I don't know when I have ever felt so weak before walking out onto a public platform but I was determined to let no one know my condition. I then proceeded to make what some of the reporters have called my best speech of the campaign.

> I woke up on the Sunday before election to begin what was to be the longest "day" of my life—a stretch of 72 hours during which I was able to manage less than five hours of sleep . . . I was tired after a campaign that had already probably been too long and too strenuous . . . In that talk, which some observers—Frank Holeman of the New York *Daily News* was one—rate the best of my campaign telecasts, I returned to the theme of my acceptance speech at Chicago.

> I knew that I was tired physically, but despite lack of sleep, I had never felt more alert mentally and none of the questions gave me any trouble. Frances Dewey (Mrs. Tom Dewey) was to tell me weeks later that the telethon was my best appearance of the entire campaign. Here again, therefore, was an example of something I had learned from long experience—that in time of stress and crisis, an individual can be at his best mentally even though he is physically exhausted.

> I was so tired at the time, for sheer lack of sleep, that I was concerned as to whether my handling of the

conference had been anything close to par. Frank
Stanton, president of CBS, called me later that
night and said he was sending me a recording of the
conference because he thought it the very best I had
ever had up to that time. I told him of my concern
and he observed that it had been his experience, often
as not, that an individual is at his very best on
radio or TV when he is physically tired. Because
of his very fatigue, he raises the level of his mental
and emotional concentration even higher, to compensate for the physical factor and thus to meet the
challenge.

Mental concentration over "the physical factor," positive
thinking over negative facts, spirit over matter—through
it all, no matter how the body flags, the mind spins on,
clear, untired, disencumbered of its weak material shell.
He rises above that puppet Nixon body the cartoonists
mock. They must think he inhabits that disjointed thing
(assembled every morning, disassembled every night).
Who did they think does the assembling, then stands back
to judge the puppet and judge all the things around it,
from a distance? They still have not found *him* under it
all—the dissembler, the inner decider, the disciplined man
pitted always against himself (as when bowling). He is the
living fulfillment of the Alger period's success manuals:

> What is it that keeps the underdog down? What is it
> that the upper ten possesses that the under ten thou-
> sand does not have? Faith, Confidence, Power, Am-
> bition, and more. Far greater than all is "THAT
> SOMETHING," which could best be defined as the
> capacity to say "I WILL." (*That Something*, by
> W. W. Woodbridge.)

Nixon's own code is suggested in the praise he metes out
to others. He introduced the members of his cabinet with
repeated reference to an "extra dimension" in the men he
chose (THAT SOMETHING). He praised his vice-presidential choice by saying, "You can look him in the eye
and know he's got it" (IT). He wrote admiringly of Rose
Woods that, however driven, she was too strong to break.

> There is a plus-entity and a minus-entity in every
> human body. To the plus-entity of a man, all things

are possible. (*The Magic Story,* by Edward Wortley.)

Nixon is the American of James Agee's description, the man who for security "dives back into the womb for pennies," who renews, purifies himself by gaining material things—not to enjoy them, just to earn them, a spiritual achievement measured in unused money, in an unused body, in a self denied:

> Success is not land, money, popularity, attention, or even influence. Success is that "something" much more enjoyable than any of these things. Success is a spiritual quality, an inward satisfaction. (*What Is Success?* by Roger Babson.)

This, in briefest summary, is the ethic now rejected by the kids—distrust of the body, divorce from one's own sensations, life in a hostile cage of ribs and itches. They have come to reclaim the body, arguing that self-denial can have a terribly literal sense, can mean obliteration of the self. And their best argument is Nixon, the man who lives in a cage of his own "caginess" and caution. He can no longer inhabit his emotional responses. Even his most famous "breakdown" proves this—the "last press conference" of 1962, where he said "You won't have Nixon to kick around any more." The press, never kind to him, had outdone itself in the California race for governor. A blast of anger at such men would not only have been natural (if ill advised); it might have made Nixon, in a Harry Truman way, more likable—showing his humanity at last.

But even in this crisis of lapse and fatigue, he only slipped gears partially, losing and gaining control in halts and jerks. There had been some early hints of danger that day, and provision taken against them. Mrs. Nixon, whose jaws almost ground each other to powder in the agony of his presidential concession speech two years earlier, did not come to the hotel this time; she was hidden at home. And Nixon himself was at first persuaded not to go down and face reporters. Herb Klein would read the telegram to Governor Brown and answer journalists' questions in his wrinkled and winking conciliatory way. So far the protective machinery was humming along nicely. But for once Nixon did not *want* it to work. Preparing to leave the hotel, he sent another aide to the podium where Klein was speaking: the defeated candidate would stop by briefly on his way out of the building, to answer questions.

Nixon entered, laboring unsuccessfully at the game smile demanded of politicians who have submitted to the judgment of voters and now must accept it. But as he advanced to the podium, his eyes picked out this or that face in the press corps; and behind the faces—behind pens slanting in a hostile scrawl, mikes held up for every slip— he could see again the words they used against him, headlines, leads, last paragraphs all stored in his retentive memory bank, that library of grievances. Now the wheels turned faster, back and forth, arguments for and against acknowledgment of his long war with the press.

His last chance, perhaps, to let them know he knew— make them understand he had known all along what they were doing to him. Klein was stepping back from the microphone. It was now or never. The machinery, under pressure, blinked faultily, not rendering a certain answer. Nixon moved on, his head down but those active eyes, insomniac with intelligence, out scouting in all directions. And inside circuit after circuit was blowing, breaking down. *Now:* "Now that Mr. Klein has made his statement, and now that all the members of the press are so delighted that I have lost, I'd like to make a statement of my own." That second clause caught his audience. The heads came up, alert. But danger signals, for the systems failed, were already ringing in Nixon: "I appreciate the press coverage in this campaign. I think each of you covered it the way you saw it . . . I have no complaints about the press coverage." Back under cover (Klein could breathe again). Nixon pushed into conventional remarks, already covered in Klein's statement. Congratulations to the winner—but no area was really safe: "I believe Governor Brown has a heart, even though he believes I do not. I believe he is a good American, even though he feels I am not." Nixon was proud of the fact that he "defended" Brown's heart and patriotism, even though— he is drawn magnetically back and back to the press— "you gentlemen didn't report it." He tells them to report it now "in the lead—in the lead" (make up for all the headlines, last paragraphs, leads).

Yet after each lurch forward he backs off: "Now I

don't mean by that, incidentally, all of you." One reporter, Carl Greenberg of the Los Angeles *Times,* is
praised because he "wrote every word that I said"—a
ridiculous claim, and hardly the right way to disengage:
if one is expressly praised, all others implicitly are blamed
—so the signals warn him off: "I don't mean that others
didn't have a right to do it differently" (that's better, back
on the track)—but Greenberg just "felt that he had an
obligation to report the facts as he saw them" (*off* the
track!—did the others not report facts as they saw
them?).

He cannot, it is clear, ease away from the subject. He
must break off: "I am saying these things about the press
because I understood that was one of the things you were
particularly interested in. There'll be no question at this
point on that score. I'll be glad to answer other questions"—which, after the compulsive things that follow, he
never gets around to doing.

He lurches once more into conventional things—praise
for his campaign team; Republican victories in other states;
chances for the party in the 1964 presidential race. Kennedy, he admits, will be hard to beat after his handling
of the Cuban crisis. But, then, there may have been
some sellout in that episode: "Is there a deal with regard to NATO? Is there going to be with regard to
NATO and the Warsaw Pact? Are we going to continue
any kind of an agreement in Cuba which means that
Khrushchev got what he said we would never agree to before he made his threat with regard to his missiles, and
that is, in effect, ringing down an Iron Curtain around
Cuba?" Again aware of danger, he withdraws: Kennedy is
all right "if he can only get those who opposed atomic
tests, who want him to admit Red China, all the woolly
heads around—if he can just keep them away from him
and stand strong and firm with that good Irish fight of
his.

"One last thing." Oh-oh, will he slide back to the subject that he closed? The press? Klein must have been
quivering inside. But no: "One last thing. People say,
what about the past? What about losing in sixty and losing in sixty-four?" Typical politician response—at least
he had "battled for the things I believed in." Now the
getaway. But he cannot leave yet; the buildup of resent-

ment in him has not been discharged. Once more, "One last thing." This must be it.

It is. "One last thing. At the outset, I said a couple of things with regard to the press that I noticed some of you looked a little irritated about." (Those eyes were catching each response.) "And my philosophy with regard to the press has really never gotten through. And I want it to get through. For sixteen years, ever since the Hiss case, you've had a lot of—a lot of fun—you've had an opportunity to attack me." But there is always, even now, an "on the other hand": television at least has been fair, keeping the newspapers more honest than they might have been. And he has not been so bitter at the press that he called editors to complain or cancel subscriptions (swipes, both of these, at Kennedy). Each time the façade cracks, the industrious apprentice inside, who has maintained this wall so long, rushes to plaster it over. Not till the very end, after fifteen minutes of worrying this loose tooth in his skull, does he let the hurt, for one moment, blurt out: those in the press "have a right and a responsibility, if they're against a candidate—give him the shaft; but also recognize, if they give him the shaft, put one lonely reporter on the campaign who will report what the candidate says now and then." At last, quick and almost furtive at the end, he said it. "Thank you, gentlemen, and good day." He moved off rapidly, before they could ask questions (the announced reason for his coming).

Had he stood there punching honorably, he might have won praise, or at least respect. But reflexes of self-protection, self-distrust—the feint and pullback of wariness reduced, now, almost to dazed cringe—gave a stingy and secretive air to his assault. There was no stature in his wrath—high showdown indignation—only a twisted spite emerging intermittently. At this moment of maximum self-revelation and humanity, his speech was riddled with formulaic insincerities. "Appreciate the press coverage." "'I think each of you was writing it as you believed it." "Covered it the way you saw it." "I have no complaints" (he said, as complaint reeked off him like sulphurous sweat). "You will interpret it. That's your right." "Right and responsibility" to give candidates the shaft! It was not irony that made the thing oblique; it was the unwilled automatic baffling of *any* spontaneous move on his part.

And the uncanny thing is that Nixon's machinery, though it failed him as a human being, did its job. Answering questions about that "blowup," during his 1968 campaign, he could truthfully say, "The parts of my speech that got so very much publicized were few . . . Comparatively little attention seemed to be directed to certain other remarks I made. I said, for instance, that I appreciated the press coverage in this campaign: 'I think each of you covered it the way you saw it . . . I have always respected you. I have sometimes disagreed with you.' " He was right; there it was, on the record. More important, his self-checking apparatus had worked with such regularity throughout the fifteen minutes that no one television clip could be isolated to confirm men's memory of the "blowup." For years it had been said that, if Nixon became a candidate again, he could be eliminated by a mere rerun of his "last press conference" on TV. But Joe Napolitan, Lawrence O'Brien's old partner in public relations, viewed the tape for Humphrey and could not find a usable segment. Tricky had evaded the trap after all. He does not know how to break down.

Part FOUR

THE POLITICAL
MARKET

(Woodrow Wilson)

1. "Self-Determination"

"In his first inaugural address, this is what Wilson told his countrymen: 'Men's hearts wait upon us; men's lives hang in the balance; men's hopes call upon us to say what we will do. Who shall live up to the great trust? Who dares fail to try?' "
—*Richard Nixon, October 2, 1968*

HENRY KISSINGER, who looks like a serious Harpo Marx, haunted the outskirts of power in Kennedy's day, but was too dour and Germanic for Camelot. In Nixon's somber capital he has the reputation of a wit—elfin, sly, a bit of a "swinger." These fluctuations in esteem match a certain flexibility in his thought. A "hard-line" strategist at the outset, he was considered vaguely dovish by the time he framed Rockefeller's campaign proposals on Vietnam. In the month of Nixon's inauguration, he published a paper in *Foreign Affairs* which proposed, in effect, that we define our way out of Vietnam: since we needed a victory of sorts to get out while maintaining "face," why not define our goal in minimal terms, aim at something we can easily accomplish? To do this, we must make a sharp distinction between military and political objectives: Kissinger would have had us leave all political questions— the fate of the Thieu regime, the future makeup of South Vietnam's government, the status of the NLF, the form and time of elections—to Saigon and the NLF. America, as an outside power, would undertake merely to have other outside powers—i.e., Hanoi—step back from this "internal" process. It was a formula for what Kissinger would later call "an elegant bugout."

Opponents of the Vietnamese war were at first

heartened when Kissinger joined Nixon in the White House. Yet their man was soon presiding over Nixon's plan to "Vietnamize" the war, help set up elections under international observers, and guarantee that self-determination would be achieved as the result of our efforts—that is, he was tangled again in the very questions his article had said we should avoid. And the Paris talks were being conducted not on the "double track" that article advised (Washington-Hanoi and Saigon-NLF) but in general sessions where every issue was discussed by every party. What had happened?

Partly, of course, Kissinger had deferred to Nixon, a technician serving his President. But the "hard-line" Kissinger had never disappeared entirely. Even in the *Foreign Affairs* article he remained true, on basic questions, to what C. Wright Mills called "crackpot realism." Kissinger, anticipating Nixon's line, said the reasons for our original involvement were now beside the point. Once involved, we must be seen to accomplish something if we are to maintain our aura of invincibility. Caught in a bad fight, we must manage to look like a winner: "The commitment of five hundred thousand Americans has settled the issue of the importance of Vietnam. For what is involved now is confidence in American promises. However fashionable it is to ridicule the terms 'credibility' or 'prestige,' they are not empty phrases; other nations can gear their actions to ours only if they can count on our steadiness." The assumption, throughout, is that America's unchallengeable might, her record of success in conflicts, is what preserves the peace. And if waging a long frustrating war is the cost of maintaining that record, then the cost must be paid. All our wars are wars against wars.

Yet a different brand of realism—Eisenhower's brand, for instance—would recognize that "tyranny of the weak" is a basic fact of modern life, that there are some wars Super Powers cannot win (and therefore should not enter). Even Kissinger had to admit that, if Hanoi would not make the gesture of stepping back from South Vietnam, we were indefinitely pinned down, trying to salvage "prestige" while at the mercy of an enemy: "If Hanoi insists on total victory, the war must continue." To fight or not to fight is not a decision left, in that case, to America. The deciding, and the timing of decision, are then in the hands of an enemy capable of detaining us as long as he likes, dismissing us only when it serves his purpose. In this servile position, we should somehow convince ourselves that we were "maintaining prestige."

A cooler realism would face the fact that future "credibility" cannot be built up so long as:

—a tiny country goes on killing American soldiers;

—while America, with all its resources, wins insubstantial (if any) victories;

—and the commitment of vast resources to this conflict inhibits freedom of response in other parts of the world;

—as, progressively, domestic problems go unsolved because of the concentration of funds, efforts, official attention on Vietnam;

—so that opposition to the war causes resistance in the young, disillusionment in their elders, deepening of the "generation gap," general fostering of discontent;

—yet this bitter experience, far from extending "credibility" to future engagements, leaves the nation less willing than ever before to undertake foreign ventures.

That is the picture a true realist would have seen by 1969. But Kissinger was a "crackpot realist," and the war went on.

What, meanwhile, of his master? Was he not serving an old Cold Warrior, who would not listen if Kissinger had counseled peace? That judgment of Nixon is part of the general caricature formed of him in the Hiss days. Nixon was never a domestic McCarthy; and he was never a foreign-policy Goldwater, trying to tame the doomsday machine for work as a "defoliant." Nixon was a Cold Warrior at the time when everyone was. He admired the scholarship of Dulles and leaned toward him (therefore to the Right of Eisenhower) during his period as Vice-President—but this was in large part because Dulles had an articulated policy, while Eisenhower seemed to drift. Like Tolstoy's earthy general, Kutuzov, Ike realized the disparity between plans drawn at headquarters and operations carried out; he responded to the hope or fear of immediate gain or loss, things one can measure and be sure of. But Nixon loves to "wargame" contingencies, do homework on the "conceptual framework" of world affairs ("conceptual" is Kissinger's favorite term). He has always preferred international to domestic politics—he indulged the taste even when it hurt him to do so, as when running for governor of California. He feels (mistakenly) that the country can run itself through local and congressional machinery, but only a President can make and carry out policy toward other nations. Nixon cannot admit the importance of presidential style and presence in easing domestic fears (Roosevelt in the thirties), arousing confidence in the young (John Kennedy in office), assuaging racial bitterness (Robert Kennedy running for office). To admit this would be to recognize his own incapacities. Better to insist that the President is on hand to steer the ship of state out on international waters. This is not a matter for charisma, but for detailed work and study—just what Nixon excels at.

His hero, Woodrow Wilson, felt the same way. For him the big questions, the true "affairs of state," were all *international* matters. Even as a lackluster graduate student, Wilson was impatient with the imposed study of domestic institutions and yearned for "the grand excursions amongst imperial policies which I had planned for myself." So, in 1968, Nixon seemed almost to long for crises, for the power to make moves on the big board: "We could put the Mideast on the fire. And you could put trade on the fire. And you put the power bombs on the fire." He talked of "linkage," of settling the Vietnam war by tying it to issues in Russo-American relations. He talked of revising all our alliances. Like Tolstoy's Napoleon, he wanted to make moves and moves and moves—on the map.

Intent on this role, Nixon had for years aimed his study, his reading, his personal contacts and extensive travel, at the acquirement of expertise on foreign nations. It is too simple to dismiss the views thus acquired as simply "anticommunist." In fact, he took a more pacific stance on the Cold War than John Kennedy did. Memory of the 1960 presidential debates has yielded to stereotypes of both Kennedy and Nixon. To read the transcript again is as surprising as instructive. Were you to scramble answers to reporters' questions, even well-informed students of the period might misattribute unidentified quotations. Here, for instance, is the way one man appraised subversive activities as an "internal threat" to the United States:

Well, I think they're serious. I think it's a matter that we should continue to uh—give uh—great care and attention to. We should support uh—the laws which the United States has passed in order to protect us from uh—those who would destroy us from within. We should sustain uh—the Department of Justice and the FBI, and we should be continually alert. I think if the United States is maintaining a strong society here in the United States, I think that we can meet any internal threat. The major threat is external and will continue.

And the other man, thus:

It is also essential to being alert that we be fair; fair because by being fair we uphold the very freedoms that the Communists would destroy. We uphold the standards of conduct which they would never follow. And, in this connection, I think that uh—we—must look to the future having in mind the fact that we fight Communism at home not only by our laws to deal with Communists uh—the few who do become Communists and the few who do become tra—fellow travelers, but we also fight Communism—at home by moving against those various injustices which exist in our society which the Communists feed upon.

The first answer, with its emphasis on "those who would destroy us from within," was Senator Kennedy's. The second, with its stress on the few who become communists and the importance of social justice, was by Vice-President Nixon. Nor was this an unusual exchange. Those who look at the treatment of civil rights in the second debate will also find their expectations baffled.

But the principal contrast came in the realm of foreign affairs, where Kennedy urged an intensification of the Cold War, and accused Eisenhower of losing Cuba, much as McCarthy had accused Truman of losing China:

Arthur Gardner, a Republican Ambassador, Earl Smith, a Republican Ambassador, in succession— both have indicated in the past six weeks that they reported to Washington that Castro was a Marxist, that Raul Castro was a Communist, and that they got no effective results.

Do you know today that the Com—the Russians broadcast ten times as many programs in Spanish to Latin America as we do? Do you know we don't have a single program sponsored by our government to Cuba—to tell them our story, to tell them that we are their friends, that we want them to be free again? . . . Which system, Communism or freedom, will triumph in the next five or ten years? . . . By 1965 or 1970, will there be other Cubas in Latin America? . . . I have seen Cuba go to the Communists. I have seen Communist influence and Castro influence rise in Latin America . . . And I don't think this administration has shown the foresight, has shown the knowledge, has been identified with the great fight which these people are waging to be free, to get a better standard of living, to live better . . . I think the Communists have been moving with vigor—Laos, Africa, Cuba—all around the world today they're on the move. I think we have to revitalize our society. I think we have to demonstrate to the people of the world that we're determined in this free country of ours to be first—not first if, and not first but, and not first when—but first.

Mr. Nixon would add a guarantee to islands five miles off the coast of the Re—Republic of China when he's never really protested the Communists seizing Cuba, ninety miles off the coast of the United States.

In this bully-pulpit-thumping mood, determined to be first without an if or a when or a but, Kennedy actually invented Nixon's 1968 argument that "parity" would mean inferiority for the United States:

The point was made by Mr. Nixon that the Soviet production is only forty-four percent of ours. I must say that forty-four percent and that Soviet country is causing us a good deal of trouble tonight. I want to make sure that it stays in that relationship. I don't want to see the day when it's sixty percent of ours, and seventy and seventy-five and eighty and ninety percent of ours, with all the force and power that it could bring to bear in order to cause our destruction.

Mr. Nixon talks about our being the strongest country in the world. I think we are today. But we were far stronger relative to the Communists five years ago, and what is of great concern is that the balance of power is in danger of moving with them. Before we go into the summit, before we ever meet again, I think it's important that the United States build its strength; that it build its military strength as well as its own economic strength. If we negotiate from a position where the power balance or wave is moving away from us, it's extremely difficult to reach a successful decision on Berlin as well as the other questions.

I'm talking about our willingness to bear any burdens in order to maintain our own freedom and in order to meet [*sic*] our freedom around the globe . . . That's how the United States began to prepare for its great—actions in World War II and in the postwar period.

I think we should st—strengthen our conventional forces, and we should attempt in January, February, and March of next year to increase the airlift capacity of our conventional forces. Then I believe that we should move full time on our missile production, particularly on Minuteman and on Polaris.

Kennedy, too, was ready to put various countries "on the front burner" to prove America could "get moving again" in the Cold War. Walter Cronkite asked him exactly *which* countries, and he answered:

One of the areas, and of course the most vulnerable area is—I have felt, has been Eastern Europe. I've been critical of the Administration's failure to suggest policies which would make it possible for us to establish, for example, closer relations with Poland, particularly after the '55–'56 period and the Hungarian revolution . . . I would say Eastern Europe

is the area of vulnerability of the uh—S—of the
Soviet Union.

Kennedy seemed determined to show as much chutzpah
toward Khrushchev as Nixon had in the kitchen debate:

> I want Mr. Khrushchev to know that a new genera-
> tion of Americans who fought in Europe and Italy
> [sic] and the Pacific for freedom in World War
> II have [sic] now taken over in the United States,
> and that they're going to put this country back to
> work again. I don't believe that there is anything this
> country cannot do. I don't believe there's any burden,
> or any responsibility, that any American would not
> assume to protect his country, to protect our security,
> to advance the cause of freedom.

In the debate set aside for domestic concerns, Kennedy
began by serving notice that the format would not divert
him from The Enemy:

> In the election of 1860, Abraham Lincoln said the
> question was whether this nation could exist half-
> slave or half-free. In the election of 1960, and with
> the world around us, the question is whether the
> world will exist half-slave or half-free, whether it will
> move in the direction of freedom, in the direction
> of the road that we are taking, or whether it will
> move in the direction of slavery . . . We discuss
> tonight domestic issues, but I would not want that
> to be—any implication to be given that this does
> not involve directly our struggle with Mr. Khrushchev.

Nixon, of course, was obliged to argue that what America
had been doing under Eisenhower was glorious, that
the administration had not betrayed Hungary and Cuba
to the Communists, that there was no missile gap, that
Ike's great contribution was keeping the peace, and that
the Republicans would keep us out of war. Yet his rhetoric
went beyond the necessary pieties. Whenever he could,
he indulged in talk of moral suasion and example:

> It is not enough for us simply to be the strongest na-
> tion militarily, the strongest economically, and also

to have firm diplomacy. We must have a great goal.
We also believe that in the great field of ideals that
we can lead America to the victory for freedom . . .
It is essential that we extend freedom, extend it to
all the world . . . It means making more progress
in civil rights than we have so that we can be a splen-
did example for all the world to see—a democracy
in action at its best.

Men find it hard to credit Nixon when he moralizes.
Arthur Schlesinger, in a 1960 campaign pamphlet, argued
that Kennedy held to basic principles, while Nixon had
swung free as a weathervane to any wind. It was an
odd claim to make. Nixon's career, whatever else one
could say of it, had been at least as consistent as Kennedy's—as that of the liberal hot-cold warrior, Catholic
secularist, McCarthyite civil-libertarian, who changed flags
often and deftly. Indeed, it was Kennedy's ease of adjustment that saved him from his own campaign promises and initial vision of the presidency. He had come
to that office preaching cold war as a crusade. Domestic satisfaction seemed almost too complete under Ike;
the country was affluent, snoozy, no New Deal rhetoric
could rouse it; poverty was undiscovered, and black unrest just stirring. Kennedy, with his call for escape from
the Eisenhower narcolepsy, had to reduce everything to a
contest with Khrushchev. If the Russians trained lots of
scientists, we would train more—would even teach Johnny
how to read. If they put up sputnik, we would shoot the
moon. If they staged a Budapest, we would have our
Bay of Pigs. At this point, Kennedy's scrambling touch-
football spirit was to the fore. Like Teddy Roosevelt,
he loved challenge, the game of politics, its clash and
maneuver, the joy of winning—and he carried this élan into
his diplomacy. Mencken said of Teddy that he "preached
incessantly the duty of the citizen to the state, with the
soft pedal upon the duty of the state to the citizen."
Kennedy, in his "Ask not what your country . . ." mood,
had the same readiness to shove citizens into conflict.
But a resilience toward principle—verging on cynicism
in his campaign acrobatics over Cuba and the offshore islands—made him, progressively, modulate this chest-
thumping attitude. After some jolts in office, he stopped
looking upon Khrushchev as a boisterous football op-

ponent; it became clear to him that there *are* some things America cannot do. By the time of the American University speech, Kennedy had backed off. He no longer insisted that the world become *all* free instead of half-free; he would settle for a world "made safe for diversity" —that is, for a position he attacked as "soft" when Eisenhower held it.

For better or worse, Nixon does not have the gift for changing his stands gracefully. Though he tries to suit himself to the needs of the moment, he is stiff—not only physically, but in his intellectual carriage. Eisenhower said that he was good at summing up the main features of a proposal in cabinet meetings, but not at suggesting new plans. He does assigned homework well, but lacks imagination. His planning is thorough but cautious, worked out within the accepted framework of things. In foreign affairs, that accepted framework has been what we may loosely call Wilsonian. We profess a devotion to freedom for all peoples, a freedom to be measured in terms of "self-determination"—which boils down to American-style elections. Right and Left are agreed on these norms for judging others (and therefore for dealing with them). We do not offer a counter-philosophy to communism, but a procedure: freedom is the machinery of suffrage, judged by the distribution, frequency of use, and access to ballot boxes; by the number of electoral alternatives put before people and actually decided by them. Measured by such standards, America scores, let us say, 70 percent, and Russia scores, say, 15 percent. That is the measure of the two systems' excellence. One land is free, the other not.

Nixon, accepting this basis for judgment, did far more than Lyndon Johnson to aim our policy at "self-determination" for South Vietnam. The May speech of 1969, his most thorough treatment of Vietnam, never moved far from the glad rephrasing of Wilson's creed:

> We have to understand our essential objective: we seek the opportunity for the South Vietnamese to determine their own political future without outside interference.

> What the United States wants for South Vietnam is not the important thing. What North Vietnam

wants for South Vietnam is not the important thing. What is important is what the people of South Vietnam want for themselves.

We are willing to agree to neutrality if that is what the South Vietnamese people *freely choose.*

We are prepared to accept any government in South Vietnam that results from the *free choice* of the South Vietnamese people themselves.

We ask only that the decision reflect the *free choice* of the people concerned . . . [the kind of settlement] which will permit the South Vietnamese people to *determine freely* their own political future.

Our basic terms are very simple: mutual withdrawal of non-South Vietnamese forces from South Vietnam, and *free choice* for the people of South Vietnam. (Italics added.)

Nor did he weary of this theme in later pronouncements, basing messages to Hanoi on it, voicing it during his tour of South Asia, returning to it in his November 3 telecast: "We have declared that anything is negotiable except the right of the people of South Vietnam to determine their own future." He went far beyond the demands of formal virtue in our pronouncements of state. Not only that: he closed off the path of retreat pointed out by Kissinger. In fact, this insistence on self-determination led to immediate contradiction: in asking for a new set of elections newly supervised, Nixon undercut the regime he was formally supporting. America claimed that free elections had already taken place, that the Saigon Constitution was validly adopted, the Thieu regime legitimate. Why, then, look to a new order, to be ushered in by new elections? If the Thieu government was not legitimate, why were we supporting it? If it was legitimate, why try to replace it?

Moreover, Nixon looked to the "Vietnamizing" of the conflict as part of his program to induce self-rule. But this meant turning our weapons and war skills over to the regime in power, giving it an edge in any future struggle for "self-determination." Instead of creating neutral conditions, we were stacking the deck.

Why would Nixon open such a can of worms, after all his homework with the master of "new concepts"? In place of Kissinger's minimal war aims, Nixon had announced a goal not only difficult but impossible to achieve (impossible, at least, to know whether it could be achieved). Those who have considered Nixon tricky and unprincipled may look for a stratagem in this. But his plan was not clever and opportunistic; it was naive and self-defeating. Why?

The answer is simple. Nixon is emphatic about the traditional moral assumptions of our foreign policy because he believes in them. It is fascinating to observe how apologists for the Vietnam war, hard pressed to explain our presence there, fall back on what is most convincing to *them*, to what they privately believe. Kissinger argued from *Realpolitik*, from the kind of stick we must wield in the world. Lyndon Johnson, in his Johns Hopkins speech, fell back on the New Deal: he would build TVA-type dams on the Mekong River (liberals applauded that speech). Humphrey defended the war as a kind of international slum-clearance: "I think there is a tremendous new opening here for realizing the dream of the Great Society in the great area of Asia, not just here at home." And Nixon voices his belief that international virtue is the best *policy*.

He has not been a convincing moralist, he does not have the preacher airs of Woodrow Wilson; but he is notable for his belief in preachers—not only in Billy Graham and Dr. Peale, but in the Horatio Alger tracts and maxims of his youth. He believes in the moral reward for effort, the spiritual quality of success—all that disappearing ethos he appealed to and is trying to resuscitate. He does not woo the Forgotten American cynically; he *agrees* with the silent majority. Those who misunderstand him simply have not listened to him, trusted him or what he says. When he writes that "Selflessness is the greatest asset an individual can have," he is the same man who told a college orator to concentrate on issues as an escape from paralyzing self-consciousness. The unmistakable note is struck in that word "asset," in the bookkeeper's approach to religion. Even the world's troubles can lead to individual peace of mind: "The bigger the problem, the broader its consequences, the less does an individual think of himself." (Wilson had said the same thing: "It was possible, when necessary, for a man to lose his own personal existence, even to seem to himself to have no individual life apart from his official duties.")

Since Nixon is a fundamentalist on domestic values, it should not come as a surprise that he holds to the moral framework of American thought about foreign affairs. When liberals have grown too clever or self-doubting to remember their own arguments, whether in defending campus order or championing freedom for other nations, Nixon can repeat them with conviction. This explains his admiration for Wilson, which is not a casual matter but a deep personal bond of sympathy and understanding. Nixon knows he is defying traditional party lines when he adopts a Democrat as his "patron saint." He was proud, while serving as Vice-President, to work at the desk Wilson used in the White House, and when he reached the Oval Office at last, he had Johnson's large desk moved out and the Wilson one brought in. He televised his November 1969 speech on Vietnam from that desk, and referred to this fact in stressing that this policy was based on Wilson's principles. He likes to quote Wilson, sometimes without identifying his source: in his inaugural address, he referred to "peace with healing in its wings," a Wilson coinage (the kind Mencken derided when calling Wilson America's *Doctor Dulcifluus*). Nixon's tracing of similarities descends even to the trivial: he has publicly remarked that Wilson, too, liked to watch football. Wilson is the only Democrat whose picture hangs (with Theodore Roosevelt's and Dwight Eisenhower's) in the cabinet room.

Nixon seems to liken himself to Wilson not only in terms of principles but of temperament—Wilson was a lonely misunderstood leader. Nixon considers himself an introspective intellectual somewhat out of place in the gladhanding world of politics. (Wilson, it is true, was a formal academician for a long period, but he was not as good a student as Nixon—he had difficulty getting his doctorate.) Both men had a pious, provincial upbringing —Nixon in Hannah's Quakerism, Wilson in his preacher-father's Presbyterianism. Both remained personally ascetic, abstract in their thinking, sensitive to criticism, sheltered by their family and entourage (both men had daughters only, and lived cushioned in feminine solicitude—Rose Woods has been, in certain periods, as protective as the second Mrs. Wilson).

It is no wonder, then, that Nixon—identifying so with Woodrow Wilson—should blunder as Wilson did. For the best, most instructive parallel to our Vietnam engagement is Wilson's disastrous Mexican involvement. He determined, early in his reign, that he would make South American republics democratic in fact as well as name, beginning with Mexico. The result is described this way by Christopher Hollis:

> An election was held in October. But its results, being favorable to General Huerta, were, Wilson decided, not a genuine expression of the will of the people . . . In his complaint that the elections were "irregularly conducted" he was right, but it only showed his ignorance of Mexico that he would have troubled to make such a complaint. The electoral machinery was treated by both sides as a tired and flagging joke and was kept in existence only out of a puzzled good nature because, for some reason quite incomprehensible, it seemed to give pleasure to the President of the United States.

But Wilson was not *sufficiently* pleased with such elections; backing various opponents of Huerta, he was drawn into two military raids on the country: "We have gone into Mexico to serve mankind . . ." In a series of moves, threats, blunders, Wilson found himself first supporting Villa, then attacking him, calling for elections, then challenging them. Soon he was mobilizing for all-out war on the country. As John Morton Blum says, "Confused as he was by his own uninformed intentions, while he championed peace and justice in Mexico, he seemed, like the jingoes, ready 'to blow up the whole place.' " Wilson had arrived at that fatal recurring moment in our country's diplomatic benefactions, the moment when it makes sense to start shooting people philanthropically, for their own good. He was as ready to do Mexicans this service as we have proved, year after discouraging year, with Vietnamese, preaching democracy with well-meant napalm, instructing (as we obliterate) children with our bombs. We believe we can literally "kill them with kindness," moving our guns forward in a seizure of de-

mented charity. It is when America is in her most altruistic mood that other nations better get behind their
bunkers.

2.   A Good Election

> *"I am going to teach the South American republics
> to elect good men."*
>
>   —*Woodrow Wilson*

AMERICA WENT INTO VIETNAM, as into Mexico,
to create the conditions for self-determination. Yet Nixon
seems not to have asked himself, on assuming power,
whether any of our actions had advanced us toward that
goal. There was an elected government in the country, to
which we gave support; its Constitution had been adopted
"according to the rules." Yet the head of that government, Marshal Thieu, needed the American army, navy,
marine corps, and air force to keep him in office—so
our measuring rod for "legitimacy" seemed inadequate.

Thieu's apologists could answer that "outside interference" was responsible for his insecure purchase on the
country. But it is difficult to say what is an "outside,"
what an "inside" force in a country divided against itself,
created in the first place by outside interference, overrun
by a mix of neighboring marauders and native guerrillas,
enmeshed in a web of American power spread throughout the area. "Self-determination" in such a case waits always on the definition of a national self to *be* determined, and there were competing definitions—on one or
more of which America was seen to be acting. At times
we held that Thieu ruled validly (which automatically
excluded the NLF from his nation). At other times we
looked to some future election (undoubtedly including the
NLF) to bring about legitimacy. Meanwhile, all our decisions and vacillations influenced Vietnam "from outside."

Our devotion to self-rule could survive disappointment in various Vietnam regimes—that of Diem, of Ky, of Thieu. It was admittedly difficult to introduce free elections in new countries, half-countries, countries at war with themselves. But the power of the vote had become suspect, in 1968, not only far off in unsettled Vietnam; it was also rendered dubious at home. What disturbed many Americans was not the fact that Thieu had been put in office, but that Nixon had. As we worked to establish our electoral system in the Saigon government, men asked if it could be made to work again in the United States. The boast of our procedure has been that it singles out the best man for our leader—and it elevated Richard Nixon. It would give us the best policies available—and we got a continuation of war in Vietnam. It would let the best party win—and Goldwater's party came to power. Stunned by this outcome, Harvard biologist George Wald, addressing 300,000 people at the New Mobe march one year after Nixon's election, said, "A man is not free who, when he votes, is forced to vote for the lesser evil"—and the crowd cheered. The assumptions of the Nobel laureate (and, it seemed, of his audience) were obvious—that elections once did more in this country than offer a choice of two evils; that men were truly free only then; and that return to such elections must be brought about if we are to regain freedom.

It is easy to call such expectations naive. Professor Sidney Hyman reminds us just how much our elections "say" or can say: "The casting and counting of the votes in a Presidential election unconditionally affirms the existence of a consensus about only two matters. First, the voting process itself states anew the preexisting consensus that is part of our constitutional morality. The second matter . . . is that a consensus exists to accept a decision of part of the community as though it were a decision of the whole." That is, the vote proves that people wanted to vote (thinking it important), and that they were willing to abide by the result (thinking it legitimate). Yet these very things—the idea that voting matters and is valid—arise from a belief that the vote does more than this, "says" more; that through it we are affecting our fate, exercising self-determination. And it was a doubt about these basic beliefs that soured the air around

1968's election, made men call in question "the whole System."

Some objections were localized, particular—discontent with the nomination conventions, the possibility that Wallace could throw the election into the House, criticism of the electoral college. Party reform, change in the college, direct election, and other proposals were aimed at curing these problems. Yet certain doubts went deeper, and would survive all change aimed merely at the mode of casting, counting, weighing, equalizing, or extending votes. Improve the mechanics as far as that is possible, basic questions still remain—including the most basic question of all: what is it, exactly, that is chosen at the polls? Is it one party over another? Yes, in a way—though voters like to claim (in presidential years, especially) that they "vote the man," not adhering blindly to their party's candidate, whoever that may be. Such voting is considered unenlightened, the result of bias or habit—after all, if citizens did nothing but repeat a party vote each year, the majority party would be returned in perpetuity by much the same margin. Better to "vote the man"—so the *candidate* is what we choose at the polls.

Yet one cannot, in choosing a candidate, disregard his stand upon the issues, his policies and proposals—cannot, that is, unless one goes solely by personal "image," the Ike smile, Nixon's bad makeup job in 1960. So an even more enlightened position is to say, "I do not vote the party or the man, but the issues." The conscientious voter, neither stuck in mere tradition nor charmed by a winning smile, asks where each man stands on the major questions he must deal with.

But how is one to find this out? If there were only one issue to be decided by a President, and only two ways of coping with it; and if two (and only two) candidates could be found to declare, unequivocally, one for each alternative; if only those concerned with that issue and informed about it were to vote—then, and only then, would a presidential election settle a policy matter. But that never happens. There are a *number* of issues, and to the extent that a voter is informed and concerned he will find neither candidate agreeing with the whole range of his views on all the issues—and probably not fully representing his views on any single issue. Suppose, for instance, a voter in 1968 favored "ending the war in Vietnam by winning it with whatever force was needed." Where would he find a candidate? Only General LeMay—rather insecurely attached to the Wallace ticket (he came in too late to be put on most states' ballots)—took this stand on this issue. But suppose, as well, that this hypothetical "hawk" disagreed with Wallace's domestic views; or, not disagreeing, thought Wallace's brand of advocacy would be demagogic and divisive. Or say that he simply knew Wallace could not win, and did not care to waste his vote on the man. On one or more of these grounds, he would be prevented from expressing his will on the major issue in foreign policy.

The same thing was true of the man who wanted an immediate peace settlement in Vietnam. It may have seemed he had a wider choice—*two* nationally known candidates who advocated instant withdrawal, Eldridge Cleaver and Dick Gregory. But Cleaver was too young to take office, Gregory is a comedian, and neither man was on the ballot in any state. With only a write-in vote possible, neither could make as strong a bid as LeMay. Thus the "dove" was in the same position as the hawk: so far as voting an issue dear to him was concerned, each was effectively disfranchised.

Yet those with more moderate views on the war were not much better off. Both Nixon and Humphrey promised the same thing—peace with honor, through negotiation; settlement, with a number of unspecified ifs. Guesses on what either wanted to do, could do, might do, were only guesses. A vote for one or the other "said" nothing specific about the conditions of acceptable settlement.

Even where candidates are more specific in their proposals, how does the voter express his will on the whole range of issues debated in an election? It would be relatively simple if the voter could say, "There are ten main issues that matter to me, and Candidate A takes my view, or approximates it, on six of them, while Candidate B takes my view on only four—so I'll vote for Candidate A." It does not work that way. For one thing, certain issues mean more to each voter; so that, to get agreement on one acutely sensitive issue, he might choose a candidate who disagrees with him on most of the other issues, or on all of them. Or a voter might consider an issue very dear to him, though it is not being formally considered by either candidate; and this issue could still dictate a choice. In 1968, for instance, some on the Left advocated a "punitive" vote for Nixon: they wanted to punish the Democratic Party—for the war, for Chicago, for rejecting McCarthy, for Meany and Connally and Daley. They wanted to wreck the old party and build a new one for future elections; and their votes would therefore say nothing on the issues immediate to this election.

Or suppose that there are ten main issues, and a voter is only aware of five of these—only aware, that is, of an apparent alternative in five matters. Though one of the hidden issues might affect him deeply, his vote will not reflect any opinion on the matter. Or say that a man has essentially no views on the issues, and goes to vote almost at random for either man, because he is assured that this is his patriotic duty. To the extent that his vote counts equally with the careful decision of an informed citizen— that is, has just as much weight when people are trying to find out what the electorate "said" with its votes—this chance act will falsify the record, give no true measure of what mattered to the electorate.

How, then, can one say that a majority vote for one candidate is a vote for his views? Is it a vote for all his views? Did all those who voted for him agree with him on all the issues? Clearly not. Then *which* ones mattered? And to which voters? Perhaps only one particularly "hot" issue mattered, and there is no "mandate" on the others—not, at least, on the majority of them. But, in that case, how tell one set of issues from the others? How measure the care, or lack of it, that went into the votes? Perhaps a lackadaisical majority, not really concerned with the issues, will put a man in office precisely as a way of avoiding difficult thought about policy. Partisans of Adlai Stevenson took that view of Eisenhower's election; by their standards, the minority vote constituted the *only* vote on the issues; so far as a mandate on policy existed, it was discernible in that minority. The Stevenson vote "said" more on substantive matters than the winning vote did.

All these difficulties would still exist, even if the candidates were trying to make their positions "perfectly clear" (the phrase they use when making their positions imperfectly clear or perfectly unclear). But of course they do not aim at such clarity—for very good reasons. On any complex issue there are likely to be more than two informed attitudes; thus, if we are to achieve precision, we must have at least as many candidates as there are respectable alternatives on that issue. But once candidacies have proliferated on that one issue, how stop them from growing on each of the other issues? And then how work out a combination of these very definite stands that has any chance of appealing to a majority, or even a healthy plurality, of the electorate? We Americans like to congratulate ourselves on the two-party system precisely because it prevents this litter of detailed alternatives without broad support behind any of them; yet the price we pay is the vapory effusion each candidate gives off when asked for his stand on a particular matter. Once you begin the process of "amalgamating" various positions into a broad general area of agreement, where do you stop? Each candidate will, naturally, try to amalgamate as many positions (and voters) as possible on his side, by artful combination of things logically incompatible.

As a result, even when analysts think they discern a "mandate" arising from an election, it is impossible to say precisely what the "mandate" is for. Richard Nixon, for instance, despite rhetoric much like Humphrey's, used signals (e.g., Agnew's nomination) to suggest he would take a "tougher" stand than his opponent on the issue of law and order. On particular matters, he slid by with meaningless gestures like the promise to have a new attorney general. Asked about the Chicago convention, he managed to avoid praising or criticizing the mayor and his police—just as Humphrey did. Nonetheless, he conveyed the impression he would be "tougher." Add to his plurality the Wallace votes for an even tougher stand, and you get —so commentators say and the Nixon team assumes—a "mandate" for rigorous law enforcement. But what does that mean? Is "law" a code word for racial repression? To some voters, probably. But not to others. How many were there of each? Who knows? Of those who did not mean to talk a racist code, yet voted for Nixon, how many favored a specific policy of law enforcement? And how many agreed on that policy? And where did they discover it? (Not, obviously, in Nixon's campaign talks.) How many voters had any idea how law might be better enforced? And if they had no idea, how can they be said to have voted for a policy? If Nixon exercises his presumed "mandate" in a specific (though previously unspecified) program, how did the *voters* choose this program? How *many* of them chose it, or knew they were choosing it?

For that matter, how much of Nixon's slim majority came from a decision on this issue? Some who voted for him did not feel strongly about it. Some, clearly, did not agree with him on getting tougher (e.g., those Democrats who voted Republican to punish their own party) or had no operative judgment about the matter (e.g., those who automatically vote Republican, no matter what). How many reluctantly chose Nixon though their views on the matter were not adequately reflected either by Nixon or Humphrey, Wallace or Cleaver?

And notice that these obstacles arise even if the public is acting in an eminently wise manner, trying to express an informed view on a variety of issues. But the authors of a study in election behavior undertaken by the University of Michigan's Survey Research Center do not limit themselves to such technical objections when they say there is no way to discover a "mandate" on the issues after an election. These men—Morris Janowitz and Dwaine Marvick—argue that the "mandate theory" of elections must be rejected because "it assumed a level of articulated opinion and ideology on the campaign issues not likely to be found in the United States."

So it does not seem, after all, that the voters "buy" one set of views, one line of approach to the issues, when they cast their ballots. They may think they do; most people prefer to think that, whatever may be said of others, *they* vote the issues. But politicians are busy making sure they do not. And social scientists, busily studying the outcome, are unable to determine just what policies may have got "bought."

Must we fall back, then, to the idea that we "vote the man," that a *person* gets bought? That is what the Survey Research Center fell back on, when it substituted for the mandate theory of election the "competitive theory." Granted, competing men are felt to stand for at least slightly different things, but these differences are not so much debated on their own merits as symbolized in the competing personalities, in their careful rhetoric, emphases, and image. This approach seems to come closer to observed reality. We may not know *what* won in an election, what the voters were trying to say. But at least we know—or usually know—*who* won. He may have won by a narrow margin, as Nixon did; by a disputed margin, as Kennedy did. But the winner cannot be mistaken for the loser. The accomplishment of the election year is clearly marked in careers made (Agnew) or furthered (Muskie), broken (Humphrey) or damaged (Rockefeller). Some men, scheming toward the election year, see it pass them by (Romney, Reagan, Percy) with barely a nod. Others have a considerable impact (McCarthy, Wallace) without being themselves elected. Even those who know nothing about the issues can, usually, identify leading candidates by the end of a national campaign. And once the winner is declared, almost every adult in America will know who his President is. So we cannot say the election decided nothing.

But what does it mean to "vote the man"? Does it mean the electorate has chosen the best man to rule them, best by the pertinent criteria and by all available evidence? That is what the myth says: since only ability counts, not mere rank and birth, "any boy in America can grow up to be President." (Yes, any *boy*. Though rank and birth were not supposed to count, sex always did.)

The Constitutional Fathers seem to have aspired to this ideal. The electors from each state were to be chosen for their wisdom, discretion, and integrity; and this expert panel was to choose, from men of its own stature, the one it most admired, the *primus inter pares*. The process even seemed to work—twice: when Washington was chosen unanimously by an unfettered college of electors. But even in that original scheme there were restrictions. Not every man in America was considered (and *no* woman was). Only gentlemen of some status, wealth, and education were in practice put forward. And there were many hidden restrictions in that attitude, most of which are still with us. At the outset, no Jew, or Catholic, or Protestant outside the mainstream had a chance of becoming President, and in some measure that is still true. Kennedy's election did not prove that religion is no longer a factor; it proved only that, given the right combination of candidate and vote concentrations, those who would vote for him because of other reasons *and religion* outweighed those voting against him for other reasons *and religion*. With another Catholic—or with a Jew—the restriction may still operate. (Goldwater was from a half-Jewish family, but had become an Episcopalian by the time he ran.)

Besides this restriction, the same amalgamating drive that leads to the blurring of issues makes for the exclusion of all but socially "central" personalities in a presidential race. That is, no blacks, no Mexican-Americans, no professed atheists, etc. Dr. King was among the greatest leaders of modern America, a winner of the Nobel Peace Prize; but he had no chance, ever, at the presidency. No matter what his other qualifications, Rockefeller was eliminated from consideration in 1964 by his divorce and precipitate remarriage. (Divorce alone would have excluded him in earlier times, and may have had some influence in Stevenson's losses. Ronald Reagan, of course, hopes that divorce and *less* precipitate remarriage will be no obstacle in the future.) And though some of these limitations (e.g., divorce) are falling away as society changes, others arise in their place. Barry Goldwater, for instance, was probably right when he said that in the future a college degree will be a minimum requirement for a presidential candidate. Goldwater was perhaps the last major candidate to be put forward without a college education (even Wallace had the edge on him in this respect). The result of such prior requirements is a nurtured blandness, an inoffensiveness in our candidates—the ideal represented in the phenomenal popularity of Eisenhower, who was presented to voters as the quintessential "good guy." When Nixon listed his reasons for choosing Agnew to run with him, the third item on the list was this: "he is a family man."

Even within the respectable "white male Protestant" range of choice, there is still a heavy sifting to be undergone, based mainly on wealth—not personal wealth, necessarily (though that helps), but access to political money, either from the party or direct from big donors, money earned by political service and promises, by ideological or other debts. The politician must, according to his place on the spectrum, be able to tap the corporations or unions, the American Medical Association or the big contributors. And this becomes increasingly true in an age of vast television and technical expenditure. In fact, the selective factor based on wealth is greater now than at the outset of our system. In Washington's day, one might choose from any educated (and therefore fairly wealthy)

man. Today we can only choose a wealthy man, or one
with access to wealth, *who is also a practicing politician.*
A candidate may commence an amateur, like Romney;
but by the time he is considered *presidentabile,* he has
moved by definition up among the pros, where the resources of the professional must be mastered and wielded.
When we set out to choose the "best man," we are not
allowed to go through our whole range of acquaintance,
direct or indirect, and choose the preacher (King?) or
doctor (Spock?) or professor (Schlesinger?) or author
(Mailer?) we might prefer. We must choose from the
politicians. And even among eligible politicians our choice
is narrowed to those left on the ballot by November. In
1968, a huge combined number of Americans wanted
Rockefeller, McCarthy, Reagan, Wallace, and even
Lyndon Johnson, not to mention the candidate removed by
an assassin's bullet in California. Some would have liked to
vote for Wallace, but on the Democratic national ticket.
Yet a final crucial sieving had taken place, after other
baffles had done their work—eliminated, screened, excluded. Even if a candidate possesses all the preliminary
qualifications—male Caucasian; of conventional religion
and family life and career; in politics; acceptable to political sources of funds—he still must get himself nominated
by one of the two major parties (or, even more difficult,
put together a viable third party). This final screening is
made on many grounds, and is essentially a matter of
compromise. Given a range of views in the party—given,
say, the spectrum from Jacob Javits to Strom Thurmond,
from Al Lowenstein to James Eastland—which "centrist"
can extend himself, simultaneously, in both directions
along the scale, to include most of the party's factions?
The last-minute "centrism" of Romney and Rockefeller
could not be stretched as far as the lifelong elasticity of
Nixon. And so the deal was, at many levels, worked out—
not by the public at large, but by party bosses, workers,
moneymen, ideologues. The essence of the two-party system is compromise, and that will remain true no matter
how each party is reformed.

Given the whole process of exclusion, laying greater
stress on conformity and compromise than on ability and
vision, it is no wonder men like Orestes Brownson and H.
L. Mencken asked whether hereditary monarchy has, by
sheer accident of birth, produced a more random set of

qualifications, a grayer level of mediocrity, than the electoral system has put into the White House. (We cover this over, of course, by our Houdonizing of Presidents in the classroom and elsewhere. Every President has had his Parson Weems; and if the ways of being Weemsified have grown more subtle, they have spread and accelerated. If present tools had been available in Washington's day, there would have been a cinerama epic on his adventure with the cherry tree, the General would have given out tie clips in the shape of hatchets.)

In what sense, then, can we say that we are voting for the best man? Not in an absolute sense, surely. Not even in an approximate sense. Only in *one* restricted sense: we are voting for what we hope, behind all the hoopla and PR work on their images, is the better man of the two men who are, whatever one's own true preference, the only remaining alternatives. Nixon was chosen by 43 percent of those who voted. But only 60 percent of the adult electorate went to the polls. So he was chosen by approximately 25 percent of the adults in America. Of those, how many actually would have made him their first choice? How many, in that slim quarter of the population, would —given the chance—have voted for Thurmond or Reagan, Rockefeller or McCarthy? With some he was the second choice; with others the seventh, or seventieth; or two-millionth (i.e., some would have voted for him if he were any American other than the Democratic candidate). Some, no doubt, voted as Mencken used to: "Let us hold our noses, and do our duty." Or as McCarthy did when returning to Hubert and the Democratic fold: "I'm voting for Humphrey, and I think you should suffer with me."

In fact, the picture I have given is a little too rosy. I have described the problem of choosing a man simply on the basis of his ruling ability, apart from complications that arise when one looks toward issues or the party. But of course that is an impossible distinction in most cases. Of the two men put up, a voter may think one has superior ability, yet suspect that those abilities would be put to work promoting things he disapproves of. To that extent, the abilities are a menace to him. So, given a poor choice in the first place, he must consciously take the poorer man. Granted, the candidates' opinions are kept deliberately vague, but some guess at them must be made—as Janowitz and Marvick admit, even while rejecting the mandate theory. Mencken professed respect for one politician, a rare admission in his life; but could not act on his respect, since the unusually defined issue of Prohibition was concerned: "The Hon. Mr. Atwood I have known for many years and hold in high esteem. He is honest and intelligent and full of the milk of human kindness. Unluckily, he is dry, and so I am forced to hatchet him."

Since the last decisive winnowing of potential candidates takes place deep inside the party system, are we not forced back to a vote cast, neither for the issues nor the man, but for the party? The party with the largest registration tries, of course, to hold its lead, by urging people to stick with a noble tradition. When Democrats lead, they claim to have a monopoly on compassion. When Republicans lead, they do so as guardians of fiscal responsibility. These emphases are supposed to reflect a difference in principle within the parties—though, when they get their principles all spelled out, with every proviso, both parties sound much the same: it becomes compassion-*with*-responsibility, or responsibility-*with*-compassion. Was Wallace right, then, in saying there is not a dime's worth of difference between the two?

Not if one looks behind the campaign rhetoric. The parties are actual and distinct, two different *bodies*. Each party has captured, to some extent, a different clientele, set up permanent negotiations with business, or labor, or farmers, or professional backers, each bloc with an investment of time and money and effort in the party, each with corresponding leverage upon it. This leverage has been earned by past services and donations, and is not lightly to be sacrificed. The laborer tends to think he will "get a better deal" from the Democrats because the Democrats owe the unions so much. The physician thinks he will get a better deal with the Republicans because the party owes the AMA so much (a debt called in when Robert Finch tried to appoint an HEW official not cleared through the doctors).

Voting the party seems, then, to make sense in terms of long-range political structure, coherence, influence. The party, even in loss, is always building, looking ahead, using a particular election to help it get in better position for succeeding elections, representing its clientele on a continuing basis. But this party influence cuts two ways. In order to get your slice of pie, you have to let others in the party get theirs. A "dove" on Vietnam, who also has a stake in the Democrats' urban welfare structure, may have to yield to George Meany's hawkish unions when the subject of a peace candidate comes up at the party's convention. The wider the coalition, the more factions there are to make claims on the party. Thus one rarely gets a "pure" choice since the parties are built for compromise, for dealing with the urgencies of human ambition and avarice—which leads to the recurring dream of an "amateur" politics that would break through the old fabric of deals and compromises.

When you vote for the Republican Party, then—or vote for it at the national level—which party are you voting for, John Tower's or Ed Brooke's? At the local level, where one actually votes for a Brooke, or a Tower, it is, perhaps, possible to know what you are getting. But a national candidate is chosen precisely to throw an umbrella over all factions, or to give the impression that he is doing so. How far can this gesture be trusted? Though a Daley or Thurmond may have been the deciding force in nominating a man, that candidate's task is to move out from his base and reach as broad a constituency as possible, appealing not only to all wings of his own party, but to Independents and even to those in the opponent party. The presidential campaign is, therefore, the least party-oriented of our races. This, you will remember, pleased James MacGregor Burns. The broad compromising "Presidential Party" of his description is contrasted with the obstructive "Congressional Party" oriented to narrow local issues. He would have us strengthen the former and debilitate the latter. Nixon may say a good word for the textile industry when campaigning in South Carolina, or for the F-111 in Texas; but it is clear that, once in office, he has too many sectors to please, too many problems transcending the pork barrel, to be held strictly accountable to local commitments, the way a congressman is. Such ritual gestures are not the *real* part of a presidential campaign, for Professor Burns. The real, redemptive part is the raising of party debate to a national level, where it is compelled to address the big issues, to hammer out principles and set large goals.

In short, Professor Burns believes in platforms. (When Professor Schlesinger told Robert Kennedy he could discharge his duty on the Vietnam war by getting a peace plank into the Democratic platform, Kennedy said, "Arthur, when was the last time millions of people rallied behind a plank?") Burns believes in committee reports and campaign rhetoric. He thinks the presidential debates are actual debates—that candidates say something. But less romantic political scientists, from all parts of the theoretical spectrum, realize it is the job of candidates to say nothing. Anyone who thinks of the Kennedy-Nixon broadcasts in 1960 as the "Great Debates" has not gone back to read the four texts. Nor does he remember the impression they gave at the time—which was that Nixon lost them because of poor cosmetics and a haggard appearance. The presidential campaign is not only the one in which issues are most submerged, but in which the manipulatory powers of modern TV and advertising are most brought into play.

Burns may call this rational debate if he wants. It does not much matter. He cannot make this quadrennial affair a *continuing* kind of debate. The problem, as he sees it, is that the presidential party comes to life only when a presidential election is taking place; he would extend that life by keeping up the discussion of goals, the drafting of platforms, the arranging of debate throughout the four-year lacuna. But who would do this keeping up? The presidential party? What, and where, is that?

Burns is right in seeing that the congressional party has a continuing life: local elections, congressional and Senate races, judicial appointments, patronage arrangements, fund collection, the payoffs, the rake-ins, the grooming of future candidates—all this goes on constantly in the state and local party. What Burns fails to see is that this *is* the party, that there is no such thing as a presidential party. Consider what happens in the nomination of a presidential candidate. Before the convention the party is committed to no one man (though an incumbent President has an advantage, there is no ban on challenges by other candidates—e.g., McCarthy and Kennedy challenging Johnson, forcing his withdrawal). Up to the convention, the party has no candidate, only several contenders. Backing each of these contenders is a personal following within the party, each one working for its man and against the party's other contenders. After the nomination, the successful contender will arrange what peace he can with his former rivals. Gestures of solidarity will be made, and the presidential campaign will be coordinated in greater or less degree with the races of candidates lower on the ticket. But the team the candidate takes on with him into the November showdown—and, if he is successful, into the White House—is still his personal entourage. With Kennedy, it was "Camelot"—the Irish Mafia, the Harvard brain trust, the network of family retainers. With Nixon, it was the law firm (Mitchell *et al.*), the "Nixon regulars" in the party (Finch, Klein, *et al.*), and the Disneyland Mafia (Haldeman *et al.*). Once its man wins, the team disappears into the Cabinet, the White House, the bureaucracy; its members do not, now, have the time or the inclination to run debate sessions outside the executive structure. Their loyalty is to the President, not to an impartial critical stance; besides, after being only loosely accountable to the party in the final bid to win the White House, this group must reopen negotiations with it when legislation is sent to the Hill, where the President proposes but Congress disposes. Nixon is not merely beholden to Strom Thurmond for his past good deeds in Miami; he is accountable to him in the present, because of Thurmond's congressional influence on the party and on the Right Wing in general; and he knows he will be accountable to him in the future, for his effort to be renominated and reelected. Yet while trying to get along with his party, the President must exist, in part, outside it—so he can deal with members of the other party in the Senate and the House. To that extent, he must avoid too close an entanglement with his congressional party; yet he does not do this by forming a *counter* party and making more trouble for himself with Congress. What makes the President stand apart from his own congressional leaders is not the existence of a presidential party but his mode of dealing with *both* parties. In handling these delicate set of negotiations, the President will hardly let his entourage go outside the Washington structure and form itself as a "presidential party" to criticize Congress.

But how about the losing candidate? What prevents him from forming a presidential party of opposition? The loser becomes, after election, a contender once more for the party's nomination. He is jockeying, along with his personal followers, against potential rivals. Each is suing for the party's favor, though the party maintains an official neutrality as the situation develops, right up to convention time. Such a contender will not set up a rival party unless he means to admit that the nomination is not available to him in the regular party.

Thus there is no such thing as a presidential party: there are only successful or unsuccessful entourages of contenders within the parties. The whole "four-party system" of Burns is a pleasant hallucination born of the days when Kennedy was going to "break" Congress (a thing he signally failed to do). What actually exists is not the four-party system, but what Willmoore Kendall calls "the two majorities"—a presidential majority voting for a national candidate who has been screened by the party, and whose claims are vague and idealistic; and a congressional majority that votes to protect an interlocking set of local interests.

Thus what the voter chooses, in electing a President, is not policy, not the best man, not the party as such, but an indeterminate muddle and stir of all three—a vague mix of issues; one of two men already chosen by a whole series of prior factors, including the final veto exercised by the party convention; and a man who is, by contrast with contenders for other office, only loosely accountable to the party during his November effort at election (when he must appeal to voters beyond the party pale) and who, in the White House, is often forced to transcend party lines (to deal with the opposing party in Congress).

There is nothing new in this analysis. Though the American people remain strikingly naive in their estimate of what elections do, political scientists have described the process in cold terms for a number of years; and observers with keen eyes (like Mencken) simply *saw* it all along. George Bernard Shaw richly enjoyed the spectacle of modern elections: "[Democracy is] a big balloon, filled with gas or hot air, and sent up so that you shall be kept looking up at the sky whilst other people are picking your pockets. When the balloon comes down to earth every five years or so you are invited to get into the balloon basket if you can throw out one of the people who are sitting tightly in it; but as you can afford neither the time nor the money, and there are forty millions of you and hardly room for six hundred in the basket, the balloon goes up again with much the same lot in it and leaves you where you were before." But the frenzied tone and ballyhoo of our campaigns was best suggested long ago, when Samuel Johnson described the voting on petitions in his time:

The progress of a petition is well known. An ejected placeman goes down to his county or his borough, tells his friends of his inability to serve them, and his constituents of the corruption of the government. His friends readily understand that he who can get nothing will have nothing to give. They agree to proclaim a meeting; meat and drink are plentifully provided; a crowd is easily brought together, and those who think that they know the reason of their meeting undertake to tell those who know it not; ale and clamour unite their powers; the crowd, condensed and heated, begins to ferment . . . all see a thousand evils, though they cannot show them; and grow impatient for a remedy, though they know not what.

A speech is then made by the Cicero of the day; he says much, and suppresses more; and credit is equally given to what he tells, and what he conceals. Those who are sober enough to write, add their names, and the rest would sign it, if they could.

Every man goes home and tells his neighbour of the glories of the day; how he was consulted, and what he advised; how he was invited into the great room, where his lordship called him by his name; how he was caressed by Sir Francis, Sir Joseph, or Sir George; how he ate turtle and venison, and drank unanimity to the three brothers.

The poor loiterer, whose shop had confined him, or whose wife had locked him up, hears the tale of luxury with envy, and at last, inquires what was their petition. Of the petition nothing is remembered by the narrator, but that it spoke much of fears and apprehensions, and something very alarming, and that he is sure it is against the government; the other is convinced that it must be right, and wishes he had been there, for he loves wine and venison, and is resolved, as long as he lives, to be against the government.

The petition is then handed from town to town, and from house to house; and, wherever it comes, the inhabitants flock together, that they may see that which must be sent to the king. Names are easily collected. One man signs, because he hates the papists; another, because he has vowed destruction to the turnpikes; one, because it will vex the parson; another, because he owes his landlord nothing; one, because he is rich; another, because he is poor; one, to show that he is not afraid, and another, to show that he can write.

To say all this is not to say our elections serve no purpose. They are a satisfying ritual with practical effects. They do not tell us What the Nation Wants in any specific way, but they indicate, in broad terms, what the citizens will put up with. They help to circulate administrative personnel, challenge or renew old loyalties, legitimate situations. If they do not effect major changes, they ratify change already made, institutionalize it, celebrate it. They make for accommodation in the rulers and acquiescence in the ruled. They stimulate the separate regions' awareness of each other. They are big business. They are show business. They amuse, sometimes they edify, in the large sense they educate (if only by effacing some illusions). But they do not create freedom, equality, or the democratic ethos. In important ways, they do not even *express* that ethos—we can bring things efficiently to a vote because everyone does *not* have an equal chance at political office, because so many people are automatically excluded beforehand. In the same way, our elections satisfy not because they offer wide options to us, but because so few things abide the decision of an electorate. We do not vote *for* democracy, for our "way of life"—as if totalitarianism were put up as an alternative. We vote *within* the particular democracy our history has made us; the material for decision can only be formulated manageably within agreement on this context. When opposed sides dig in on life-or-death issues, adjudication by the ballot is not normally acceptable—e.g., we found no way to settle the issue of slavery by the vote; it was put to the arbitrament of arms.

We like to say we are "open" to all views in the political arena, as in the academic one; but we are not, and could not possibly be (the question of slavery is no longer "up" for anyone to vote on here). The nature of our freedom is not shown by our actual choices in the voting booth, but by the kind of questions we have settled before we reach that booth. We vote the way we do because (in some measure) we are free. We are not free because we vote the way we do.

Thus our basic norm for judging other nations has been false. Russia is the kind of country she is, not because of one-party elections poorly attended, but because of large and complex historical circumstances. These circumstances have bred freedoms and inhibitions not marked off on our simple yardstick. If a nation wishes to bring in Hitler, it can do that through election as easily as by other means. If a nation wishes to have free elections *and* slavery, it can manage that—as our Founding Fathers did. Conversely, traditional freedoms can be maintained where elections have not penetrated.

Thus, to return to Marshal Thieu (or whoever will preside over Vietnam's "self-determination" in the future): it is said that Thieu was not validly elected because certain men (communists) were denied suffrage, certain pressures (American) were exerted, so that certain subjects could not be debated. All very true. But as true of our elections as of Vietnam's. Certain issues were excluded in our 1968 election—not dead historical ones (like slavery), but live important ones (like whether to fight on in Vietnam). Major problems are not often settled by elections. They must, usually, be settled before elections are held (e.g., whom to admit to the roll of candidates or the roll of voters), or they must abide the workings of the whole political process (e.g., our Vietnam policy). A nation has already expressed itself, before it goes to an election, by deciding which people should be allowed to vote or to run (communists? criminals? women? illiterates? adolescents? the poor? resident aliens?) and by deciding what issues will be voted on (can one vote to dissolve a country? to reunite with another part of the country? to divide one sector from another?—such matters are not determined by the vote, though they dictate how votes will be cast in the future).

It is said, too, that elections in Vietnam are only crippled by the fact that outside influence, communist or American, pervades the area. But all elections take place in situations of foreign challenge or opportunity, under influences exercised or desired or resented. Men and nations act in context, or they do not act at all. The problem with Thieu's election was not that it was a "bad election" (as Wilson called Huerta's), but that it was an *election;* and elections can only do certain things. They cannot do what we ask them to do. They cannot remake the world in our image (or, rather, in that mirror-image we imagine for ourselves). Nixon committed us to remain in Vietnam till that country holds elections like ours. It was a commitment to remain there forever.

The error of Wilson in Mexico, of Nixon in Vietnam, of our whole quest for "self-determination," is clear: we have reversed the order of cause and effect. Free elections are created by free men, not vice versa. The machinery of election will not call up, establish, or guarantee political freedom. The belief that it will reveals our trust in "the market," our belief that *competition* of itself makes excellence prevail. Our faith in the electoral process is based entirely on myths of the market. We think we can be "open" to all political alternatives (we cannot). We think we welcome all competitors for power (we do not). We think this will give us the best rulers available (it does not). We think the freedoms we possess were wrought by this process (they were not). We think the process will work automatically for others (it will not). If our freedoms are impaired, we think—as Dr. Wald did—this comes from some failure in the voting process (it does not). And we hope to cure all such discontent by repairing, restoring, or improving the process (we cannot). We think that voting is freedom's "invisible hand." In several senses, all deeper than the one he intended, Americans agree with Nixon's statement in 1968: "There is nothing wrong with this country that a good election cannot cure."

3. The Covenant

"Let us press toward an open world—a world of open doors, open hearts, open minds—a world open to the exchange of ideas and of people, and open to the reach of the human spirit—the world open in the search for truth and unconcerned with the fate of old dogmas and isms—a world open at last to the light of justice, and the light of reason."

—President Nixon, Wilsonizing

WOODROW WILSON, reelected in 1916 because "He Kept Us Out of War," took the nation into war just one month after his second term began. In this short time he traveled all the way from nonintervention and official neutrality to complete dictation of the terms for surrender, for peace, and for the postwar organization of nations. Mencken thought this "conversion" a cynically staged thing. Others fasten on one or other point in the process as, admittedly, "expedient"—e.g., Richard Hofstadter shows how carefully the first "neutrality" was framed to be a neutrality *against* Germany.

But Wilson felt he had been true, always, to his vision of a higher noninterventionism—even in the act of sending troops to Europe. The war had been caused, after all, by aggressive alliances, secret pacts, competing power combines—what he called "the great game, now forever discredited, of the balance of power." Thus the thing to do was join the world spasm and direct its energies toward a clearing of the board: no more special alliances, colonial bonds, power blocs. True, an international Covenant would be needed (Wilson, proud of his Presbyterian background, descended from Scotch Covenanters, liked the biblical majesty of the term *Covenant*, and insisted on its use for the founding document of the League of Nations). This would be a Covenant against covenants, as the First

417

Commandment establishes a Religion against religions. Signatories to the League would "have no strange pacts before them." Only the League should claim men's extranational allegiance. A continental pact—e.g., that defined by the Monroe Doctrine—was, to the League, what the cult of idols had been to the worship of the One God. Wilson had, eventually, to soften his criticism of the Monroe Doctrine—as John Foster Dulles had to give in to Nelson Rockefeller's defense of inter-American pacts when the United Nations was founded. But there was hope, in both cases, that the overarching organization would eventually supersede all lesser pacts. It was in this sense that Wilson promised deliverance from "entangling alliances":

> We still read Washington's immortal warning against "entangling alliances" with full comprehension and an answering purpose. But only special and limited alliances entangle; and we recognize and accept the duty of a new day in which we are permitted to hope for a general alliance which will avoid entanglements and clear the air of the world for common understandings.

> If the future had nothing for us but a new attempt to keep the world at a right poise by a balance of power the United States would take no interest, because she will join no combination of power which is not the combination of all of us.

> I am proposing that all nations henceforth avoid entangling alliances which would draw them into competitions of power . . . There is no entangling alliance in a concert of power.

> Special alliances and economic rivalries and hostilities have been the prolific sources in the modern world of the plans and passions that produce war. It would be an insincere as well as insecure peace that did not exclude them in definite and binding terms.

An Alliance against alliances was, after all, the logical outcome of a War against war (which had been preceded by a Neutrality against neutrality).

In sweeping away all partial alliances and aiming at a

single solution to world problems, Wilson was acting in true American style. We have tended, always, to form policy in terms of "all or nothing"—absolute neutrality and isolationism, on the one hand, or "total surrender" and a *novus ordo seclorum*. This is the mood Wilson expressed, both in his neutral and his interventionist ecstasies:

> There can be no compromise. No halfway decision would be tolerable. No halfway decision is conceivable. These are the ends for which the associated people of the world are fighting and which must be conceded them before there can be peace: I. The destruction of *every* arbitrary power anywhere that can separately, secretly, and of its single choice disturb the peace of the world . . . II. The settlement of *every* question, whether of territory, of sovereignty, of economic arrangement, or of political relationship, upon the basis of the free acceptance of that settlement by the people immediately concerned . . . III. The consent of *all* nations to be governed in their conduct towards each other by the same principles of honor and of respect for the common law of civilized society that govern the individual citizens of all modern nations in their relations with one another . . . IV. The establishment of an organization of peace which shall make it *certain* that the combined power of free nations will check *every* invasion of right . . .

Wilson's dream of the League was based on the great myth of the Social Contract, of society as a juridical entity brought into being by grant and codicil, by definition and subscription. The concept of a Social Contract is now the companion, in politics, of the Free Market in the realm of economics. The Market deals with autonomous and equal entrepreneurs, brought together on a field of competitive trading. The Social Contract deals with the introduction of autonomous individuals into society. In society, each man's sovereignty over himself is challenged by the next man's, with consequent friction, right clashing with right, privilege shouldering privilege. A neutral arbiter of some sort is needed to adjudicate these conflicts; yet this agency can have no power over the individual

which that individual did not freely surrender. The aim
of the Contract is to bring about this surrender under
conditions that keep the loss of the individual's power
minimal. The Contract pares away the smallest necessary
part of the individual's authority over himself, and, by
accumulation of these slivers, attains the minimum powers necessary to keep political intercourse peaceful. The
contractual terms are designed both to limit the arbiter
and to safeguard all the residue of the individual's sovereignty—just as the aim of free-market rules is to keep
each entrepreneur as independent, active, unimpeded as
possible, while maintaining the processes of trade.

Every branch of social inquiry conspires to indict this
mythical pattern of society formed by compact. The individual sovereign over himself exists neither in history nor
in any reasonable theory of human development. It is
clear that political mass precedes the political unit—the
tribe precedes the citizen; status precedes contract; shame
culture and "objectivity" occur before the birth of guilt
culture and an expressed human subjectivity. The Lockean
world of free agents bargaining to "enter society" is as
false—and as deeply falsifying of all subsequent inquiry—
as the picture of a ghostly starting line at which all economic competitors somehow line up and begin the race of
life with an "equal start." The theory proposes a *mechanics* of society: preformed parts are assembled
(atomic individuals brought into contact with each other)
and the machinery is tinkered with to make free interaction possible, eliminating friction. But the individual
emerges from what might better be imagined as a *chemistry* of society—just as the poems of Shakespeare can
emerge only from the rich matrix of speech, words,
meanings developed by mankind.

But myth is undisplaceable by argument, and the image
of the Contract is as constant (though often unconfessed)
an element in modern thought as the concept of a human
Marketplace. This makes for confusion and error, with results bad enough at the domestic level. But the contradictions have an even more disastrous effect on the study of
international relations. For at that level, Social Contract
theory becomes Wilsonian Covenant theory—the atomic
individual subscribing to the Contract becomes any self-
determined people entering into the Covenant. We are
faced, at that point, with the paradox that liberal inter-

nationalism fosters the spirit of nationalism—and this for three reasons.

1) Self-determination presumes that there must be a self to be determined. The whole idea of the Social Contract was based on the sovereignty of the individual—his irreducible dignity and rule over himself: no authority can assume a power over him that has not first been freely surrendered. In the same way, Wilson declared that no one can have authority over a nation, a people, but that nation itself. No one can interfere with its "inviolable rights." The difficulty with extending the Rights of Man to become Rights of a People is obvious. The atomistic individual, existing prior to the social arrangement, is a myth—but a myth attached to some concrete phenomena: there *are* human units, all about us, easily identified, whose needs government must serve. One man cannot split himself into two men, alienate his inalienable rights by merging with another man to become a single human being. But where is the nation, the people, on which Woodrow's Presbyterian deity can bestow "God-given rights?" Is "the people" any concrete, observable government? But what if that government is not expressive of the people's will? What if the people have been denied self-determination—like the Mexicans Wilson ministered to? Once the forces of oppression are removed, how do we know the people—the national self to be determined—will be boundaried within the oppressing government's former precincts? Once, that is, French colonial rule is removed from Indochina, how many peoples are there to be self-determined—one, ruled from Hanoi; two, ruled, from Hanoi and Saigon; or three, counting the NLF; or more? What makes a single people? Is Ireland, is Canada, one people or two? Were the Ibos, despite their own protestations, simply part of the Nigerian people? Are the East Germans a separate people?—and, if not, should they absorb West Germany or be absorbed by it; or should they enter an entirely new configuration, one not bounded by the prior lines of either or both German regimes?

The answer to such questions has been given, in the past, through a conjunction of pressures: as Walter Lippmann put it, "By conquest, by royal marriages, by providing protection to weaker principalities, the large national unions were gradually pulled together." Wilson's concept of national self-determination is aimed at removing such arbitrary, random, external factors; the nature of the people's political regime should arise from the free expression of that people's character. But the existence of such a national "self," standing free of external influence, is as legendary as the existence of Locke's precontractual man. The nation-state can no more preexist the shaping pressures of the nation-state system than the human individual can preexist human society or the poems of Shakespeare preexist common speech. Wilson imagined a world where an indeterminate number of peoples slip, like homeless spirits, in and out of available or contrivable governments. A "ghost in the machine" duality is thus established—a duality as of soul and body—between peoples and their governments. The scene is surrealistically fluid—several ghosts in one body, or one in several bodies, or bits of national soul yearning through broken torsos and stray governmental members until each people becomes appropriately "fleshed" through a process of self-determination.

How do we capture this volatile essence of a people, find it and give it a home? Is the determining bond one of language, of blood, of geographical containment, of prior political union? All such norms are inadequate. Classical liberal theory has only one way of deciding what should constitute a separate nation: those are a people who *say* they are a people (what else is self-determination, after all?). John Stuart Mill formulated the proposition in *Utilitarianism:* "Where the sentiment of nationality exists in any force, there is a *prima facie* case for uniting all the members of the nationality under the same government, and a government to themselves apart. This is merely saying that the question of government ought to be decided by the governed." Thus, when the English colonies in America *declared* themselves to be independent, they *were* independent (though, for some reason, when the elected representatives of a bloc of American states declared themselves independent, by means of congresses of secession, America's federal government informed them that, no, they were *not* independent). Where two or three are gathered together in the name of Nationhood, there is It in their midst. Thus internationalism must seek the authentic voice of each separate people, each national soul yearning for a body.

2) Liberal theory calls not only for a national self to

be determined, but for a representative of this self to enter into the global Covenant with other peoples. Wilson had to make sure the Mexican government was truly chosen by the Mexican people, not only for the Mexicans' own good, but in order to have a responsible signatory to international agreements. The Covenant is meant to protect peoples, to guarantee their self-determination, so it cannot receive into its workings those governments that thwart a people's self-expression, that are not proper moral agents of the *Volk*. On the basis of this argument, dictators should not be allowed to function within the Covenant, which is dedicated to their overthrow. That is why there was opposition, at San Francisco, to admitting Perón's government into the UN. That is why America for years has blocked the entry of Red China into the UN (though we admit Russia). And if there are contending governments, or divided countries, the Covenanters find themselves in a very difficult situation: they must decide which is the true government, and deal only with that— or, if necessary, set up a true government (in the Congo, say, or Korea). Where no "representative" government can be found or created, there is no way of dealing with the people.

This explains the liberal longing for a *true* national leader, one who can express his peple's will in the Organization that exists to protect that will. A Fidel Castro, a Patrice Lumumba, is hailed as the George Washington of his country; for if such men are *not* the George Washingtons of their people, then we have no one we can deal with. If Diem was not the George Washington of South Vietnam, then we had to hope for his fall so that a true leader could take his place. Roger Hilsman, who worked in the State Department for Diem's overthrow, said we must be patient and wait for the *real* George Washington to stand up: "Like Egypt, Vietnam would find her Nasser the second time around—or the third—or the fourth." In this way Wilson tried to install the true leader in Mexico —not Huerta, but maybe Villa; if not Villa, then maybe Zapata; if not Zapata, then Carranza. The paradox reasserts itself: internationalism encourages the rise of leaders who express a pungent nationalism.

3) Nationalism is necessary, in this liberal scheme of things, not only to guarantee internal legitimacy and to supply a responsible agent for external negotiations, but to

THE POLITICAL MARKET

give that foreign agent a juridical equality with all other parties to the Covenant. The force of the Social Contract is based on the doctrine of men's equality: all men were equally sovereign over themselves prior to the Contract, and each enters by surrendering the same amount of this "original" self-rule to the state. The state therefore has authority only in those ceded areas, an authority that is the same for all.

Wilson applied the contractual model to his international Covenant, and came up with a doctrine of the equality of *nations:* "Only a peace between equals can last." Yet nations differ not only in size and resources (as individuals do), but in stability, social complexity, solidarity, unity, presumption of legitimacy, modes of representation and basic self-definition. They seem to differ in every way; so in what way are they equal? There is only one possible ground for such equality—their very nationhood. Whatever else they are (goes the argument), they are all *nations,* sovereign over themselves. Thus a mystique of nationhood, an emphasis on original sovereignty, lays the basis for juridical equality in Wilson's internationalism. Each nation is to have an equal vote in the General Assembly, the "liberal" branch of the UN. And the UN, the very temple of internationalism, puts a consequent pressure on emerging or potential nations to achieve separate, equal station with all other countries. The tendency to form federations, or larger and more complex national units—e.g., in the friable postcolonial worlds of Africa or Southeast Asia —is countered by this pressure for independence. The internationalist mentality has contributed to the proliferation of new countries, the division of old nations.

At the end of World War II, a strong sentiment for what was called internationalism, a tendency to blame the world's past troubles on "nationalism," led to the expectation that there would be greater cohesion in the world, an amalgamation of groups (e.g., a United States of Europe), experiments in federalism leading eventually to World Government. But the very steps taken to promote this movement seem to have had an opposite effect. Not only were many new nations born, but "double nations" arose (Germany, China, Korea, Laos, Vietnam, Nigeria). Liberals, forced to explain these unintended effects, tried to distinguish Bad Nationalism (attacked in propaganda for the UN) from Good Nationalism (nurtured by the UN). Professor Schlesinger was ready to oblige: "The nationalism that arose after the Second World War was, in the main, not the aggressive and hysterical nationalism that had led nations before the war to try to dominate other nations. [That is: It was not Bad Nationalism.] It was, rather, the nationalism generated by the desire to create or restore a sense of nationhood. [That is: It was Good Nationalism.]" Yet this Good Nationalism had all the marks of the Bad— jealousy of one's own sovereignty, prickliness toward neighbors, militarism. Most of the nationalist leaders were generals, guerrillas, men of war. The fact that their wars were contained was more the result of nuclear stalemate and "the balance of terror" than of some new strain of jingoism that inoculated one against the old strains.

Schlesinger's nondistinction was based on the assumption that nationalism *is* an anomaly in the framework of liberal internationalism. But it is not; it was implicit in liberal theory from the outset—a point recently stressed by Professor Seliger of the University of Jerusalem (in *John Locke, Problems and Perspectives,* edited by John W. Yolton): "To the extent that liberalism provides foundations of modern democracy, it does so also with regard to modern nationalism," since "collective is derived from individual self-determination."

Now we see why it was so urgent for Wilson to demand open elections everywhere in the world as a necessary condition for peace anywhere in the world. We need some uniform mechanism to discover what the people want, who the people are, who shall represent each people in the Covenant. Where the ballot does not exist, we must introduce it; where voting is restricted or rigged, we must supervise the elections; and then, having created the conditions for free choice, we must abide by the results. Which means there must *be* results. Clear results—some policies and leaders chosen, others rejected. If there is no popular will expressed through this machinery, there is no certifiably existing people. If two wills are expressed, there are two peoples. If more than that, then more peoples. If an ambiguous will is expressed, then there is no moral agent for the nation, no body to house the ghostly rights of nationhood. That is why we must have faith in the power of elections to "settle matters." We must believe, even, that where no clear popular will existed previously, election can create one (not just reflect it)—can, in that sense, create nationhood, call a people into being. So Nixon summons a new nation to arise in South Vietnam, the result of an election internationally supervised. Though the power of elections is in many respects limited, even fictive, we must hide that fact from ourselves (and we *do* hide it, with amazing success), or we make the whole liberal approach to foreign affairs impossible.

A false analogy underlies this whole complex of beliefs. The analogy runs: as the individual is to the nation-state, so the nation-state is to the international organization. We have already seen Wilson's expression of this equation: he said nations must be "governed in their conduct toward each other by the same principles of honor and respect for the common law of civilized society that govern the individual citizens of all modern nations in their relations with one another." The analogy suggests that each country has a unitary national will, expressed in the result of its elections. This leads to difficulties already mentioned in the case of inchoate or crumbling or questionably existent nations. But it leads to even more pervasive (and less suspected) misunderstanding in the *established* nations, those which have apparently successful electoral systems. America, for instance, is presumed to have a machinery capable of expressing the national will, at least on matters of great importance to the nation. That is why Nixon refers to "what America wants in Vietnam." Yet it is clear, from an analysis of the 1968 election, that the American people had no way of indicating what they wanted in Vietnam—that no one can know for sure what they want there, or know whether *they* know what they want. And if America, with an electoral system as open and flexible as any in the world, cannot say with confidence what its national will is on such a crucial issue, how can countries without settled constitutional processes arrive at knowledge of the popular will?

Yet the concept of a unitary popular will cannot be shed by liberal thinkers. That is why, despite his anti-authoritarian philosophy, the liberal so often yearns for a strong executive—the Super-President of Richard Neustadt, of all those liberals who canonize maximum leaders like Wilson, FDR, and John Kennedy. The clash of blocs and interests in Congress is a constant reminder that there is no such thing as a single will in the nation—and this is an embarrassment to the theories of a fully determined national self. Congressional debate and division reflect the fact that "the people" differ, vary, are divided on many issues. Liberals have preferred to think that Congress is divided only by party duels or selfish interests—by things unrelated to the National Will. Then where does one find that will? In a Champion who rises to embody, at home and abroad, the "true" objectives of "the people," a man who stands above party and speaks with a single voice. Indeed, his unitary voice is the sign and vindication of belief in one National Will, and as such it takes on a sacred character.

Wilson, toward the end, was certain he embodied the people's will in his struggle with Congress—he would take the matter to the voters and they would reelect him in a plebiscite on the League. Nixon, of course, has no such messianic self-regard; but he works from the intellectual assumptions of Wilsonianism. He talks as if he knew and could say "what America wants" in Vietnam. He talks of giving South Vietnam what *it* wants, as if he knew what that is and could bestow it. In a subtle way, all Nixon's years of foreign study were distorted by this abstract language about nations and their wants. Only so could he come to office in 1969 still believing in what he called "linkage" as the best tool of diplomacy.

His argument was that if Point A is vital to Russia, then that country, "knowing its own mind," will yield less vital things (like Point B and Point C) if we assure her that Point A will thus be protected. The trouble with this approach, as seasoned diplomats know, is that different groups in any nation (even a nation like Russia) have differing degrees of influence over the national reaction on Point A, say, or Point B. There is not perfect agreement, or even full communication, between all parts of the bureaucracy, between generals and commissars, factions of the Party, ideologues and pragmatists, intellectuals and the people. The matter is not subject to one National Will. That is why shrewd bargainers like to isolate issues and treat each one on its merits in negotiation between nations—the very opposite of Nixon's long-credited philosophy of foreign affairs.

Nixon also treated nations as simple units when he talked of "neutral" arbiters to oversee Vietnamese elections. The idea that a nation-state can disinterestedly settle the affairs of another nation-state is absurd. In the first four decades of this century, we helped set up ninety-seven treaties providing for neutral arbiters, yet arbitration took place only twice, in circumstances where it would have taken place without the treaties. It was, after all, our attempt to act as a neutral force during French withdrawal from Indochina that involved us in a war where we are, alternately, referee, interested party, rival, aggrieved party, aggressor, creditor, debtor, captive, captor, wooer and wooed, pursuer and pursued, to all the neighboring South Asian nations—but never truly neutral toward any of them. To achieve such neutrality we would, first of all, have to neutralize contending opinion within our own borders (hawks, doves, anticommunists, do-gooders, etc.)—that is, silence all dissent from the "neutral" actions taken by our rulers in the nation's name. Nixon admitted as much when describing his pledge to bestow self-determination on Vietnam. In the November 3 telecast, he said: "I have initiated a plan of action which will enable me to keep that pledge. The more support I can have from the American people, the sooner that pledge can be redeemed." Some Americans, that is, can impede the fulfillment of the National Will by opposing it—opposing America, as it were: "North Vietnam cannot defeat or humiliate the United States. Only Americans can do that." If you believe in one National Will, then all who act apart from that Will are outside "the Nation"—which is apparently Agnew's doctrine on demonstrations. Critics of the war, by prolonging the war, are in effect killing American soldiers, acting as traitors, as enemies to their own people.

But what if growing numbers of the people oppose our officially announced National Will? It is supposed to be *their* will, after all, and Nixon, who claimed to be listening to the 52,000 people who sent telegrams supporting his November 3 speech, *refused* to listen to the 300,000 people who, a week later, came in person to demonstrate against the war, (It helps, at times like that, to believe that America has a "silent majority"—all vocal expression of opinion then becomes, by definition, the noises of a minority.) At this juncture it is common for rulers to retreat to the position that the National Will is what people *should* want. That was Wilson's claim when he said the nation supported the League. The people's will becomes what National Destiny imposes on that people as a duty.

As Nixon said on November 3: "I know it may not be fashionable to speak of patriotism or *national destiny* these days, but I feel it is appropriate to do so on this occasion . . . [because] the wheel of *destiny* has turned so that any hope the world has for the survival of peace and freedom will be determined by whether the American people have the moral stamina to meet the challenge of free-world leadership." It is not simply a question of what the nation wants, but of what it *must* do to meet its obligations, its call to greatness. The highest use of the will becomes asceticism, denial of the will. That, too, was part of Wilson's teaching. On his way to Versailles he said that America would be "the only disinterested people at the Peace Conference." America, as the most fully self-ruled nation, had the greatest resources of self-discipline. All our factions were thus subsumed in one overriding Purpose. "We manifested one hundred years ago what Europe lost, namely self-command, self-possession . . . Only free peoples can hold their purpose and their honor steady to a common end and prefer the interests of mankind to any narrow interest of their own." As, in Emerson's moral marketplace, the self-*made* man is the self-*mastered* one, so, in Wilson's scheme of things, the self-*determined* nation is the self-*denying* one, not to be wearied in its worldwide missions of benevolence. Nixon put it this way in his telecast: "Let me be quite blunt. Our fighting men are not going to be worn down; our negotiators are not going to be talked down; our allies are not going to be let down." Or, as he said late in 1969: "The peace that we will be able to achieve will be due to the fact that Americans, when it really counted, did not buckle, did not run away, but stood fast so that the enemy knew that it had no choice except to negotiate . . ."

4. Universalism

"I wish there were some great orator who could go about and make men drunk with this spirit of self-sacrifice."

—*Woodrow Wilson*

BY THE EARLY FIFTIES, heresy had reared its head in the liberal camp; men ventured on a "realist" critique of progressive ideals. There was a vogue for hardheadedness and pragmatism, for Reinhold Niebuhr's attacks on the idea of man's perfectibility. In the area of diplomatic history, realists like George Kennan, Hans Morgenthau, and Walter Lippmann dismantled what had been one of liberalism's finest exhibits, the international vision of Woodrow Wilson.

The heretics, of course, were thundered against by guardians of the old faith. A good example of this reaction was *The American Tradition in Foreign Policy* (1955), by Professor Frank Tannenbaum of Columbia. He said the realists were deserting all that was best in American foreign policy, and restated the creed intact. American policy, he claimed, has always been:

—*Based on the doctrine of the equality of nations:* "The international relations of the United States have unconsciously been dominated by the belief that the relations between states can be made to rest only upon the ideal mutuality, the equal right to abide in freedom and the dignity of all nations—great and small."

—*Based on a laissez-faire model of single nations competing peacefully:* "It [the world imagined by American policy] accepts the doctrine of live and let live as a matter of course, for its own life is conceived of as a process of continuing accommodation within a world of nonviolent friction."

—Based on a renunciation of "monopolistic" blocs of nations: "That is why the concept of a 'balance of power' is alien and repugnant to the American people. We have condemned in others the policies derived from that concept and have rejected them for ourselves."

—Based on the belief that, just as individualism leads to its apparent opposite (social solidarity), so nationalism will lead to internationalism: "Cooperation is possible only among equals, so that equality eliminates the basic reason for political disruption because equals politically are 'coordinate' in rank, and this common identity is essential for different states to achieve that unity which makes them members of the same political family."

—Based on a conviction that international justice is to be achieved "all or nothing": "To the American people, it is inconceivable that military security can rest upon injustice, upon power, upon the ill-gotten fruits of imperialism and oppression."

—And, of course, based on the understanding that America should be the model for the world: "Benjamin Franklin was sagacious and experienced beyond most men and he not only knew the United States but had deep knowledge of England and the Continent. In the ripeness of his years, after helping frame the American Constitution he felt that it represented a political system that Europe might well adopt for itself. In the year 1787, Franklin wrote to a European friend: 'I send you enclosed the proposed new Federal Constitution for these States. I was engaged four months of the last summer at the Convention that formed it . . . If it succeeds, I do not see why you might not in Europe carry the project of Good Henry the Fourth into execution, by forming a Federal Union and One Grand Republic of all its different States and Kingdoms; by means of a like Convention; for we had many interests to reconcile.' "

A wonderful breed, those eighteenth-century rationalists. All their thoughts were not only true; all their truths were "self-evident." It took Jefferson only "two or three nights," after his regular working day, to divide legend from fact in the New Testament. Franklin cannot understand why his country's plan will not work everywhere. After all, he spent four months drafting it (more time or labor, one is made to feel, would have been mere ostentation). Wilson would have been at home with men like these. Except that he made pikers of them. They believed in the God-given rights of Man. He believed in really *hard* things, like the God-given rights of the Nation.

In nothing is Tannenbaum more the true, if naive (true because naive) spokesman for "Americanism" than in his belief that any departure from the ideals he enunciates is an attack on morality itself: "This doctrine [of diplomatic realism] is confessedly, nay gleefully amoral. It prides itself upon being realistic and takes Machiavelli as its great teacher." Nothing exceeds a Tannenbaum's credulity—not even the picture of George Kennan being gleefully amoral. Morality is heroic, in the puritan, or nonexistent; one is among the elect or the damned. In the individual this leads to a perpetual self-questioning and search for one's own motivation, along with unwillingness to accept any but the noblest explanation for one's acts—e.g., Nixon reasoning to others (and no doubt to himself) that he accepted political donations in 1951 so he could give work to deserving girls in Washington. Unless the Calvinist is convinced that the grace of predestination lifts him to heights of virtue, he must suspect that his deity has consigned him to damnation. The "Something Else" of success is the mark of salvation. "Morality" is absolute and selfless virtue; anything else is immorality. All or nothing.

Again and again this puritan trait shows up in our national attitudes. It was Wilson's constant theme. "I have uttered as the objects of this great war ideals, and nothing but ideals, and the war has been won by that inspiration." "The force of America is the force of moral principle . . . there is nothing else that she loves, and . . . there is nothing else for which she will contend." But the theme was not unique to Wilson; it is infectious, it lives on. Dean Rusk was smitten by it when he said, of Vietnam, "We have no quarrel with the Communists, all our quarrels are on behalf of other people." And this plague of nobility descends, now, upon Nixon: "The United States has suffered over one million casualties in four wars in this century. Whatever faults we may have as a nation, we have asked nothing for ourselves in return for these sacrifices." Nixon seems especially interested in the concept of generous warfare. Not only did he say in his May 1969 speech: "History will record that never have American fighting men fought more bravely for more unselfish goals than our men in Vietnam." He also said, during his visit to

Vietnam: "Out here in this dreary, difficult war, I think history will record that this may have been one of America's finest hours"—apparently on the Tennysonian principle that the more senseless a charge is, the more selfless it is bound to be (noble Six Hundred).

The National Will, to be glorified, must be more than mere willfulness; it must have a transcendent goal. In the very act of asking Congress to declare war, Wilson had insisted on the altruistic manner in which we were to shed blood: "The world must be made safe for democracy. Its peace must be planted upon the tested foundations of political liberty. We have no selfish ends to serve. We desire no conquest, no dominion. We seek no indemnities for ourselves, no material compensation for the sacrifices we shall freely make. We are but one of the champions of the rights of mankind. We shall be satisfied when those rights have been made as secure as the faith and the freedom of nations can make them." For Wilson, as for Nixon, he who would gain a self must lose the self, even when it is a national self.

No wonder Wilson was helpless in the hands of his European counterparts. At the very least his "selflessness" robbed him of bargaining tokens. He could not, to make Orlando of Italy give up something Italians wanted, sacrifice something that Americans wished to achieve from the treaty—since Americans, he said loftily, wished for *nothing* for themselves. (Nixon put himself in the same position with regard to Vietnam—Hanoi had very definite interests of its own, while Nixon professed a detached and unselfish attitude toward the war's outcome.)

Wilson's position not only left him without chips to play; it was taken as a standing insult to other nations, which professed legitimate interests of their own. But worst of all, Wilson's approach destroyed America's credibility. Ethereal profession, it was felt, would yield at some future point to baser instinct. Other nations were bound to act on the assumption that Americans had not yet become angels. In others' eyes, a country becomes more reliable insofar as its own interests are recognized, stated, built into the fabric of a peace, made the basis for long-term commitments. Only then do men feel they have something they can trust.

But Wilson's fundamental problem was not merely strategic or psychological—how to win points and gain

trust at the bargaining table. The problem was moral. He
had staked his whole case on an appeal to morality, and
the doctrine of national selflessness is an immoral one—
an irrational one, based on the sacrifice of other men to
certain men's ideals. It is, admittedly, against the whole
grain of Tannenbaum's tradition to say that national altruism is an immoral stance. We have assumed that the self-
sacrifice we honor in individuals is equally admirable when
attempted by nations. We have even used a slogan misquoted from Stephen Decatur—"my country right or
wrong"—as a summary of all that is *im*moral in foreign
policy. But even in individuals we do not admire an unlimited self-sacrifice. The man who throws his life away
too lightly may be wronging his family, or others who
depend on him, or those who will be killed in the train
of his act's consequences. Nonetheless, within these limits,
we respect the heroes who place their lives at the disposal
of a cause more dear to them than life—men, say, who
volunteer to fight for and with an oppressed people, or
what they conceive to be one (the Lincoln Brigade, those
who tried to aid the Hungarian freedom fighters, those
who flew relief to Biafra).

The leader of a nation, however, is in a different position. He is not sacrificing himself when he declares a war;
he is sacrificing others' lives—either because those lives
are endangered anyway (a war of self-defense) or because
some principle or interest is at stake and the leader feels
it important enough to defend with his countrymen's lives.
Of course the leader claims that "the country" sacrifices
itself—and here we see how necessary is the myth of a
discernible National Will. That is what makes it possible
for a Wilson, or a Nixon, to feel that he is not sacrificing
men to his own ideals. (Richard Hofstadter has noticed
how, as American entry into World War I became im-
minent, Wilson began insisting on the distance between
his office and himself, "to relieve himself of some of the
burden of responsibility.") Even before Wilson took the
nation into a world war, he had mobilized the army
against Mexico to make it "self-determined." He could
put himself in this position only because he thought an
American ruler's task was, precisely, to do good for others, not to protect the nation's legitimate interests. One
of the effects of national selflessness is to give our rulers

an almost unlimited mandate abroad—which helps explain the doctrine's attractiveness to those rulers.

Wilson sacrificed other men (not himself) to self-determination in his raids on Mexico, killing both Americans and Mexicans—it is hard to say which was the greater crime. Wilson had a deeper responsibility to Americans; but for that very reason he had less right to interfere in the fate of Mexico. In the case of his own country, let us suppose what is indeterminable—that he had a majority of the nation behind him in his Mexican policy. This is indeterminable, first of all, because Wilson's policy was not very clear even to himself, it often fluctuated. Beyond that, there were much the same obstacles to finding a National Will in Mexico as there were, in 1968, to finding "what the people want" in Vietnam. But let us *suppose* a majority in Wilson's favor: even then he had no right to risk the nation's resources and safety as if the minority opinion did not exist. The fact that he was put in office by an electoral-college majority does not make his actions *America's* actions. An election cannot establish a unitary National Will. The belief that it does so leads to the belief that the Nation is deciding whatever Richard Nixon decides should be done, with American bombs and American lives, in Vietnam. Yet even if a President could embody a unanimous National Will—even if we grant that impossible hypothesis—what right does a Wilson or a Nixon have to impose that will on another country? If Wilson *had* embodied the National *Will* of America, he obviously was not the embodiment of Mexico's will, any more than Nixon can embody the will of South Vietnam.

Under plangent declarations of our disinterestedness, one sometimes hears a "roundabout" argument from self-interest: only if *every* nation is free, self-determined, prosperous, protected against aggression, can *any* nation be at peace. This is the "enlightened" argument from self-interest, which says that it is in our interest not to act in our interest—thus calling on several deep instincts, the desire to take an all-or-nothing approach to foreign affairs, the bustling succeeder's hope that "honesty is the best *policy*," the Nixonian formulation that "selflessness is an *asset*," and the belief that we should not let our left hand (while giving) know what our right hand is doing (namely, taking).

Professor Schlesinger, who likes this argument from a

higher self-interest, has given it a name, *universalism:* "By 'universalism' I mean the belief that the United States has an active and vital interest in the destiny of every nation on the planet . . . all nations share a common interest in all the affairs of the world." This policy, he assures us, has "produced acts of national generosity unparalleled in the history of man." (He is verging toward Nixon's concept of the generous war.) Schlesinger admits, however, that universalism led us into Vietnam—but only by an "illegitimate extension" of a concept "entirely sound and necessary" in itself. The fact that the war is simply an extension of this valid premise explains "why decent men [including Schlesinger] should therefore have defended that involvement with such invincible self-righteousness."

The trouble with this doctrine is twofold, theoretical and practical. The theoretical objection is based on the fact that honesty is not, in itself, the best policy—that a natural "market" does not guarantee success to virtue. The practical objection is that a nation embarked on profitable altruism never knows quite what it is up to, and neither do other countries. Take foreign aid, for instance: our "selfless" side makes this a matter of charity, given with no strings attached. But our calculating side says that such virtue will have a reward, and estimates the *amount* of reward likely to result from this or that bequest. The upshot is a policy that has no clear rationale, seems alternately quixotic and capricious, Machiavellian and exploitative (far more so than would a plan of *confessed* bribes to allies). We never seem able to answer, even to ourselves, the question, Are we buying allies or simply doing good to others? Our actions suggest the former, our arguments claim the latter, and the result is that we are not credible to anyone, including ourselves. Lippmann points out that it was Wilson's very "selflessness" that made it impossible to mobilize America behind the League of Nations: since he had defined no clear national interest for Americans in the war, his countrymen felt they had no stake in the peace settlement. Americans wanted nothing for themselves, said Wilson; so the country shrugged its shoulders and let others squabble for what *they* wanted at Versailles and Geneva. Wilson felt that just *because* we had no selfish ends, we would be *more* active and interested in working for global justice. But when it came time to prove this, Americans could not believe they were that noble. No one else could, either.

Schlesinger, with his own brand of partial realism, says that Vietnam was an "illegitimate extension" of our legitimate doctrine of universalism. He says that we should have restricted our intervention to nations and issues that clearly affect world peace. Yet the universalist doctrine, even as he states it, is that *all* countries and issues affect the world order. "Universalism," his own term, is expressly all-encompassing. One cannot "extend" a universal—there is nothing left over to extend it to. It is typical of Schlesinger to choose the term, and then desire its contradiction—a *partial* universalism. Perhaps he means that mere consistency to an idea is an illegitimate extension of it—as we have seen, he likes his principles "submerged," unconfessed, not "dogmatically" adhered to. A principle adhered to consistently becomes, in his eyes, an "ideology" instead of an "idea."

Yet, granted this principle of having no clear principles, how do we determine the point at which we should abandon principle? Where does consistency become an "illegitimate extension"? In Vietnam, for instance, Schlesinger himself did not become aware of the illegitimacy until well into Johnson's regime; he was still defending the war during the successful antiwar "teach-ins." Now he tells us that we "went too far" in Vietnam, but his norms seem merely quantitative—he falls back on the "just war" concept of proportionality: "I do not see that our original involvement in Vietnam was per se immoral. What was immoral was the employment of means of death out of all proportion to rational purposes." It was not wrong to kill Vietnamese (or Americans); but we should not have killed *so many*. Bombs away, but sparingly. It is easy to see how such a view leads men imperceptibly—one bomb at a time, as it were—into situations that are not, for a long time, repugnant to their original principles, but which become, at some stage of the carnage, more than they can stomach.

But it is dangerous to let one's mind wait upon one's stomach for moral guidance. Others, unlike Schlesinger, have found in the large-scale enacted folly of Vietnam an indictment of the principles that led us there. Once we commit national resources—money, aid, influence, favor, threats, "advisers"—to a selfless goal we have been insist-

or some time, it is easy to move from "moral ... economic pressure, from economic alliance to military pledges, and from military pledges to bombing runs. The more selfless our efforts have been, the more evil, indeed inexplicable, becomes any force that would frustrate them. When Wilson's efforts in Mexico were thwarted, it was easy for him to think of those opposing him as monsters, so evil that they must be disposed of sooner or later. Then, once the firing starts and war-fever takes hold, it is easy for battle to escalate toward all-out war. There is, at each new stage of this process, an increased amount of prestige already committed, needing defense by slight *further* commitment.

Our Vietnamese war—attacked, finally, by liberals—merely demonstrated the error of principles that liberals continue to hold in other matters (for instance, in the area of foreign aid). The attempt to be nationally "selfless" is not only confused and confusing, but wrong. The state should not take any position toward other states except from "reasons of state." It is immoral—not reasonable—for the state to act as something other than what it is. Presidents are not elected, as Wilson thought he was, to create a new world in the American image, but to administer the country's resources in the country's interest.

Wilson said that America's doughboys fought for the Fourteen Points. Roosevelt said the GI was fighting for the Four Freedoms. Johnson and Humphrey sent men out to die for the planting of dams in Vietnam. Nixon preaches a war of generosity. Each time we have fought in this century, our leaders have denied that we did it for ourselves. But the men who do the actual killing cannot live on such flowers of rhetoric. In World War II, the morale builders tried to assure men they fought for "the girl back home" or for "Ma's homemade pie." It is absurd to kill men for a pie, but that argument was groping toward the right nerve. The soldier had to believe he was fighting, if not for Ma's pie, then for *Ma*, for her safety and his girl's. Talk to any soldier who believes in what he is doing in Vietnam, and you will get no nonsense about America's lack of vital interests there. He has been led to believe that he is crippling a communist monster before it has time to swallow America. Each man fights, if he is fighting with conviction, for his country, and that in the most concrete sense. For anyone at the battle line realizes it would be immoral to go around killing men for a Cause.

5. Our Country!

"When men take up arms to set other men free, there is something sacred and holy in the warfare. I will not cry 'peace' as long as there is sin and wrong in the world."

—*Woodrow Wilson*

WOODROW WILSON was readier to do battle than many a jingo or general. The moralizers, it turns out, are not necessarily moral, any more than rationalists are rational. So perhaps the "immoralist" doctrine is a sound one—or can be interpreted in sound ways.

At the very least, the man who says "my country, right or wrong" is admitting that his country *can* be wrong. He does not identify his country with the cause of righteousness itself. He is obviously thinking of his country *as* a country, not as an individual (usually himself) writ large, nor as an abstract proposition he is asked to demonstrate, a creed he must say his Credo to. The liberal tends to think his country is in the right or it ceases to be his country (his consent, after all, is what constituted it a country in the first place). This leads, with some men, to an integrity so lofty as to be irrelevant; whose country, after all, can be right very much of the time? With other men, it leads to the easier assumption that their country must, in any case, be in the right. And a third class mixes the first view with the second—Wilson, for instance, sincerely thought his country was the last best hope of democracy, yet had to keep hiding from himself the economic factors that cooperated in our drift toward war. Once let a man identify his country with his fondest beliefs, with the very fate of freedom, with the hopes of mankind, and he is tempted to guard its moral claim at all costs, to rationalize failings, to invent lofty motives for the nation's policy. Puritan self-scrutiny turns, at that point, into puritan hypocrisy—a hypocrisy more easily adopted since it does not puff oneself, but one's Cause. Wilson reached the point where he could not admit to himself that America might wage war for something less than universal liberty.

Decatur's formula does not seem so unreasonable after all—especially when we recall its authentic form (so often misquoted): his toast was, "Our country! In her intercourse with foreign nations may she always be in the right; but our country, right or wrong!" Can that toast be a moral guide? Perhaps. Our history contains a famous instance of a man choosing his country though he knew her course was wrong. Colonel Robert E. Lee was no secessionist in 1860—he said that if he owned all the slaves in the South, he would give them up to save the Union he had fought for. Yet, as a professional soldier, he had only three choices—(a) to remain in the federal army and help destroy his own state, in the process killing his friends, his relatives, the countrymen closest to him; or (b) to resign his commission and stand by idle, watching others ravage his homeland and kill his friends; or (c) though convinced of the futility of secession, to stand, once it came, between his people and those who would harm them. The first choice he had to reject (refusing, in the process, Lincoln's offer that he lead the new Union army being raised). Having resigned his commission—he could not take part in preparations to invade his native state—he hoped that his military career was at an end, that the conflict would be averted and he could remain a civilian. It was in this period that he refused command of the new Confederate army being raised. But when his native state seceded (men cheered crazily in the streets of Alexandria while Lee's Arlington home went into mourning), he could not refuse his governor's request that he lead the troops of Virginia. He chose his country, right or wrong—rather, he chose his country, wrong. It is impossible to think this an immoral decision, especially when we read the anguished letters he wrote to friends, justifying it.

With all my devotion to the Union and the feeling of loyalty and duty of an American citizen, I have not been able to make up my mind to raise my hand against my relatives, my children, my home. I have therefore resigned my commission in the Army, and save in defence of my native state, with the sincere hope that my poor services may never be needed, I hope I may never be called on to draw my sword.

After the most anxious inquiry as to the correct course for me to pursue, I concluded to resign . . . I am liable at any time to be ordered on duty, which I could not conscientiously perform . . . I am now a private citizen, and have no other ambition than to remain at home.

Tell Custis [his son, also in the army] he must consult his own judgment, reason and conscience as to the course he may take. I do not wish him to be guided by my wishes or example. If I have done wrong, let him do better.

It might be objected that Lee was not choosing his country—the United States, the Union—but something *opposed* to his country. Yet Lee did not think of the nation as a legal unit indivisible, a judicial entity with one National Will (that Will ordering him to fight). Nor did he justify his choice on the grounds that he had a new country, the Confederacy, established by the right of self-determination. This whole cast of thought was foreign to him—as would have been E. M. Forster's famous dictum: "I hate the idea of causes, and if I had to choose between betraying my country and betraying my friend, I hope I should have the guts to betray my country." Forster equates, in the modern manner, country with Cause. Lee did not. He was not fighting for any Cause, for slavery or the Confederacy. For him, country *meant* one's friends— the bond of affection that exists among countrymen; and when a rift opened in this union of persons, he had to choose those to whom he was bound by primary rather than secondary ties.

The Wilsonian turns his country's citizens into a Cause, and then—having performed that depersonalizing operation—he personifies the Cause, gives it a "self" to be determined from within or repressed from without, to act selflessly or selfishly. But Lee's people were actual persons, not a personified idea. He did not ask whether they were

acting selflessly or selfishly; they had no unitary self to
surrender or impose on others. They were a social complexus of erring, noble, idiotic men. He knew it was in their
interest to remain part of the Union, part of a larger
band of countrymen. Choosing between these two levels
of his own people was an insane thing—but he was put
by war (an insane thing) in a position where he *had* to
choose. Forster, by thinking of his country as an abstrac-
tion, evades the point of his own dilemma—would he, for
instance, "betray" his country to a friend who meant to
torture and kill thousands of his countrymen? The choice
is not between a friend and an abstract Cause, but—more
often—between one's best friends and some not-so-good
friends; and, put in those terms, the matter becomes more
complex—one's choice depends very much on what one's
best friend means to do. Ironically, attacking Causes,
Forster has turned his friendship into a Cause that cannot
be questioned or doubted.

Lee did not help his fellow Virginians because they
were right, or because he approved of anything they
wanted to do as a body. He joined them only when it
became a choice of killing one's own, or watching them
be killed, or protecting as many of them as he could at the
risk of dying with them. Only at that last extremity was
he edged over to their side. Ironically, those who best
grasp the moral norms of the Old South's general are
some of the New South's blacks. Loyal to America, convinced that their people are far better off in the larger
complexus of American society, many black leaders strive
to prevent division between the races; but they are forced
to say candidly that, if intransigence on either side forces
an insane choice upon them, they must stand with their
people.

The most important aspect of Lee's choice is that, since
he did not conceive of his state as a Cause, or as himself
writ large, or as a Will that absorbed his, there were no
grounds left for justifying war except the argument of
self-defense. Killing others is justifiable if they are about
to kill oneself or one's family or one's people—not to
prove a point, or spread some creed by the sword. Lee
has become something like a secular saint, a holy warrior
in our history, because he did not fight a Holy War. Men
who abominate slavery can admire him, since he did not
fight for slavery—or for anything but protection of his

people. It is the only honorable motive for a war. To take this view is to have a moral standard far more stringent than Schlesinger's limited-universal, partial-encompassing idea-not-dogma about the acceptability of battle. Schlesinger was left with clumsy quantitative tests—it was all right to get involved in Vietnam, but *not too far;* to bomb, but *not too much;* to engage in minor warfare *but not with major casualties.* Yet killing is never minor—there is no minor war, any more than there is minor murder. The question is, Do you kill out of self-defense or not? Is there a real threat to the people's existence? When that threat becomes actual (not merely possible), we can take the minimum necessary means to preserve ourselves. When the threat ceases, so should our response.

In the case of Vietnam, did we ever have a legitimate national interest there, on a scale that justifies massive killing? The only thing that could justify the bombs was a threat to our own national life. Some, of course, maintain that such a threat existed. By the domino theory, Vietnam was just one step along a course that would lead to our destruction. But if that argument is to be made, it must be based on solid evidence. Unfortunately, other arguments—idealistic talk about saving Asia for Asians, setting up elections in Saigon, planting dams on the Mekong—furnished easier excuses for our bombers. In this fog and mist of crusade and noble sentiment, no one had to analyze the facts, make warhawks *prove* their case. The argument from self-defense was allowed to slide off into suggestions that "saving Asia" is, in the long run, saving a world order that will, in the long run, save America; we were back in the "universalist" posture, where saving anything is equivalent to saving everything. That is too easy an excuse for any war, and especially for warfare in our time.

In this complicated world of power and tension, where American life and property are at stake around the world, the question of national self-defense is admittedly intricate. That is why we should not permit the "overmotivating" of acts like the Vietnamese war—using this reason when it serves our purpose, that reason to serve another purpose, and a third when *that* serves; and throwing the whole pack of reasons at people to evade the necessity for giving any one reason a good hard look. The question of self-defense *is* complex in itself—and that is why we must not further confuse inquiry by shifting our focus, changing our norms, jumping from one position to another, saying part of the time that we have no self-interest in Vietnam, at other times that we have some interest; and, when pushed, finally claiming that we have a vital interest there, though previous statements denied this.

Muddled idealistic talk about Vietnam disguised the ugly fact that what we attempted there was a form of preemptive strike. Naturally, that is not what it was called, even when one of our "realists" was speaking. They talked of "living up to our commitment," keeping our word, not breaking our promises. That sounds very noble, as if we were serving simple truth and honor—until we push the analysis: then it becomes evident that a failure to our commitment would be evil because it would hurt American prestige. That seems a little less lofty motive for napalming Asians; but Kissinger could answer that our prestige is a very important thing, to be carefully guarded, because serious injury to that would put us in peril—would make us less credible to allies, less intimidating to enemies. Only at this stage of the argument do we touch on the real argument for war, the argument from self-defense. Once we have reached this level, we can ask the pertinent questions. How *much* peril would it put us in—would it cripple us, or merely inconvenience us? And if it would merely inconvenience us, are we justified in obliterating villages and burning off countrysides and sacrificing the lives of our own men to avoid an inconvenience? Our courts say that one man can kill another in self-defense; but that does not mean he can slaughter three people ahead of him in a line because they inconvenienced him.

Our generals maintained that if we did not block the communists in Vietnam, we would lose more lives blocking them elsewhere, later; and if we did not block them at that later date, we would be consumed by them. That was their argument; but it could not be analyzed while we let politicians pretty-talk us with TVA and freedom-through-elections and the Great Society for Asia. To treat such a matter with the proper seriousness, one must be fully aware of the moral issue posed by a preemptive strike. That issue is: may we engage in actual bloodshed today to reduce (or avoid) hypothetical bloodshed tomorrow? And before we make that decision, we must weigh, to the best of our ability, a number of crucial matters. We must come to the reasoned conclusion that:

1) our prospective enemy will reach a position, unless we block him at this key point, from which it is possible to destroy us; and that

2) having reached that position, he will have and exercise the intention of destroying us; because

3) we shall be unable, at that point, to exercise an effective deterrent; and

4) being unable to defend ourselves, we shall not receive sufficient help from others.

Large questions, all four, not easily resolved. They may even look rigged to deny the possibility of a just preventive strike—after all, an enemy's intention can be reversed any time up to its actual execution. For that matter, a man who has already begun to swing his fist at an individual may check himself at the last moment—is the *individual*, then, not justified in hitting a preemptive blow? Obviously he is. One cannot have the same kind of knowledge about the future that is possible for the present or the past, but we must make rational conjectures and act on them or stop living. Preemptive strikes are not immoral in themselves, so long as one h˙s made a responsible judgment on the points listed above. But it is clear that this kind of inquiry did not shape our Vietnam policy; we limped into that impasse babbling a mishmash of "universalist," "selfless," and self-interested arguments. In fact, careful consideration of the need for self-defense, the only moral justification for war, is rare in American politics. This is equally true on the Right and on the Left. Most discussion of our policy is a debate between rival Causes, not an attempt to move away from the concept of holy war. Some leftists who opposed the Vietnam intervention seem ready to leap into war in the Middle East. Rightists who did not want American troops to join the UN forces in the Congo were willing to take America into the Hungarian Revolution. The man of the Left is not prepared to unseat Fidel in Havana; but he will gladly topple a Diem in Saigon—or, given half a chance, he will knock off Haiti's Papa Doc. The Left feels called to a crusade against dictators holding power anywhere on the globe, and itches to "do something" about Franco or Chiang; while the Right yearns to engage communism, under any guise, wherever it is encountered. Each side is checked by practical obstacles and risks—prudence tempering principle; but if the risk is retired, we find the principle still there, unchanged. Each side, too, can argue that, off at the end of a long chain of connections, it is to our *interest* to overthrow dictators or halt the advance of communism. But this is not the primary motive in either case—willingness to intervene is not nicely calibrated to the actual threat offered us, at any point, by a Papa Doc or a Fidel. The dictator or the communist rebel is hated, respectively, as an affront to a particular view of World Justice, something that moral sensibility cries out against and would obliterate. The readiness to send American soldiers out to serve one or the other of these visions—or, God help us, both at the same time—is the most terrifying thing about America's power in the world.

The normal response to critics of the Vietnam war has been the charge of "neo-isolationism"—it is Nixon's response, as it had been Rusk's. This, too, is part of our desire for all or nothing, our determination to "link" all issues and *settle* them (if necessary, by force), to make the world *henceforth* safe for democracy. The implied premise is that we cannot have *any* relations with a country unless we are willing to go to war for that relationship. This attack on "isolationism" is difficult to put in the form of argument—it is, rather, an outpouring of lofty emotions expressing a mood, a tone, of moral absolutism. But the charge performs one useful service—it directs our attention back to the *locus classicus* of American "isolationism," George Washington's policy during the French Revolution.

Washington's noninterventionism has often been exaggerated in our histories. He supported the aggressive commercial policy of Hamilton, which made "noninvolvement" impossible. Besides, we were not physically isolated from the rest of the world in his day—British and French forts bounded our territory to the Northwest and Southwest, and threatened our Western flank through various Indian alliances. Washington did not even give us that dire phrase "entangling alliances"—as most Americans (including Woodrow Wilson, Washington's biographer) seem to think. That phrase came from the inaugural address of the nation's greatest (if wildest) phrasemaker, Thomas Jefferson, who was a troublesome "interventionist" during Washington's term of office, but cooled down when he had to face the realities of holding power.

What is most important about Washington's testamentary address to his country is not its supposed isolationism, but its antiwar sentiment, its warning against militarism ("those overgrown military establishments which, under any form of government, are inauspicious to liberty, and which are to be regarded as particularly hostile to republican liberty"). It is appropriate that Eisenhower, the second most popular leader of armies in our nation, should have left office with the same warning: Eisenhower had, from childhood, an admiration for Washington not shared by modern intellectuals, who prefer the romantics of our history, Jefferson and Jackson, Lincoln and FDR. Eisenhower, like Washington, saw no romance in warfare. Washington, defending his neutrality in the French campaigns against European monarchy, said: "The duty of holding a neutral conduct may be inferred, without anything more, from the obligation which justice and humanity impose on every nation, in cases in which it is free to act, to maintain inviolate the relations of peace and amity toward other nations." War is justifiable only when we are no longer *free to act* in any other way—as Lee was no longer free to take any course but the one forced on him by history. Washington, too, saw the morality of war in terms of strict self-defense. In his own draft of the Farewell Address (he published Hamilton's reworking of it), he prayed "that we may be always prepared for war, but never unsheath the sword except in self-defense." This was a characteristic thought: in his will, he bequeathed his best swords to five nephews, on condition that they were "not to unsheath them for the purpose of shedding blood except it be for self-defense, or in defense of their country and its rights." The greatest generals of our political history—Washington, Grant, Lee, Eisenhower—have been notably unwarlike men. (MacArthur, thank God, existed outside our political world, outside any world but that bounded by Autobiography.) These supreme commanders have been less bellicose than our Little Colonel, our artillery gunner, our PT boat commander, or—now— our naval supply officer.

The principal burden of Washington's valedictory address is not that America should remain isolated, but that it should avoid war. His moral opposition to warfare has been blunted by those who read, and then dismiss, the address as an attempt to forestall dealings of any sort with other nations. The Address expressly rejects that impossible ideal. Washington's own draft prays "that we may fulfill with the greatest exactitude all our engagements, foreign and domestic, to the utmost of our abilities"—which assumes, of course, that we *have* foreign engagements. The final Hamilton draft, corrected by Washington, argues not only for "fidelity to existing engagements" but for "liberal intercourse with all nations" and for flexibility in "establishing with powers so disposed . . . conventional rules of intercourse, the best that present circumstance and mutual opinion will permit, but temporary and liable to be from time to time abandoned or varied as experience and circumstances shall dictate."

What Washington objected to was the establishment of rigid blocs, forever at enmity, the situation of "cold war": "Nothing is more essential than that permanent, inveterate antipathies against particular nations [*read, today: Russia?*] and passionate attachments for others [*read, perhaps: South Vietnam?*] should be excluded." Washington's text argues that "the nation which indulges toward another an habitual hatred or an habitual fondness is in some degree a slave." The plight of America, at the mercy of either Saigon or Hanoi, or of both at the same time, is a perfect example of this situation. Washington's Address is meant to defend his neutrality act of 1793, when he refused to be stampeded into the French struggle for the Rights of Man. He was not willing to engage in war for such Causes, and he dismissed any talk of national selflessness. In his own draft of the Address, he wrote: "Whatever may be their professions, be assured fellow citizens—and the event will (as it always has) invariably prove—that nations, as well as individuals, act for their own benefit and not for the benefit of others, unless both interests happen to be assimilated." Hamilton rephrased this point to read: "It is folly in one nation to look for disinterested favors from another . . . There can be no greater error than to expect or calculate upon real favors from nation to nation. It is an illusion which experience must cure, which a just pride ought to discard." Nor did Washington accept this as a "gleefully amoral" doctrine. On the contrary, he thought the norm of morality in

rulers was to protect the nation's legitimate self-interest—
in his words, "our interest, guided by justice."

Naturally, Washington knew that an illusion of selfless
devotion could sway nations—he had experienced the
pressures of those who would join France's crusade in
Europe for *liberté, fraternité, égalité*. But he deplored
such instincts, which run counter to the sober estimate of
national interest, set up conflicting standards, and make
for erratic policy, for diplomatic instability. He predicted
the outcome of such idealistic belligerence. The words can
be applied directly to our involvement in Vietnam:

> A passionate attachment of one nation for another
> produces a variety of evils. Sympathy for the favorite
> nation, facilitating the illusion of an imaginary com-
> mon interest in cases where no real common interest
> exists, and infusing into one the enmities of the
> other, betrays the former into a participation in the
> quarrels and wars of the latter without adequate in-
> ducement or justification . . . And it gives to ambi-
> tious, corrupted, or deluded citizens (who devote
> themselves to the favorite nation) facility to betray
> or sacrifice the interests of their own country with-
> out odium, sometimes even with popularity, gilding
> with the appearances of a virtuous sense of obliga-
> tion, a commendable deference for public opinion,
> or a laudable zeal for public good the base or foolish
> compliances of ambition, corruption, or infatuation
> . . . Excessive partiality for one foreign nation and
> excessive dislike of another cause those whom they
> actuate to see danger only on one side, and serve to
> veil and even to second the arts of influence on the
> other.

That reads, today, like a history of our long descent into
the Vietnam darkness. And other passages strike home,
too. The Address says that once we "implicate ourselves
by artificial ties in the ordinary vicissitudes of her politics," it becomes difficult "to guard against the impostures
of pretended patriotism." Critics of the war in Vietnam
were regularly branded as men lacking in patriotism, in
courage (Johnson's "Nervous Nellies"), in concern for
the world. President Nixon used this whole repertoire of
charges in his address (June 1969) to the Air Force

Academy at Colorado Springs. Patriotism? "Patriotism is considered by some to be a backward fetish of the uneducated and the unsophisticated." Courage? "They observe the problems that confront us, they measure our resources, and then they despair." Concern? "Those who think that way have grown weary of the weight of free world leadership . . . They have lost the vision indispensable to great leadership." Nixon told the Air Force officers that "the American military should never be anybody's scapegoat"—especially not the scapegoat of "the sceptics and the isolationists," with their "simplistic slogans." The airmen, like their President, should refuse "to buy some popularity by going along with the new isolationists." They should hark back to the success literature that made our country great: "Sceptics do not build societies. The idealists are the builders." Then, after Dr. Peale, a touch of Captain Armstrong in the night: "When the first man stands on the moon next month, every American will stand taller because of what he has done."

With a characteristic sense of hierarchy in his values, Nixon rose from considerations of policy to the supreme importance of building one's character, making one's self. Our war in Vietnam is not only good for the Vietnamese, but, even more important, doing good to them is good for us:

> We stand at a crossroad in our history. We shall reaffirm our destiny for greatness or we shall choose instead to withdraw into ourselves. The choice will affect far more than our foreign policy; it will determine the quality of our lives. A nation needs many qualities, but it needs faith and confidence above all . . . Every man achieves his own greatness by reaching out beyond himself. When a nation believes in itself—as Athenians did in their Golden Age, as Italians did in their Renaissance—that nation can perform miracles. Only when a nation means something to itself can it mean something to others. That is why I believe a resurgence of American idealism can bring about a modern miracle in a world order of peace and justice.

Our trumpets blow only for the loftiest—and most questionable—motives: as the success handbooks propose millionaires for our imitation, Nixon asks us to imitate imperialist Athens (which overreached itself so rapidly and disastrously) or the Renaissance city states (which turned all Italy into one bloody cockpit). We fight not for self-aggrandizement, but from even more suspect puritanical motives, to improve the world as a means of self-improvement. And in the process we make our country a Cause (instead of a toast), a Cause to which we sacrifice our countrymen.

Our country, right or wrong?—we can hardly be thinking in those terms when (as the Maryland Secretary of Health has put it) "the average American pays $402.08 a year in taxes for armaments but only $2.52 for food to feed his fellow citizens"; when we are willing to "send the gunboats" to "protect the flag" when one American citizen is threatened abroad, by foreigners, but are unwilling to think of the national prestige as engaged in the protection of American children from rats in this country's slums. The competitive ethic makes us think of any American as "on our team" when we are competing abroad, with other countries, but reduces that same American to a rival, a potential enemy, in our domestic competition, our struggles against each other in the marketplace; so that patriotism is degraded from love of countrymen to mere hatred of foes, mere xenophobia, and men consider it "patriotic" to prefer the muddled abstractions of "confrontation with Communism" in Vietnam to the lives of our young men. We no longer know what "our country" is—as Lee knew, in the tragedy of 1860, what his country was, that it was his country*men*, his erring Virginians. We need a new, more humane concern for our country (right or wrong)—and Vietnam is not our country.

Part FIVE

THE FUTURE
OF LIBERALISM

1. Saving the System

> *"Many people are prepared to rebel against the entire system that has brought us to our present state of affairs."*
>
> —Richard Goodwin

"MID-AMERICA," with some wistful glances at Wallace, voted Nixon into office in 1968. The liberal Eastern Establishment found it was not needed on election day—which made its leaders take a second look at the Forgotten American, at an angry baffled middle class that, paying the bill for progress, found its values mocked by spokesmen for that progress. These voters felt cheated, disregarded, robbed of respect; and unless their support could be reenlisted, the Establishment's brand of liberalism would perish as a political force—just what Kevin Phillips was predicting.

It was time for the intellectual, compassionate toward blacks and students and war-protesters, to rediscover the working man, show compassion for his woes. Pete Hamill in the New York *Post* (along with his colleagues in the *Village Voice*), Marshall Frady in *Harper's*, Norman Mailer in his New York campaign for mayor considered what honorable appeal might be made to men left otherwise to Wallace's dark summonings. Out of this ferment came many suggestions, two of them notable for their scope and backing. The first plan was to extend the idea of "participation" from blacks and the poor to the working-class voter, turning him into a political "activist." Thus more people would be drawn more intimately into the political process; that process would, at the same time, have to be decentralized—the action split up, divided, spread around—in order to give these people something to do; and the result of both trends would be a revitalization

455

of the whole system. The best spokesman for this approach was Richard Goodwin, in several places starting with a long piece in the *New Yorker* of January 4, 1969.

A second approach, sponsored by Daniel Patrick (Pat) Moynihan, rejected the idea of drawing people deeper into politics; it looked outside government to the creation of a new voluntarism, to social action with greater freedom, spontaneity, autonomy than the political process allows. The seventies will undoubtedly witness some debate between these approaches, Democrats tending to favor the former, Republicans the latter. Yet both are essentially sterile.

The deficiencies in these plans would not be so striking were the credentials of their sponsors less compelling. The future of liberalism could hardly be put in more vigorous hands than those of Dick Goodwin and Pat Moynihan. Both entered politics under John F. Kennedy, and both were still working for the Restoration as Robert Kennedy campaigned his way to death. They had shared in the most exciting political experience since the New Deal, the bright first days of the New Frontier, and they have much of the youth and brillliance, the versatility and toughness associated with that time. Yet both have moved on, have rejected the Neustadt conception of presidential power that gave us Maxwell Taylor's counterinsurgency and Robert McNamara's military-industrial complex.

Goodwin is an especially important man to watch, since he has a discriminating feel for where the action is going to be, an almost automatic way of slumping toward the action's center, and a gift for focusing everyone's attention on it. No one is quicker with a phrase or a program. He christened JFK's "Alliance for Progress" (though Sorensen rather petulantly says that *he* thought of "Alliance" and Goodwin merely added "for Progress"). Goodwin gave LBJ "the Great Society" (though Johnson at first tried to claim the phrase was his) and "The War on Poverty." He suggested the title for Manchester's *The Death of a President*. Goodwin was the road rhetorician for Kennedy's campaign of 1960 and Johnson's of 1964. Johnson said of the speech writer who gave him his "We Shall Overcome" paragraphs: "He cries with me whenever I need to cry over something." Goodwin works well with a variety of people; in 1968 he even supplied a speech to Robert Kennedy while he was still on Eugene

McCarthy's rival staff. William Manchester, at the outset of his fracas with Jacqueline Kennedy, could not decide whether Goodwin was on his side or hers. LBJ had the same uncertainty about him, and so did McCarthy.

Goodwin has an oblique rapid manner; his crinkled face and suits combine ease and intensity; his omnipresent cigar seems casual yet, at the same time, as purposeful as a smokestack. He was at the top of his class when he graduated from Tufts; still at the top—and editor of the *Law Review*—when he left Harvard Law School. Within a year he had done time as a favored clerk to Justice Frankfurter; skipped over to the Commerce Committee just as its TV investigations reached their climax (Goodwin persuaded Charles Van Doren to confess in the "Sixty-Four Thousand Dollar" quiz scandal, then wrote the affair up for *Life*); and, before the year was out, moved on to the office of Senator Kennedy, arriving there just as JFK began his successful bid for the presidency.

In the brief three years of JFK's administration, he was appointed Deputy Assistant Secretary of State for Inter-American Affairs, the head of the Peace Corps International Secretariat, and Special Presidential Assistant for Cultural Affairs (the last post was announced November 2, 1963, and he never took office). Before he was thirty years old, he had been involved in consultation on the Bay of Pigs invasion, created a Latin American program, and engaged in diplomacy-by-gossip with Che Guevara. As a fix-it man he served the Kennedys as well and as often as Abe Fortas served Johnson. He handled tasks like the ransoming of Cuban invaders, the Lincoln ritual of Kennedy's burial, the rush acquirement of an "eternal flame" mechanism, the pressuring of Harper & Row over Manchester's book, the announcement of Bobby's intentions to Gene McCarthy, McCarthy's last-minute offer to step aside for Teddy, and the distribution of candles for a mourning procession at the Chicago convention. At that convention, he was trying to broker a ticket that would have healed the rifts in the Democratic Party—Governor Connally to serve as Vice-President to McCarthy. It is not surprising that he showed up at Hyannis Port after Ted Kennedy's car accident; his established pattern of showing up where the action is hottest had even taken him to the Pierre Hotel when Nixon was choosing his administration. Men were beginning to feel that Goodwin was not trustworthy. As Gore Vidal said of him, "Goodwin is forever an Iago in pursuit of an Othello."

No one can doubt, though, that Goodwin has an instinct for useful issues and the right way to exploit them. The number of phrases he has made part of the public consciousness demonstrates that what he is saying today a great many people may be saying tomorrow. And what he was saying in 1969 was "the politics of participation"—participation for the alienated majority, which he thinks even more deeply wounded than our country's angry minorities. The latter have, at least, a goal and an ideal, for which they are willing to work purposefully, to make sacrifices. But the dissatisfied, half-affluent laborer is psychically crippled; he cannot even define his own troubles. *"Somehow, the crucial aspects of his environment seem in the grip of forces that are too huge and impersonal to attack."* This produces a *"malaise of powerlessness."* Men want to *"regain control of and play a real part in the enterprises of society . . . For individuals have a fundamental, instinctive need for a degree of personal mastery over their lives and environment."*

The way to regain this sense of direction, of mastery and power, is—as the kids put it—to become "politicized." Men must *"share in the political process"* and *"personally affect important issues."* This can be accomplished in two ways—by simultaneously narrowing the theater of power and broadening the vision of power. First we must scatter and divide responsibilities, creating local control: Goodwin stresses *"the need for decentralizing the operations of government—allowing communities, private groups, cities and states to make public decisions that are now vested in the central government . . . Increasing the individual's power over the conditions of his life involves the blended methods of transferring authority, creating it where it does not exist, and lessening the coercive weight of the state."*

It is difficult to see how this can be accomplished in the modern world. It is true that centralization reaches a point where it is inefficient; many operations must be farmed out. But the more a government farms out special operations, the more is true decision-making centralized. For special tasks to be performed and integrated with other social efforts, there must be coordination at the top, through just those *basic* decisions that Goodwin would return to the local level, the decisions on ultimate direction, on the overall shaping of environment. If these large issues are to be handled by separate communities—each making as many decisions as possible—the natural result will be duplication of effort, the joining of forces only after incompatible procedures are adopted, and an increasing machinery of adjudication between these procedures. In this sense, as Gunnar Myrdal has pointed out, decentralization in modern governments will add to the spare wheels and redundancies of bureaucratic process, not diminish them.

Goodwin does not address himself to these practical obstacles. Indeed he does not even try to reconcile the *"lessening of the coercive weight of the state"* with admissions like this: *"Many conservatives have welcomed the idea of decentralization, hearing in it comforting echoes of old battle cries about states' rights. They are mistaken, for decentralization, if it is to work, will require even larger public programs and even more money for public needs. Otherwise, the momentum on which local interest and involvement depend will be lost. Nor does decentralization mean the absence of rigorous national standards for the use of national revenues. For example, money given for education must in fact be used for education open to all. Such standards are necessary to protect citizens against unresponsive government, and local government against the pressures of private interests."* More government funds will be needed, and that means more government standards. In other words, local control will exist unless the local people want to control things in a way that departs from the desires of a central authority. This sounds suspiciously like the managing of *illusions* about local control—the federal funds are, you notice, meant to keep up *"local interest and involvement."* Any approach to power which is primarily therapeutic tends to get separated from the realities of power and concentrate on the feeling of power, something much more easily created as an illusion than supplied as a reality.

Misgivings about Goodwin's first prescription, the narrowing of the theater of power, are deepened when he adds his second, the broadening of the vision of power. Although people are, more and more, to control their own segment of the environment, they must not get compartmentalized within it. On the contrary, they should feel they are controlling other segments as well, if their malaise is to be treated adequately: *"It is equally important that the individual be given freedom to participate in the important enterprises of our society, from working in the underdeveloped world to improving the life of the ghettos. If citizens are to find a purpose beyond their daily lives, it will come from having a personal share in important public causes, and the causes must be large and worthy enough to tap moral will and energy."* How large should the concerns be? Worldwide, no less: *"A foreign policy actively devoted to social justice, increased liberty, and the institutionalization of peace on a worldwide scale can enlist the best impulses of the American people."* Even foreign policy is to be a matter of personal therapy: *"A foreign policy founded on traditional American values* [which he has described as one that fulfills *"popular needs and desires"* in other countries—i.e., Wilson's foreign policy] *not only is wise but is essential to our domestic well-being, since shared purpose is the only enduring cement of national unity. In it lies our only hope of finding a moral equivalent of war—or, in this case, a partial alternative to domestic unrest and division."* Having no peace, we will give it to others; and distract ourselves, in the process, from the fact that we have no peace. *"The nature of our role in world affairs must pervade every man's sense of himself as a citizen."* Every man his own Peace Corps.

All this grandiose talk of an overarching vision in which one participates is at odds with the earlier claim that only local control and decentralization can give man a sense of participating. Put in simple terms, Sector A must run its own affairs with a gratifying sense of autonomy; yet must sense its power, also, over Sectors B and C and D— indeed, over the whole world—without, somehow, destroying the sense of autonomy within those sectors. And each of those sectors, at the same time, must be exercising a pleasant mastery (presumably unsuspected, because unresented) over Sector A! Goodwin is engaged in a sleight-of-hand act. We are all to participate in foreign affairs. How? The local communities are not, presumably, going to conduct foreign policy, each town hall drawing up its special treaty with Russia. Yet we were earlier told that politics *must* be reduced to the local level if participation is to be experienced. We cannot make our individual

voices heard at the *national* level (so we must decentralize)—yet a few pages later we are told to make our
individual voices heard at an *international* level.

This contradiction is symptomatic; it reveals the basic
strategy of Goodwin's mind—which is not to solve problems, but to displace them. We cannot rule the nation?
—all right, rule the world. Or, alternatively, rule the village. The solution to our inability to rule the nation is
simply to look somewhere else. We have no satisfaction
in suburbia?—all right, then create satisfaction in *"the underdeveloped world"* or *"the life of the ghettos."* This will
make one stop looking at the suburbs, and their problems
will consequently disappear. We feel no sense of direction in our personal lives?—all right, then direct the lives
of others. A man has no idea which way to go? Good,
rush him to the helm: perhaps the mere excitement of
steering will distract him from the fact that he has no
course to steer. The whole is an exercise in humoring the
invalid, in hoping that, rushed off to care for everyone
else's problems, he will forget that nothing has been done
for him—will fail, in fact, to notice that his illusion of
power over the problems of others is only an illusion. The
emphasis throughout is not on facts but on feelings:
*"The nature of our role in world affairs must pervade
every man's sense of himself . . ."* One must induce these
feelings, and the best way to do that is through modern
devices for manipulation—Orwellian TV sets to "turn
men on" politically.

It is obvious that Goodwin does not know what he is
recommending, that he would be horrified at the thought
of Orwellizing people in order to cure their malaise. But
that is where his program tends: since his recommendations are contradictory, and do not accommodate the realities of power, they must deal in illusion. If therapy is
the aim, centered around a subjective craving for power,
that craving, further stimulated, must be fed; and there is
only one way to feed it. If, indeed, it can be fed at all—
for the great danger of the whole process is that, given a
busy-work scheme of simulated participation, the patients
will see through the pretense, and become even more
angry at being duped.

Goodwin is riding a trend, but a vague unreasoned one,
when he treats "participation" as a wonder drug for the
body politic. The "New Politics" is an attempt to cure

liberalism with a tempered dose of radicalism. Yet old liberal beliefs haunt and invalidate the scheme. All our "new politicians" share the assumption that modern man's trouble comes from the fact that he is not participating in affairs, either because he was never given the chance (he is *un*politicized, like blacks in the South) or because new conditions prevent him from continuing his participation (he is *de*politicized, like the discontented middle class). In any case, the solution is to politicize him. The assumptions in this line of reasoning are:

1) that the American individual once had political control of his fate; but that

2) somewhere along the way, he lost it—whence his current "malaise of powerlessness." So

3) "regaining control" will dispel the malaise.

The first step is the fatal one—the myth that the political marketplace once did work as it is supposed to, giving individuals a sensed power over political decision. The myth has no answer to the simple question, when and where did this successful participation take place? Was it in the nineteenth century, when property and literacy qualifications, stiffer age and residency requirements, bars to female suffrage, the disfranchisement of slaves (and, later, of the freed blacks in the South) were all observed? Or was it in the earlier part of our own century, when former restrictions were only slowly removed? The year 1968 did not represent the limiting of participation in the electoral process. Just the opposite: with heavy new registering of black and Mexican-American voters, with increased tools for communicating with the public and accurately tabulating the vote, 1968 represented the closest approach in our history to a full, informed, open popular vote. What failed was not our embodiment of the electoral ideal, but that ideal itself. The closer we come to meeting its demands, the more clearly we see that it cannot perform as we want it to.

But Goodwin, it is clear from his essay, would supplement participation in elections with a more vital contribution to local politics. Is it true, then, that the individual had more power over his local environment in the past? Again we have to ask, where? The national limits on suffrage (and on political activity in general) were all observed at the local level, where they were supplemented by a community structure based on social pressures toward conformity. The smaller the locale, the stricter the code; and this code—taking its most obvious legal form in blue laws, censorship statutes, gambling restrictions, regulation of liquor's sale and consumption—has always been at odds with the social openness, the chances for initiative, praised by liberals. Which is, of course, why liberal legislation has been winning a long war with these prejudices (these prejudgments, closing the intellectual market) of the local community. Seen in this light, the age of maximum participation, of ability to change one's environment, to overcome social inertia and community pressures toward conformity, is just dawning, not disappearing. Where does Goodwin find the ideal of participatory democracy in our decentralized past? In the East remembered by the older characters in Marquand, Auchincloss, Cozzens? In the South of Faulkner or Tom Wolfe? The lingering Pennsylvania of John O'Hara? The Chicago of Upton Sinclair, or Midwest of Sinclair Lewis? The Southwest of Edna Ferber? The northern California of Steinbeck? Any attempt to capture the folkways of our local centers has told a story not of participatory democracy but of closed social corporations, the rules of climbing in them quite rigid, the pinnacle of power monopolized by various social and business combines. That situation has gradually been changing; and—is it accidental?—now we hear a lament for the decline of community, a decline which the new politicians would remedy by further atomizing society, "politicizing" each man, urging him to "do his own thing." They seem to believe that community is merely the sum of individual "own things."

Or, since much of the modern malaise of powerlessness spreads out from urban problems, should we look back, to find widely distributed power and political initiative, toward the New York of Tweed or Tammany, the Boston of Curley, the Jersey City of Hague, the Kansas City of Pendergast, the Memphis of Crump, the Richmond of the senior Byrd? It is true that a number of social scientists trace a growth of urban discontent to the decline of city machines. Lloyd Ohlin, for instance, reported to the Ford Foundation that "the diminishing vitality of the local political machine, with its autocratic and attentive political boss, eliminates an important interpretive link to the new world for migrants." But the machine's responsiveness to people's needs was not the result of those people's participation in power. The machine was precisely a device for monopolizing power, concentrating it in the hands of the boss (whom Ohlin calls "autocratic") and his cronies. What the people got from this arrangement was not power but services. It was by guaranteeing the services that the boss retained his power. And liberal assault on that power contributed to our cities' inability to render services. The prospectus of the Ford Foundation's Mobilization for Youth noted that "the machine humanized and personalized its services. It provided help and favors rather than justice and assistance." This went against all liberal theory, which demands rights not favors. As Moynihan points out, even black Harlem once had its own effective machine—one that was, like Tammany, destroyed by liberal reformers. Thomas Blau writes, "In a nominalistic sense, reform in New York, like reform before it, has favored greater mass participation, but in terms of many unconnected individuals, each having no power of any importance. 'Participation,' either as taking part in insurgency or having an institutionalized share of authoritative decision making, may thus be a mechanism for reducing autonomy as easily as for engendering it."

People often prefer the services a boss can render to the freedoms a reform can give. This was proved by the kind of boss, who, for much of America's working class, replaced the city boss: a labor boss like Hoffa can monopolize power within the Teamsters Union because he is able to render just those services—legal, medical, economic, social—the city machines had supplied. (The appeal of Huey Long's paternalistic populism, of the I.W.W. in its first rural stage, and of Cesar Chavez suggests the possibility of a rural "machine" rendering the same services.) Nor does one have to go to the notorious "bosses" of labor to see what the working man prefers: even the most respectable, least boss-ridden unions put delivery of services over market openness and individual initiative when they promote the union shop. It is no accident that the legal and other harassment of union bosses is accompanied by a decline in the unions' power and a growth of workers' discontent. It is a modern analogue of the reform movement that broke Tammany.

Machines were not models of participatory democracy,

or of any kind of democracy—even when operating "for the people," their decisions were not made "by the people." What were the machines, then, if not democracies? The answer can be found in their function: they were instant, artificially formed aristocracies, performing the tasks of a traditional aristocracy in return for personal privilege and status. The machine man was a *padrone*. The machine's operations—its deals, favors, interests—were a crass version of the subtler, traditional, understated social arrangement whereby an aristocracy performs services for others in order to retain privilege for itself. The aristocracy can be middle-class, as in Lewis' Gopher Prairie (or commercial, as in his Zenith); rural, as in Faulkner's Jefferson; exploitative, as in Sinclair's Chicago; fading, as in Marquand's Boston. But it exists to give stability to society, and it can only strengthen itself by making the advantages of this stability apparent to non-aristocrats.

The city machine was an accelerated, stripped-bare version of this social arrangement. It had to perform its function for people who had not existed in the traditional arrangement, whose immediate absorption was necessary —immigrants with foreign customs and language; rural migrants to the city, lost there; a proletariat without the ties of a peasantry to its own aristocracy.

The case of the workers' "machine," the union, is even clearer than that of the urban organization. The theory of American business was precisely the nineteenth-century liberalism of Bentham and Mill—individualist, therefore competitive and open. The entrepreneur was a worker for himself, and therefore was—in theory, not merely in greed —forbidden to supply the social services of an aristocrat. To form social structures would be to "close the market" in various ways. Workers should not be bound to their employers by loyalty, favors, and long-term advantage; that would reduce flexibility, efficiency, and day-by-day innovation; it would weaken reliance on the market value of labor, reduce men's readiness to seek new jobs, methods, products—it would, in short, blunt the instruments of the Invisible Hand in promoting ultimate prosperity (at the cost, it may be, of short-term want). Ruskin attacked this concept of the businessman in the period of Mill's market orthodoxy; he said that no peace would come to society unless employers provided the social services (and enlisted the social loyalties) that go with privileged status. That was the point of his scathing first essay in political analysis, "The Roots of Honour"—and it was dismissed as sheer romance. But Ruskin had stated a basic human need, and the unions vindicate him. Since the employer would not be a boss in the sense of a *padrone*, union leaders created a new machine. Their organizations did not aim merely at better pay for the workers, but at job tenure, welfare security, social stability—all the services that arise from a sense of community. The unions were, therefore, conservative and aristocratic, counteracting the openness and liberalism of free-agent entrepreneurs. This function of unions, so often ignored, has been well stated by the conservative sociologist Will Herberg, who wrote in *National Review:* "The way Western bourgeois society developed to cope with massive proletarian alienation was that most bourgeois of bourgeois institutions, the labor union. We still have not learned to appreciate properly the conservative, anti-disintegrative service that the labor unions, despite all their faults and shortcomings, have rendered to the social order." The unions' conservatism reveals itself in many ways—in a stress on rank (apprenticeship, seniority, offices), on loyalty (to "the brothers" but also to the bosses, and to a structure of fraternal-lodge gradations within the union), on bourgeois values (like patriotism, thrift, religion).

Thus the first assumption in Goodwin's argument—that we once possessed political power over our destiny—depends on myth, not history; on the myth of a "golden age" of Jeffersonian democracy at the local level. This myth—of a political "free market" once realized, or capable of realization—lies behind most social analysis on the American Left, just as the myth of a golden age of entrepreneurial liberalism animates the American Right. The Adam Smith free market never existed in America—first, because its basic assumption is false (that fair competition, based on equal opportunity, can be arranged); second, because the rigid local structure of American society limited the pure economic liberalism of the entrepreneur just as it did the pure political liberalism of free suffrage; third, because influential businessmen did not *want* the market to work (they could get much greater rewards from monopoly, protectionism, and government contracts than from the ministrations of the Invisible Hand); and fourth, because self-protective devices (e.g., the trade unions) were erected where laissez faire did make some inroads.

The growth of American business has little to do with the free market. The reality behind that growth was governmental favoring of manufacture over agriculture (e.g., in the great preferential tariff fights that led up to the Civil War), governmental expansion at the proddings of commerce (e.g., in the political deals for rail rights and land grants that determined the westward expansion), governmental protection of capital risks abroad by "gunboat diplomacy," governmental shelter for big combines in turn-of-the-century Supreme Court decisions. Big business and big government grew in the past by feeding each other—and they still do. That is why Republican fundamentalists, who took the strictures against big government seriously, were regularly defeated by the party's Eastern Establishment. Senator Taft, defeated in 1952, huffed that "Every Republican candidate for President since 1936 has been nominated by the Chase National Bank." And now, as money shifts westward following population trends, Richard Nixon combines old-fashioned attacks on "Big Government" with the promise of big government contracts to the military industries of the Sunbelt.

But though the businessman did not live by his theory of laissez faire, it was all the theory he had. He pretended to live by it, and often thought he did. Besides, though the theory was abandoned when it was to the businessman's advantage to abandon it, it was religiously adhered to and trumpeted when *that* led to his advantage. Businessmen who were very protectionist with regard to their tariffs, interests, and government shelter became evangelists of free competition where the worker was concerned. In *getting* favors, businessmen did not believe in equal opportunity; but in *providing* them, they were careful not to interfere with the workers' competitive flexibility and openness to opportunity: they would not "pin a worker down" with long-term contracts, retirement and welfare stakes in his present position, health care and other forces making for inertia in the labor market. (Carlyle, in *Chartism*, perfectly caught the attitude of such employers: "The master of horses, when the summer labor is done, has to feed his horses through the winter. If he said to horses: 'Quadrupeds, I have no longer work for you; but work exists abundantly over the world: are you ignorant (or must I read you Political-Economy lectures) that the steam engine always in the long run creates additional work? Railways are forming in one quarter of this earth, canals in another, much cartage is wanted; somewhere in Europe, Asia, Africa, or America, doubt it not, ye will find cartage: go and seek cartage, and good go with you.' They, with protrusive upper lip, snort dubious; signifying that Europe, Asia, Africa and America lie somewhat out of their beat; that what cartage may be wanted there is not too well known to them. They can find no cartage. They gallop distracted along highways, all fenced in to the right and to the left.")

Since laissez faire was the only theory the businessman knew, he ended up thinking that he must have lived by it, after all, to get where he is. If sacred dogma asserts that growth comes from open market competition, then the fact of growth will establish, retroactively, the fact of competition. If big business became big, it must have done so by observing the rules of Adam Smith. Thus myth replaces history.

And, in an exactly parallel way, Goodwin lives with a mythical golden age of Jeffersonian liberalism—the town meeting, maximum individual participation, a political individualism that gave scope to initiative, made anyone who was interested in politics the master of his political destiny (as the diligent apprentice became a master of the economy). Yet what our history actually reveals, at the community level, is local conformity, rigid mores, religious and other prejudice, aristocracy and control—not atomistic mobility and initiative.

Because the first step in Goodwin's argument is based on illusion, the second step is bound to be invalidated. Out of his misunderstanding of the past, Goodwin creates a whole series of false correlations in the present.

He equates, for instance, individual satisfaction with the possession of political power. Yet the lesson of the unions and the urban machines, as well as of more traditional community structures, is that satisfaction arises more from services received, from security and stability, than from competitive rights in the political market.

Having established the first equation (satisfaction = power), he can reverse it to read: dissatisfaction = powerlessness. And since he has defined our dissatisfaction as a form of anomie (the inability even to define one's trouble), he can make this substitution: anomie = powerlessness.

But this last equation, as Moynihan points out, has been tested by the social scientists and found wanting. Melvin Seeman found that anomie and powerlessness can be separated; that, in fact, they tend in different directions. Anomie leads toward violence and antisocial acts, whereas powerlessness, in itself, does not. The client of the city machine did not have power; the boss did. Yet when a boss supplied the desired services, the client, though powerless, was contented. Anomie, on the other hand, can exist in conjunction with power—which is the point of all our stories about empty success; about loneliness, loss of direction at the top of the corporate structure; about suburban despair, where privilege exists without purpose.

It is easy, after looking at Goodwin's analysis of the present, to predict his recommendations—the third step in his argument. We are afflicted by anomie (i.e., loss of direction) because we are powerless (i.e., have no hand on the helm). To cure the first state, we need only alter the second—when a man's hand is put on the helm, the combined tugs and shovings of all hands will "self-correct" to the desired course. Everyone's hand on the helm becomes a political Invisible Hand steering us home. Democracy, which is essentially a voting *procedure,* will be cured by procedural adjustments—the increase of men's activities in the voting and campaigning marketplace, a sense of purpose born of this increased scurry, a sense of community born of the equal chance to scurry, a sense of justice achieved by removing some inequities from the process. The proper repairs will make this machinery "work" again, and that is all man needs to make him happy.

Goodwin's attitude toward political unhappiness turns out, on examination, to be much like Professor Schlesinger's approach to campus unrest: if people are dissatisfied with the liberal system, this merely shows they want *more* liberalism more consistently applied—reform, updating, renovation. In politics, this means that elections must once again supply what George Wald demands of them—the best men and policies and parties to rule us. But this they have never supplied, and never will.

If the source of man's unhappiness is politics, then the

cure must be sought in politics, in power, in the satisfaction of controlling others, of ordering events, not only in America but around the world. That sense of mastery is what makes a Goodwin happy, or a Nixon, or a Woodrow Wilson. But it will not satisfy the mass of men, even if they could be hypnotized into believing they wield such power. Elections, which did not even forge our political freedoms, certainly do not extend to more general sources of man's joy or sorrow. They do not supply the individual with dignity, self-respect, or purpose (other than the purpose of voting periodically), with a stable set of values, with a margin of opportunity within a framework of predictability, with a sense of community reciprocated by others. If men do not take these things to the polls with them, the voting process will not produce them. What the schools, the churches, the home cannot do, the political process will not be able to accomplish. Yet, having given up on direct attempts to resuscitate these other institutions, we are in effect asking politics to supply them with artificial respiration, or to take their place. Politics can do neither.

There is a lesson to be learned from the history of the first group urged to "participate" in politics—the Southern blacks registered by Tom Hayden and his friends. The vote has not proved a panacea to the blacks—how could it? They make up only 11 percent of the population, and they must use this slim minority power at the polls against massive historical and social prejudices and inhibitions. Total enrollment and bloc voting could accomplish some things for them at election time—though it would be facing a pattern of counter-voting by blocs in the white majority. Thus black leaders have had to look beyond the vote for nurturing pride, purpose, and satisfaction in their community (learning something, in this way, that many whites have yet to discover). They have begun to formulate ideals—of negritude (black is beautiful), of society (the brothers), of identity (Afro-Americanism)— that have little to do with Goodwin's "Jeffersonian" vision of hyperthyroid individualism. The world of black power, first and most fully proposed by the Muslim organization, is not a world of participatory democracy—any more than the city machine was—but of authority, discipline, and social services. It even adopts some of the old machine's instruments—the farming of jobs back and forth among one's own, the declaration of spheres of influence, "protection" within these spheres, internal enforcement and patronage, hierarchical privilege and group solidarity, the massing of purchasing power to make an impact on society. Far from being participatory, this black strategy is "separatist," a withdrawal (partial, at any rate) from areas where the cards are stacked against the black man, in order to enrich with community the lives of people who were undifferentiated units before, and to give the community thus formed more buying power, more social recognition, more united moral suasiveness and other kinds of leverage that go beyond the formal right of the individual to vote.

"Participatory politics" is not the way to make men happy, whole, humane. We should have learned that long ago, simply by observing the effect of politics on its most intimate participants—the pros, the politicians themselves. If anything, politics is a drain upon the humanity of its practitioners, not a heart-pump to restore it. The most fully "politicized" man in the world may well be Richard Nixon.

2. Refiguring the Calculus

"With a view to increase of the means either of subsistence or enjoyment, without some special reason, the general rule is, that nothing ought to be done or attempted by government. The motto, or watchword of government, on these occasions, ought to be— Be quiet."
—*Jeremy Bentham*

"The time may have come when the issue of race could benefit from a period of 'benign neglect.'"
—*Daniel Patrick Moynihan*

ON JUNE 4, 1965, President Lyndon Johnson was scheduled to deliver a speech at Howard University. All the night before, into the morning and toward delivery hour, two men drafted the speech with a sense of history upon them. They were going to make the President who had completed the civil rights legislation call that achievement inadequate. They were going to put the President out ahead of "respectable" Negro pressure groups, seizing the initiative, offering more than had so far been asked. The government itself would voice grievances against the government. The right to eat at an integrated lunch counter, buy a home in an integrated neighborhood, go to an integrated school, join an integrated work force —all these things had been vindicated without giving men the money to buy hamburgers or a home, the discipline needed to get an education or a job, the means to overcome social pressures still hemming men in after laws have set them free.

The civil rights laws had been based on a concept of equal opportunity, to be achieved by making sure the "rules of the game" are equitably enforced. But that has never been enough to make men succeed. Even when men play under a just set of rules, fairly administered, some of them are eliminated from the game, through no fault of their own, because of prior disadvantages. The classic response to this has been the handicapping system—moving out from a guarantee of equal place at the starting line to the creation of a systematically staggered starting line. This approach had been standard in the treatment of whites' aspirations. But by 1965 blacks had just been admitted to the track, given the protection of the game's rules. Now President Johnson, who liked to think of himself as the heir to Franklin Roosevelt, was going to move blacks straight from stage one (equal rights) past stage two (equal opportunity) into stage three (equal results): "You do not take a person who, for years, has been hobbled by chains and liberate him, bring him to the starting line of a race and then say, 'You are free to compete with all the others,' and still justly believe that you have been completely fair."

People must not only be admitted to the race; they must also be equipped for the race. The speech writers committed Johnson to furnishing "not just equality as a right and a theory, but equality as a fact and as a result." And it was clear that the effort involved would be of a scale and complexity not dreamed of in earlier programs.

A job was no longer enough; job training was necessary. Nor was job training enough; general education had to precede that. And even education was not enough unless a good home made children susceptible to the discipline of education. All right, if that was what the situation demanded, the "President of all the people" would furnish it: "Unless we work to strengthen the family, to create conditions under which most parents will stay together—all the rest, schools and playgrounds, public assistance and private concern, will never be enough to cut completely the circle of despair and deprivation." It was a daring promise, issued by a confident and popular leader, drafted by two clever men—and it was greeted effusively by black leaders and white liberals alike. White House aides read the speech, over the telephone, to Martin Luther King, Roy Wilkins, and Whitney Young—who all praised it. An Urban League statement endorsed it. Robert Carter, general counsel of the NAACP, said: "The President had an amazing comprehension of the barriers that are present in our society to the Negro's progress."

One of Johnson's two speech writers we have already met—Richard Goodwin. His touch is evident all through the speech, his gift of phrase ("the walls are rising and the gulf is widening . . . [but] inherited gateless poverty . . . [must] finally yield to our unyielding will"). There is even a forecast of Goodwin's later strategy for middle-class whites—to find meaning in their own lives by giving meaning to others' lives: "It is the glorious opportunity of this generation to end the huge wrong of the American nation and, in so doing, to find America for ourselves." Most of the research used in the speech came from Goodwin's collaborator, but one part he added himself—the announcement of a public conference to formulate government policy toward the blacks. This was a bold proposal, even bolder than the President seems to have realized. Officials usually formulate their program, then call the public to briefings and sessions where support for the program can be generated. Goodwin's scheme offered a blank check on the President's political account, to be filled in by a public panel. The idea was either very good or very bad; in any case, startling.

The other man responsible for the Howard speech was Daniel Patrick Moynihan, Assistant Secretary of Labor, at that time the youngest Assistant Secretary in the administration. Like Goodwin, he graduated from Tufts; and, like him, he left Washington after the Kennedy years to teach at Wesleyan University (later he moved to MIT and Harvard). These accidental points of resemblance, however, do not hide the men's great differences in character and background. If, in his brashness, Goodwin sometimes suggests a Left-Wing Roy Cohn, Moynihan, once a director of Americans for Democratic Action, has become a Right-Wing Kenneth Galbraith—a wit and a romantic, not just a scholar, making his mark by all three gifts. He does not, of course, have Galbraith's dour Scottish humor; a joshing Irish one, instead, pugnacious but magnanimous—a Galbraith, as it were, inflated with laughing gas and bobbing giddily. He obviously thinks an urbanist should be urbane—the bow tie and startled eyebrow arcs bend toward others at cocktail parties as the florid raconteur nudges his points home. Goodwin, who can rasp in person, is a superb tactician of the written word (he told a fellow McCarthy speech writer, early in 1968, "With these two typewriters we are going to overthrow a President of the United States"—a President whose best moments of oratory he had already created). Moynihan, by contrast, writes a clumsy prose that almost begs to be misunderstood; yet he is a useful ally in any situation where force of personality can be exerted. This may come from the fact that, while Goodwin was blazing his way through classrooms in the approved course of academic advancement, Moynihan was living the urban sociology he would later write. He is the product of that matriarchal Irish home formed when an irresponsible father—in this case, an Oklahoma journalist—deserts his family. In a Catholic atmosphere like Moynihan's, the gravity of this offense was obvious—and the son has become famous for his emphasis on the role of unstable families, especially of the matriarchal sort, in creating social unrest. His mother brought her children to New York, where Moynihan became a shoeshine boy in Times Square, attended school in Harlem, held bit jobs as longshoreman or bartender—and his first book was on New York's checkered ethnic pattern, its crazyquilt of living styles: he collaborated with Nathan Glazer on *Beyond the Melting Pot*, a book that undermines the slogan used for its title. (The book is a favorite with another connoisseur of ethnicity, Kevin Phillips.) Moynihan possesses what he has described as the New York style ("fascinated by racial, ethnic, and religious diversity"). He tends to sort out the work of his fellow scholars in terms of their family and religious background: "Could it be that where the Jewish scholars Cohen and Miller watched the antics of the *goyim* with wonder and detachment, the Protestants Cloward and Ohlin, suffering servants of the Lord, had to perceive in the whole miserable business the morally autonomous individual struggling for salvation?" It was, in fact, this interest in family backgrounds that brought him to Goodwin's office for the all-night job of writing Johnson's speech.

Moynihan had just prepared, as an "internal document" of the Labor Department, a challenge to the belief that "the nature of family life is about the same throughout American society." The Negro family, he maintained, has problems different in kind and deeper in effect than other families have. These are derived from the Negro's unique background of slavery on this continent (males and females sold separately, children bred from them indiscriminately as accretions of property). Such disadvantages could have been overcome, but Southern oppression and Northern rootlessness, white fear or hate of Negro males (leading to disproportionate employment of females), along with cruel welfare laws promoting husband absenteeism, prevented the black family, weak to begin with, from growing toward strength.

It was an old tale, often told—best, perhaps, by Negro sociologist E. Franklin Frazier. All Moynihan did was work up a long memorandum on the situation, using the tables and statistics available at the Department of Labor. His aim in doing this was to promote better funding of accepted programs—mainly of employment and housing —not to encourage "meddling with the family" (an ambition against which his Catholic social training militated). Yet, because of his desire to shock government officials into action, he had been blunt and dramatic—describing the black illegitimacy increase as "drastic," the Negro family as "approaching complete breakdown," and that family's situation as a "tangle of pathology." Nor did his clumsiness with the written word help: he described four different things as "the fundamental problem"—and these were not so much *causes* of the Negro's plight (e.g., the work of white slave owners, employers, welfare workers) as *effects* of the suppression and discrimination (family structure, breakdown of community, female dominance, male unemployment).

Moynihan's report was not known to the public when the Howard speech was delivered. But White House aides, trying to prove to newsmen that the speech was a serious one, to which serious thought had been given, began to leak accounts of the report—accounts which, distorted, caused angry reaction among black leaders. Finally, to prevent worse distortion, the report itself was released, but in its "internal" form, without explanatory preface or policy recommendations. What had been aimed and effective as an administration memorandum became a public relations disaster as a public document, discrediting Johnson's speech in retrospect, and sabotaging in prospect the conference Goodwin had suggested. The ensuing controversy brought out the worst in all participants. Many black spokesmen, triggered by the term "pathology," took a "so's your old man" position. If Moynihan was going to call them sick, then they would call him sick:

> One can't talk about the pathologies of Negroes without talking abut the pathologies of white society. If Negroes are sick socially, then whites are sick morally. (Whitney Young)

> Most recently, in a new and all embracing canard, we hear about the "pathology" of the Negro family instead of the sickness of America. (Core report.)

The scheduled conference now became an administration embarrassment. Preparation for it was shoved over to Hubert Humphrey, who relies on blarney instead of doing his homework. Thus, as conference time drew near, sloppy planning threatened to make it the Johnson regime's Waterloo. At this point the fall meeting was turned into a drafting session preliminary to the *real* conference, which was scheduled for the spring of 1966. The result was that two disastrous conferences were held, instead of one. Moynihan and his report were disowned; leaders did not want to discuss the family at all; the discussion became a general gripe session; wounds were opened and rubbed for the thousandth time, without hope or thought for their proper medicine. It was a dismal sequence, one that gave

Moynihan an undeservedly bad name among blacks, wiped out the credit Johnson had built up with black leaders, and destroyed any administration chance for moving out "beyond civil rights." A perfectly sound set of social statistics, carried into the electric atmosphere of politics, exploded in their compiler's hands.

It is no wonder Moynihan displayed, in his next book, a rather gloomy satisfaction at the failure of another social theory translated into political action during the Johnson years: *Maximum Feasible Misunderstanding* chronicles the breakdown of the War on Poverty (another flapping pennon of Goodwin rhetoric) as it was conducted by the Office of Economic Opportunity (OEO)—more especially, the failure of the OEO's Community Action Programs (CAP). The book was written in the aftermath of Moynihan Report battles, and reads like the work of a wounded man. It is an odd book, spluttery, jerky, erratic, intense, satirical, inarticulate with unfocused passions. The very prose is limp, mangled, loose-jointed. Page after page we get broken-limbed sentences like this:

> Two unusually gifted and successful elected officials, working in the tradition of New York ethnic politics, their shared view, contrasting as they do with those of the professional reformer is to be noted.

But the book's deeper malady is logical. There is a great deal in it that makes no sense unless we remember that Moynihan is talking as much about the flap over the Negro family as he is about the OEO controversy. Just as Moynihan put forth a scholarly hypothesis which, introduced directly into the political wars, caused unproductive anger and reaction, so the Richard Cloward and Lloyd Ohlin theory of opportunity, directly adopted by drafters of the poverty legislation, was bound to end in disaster. Conclusion? The hypotheses of social science should not become the programmatic basis of political projects. Yet Moynihan's implicit analogy is faulty. His own report, and nothing else, was the basis of the Howard speech; and his report was the sole cause of those complaints that sabotaged the Johnson-Humphrey-Goodwin conference. Many things, by contrast, went into the poverty program besides the opportunity thesis: that program went through a long period of incubation, formulation, adaptation, administration. The program showed the influence of bureaucrats primarily interested in budgeting and efficiency, of ideologues interested in "participatory democracy," of politicians working in classical pork barrel terms, of hacks and prophets and compromisers, of people at the local level who would "do their own thing" no matter how the law was drafted in Washington. Moynihan's own account of the legislation's vicissitudes, although one-sided, is enough to refute his key assertion: "In sum, the [poverty] bill incorporated the purest doctrine. It represented the direct transmission of social science theory into governmental policy."

Furthermore, even if the opportunity theory had been as purely transmitted as Moynihan supposes, this would not have explained the emphasis on participatory programs in the poverty bill. The Cloward-Ohlin thesis is that deviant behavior in delinquents does not come from the possession of ideals that differ from middle-class standards. Slum dwellers in our culture have, according to this theory, the same ideals as most Americans; but they do not have the *opportunity* to reach those goals. The kids will conform if they are just "given a chance." This hypothesis, though it can accommodate the ideal of participation, does not *demand* it with any cogency. Paternalistic guidance is logically just as acceptable as "self-direction" by the poor themselves—there is no coercion, on this hypothesis, since final conformism to middle-class patterns is all along envisaged. The passion for participation did not come only or mainly from the academicians admitted to consultation with the bill's drafters: this passion had been built up in many places—the South of the civil rights workers, the militant circles of SNCC, Catholic Worker projects like those that gave Michael Harrington his training. Cloward and Ohlin did not write Tom Hayden's manifesto for "participatory democracy," any more than they wrote Richard Goodwin's *New Yorker* article on local control. Moynihan completely ignores these sources of the participation mystique, and derives it all from an academic conspiracy to "mastermind" legislation. In a bit of unintentional self-revelation, Moynihan describes the poverty program and its failure as a struggle between New York (speculative, interested in theory) and Washington (pragmatic, responding to actual pressures of the moment). That symbolic picture does enclose Moynihan's own mental cosmos.

He is a New Yorker in Washington, and the rest of the nation, to judge from *Maximum Feasible Misunderstanding,* might just as well not exist. Professor Sar Levitan has pointed out that Moynihan's entire judgment on the failure of CAP is based, in his book, on two New York City programs and a well-publicized scandal in Syracuse.

Even if the opportunity theory of delinquency had played the role in policy-formation that Moynihan claims, this still would not establish his thesis—that social scientists should not take part in the formulation of policy. It might prove, instead, that this *particular* theory was faulty. This is a possibility Moynihan plays with but never faces squarely—once again because he is thinking of his assumed analogy; even a sound set of hypotheses, *even the Moynihan Report,* does not provide the material for political judgment. Yet this, too, is a position one cannot derive from the poverty program. Perhaps the only moral to be drawn from it is that politicians should be more careful in handling the data of social study (not that they should be deprived of that data). But Moynihan would keep social scientists away from *any* discussion of future projects: "The role of social science lies not in the formulation of social policy, but in the measurement of its results." *Past* programs can be studied; and the statistics that result from such study can be made available to politicians (passed, apparently, through some decontamination chamber). These strictures go beyond the common sense view that no one knows the future, that every branch of knowledge is limited. Moynihan is zealous for "research purity" on the part of academicians (who must give up their social-engineering ambitions), and for skeptical toughness on the part of politicians (who must refuse to lean on the guesses of scholars).

By turning social study back to pure research, Moynihan adopts a fundamentalist view of academic freedom. No theory is more than a hypothesis. To act on it, to use public funds to support it against other theories, is to "close the market" of ideas. Such theories should be kept in a rarefied world where their "free play" is guaranteed; one should not allocate funds to a theory's advocates because that implies a judgment that they alone have the truth: "Professional persons were too willing by half to see public funds, and tax-free private funds, employed on a vast scale to further what was in effect a political agenda of a fairly small group of individuals." This retreat to a fundamental reading of liberalism is the strategy that emerges throughout Moynihan's work.

But an obvious question arises: If social scientists have no part to play in the formation of policy, what is Moynihan himself doing in the basement of the White House? His answer is that he wears a different hat there, a politician's. His academic background is useful, but only because it has taught him the tricks of snake-oil peddlers from the academic grove; he can warn politicians against them. He is the administration's academician for standing guard against academicians. Even before Nixon's election he had advocated the hiring of such an academic watchdog to bark scholars away from unsuspecting pols: "The President needs a social science gatekeeper . . . The liberal lawyers who typically make up most of the White House staff don't understand social science . . . They tend to believe anything that sounds right."

But if social scientists have their limits, so do politicians, and there seems no reason why the politician should not supplement his own kind of knowledge with that of the scholar—throwing in a grain or more of salt, steeling himself against any presumption of sociologists' infallibility; tying himself to the mast, if need be, while he listens to the song of academic sirens, but at least listening to what they might suggest—as he would listen to any interested and intelligent observer. Moynihan will not allow even this; and to understand *why* he will not, consider what other voices he would silence. He does not like to hear "reform professionals" speak for the poor. In fact, contempt for such meddlers bursts from him again and again in the book, where "middle-class reformers" is a formula of disdain:

> If middle-class reformers ceased to mind other people's business they would cease to be reformers.

Sometimes it is the crime of such reformers that they are more interested in attacking their own class than in helping another class:

> However scientifically sound, Miller appeared to be politically conservative, and therefore, one is led to suspect, did not meet the needs of the private agenda

of the middle-class reformers, namely, to prove a case against middle-class society.

Yet Moynihan himself is careful to pin the scornful "middle-class" tag on his reformers, and seems to show a good deal of contempt for that class himself:

> [The Peace Corps] was (and is) a program almost exclusively designed for well-educated middle-class youth, and involves not an inconsiderable subvention for them . . . As the 1960's passed, signs increased that the various forms of public disorder either sanctioned, induced, or led by middle-class liberal-radicals had begun to acquire an ominous, even sinister cast in the mind of the public at large.

Who or what is this "public at large," on whose behalf Moynihan often speaks? The answer is given in passages like this:

> And here the personal qualities of the middle-class professional reformers, elite academics and intellectuals for the most part, contributed not a little to the mounting tension. For if capable of the deepest empathy, the purest Christian compassion for the poor, too frequently they had nothing but contempt for the working class, lower-middle-class bureaucratic and political cadres that ran the city.

In short, the middle-class do-gooder is teaming up with the poor to do in the Forgotten American, the lower middle-class hard-working man who is drawn toward Wallace, if not Nixon:

> Social scientists love poor people. They also get along fine with rich people. (Not a few are wealthy themselves, or married to heiresses. In any event, in the 1960's, persons of great wealth have been a major source of support not only for social science research, but for radical political activity.) But, alas, they do not have much time for the people in between. In particular, they would appear to have but little sympathy with the desire for order, and anxiety about change, that are commonly enough encoun-

tered among working-class and lower middle-class persons. The privileged children of the upper middle classes more and more devoted themselves, in the name of helping the oppressed, to outraging the people in between.

These privileged villains were not willing to stay in the slums doing good; they turn their assault on City Hall:

> Just possibly the middle class reformers felt more at home at such levels—their turf.

They would not work through the churches and other "native" institutions of the poor:

> Was it that hymn shouting and bible thumping somehow does not elicit in the fancies of the white radical quite the same fascination as does the black demi-monde?

And then the reformers were upset when "backlash" occurred:

> One of the least attractive qualities of some of the early middle-class practitioners of conflict-oriented community action was the tendency to cry "Foul" when the animal defended itself.

In this spluttery attack on middle-class reformers, satire replaces social science, and Moynihan showers his target with all kinds of charges—self-contempt, class betrayal, fascination with the demi-monde, an itch to make trouble. But the heart of his charge against them is that they pretend they can speak for others:

> The presumption of superior empathy with the problems of the outcast is surely a characteristic, and a failing, of this liberal mindset.

> New York's Mobilization for Youth was a plan devised by a group of middle-class intellectuals to bring about changes in the behavior of a group of lower-class youth who differed from them in ethnicity and religion, in social class and attitudes, in life styles, and above all, in life prospects.

It is clear that Moynihan thinks we have a large group of paid academic poor-people-watchers, and a large social worker group of paid poor-people-improvers, and in the Babel of their (at best) learned and crusading voices, their (at worst) dithering and self-interested voices, the true voice of the poor people is drowned out.

He overemphasizes the role one theory played in the shaping of the poverty program because he exaggerates the extent to which theorists have begun to anticipate problems, to supplant the voicing of actual grievances with the prediction of future grievances. He sees the social scientists as greasing wheels before they squeak, out of a certitude that they know which wheels are going to squeak. The result, however, is that their bustle of oiling and prediction draws attention to the wheel and, in effect, *makes* it squeak. Thus, progressively, the prophets of trouble desire to see their prophecies confirmed:

> The intellectual group had acquired an interest in the political turmoil of the moment and came very near to misusing its position to advance that interest.

> The reaction among many of the more activist social scientists (obviously this risks labelling a vast number of persons from a smallish number of incidents) was not to be appalled by disorder, but almost to welcome it.

Moynihan's convictions on this score are almost fanatical, and that is why he must insist that the poverty program was concocted in classrooms, not in the slums:

> The war on poverty was not declared at the behest of the poor; it was declared in their interest by persons confident of their own judgment in such matters.

> Whatever exactly is meant by the term "poor," it will be clear enough that they had almost nothing to do with the process.

> The various planning groups were made up exclusively of middle-class whites. At no time did any Negro have any role of any consequence in the drafting of

the poverty program. Nor did any Negro have any role of any consequence in the drafting of the CAP guidelines . . . It is clear that to the degree that risks were involved, whites were taking them for blacks.

For Moynihan, it is a procedural error to anticipate the squeaking wheel. If it is anticipated, one of two things happens—either (a) the wheel, oiled beforehand, never does squeak, so we cannot know whether it *would* have squeaked, or (b) the wheel squeaks, but does so only in the artificial situation created by the certitude that it was about to squeak (so we cannot know whether it would have squeaked without this focusing of attention). We cannot know which wheels will squeak of themselves unless we permit them to reach the squeaking point—unless, that is, we benignly neglect them. Acting on theories that *anticipate* the squeak is unscientific procedure, since our interventions destroy the possibility of testing the theory in a laboratory situation. That is the *scientific* fault in the predictive use of social studies for formulating policy. The *political* fault is that the theories destroy the possibility of drawing up an accurate calculus in the Bentham manner. That calculus depends, remember, on each person's seeking his own good. If do-gooders try to do good for others, they will do harm, by introducing an element of falsehood into the equation—they have not sought their *own* true interest. No rational balance can be struck between competing interests if people make others' interests their own. It is this fundamentalism of the nineteenth-century progressives that drives Moynihan, making him furious with those who try to speak for others—those who "play God with other persons' lives," those who claim "the ability to anticipate problems, and to know best." A populist fervor for "authentic" protest pervades Moynihan's attack on stimulated or artificial protest:

A certain gushiness comes through, in the manner of well-to-do benefactors thinking up a nicer life for the poor.

It is this regard for authentic protest that makes Moynihan speak so well of the professional protest leader, Saul Alinsky. At first, such praise seems anomalous: is not Alinsky a middle-class do-gooder speaking for others, arranging protest, creating squeaks? Yes, he is—and to that extent Moynihan has misgivings about him. But, by contrast with the theorists who try to work out of Washington, Alinsky mocks those who use City Hall funds to fight City Hall. Alinsky does not expect rebellion to be a government program; he recognizes the fact that, in Moynihan's words, "social radicalism is not a civil service calling." Above all, Alinsky seeks to get *paid* for his services, and solicits funds, not forcefully through taxation but on the open market: thus, in Benthamite terms, he appeals to self-interest at various levels—he must attract free "investors" in his plans for social improvement, keep costs down, convince the poor his agitation is fruitful in its own terms (not simply as a welfare boondoggle from the government). He is, at least by comparison with governmental do-gooders, an authentic voice of protest, expressing true local interests (not the distorting, altruistic "interest" of social theorists):

> Alinsky emerges from the 1960's a man of enhanced stature. His influence on the formulation of the anti-poverty program and its predecessors was not great. Indeed it was negligible, in that a primary motive of these efforts was to *give* things to the poor that they did not have. Alinsky's law, laid down in *Reveille for Radicals,* which appeared in 1946, was that in the process of social change there is no such thing as give, only take . . . Throughout his career he had begun his organizing campaigns with cash in hand, completely independent of the power structure with which he wished to bargain.

Where Goodwin would decentralize government and reintroduce individual initiative into modern life by *politicizing* everyone, Moynihan seeks the same results through a *de*politicizing process. Goodwin would limit government by spreading political power around, Moynihan by keeping things outside the grasp of the government. Both men return to the ideals of an older, individualistic liberalism, but Moynihan is more orthodox in his attempt to limit government and rely on "private-sector" competition. He admits that the government has a key role to play—largely in the collection and dispersal of money. But he thinks it should be restricted to that role. Government plans poorly, and administers poorly; thus its money-dispersing function should be as automatic as possible. Even though he considers the health of the family unit the secret of social stability, Moynihan's report was not meant to promote plans for building up the family. He thinks the way to help the family is to get the government out of the family's business—as the old-style liberal thought the way to foster individual initiative was to keep government out of the individual's affairs. At a Berkeley conference in 1965, Moynihan expressed his view on the relation between welfare and the family:

It became more obvious that the primary function of community welfare programs is to provide surrogate family services. The logic of this relationship has taken us well beyond the original provision of food and clothing and money to far more complex matters of providing proper attitudes toward work, reasonable expectations of success and so forth. Obviously these are matters which for most persons are handled within the family system, and most of us would risk the speculation that the traditional family arrangement is probably the more efficient one.

The language of Left and Right has been almost totally misleading in America, at least since the thirties; but in few cases has it been so deceptive as in the discussion of Moynihan's welfare views, which were embodied in the Nixon plan for a New Federalism. This plan was treated as a Nixon "zig" to the Left, meant to balance his frequent "zags" over to the Right side of the field, where Strom Thurmond calls the signals. James Reston, for instance, who fell for the Nixon New Alignment in 1968, swallowed the hook of the New Federalism in 1969: "Mr. Nixon has taken a great step forward. He has cloaked a remarkably progressive welfare policy in conservative language . . . He has repudiated his own party's record on social policy at home."

No such thing. Moynihan's welfare extensions are aimed, ultimately, at eliminating welfare workers. It is welfare used against welfare by this professor-against-professors. That is why one of the leading advocates for this kind of program has been "Right-Winger" Milton Friedman. If one must pay a dole to the poor, the argument goes, it should be done in as neutral and automatic a way as possible. The role of government is to pay out, not to play at social planning. If welfare is spent to bring about a new social alignment, to enrich the slums or abolish the slums, to help the Negroes or the jobless, to help fatherless families or families with fathers, then government is forcing the "natural" processes of change, making it impossible to figure an accurate Calculus. But if welfare is given on a simple, standard economic basis, to workers and non-workers alike, to black and white, to anyone who falls below a fixed income, the effect of the plan is simply to provide an economic plateau, below which men cannot fall, with minimal influence on the actions of these men beyond the bare economic boost. The aim is to let everyone spend the money himself, so that *true* interests and desires will be expressed.

Thus the New Federalism did not indicate a Leftward turn on Nixon's part, or a shrewd trick played on Strom by Moynihan's aides. The rationale on which the welfare money is to be spent is more important than the fluctuating amounts of money voted or the number of men on the welfare rolls at any one time. And the Moynihan rationale is competitive, individualist, based on the beneficence of the market, aimed against the sociologists and bureaucrats and do-gooders. He is willing to spend a little more government money to prevent any more government planning.

Yet it should be noted that only two of the New Federalism's original three features were based on the Moynihan logic. The elements of that program, as it was carpentered by Secretary of Labor George Shultz, are: (1) a return of federal funds to the states, on a gradual basis; (2) standardization of welfare payments; and (3) a requirement of work training and job placement for those on welfare.

1) Return of federal funds to the states reduces the amount of social planning and God-playing that can be done out of Washington. It tends to remove the machinery that future Lloyd Ohlins might use for imposing their theories on the nation. It makes the political process responsive to local pressures, to the play of interests out across the nation, the things that interact in working out the Calculus.

2) While the first provision limits the sphere of social

scientists in Washington, the second one limits the powers of social workers out in the slums: standardization reduces the scope of their discretionary power over *who* receives welfare, and under what *conditions*. The single standard of economic income makes unnecessary much of the visiting, investigating, amateur psychology sessions, and general slum-crawling of middle-class meddlers. Moynihan's war on them is effectively waged in this part of the program. *Maximum Feasible Misunderstanding* diagnosed the unrest of society as growing from a squeeze put on the lower middle class by the pressure of white reformers from above and poor blacks from below. The standardized welfare plan would not only limit the role of the reformers but—by making no distinction between worker and nonworker in its guarantee of a minimum income—it would include a new slice of the working white population, thus defusing the objection that welfare is only a program for supporting black nonworkers.

3) The third feature of Nixon's plan, however, is neither neutral nor beneficial, according to the Moynihan scheme of things. The New Federalism proposes not only work incentive (by continuing welfare up to a certain "floor," even for those working), but work *requirements* (compulsory job training for those on welfare, compulsory job placement where suitable work can be found, and day-care for the children of single women thus trained and placed). The individualist objection to such a program is that it brings the social worker back on the scene—to do the training, placing, and baby-sitting; to decide which men and women are fit to work, and what jobs are "suitable" for them to work at. The plan's neutral and automatic features are clogged again with discretionary meddling. Furthermore, in yielding to the indignation of those who think welfare without work an immoral situation, the plan refuses to one class what it does for others —public money supports colleges to keep young people off the work market, and taxes are paid back to farmers for not farming, to oilmen for not taking oil out of the ground. The principle of buying people out of the market for the market's good is established for many people who complain that the government "pays the *poor* to do nothing."

Aside from such theoretical objections, the compulsory work plan is bound to fail. Those who do not want to work, or do not want to work efficiently and zealously, cannot be forced to do either. Efforts in this direction are wasted and frustrating. Employers would prefer not to have the inefficient, the lazy, the undependable foisted off on them by government programs. Besides, even if it were possible to instill the work-ethic in every poor person—out of a zeal for the good of his "lazy good-for-nothing" soul—it is not likely that society could find the jobs to keep all the poor busy. Unemployment, in our economy, is not merely a function of the unwillingness to work, but also of the unavailability of jobs—a situation that will become more marked as automation advances and workers in general achieve (or submit to) shorter hours.

Nixon's work requirement provisos are a good example of moral indignation running wild and undoing what it most desires. The logic of competitive individualism—which is Moynihan's logic, no less than Friedman's—must admit a place to those who do not *want* to get ahead, must feed them (on humanitarian grounds) yet leave them stigmatized as "nonproducers." The clearer it is made that the dole is a dole, the more are the rewards of incentive set off and honored. One better preserves the sanctity of competition by refusing to disguise the "handout" with busywork schemes of character formation or job preparation. Yet logic and consistency desert men in the grip of a fanatical belief, and the American fanatic has always suffered moral disorientation at the mere thought of anyone's "getting something for nothing." The phenomenon is much like the madness of a backwoods preacher whose whole gospel depends on the existence of sin, yet who is so affronted by sin's existence that he must destroy either the sinner or himself. It is no wonder, then, that Nixon had to recognize "conservative" voices like that of Arthur Burns, and include an anomalous work requirement in the welfare plan, though this violates its Moynihan logic and balance. Nixon would depart from classical liberalism in order to save classical liberalism, recruit support for the individualist logic by throwing sops, along the way, to individualist passions.

3. "Left" and "Right" in America

"If America is not to have free enterprise, then she can have no freedom of any sort whatever."
—Woodrow Wilson

IN 1967, Professor Moynihan addressed the Americans for Democratic Action, an organization formed twenty years earlier to protect the American Left from the American Right by taking a severely anticommunist stand in the Cold War. But now Moynihan was asking the organization to open its arms to the Right: the pretensions of Big Government had created disillusionment among the people, and intelligent men on both the Left and Right should unite to combat this development. It seemed heresy at the time—though two years later, many others would (like Richard Goodwin) discover the anguish of the middle class and the need for decentralization. In retrospect, Moynihan has been considered an opportunist even sharper-eyed than Goodwin; at the time, he was just a traitor. Neither charge is just: he has been consistent throughout, consistently liberal because a classical liberal.

Moynihan was always a minimalist about the government's ability to deliver and perform, because he was a maximalist about the nature of ethnic conflict in America. He bore certain scars out of the poor-white Harlem of his childhood, wounds liable to twinge vicariously when government does for one segment of the population things that other segments resent. He believed in *minimum* government because he paid more than lip service to the liberal ideal of *neutral* government. A particular concept in the social sciences should not be given undue advantage by the government, any more than one ethnic group should be favored. The fundamental rule of government, for Moynihan, is what might be called the Principle of Interchangeability—the government must never do for

490

Citizen A what it is unwilling at the same time to do for Citizen B. This principle has, of course, a built-in provision against Big Government, because it automatically eliminates so many programs. One cannot form a plan for poor Negro families that does not apply to poor white families: as Moynihan said in a *Dædalus* conference, "In order to do anything about the Negro Americans on the scale that our data would indicate, we have to declare that we are doing it for everybody." Normally, special problems on a large scale would lead to aimed and intense programs for the needy segment of the population; but that would offend against the Principle.

Moynihan is very good at using this Principle of Interchangeability to revive classical liberalism among modern welfare liberals—he urges them, for instance, not to use government money on Left-Wing schemes unless they are willing, in the same area, to see the voters turn around and use such money for Right-Wing schemes:

> Professional persons were too willing by half to see public funds, and tax-free private funds, employed on a vast scale to further what was in effect a political agenda of a fairly small group of intellectuals. At just that time when their colleagues, and students, were raising the utmost rumpus about the intrusion of Federal money, and *therefore* influence into universities via national security and space programs, these professors were enthusiastically pressing for ever more public money to be expended in urban and rural neighborhoods in such a way as to change the political and social attitudes of the residents thereof. The precedent in either case is a questionable one. The next President of the United States as I write, will not be Lyndon Johnson. It could be George C. Wallace. How much public money would American liberals be willing to see President Wallace expend for the purpose of increasing the participation in public affairs of those elements in the population he regards as simultaneously deprived and underorganized?

If the federal government should stay out of plans aimed only at one segment of the population, so should local governments (like the City of New York):

In the summer of 1968, the City of New York, with the assistance of a Yale summer interne and the fullest cooperation, as it were, of the *New York Times,* launched a monster registration campaign in the poorer areas of the City. (Had a Tammany Mayor undertaken to spend public funds for such a purpose the *Times* might have seen the matter differently. But this was a reform Mayor, and in any event the poverty program had legitimated such efforts, and they were not yet being resorted to by outright reactionaries.)

And even the foundations should observe the purity Moynihan expects of government:

In effect, the Public Affairs Program of the Ford Foundation invented a new level of American government, the inner-city community action agency. The idea that a private, tax-free organization, responsible to none but its own wishes, should attempt anything of the sort would surely have given rise to not a little consternation in liberal circles had the organization been seen as politically conservative.

Once Moynihan has applied his neutralizing Principle, the only agent left for social mobilization among particular ethnic or economic segments of the community is the lone Saul Alinsky type—and Moynihan even has misgivings about him.

The Principle of Interchangeability is limitlessly applicable. Black Studies, for instance, should not be allowed in schools supported by taxes unless Irish Studies are also provided for. A quota to boost black registration at a school cannot be permitted because a similar quota applied to Jews would decrease the number of Jews let in. Desegregation plans cannot be drawn up specifically for the South; they must be made to apply just as stringently to the North, even when this means a scattering of manpower and diffusion of effort. In all ways the government must treat men simply as citizens, "regardless of race, creed, color, or sex."

It is absurd to see candidates whose campaign tickets have been "racially balanced" promising to disregard eth-

nic considerations in their administration of government.
(Lindsay tried this for a while, but by 1969 he was deploring Nixon's nomination of a non-Jew to the "Jewish
seat" on the Supreme Court.) Applied with any rigor, the
Principle of Interchangeability would prevent a congressman from giving more attention to a constituent than to a
man from outside his district—why distinguish by mere
region when one cannot do so by race or sex?

Actually, the law will favor some—and this must, of
necessity, be done at the expense of others. Moynihan
knows these facts of life, but he wants the best balance
to be struck; the maximum favoring of any one set of
citizens to be tempered by minimum imposition on others.
He wants, in other words, the greatest good for the
greatest number. He wants the Calculus. And this is not
to be achieved by theorizing about the Good Society.
Social scientists may think they know what the Good
Society is, but they have no right to impose their vision on
the rest of us. Only the politicians should conduct our
politics. "Trust the politicians," Moynihan said in an interview just before Nixon's election. "They know what
they know." And what is it they know? How to get votes.
Not a very lofty sort of knowledge?—not, perhaps, in
itself. But the combined efforts of politicians to soothe,
entice, or placate voters is like businessmen's combined
knowledge of how to make sales—it creates a general
availability of desired commodities. And the pleasing of
political "consumers" all across the board makes for the
articulation of our Calculus. The trouble with the imposed
solutions of "reform professionals" is that they destroy
this delicacy of response:

> As such decisions become more professional, they are
> likely to become less political, in the sense of re-
> sponding to existing power configurations.

Response to "power configuration" is all-important for
Moynihan: one cannot believe in the Calculus without
being forced to believe in some machinery sensitive
enough to register the true balance of interests; and in
our politics that instrument is the electoral system.

Moynihan appeared, in his ADA speech, to be a heretic,
but he was the voice of orthodoxy calling others back
to true belief. His fellows in the room believed in the

electoral system, but refused to see that if the electoral system really worked as these men said it did, then social planning was not only unnecessary but an unnecessary evil. Activist social scientists are, in politics, what economic planners are to the free market—people whose meddling cancels the work of the Invisible Hand. The liberals attending Moynihan's speech professed a devotion to neutrality in government—without seeing that a truly neutral government would have to be a minimal government. These men claimed that only the free play of ideas would lead to truth, yet they gave some ideas a social monopoly by supporting the efforts of planners with tax money and tax-exempt funds. For all these reasons, a consistent liberalism would drive the political scientists out of advisory roles in our democracy as ruthlessly as Plato drove the poets out of his literary Republic.

Yet we tend to think of such consistency as anachronistic (*nineteenth-century* liberalism) and of its supporters (Moynihan or Friedman) as rather fanatical. Unless the "nineteenth-century" tag is carefully placed on their liberalism, each time it is mentioned, we feel that an intolerable confusion will be the result. History has now made laissez-faire economic theory a phenomenon of the Right, Lockean insistence on individual civil liberties the possession of the Left. Moynihan, if he believes in the marketplace of usage, must go along with this dismembering of liberal beliefs once unified in Mill. What history has put asunder let no man join together.

Yet by 1969, Moynihan the anachronism was being treated, in places, as Moynihan the prophet. The Left was worrying about local control and Big Government, decentralization and the tax burden. Middle-class striving was reassessed, and looked no more disreputable than the agitation of the poor. Signs like this should remind us that "nineteenth-century" liberalism was very much a *twentieth-century* school of thought, right down to—indeed, well into—Franklin Roosevelt's first term. Classical liberalism was, until the New Deal took hold, not only an integral or triumphant philosophy, but—for the whole period since the Civil War—a practically unchallenged one. Different men, of course, drew differing practical lessons from the theory, gave different emphases to its components; but almost all Americans subscribed to it, the middle-class striver and the millionaire, the reformer and the banker, the Populist small farmer and Progressive small businessman, the Democrats and the Republicans, Wilson and Cox no less than Harding and Coolidge. Herbert Hoover, the last Republican President before the New Deal, stoutly professed this philosophy in all its aspects; but so did the last Democratic President before the New Deal, Woodrow Wilson.

In the anguish of the Depression, this integral faith was shattered—its elements flew apart, and men not only did not join them again, they could not imagine that they had ever been securely joined. Former components of the liberal system were now arrayed against each other, portrayed as antithetical in origin, motive, and end. It became psychically necessary to forget that the liberal Wilson was a laissez-faire economist in his domestic policy, or that the conservative Hoover was an internationalist in his foreign policy. The two men were very close, both in their esteem for each other and in their basic views. Each stood with the Progressive wing of his own party. Hoover had Bull Moose sympathies, and ran for the Senate in 1920 as a maverick Republican candidate supporting the League of Nations. His international charities and penchant for efficient organization made him suspect, at first, to Wall Street; he was known as the most liberal man in the Harding-Coolidge cabinets, and the big bankers (who wanted Coolidge to run again) tried to block his nomination in 1928.

Wilson, for his part, defended the true economic faith against Teddy Roosevelt's assaults. The Wilsonian Progressives opposed trusts on laissez-faire grounds, because they closed the market to individual competitors. As Wilson put it, in *The New Freedom*, "Monopoly always checks development, weighs down natural prosperity, pulls against natural advance." One must "bust the trusts" to protect the market, to foster competition, to promote efficiency: "A trust does not bring efficiency to the aid of business; it buys efficiency out of business." Theodore Roosevelt, though he engaged in his own slight trust-busting with characteristically grand gestures, took issue with Wilson's New Freedom. His own program, the New Nationalism, proposed to use government power for regulating big combines, not for breaking them up: "This is an age of combination, and any effort to prevent all combination will be not only useless, but in the end vicious, because of the contempt for law which the failure to enforce the law inevitably produces . . . They [the democrats of the Wilson-Brandeis persuasion] tried by the Sherman-law method to bolster up an individualism already proved to be both futile and mischievous, to remedy by more individualism the concentration that was the inevitable result of the already existing individualism."

A glimmer of the truth had reached Roosevelt—that the market did not *work*, that Wilson was trying to run a race in which there should be no winners but only perpetual *striving* to win. In the same passage that attacks trusts as inefficient, Wilson goes on to praise the man who can "make his way," even though it is clear that this will be done at the expense of others: "Any man who can survive by his brains, any man who can put the others out of the business by making the thing cheaper to the consumer at the same time that he is increasing its intrinsic value and quality, I take off my hat to, and I say: 'You are the man who can build up the United States, and I wish there were more of you.'" Wilson was engaged in the old Market juggling act that promises a simultaneous equal chance and competitive rating. He said we must return to the past when "eager men were everywhere captains of industry, not employees; not looking to a distant city to find out what they might do, but looking about among their neighbors, finding credit according to their character not according to their connections." This exercise in Progressive nostalgia neglected the fact that men become *captains* of industry only by making other men serve them as *privates*. The world of Wilson's theory is all captains and no privates, all employers and no employees, all character (promising future performance) and no connections (based on past performance), all runners but never a loser (and so never a winner).

Wilson was, in short, a devout believer in the free market and "the forgotten American." Hofstadter points out that "Wilson's speeches, the best parts of which are printed in *The New Freedom*, sound like the collective wail of the middle class." The speeches he refers to form a solid bridge across our recent history, a bridge that leads from Horatio Alger straight to Richard Nixon:

What this country needs above everything else is a body of laws which will look after the men who are

on the make . . . The originative part of America,
the part of America that makes new enterprises, the
part into which the ambitious and gifted working
man makes his way up, the class that saves, that
plans, that organizes, that presently spreads its enterprises until they have a national scope and character
—that middle class is being more and more squeezed
out . . .

The man who is on the make is the judge of what
is happening in America . . . I know, and every man
in his heart knows, that the only way to enrich America is to make it possible for any man who has the
brains to get into the game . . . Are you not eager
for the time when the genius and initiative of all
the people shall be called into the service of business?

Every great man of business has got somewhere a
touch of the idealist in him . . . Business underlies
every part of our lives; the foundation of our lives,
of our spiritual lives included, is economic.

No wonder Nixon feels an affinity for Wilson. Believers in
the self-made man at home, both dealt in the "self-
determined" nations abroad, and gave an evangelical flavor
to their exhortations for an "open world" of peaceful
competition between such nations. The connection between
their domestic and international policy was suggested by
Louis Hartz: "Wasn't Wilson smashing the Austro-
Hungarian Empire into bits much as he would smash an
American trust? Wasn't he depending on an automatic
harmony as clearly in the one case as he was in the
other?"

Theodore Roosevelt toyed with the insight that the Market was not working, never had worked as men claimed.
But, by skills long nourished, Americans continued to believe in the Market even when their practice accommo-
dated realities destructive of its myth. A good example
of this, in men of undoubted sincerity, was the collaboration between Wilson and Hoover to regulate food sales
during World War I. Hoover says, of such governmental
control: "He [Wilson] yielded with great reluctance to the
partial and temporary abandonment of our principles of
life during the war, because of the multitude of tasks with
which the citizen or the states could not cope. But he

often expressed to me the hope that our methods of doing so were such that they could be quickly reversed and free enterprise restored." The measures were temporary, caused by the need for increased efficiency. Yet it had all along been the boast of the Market—and a staple of Wilson's rhetoric—that a free economy is the most *efficient* one imaginable. If a spectacular emergency, like war or hurricane or flood, throws off the Market spectacularly, why do not the thousand accumulating accidents of life throw it off subtly yet persistently at all times? The answer is, plainly, that they do. Death, sickness, luck, accidents of all sorts, the manifold interventions of human perversity, make it impossible to correlate success with quality or virtue. Yet both Wilson and Hoover were on record as desiring, after the war, to restore this inefficient system *in the name of efficiency*. They did not see —Americans *will* not see—the truth that has always surrounded them.

The psychological need to deny this truth is very great. Inefficiency is a charge that should be fatal to Market thinking, deep as that is in the whole American language of business and politics and education. What worse thing, after all, can you say about a system built on the cult of *success* than that it *fails?* The Manchesterian economic policy was just one dogma in the nineteenth-century religion of progress. If all things worked together unto enlightenment, if evolution was the law of life, then automatic progress was to be expected in man's economic activity also. The Invisible Hand of Adam Smith's celestial Providence became, in the utilitarian world of Bentham and Mill, the machinery of earthly Progress. Darwin confessed that his model for natural selection had been Smith's concept of market competition; so men were just retracing Darwin's steps when they brought biological "laws" back into the world of economics to create "Social Darwinism."

But the nineteenth-century English liberals had been consistent in their thinking. If one progresses by survival of the fittest, then, as a consequence, the less fit do *not* survive. If the race is never finally won, at least some competitors are forever eliminated. Malthus made this clear when he said that, since the Invisible Hand provides the maximum food intended by Nature and Nature's God (Malthus was a clergyman), it was the will of Nature that population in excess of this divine provender should starve (if it were allowed to come into the world). This cruel consistency in the great originators of liberal thought came from the fact that they were considering the *whole* of their system, writing in social terms of the *race's* progress. They lived with the fundamental paradox of laissez faire, that it was other-oriented, with the stress on live and *let* live. Out of this paradox come the Orwellian formulations that still plague liberalism—the tenet that individualism is the basis of society, that confessed self-interest leads to the best-calculated balance of public interest, that selfishness is the highest charity, that (as Mr. Dooley put it) "Th' worst thing ye can do f'r anny man is to do him good."

But in America there was, from the outset, a different emphasis in the liberal creed. Men were not only interested in the efficiency of the system, but in the Market's use as a school of moral formation. Business molded character. It was to this belief that Wilson addressed himself when he said that the American economy was the secret of America's spiritual life. So, even though Wilson routinely attacked the trusts as inefficient, what really disturbed him was their impersonality, an amoral stress on the material results of manufacture rather than the spiritual results of trade. The entrepreneur of our mythology succeeds by pluck, ingenuity, persistence, diligence, hard work, brains, and calculated risk. But what happens when the adventurous entrepreneur becomes a mere stockholder? Wilson gave this rueful answer: "He is merely contributing money for the conduct of a business which other men run as they please . . . He cannot even inquire or protest without being told to mind his own business—the very thing he was innocently trying to do."

Thus there was a certain tension, in the American ideal of business competition, between the assumption that it is the most efficient system and the belief that it is a morally uplifting system. And there is still a difference of emphasis between fundamentalists of the Market who (like Milton Friedman) claim that welfare programs will throw off the operation of a free economy and those who (like Barry Goldwater) insist that it will soften the moral fiber of its beneficiaries.

And in Americans' eyes there was a *third* justification for the free-market ethos: individual initiative is considered a check on the ambitions of those in authority. Our constitutional system, based on the reservation of powers at successive levels of government, works out, ultimately, from the primary reservation of powers to the individual. The vigor of initiative and enterprise have long been considered a hedge on Big Government—as in Goodwin's argument, where the desire for mastery over one's own life works against the concentration of power in Washington. This argument would remain valid even if one were led, by it, to certain inefficiencies. Democracy, goes the boast, may not be as efficient as totalitarian government. But the gain in liberty is more than worth any loss in efficiency. It was this instinct that led Wilson to say, "If America is not to have free enterprise, then she can have no freedom of any sort whatever."

Given these three arguments, in theory supplementary, though in practice alternative, the justification for the Market staggered along like a three-legged cripple, no one limb very strong and each one buckling from time to time, but balancing itself, if unsteadily, on this or that pair of legs—even, for a period, on one leg, if need be. The teetering deathless thing seemed forever rickety but indestructible. The only way to bring it down was to kick all three legs out from under it, decisively, at once.

And that is what men either feared or hoped had happened in the Depression. Millions of Americans seem to have realized, as in a flash, that the Market did not work, that starvation was not necessarily good for one's character, and that it was not slavery to have a government that governed. The first impression is of the rickety old scheme's sudden and total collapse. Hoover, who had seemed a wizard of logistical expertise, engineering intelligence, and managerial skills, became overnight a silly incompetent. To those who repined for the three-legged monster, the New Deal was a traumatic break with the past. The tradition of political thought bequeathed to America had undergone a long-overdue and violent fission. In the thirties and forties, Adam Smith and Locke, once joined in the Mill synthesis, seemed not only to have parted ways but to be natural and inveterate enemies. It was hard for men to remember how impregnable the union had seemed, so recently; how united both parties had been in their allegiance to the original amalgam, how integral had been both Wilson's and Hoover's faith in it.

Yet this appearance of total opposition between the two components was deceptive. FDR himself began with an orthodox view of economics. His first platform promised a balanced budget, and he blamed the Depression in part on Hoover's extravagant expenditures. He groped into his regulatory schemes on an experimental basis, working out from TR's recognition that the market was not working. (The New Deal was heir to the Republican New Nationalism, not the Democratic New Freedom— FDR, as a young Secretary of the Navy, an apostle for naval supremacy, had been a great admirer of his wife's uncle, the Rough Rider.) Yet though Franklin Roosevelt saw the limits of market efficiency, he did not attack the other two justifications for individualism, its role in forming character or inhibiting despotism. On the contrary, like TR before him, FDR's aim was to save capitalism, not destroy it; and Roosevelt was bewildered when some businessmen did not get the point (though others did). He said capitalists were like a drowning man who, dragged out of the surf, attacks the lifeguard for not also saving his hat.

If Roosevelt departed from (without destroying) the ideals of the economic market, he did nothing to weaken the complementary ideals of the political market and the academic market. As we saw earlier, he expressed the solidarity of the first two markets in his second presidential acceptance speech, when he said, "If the average citizen is guaranteed equal opportunity in the polling place, he must have equal opportunity in the market place." The Left continued to be individualist in its attitude toward civil liberties, suffrage politics, academic freedom, and international self-determination—though it forgot that these were all part of Hoover's program as well as Wilson's. The objective result was liberalism-as-before but with key adaptations in the area of economics—though one must never forget the subjective feelings of division and trauma that accompanied even this degree of departure from the ancient faith. One could regard this as a liberalism finally come to grips with reality, a philosophy that had made the adjustments necessary for survival, losing some of its illusions along the way. (That is the version Professor Schlesinger celebrates in his Roosevelt volumes.) Yet, to the extent that Roosevelt kept alive the game-metaphor of economic competition, his was a maimed liberalism, disguising its theoretical weakness rather than resolving them. Worse than that, the failure to face up to contradiction in the sphere of economics meant that the mythical nature of our other markets was not even suspected. Emersonian competition in the business world had not worked; but it had to fail spectacularly before men would admit its inefficiencies, and the dysfunctioning of our other markets was not forced on men's attention with such vividness. If a captain of industry succeeds on the economic market, privates must serve him. But if one decides, in the "free market" of ideas, to live with *this* idea today, it is easy to fool oneself and others by saying that *other* ideas have an equal chance to reassert themselves tomorrow. An idea does not starve or surrender—it does not become the victim or the employee of more efficient ideas—as an economic competitor would. The game of academic freedom is so easy to play because "survival of the fittest" can be professed without admitting that the fittest survive, in Darwin's scheme, by elimination of the *less* fit. Ideas are easily thought of as "preserved" in an intellectual limbo, ready for reconsideration. In the political market, too, we can pretend that all votes "matter" in the end, that each leads to the subtle final adjustment, the ultimate calculus of the ballot box. In that sense, no one loses; each factor contributes to the final equation. Thus the New Deal, while tempering the economic market with some controls, did not unsettle belief in the academic and political "free play of ideas."

If the Left was maimed by separation from the integral body of liberalism, the Right was even more impoverished. Theoretically, the surviving champions of laissez faire could have kept the liberal faith intact, and its best representatives tried to. Milton Friedman, for instance, sustained many views treated, in the forties and fifties, as proper to the Left—regard for civil liberties (including those of Negroes), moderate anticommunism (one based, that is, on opposition to despotism, not on a religious crusade against atheistic regimes), internationalism (based, as Wilson's was, on the ideal of free trade, which involves an "open world," the dissolution of imperial blocs and colonial ties, the reduction of everything to the political unit of single nations "self-determined"). Nonetheless, the logistics of competition within the two-party system made Friedman, in his effort to defend

Market fundamentalism, ally himself with the mishmash of Right-Wing forces behind Barry Goldwater in 1964. This was an alliance that had no true theoretical bond at all.

The confusion of modern politics is based on this unconfessed split in liberalism of the Wilson-Hoover sort. Once the split occurred, the two parts could become nuclei for two radically different systems, rationally opposed to each other. This would have involved a real departure from the tempered individualism of liberal theory—a move toward absolute individualism on one side, toward tight social cohesion on the other. But each fragment of the original whole lingered near the point of fission, and even showed antinomian tendencies to change sides on certain issues, the Left being anticohesive on matters like dissent and loyalty oaths, the Right being conformist and "socializing" when it gave government the muscle to defeat communism at home and abroad. What is surprising in terms of pure logic is natural enough in the sphere of political reality. The New Deal, admittedly, might have based its recognition of the need for economic planning on a political philosophy of broad social control. But deeper liberal instincts were opposed to socialism in any form. Since economic planning was meant to revitalize the competitive "race" of American life, not abolish it, the Lockean mystique was untouched by the New Deal. Indeed, that mystique was held with a new fervor in noneconomic areas, as a sign of sustained loyalty to liberal individualism. Liberals became even more insistent on the right of dissent, on freedom for all to engage in the activities of the political and academic marketplace, on opposition to censorship and any control of ideas. Only in economics was "individualism" considered a bad word. Systematic Marxians and socialists who tried to bend the New Deal to their purposes were frustrated—an outcome so satisfactory to Americans that little regret was expressed over the philosophical contradictions it caused in the liberal view of things.

The picture on the Right was even more confused. If logically, the Left was expected to adopt socialist underpinnings for its new experiments in control, the Right should have moved toward an unfettered individualism, toward philosophical anarchism. Even the moderate liberal state had been unable to prevent economic planning on the New Deal scale, so why feel bound by the state at all? This line of thought *has* been followed by a few, by those who adopt Ayn Rand's laws of the jungle. But there is a great force inhibiting such a development. Though "rugged individualism" is native to America, it is held in check by an emphasis on moral orthodoxy, social conformity, and community solidarity—the spirit that creates local blue laws, on the one hand, and founds stable labor unions on the other. This authoritarian *sentiment* is not based on articulated political *theory*. Indeed, the conformist faction in American life has used, for its own purposes, the dominant liberal philosophy. It uses Locke to restrict the federal government, yet does this only so it can impose rigid controls at the local level. The classic instance of this was Southern devotion to states' rights arguments (arguments based on opposition to governmental encroachment) used to protect segregation laws (which typify governmental interference in private life). In Washington, a Southerner sounded as if he were for free enterprise, but back in Mississippi there were laws to say who could and could not be served by any businessman.

Thus an extraordinary alignment came about on the Right. Those who professed the purest form of individualism (libertarians like Milton Friedman) were thrown into a political redoubt with those who held the most authoritarian and conformist views (Southerners, religious fundamentalists, sentimental traditionalists). This conjunction of extreme social atomists with extreme social conformists would have been unthinkable but for one thing —the large dose of religiosity that had been mixed, historically, with the American cult of free enterprise. Academic economists conceived their individualism in terms of Locke and Mill; but the emulative ethic, as it was glorified out among the American people, was based on the pursuit of success as a form of spiritual discipline. Horatio Alger represented a union of economic opportunity with deep religious compulsion—the free linked with what is forced. And in that juncture lies the secret of the Right-Wing alliance.

Yet that alliance remained *only* an alliance, and of disparate things, an uneasy combination of men working from the most various motives. The purists of the Capitalist point of view were not only indifferent to Christianity, but often hostile to it (e.g., Ayn Rand or Max Eastman), while fanatics of the Christian point of view (e.g., Carl

McIntire or Fred Schwarz) were willing to abandon libertarian standards whenever these made the pursuit of communism difficult. Meanwhile, a wide spectrum of people in between these extremes rallied to the Right-Wing standard for want of a better: traditionalists of the local mores, those favoring censorship or control of the schools, those wanting to protect the social bias toward theism, those critical of liberal theory, those opposed to larger taxes or bigger government on a pragmatic basis. Some of these wanted minimum governmental activity so they could retain maximum social control of their communities. With all these elements to be satisfied, the Right could formulate no basic philosophy of politics. The best-articulated scrap of theory available to them, one that almost everyone could find some use for, was the free-market economy. Other components of Right-Wing thought were often mere instincts, prejudices, unformulated preferences. Only the economists maintained a respectable academic base and an intellectual tradition of any rigor. Thus, though their fragment of the American liberal tradition was not the most characteristic thing about the Right, it was the most useful, that which most *united* the Right. Barry Goldwater was supported by racists, states-righters, monarchists, and God knows what else; but when he had to start thinking in practical terms of an actual campaign and administration, he turned to the traditional liberals in his camp—to Milton Friedman and Warren Nutter and Harry Jaffa.

It is easy to see why socialists or communists might lend peripheral support to welfare liberals of the New Deal. It is not so easy to see why authoritarians felt drawn to the libertarian Right. To understand that, one has to have a sense of the manifold and volatile nature of this combination—a sense lost by those who analyze the Right as if it were one thing, explicable by one theory (the authoritarian personality, status resentment, Cold War anxiety, the residue of Populism, etc.). One also has to discern, beneath the conflicts and multifariousness, a historical force that made the alliance possible (a religious fundamentalism that had been grafted onto the ideal of free enterprise). This, in turn, involves an understanding of the degree to which free-market theorists offer an *excuse* to the Right, rather than a philosophy. And, finally, in order to "place" the Right, one has to remember that this covering theory of the free market is part of an original, broader liberalism held in the past.

When, in the fifties, an attempt to sort out America's ideological framework was begun, there was great confusion in the terminology of Left and Right, liberalism and conservatism, Democrats and Republicans. And the source of the confusion was not clearly grasped—the original union of Left and Right theories in one consistent system. The parts tended back toward each other, yet fought this tendency. The New Deal did not become socialist; in fact, it became even more libertarian on questions of academic freedom and the toleration of dissent. The apostles of a free market did not become anarchistic; instead, they were thrown together with religious and social authoritarians, who tried to introduce the force of social custom (e.g., the social bias that makes life hard on atheists, homosexuals, communists, and other nonconformers) into the realm of law. Incomplete, the two half-theories were vulnerable, their contradictions easily exploited. Those who tried to think consistently, on either side, were forced back toward the liberalism of their common origin. But by now the "other side" was an enemy camp, hostile because of historical clashes, and it was necessary to avoid Left or Right "deviationism." A natural bias of the two parts toward each other was therefore countered by deliberate effort to invent or stress differences between them.

The resulting tug and counter-tug gave postwar politics an unreal lunar quality, a half-light proper to such half-theories. Americans thought they had broken the liberal philosophy's circular perfection into two contained parts, that each side had gone off with its own smaller moon to live under different skies. But the moon was never broken. The half-moons were created by darking out part of the theory; and if one looked hard enough, the thin completion of the circle was still visible, implicit in the dark half. The individualist economy was still implied in the individualist politics, and vice versa. Americans were not inhabiting separate universes; only some of them looked at their sky's "half-moon" as in a photo, and others saw it as in a negative. It was a black and white world in either case; but what was white for one was black for the other.

4. "Beyond Left and Right"

> "In the Western world . . . there is today a rough consensus among intellectuals on political issues: the acceptance of a Welfare State; the desirability of decentralized power; a system of mixed economy and of political pluralism."
>
> —Daniel Bell (1960)

DURING THE NINETEEN FORTIES, the problem of America's fragmented liberalisms did not attract much attention. World War II and the burgeoning Cold War absorbed men's energies and eased domestic conflict. War spending settled the question, still unresolved by 1939, whether New Deal programs would justify themselves economically. Military need laid a patriotic base for programs the Right had objected to in peacetime. The New Deal was absorbed into the nation's life; old wounds were healed; in a crisis men tacitly agreed the various markets did not work (controls were exerted over thought and political dissent as well as over the economy).

But as things eased in the fifties, new problems arose; and they could not be explained in terms of a fundamental clash between Left and Right. Republicans returned to office in 1952, but not to abolish the welfare state or make the Cold War a hot one. A sense of continuity came over men with the force of anticlimax. It seemed that one of the decade's main problems was a lack of problems—silence from the young generation on the campus, silence from the White House, strange harmony among intellectuals. The Left and the Right had for years been cranking up their rhetoric for battle, and now had nothing substantial to fight about. Both sides accepted the New Deal—whether too little or not enough was only a matter of degree, not of basic difference. Both sides were anticom-

munist—whether too little or not enough, again, was a
question of degree only. One of the best books of the
decade, *The Liberal Tradition in America* by Louis Hartz,
could reach the conclusion that "the age of purely domestic crisis apparently is over."

Thus was born the great fifties issue of conformism—
concern for all our little men in gray flannel suits. Only
Joseph McCarthy broke the mental hush of the time; but
that was a striking exception. Hartz wrote, just after his
claim that domestic crisis had ended, "There can be no
doubt that it [McCarthyism] represents the most frightening closing down of 'Americanism' at home that we have
yet experienced." Those who deplored our too tranquil
domestic life had simultaneously to deplore this savage
conflict. Critics of conformity had to say McCarthy was
not to be tolerated.

Nothing in the period, neither its tumult nor its calm,
seemed understandable in terms of class, party, ideology,
or class interest. So theorists of the fifties launched an
effort to describe America in terms that preclude theoretical conflict. There was an American *consensus,* they
argued; and McCarthy was outside that consensus, out of
the mainstream, off on the fringe. It was this approach
that gave such crucial importance to terms like "ultra,"
extremist, radical. What was wrong with the Radical Right
(as Seymour Martin Lipset christened it) was not that it
was Right, but that it was Radical. The Super-Americans
were not wrong because of their Americanism, but because of their super quality (to be super anything, it was
decided, is un-American). To understand what happened,
we must watch the currents of "mainstream" thinking converge—in history (the consensus historians), in political
science (the end-of-ideology movement), in social psychology (the status-politics school of thought), in sociology
(the reconsideration of individualism), in public planning
(the writers for *The Public Interest*), in Republican circles
(the "New Conservatism"). Needless to say, these lines of
thought meet, mingle, run parallel, so that theorists in one
current contribute to the others. But the themes can be
separated, and their contribution to the whole assessed.

Perhaps the most striking attempt to recapture the
unity of liberal theory was made by the consensus historians, most notably Daniel Boorstin and Louis Hartz.
Boorstin realized that there was fundamental agreement

between, say, Hoover and Wilson; but instead of tracing the shape of this shared philosophy, he argued the two men were united by a common (and laudable) *lack* of philosophy. America has had no great political theorists because it has had no political theory at all—at least, not in the European sense. Our "tradition" was a response to the "givenness" of the American situation; realistic contact with the land's given things has made theory unnecessary and downright evil. Americans have undergone a historical "preformation" that gives a prior framework to their politics; all differences are thus contained, all opponents share common ground. The American way of life is, politically, "the American way of *not* philosophizing about politics." Boorstin's polemical aim, in *The Genius of American Politics*, was to moderate some of the passions of the Cold War: how can we counter communism with our own philosophy of government when we *have* no philosophy of government? But the larger effect his approach had on American history was to damage the assumption that there had ever been basic disagreement between the political parties. If we have no theory of politics, how can there be theoretical differences? All we have is a shifting consensus in our reaction to America's givenness: Republican opposition to the New Deal was simply a matter of time-lag, the minority moving along in the train of the majority. By the time the Republicans regained office—*in order* to regain office—it was necessary for them to catch up with the consensus. Eisenhower came to administer the welfare state, not dismantle it.

But Boorstin must use language very carefully, even trickily, to advance his theory that we have no theory. After all, if we have a consensus, that consensus must have some content, a point that slips through Boorstin's careful guard on occasion—e.g., when he speaks of the consensus as "an implicit political philosophy," or says, "We do not need American philosophers because we already have an American philosophy, implicit in the American Way of Life." Even an implicit theory is a theory; and to say we have no need of philosophers because we have a philosophy is much like saying we need no artists to have a national art. When Boorstin trumpets "the American Way of Life," he shows the dangers of keeping our theory implicit: an unexamined consensus is forced on men, and any departure from it becomes "un-American."

Boorstin began by attacking the chauvinism of Cold Warriors, but he ends up celebrating "the American Way of
Life" in a way very useful to chauvinists.

Louis Hartz was a better spokesman for consensus; facts
that were fatal objections to Boorstin are incorporated into the Hartz approach. His *Liberal Tradition in America*
meets the two main objections head on: he not only admits but insists that the liberal tradition has a theoretical
content—that it is, in fact, Locke's theory. We began with
Locke, according to Hartz, and after every historical scuffle we find, as the dust settles, that we have ended with
Locke. The second objection is confronted just as calmly:
he not only admits but insists that universal subscription
to this theory has made it an orthodoxy, the source of
America's conformism. According to Hartz, we have a
liberal theory supported by conservative instincts—
Locke's arguments maintained for Burke's motives of loyalty. Thus, what is wrong with the liberal tradition is not
its liberal content but the fact that it *is* a tradition, that it
forms "a colossal liberal absolutism." A liberalism thus
established is not challenged to reexamine and renew itself. Indeed, philosophical self-examination can no longer
be achieved in purely American terms—there is no vantage point *outside* Locke from which to view our Lockean
orthodoxy. The theory is everywhere, made invisible by its
omnipresence. The solution is to go outside America—
in historical analysis, by placing American liberalism
against the broader spectrum of European political philosophies; in practical terms, by pursuing a course of international involvement. Only intimate dealings with other
nations can make us recognize the nature of our own
theory. In effect, by learning how bad *they* are, we learn
how good we *should* be. Hartz does not regret that the
liberal tradition has prevailed in America, but that it did
so without a fight. Only by fighting for what we have can
we truly have it. (Hartz's view is circular, however; he
wants America to spread liberalism to the rest of the
world—where, if it prevails, worldwide unanimity would
make self-knowledge impossible for all nations, not just
for America. Then we would *truly* have "a colossal liberal
absolutism." Hartz, without realizing it, executes a tricky
series of maneuvers that cancel each other out and bring
him back to Boorstin's side: "If America is the bizarre

fulfillment of liberalism, do not people everywhere rely upon it for the retention of what is best in that tradition? The hope for a free world surely lies in the power for transcending itself inherent in American liberalism.")

Hartz admits that there has been some conflict in American history, though it was mostly shadowboxing—men did not recognize their shared assumptions. A pattern (and Hartz loves patterns) keeps emerging, of tension around two poles—the "Whigs," heirs of Hamilton, who stress the overall process of liberalism as an *efficient* one, its blessings totted up in a rather cold Benthamite way ("anything which enhances the 'total mass of industry and opulence' in a country 'is ultimately beneficial to every part of it' "); and the "Democrats," heirs of Jefferson, who stress the scope given to individuals within the system.

Hartz was flirting with a recognition that Left and Right, in the fifties, were originally parts of a whole; but he did not grasp the precise nature of their complementarity, because he underestimated the importance of the thirties, of the moment when the whole broke into its parts. For him, the New Deal was just another bout in history's shadowboxing match between Whigs and Democrats. This is false to the events, in several ways:

1) For Hartz, political theory and political reality are coterminous; indeed, American political theory soon becomes synonymous, in his book, with the whole of American social reality. If our theory is everywhere, then it must explain everything, even things apparently opposed to it—and, true to his premise, Hartz even explains McCarthyism as a product of the liberal tradition. "Liberal hysteria" emerges whenever a conformist stress on the fact that our liberalism is a *tradition* gets the upper hand over that tradition's individualist *content*. In this way Hartz performs the welcome trick of placing McCarthy within the consensus (so he could typify the evils of conformism) while establishing grounds for his condemnation (conformism is an evil side effect of liberalism, which must be purged —i.e., McCarthy must be shut up to protect free speech).

But Americans have regularly contrasted "society" and "government," and if the theory of *government* has been liberal, the practices of *society* have been decidedly illiberal. Some men, in fact, have held the liberal theory of government in order to maintain illiberal practices in society (Southerners invoking states' rights). This whole side of American life is missing from Hartz's arid scheme of American history. The conformist local community, the authoritarian check on mores, the communitarian impulses (manifest in the growth of labor unions)—none of these is considered as a source of conformism separable from agreement on our theoretical tradition. Yet it was a mixture of these forces that erupted in the McCarthy movement, not an excess of devotion to Locke on the part of Wisconsin's senator.

2) Hartz reduces the complexity of the very theory he would stretch to cover American life. For him, its only complication is the play between two poles of apparent conflict. Yet we have seen that Wilson stressed at least three justifications for the liberal market—that it is efficient (Hartz's Hamiltonian Whiggery), that it protects men from creeping despotism (Hartz's Jeffersonian Democracy), and that it *forms character*. This last aspect of the tradition, so characteristic of Locke's views as they became Americanized, is outside Hartz's purview. He devotes a whole section of his book to the Horatio Alger ethic, but does not see its close connection with religious fundamentalism, with methodist morals and baptist fervor and puritan rhetoric. Hartz views his Locke in a cool secular light which does not reach to the dark things, the self-punishment, behind America's abject devotion to success. One must "earn one's way," and the earning must *hurt* (sit in *hard* chairs to do one's thinking). Hartz cannot explain the deep hold liberalism has upon the American mind, because he does not see that we have made a secular religion of liberal thought.

3) Because he reduces the complexity of the tradition he is emphasizing, Hartz scants the crucial nature of the split that took place in that theory under Roosevelt. (Consensus history, as its critics have successfully urged against it, underestimates conflict in general—during the Federalist period and Civil War no less than at the New Deal; but the New Deal is the conflict most relevant here.) Hoover was not Hartz's ancient Whig calling for efficiency and order. If anything, the recognition of our system's actual breakdown, the pragmatic attempt to restore its operation, made FDR that kind of "Whig." Both the poles of Hartz's *schema* were encompassed by the New Deal. What was left out is what Hartz leaves out—individualist

religiosity, the belief that welfare destroys a man's character, the spiritual ideal of "man on the make." The fact that religion had fastened itself most directly to the economic features of the liberal creed gave those features their almost magic importance, caused a sense of betrayal when this economic code was modified. Such modification was not only a departure from the past, but seemed almost a loss of faith. Mid-America's scandalized religiosity led to charges like McCarthy's—"twenty years of treason." And this same scandal caused the wider, milder belief that Left and Right were fundamentally at war on the meaning of human life. Hartz was right in sensing that this war did not exist; but wrong in concluding that therefore no break at all had occurred within American liberalism.

If the fifties historians found consensus everywhere in America's past, the "end of ideology" political scientists had an even grander vision of the "mainstream," which they thought ran clear around the globe. The primary theater for expression of this view was the Congress for Cultural Freedom (CCF), founded in 1950. At its first meeting, held in West Berlin, Sidney Hook foresaw "the era when references to 'right,' 'left,' and 'center' will vanish from common usage as meaningless." This was the postwar period of *Angst*, of the vogue for Existentialism in Europe. There was a feeling of loss and disillusion on the Left, weary readiness to admit that, because of "the God that failed," there had indeed been a *trahison des clercs*. In *The Opium of the Intellectuals*, Raymond Aron said his contemporaries must give up the narcotic of utopianism, and greet instead "the end of the ideological age."

Meanwhile in this country, the quintessential liberal, Arthur Schlesinger, congratulated his own generation because it did not grow up, as earlier Leftists had, blinded by dreams.

[This generation's] prophets were the writers who refused to swallow the fantastic hypocrisies involved in the defense of totalitarianism: Silone, with his profound moral sensibility; Gide, with his quivering sense of freedom; Koestler, with his probing, insatiable intellectual curiosity; Hemingway, who disliked people who pushed other people around; Reinhold Niebuhr, with his tragic sense of the predicament of man;

George Orwell, with his vigorous good sense, his
hatred of cant; Edmund Wilson, with his belief in
moral and aesthetic taste.

The Existentialists' opposition to arid theories could be
wedded, Schlesinger felt, to "tough-minded" American
pragmatism—he pointed to Reinhold Niebuhr as a prophet
of this union. Schlesinger, who was active both in the
CCF and its American subsidiary, the American Committee for Cultural Freedom, had already sounded the
Congress's theme in 1949, with his book *The Vital Center*.
There he hailed the "inspired suggestion" of De Witt C.
Poole that Left and Right no longer stood at opposite
ends of a line, but were like two sides of a circle, with
liberalism at the top and totalitarianism at the bottom.
The moderate Left and Right, converging toward each
other above, thus stand allied against (and at an opposite
pole from) both communism and fascism at the circle's
bottom. This "ingenious solution," which does justice to
"the complexities of this ghastly century," suggested that
men of the Left and Right should meet along the circle's
top periphery, where their consensus becomes (by a
scrambling of the metaphor) "the vital center."

The term "end of ideology" emerged at the 1955 CCF
meeting in Italy. The journal of the Congress, *Encounter*,
summarized that meeting in a report titled "The End of
Ideology?" By 1960, Seymour Martin Lipset was using the
phrase to sum up the last chapter of his book, *Political
Man*, and Daniel Bell had published his volume called
The End of Ideology. The body of thought taking shape
under this banner was directed to other (and to more)
objects than was consensus history. In some ways the two
were at odds, their spokesmen disagreed. Schlesinger, for
instance, had a stake in preserving the picture of conflict
between Leftist champions and Rightist villains in the Age
of Jackson and the Age of Roosevelt—so the vital center
had to be a recent phenomenon, the mark of his generation. Louis Hartz, on the other hand, was sending America
out into the world to discover the difference between a
real Left and Right just as the CCF declared that this
difference no longer existed.

The point to be explained, by either party, was the
fact that "Left" and "Right" did not seem to mean much
anymore. Boorstin and Hartz sought explanations in Amer-

ica's own past. The CCF tried to find its explanation in a mood essentially alien to America: despite superficial congruity, European Existentialism and American Pragmatism were uneasy bedfellows. Europe's disillusionment came from the fact that ideology had been so burningly important there, the lines clearly drawn, the battle intensely engaged: even the end of ideology could only be explained *in terms of* ideology, as the dream's failure, the intellectuals' treason, the loss of something dear. Arthur Koestler expressed this view, at the first CCF meeting, when he said ex-communists were best equipped for coping with the modern world. Only "burnt-out cases" of ideology could resist its lure, guide men past its snares. Whittaker Chambers took the same position in America, and his writings show how futile it is to equate the anti-ideological hangover of Europe with the nonideological temper of America. Chambers lived in a European underground of the mind, and did not understand his own country at all. Investigators of un-American activities never came across a more un-American mind than that of their prize Witness. All the heroes and villains of his thought were European—revolutionary idealists and totalitarian commissars. It is no wonder Chambers made CCF types uncomfortable; he dramatized the absurdity of their own quest for explanations of America in terms of Europe.

Ideological symmetry had been effaced in America, but not by the bitterness of disillusioned revolutionaries. It was effaced by the split within our moderate liberalism, and by strange alliances formed around the fragments of that theory. The consensus historians were right to look for the explanation of America's ideological muddle in our own history; and their argument, for all its shortcomings, has stood up better than the CCF thesis—Hartz has more to offer us than Bell. But the interesting thing is that both schools had to deal with the same problem, the bafflement of ideological analysis; and both sought, by different routes, to solve the problem in terms of consensus, a "mainstream," a "vital center." Both sensed a need for "putting the pieces back together" after liberalism's breakup.

A third attempt at the same task was the development of "status politics." This was not identical with the trends already considered; but its starting point was the same.

Seymour Martin Lipset (in *The New American Right,* 1955) distinguished status politics from class politics (the latter "based on the discord between the traditional left and right"). If "Left and Right" have become meaningless in America because of political consensus, how does one explain whatever conflict *does* occur in our history? Lipset—and, even more thoroughly, Hofstadter—explained this conflict as arising, not from theoretical differences but from status anxieties. Since America has an "open" social system with no stable classes, men do not have fixed social identities; they must earn their position in society, their status. Yet in a fluid world of opportunity, status is insecure, always slipping, unless men earn it again, perpetually reestablishing themselves. This leads to resentment, the desire to be more American than the next man, more superlatively common, less questionably alien.

Hofstadter's analysis, first centered on the fifties and McCarthyism, was traced backward throughout our history in *Anti-Intellectualism in American Life.* Since the American creed says that any man's vote is as good as the next on the political market, it has tended—through the all-important equation of the political and academic markets—to say that any man's political opinion is just as good as the next, and to create resentment when some opinions (those of "intellectuals") are treated as more important than those of the common man:

> As Walter Lippmann observed, the religious doctrine that all men will at last stand equal before the throne of God was somehow transmuted in [William Jennings] Bryan's mind into the idea that all men were equally good biologists before the ballot box of Tennessee. In effect, Bryan proposed to put the question of evolution to the vote of Christians, and the issue was metamorphosed into a question of the rights of the majority . . . "The one beauty about the word of God," said Bryan, "is that it does not take an expert to understand it." When some metropolitan newspapers suggested that a jury of Dayton residents might not be competent to pass on the issues at stake, Bryan commented: "According to our system of government, the people are interested in everything and can be trusted to decide everything, and so with our juries."

Hofstadter saw an essentially popular basis behind McCarthyism—indeed, he treated McCarthyism as the new Populism. He agreed with Hartz that conformism was a by-product of democratic liberalism; but he made an essential improvement on Hartz by allowing for the impact of fundamentalist theology on this intolerance. His error is that he does not see, any more than Hartz did, the essential authoritarianism in *society* as distinct from our liberal theory of *government*. He too derived McCarthyite intolerance directly from liberalism, not from authoritarian communal structures *using* the liberal theory of government *against* government. The American anti-intellectual may think "one man's opinion is as good as another's" when he is talking about a "Left-Wing professor." But he does not think that when he is censoring films at the local movie house. He may think "one man is as good as the next" when he is talking to a federal marshal in front of his school; he does not think it when he joins the Ku Klux Klan. He may claim that every man should decide his own mode of life; but not when he is passing prohibition and antigambling laws at the state level. McCarthyism was not an aberration of Lockean democracy, though it used some Lockean rhetoric as a cover for basically anti-Lockean instincts.

Status politics performed its function—it supplied a nonideological explanation for domestic conflict. That is why so many people groped to much the same view of McCarthy at much the same time—not only Lipset and Hofstadter, but Daniel Bell, Peter Viereck, and David Riesman. And that is why a theme cognate to that of status politics—the individual's "search for identity"—produced an even larger body of writings. Pop sociology of the fifties was full of organization men, men with the mass mind, pyramid climbers, those caught in the lonely crowd. There was a vogue for Ortega y Gasset and Tocqueville, a yearning back toward aristocratic ideals of taste. Erich Fromm's distinction between selfishness (a weak self crying to be propped up by the good opinion of others) and self-love (a strong self grounded on rational pride) was developed into David Riesman's theory of "other-directed men" vs. "inner-directed men." The mood of the time is conveyed by Riesman's "Individualism Reconsidered." Liberals had for years made fun of Herbert Hoover's "rugged individualism." Now Riesman said that the proper target should not be individualism as such, but the excesses of an earlier capitalism. The New Deal, when it drove free market purists out of the liberal amalgam, assailed, also, our fervent belief in the lone man's inner resources. By bringing back a sanitized ("re-considered") individualism, Riesman was helping re-create the Hoover-Wilson quasi-theology. It is no wonder, then, that pop psychology went hand in hand with pop religi-osity. Billy Graham started playing golf with Ike's busi-nessmen at a time when *The Power of Positive Thinking* simplified "inner-direction" down toward a Coué brand of self-hypnosis, when Bishop Sheen on TV and Thomas Merton on the best-seller list told men to withdraw from "the lonely crowd" into a busy new self, meditatively inner-directed, to find peace of soul. Those in better touch with the people were supplying the religious element lacking from Hartz's secular analysis of American liberalism.

Another force making for consensus was the "New Con-servatism" of the fifties. Clinton Rossiter would play Ham-ilton to Arthur Schlesinger's Jefferson, reestablishing the poles of tension within consensus. Hartz had argued that Locke's views were held for Burke's motives; but he stressed that this *was*, despite the burdensome character of all traditions, *Locke's* theory after all. By a slight change in emphasis, Peter Viereck could argue that the *important* thing was the *tradition* that sustained our liberal views—so that, accepting Hartz's thesis, he found grounds in that very thesis for calling himself a conservative. Ros-siter said he aspired to stand at that point where the most conservative liberal and the most liberal conservative find themselves agreeing—i.e., at the top of Schlesinger's play-ground drawing of the circle, on the "consensus-point." Reviewers said of Rossiter that his conservatism differed barely, if at all, from America's most fashionable liberal-ism; and Viereck's ideal conservative was Adlai Steven-son. It seemed accidental, in this world, whether one called oneself liberal or conservative—which is the point of consensus thinking. Many liberals were rediscovering "conservatives" like Burke or Metternich. Schlesinger him-self helped along a revival of interest in John Calhoun, and made Winston Churchill one of the heroes of *The Vital Center*. Anyone who would submit gracefully was being herded into the great cleared space in the Middle.

A younger group of historians and political thinkers

now accuses liberals of "selling out" in the fifties, of growing too cozy with power, losing the intellectual's distance, alienation, radical posture of dissent. Exhibit A for the prosecution is the fact that one of the large trends considered above—the end-of-ideology thesis, upheld by *Encounter* (and the CCF)—was secretly financed by the Central Intelligence Agency. This, we are told, was a Cold War operation, with intellectuals the tools of government, cranking out propaganda. But the congruence of this trend with all other currents of the time suggests that the same thoughts would have been voiced without government funds. The fundamental themes had all been expressed before the CCF was founded—e.g., in *The Vital Center*—and they were repeatedly arrived at by men unconnected with *Encounter*. Writers should not, admittedly, be lied to; and those who wrote without knowledge of any government backing—i.e., most of those involved—were deceived. But they are *self*-deceived if they cast their "independence" in the narrow terms proposed by their critics. Government support for higher education, the tax-exemption of foundations, the mystique of a liberal society in which the political and academic markets are meant to support each other—all this implies the closest contact between education and government. Liberalism assumes that freedom will be found within the political process, not apart from it. If this involves a sellout, then that occurred long ago, not in the fifties; and the academicians who were most censorious have not been known for turning down government money at their universities. If the relationship between government and the intellectuals was a false one during the fifties, this was not because liberals were then being false to their principles. The fault lies in those principles themselves.

The New Left attack on consensus thought, triggered in 1960 by a C. Wright Mills article, did not come till the decade had run its course; but another charge hovered over "the vital center" from its earliest formulation, the charge of bland compromise, the suspicion that its spokesmen were just rationalizing postwar weariness, that they offered nothing new or adventurous, only a mood of dead end, of defeat—timorousness masked as prudence. This was a charge to which intellectuals were especially sensitive during the period when they accused Eisenhower of a trancelike reign that fed on apathy. The only way to answer this charge of blandness was, apparently, to "out-tough" its proponents; the intellectuals would present themselves as the *realists*, men acquainted with the hard facts of power. The truly timid ones were those who fled toward utopias, toward safe pure doctrines unconnected with the task of real *men* in a real world. The typical liberal professor of the fifties had served in the military during the forties—usually as an officer, often in intelligence (OSS for men like Schlesinger, CIA for a William Sloane Coffin, both units for men like CCF's Michael Josselson). They had seen through the PR operations of the war to its dirty underside, to the actual fight that preserved the world's freedom from Hitler. This experience was oddly satisfying to academicians, who could now voice the old charge used against them, that "ivory-tower types do not know what it is all about." They went back to the campuses with their OCS crew cuts and their wartime slang, ready to give the intellectual world a tough-minded going over. When Daniel Bell wrote *The End of Ideology*, he included in his acknowledgments special thanks to "Michael Josselson . . . whose practical political wisdom was often ballast for intellectual fancies." It was a note often struck at the time.

As usual, the typical voice was Schlesinger's. Already in *The Vital Center*, he had found the tone that would be useful all through the fifties, and he obviously enjoyed writing Bogart stuff out of the corner of his pen. After adopting Hemingway as his political guide, Professor Schlesinger said that modern liberalism's "political leaders brought a new virility into public life," a sense of "the gusto of democracy," to rescue us from the "political sterility" of the older (classical) liberalism and the "frenzied flight from doubt" on the part of doctrinaire Leftists. The older-style Leftists, because they did not rely on a "hardboiled reading of our own experience," overestimated "the political courage and will of the capitalists," and underestimated "middle-class cowardice." They did not see that "the businessman . . . rescued society from the feudal warrior, only to hand it over to the accountant. The result was to emasculate the political energies of the ruling class." In fact, "neither the capitalists nor the workers are so tough and purposeful as Marx anticipated."

Since the radicals were not tough enough to stand up

to the capitalists, to trade with them and do business, to call their bluff, they preferred to sit by and criticize those who, leaving the shelter of doctrinal purity, accomplished things for liberty: "Where the doer is determined to do what he can to save free society, the wailer, by rejecting practical responsibility, serves the purpose of those who wish free society to fail—which is why the Doughface so often ends up as the willing accomplice of Communism . . . Life, in short, is not a form of political soap opera; it is sometimes more complicated than one would gather from the liberal weeklies." The tough-minded politicians worked for freedom while "the radical intellectual dallied with Communism." These tough minds did not succumb to the "self-love which transforms radicalism from an instrument of action into an expression of neurosis."

The ideologue is "sentimental" in his approach to the political realities—"soft, not hard," because "he has rejected the pragmatic tradition of the men who, from the Jacksonians to the New Dealers, learned the facts of life through the exercise of power." Not wielding power, they are overcome by fear of it and display "the weakness of impotence," "the failure of radical nerve." These are the people who run to Russia as "invalids" hoping to "throw away their crutches as they leave the Soviet shrine," but they end up "whimpering and crawling a little way down the road." Even those who suffer totalitarianism often bring it on themselves by their weak-nerved simpering: "For every Mayakovsky, who kills himself, a thousand exhibit masochistic delight in accepting correction . . . The [concentration] camp is the culmination of dominance and surrender, of sadism and of masochism." In fact, totalitarian politics is simply unmanly—"something secret, sweaty and furtive like nothing so much, in the phrase of one wise observer of modern Russia, as homosexuality in a boys' school."

These phrases, all taken from one short book, set up the desired contrasts for a decade. On one side, virility, gusto, the facts of life, men hard-boiled and tough-minded, the doers. On the other side, emasculation, impotence, sterility, failure of nerve, hysterical flight, neurosis, masochism, soap-opera addicts who become "willing accomplices" of cruel totalitarianism, whimpering, crawling, soft invalids and sweaty school queers. It was time for the swaggering officer-professor to come into his own. This

type called the fifties his supreme period of trial (Mc-
Carthy, you know)—but this persecution was just what
he needed to bring out his martial heroism. The intellectual has never received as much attention and respect as he
did in the fifties.

And by no accident, this era of the Bogart Professor
was also the time of the "silent generation" among students. McCarthy, no doubt, scared all the young ones'
eloquence back down their throats? Yet there was every
encouragement, from the crew-cut teachers, for kids
to scorn McCarthy—as if they needed encouragement. No
one on the faculty seemed to get the point—that the students were quiet because they were *noncoms*. The whole
basis of this shrewd fifties consensus on the importance of
consensus was belief that only *experience* counts, the tested
response of seasoned pilots, the "cool" of men who had
called many bluffs, wielded power, proved their manhood.
If that is the norm of performance, then what do students
and the young have to offer—their freshness (soft-minded),
their enthusiasm (sentimentality)? The only way they can
become old pros themselves, and some day talk as tough
as Professor Schlesinger, is by careful service as novices
—the inexperienced quietly giving their attention to the
experienced. Professors barked to the silent generation
that they should "sound off," never suspecting that this
bark was the cause of the kids' silence. Even when the
kids spoke up, finally, the message was lost on their men-
tors. The principal student manifesto, at last written by
Tom Hayden, did not blame the authorized villains. It
turned on the academy's own captains and colonels: "To
be idealistic is to be considered apocalyptic, deluded. To
have no serious aspirations, on the contrary, is to be
'tough-minded.' " Out "beyond Left and Right," out in Consensus Land, the students had nothing to contribute—
which is one reason Consensus Land was bound to disappear.

5. Nixon Triumphans: The Self-Made Man

"Expect to be hearing a good many more hymns on television."

—Richard Goldstein (1969)

THE CONSENSUS OF THE FIFTIES was rent by the violence and division of the sixties. But at first, back in 1960, John Kennedy seemed the vindicator of "mainstream" concepts. Since domestic conflict was no longer a problem for proponents of the consensus, James MacGregor Burns could dismiss the need for congressional checks and balances; Neustadt's President was to be the voice of a nation at one with itself, all its energies fused and working outward, facing the world with brash nonideological savvy and self-confidence, blazing a new spiritual frontier with Natty Bumppo shrewdness and nerve.

Schlesinger's professorial tough talk, originally a defense against "extremists," now went on the offensive, adopted a nationalistic strut and swagger. Ideology had been replaced by "style," yet that style was aggressive, ready to "bear any burden," determined the world should not remain "half free, half slave." America, youthful, vigorous in a nondoctrinal way, would charm or bluff people over to its (nondoctrinal) cause. Jack and Jackie were going to seduce the world, as their way of conquering it. The early symbol of this stylistic imperialism was the Peace Corps—wholesome youths sent everywhere, not to preach, but to win converts by their personal energy and concern. They were to be walking epitomes of Boorstin's American Way of Life, and those who inspected these samples were expected to buy the complete line of American wares. Thus the crew-cut professors of the fifties were given a "corps," their very own intellectual shock troop. The imagery was military, an *army* for peace, to wage war on war while

Goodwin blew his trumpets of paradox. Professors sniffed Washington air and remembered their youth, their days as young second lieutenants. Now they could issue orders again, tell a silent generation of Peace Corps students what to say in Guatemala or Uganda.

Jack Kennedy would out-tough Khrushchev politically, as Arthur Schlesinger had out-toughed domestic Leftists rhetorically, or as Michael Josselson had out-toughed "doctrinaires" in the CCF. The Kennedy team could take on the world. It would even take on the Pentagon, where Republican Robert McNamara seemed the essence of non-partisan hardheadedness—the wire hair bent around his iron ball of a head, his body kept lean in murderous squash games, his blazing eyeglasses wired to receive computer data. It was a time of touch football, of rough baptism in Kennedy swimming pools, of fifty-mile hikes; even Pierre Salinger puffed and jiggled along Potomac footpaths.

Then the blows came: Bay of Pigs, Vienna conference (where Kennedy, for all his style, was upstaged by the more colorful Khruschchev), Berlin Wall, Laos, missiles in Cuba, premonitory rumblings in Vietnam. The "permanent" consensus melted with magic speed; blacks and young rebels called for radicalism. Dallas shattered the myth of domestic unanimity; a new period of suspicion and denunciation arose, Mark Lane its mini-McCarthy with his hat full of conspiracies. Then, even as expiatory civil rights and poverty bills were passed under Lyndon Johnson, a deeper sense of disappointment, disorientation, set in. The Peace Corps, the Alliance for Progress, tough in their rhetoric, had proved soft, elusive, ambiguous in their performance. "Style" began to look a poor substitute for thought. RFK's "guerrillas" declared "total war" on poverty, and lost. The hard managerial approach of McNamara, far from curbing the Pentagon, streamlined the military-industrial complex, gave it new powers. Liberals began to shake their heads sadly over Sorensen's inaugural address and General Taylor's "counterinsurgency"—preludes to Vietnam. The New Frontiersmen were packing up and leaving town. Nothing was left of Camelot but a dream; and the princess shattered even that when she remarried. The fifties had produced the sixties only, it seemed, to suffer parricide at the new decade's hands.

But this short-term reversal was illusory; deceptive because based on *self*-deception at work from the outset in "enders of ideology." The Goodwins and Sorensens and Schlesingers, cigar-chewing intellectual top-sergeant types, thought they were realists moving out "beyond Left and Right" to a new era of shrewd wheeling and dealing within an easy consensus; but in fact they covered a retreat. Since no one wanted to admit this was a turning back toward the past, a covert reaching out toward "the other side," the whole thing moved softly under loud talk, sounding no alarms. Capitalism could not be reintroduced into the liberal scheme as a systematic cause and militant philosophy; the palely-lit half-moon wars of the New Deal, all the morally satisfying drama of "the age of Roosevelt," made that impossible. But "consensus" and "the end of ideology" made it possible to say that one should neither accept *nor reject* capitalism as an ideology. Therefore "tough-minded" pragmatism could sneak free-market thinking back onto the "Left" side of American politics. In 1952, Galbraith's *American Capitalism* urged men to look at "capitalism as a practical matter rather than as a system of theology," and the result was a quite visible reappearance of our old friend, the Invisible Hand. Only this time it called itself Countervailing Power: "Given the existence of private market power in the economy, the growth of countervailing power strengthens the capacity of the economy for autonomous self-regulation and thereby lessens the amount of overall government control or planning that is required or sought." At the same time, old New Dealers like David Lilienthal and A. A. Berle Jr. were finding a new maturity and social conscience in managerial capitalism, while Peter Drucker elaborated his plan for "reprivatizing" the economy. Thus the foundation was laid, on the Left, for the "reverse muckraking" of Irving Kristol and his associates at *The Public Interest:* during the sixties, these men did to governmental incompetence and bureaucracy what the Progressive muckrackers had done to capitalist "robber barons." The emphasis, throughout this transition, was on the realism of liberal intellectuals who were so "undoctrinaire" as to adopt programs normally thought of as Right-Wing.

Horatio Alger was being called back onto the raft, but he had to be called softly, by signals no one would admit he saw. Too many liberals had spent too much time laughing at the mystique of the "self-made man" for them to welcome Alger back in his familiar guise. But the liberals could argue that "status resentment" is the by-product of our nonfeudal democracy, that the American's mobility, his lack of social identity derived from a class system, make it necessary for the democratic personality to be "tough," to have a certain inner-direction suitable to this "land of opportunity." Such a line of thought carried us more than halfway back to individualism and the whole ethic of earning. It was easy for Richard Goodwin to add that Jefferson would have understood middle-class discontent at a time when men are not masters of their own fate. Initiative, individualism, "middle-class values" were respectable again. Of course, there had been a lot of rhetoric over the dam, "Left" rhetoric aimed at the bourgeois way of life; but the liberals could forget that by calling unhappy Mid-Americans their spiritual "proletariat," a group not materially but spiritually deprived, starving for power over their lives. And it is the job of the intelligentsia to give the "proletariat" what it clamors for.

In the same way, it would have been difficult for liberals to welcome back, directly and in one operation, "conservative" emphases on stability and property. Thirties rhetoric against "standpatters" and "vested interests" had obscured the fact that Locke's liberalism was founded on his concept of property. But "mainstream" thinking came to the rescue again, blunting ideological hostility. Burkean continuity was not to be seen as a separate "ideology" but as the vehicle carrying our Lockean consensus down through history. The New Deal was no longer the "revolution" its enemies called it (and some of its friends imagined it); it was now the Establishment. Attacks on it were radical, and defenders of it could be accepted, in a sense, as Tories. Thus, surprising as Moynihan's speech seemed in 1967, the ground had been laid for it in the fifties: he could defend stability because he was addressing an audience with a stake in the liberal Establishment. The consensus thinkers had described a Lockean theory upheld by Burkean loyalties; in just their sense Moynihan described his welfare plan as a Whig measure proposed by Tory men, and tried to make his own hero, Disraeli, the patron saint of the Nixon administration.

The consensus thinkers believed they were describing a permanent feature of American life when in fact they were returning to a specific period and its doctrines, to

America's pre-Depression classical liberalism. They could not admit this, even to themselves—especially to themselves. The note of self-deception can be seen in all the liberals' attacks on Eisenhower, who was blamed for the blandness of the fifties, for the silence of the students, for the homogenizing effects of "Madison Avenue," for the Mass Culture criticized by Dwight Macdonald. Yet the real intellectual basis for the decade's muted tone, its ideological retardedness, had been laid before Eisenhower ever took office. *The Vital Center* was published three years before Ike's election; the CCF was founded two years before; the ADA had, back in 1948, tried to make Ike its candidate, a national hero to embody a nontheoretical national consensus.

What liberals did not like about the Eisenhower regime was that, under him, the imagined consensus became actual; and the reality was more dispiriting than theorists had been willing to expect. In their own descriptions of the consensus, a good deal had been left out—all those things the Eisenhower regime supplied. Here were business types convinced that what was good for General Motors was good for America (why not?—another Wilson would have agreed with "Engine Charlie" on this). Here were Horatio Alger heroes who seemed (like Nixon, in his Checkers speech) sanctimonious con men. Here was middle-class religiosity (golf-course apocalypses of Billy Graham). These were the realities of American individualism, enterprise, and competition. If there was a consensus, these men were its embodiment. Just as the fifties thinkers had hidden from themselves the doctrinal orthodoxy they were reassembling, so they conveniently forgot the pungent human types that would uphold the orthodoxy.

For, make no mistake about it, if our way of life derives from America's "givenness," Nixon is what will be given us. We do not, as Hartz thought, have our Locke preserved for us by Burke, but by Horatio Alger. And if ideology is to end at the roots of American character, it will end in agreement on the sacredness of earning. "Status resentment" is not an accidental by-product of liberalism, but the essential fuel for all our competitive races. And if a New Conservatism looks for an American version of Metternich, it will not find him (as Viereck thought) in Adlai Stevenson; it will find him where Henry Kissinger, another Metternich admirer, now seeks him, in Richard

Nixon. It will find him in Moynihan's miniature Yankee
Disraeli. Another conservative, Ralph de Toledano, tried
to describe Nixon as a modern Disraeli during the fifties;
but that attempt was made too early. The fifties could
not quite accept Nixon because the work of the fifties had
not been completed.

Nixon was the most distasteful part of the Eisenhower
regime, because he epitomized all those traits liberals
wanted to ignore when they celebrated the American
"mainstream." He was more self-made than Eisenhower.
He was more religious—Ike started going to church when
he sought office; Nixon "brought the church home with
him" when he entered the White House. He was more
competitive, *much* closer to the common man, and full of
that resentment our emulative ethic breeds. And—here
was the true scandal, the stumbling block even brightest
analysts could not get over—Nixon logically completed
the picture by being more deeply and consistently liberal
than Eisenhower. Phrases like "equal opportunity" and
"self-determination" mean something to Nixon. To Eisenhower, they were just phrases; he had not been educated
enough to believe in the learned myths. Nixon is a politician, and—like all politicians—he must use every margin left him for maneuver. But his basic beliefs are in that
very system toward which the fifties thinkers groped their
way. Nixon is at one with Woodrow Wilson and Herbert
Hoover in all things that united those earlier Presidents.
He believes in, he summarizes, he is the apt spokesman for
(and the final product of) classical liberalism. Eisenhower
was a cover, like so much else in the fifties—he disguised
the basic shift taking place, a shift back toward the man
Eisenhower thought so little of, toward his own Vice-
President.

Even now commentators do not see that Nixon is the
authentic voice of the surviving American liberalism. They
speak of his policy as a matter of zigs and zags, a welter
of compromises, a muddling through the moment under
prods of hope or fear. "Conservatives" (i.e., Thurmond
and Mitchell) are played off against "liberals" (i.e., Finch
and Moynihan), North is pitted against South. Nixon is
guided, we are told, not by principle but by an inbuilt
instinct for omnidirectional placation ("Give him a choice
from one to ten and he will always choose five"). Yet
there has been a connectedness in the programs Nixon

personally espoused. "Black capitalism," for instance, is not a mere sop to the Negro community (ineffectual sop) —Nixon believes in civil rights, only he believes man's first right is the right to earn. His diversion of civil rights energy into the North, though it may soothe Senator Thurmond, is based on the liberal principle of Interchangeability, a principle Nixon, no less than its major spokesman (Moynihan), accepts. A tough line toward student protesters and marchers is part of John Mitchell's strategy for winning Wallace types to Nixon, but it is in perfect accord with Nixon's own compulsive sense of tidiness and order. The President's devotion to "self-determination for the Vietnamese" is not a mere cover for our actions in Vietnam; it is a Wilsonian ideal very dear to Nixon. The voluntarization of the draft is meant to buy off student opposition to the war—but it is also in line with Nixon's general hope (officially handed over to George Romney and Mrs. Nixon) that private action can make governmental compulsion unnecessary in many spheres of life.

The coherence of Nixon's own views has not generally been recognized, and for an important reason: this would involve the admission that American liberalism and the emulative ethic cohere—inhere, rather, in each other. All our liberal values track back to a mystique of the earner. Each of this book's preceding parts was devoted to one aspect of that earning ethic. Part Four dealt with the political market, national and international, which is based on a contractual tie between individuals (or nations) originally sovereign. The precontractual individual or state enters into "human commerce" for the advantages this commerce offers, advantages to be realized through a vigorous but peaceful competition that puts reason, excellence, and persuasion to work. The individual's participation in this process is guaranteed by the umpire-state's attention to his civil liberties (those pertaining to the Contract), just as the nation's participation is guaranteed by attention to each one's right of self-determination (secured in the Covenant). Competition in this area of politics leads us to adopt the best men, policies, and parties available. This is "the System" that seemed, in 1968, to be failing; a system that some tried to save by renewal or purification, by a return to the source. That return was partial and incomplete (e.g., Goodwin's attempt to revive the emulative process by "spreading government around"), or total and consistent (e.g., Moynihan's attempt to revive the emulative process by making government minimal and neutral, the mere umpire of contractual theory). The advocates of an entire return went to the proper patron, to Richard Nixon, whose belief in this whole fabric of myth is as unquestioning as Woodrow Wilson's.

Part Three dealt with the world of ideas, the academy, where "education for democracy" nourishes with free thought the arena of politics. In the eyes of the young, this "nourishing" support of the government has become the academy's crime. Thus liberal professors find themselves improbably defended by Spiro Agnew as they try to control their own students. The traditional liberal must, in the academy, be a "law and order" man, since Academic Freedom demands that loyalty be invested not in specific ideas but in the *process* of their airing and exchange. Nor does academic freedom preclude close ties with the electoral machinery of government, since that too is a process of peaceful competition, one parallel and complementary to the academy's. The governmental spokesmen for academic liberalism were in Chicago, and they certainly did not sympathize with Mayor Daley. But neither were they with the kids in the parks—despite McCarthy's late passage (bodyguarded by Dick Gregory) across the street to quote Péguy into the bullhorns. The more energetic liberals (e.g., Moynihan) were with McCarthy, the tired liberals (e.g., John Roche) with Humphrey, while the Kennedy men (e.g., Schlesinger) were temporizing with McGovern. All these men would like to be on the kids' side of the barricades, but their philosophy forbids it, tells them to look solely to the processes of intellectual exchange—which boils down to school *administration*. They believe in the neutral marketplace of ideas, where that market blends with the world of electoral choice; and their true though unwelcome champion is—if not Mayor Daley or Vice-President Agnew—Richard Nixon.

Part Two dealt with businessmen, with those Joneses we try to keep up with, whom we envy but imitate. We are told that it is easy to join their ranks—but that means it is easy, also, for them to slip down to our level, a fact that gives them their oppressively *scrambling* air. They are all runners who can never win the race, long distance runners, well-fed worriers; and they went to Miami to choose their very archetype, the longest distance runner of them all.

Part One dealt with the internal race man must run with himself in America. Every American is told that this land guarantees him "opportunity"; if he fails, it is his own fault—so he *must not fail.* Yet if he succeeds, it must be as a "common man," one who moved out from an equal starting place and who is not blocking an "equally equal start" for all those around him. He must start the race again every day, doubt past achievement, justify his success by repeating it. As Wilson put it, he must forsake "connections" and rely only on "character" for his moral credit.

Here, in active trading on this moral market, is energy generated for all other activities. This has been recognized by many critics, admirers or reformers of the American ethos. David Riesman says, "Americans have always sought that good opinion [of others] and have had to seek it in an unstable market, where quotations on the self could change without the price-pegging of a caste system or an aristocracy." Back in the Populist days, a reformer like Benjamin Flower could say that America must spiritually "keep the market open":

> Law-bulwarked privilege, possessing monopoly power, has always fattened off of productive industry . . . But baleful as is the influence of privilege in the realm of commercial activity, the evil dwarfs into insignificance when compared with its influence in fields that are largely speculative or theoretical; for here, while exerting the same impoverishing and demoralizing effects that mark it in the domain of material life, it encroaches on things intimately personal.

In that easy transition from "the material" to "the moral," in the attack on any "monopoly" of speculative ideas, in the praise of "productive industry," is the whole genius of America, our central conception of human achievement. Proving oneself in the free arena of competition is the test of manhood, truth, and political wisdom. And this is always, in the end, a way of proving oneself to *oneself.* The striver can never stop striving. It is because Nixon is so totally this sweaty moral self-doubting self-made bustling brooding type, that he represents the integral liberal-

ism that once animated America and now tries to reassert
itself.

The concept of the self-made man has been the key to
America's liberalism. The central tenet of the great historical school of liberal thought has been a belief in self-
regulation. If one simply removes imposed controls, the
economy can be self-regulating (Smith), as the ecological
balance (Malthus) and the animal world (Darwin) are self-
regulating. If one removes controls, man can be self-
regulating (Locke); even ideas can be self-regulating
(Mill). If colonial and imperial controls are removed, the
nations can be self-regulating (Wilson). But the problem
with the concept of self-regulation is that it *is* a form of
regulation—that is, of control; and, among men at least,
the regulating powers belong to a part of the community,
not to the whole. Yet since the whole of the community is
the "self" at issue, how can we say that the system is self-
regulating unless the *whole* governs? The quest for a
system of self-regulation thus becomes the quest for a
"self" able to act for the whole. Locke argued toward the
view that, mystically speaking, the majority *is* the whole.
Subtler trackers on this spoor have argued that a con-
catenation of branches and houses is ("representatively")
the whole ("Publius"), or that a "concurrence" of numbers,
interests, and geographical areas is the whole (Calhoun).
Modern variations are continually played on this theme:
diversity-rule (Burns), "minorities rule" (Robert Dahl),
"countervailing" rule (Galbraith). None of these equations
is satisfying—cannot be, since the basis of the discussion
is that liberal complex of metaphors (the Market, the Contract, the Starting Line, the National Self) which forms a
neat cluster of mutually reinforcing arguments, but never
did correspond with social reality. The belief in self-regulation runs into the same difficulties that plague the idea
of self-determination—the impossibility of finding a "self"
to do the regulating.

If this problem cannot be resolved in theory, it can be
coped with psychologically. Since, in liberal theory, the
community is based on the individual, the solution to the
problem of self-determination can be found by making the
individual equal the whole, a "majority of one," each man
king over himself. Self-regulation has been internalized in
the American moral system; each man is a *self-made*
man to the extent that the problem of control becomes

irrelevant through individual restraint. Here is the only way of mastering one's fate: self-mastery. One must not only be industrious but self-denying—no "kid gloves." The code of the McGuffey Readers is a hard one; it opposes trivial culture and frills, the dilettantes, the "fancy-pants" —what Agnew, that resolutely McGuffeyized disciple of Nixon, calls the "effete" ways of intellectual "snobs." Handsome is as handsome does; and the doers are almost proud of ugliness in all but their handsome deeds. Our hero is the "snuff colored Ben" of D. H. Lawrence, moralizing Ben Franklin who cramped America's spirit with the calculations of self-improvement: "Absolutely got down by her own barbed wire of shalt-nots, and shut up fast in her own 'productive' machines, like millions of squirrels running in millions of cages."

"Self-government" is primarily a personal morality in America, not a political philosophy. If we do not "govern ourselves," we shall need a king to govern us, like recalcitrant ancient Israel. But if we do "govern ourselves" —our appetites, our desires—then Democracy is safe. Thus does our individualism reduce social problems, always, to the level of private morality, to things outside the scope of legislation. No one can make life better for others except those others themselves. A man can be self-made only by himself. Even when there are tasks that must be done by a communal effort, these should be left to "voluntarism." Turning the job over to government is a confession that one *needs* government, a confession of weakness, an admission that *self*-government has failed. As Nixon likes to put it, people do not become great by what the government does for them but by what they do for themselves.

These beliefs, deeply held (however men fail to live up to their own standards), return us to this book's starting point—to the moral horror felt by Mid-America as it looked at the militant blacks and "hippies" of the late sixties, to the sanctimonious air of Wallace rallies, the shocked righteousness of Chicago police who saw their city's parks fouled with four-letter words and liceridden hair and unnamable couplings. The American's insistence on self-regulation makes him see chaos come again when the young, or the blacks, refuse to honor self-restraint. It is one thing to fail at self-restraint; it is a totally different and terrifying thing not even to try for it, aspire toward it, honor its imperatives. If the ideal of moral self-government is dishonored, then all other meanings of the word "self-government" become a mockery to Americans. Faced with this cosmos-unsettling spectacle, white Mid-America fears even the smallest minority of militant blacks or kids. This is what made men in bars and taxicabs cheer the clubbing of young people with moral fervor, as if Christians were tearing lions in the arena. The agony of the lower middle class, Goodwin surmised, lies in its sense of powerlessness. But this is not to be diagnosed in Goodwin's mechanical terms (the individual has dropped below the tolerable minimum of leverage upon government); and it is certainly not to be cured by his remedy (increase the degree of leverage up to the tolerable). The agony comes from a crumbling of the moral ethos that upheld our mystique of government, freedom, opportunity, dignity, and excellence. "Law and order" is not merely a code phrase for racism. It is the last clause left from our old moral creed. And the cry of the middle class is not for Goodwin's "participatory" moderation of the kids' own demands, realized in local democracy. It is a call for the return to fundamentals, to earning, to "something for *something*." American liberalism has always been based on this and must, when its survival is at stake, return to this—to the ideal of self-government, of the self-disciplined self-made man.

6. Nixon Agonistes: The Last Liberal?

"He is the most perfect example we have of the culture which has failed and is dying out."
—Lincoln Steffens
of Woodrow Wilson

MOYNIHAN TRIES to cast Nixon as Disraeli; Kissinger would like him to be Metternich; Nixon himself yearns for

Woodrowfication. But the historical parallel that must be most convincing to Nixon himself is still Len Garment's— Churchill: the man and the moment came together. Nixon seems the logical product of our recent history. If our system does not choose "the best man," its winnowings tend to produce an *appropriate* man to lead us, one amenable to the merchandizing trends of the moment; one who, if not really answering the needs of popular symbolism, can nonetheless be given the requisite garb of relevance. He becomes our "man of the moment" by accommodating the moment.

But there was no need to do an image job on Nixon— the "selling of the President" is a process all candidates must undergo now (so an expertise in all camps tends to cancel itself out); yet the process affected Nixon much less than it would others. The things that spoke to and for the Forgotten American of the 1968 campaign were always present in Nixon, completely, interconnectedly— so much so that the last two decades seem almost to bear witness to a single trend: the inevitability of Nixon.

Yet if a certain logic has driven men back to the essentials of American individualism, it is the logic of desperation. If Nixon is proper spokesman for that ethos, then nothing could prove better how shrunken, small, how unheroic that ideal is. This politics will not summon us with trumpets. The tone of our public life is not the old one—"These qualities made America the great country it is, and we must be true to them." The present tone is, "These qualities made the country what it is, and we must settle for them." There is a forlorn air to arguments in favor of Nixon's leadership: there may be things wrong with the American spirit, men grant, but Nixon can at least deal with the authentic national character. He knows it. Here is one thing we can rally to when the nation seems agreed on little else. Nixon can "bring us together again" because he can find the ground where we last stood together years ago.

The new liberalism has a cowed apologetic air. Even things that were once sources of legitimate pride have a faded mousy look. Things like Hannah Nixon's undemonstrative piety and sensitive concern for others. Or the bite of Frank Nixon's individualism, aimed at achievement, trying for success, but a bit too fine to succeed. Or homely uncomplaining industry, a quiet patriotism running deeper than xenophobia. Or a "Faustian" willingness to take great risks on the chance of making great progress. Traces of all these qualities are left in Nixon, in the new Americanism. But they are a residue only, dilutions of what had once been strong. Weariness and compromise—the workings of the Mixmaster "market"—have puréed all Nixon's separate virtues to an unoffending mush.

Even some Democrats urged the election of Nixon in 1968, on the grounds that he was the best we had for the time—for a time of retrenchment and cooling off, for a time of lowered voices and hopes. He was more palatable than Wallace. He was closer to the people than Humphrey, closer to the American mainstream. Descriptions of that "mainstream" used to be triumphal in the fifties, but no more. Now arguments from the "mainstream" tend to be consolatory, urging acquiescence, resignation. Nixon is not pretty, inspiring, heroic, grand. But those who support him (men like Stewart Alsop) make virtues of every deficiency: he will not feed the people on movie-star daydreams, as Jack and Jackie did. If Nixon is lacking in stature and all too human, that will teach the country that it must be great on its own, not vicariously, not leaning on its ruler's strength. A great country will be great no matter who comes and goes in the White House. A people is greater because of its own actions, not by virtue of what government does for it.

But this nation does not feel great, does not contrast some true communal stature with the President's "low profile" of power. Nixon's victory was the nation's concession of defeat, an admission that we have no politics left but the old individualism, a web of myths that have lost their magic. We cannot convincingly proclaim that where we stand is a "vital center." Our "mainstream" is a sludge. The "consensus" is no longer a matter of compromise but surrender. Our archetypal "self-made man" is not only self-effacing but almost self-obliterating.

It had to be. The "markets" Nixon represents were always at war with reality, were a thing of liberal fancy. But they were *usable* fancies in the past; we did not see through them, then. Now we cannot hide their emptiness. One by one, they fail us:

1) The *moral* market proposes an Emersonian self-creation that is really self-destruction. One rises over sacrificed earlier selves (the very history of Nixon), putting

even self-contempt at the service of lofty disanimating ambition. The chill in Emerson's words has entered Nixon's bones; he creaks with it when he moves. The real evil of Horatio Alger was not that he made an apprentice bustle sycophantically in the wake of millionaries, but that he distilled the poison that (only a touch of it) turns the saintly (e.g., Hannah Nixon) into the sanctimonious (e.g., Richard Nixon).

In the past, we could believe that no one gets "something for nothing," that the sole spring of achievement is man's willingness to *earn*, that "anyone can make good." Our society was not then so manifestly interdependent, its socializing processes so compulsory; "earners" seemed more autonomous and imitable, while nonearners were not only neglected but almost invisible (when we said "Any boy born in America can grow up to be President," of *course* we did not mean black boys—and we did not find it odd or embarrassing that we did not). Now only the most resolutely self-deceived "earner" can make the boast "I never got something for nothing." And only by a cultivated solipsism can parts of the middle class keep saying, "*We* made it on our own, why can't *they?*" No one makes it on his own. The whole American myth of what Wilson called "the man on the make," the self-making man, is a cruel hoax. The middle-class earner, given initial advantages, uses them to build walls of security, forgoing risk —medicare, social security, pensions, free schools, government unemployment checks, union guarantees of a job or a wage. Those Wallace supporters who cry out against welfare live in a network of interdependency, clinging to it, keeping others from it. Yet they live, too, with the old lie—not merely to keep down today's menacing, more visible "non-earners," but to feed self-respect on the only food it has known in America. The earners have to *feel* that each "made it on his own," or their whole moral code unravels, leaving them no pride. Yet their ears must hear, finally, involuntarily, a hollowness in their own voice. So self-contempt grows in them; they find themselves guilty of the thing they curse in others—*dependence*, reliance on other men, the lack of self-made autonomy. Self-made men are not the bold swashbucklers imagined once, laughing, spontaneous, free. They are cramped, full of pretense, diminished things—Dick Nixons.

2) The "moral market" is what Wilson referred to when

he said free enterprise forms character. The *economic* market is what he had in mind when he said the free enterprise system is the most efficient one. Maximum freedom means maximum productiveness; our "openness" is to be the measure of our stability. Fascination with this ideal has made Americans defy the "old world" categories of settled possessiveness versus unsettling deprivation, the cupidity of retention versus the cupidity of seizure, a "status quo" defended or attacked. America, it was believed, had no *status quo ante*. Our only "station" was the turning of a stationary wheel, spinning faster and faster. We did not base our system on property but opportunity —which meant we based it not on stability but on mobility. The more things changed, the steadier we would be. It is this ideal that first made it so hard to talk of a European "Left" or "Right" in America (even before the added confusion of liberalism's split during the thirties). The conventional picture of class politics is composed of the Haves, who want stability to keep what they have, and the Have-Nots, who want a touch of instability and change in which to scramble for the things they have not. But Americans imagined a condition in which speculators, self-makers, *runners* are always using the new opportunities given by our land. The society's leaders (*front*-runners) would thus be mainly agents of *change*. The nonstarters are the ones who want stability, a strong umpire to give them some position in the race, a regulative hand to calm manic speculation; an authority that can call things to a halt, begin things again from compensatorily staggered "starting lines."

"Reform" in America has been sterile because it can imagine no change except extension of this race-metaphor, wider inclusion of competitors (Nixon's "piece of the action" for blacks). There is no attempt to call off the race. Since our only stability is change, America does not honor the quiet work that achieves social interdependence and stability. There is, in our legends, no heroism of the office clerk, no stable industrial "peasantry" of the men who actually make the system *work*. There is no pride in being an employee (Wilson asked for a return to the time when everyone was an employer). There has been no boasting about our social workers—they are merely signs of the system's failure, of opportunity denied or not taken, of things to be eliminated by Moynihan's return to small-government individualism or Goodwin's return to self-mastery (every man his own foreign office, the new reading of Wilson's "every man his own employer"). We have no pride in our growing interdependence, in the fact that our system can serve others, that we are able to give those in need "something for nothing"; empty boasts from the past make us ashamed of our present achievements, make us try to forget or deny them, move away from them. There is no honor but in the Wonderland race we all must run, all trying to win, none winning in the end (for there is no end).

3) The *academic* market is based on the pretense that real intellectual neutrality toward ideas can be maintained; that ideas will, of themselves, join, struggle, clash in the blank arena of the mind. The liberal intellect should first be a mere observer, detached and impartial ("may the best idea win"), so that it may finally be the arbiter, raising the glove of the victorious idea. Yet it is only the mind that can conceive ideas, be their vehicle, urge them, reject them. Ideas will not carry themselves into battle, act by some inner energy upon the passive observing mind. The picture of the mind as somehow above ideas, arbitrative over them, is one of the attempts to find a mechanism *in* nature that will yet be *above* it, an invisible hand "self-regulating." Thus truth is said to reside in the mind's openness toward ideas, yet also in the ideas that prevail; and the mind gets from its first impartial stance to its later acceptance without ever being quite responsible for the outcome. It was not an *advocate* of the winning idea at the outset, but a *judge*, finally, of the outcome—which leaves the ideas without *any* original advocates.

It is this lack of responsibility for its own ideas that the kids sense in the academy, and condemn. As Tom Hayden put it in 1962: "The message of our society is that there is no viable alternative to the present." Thus, though Vietnam is "the professors' war"—we have never undertaken hostilities under such firm scholarly guidance, such reliance on academically certified expertise—the academy is not felt to be responsible for the advice and advisers it gave the politicians. There is an inevitability about the market's workings. Schlesinger will admit that liberal principles were "overextended" in Vietnam, but not that they were basically erroneous. How could they be? They were the *prevailing* thoughts; they had proved their worth, against other alternatives, in the competitive give and take of academic freedom. They were, by definition, the best we had or could have at the time. The arbiter never admits to advocacy.

And, after all, what other approach is there, what "viable alternative"? Should not the best theory be made available to the political market in *its* search for the best practical policy? And is it not the interaction of the two markets that keeps both "honest" and fruitful? Schlesinger is sure of it: "The assumption that power will inexorably subvert intelligence exhibits a fatal lack of confidence in the force of facts, ideas and reason . . . The breach is closing between mind and state, and this will not necessarily mean the capitulation of intelligence to power. It may well mean rather a resumption in contemporary terms of the partnership between ideas and responsibility that gave the early republic its lustre." These two markets were meant for each other.

4) The *political* market is what Wilson had in mind when he said free enterprise checks any tendency, in America, toward despotism. It has another effect, not often recognized. Americans have shown, in the past, a strange confidence in their country's power, amounting almost to belief in its omnipotence. Various reasons are given for this—the country has not been invaded over the last century and a half, nor ever (until Vietnam) lost a war. But a deeper force is at work as well. Since a people becomes great, not by what government does for it but by what that people does for itself, we are bound to be greater than countries which need kings, strong rulers, strict controls. If our self-discipline failed, we would need a despot, and be as weak as others; but, as things stand, our government is only a market mechanism that allows us to develop all our potentialities. Freedom puts men's energies to most efficient use; that is what our electoral "free system" is all about—and though we think everyone else should adopt it, *until* they do we are their superiors. We are people not restrained by government but only by ourselves, a country in the true sense self-determined; and there is about such self-determination some of the mystique attached to the self-made man, the man who can do anything because he has "that extra SOMETHING" of the success manuals.

This was the last of our beliefs to be shaken; but Vietnam shook it. Americans were dying by the thousands to initiate free elections in Vietnam at the very time when those elections had yielded so little satisfaction at home, had given us the anachronism, Nixon. He was as obviously not our "best man" as the Vietnam decisions had not been the "best policy" for this country. Belief in the competitive triumph of excellence was bound to be shaken.

There, in their original interlocking cluster (with Nixon at the center), are all the liberal things we believed in once, now grown unbelievable. Even defenders of that old faith say merely that it is what we must work with. They are engaged in a holding action: bad as the system is, how are we to abandon it without getting something worse? Not liberalism only, but liberty itself, would be at stake if we were to abandon our elections, academic freedom, and the individual disciplines of thrift and industry.

That defense misses the point. Criticism of liberalism does not lead logically to the destruction of its many achievements. In the ingenious quest for "self-regulating" mechanism, liberalism did give us marvelously improved regulating devices. It is only the pretense that these are *self*-regulating—automatic, the producers of freedom rather than its product—that must be abandoned. Not the machinery, but the rationale behind it, has proved untenable, and has embittered men. The mystique of earning has inflicted a crippling sense of inferiority on our nation's nonearners. The belief that our electoral system guarantees the choice of the best men and policies can only give voters a sense that the whole operation is a mockery when Richard Nixon is freely chosen to preside over the course of war in Vietnam. The belief that a real neutrality of the mind can exist toward ideas leads to the aridities of academe. Considered on their own terms, the techniques developed under liberalism are not only admirable but can be put to better use when we abandon liberal efforts to reduce all social life back to individualist terms. For instance:

—I have given, in an earlier place, the reasons I think our electoral system an apt means of orderly government for our society, involving as it does a ritual of recommitment to the social body. It is only when election is con-

542 THE FUTURE OF LIBERALISM

sidered as a market machinery that makes excellence prevail that it cheats men with false promises and tempts them to retaliate against the system. It is only when Goodwin makes divided responsibility mean every man is his own foreign office that liberal "self-government" becomes a flattering lie, a promise that all can be rulers and none ruled.

—No one, so far as I know, suggests that we should give up free market concepts right down to the refusal to pay more for better goods. There is much that governmental bureaucracy cannot accomplish and private enterprise can. But the view that this enterprise can be self-checking, automatically self-regulating, only leads in the end to compensatory excess of governmental control.

—In the same way, no one denies that thrift, prudence, industry, and self-discipline are components in any balanced approach to human virtue. What was evil about the ethic of earning was the belief that the degree of man's success was the measure of his human worth, that true success meant one must accomplish everything for oneself, that those who accept "something for nothing" are inferior beings.

—Many of the rules invented to protect academic freedom have been conducive to free speculation. But the pretense that all ideas were aired equally led to subtle failures in the protection of dissent. Officially, there was no "orthodoxy" in any field, and so no specific measures were needed to protect dissent from that orthodoxy. In theory, dissent was itself the only orthodoxy; and, reality not corresponding with that theory, the rules sometimes backfired, or drained real dissent of its challenge.

The historical achievement of liberalism is a great one, and even its severest critics would not systematically raze all its monuments. That these great deeds were accomplished by men acting, often, out of self-delusion means only that we are looking at the history of men—the same could be said of any school of thought that led to large actions in the world. One cannot even indulge in "hypothetical history" by saying a different course would have been a better one. This is our history, its good and bad intermixed; we cannot choose another.

But one thing we can do—we can *make* history by refusing to rest in liberalism's self-deceptions, once exposed. Whatever usefulness classical liberalism had in the past came from men's devotion to it as the best they could imagine or devise, from human generosity and idealism expended in its name. That claim cannot be made for the current return to liberal individualism. There is an air of pusillanimity about it, of flight from pursuing truths. It refuses to take uncomfortable realities into account, whether these be in the realm of social theory, of political fact, or of psychological challenge. Its symbol is Nixon's refusal even to deal with blacks or dissident students, as if "the silent majority" were the whole of society.

If Americans muster the nerve and honesty to face these new problems, no one can be certain what shape our politics will take; but one thing is certain—nerve and honesty would, of themselves, shatter the individualist basis of our politics. This country has not taken very seriously the aim enunciated in the Preamble to the Constitution—"to form a more perfect Union." Today there is a desperate thirst for community, for social bonds, new "families," communes. There are wild versions of the social impulse wandering free, and a tendency, in small communities, toward separatism from the rest of national life. If these yearnings are ignored, there can be nothing but pitched battle between their spokesmen and our official individualism. But if they are taken seriously, then the great lack in our political theory—its blindness to the facts of community life—can at last be repaired. The denseness of local conformism and dictated mores, the sources of authoritarian structure, have been conveniently left out or distorted in liberal theory. This side of life has not been understood, its energies made fruitful, its dangers realistically countered. When liberals did bother to notice such phenomena, they tried to explain them away—as primordial base "matter" not yet etherealized toward liberalism (e.g., city machines), or as a by-product of the liberal tradition itself (Bryan calling for "majority rule" over the biological facts of life). Sometimes the facts were wildly colored to fit liberal theory—as when labor unions were considered primarily as "Leftist" forces unsettling property with revolutionary ideas, rather than as efforts at stability. Rarely was liberal theory enlarged or altered to accommodate these facts, so reluctant to it, so eloquent of man's need for a fixed social environment, so destructive of the myth that man is a self-determining atom moving free toward a lone encounter with his fate. The communal side of life was either ignored, or condemned, or consigned to inferior ages and cultures (none of them ready for the self-rule that is America's source of pride). Thus even when liberals "rediscover" the middle class and its discomforts, they try to cure that malady with further doses of the competition that tortures men, not with new kinds of security and communal affection. Even when a politician (like Nixon) panders to this unknown (and therefore rather frightening) aspect of American life, he must do it in misleading liberal formulae. There is a vast underside of American life, never explored or tamed, which is at odds with individualist standards, yet has been fatally linked with them in the past.

Already new social units force themselves on our attention, demanding a new kind of attention. What would happen, for instance, if we took seriously the college campus as a community (not as one more "market" of individuals and ideas, but as a social structure with its own identity and interests)? In the past, the basic assumption was that colleges were simply collections of individual children, all of whose parents had hired the same set of teachers to act temporarily in their place. Now teachers have lost the authority they held *in loco parentis,* but they have not acquired another authority, that of leaders in a social subunit. Instead, they try to pretend the academy's authority rests solely in ideas, not in men. They wait upon the ministrations of the Invisible Hand—and wait in vain.

Or what if we took seriously black ghettos as special communities, in need of indigenous leaders with appropriate leverage upon society as a whole? Norman Mailer campaigned for mayor of New York, in 1969, on a platform that would have made the city (itself a checker of new social units) "the Fifty-First State." That may prove too cautious a view of the social regroupings that must take place if we are to express the reality of our communal ties in the future. Geographical representation is often nonrepresentation today. The future may lie in an approach to "constituencies" not merely defined by locale. Only a period of intense experimentation, and close observation of the actual way society is sorting itself out, can give us social tools corresponding to our needs. We have reached a point of technological interdependence and psychological division that calls for as much wisdom and ingenuity as the nation's founding period. But the "new federalism" must not, like Nixon's, merely return to earlier units of rule. Those units have already failed—the reason for our departure from them in the first place. And we shall not know or honor *re*founding fathers until we break our philosophical bondage to the past—as the Colonies could not forge the Constitution until they withdrew from British rule.

The great temptation is simply to drift, "lower our voices," settle for what we have, we are; say it is too late for change, we lack the resources, all we can do is keep our heads above the wave, treading water. History has made us, we cannot remake ourselves. To say this is to say that we are not the heirs, merely, but prisoners of our past thoughts, that we cannot break through them and be free, even when we recognize their delusive aspects. If this is so, then we must perish, feeding on recognized falsehood, our fate the fate of our exposed, exploded theories. But it is not so. Even in the past a great deal of our national life was left out of the accepted theories, and this becomes increasingly true as liberalism fails to enlist the energy and hopes of the young. At any rate, history never rests, never leaves alone the thing it makes; and there are signs that history, having made ours a great nation, may now be in the process of unmaking us—unless we can tap some energies for our own renewal. It is the scale of this task that has frightened men, made them withdraw to Nixon's faded standard. But we have no safe haven of escape—least of all there. If our liberal system is coming apart at the seams, it is not because of "subversive" nibbling moths and underminers. It is because the seams, of themselves, will not hold; the fabric is old, worn, unrenewable, and must be discarded. If we have a chance to create a newly articulated community, it will not be given us on the road Nixon travels.

Nor is renewal to be found in mere self-flagellation; the attack on error must go beyond bitterness over lost myths, our lost (rather, our imagined) selves. We must not, even, despise Nixon, but forgive him—absolve ourselves. We were *not* such supermen, after all; only vanity can make us hate that fact, or the things that remind us of it. We must accept our own past, not consoling ourselves longer with national legend. As Murray Kempton says, the final test of maturity is the forgiveness of one's elders—all those Mc-

Guffeyized aunts and ancestors to whose teaching Nixon would call us back.

Forgive our elders; this does not mean we should try to *be* them—for they are dead. And it is only a calm realization that our main myths are dead or dying that can make us, as a nation, live on. We were shaped by those beliefs, but we are something more than they ever were, we can outlive them. We remained more than our self-flattering tenets—our individualism, self-regulation, discipline, achievement, "markets," Causes. It is comforting—needed comfort—to reflect that this is so, that we can survive our own creed's dissolution; for Nixon, by embodying that creed, by trying to bring it back to life, has at last reduced it to absurdity.

Afterword

Richard Nixon ran the first counterinsurgent Presidency. He came to Washington not only to do war with the "counterculture" of rioting kids and peaceniks, but with the Establishment the kids were rioting *against*. He did not trust the bureaucracy in place. Later he would claim that FBI and CIA recalcitrance made him hire private teams of "plumbers" to plug government leaks. But a mere two months after his inauguration, his aide Bob Haldeman put on the President's secret payroll the security man, John Caulfield, used during his presidential campaign.

Caulfield hired others, e.g., Tony Ulasewicz and Tony LaRocco, to do some spying for the White House. Their first big assignment came in the aftermath of Edward Kennedy's accident at Chappaquiddick. Nixon was certain that the press would cooperate with any Kennedy hiding a crime, so his private gumshoes were dispatched to Martha's Vineyard in the summer of 1969. Later they spied on Senator Kennedy, trailing him, questioning any who might revile him (even Bobby Baker, the convicted associate of Lyndon Johnson). Later, Charles Colson directed some White House dirty tricks, using his "operative" Howard Hunt. When the Nixon obsession with Kennedy called for a leak implicating John Kennedy in the assassination of South Vietnam's president Ngo Dinh Diem, Hunt tried to forge diplomatic cables, creating the "evidence" of Kennedy's guilt.

From the very first months of his Presidency, Nixon found chores for a growing army of private spies and political saboteurs. They plotted against the press—tapping columnist Joseph Kraft's telephone, trying to discredit Jack Anderson. Hunt used a wig and a voice-distorter to question one of Anderson's sources. When Daniel Ellsberg leaked the Pentagon Papers to *The New York Times*, gumshoes gave him the Ted Kennedy treatment. They broke into a psychiatrist's office to find the stuff for smearing him. The files illegally gained were meant to be leaked, of

547

course—though the White House was piously attacking leaks.

When this bungling crew finally got caught breaking into the Democratic National Committee headquarters in 1972, there could be no hesitation in the White House over the need to cover up. It puzzled some that Nixon should compound one error with a greater one, the cover-up of a third-rate attempt at burglary. But these observers did not realize how many third-rate attempts might come out—not only what was done, but what was planned and never consummated, like firebombing the Brookings Institution to get some of its files.

The Watergate break-in, coming in a campaign year when Nixon led all rivals in the polls, seemed undermotivated and overbungled. Conspiratorialists of many stripes were bound to conclude that the break-in had some bizarre purpose not yet discovered, one that was deliberately sabotaged. But the Ellsberg break-in was undermotivated and overbungled. So were Hunt's forays in a wig and Ulasewicz's schemes against Edward Kennedy (including a plan to seduce, seriatim, all the girls at the Chappaquiddick party in order to blackmail them into blackmailing Ted Kennedy). Bob Haldeman plausibly claimed, from prison, that he blocked many petty schemes Nixon invented on the spur of the moment. In his own memoirs, Nixon says he considered faking further break-ins and blaming them on the Democrats. He was clumsy at everything else, why not at crime?

Indeed it was his clumsiness, his distrust of others, that blunted and contained his threat to the Republic. Nixon claimed that other Presidents of recent memory had done the things he did; and it is quite true that modern presidents misused their power over the FBI and CIA and IRS. What set Nixon apart was his inability to rest content with such abuses. He felt these agencies were not serving him well enough in his illegal acts of self-protection. He had to hire his own spies to spy on the official spies. The CIA was used against Ellsberg; *but Howard Hunt was used against the CIA*. Thus Nixon got caught in his own "third murderer" problem—he had to hire new crooks to control his crooks, in an infinite regression. The quintessential loner was trammeled in a huge cast of characters created by his need to be alone. He was pitted at last not only against the Establishment culture and the radical counterculture, but against his own counterinsurgency.

Nixon remained an outsider even at the peak of "inside" power. Though he should have presided over the country's establishment, he approached it like Green Beret troops sent over to prop up Diem—distrusting their own instrument even as they fought savagely against insurgents. Nixon's mind was perfectly revealed in the summer of 1970 when Charles Manson was on trial for ritual murders performed in California. Nixon almost caused a mistrial with his impassioned outburst inspired by a viewing of John Wayne's *Chisum,* the story of a man who takes the law into his own hands to kill off an outlaw menace. Nixon said that the permissiveness of the press would lead to another *Chisum* experience.

Yet Manson was caught, tried legally (no thanks to Nixon), and sentenced. Justice prevailed. Nixon, you see, distrusted the courts as well as the bureaucracy. To be a hired gun for good—to ride in and rescue where there is no sheriff (or only a weak one)—that is the outsider's dream. But what happens if the sheriff himself continues to dream that dream? Nixon was still making raids on the government even when he *was* the government.

That is the reason he still fascinates and teaches. He is always the lone man testing himself and others in a battle for survival. He realized the dream of American individualism as expressed in the private eye or rootless cowboy, the traveling norm in an aberrant world, an entirely private agent of public order. Nixon wrote in his 1978 memoirs: "Washington is ruled by Darwinian forces, and if you are in serious political trouble, you cannot expect generosity or magnanimity for long." And Nixon was always in serious trouble, no matter what the polls said about his chances against George McGovern. Life is one long trouble, one long testing in the marketplace of survival. William Graham Sumner, the American prophet of social Darwinism, said it best: *"The relation, therefore, between each man's needs and each man's energy, or individualism, is the first fact of human life."*

Sumner also wrote: *"It is a humane and rational view of things that each life shall stand for itself alone and not be weighted by the faults of another."* Nixon, drawing on Theodore Roosevelt's phrase, repeatedly called his the life of "man in the arena"—the center of all eyes, exposed, ringed with distancing space. *"I have shown already that a free man cannot take a favor. One who takes a favor or submits to patronage demeans himself."* No one can reach across the cleared space to help this embattled individual.

But Sumner had to admit that the survival of the fittest could be hampered by intrusion of sheer accident into the competitive market that establishes human worth: *"There is no man who is honest and industrious who cannot put himself in a way to maintain himself and his family, misfortune apart, in a condition of substantial comfort."* Nixon failed, against John Kennedy, in the campaign of 1960, but he felt he was the fitter to survive. So the market must have been tampered with. Survival would thenceforth mean "correction" of the market with tactical counter-tampering. This passage from Nixon's memoirs shows why Watergate was inevitable:

> We were faced in 1960 by an organization that had equal dedication to ours and unlimited money, that was led by the most ruthless group of political operators ever mobilized for a presidential campaign. Kennedy's organization approached campaign dirty tricks with a roguish relish and carried them off with an insouciance that captivated many politicians and overcame the critical faculties of many reporters. I should have anticipated what was coming as I observed some of what went on in Kennedy's brilliant but coldly mechanical destruction of Hubert Humphrey in the primaries . . . From this point on I had the wisdom and wariness of someone who had been burned by the power of the Kennedys and their money and by the license they were given by the media. I vowed that I would never again enter an election at a disadvantage by being vulnerable to them—or anyone—on the level of political tactics.

One of the Kennedy operatives remembered and feared from the 1960 campaign was Lawrence O'Brien. It was to tap his phone and search his files that Nixon's operatives raided the Watergate office of the Democratic National Committee. Nixon had made himself a pledge whose keeping would be his undoing. The anti-Establishment administration, still counterinsurgent in victory, staged a bloodless coup against itself, trying to steal votes in an election it had already won. Richard Nixon, from his need to struggle, stole the White House from Richard Nixon.

Index of Names